SERVICE BOOK

OF THE

HOLY ORTHODOX-CATHOLIC APOSTOLIC CHURCH

COMPILED, TRANSLATED, AND ARRANGED FROM
THE OLD CHURCH-SLAVONIC SERVICE
BOOKS OF THE RUSSIAN CHURCH
AND COLLATED WITH THE
SERVICE BOOKS OF THE
GREEK CHURCH

BY

ISABEL FLORENCE HAPGOOD

REVISED EDITION
WITH INDORSEMENT BY PATRIARCH TIKHON

ASSOCIATION PRESS

NEW YORK: 347 MADISON AVENUE

1922

ПАТРІАРХЪ МОСКОВСКІЙ
И ВСЕЯ РОССІИ
ТИХОНЪ.

Троицкое Патріаршее
Подворье.
Москва.
1921, Ноября " " дня.
№ 753

*Facsimile of
Patriarch's
Endorsement*

Въ Американскій Христіанскій
союзъ молодыхъ людей.
НЬЮ-ЙОРКЪ.

Миръ вамъ и миръ отъ Бога Отца
и Господа нашего Іисуса Христа!

Глубоко тронуло меня Ваше
добородное истинно христіанское желаніе
и рѣшеніе перевадъ настоящую книгу
"Orthodox Eastern Church", плодъ многолѣтней
работы Miss I.F. Hapgood.

Искренно, воздушно при-
зываю Вамъ Божіе всеблагостное благословеніе
и это благостное вниманіе, имѣвшее
въ виду распространеніе Христовой вѣры
и знаній и собействіе явному общенію
вѣрующихъ во Христа отъ нашего Господа
и Спасителя, имѣвшемъ во Святомъ Своемъ,-
и всякаго благодатнаго преуспѣянія и
радости о Духѣ Святомъ всѣмъ трудящимся
въ этомъ великомъ дѣлѣ.

Выражаю отрадную увѣренность,
что, при внималомъ предприиятаго изданіе
ніе, глубоко мною уважаемой д-ръ Джонъ Р.
Моттъ и его сотрудники не обойдутъ своимъ

любезнымъ вниманіемъ г-жу Хапгудъ, и при-
гласятъ ее къ лучшему и полезному участіе
въ дѣлѣ исправленія неточностей, опущен-
ній и корректурныхъ погрѣшностей, вкравшихся
себѣ мѣсто въ первомъ изданіи и, сколько
мнѣ извѣстно, собранныхъ уже ею въ особой
перечень, на случай второго изданія
ея книги.

Слава Богу за все! Его промысли-
тельному изволенію вибрая совершенно
вручаемаго во славу Его дѣла, будемъ
счастливы, если Господь судитъ мнѣ
еще со всѣми ревнителями этого, что
стало потребнымъ къ уразумѣнію ученія
Святой Православной Апостольской Церкви
книгѣ изданія, во свидѣтельство ревно-
сти Христіанскаго Союза Молодыхъ Людей
о благословенномъ Христовой Истины.

Патріаршее благословеніе наше
всегда близкому сердцу нашему Американ-
ской паствѣ нашей, незабвеннымъ нашимъ
американскимъ друзьямъ, и всѣмъ Вамъ!
Патріаршее благословеніе наше и молит-
венный привѣтъ!

+ Тихонъ, Патріархъ Московскій
и всея Россіи.

PREFACE TO THE SECOND EDITION OF THE SERVICE BOOK

HAD communications with Moscow been less complicated, His Holiness, Patriarch Tikhon would have received a complete set of the new proofs for his inspection. On January 1st (the 14th N.S.), 1917, I discussed with him, in Petrograd — he being then Archbishop of Vilna and Lithuania — the possibility of a much needed new edition, my own efforts to secure such an edition and a list of corrections which I had already prepared. The first edition was prepared and published under his supervision, while he was at the head of The American Mission, as Archbishop of the Aleutian Islands and North America.

From beginning to end the preparation of this second edition of The Service Book has been unreservedly and exclusively entrusted to me by the Young Men's Christian Association. I have made no changes whatsoever, beyond the correction of accidental errors and omissions — none of them important — natural in the first edition of an exceedingly difficult work; with one exception:

The word "Ruler" has been substituted for any more specific title in the prayers, litanies and hymns. This renders it easy for any one of the score of autonomous churches belonging to the Eastern Orthodox Confession to supply the appropriate Official title for the head of the State, wherever occasion may be found to use this version at their wonderful services.

The Services, as herein set forth, are regularly and officially used, with unimportant local differences, in all the branches of the Orthodox Catholic Church. They are, also, used in one branch of the Roman Catholic Church, known historically as the "Uniat," or "Greek-Catholic" (Roman Catholic of the Greek Rite). The most considerable section of this Uniat Church is that which, at the close of the XVI. century, in South-West (Little) Russia, broke away from its Mother Church, the Russian, and became "Uniat" by recognizing the headship of Rome. It has retained the Old Church Slavonic language and all the Service Books of the Russian Church; but the divergent dogmas and most of the customs of the Roman Church have gradually been substituted for those of the Mother Church. Since the World War this branch of the Roman Catholic Church has adopted the title of "The Ukrainian Church."

(Signed)   ISABEL F. HAPGOOD

January 14, 1922.

PREFACE

SOME explanation is necessary touching the aim and scope of this Service Book, and my methods in compiling it.

It has always been the policy of the Holy Orthodox-Catholic Apostolic Church of the East to have her services celebrated in the languages of the countries inhabited by her members. In accordance with this policy it is desired, eventually, to make English the language, in this country, of the Russian Church, which was the first to bring Christianity to Alaska, and now has more parishes in all sections of the land than either of the other representatives of that Communion, — the Greek and Syro-Arabian branches.

Moreover, the adoption of the English language is the sole solution of many difficulties encountered by the priests of·that church in administering to the spiritual wants of their flocks, who come from many countries, each of which has its own language or dialect, — Great Russia, Little Russia, Galicia (in Eastern Austria), Hungary, Servia, Montenegro, Bulgaria, Rumania, Syria, Greece, and, possibly, other localities. English is the Pan-Slavonic language in America, as German is the Pan-Slavonic language on the Continent of Europe. The children are reared in our American public schools, as a rule, and it will be difficult to teach them their church services in the original tongue, under the prevailing conditions. An English version of the services is also desirable for the pupils in such parish schools as exist, where much attention is given to instruction in English.

I have used the Old Church-Slavonic books of the Russian Church, rather than the original Greek, because my work has been done, primarily, for the use of the Russian Church in America. Slight differences in arrangement and practice (not in dogma) have arisen between the Russian Church and the Greek Church, similar to those between the Church of England and the Protestant Episcopal Church in America. I have carefully compared everything with the original Greek.

My object has been to make a book which shall show, as precisely and clearly as possible, all the services in general use ; and that in a manner which shall be practical, not only for the ecclesiastics who are familiar with them and their congregations, but also for students of Liturgies and for travellers in the various lands where the Orthodox Church exists, as well as visitors to the churches in America and in numerous capitals and cities of Europe. To that end I have adopted an arrangement of my own devising. The difficulty and intricacy of the undertaking have been very great, owing to this arrangement and to other factors in the case. The treasure of services in the Orthodox-

Catholic Church is so vast and so rich that a complete version, within a reasonable, convenient compass, is utterly out of the question. Accordingly, I have selected those services which are generally used, and include, practically, all that are ordinarily required. For instance, I have omitted even the skeleton of such services as the Midnight Service (*Polunóshtchnitza*), Little Vespers, the Blessing of a Ship (at launching), and many of a private nature, such as the Blessing of a Pectoral Cross, the Blessing when a Well is dug, and so forth.

In the original the Litanies, Prayers, and certain of the Hymns in the unchanging framework of the Liturgies, Vespers, Compline, and Matins are printed consecutively. The movable portions and specially appointed Hymns are inserted according to the rubrics, at the proper points, from various other volumes.

I have combined the fixed parts and have arranged them in such way as to show what takes place simultaneously within the Sanctuary and outside. I have also indicated the usual variations during Pontifical Services, Feasts, Fasts, and so forth, selecting these and the most important representative Hymns for various occasions from the numerous volumes in which they are dispersed.

For the sake of convenience, I have combined the Liturgies of St. John Chrysostom, St. Basil the Great, and the Pontifical Liturgy, thus avoiding repetition, but keeping them as distinct, otherwise, as in the original.

I have been obliged to leave the service for Vespers almost in a skeleton state, as it appears in the original service books (instead of filling it out, as in the case of the other services), because of its very great flexibility, which causes immensely wide variations dependent upon the seasons — the proximity of Fasts, Feasts, and so forth.

If in actual practice it shall prove desirable to have the more infrequent services (or others, which are abbreviated here) in fuller form, I shall endeavour to complete them, either in a new edition of the present work, should there be a demand for it, or in special volumes. In that case I shall hope to take advantage of all competent and unprejudiced criticism for the perfecting of a book which has long been so near my heart; also of any new translation into the Old Church-Slavonic, or revised edition of the Russian Service Books. In several cases I have preferred for this volume the older, rather than the more recent, editions.

It has seemed practical and advisable to retain the Slavonic nomenclature for the parts of the service, in addition to the corresponding English terms. Had I introduced the original Greek terms also, great confusion would have ensued. But the omission of the Greek is unimportant. Most of the Slavonic terms are sufficiently near those from which they were borrowed to make comprehension perfectly easy. In the exceptional cases there is no difficulty in determining the correspondence. Thus the book will be as useful for a comprehension of the Greek services as of those in the Slavonic countries.

There have been two or three previous translations, from the Greek or Slavonic, of portions of these services, by other persons than myself. But in practice they have proved unsatisfactory, either in language or arrangement or both, or because neither singly nor combined do they furnish the services in that completeness which is imperatively necessary. My aim has been to remedy these defects.

A list of the service books which have entered into the composition of my volume will afford some idea of the difficulties of the problem.

(1) The *Sluzhébnik*, or Service Book, which contains most of the fixed portions of the Liturgies of St. John Chrysostom and St. Basil the Great, and of the Presanctified Gifts ; also the Litanies and Prayers of Vespers and Matins, together with the Graduals and Benedictions appropriate to all occasions. This is used by the Priest and the Choir.

(2) The *Tchásoslov*, or Book of the Hours (Horologion), which contains, in addition to the Hours and the Typical Psalms, those fixed portions of Vespers, Compline, Matins, Midnight Service, and so forth, which are used by the singers and the readers ; also a selection of Hymns for various occasions.

(3) The Pontifical Service Book (*Tchinovník*), which contains the fixed portions of the Liturgies above mentioned, as celebrated by a Bishop ; together with all the Offices of Ordination, ecclesiastical promotion, the blessing of an *Antimíns* (corporal), and so forth.

(4) The *Októikh*, or Book of the Eight Tones, which contains the Canons and certain of the Hymns used during Little and Great Vespers, Compline, Midnight Service, and Matins ; the Hymn for the Day and the Collect-Hymn from the Canons being used also at the Liturgy on the following morning. There are eight complete sets for each service mentioned, for every day in the week, all during one week being sung in the same Tone.

(5) The Monthly *Minéya*, in twelve volumes, which contain the order of services for all the fixed days in the year celebrating some special event in the history of the Faith or the Church, or commemorating a Saint or Saints. All the *Minéya* contain the Prayers for Vespers and Matins, while some have special Prayers for the Hours, Liturgies, Compline, and the Midnight Service.

(6) The volume known as the *Anthológion*, or *Prázditchnaya Minéya* (Festival *Minéya*) contains the Services for the Twelve Great Feasts.

(7) The Fasting Triódion (*Póstnaya Triód*) contains the variable portions of the services on the movable days which constitute the preparation for the Great Fast (Lent), and during the entire Great Fast. It is so called because the Canons have only Three Odes (or Theme-Songs), instead of the customary nine — practically eight — which are in the Book of the Eight Tones (*Októikh*).

(8) The *Tzvyetnáya Triód* (Flowery Triódion), or *Penticostárion*, contains the order of services during Easter-tide, beginning with Easter and ending with Pentecost, including the following day, — Whitsun

Monday, — which is the real Pentecost, or Day of the Spirit, Sunday being called Trinity Day.

(9) The *Apóstol* contains the Acts of the Apostles, the Epistles, and the Graduals, Introits and Anthems for the Feasts.

For their guidance in the use of these complicated volumes the ecclesiastics have a volume entitled the *Typikón, Ustáv*, or Rule, which provides regulations for all possible contingencies.

(10) The Great *Trébnik*, or Book of Needs, which contains all the Sacraments (except the Holy Communion and Ordination), — Baptism, Chrismation, Confession, Matrimony, Unction of the Sick; together with various other services, such as the Reception of Converts from various other Churches, the Tonsure of Monks, and so forth; also private services, such as Prayers at the Birth of a Child, the several Funeral Services, the Consecration of a Church, the Blessing of a New Dwelling, and so forth.

(11) A Book of *Te Deums* and Prayer Services (*Moliébny*) for different occasions.

(12) The *Irmológion*, which contains the Theme-Songs of the Canons, and certain Services of Song in honour of Our Lord, the Birth-giver of God, St. Nicholas, and others.

It will be seen that I have been confronted with the problem of rejection, as well as of judicious selection. I may add, that many things are done or said " by custom " which are not mentioned in the printed books. These I have included.

I have used the King James version of the Bible for the Scripture lessons ; and the Psalter contained in the Book of Common Prayer for the Psalms and Verses, with occasional exceptions, when the exigencies of the Slavonic version or adaptation to special cases or services required slight changes.

My book has been revised by a very able and thoroughly competent priest, to whom I am greatly indebted for indispensable services in supplying me with the unrecorded points of the ritual (established by usage) referred to above, and for making sure that I have accurately expressed the dogmas of his Church, and have properly carried out the complicated arrangement entailed by my plan for rendering the services intelligible.

I alone am personally responsible for everything : the suggestion that the book was needed, and the plan without which it would have been impossible; for the execution ; for occasional invented words, and for the language, in general and in particular, except in the case of the incomparable rendering of the Prayer of St. Chrysostom, which I have taken from the Episcopal Book of Common Prayer ; and of course the passages from the Bible, as above stated.

His Grace, the Most Reverend Tikhon, Archbishop of North America and the Aleutian Islands, has, by his deep interest and practical aid, been of inestimable service, and I thank him most warmly.

His High Excellency, K. P. Pobyedonostzeff, formerly Procurator of the Holy Synod of Russia, has for years past shown sympathetic and practical interest in my work, which has encouraged me during serious difficulties, and has been profoundly appreciated.

The Holy Synod of Russia has defrayed in part the cost of publishing this volume ; and his High Excellency Count Sergius I. Witte has contributed very liberally to this object.[1] I am sincerely grateful to them.

I wish, also, to express my obligations to the late mitred Archpriest, Father Feodor Pavlovitch, of Tzárskoe Seló, for many books and much important information. Memory Eternal!

It is fitting that I should commemorate last of all my book's first friend, — his Grace, the Most Reverend Archbishop Nicholas, formerly Bishop of Aleutia and Alaska, now appointed a member of the Council of the Empire, and of the Holy Synod. He was the first person to whom I imparted my intention of making this gift of love to his Church, the first to see and to approve of my systematic arrangement and of the manuscript. He gave me a complete set of the valuable Slavonic Service Books above mentioned, and others, and has constantly used his power to the fullest extent to render possible this publication, affording me, meanwhile, the invaluable help of his fervent sympathy in my long and difficult task.[2]

To all these friends I now say, with sincerest gratitude, in the language of the Church which they love so well, Many Years !

It is my earnest hope that this Service Book may not only be of some use to the Russian Church in North America, for the use of which, in public worship, it is designed, but that it may help the other Churches — especially those of the Anglican Communion, to one of which I am myself attached — to a right understanding of the Holy Orthodox-Catholic Apostolic Church of the East.

ISABEL F. HAPGOOD.

NEW YORK, October, 1906.

[1] The money came from the late Emperor Nicholas II.
[2] He died, at Petrograd, in the autumn of 1915, as Archbishop of Warsaw. Memory Eternal!

CONTENTS

xiv CONTENTS

THE FEASTS AND FASTS OF THE CHURCH

(The Church Year begins on September 1–14.)
The Feasts are divided into several categories, consisting of three principal grades, which, again, are subdivided into Lesser and Greater.
The TWELVE GREAT FEASTS *are classified as follows :*

THE FEASTS OF OUR LORD AND SAVIOUR JESUS CHRIST.

†THE FEAST OF FEASTS, EASTER.

a. The Nativity of our Lord Jesus Christ. December 25 (Jan. 7, N. S.).
b. The Manifestation of God (Epiphany). Jan. 6–19.
c. The Meeting of the Lord. Feb. 2–15. (The Purification of the Virgin.)
d. †Palm Sunday.
e. †The Ascension of our Lord Jesus Christ.
f. †Pentecost. (Trinity Sunday, and the Day of the Spirit.)
g. The Transfiguration of our Lord Jesus Christ. Aug. 6–19.
h. The Exaltation (Setting-up) of the Precious and Life-giving Cross. Sept. 14–27.

† Movable.

THE FEASTS OF OUR MOST HOLY LADY, THE BIRTH-GIVER OF GOD, AND EVER-VIRGIN MARY.

a. The Nativity of the Birth-giver of God. September 8 (21, N. S.).
b. The Presentation in the Temple of the Birth-giver of God. Nov. 21 (Dec. 4, N. S.).
c. The Annunciation of the Birth-giver of God. March 25 (April 7, N. S.).
d. The Falling-asleep (Assumption) of the Birth-giver of God. Aug. 15 (28, N. S.).

OTHER FEASTS AND HOLY DAYS

OF THE CHURCH.

Jan. 1–14. The Circumcision of our Lord Jesus Christ, and the Feast of St. Basil the Great.

Jan. 30 (Feb. 12, N. S.). The Feast of the Three Saints (Basil the Great, Gregory the Theologian, and John Chrysostom).

May 9–22. The Translation of the Relics of St. Nicholas, the Wonderworker, from Myra in Lycia to Bari in Italy, A. D. 1096.

May 11–24. The Feast of St. Cyril and St. Methodius, the Evangelizers of the Slavic races.

June 24 (July 7, N. S.). The Nativity of St. John the Forerunner.

June 29 (July 12, N. S.). The Feast of St. Peter and St. Paul.

July 15–27. The Feast of St. Vladímir, Equal-to-the-Apostles, the Evangelizer of Russia.

Aug. 29 (Sept. 11, N. S.). The Beheading of St. John the Baptist.

Sept. 26 (Oct. 9, N. S.). The Death of St. John the Divine.

Oct. 1–14. The Protection (Intercession) of the most holy Birth-giver of God.

Nov. 8–21. The Feast of St. Michael the Archangel, and of the other Bodiless Powers of Heaven.

Dec. 6–19. The Feast of St. Nicholas the Wonderworker.

In addition to the Feasts enumerated above, every day in the Church Calendar is a minor feast, dedicated to the memory of various Saints, Apostles, Martyrs, sacred events, and so forth.

The Designations of the Church Movable Seasons are as follows:

The Sunday of : The Publican and
  the Pharisee   Ten weeks
 The Prodigal Son   is   Nine weeks
 Meat Fast   Eight weeks
 Cheese Fast   Seven weeks   Before
   The Great Fast (Lent) begins   Seven weeks   Easter.
 Orthodoxy   Six weeks
 The Adoration of the Cross   is   Four weeks
   Lazarus's Saturday, and   One week
 Palm Sunday   are

EASTER.

The Sunday of : St. Thomas   One week
 The Myrrh-bearing Women   Two weeks
 The Impotent Man   Three weeks
 The Woman of Samaria   Four weeks
 The Blind Man   Five weeks
   Ascension Day   (Thursday)
 The Holy Fathers of the Coun- is   After
  cil of Nicæa   Six weeks   Easter.
 Trinity Day   Seven weeks
   The Day of the Spirit
    (Pentecost)   (Monday)
 All Saints   Eight weeks
   The Fast of St. Peter
    and St. Paul   (Monday)

THE FASTS AND SEASONS OF THE CHURCH

The Movable Feasts and two Fasts are regulated by the date upon which Easter falls. At times this coincides with its date in the Western Church. See the table for Easter, page **xxi.**

THE GREAT FAST (Lent) begins on Monday; not, as in the Western Church, on Ash Wednesday. (There is no Ash Wednesday.) It lasts for forty-eight days. As a chieftain, before the battle, encourages his warriors with wise and timely words, so the Church prepares us in advance for feats of fasting and penitence, and then bids us to the performance of those feats. This preparation begins on the Sunday preceding that which is known in the Western Church as Septuagesima Sunday, and is called "The Sunday of the Publican and the Pharisee." Because pride, conceit of one's own righteousness, and scorn of his neighbour is the first and chiefest obstacle to repentance, the Church has appointed the condemnation of this sin as the theme of her hymns and readings on that day, taking the Gospel narrative of the Publican and the Pharisee as the key-note.

In like manner, the next week of preparation (coinciding with Septuagesima Sunday) is called after the Prodigal Son, and the sinner is reminded that, when he scrupulously examines his evil deeds, he will perceive how deeply he has offended God. Hence he is encouraged to repentance and confession. The Prodigal Son is made the theme of the hymns and readings for the day.

On the Saturday preceding the following Meat-fast Sunday a Requiem Liturgy is celebrated for all Orthodox believers departed this life, who are awaiting the Last Judgment. Therefore this Saturday is known as "Ancestors' Saturday."

On the Sunday corresponding to Sexagesima Sunday begins the Meat-fast Week. After this day no more meat may be eaten. The Second Coming of the Lord, founded upon the Lesson from the Gospel about the Last Judgment, is the special theme of this Sunday: in order that the sinner may not fall into carelessness concerning his salvation through too secure a trust in the ineffable loving-kindness of God, but may call to mind that the Lord God is also a righteous Judge.

After the Sunday (corresponding to Quinquagesima) on which begins the Cheese Fast, no more cheese, eggs, butter, or milk may be eaten. The services of this Sunday aim to impress upon us that only by strict abstinence can we hope to recover that Paradise which Adam lost through the lack of abstinence. Therefore Adam, fallen and banished, is the special theme of the Church. It is customary on this day to ask and accord mutual forgiveness, and to effect mutual reconciliation. This custom is founded on the words of Jesus Christ in the Gospel lesson for the day: "For if ye forgive men their trespasses, your heavenly Father will also forgive you." Hence it is generally called "Forgiveness Sunday."

More reverences to the earth are appointed for the Great Fast (Lent) than for the services at other seasons, and the penitential character of the Offices is augmented. In the songs and prayers the moan of the contrite soul, bitterly bewailing its sins, is audible. The first week is the most severe of all as to restrictions upon food and drink : and the Offices have less of a triumphal and festival character than during the remaining weeks. Hence, during the Fast the full Liturgy is celebrated only on Saturday and on Sunday, while on the remaining days the Liturgy of the Presanctified Gifts is used. The strictest fasting is prescribed, although the Orthodox Church usually prescribes abstinence during all fasts, not only from meat, but also from cheese, eggs, milk, butter, and so forth.

On the evenings of Monday, Tuesday, Wednesday, and Thursday of the first week of the Great Fast, the Great Canon — the Penitential Canon — of St. Andrew of Crete is read.

The first Sunday in the Great Fast is known as "Orthodoxy Sunday," and thereon is celebrated the triumph of the Church over the Iconoclasts, and the reëstablishment of reverence for Holy Pictures (Images — *Ikóni*), in the year 842 ; as also the victory of the Church over other heresies. In some Cathedral Churches the *Office of Orthodoxy* is celebrated by the Bishop before the Divine Liturgy, or near the end thereof. In this Office athletes and champions of Orthodoxy are extolled, and Anathema is proclaimed upon their opponents.

On the third Sunday, and during the week which follows, is celebrated the Adoration of the Holy Cross, which is brought forth from the Sanctuary for the refreshment and strengthening of the faithful.

On the evening of Saturday in the Fifth Week is chanted the Canticle (*Akáfist*) of the most holy Birth-giver of God, in especial commemoration of her aid during two assaults from the Saracens upon Constantinople, in the years 673 and 716.

On the Saturday before Palm Sunday the Church commemorates the resurrection of Lazarus, wherein the Lord Jesus showed forth His divine might to the people before His suffering and death ; thus assuring them of His own Resurrection, and of the universal Resurrection of all the dead. On the Eve of Lazarus's Saturday the Great Fast proper (called "the Forty Days ") comes to an end, and on the Monday next following the "Fast of Christ's Passions " begins, lasting until Easter.

OTHER FASTS.

On Monday after the Sunday of All Saints, which follows Pentecost, begins the Fast of St. Peter and St. Paul, ending on June 29 (July 12, N. S.). The length of this fast is regulated by the date of Easter and of Pentecost ; and therefore it varies from two weeks to five weeks and five days.

The Fast which precedes the Feast of the Falling-asleep of the Holy Birth-giver of God (called "The Assumption" in the Western Church), on August 15–28, begins on August 1–14.

The Feast of the Exaltation of the Cross (the Setting-up), that of the Beheading of St. John the Forerunner, and the Eve of the Baptism of Christ (Epiphany), are reckoned as fasts. (See the Table, for the dates).

The Fast preparatory to Christmas, corresponding to Advent, is called "The Christmas Fast," and begins on November 15–28.

In addition to these Chief Fasts and the Great Fast, all Wednesdays and Fridays are fast-days, except during what are known as the "compact weeks;" from Christmas to the Eve (Fast) of the Epiphany; the Week between the Sunday of the Publican and the Pharisee and the Sunday of the Prodigal Son; Meat-fast Week, when cheese, eggs, and milk are permitted; the Bright Easter week; and the week preceding the Fast of St. Peter and St. Paul.

The joyous character of the Offices at the great Feast of Feasts, Easter, can be seen on page 226.

The second Sunday after Easter Day is called St. Thomas's Week, or "Anti-Paskha," from the Gospel Lesson for the day, and commemorates the appearance of the Lord to His disciples after the Resurrection, and the viewing of His wounds by Thomas.

The third Sunday after Easter is called after the Myrrh-bearing Women, who witnessed the burial and resurrection of Christ. And with them are commemorated Joseph of Arimathea and Nicodemus. Here, as on the Sunday which precedes and the Sundays which follow, the special title is derived from the Gospel Lesson for the day.

On the fourth Sunday is commemorated the Impotent Man whom Christ healed at the Pool of Bethesda.

The Lesson for the fifth Sunday, about the Woman of Samaria, shows Jesus Christ as One who knows the secrets of the heart, and as the true Messiah.

The Sunday of the Blind Man (the sixth after Easter) commemorates the healing by Christ of the man who was born blind.

Ascension Day falls on the following Thursday, and, as in the Western Church, is followed, ten days later, by the Feast of Pentecost. But what is called Whit-Sunday in the Western Church is Trinity Sunday in the Eastern Church, and the next day is The Day of the Holy Spirit (or Ghost), that is Pentecost.

The seventh Sunday after Easter is the Day of the Holy Fathers of the Council of Nicæa.

The first Sunday after Pentecost is All Saints' Day.

TONES.

There are eight Plain Chants, or Tones. During the Bright Easter week the Tone changes in regular order every day. On the second Sunday after Trinity Sunday (Pentecost), and during the week which follows, the First Tone is used, with its appointed Gradual (*Prokímen*), Canon, Hymns (*Tropari*), Verses (*Stikhéra of the Stikhóvni*), Hymns to the holy Birth-giver of God (*Bogoróditchni*, or *Dogmátiki*), Collect-Hymn (*Kondák*), and so forth. Thereafter the Tone changes on each successive Sunday, until all eight Tones have been used. On the tenth Sunday after Pentecost, the First Tone is used again; and so on, throughout the year.

A TABLE TO FIND EASTER DAY

Easter Day, on which all the Movable Feasts and Holy-days depend, is the first Sunday after the Full Moon which happens upon or next after the Twenty-first of March; and if the Full Moon happen upon a Sunday, Easter Day is the Sunday after. This is the same rule which is used in the Western Church, but Easter Day does not always coincide in the Holy Catholic Church of the East with that Feast in the Western Church. The Eastern Church still observes the rule laid down by the Council of Nicæa (A. D. 325), and now disregarded by the Western Church, that the Christian Easter shall never either precede or coincide with the Jewish Passover, but must always follow it. Easter cannot fall earlier than March 23, O. S., or later than April 25, O. S. The Eastern Church still uses the Julian Calendar, which, since March 1, 1901, has been thirteen days behind the Gregorian Calendar.

The years in which the Easter Feast falls on the same day in the Eastern and the Western Churches are indicated by a cross in the following Table. The Full Moon used for the purposes of the Easter reckoning is the Fourteenth Day of a Lunar Month reckoned according to the ancient Ecclesiastical computation, and not the real Astronomical Full Moon.

YEARS	NEW STYLE	OLD STYLE	YEARS	NEW STYLE	OLD STYLE
†1906	April 15	April 2	1926	May 2	April 19
1907	May 5	22	1927	April 24	11
1908	April 26	13	1928	15	2
†1909	11	March 29	1929	May 5	22
1910	May 1	April 18	†1930	April 20	7
1911	April 23	10	1931	12	March 30
†1912	7	March 25	1932	May 1	April 18
1913	27	April 14	†1933	April 16	3
1914	19	6	1934	8	March 26
†1915	4	March 22	1935	28	April 15
†1916	23	April 10	†1936	12	March 30
1917	15	2	1937	May 2	April 19
1918	May 5	22	1938	April 24	11
1919	April 20	7	†1939	9	March 27
1920	11	March 29	1940	28	April 15
1921	May 1	April 18	1941	20	7
†1922	April 16	3	†1942	5	March 23
1923	8	March 26	†1943	25	April 12
1924	27	April 14	1944	16	3
1925	19	6	1945	May 6	23

YEARS	NEW STYLE	OLD STYLE	YEARS	NEW STYLE	OLD STYLE
†1946	April 21	April 8	†1974	April 14	April 1
1947	13	March 31	1975	May 3	20
1948	May 2	April 19	1976	April 25	12
1949	April 24	11	†1977	10	March 28
†1950	9	March 27	1978	30	April 17
1951	29	April 16	1979	22	9
1952	20	7	1980	6	March 24
†1953	5	March 23	1981	26	April 13
1954	25	April 12	1982	18	5
1955	17	4	1983	May 8	25
1956	May 6	23	†1984	April 22	9
†1957	April 21	8	1985	14	1
1958	13	March 31	1986	May 3	20
1959	May 3	April 20	†1987	April 19	6
†1960	April 17	4	1988	10	March 28
1961	9	March 27	1989	30	April 17
1962	29	April 16	†1990	15	2
†1963	14	1	1991	7	March 25
1964	May 3	20	1992	26	April 13
1965	April 25	12	1993	18	5
†1966	10	March 28	1994	May 1	18
1967	30	April 17	1995	April 23	10
1968	21	8	1996	14	1
1969	13	March 31	1997	27	14
1970	26	April 13	1998	19	6
1971	18	5	1999	11	March 29
1972	9	27	2000	May 1	April 17
1973	29	16			

A TABLE OF THE SELECTIONS OF PSALMS

1. Psalms i.–ix.	8. Psalms lvi.–lxv.	15. Psalms cvi.–cx.
2. ix.–xviii.	9. lxv.–lxxi.	16. cx.–cxix.
3. xviii.–xxv.	10. lxxi.–lxxviii.	17. cxix.
4. xxv.–xxxiii.	11. lxviii.–lxxxvi.	18. cxx.–cxxxv.
5. xxxiii.–xxxviii.	12. lxxxvi.–xcii.	19. cxxxv.–cxliv.
6. xxxviii.–xlvii.	13. xcii.–cii.	20. cxliv.–cl.
7. xlvii.–lvi.	14. cii.–cvi.	

The whole Psalter is read through every week. During seasons of more fervent devotion, as in the Great Fast, it is read through twice every week. On Feasts less is read. On Easter Day and during Easter Week none is read.

A TABLE OF LESSONS OF HOLY SCRIPTURE

TO BE READ AT MATINS AND THE LITURGY, ON SUNDAYS, THROUGH-
OUT THE YEAR. THE PORTIONS OF SCRIPTURE APPOINTED FOR THE
EPISTLES AND GOSPELS

EASTER.   **Liturgy:** Epistle: Acts i. 1–8.   Gospel: John i. 1–17.
            Vespers: John xx. 19–25.

MATINS	THE LITURGY	
THE GOSPEL: (Saturday Evening.)	EPISTLE	GOSPEL
For the		
First Week after Easter Matt. xxviii. 16–20	Acts v. 12–20	John xx. 19–31
Second Mark xvi. 9–20	Acts vi. 1–7	Mark xv. 43–xvi. 8
Third Luke xxiv. 1–12	Acts ix. 32–42	John v. 1–15
Fourth John xx. 1–10	Acts xi. 19–26; 29–30	John iv. 5–42
Fifth John xx. 11–18	Acts xvi. 16–34	John ix. 1–38
Sixth John xxi. 1–14	Acts xx. 16–18; 28–36	John xvii. 1–13
Seventh John xx. 19–23.	Acts ii. 1–11	John vii. 37–52; viii. 12
First Week of All Saints Matt. xxviii. 16–20	Heb. xi. 33–xii. 2	Matt. x. 32–33; 37–38; xix. 27–30
Second Mark xvi. 1–8	Rom. ii. 10–16	Matt. iv. 18–23
Third Mark xvi. 9–20	Rom. v. 1–10	Matt. vi. 22–33
Fourth Luke xxiv. 1–12	Rom. vi. 18–23	Matt. viii. 5–13
Fifth Luke xxiv. 12–35	Rom x. 1–10	Matt. viii. 28–ix. 1
Sixth Luke xxiv. 36–53	Rom. xii. 6–14	Matt. ix. 1–8
Seventh John xx. 1–10	Rom. xiii. 1–7	Matt. ix. 27–35
Eighth John xx. 11–18	1 Cor. i. 10–18	Matt. xiv. 14–22
Ninth John xx. 19–31	1 Cor. iii. 9–17	Matt. xiv. 22–34
Tenth John xxi. 1–14	1 Cor. iv. 9–16	Matt. xviii. 14–23
Eleventh John xxi. 15–25	1 Cor. ix. 2–12	Matt. xviii. 23–35
Twelfth Matt. xxviii. 16–20	1 Cor. xv. 1–11	Matt. xix. 16–26
Thirteenth Mark xvi. 1–8	1 Cor. xvi. 13–24	Matt. xxi. 33–42
Fourteenth Mark xvi. 9–20	2 Cor. i. 21–ii. 4	Matt. xxii. 1–14
Fifteenth Luke xxiv. 1–12	2 Cor. iv. 6–15	Matt. xxii. 35–46
Sixteenth Luke xxiv. 12–35	2 Cor. vi. 1–10	Matt. xxv. 14–30
Seventeenth Luke xxiv. 36–53	2 Cor. vi. 16–vii. 1	Matt. xv. 21–28
Eighteenth John xx. 1–10	2 Cor. ix. 6–11	Luke v. 1–11
Nineteenth John xx. 11–18	2 Cor. xi. 31–xii. 9	Luke vi. 31–36
Twentieth John xx. 19–31	Gal. i. 11–19	Luke vii. 11–16
Twenty-first John xxi. 1–14	Gal. ii. 16–20	Luke viii. 5–15
Twenty-second John xxi. 15–25	Gal. vi. 11–18	Luke xvi. 19–31
Twenty-third Matt. xxviii. 16–20	Eph. ii. 4–10	Luke viii. 26–39
Twenty-fourth Mark xvi. 1–8	Eph. ii. 14–22	Luke viii. 41–56
Twenty-fifth Mark xvi. 9–20	Eph. iv. 1–6	Luke x. 25–37
Twenty-sixth Luke xxiv. 1–12	Eph. v. 9–19	Luke xii. 16–21
Twenty-seventh Luke xxiv. 12–35	Eph. vi. 10–17	Luke xiii. 10–17
Twenty-eighth Luke xxiv. 36–53	Col. i. 12–18	Luke xiv. 16–24
Twenty-ninth John xx. 1–10	Col. iii. 4–11	Luke xvii. 12–19
Thirtieth John xx. 11–18	Col. iii. 12–16	Luke xviii. 18–27
Thirty-first John xx. 19–31	1 Tim. i. 15–17	Luke xviii. 35–43
Thirty-second John xxi. 1–14	1 Tim. iv. 9–15	Luke xix. 1–10

MATINS	THE LITURGY	
THE GOSPEL	EPISTLE	GOSPEL
Sunday before the Exaltation of the Cross	Gal. vi. 11–18	John iii. 13–17
Sunday after the Exaltation of the Cross	Gal. ii. 16–20	Mark viii. 34–38; ix. 1
Sunday before Christmas	Heb. xi. 9–10, 17–40	Matt. i. 1–25
Sunday after Christmas	Gal. i. 11–19	Matt. ii. 13–23
Sunday before Epiphany	2 Tim. iv. 5–8	Mark i. 1–8
Sunday after Epiphany	Eph. iv. 7–13	Matt. iv. 12–17
Week of Publican and Pharisee	2 Tim. iii. 10–15	Luke xviii. 10–14
Week of Prodigal Son	1 Cor. vi. 12–20	Luke xv. 11–32
Meat-fast Week	1 Cor. viii. 8–ix. 2	Matt. xxv. 31–46
Cheese-fast Week	Rom. xiii. 11–xiv. 4	Matt. vi. 14–21
Great Fast (Lent): First Week	Heb. xi. 24–26, 32–xii. 2	John i. 43–51
Second Week	Heb. i. 10; ii. 3; vii. 26–viii. 2	Mark ii. 1–12 / John x. 9–16
Third Week	Heb. iv. 14–v. 6	Mark viii. 34–ix. 1
Fourth Week	Heb. vi. 13–20	Mark ix. 17–31
	Eph. v. 9–19	Matt. iv. 25–v. 12
Fifth Week	Heb. ix. 11–14	Mark x. 32–45
	Gal. iii. 23–29	Luke vii. 36–50

(The Gospels in the regular Weekly Sequence of eleven Lessons — as shown above — beginning with All Saints.)

PASSION-WEEK:	MATINS	LITURGY
Monday	Matt. xxi. 18–43	Matt. xxiv. 3–15
Tuesday	Matt. xxii. 15–23; 39	Matt. xxiv. 36–xxvi. 2
Wednesday	John xii. 17–50	Matt. xxvi. 6–16

For Thursday, Friday, and Saturday, see the Special Services for these days.

EPISTLES AND GOSPELS FOR REQUIEM SERVICES

LITURGY

	Epistles	*Gospels*
Monday	Rom. xiv. 6–9	John v. 17–24
Tuesday	1 Cor. xv. 39–57	John v. 24–30
Wednesday	2 Cor. v. 1–10	John vi. 35–39
Thursday	1 Cor. xv. 20–28	John vi. 40–44
Friday	1 Cor. xv. 46–57	John vi. 48–54
Saturday	1 Thess. iv. 13–17	John v. 24–30

A TABLE OF LESSONS FOR THE TWELVE GREAT FEASTS

NATIVITY OF THE MOST HOLY MOTHER OF OUR LORD.

Matins. Luke i. 39–49, 56.   **Liturgy.** *Epistle.* Phil. ii. 5–11.
                                              Gospel. Luke x. 38–42; xi. 27, 28.

EXALTATION OF THE HOLY AND LIFE-GIVING CROSS.

Matins. John xii. 28–36.   **Liturgy.** *Epistle.* 1 Cor. i. 18–24.
                                              Gospel. John xix. 5–11, 13–20, 25–28, 30–35.

PRESENTATION OF THE VIRGIN.

Matins. Luke i. 39–49, 56.   **Liturgy.** *Epistle.* Heb. ix. 1–7.
                                              Gospel. Luke x. 38–42, xi. 27–28.

CHRISTMAS: THE NATIVITY OF JESUS CHRIST.

Matins. Matt. i. 18–25   **Liturgy.** *Epistle.* Gal. iv. 4–7.
                                              Gospel. Matt. ii. 1–12.

EPIPHANY.

Matins. Mark i. 9–11.   **Liturgy.** *Epistle.* Titus ii. 11–14; iii. 4–7.
                                              Gospel. Matt. iii. 13–17.

PRESENTATION OF CHRIST IN THE TEMPLE (PURIFICATION OF THE VIRGIN).

Matins. Luke ii. 25–32.   **Liturgy.** *Epistle.* Heb. vii. 7–17.
                                              Gospel. Luke ii. 22–40.

THE ANNUNCIATION.

Matins. Luke i. 39–49, 56.   **Liturgy.** *Epistle.* Heb. ii. 11–18.
                                              Gospel. Luke i. 24–38.

THE TRANSFIGURATION

Matins. Luke ix. 28–36.   **Liturgy.** *Epistle.* 2 Peter i. 10–19.
                                              Gospel. Matt. xvii. 1–9.

FALLING-ASLEEP (ASSUMPTION) OF THE VIRGIN.

Matins. Luke i. 39–49, 56.   **Liturgy.** *Epistle.* Phil. ii. 5–11.
                                              Gospel. Luke x. 38–42; xi. 27, 28.

ENTRANCE OF THE LORD INTO JERUSALEM (PALM SUNDAY).

Matins. Matt. xxi. 1–11, 15–17.   **Liturgy.** *Epistle.* Phil. iv. 4–9.
                                              Gospel. John xii. 1–18.

THE ASCENSION OF THE LORD.

Matins. Mark xvi. 9–20.   **Liturgy.** *Epistle.* Acts i. 1–12.
                                              Gospel. Luke xxiv. 36–53.

HOLY PENTECOST (TRINITY DAY, AND THE DAY OF THE SPIRIT).

Matins. Trinity Day. John xx. 9–23.   **Liturgy.** *Epistle.* Acts ii. 1–11.
Day of the Spirit.   *Gospel.* Luke xvi. 15–18; xvii. 1–4.
                                              Epistle. Eph. v. 9–19.
                                              Gospel. Matt. xviii. 10–20.

TABLE OF EPISTLES AND GOSPELS FOR THE SAINTS IN GENERAL

SERVICE OF THE MOST HOLY BIRTH-GIVER.

Matins.

Gospel. Luke i. 39-49, 56.

Liturgy.

Epistle. Phil. ii. 5-11; *or* Heb. ix. 1-7.
Gospel. Luke x. 38-42; xi. 27, 28.

SERVICE OF ALL THE HOLY BODILESS POWERS OF HEAVEN.

Liturgy.

Epistle. Heb. ii. 2-10.

Gospel. Luke x. 16-21; *or* Matt. xiii. 24-30, 36-43.

GENERAL SERVICE OF THE HOLY PROPHETS.

Epistle. 1 Cor. xiv. 20-25; *or* Heb. vi. 13-20; *or* James v. 10-20.

Gospel. Matt. xxiii. 29-39; *or* Luke xi. 47-54.

GENERAL SERVICE OF THE HOLY APOSTLES.

Epistle. 1 Cor. iv. 9-16.

Gospel. Luke x. 1-15; *or* x. 16, 21.

SERVICE OF A SAINTED PRELATE.

Epistle. Heb. vii. 26-viii. 2.

Gospel. John x. 9-16.

GENERAL SERVICE OF SAINTED PRELATES.

Matins.

Gospel. John x. 1-9.

Liturgy.

Epistle. Heb. xiii. 17-21.
Gospel. Matt. v. 14-19; *or* John x. 9-16.

SERVICE OF VENERABLE SAINTS, AND OF FOOLS FOR CHRIST'S SAKE. (1 Cor. iv. 10.)

Liturgy.

Epistle. Gal. v. 22-vi. 2.

Gospel. Matt. xi. 27-30; *or* Luke vi. 17-23.

SERVICE OF A MARTYR.

Liturgy.

Epistle. 2 Tim. ii. 1-10.

Gospel. Luke xii. 2-12; *or* John xv. 17-xvi. 2.

GENERAL SERVICE OF MARTYRS.

Liturgy.

Epistle. Rom. viii. 28-39; *or* Heb. xi. 33-40.

Gospel. Matt. x. 16-22; *or* Luke xxi. 12-19.

SERVICE OF A MARTYRED PRIEST.

Liturgy.

Epistle. Heb. xiii. 7-16.

Gospel. Luke xii. 32-40.

GENERAL SERVICE OF MARTYRED PRIESTS.

Matins.

Epistle. Heb. v. 4-10; *or* Phil. iii. 20-iv. 3.

Liturgy.

Gospel. Luke vi. 17-23; *or* x. 22-24; *or* xiv. 25-35.

SERVICE OF A MARTYRED MONK OR NUN.

Liturgy.

Epistle. 2 Tim. i. 8-18.

Gospel. Mark viii. 34-ix. 1.

GENERAL SERVICE OF MARTYRED MONKS OR NUNS.
Liturgy.

Epistle. Rom. viii. 28–39.   *Gospel.* Matt. x. 32–33, 37, 38; xix. 27–30; *or* Luke xii. 8–12.

GENERAL SERVICE OF HOLY WOMEN MARTYRS.
Liturgy.

Epistle. 2 Cor. vi. 1–10; *or* Gal. iii. 23–29.   *Gospel.* Matt. xv. 21–28; *or* Mark v. 24–34.

GENERAL SERVICE OF MARTYRED NUNS.
Liturgy.

Epistle. Gal. iii. 23–29.   *Gospel.* Matt. xxv. 1–13; *or* Luke vii. 36–50.

SERVICE OF CONFESSORS.
· Liturgy.

Epistle. Eph. vi. 10–17.   *Gospel.* Luke xii. 8–12.

SERVICE OF UNMERCENARIES.
Liturgy.

Epistle. 1 Cor. xii. 27–xii. 8.   *Gospel.* Matt. x. 1, 5–8.

THE SYMBOLISM OF THE CHURCH *

The Exterior. A Temple has sometimes a single dome, sometimes many domes. One dome serves as a symbol of the One Head of the Church, Jesus Christ. Three domes typify the three Persons of the Holy Trinity. Five are symbolical of our Lord Jesus Christ and the Four Evangelists.

Each dome — and where there is no dome the apex of the Temple — is crowned by a Cross, the emblem of victory.

Bells. A Belfry is generally constructed in connection with the church, either in a separate tower or in one of the domes. The direct use of the belfry is to summon the faithful to worship, although the rubric concerning the use of the different bells and their manner of chiming and pealing is very detailed and complicated. It is impossible to make it clear, in a foreign language, to those who are not personally acquainted with the beautiful Russian bells, which are treated in a peculiar way, wholly unknown in the Western Church. They are rung at certain points in the service, in order that the faithful who, for any reason, are not in church, may unite their prayers with those of the worshippers in the Temple at the most solemn moments. At Matins, for example, they are rung before the Gospel is read, while the lights are being kindled, and the choir is singing: Praise ye the Lord. At the Divine Liturgy one bell is rung while the Holy Gifts are being consecrated.

The Interior. The Temple is usually built in the form of a ship (the ship of salvation), or of a cross (the emblem of salvation). The Temple is divided into four parts: 1. The Sanctuary (Altar), beyond the Image-screen (*Ikonostás*). 2. The pro-

Altar

* These explanations are derived chiefly from the valuable work of Archpriest Konstantín Nikólsky: *An Aid to the Study of the Orthodox Church.* St. Petersburg, 1894.

longation of the Sanctuary platform outside the Image-screen, called the *Soleá*, which consists of : (a) the *Amvón*, or Tribune, which is the portion immediately in front of the Holy Door, in the centre of the Screen, and (b) the railed *Klíros*, or places for the two choirs, on either side of the Amvón. 3. The Body of the church. 4. The Porch (*Pritvór*).

The Sanctuary must be built, except when that is impossible, at the eastern end of the church.

The Altar (*Prestól*) represents the throne of God in heaven, and the

Corporal

Lord God Almighty himself is present thereon. It also represents the tomb of Christ, since his Body is placed thereon.

The first covering of the Altar, the white linen *Sratchítza*, represents the winding-sheet in which the body of our Lord was wrapped. The upper Altar-cloth (*Indítia*), of rich and brilliant material, represents the glory of God's throne. Both cloths cover the Altar to the ground.

On the Altar is placed the Corporal (*Antimíns*), a silken (formerly a linen) cloth, having upon it the representation of the Deposition of Christ in the tomb and the four Evangelists. This is spread out only in the Divine Liturgy, at the beginning of the Liturgy of the Faithful, and is folded up again as soon as that is finished. If any accident should happen to the holy Altar, the Holy Oblation can be made upon the Corporal alone, in an unconsecrated building or suitable place. In this Corporal (*Antimíns*), or Vice-Altar, are placed relics of the Saints. Other relics are placed under and in the Altar itself, in a specially prepared coffer; because the blood of the Martyrs, after that of Christ himself, serves as the foundation of the Church. And also because, in the early days of Christianity, the Holy Eucharist was celebrated in the Catacombs, on the tombs of the Martyrs.

Dikíri   Trikíri

Under the Corporal, and upon the upper Altar-cloth is placed a square of fine linen or rich material called the *Ilitón*, which symbolizes the swaddling-clothes wherein the Lord was wrapped after his birth; and also the winding-sheet wherein his body was enveloped in the tomb, as the Altar represents the gravestone.

Behind the Altar a seven-branched candelabra is usually placed (seven being the customary sacred number); and, sometimes a large Cross, for carrying in processions.

The Book of the Holy Gospels, being the Word of God, is laid upon the Altar, to denote that God himself is mystically present thereon; and the Cross stands on the Altar as upon the place where is celebrated the unbloody sacrifice offered up to God.

As the Altar represents the sepulchre of the Lord, an Ark (*Kovtchég*) is set thereon, being the Tabernacle in which are placed the Holy Gifts, the Body and Blood of Christ reserved for the sick, and (during the Great Fast — Lent) for the Liturgy of the Presanctified Gifts.

Upon the Altar is kept the Holy Chrism for Chrismation after Baptism. Tapers are placed upon the Altar to typify the light of Christ, which illumines the world; and, at Pontifical Services, the double and triple branched candlesticks (*Dikíri, Trikíri*) — representing, respectively, the dual nature of Christ (human and divine) and the Holy Trinity — wherewith the

Table of Oblation

Sacramental
Fan

Bishop bestows his blessing on the people. It is strictly forbidden to place anything whatsoever on the Altar save the objects which are here enumerated. A sponge is usually placed beside the Corporal, for the more careful brushing off of the particles from the Paten into the Chalice. In some places a Canopy (*Syén*) is suspended over the Altar, to represent the heavens outspread above the earth, upon which was offered up the sacrifice for the sins of the world.

Behind the Altar is the High Place (*Górnoye Myésto*), an elevation upon which stands the Bishop's throne. At certain times during the service the Bishop sits thereon, representing the King of Glory. On either side of the "High Place" are seats for those who celebrate with the Bishop, and represent the Apostles and their successors. At either side of the "High Place," during Pontifical services, are placed the Sacramental Fans (*Rípidi*), representing the six-winged Seraphim, with which the Holy Gifts are fanned to keep away insects.

The Credence (Table of Oblation — *Zhértvennik*) is in the northern part of the Sanctuary, and on it the Holy Gifts are prepared for consecration.

Paten

Star-Cover

Altar-Bread

For their preparation and for communicating them the following sacred vessels and implements are used :

The Paten (*Dískos*), for the bread; the Star-cover (*Zvyez-dítza*), which supports the Veil above the Paten so that it may not touch the Holy Body; the Chalice (*Potír*), for the wine; the Spear (*Kopyó*), with which the particles are taken from the Altar-breads (*Prosforí*), and represents the spear with which the Saviour's side was pierced; the sacramental Spoon (*Lzhítza*), with which the Holy Body and Blood are administered to the laity; the Sponge (*Gúbka*)

Chalice   Spear   Spoon

with which the Chalice is wiped out at the end of the Communion; three Veils (*Pokróvy*); two smaller, for covering the Paten and Chalice, and one which is called the Air (*Vózdukh*), for covering both Paten and Chalice; the Ladle (*Kovsh*), in which the holy tepid water and wine are offered (together with portions of the bread), to the communicants, after they have received the Holy Gifts; two salvers for the Altar-breads.

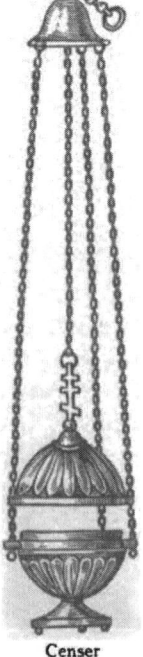

Ladle

The Censer (*Kadílo*), which, with the incense placed therein, is symbolical of the gifts offered by the Wise Men to the infant Christ, — gold, frankincense, and myrrh, — is also necessary for most services.

The southern side of the Sanctuary is usually appointed as the Repository (*Diákonnik*) for the vestments, church books, and the vessels used in the divine service.

The Sanctuary is separated from the choir-place and the body of the Temple by a solid Image-screen (*Ikonostás*), which corresponds to the chancel-rail in the Western Church. Three doors give access through it to the different parts of the Sanctuary above mentioned.

The central opening is called the Royal Gate (*Tzárskiya Vratá*), because through it, at the Divine Liturgy, the King of Glory comes forth to feed his faithful people with his own Divine Body and Blood; or the Holy Door (*Svyatýa Vratá*), because the Mystery of the Eucharist is celebrated in the Sanctuary, and through this door (or gate) the Holy Gifts are brought forth. Unordained men are not permitted to pass through it. No woman may enter the Sanctuary at any time.

The opening and closing of the Holy Door, at different points of the various services, signify several things: sometimes the opening of the gates of Paradise; sometimes the throwing open of the entrance into the Kingdom of Heaven. The Entrances and Exits through it of the clergy symbolize the progress to and from those places where the Saviour of the world abode; since the priest, at different points, represents the Saviour himself or the Angel of God proclaiming the Resurrection of Christ; while the Deacon represents the Angel of the Lord, or John the Baptist.

The Curtain inside the Holy Door is drawn or withdrawn at appointed times during divine service. The

Censer

Image-screen (*Ikonostás*) portrays those who dwell in heaven. In the Image-screen are the Holy Pictures (Images — *Ikóni*) of the Lord God magnified in the Trinity; of the most holy Birth-giver of our

Lord; of the Holy Angels, Prophets and Apostles, and other Saints of God; and presentments of sacred events which have happened for our salvation. The customary arrangement of the holy Images is as follows : On the right of the Holy Door is placed the image of the Saviour, and next it (or next

the south door, if that be next), the Image of the Temple, or of the Patron Saint of the Temple. On the left of the Holy Door is the Image of the holy Birth-giver of God. On the leaves of the Holy Door itself (which represents the Entrance into Heaven) is the Image of the Annunciation, that being the forefront of our salvation ; together with the Images of the Four Evangelists, who also, like the Archangel Gabriel, announced to the world the glad tidings of the Saviour.

Over the Holy Door is the Image (*Ikóna*) of the Last Supper ; because in the Sanctuary is celebrated the Mystery of the Eucharist, reminding us that those who wish to follow Christ and obtain entrance to the kingdom of heaven must be accounted worthy to partake of the Lord's Supper,

Banner

which is prepared within the Holy Door, and offered to the laity in front of that door.

On the northern and southern doors are depicted the messengers of God, the Angels, sent to serve those who desire to follow after salvation ; or holy Deacons, the types of the Angels, who have charge of those parts of the Sanctuary into which these doors lead.

At each *Kliros* (Choir-place) stands a holy Banner (*Khorúgv*); that is, a holy picture mounted upon a staff, typifying the victorious Banner of Christ's Church, which wages incessant warfare with the enemies of salvation.

In large churches, in line with the Images of the Saviour and the holy Birth-giver of God in the Image-screen, are placed Images of the more especially revered Saints. Above them, in the second row, are the Images of the Feasts of our Lord, and of the holy Birth-giver of God. In the third row are the Images of those Saints who, on earth as in heaven, were deemed worthy to be nearest to the Saviour, namely : Over the Image of the Last Supper is placed the Image of Jesus Christ himself, in royal or episcopal robes, having on his right hand the holy Birth-giver of God, and on his left St. John the Baptist. This Image is called the *Déisis* (Prayer), the Holy Mother and St. John being turned toward the Saviour in supplication ; and on either side it has the Images of the Apostles. In the next row are placed the Images of the Old Testament Saints,

— the Prophets : and among them is placed the holy Birth-giver of God with the Divine Child, who is from everlasting, and who was their hope, their consolation, and the subject of their prophecies.

Images and the fittings of the Temple are used in accordance with the command of God : Exodus xxv. 18–20; xxvi. 1, 31.*

The Body of the Church. The space extending from the Sanctuary platform (*Soleá*) to the Porch (*Pritvór*) is appointed for the lay worshippers, who generally stand throughout the service, — usually in two groups, — the men on the right and the women on the left. In this part of the church, during Pontifical services, in the centre there is placed a raised dais, called the *Káthedra*. Here the Bishop is vested, and here, also, he performs a portion of the service; and sometimes, even, the entire service, praying like a father surrounded by his children.

Winding-Sheet

In spacious churches, there is also placed, close to the Sanctuary platform, the Tomb for the Winding-sheet (*Plashtschanítza*); and a small table for Requiem services, with the Requiem-stand (*Panikhid-nik*),† with places for tapers and a vessel for grain.

The Vestibule (*Pritvór*), or inner porch, was appointed, in early times, for the Catechumens, or learners, and for penitents. Here they listened to exhortations and instruction, and here they prayed. The rubric decrees that the *Office for the Reception of Converts* shall be performed in this Vestibule. Several of the penitential Offices, also, are appointed to be said here, such as the *Litiyá* (a litany of fervent supplication, with oft-repeated " Lord, have mercy " in response) at Vespers.

Lights. Lights are always used during divine service, even though it be performed in full sunlight. This is done not only for illumination, but also to show that the Lord, who dwells in light ineffable, illumines the world with spiritual radiance ; to denote that the hearts of faithful believers are warmed by a flame of love toward God and his Saints ; and, also, to show forth spiritual joy and the triumph of the Church.

Wax and olive oil, as the purest of substances, and free from animal

---

* Concerning the use and significance of these Holy Images (*Ikóni*), see the Office for the Reception of Converts.

† See Appendix B, XII.

matter, are used for lighting before sacred things. Artificial light also is permitted, but only for illumination. The wax and oil are symbolical of the purity and sincerity of the gifts which provide them, made in the holy Name of God.

The lights in the Temple are kindled in accordance with the songs and services. The more vivid the joy of the Church in the Lord, the more solemn the service, the more numerous are the lights. On Great Feasts all the lights are not kindled at the beginning of the service, but at the approach of the most solemn hymns and readings. The rubrics on these points are detailed and precise. More lights are used at the Divine Liturgy than at the other services, as a rule.

Attitude. Only two attitudes are recognized as befitting the house of God : standing and kneeling. There are some moments of the service when sitting is proper. But usually it is tolerated only as a concession to physical weakness. On Sundays and Feast Days, with few exceptions, the rubric of the Church does not permit kneeling ; that is, reverences to the earth. From holy Easter Day until Pentecost (Trinity Sunday) no kneeling is appointed. The joy of the worshippers at that season is held to outweigh even their sense of lowly penitence for sin, which prompts to kneeling.

The Sign of the Cross is made with the thumb and the first two fingers of the right hand joined at the tips (the third and fourth fingers being closed on the palm), as a symbol of the Trinity, by touching the

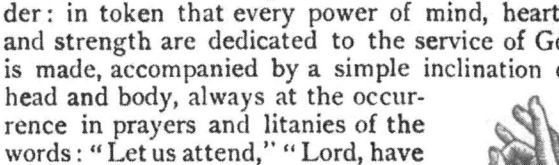

brow, the breast, the right shoulder and the left shoulder : in token that every power of mind, heart, soul and strength are dedicated to the service of God. It is made, accompanied by a simple inclination of the head and body, always at the occurrence in prayers and litanies of the words : " Let us attend," " Lord, have mercy," " Grant it, O Lord," " Come, and take up thine abode in us," " Let us pray to the Lord," and so forth.

The sign of the Cross, accompanied by a reverence to the very earth, is made when the following words occur : " Let us worship and fall down ; " " Let us give thanks unto the Lord ; " or when the singers sing, " Meet and right is it to adore thee," " We praise thee, we bless thee ; " " Our Father, who art in heaven ; " and when the holy Chalice is brought forth, during the Divine Liturgy, with the

Position of the fingers of the right hand in making the sign of the cross

Position of the fingers of the right hand for Bishops and Priests, in bestowing the benediction. The letters IC, XC, Jesus Christ, are formed

words : " Always, now, and ever, and unto ages of ages ; " " In the fear of God and with faith draw near."

A reverence, unaccompanied by the sign of the Cross, is made when the Priest pronounces the words, "Peace be with you all," "The grace of our Lord Jesus Christ be with you all," "The blessing of the Lord be upon you ;" or when he exclaims, " Bow your heads unto the Lord."

Bishops and Priests, in bestowing the Benediction, hold the fingers in such a manner as to represent the Greek letters IC, XC — the first and last letters of Jesus Christ.

Incense. The Holy Images (*Ikóni*), the Holy Things, and the people who are present at the divine service, are honoured with incense. The censing before the Holy Door signifies the desire of the worshippers that their prayers shall be borne up to the throne of God, as the incense from the censer is wafted heavenward ; and that their petitions shall be well-pleasing to God like fragrant incense. The censing of the people is symbolical of the grace of the Holy Spirit, which is shed abroad everywhere, upon all men. The censer (*Kadílo*) represents the Divine Ember, even Christ.

For the special significance of the censing at different points of the services, see the Explanations provided in Appendix B.

SACERDOTAL VESTMENTS.

Reader. A short Tunic (*Felón*), which barely covers the shoulders, is put upon the Reader when he is set apart by the Bishop, and (at the

present time) is rarely worn except upon that day. It symbolizes his coming under the yoke of the Priesthood, and his dedication to the service of God. His usual vestment is a Dalmatic (*Stikhár*).

Sub-Deacon and **Deacon.** The Dalmatic (*Stikhár*) and the Stole (*Orár*). The Dalmatic, a long, straight vestment with wide sleeves, which covers the whole person, is called "the robe of salvation and the garment of joy." It is symbolical

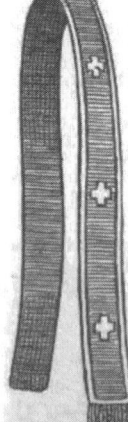

Dalmatic (*Stikhár*)   Stole (*Orár*)

of a pure and tranquil conscience, a spotless life, and the spiritual joy in the Lord which flows therefrom, in him who wears it. The Stole is a long, wide band of material which is sometimes worn over the left

shoulder, sometimes crossed upon the breast and back, in the case of the
Deacon. The Sub-Deacon wears his Stole always crossed, for convenience in the fulfilment of his duties. But the Deacon binds his Stole
about him in the form of a cross shortly before the Holy Gifts are consecrated, thus typifying the wings of the Angels who serve about the
Altar, as the Deacons themselves typify the Cherubim and Seraphim.
Sometimes the Angelic song, "Holy, Holy, Holy," is embroidered
upon the Stole. The Stole is bound about the Sub-Deacon in the form
of a cross at his Ordination, as a symbol that, through the meekness
and continence of his members and the purity of his heart, he is to
put upon him the robe of purity. The Deacon wears, also, the Cuffs

Cuffs

Zone, or Girdle   Cassock   Stole (*Epitrakhíl*)

(*Pórutchi*), for convenience during the service, and to remind him that
he must not put his trust in his own strength alone, but in the right hand
of the Lord, the Almighty and merciful God, and in His strength and aid.

Priests. The Priest's *stikhár*, or cassock (*Podríznik*), has close
sleeves. His Stole (*Epitrakhíl*) consists of a long piece of stuff like
the Deacon's, but broader than the latter, which passes round his neck,
is joined in front for its entire length, and falls low upon his cassock.
It typifies the consecrating grace of the Priesthood. The Priest, like the
Deacon, can celebrate no Office without his Stole. In it, without the
Chasuble, he celebrates the less solemn Offices : Lesser Vespers, ordinary Compline, Lauds (*Polunótchnitza*), the Hours (if the Gospel be not
appointed to be read in them) ; also various Prayer-services in private
dwellings, such as that at the birth of a child, and the like.

The Zone (*Póyas*) is sort of belt wherewith the Priest girds himself above his cassock and stole, for convenience in serving the Altar. It is symbolical of the gift of strength, wherewith God aids him in his service, and exhorts him to blamelessness of life. His Cuffs (*Pórutchi*) typify the bonds wherewith the hands of our Lord were bound.

The Epigonátion (*Nabédrennik*) is an oblong piece of brocade, which is suspended upon the hip of a priest, and signifies the Sword of the Spirit, which is the Word of God. It is also explained as being symbolical of the towel wherewith the Saviour girded himself to wash the disciples' feet.

The *Pálitza* is identical with the *Epigonátion*, except that it is sus-

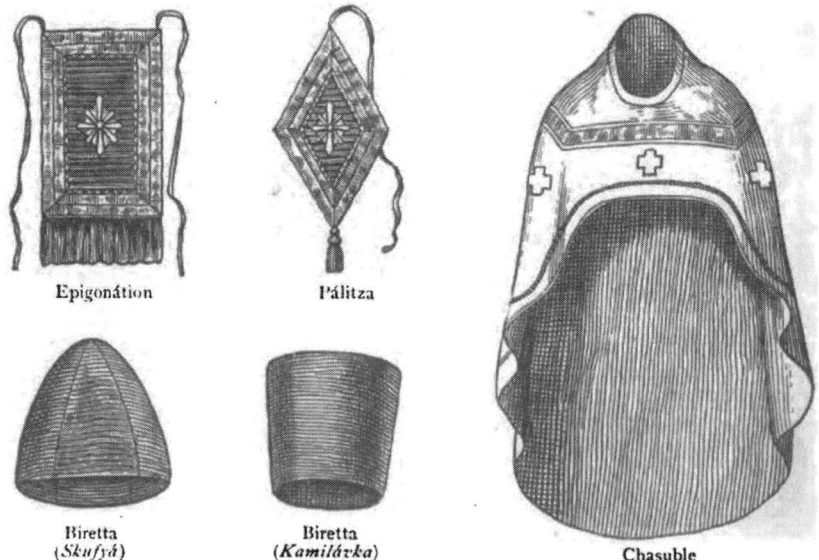

Epigonátion   Pálitza

Biretta
(*Skufyá*)   Biretta
(*Kamilávka*)   Chasuble

pended by one corner instead of by two corners. It is always worn on the right hip. The Epigonátion is worn on the right hip; but if the Priest have also a Pálitza, the Epigonátion is worn on the left hip. Both the Epigonátion and the Pálitza are typical of profound zeal for the faith, and for the salvation of Christ's flock, and are conferred as rewards of honour.

The distinguishing vestment of the Priest is the Chasuble (*Felón*), a long, ample garment without sleeves, short in front and with an opening for the head, which is put on over the other vestments.

Archpriests and Priests also receive, as tokens of distinguished service, the pointed and the upright Biretta — the *skufyá* and the *kamilávka*.

A Bishop wears all the vestments of a Priest, save the Chasuble and Epigonátion, his biretta being perpendicular, black, and draped with the monastic veil or cowl. In place of the Chasuble a Bishop wears a Dalmatic, which closely resembles the wide-sleeved Dalmatic of the Deacon. This Dalmatic (*Sákkos*) is symbolical of Christ's coat without a seam, woven from top to bottom. The Bishop's Stole (*Omofór* — Pall) is very broad, and hangs down in front and behind over his other vestments. His Pall typifies the wandering sheep, and the Prelate, when arrayed in this vestment, bears the image of the Saviour Christ, who, as the Good Shepherd, took upon his shoulders the wandering sheep and bare it to those who wander not; that is, to the Angels, in his Father's house. The Mitre is typical of a diadem or crown, and serves as an emblem of the power bestowed upon a minister of the Church. (The Mitre is conferred also

A, Dalmatic (*Sákkos*).   B, Pall

upon Archimandrites, or Abbots, and upon certain Archpriests.) The *Panagía*, which is worn on his breast by a Bishop, is generally a small, circular Holy Image, or *Ikóna*, of our Saviour and the Birth-giver of God. The *Panagía* (or "all-holy") reminds the Bishop that he must always bear in his heart our Lord and his holy Mother, the Intercessor with God; and, to that end his heart must be pure, and his spirit upright.

Mitre

The Bishop's Mantle (*Mántiya*) is a monastic vestment, which covers the whole person with the exception of the head. Its freely flowing lines typify the wings of the Angels; hence it is called "the Angelic vestment." The folds of the Mantle are symbolical of the all-embracing power of God; and also of the strictness, piety and meekness of the monastic life; and that the hands and other members of a monk do not live, and are not fitted

Pectoral Image (*Panagía*)

for worldly activity, but are all dead. All monks, when present at divine service, must be robed in their mantles.

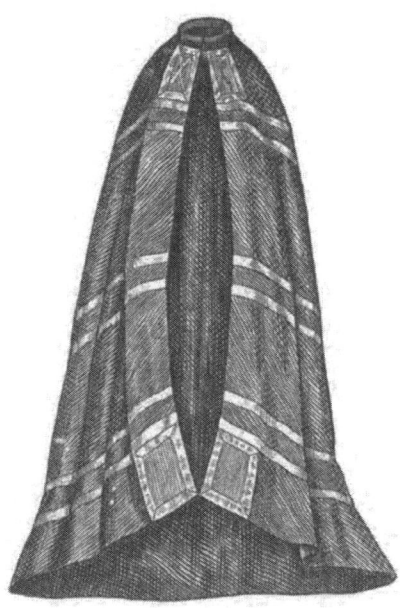

Bishop's Mantle

The peculiarity of a Bishop's mantle is that it is not black in hue, like the monastic mantle, but of purple, or some other colour; and upon it are sewn the so-called "Tables of the Law" (*Skrizháli*), and, in particular, the "Fountains" (*Istótchniki*). The *Tables* (squares of velvet at neck and foot) typify the Old and the New Testament, whence the ministers of God should draw their doctrine. The "Fountains" are ribbons, usually red and white in hue, sewn horizontally round the Mantle, and represent the streams of teaching which flow from the mouth of the Bishop. Small bells are attached to the Mantle of a Bishop, and to his Dalmatic, as to the upper robe of the High Priest of the Jews.

The Crozier, or Pastoral Staff (*Pósokh*), is given to Bishops and to Archimandrites, in token of their spiritual authority over the monasteries or cities which they rule; and as a sign that it behooves them to feed the flock of Christ.

The Eagle (*Orlétz*) is a small circular rug, with the representation of a one-headed eagle soaring over a battlemented city. A

Eagle

Crozier

Bishop stands on this rug during divine service, and to him alone is its use accorded. He is led upon a large "Eagle" at his Consecration, as the Office of Consecration sets forth. (See that Office.) The view of the city betokens the Prelate's rule over the city; the Eagle denotes the loftiness and purity of his teaching. Thus the Eagle-rug spread for a Bishop to stand upon signifies that he, by his life and doctrine, must resemble the eagle, which soars above all lower things, and aspires unto heaven.

THE ALL–NIGHT VIGIL SERVICE (1)*

The Holy Doors are open. The Priest standeth before the Altar with the censer, and the Deacon with the taper.

GREAT VESPERS

Deacon. Arise, Master, give the blessing.

Priest. Glory to the Holy, Consubstantial, Life-giving and Undivided Trinity always, now, and ever, and unto ages of ages. (2)

Choir. Amen.

Priest. O come, let us worship God our King. O come, let us worship and fall down before Christ, our King and our God. O come, let us worship and fall down before the Very Christ, our King and our God. O come, let us worship and fall down before him. (*Three reverences.*)

From Easter until Ascension Day, in place of, O come, let us worship, *shall be sung:*

Christ is risen from the dead, trampling down Death by death, **Easter-tide.** and upon those in the tomb bestowing life.

Then shall be said or sung PSALM CIV.; *and the Priest, preceded by the Deacon bearing a taper, shall cense the whole temple, after which the Holy Door is closed.* (3)

PSALM CIV.

Praise the Lord, O my soul. Blessed art thou, O Lord. O Lord my God, thou art become exceeding glorious. Blessed art thou, O Lord. O Lord, how manifold are thy works: In wisdom hast thou made them all. Glory to thee, O Lord, who hast made them all.

Thus much is generally used. But sometimes the whole is read or sung, as followeth:

Praise the Lord, O my soul: O Lord my God,

The Priest now taketh his stand before the Holy Door, with head uncovered, and reciteth the PRAYERS OF LIGHT, *secretly.* (4)

A.

O Lord, bountiful and compassionate, long-suffering and plenteous in mercy, give ear unto our prayer, and attend to the voice of our supplication. Work upon us a sign for good. Lead us in thy way, that we may walk in thy truth. Make glad our hearts, that we may fear thy holy Name. For thou art great and doest wonders. Thou alone art God, and among all the gods there is none like unto thee, O Lord, mighty in mercy, gracious in strength, to aid and to comfort and save all those who put their trust in thy holy Name.

Secretly.

* For an explanation of the Symbolism indicated by reference-numerals in the text, see Appendix B, I.

thou art become exceeding glorious; thou art clothed with majesty and honour. Thou deckest thyself with light as it were with a garment, and spreadest out the heavens like a curtain. Who layeth the beams of his chambers in the waters, and maketh the clouds his chariot, and walketh upon the wings of the wind. He maketh his angels spirits, and his ministers a flaming fire. He laid the foundations of the earth, that it never should move at any time. Thou coveredst it with the deep like as a garment; the waters stand in the hills. At thy rebuke they flee; at the voice of thy thunder they are afraid. They go up as high as the hills, and down to the valleys beneath; even unto the place which thou hast appointed for them. Thou hast set them their bounds, which they shall not pass, neither turn again to cover the earth. He sendeth the springs into the rivers, which run among the hills. All the beasts of the field drink thereof, and the wild asses quench their thirst. Beside them shall the fowls of the air have their habitation, and sing among the branches. He watereth the hills from

For unto thee are due all glory, honour and worship, to the Father, and to the Son, and to the Holy Spirit, now, and ever, and unto ages of ages. Amen.

B.

O Lord, rebuke us not in thy displeasure, neither chasten us in thy wrath: but deal with us according to thy mercy, O Physician and Healer of our souls. Guide us unto the haven of thy will. Enlighten the eyes of our hearts to the knowledge of thy truth, and vouchsafe that the residue of this day and our whole life may be peaceful and without sin; through the intercessions of the holy Birth-giver of God, and of all the Saints.

For thine is the majesty, and thine are the kingdom and the power and the glory, of the Father, and of the Son, and of the Holy Spirit, now, and ever, and unto ages of ages. Amen.

C.

O Lord our God, remember us sinners and thine unprofitable servants when we call upon thy holy Name, and put us not to shame in our expectation of thy mercy: but grant us, O Lord, all our petitions which are unto salvation, and vouchsafe that we may love and fear thee with all our hearts, and do thy will in all things.

For thou art a gracious God, and lovest mankind: and unto thee do we ascribe glory, to the Father, and to the Son, and to the Holy Spirit, now, and ever, and unto ages of ages. Amen.

D.

O thou who, with never-silent hymns and never-ceasing songs of praise to thy glory, art hymned by the holy Powers: Fill our mouths with thy praise, that we may magnify thy holy Name. And

Secretly.

above; the earth is filled with the fruit of thy works. He bringeth forth grass for the cattle, and green herb for the service of men; That he may bring food out of the earth, and wine that maketh glad the heart of man: and oil to make him a cheerful countenance, and bread to strengthen man's heart. The trees of the Lord also are full of sap, even the cedars of Libanus which he hath planted; wherein the birds make their nests; and the fir-trees are a dwelling for the stork. The high hills are a refuge for the wild goats; and so are the stony rocks for the conies. He appointed the moon for certain seasons, and the sun knoweth his going down. Thou makest darkness that it may be night; wherein all the beasts of the forests do move. The lions, roaring after their prey, do seek their meat from God. The sun ariseth and they get them away together, and lay them down in their dens. Man goeth forth to his work, and to his labour, until the evening. O Lord, how manifold are thy works! in wisdom hast thou made them all; the earth is full of thy riches.

grant unto us part and inheritance with all those who fear thee in truth and keep thy commandment; through the intercessions of the holy Birth-giver of God, and of all thy Saints.

For unto thee are due all glory, honour and worship, to the Father, and to the Son, and to the Holy Spirit, now, and ever, and unto ages of ages. Amen.

E.

O Lord, Lord, who upholdest all things in the all-pure hollow of thy hand; who showest long-suffering upon us all, and repentest thee at our calamities: Remember thy bounties and thy mercy. Visit us with thy loving-kindness: and grant that, through the residue of thy day, by thy grace, we may avoid the divers subtle snares of the Evil One, and preserve our lives unassailed; through the grace of thine all-holy Spirit.

Through the mercy and love toward mankind of thine Only-begotten Son, with whom thou art blessed, together with thine all-holy, and good, and life-creating Spirit, now, and ever, and unto ages of ages. Amen.

F.

O God, great and wonderful, who with wisdom inscrutable and great riches of providence orderest all things, and bestowest upon us earthly good things; who hast given us a pledge of the promised kingdom through the good things already bestowed upon us, and hast made us to shun all evil during that part of the day which is past: Grant that we may also fulfil the residue of this day without reproach before thy holy glory, and hymn thee, the only good one, our God, who lovest mankind.

For thou art our God, and unto thee

Secretly.

So is the great and wide sea also; wherein are creeping things innumerable, both small and great beasts. There go the ships, and there is that Leviathan, whom thou hast made to take his pastime therein. These all wait upon thee, that thou mayest give them meat in due season. When thou givest it them, they gather it; and when thou openest thy hand, they are filled with good. When thou hidest thy face, they are troubled; when thou takest away their breath, they die, and are turned again to their dust. When thou lettest thy breath go forth, they shall be made: the Lord shall rejoice in his works. The earth shall tremble at the look of him; if he do but touch the hills, they shall smoke. I will sing unto the Lord as long as I live; I will praise my God while I have my being. And so shall my words please him: my joy shall be in the Lord. As for sinners, they shall be consumed out of the earth, and the ungodly shall come to an end. Praise thou the Lord, O my soul. Praise the Lord.

Glory . . . now, and ever. Alleluia. (*Thrice.*) Glory to thee, O Lord, glory to thee.

we ascribe glory, to the Father, and to the Son, and to the Holy Spirit, now, and ever, and unto ages of ages. Amen.

G.

O great and most high God, who alone hast immortality, and dwellest in light unapproachable; who hast made all creation in wisdom; who hast divided the light from the darkness, and hast appointed the sun to rule the day, the moon and stars also to rule the night; who hast vouchsafed unto us sinners at this present hour also to come before thy presence with confession, and to offer unto thee our evening sacrifice of praise: Do thou thyself, who lovest mankind, direct our prayer as a censer before thee, and accept it for a savour of sweet incense; and grant that we may pass this present evening and the coming night in peace. Endue us with the armour of light. Deliver us from the terror of the night, and from everything that walketh in darkness; and grant that the sleep, which thou hast appointed for the repose of our weakness, may be free from every imagination of the Devil. Yea, O Master, Bestower of all good things, may we, being moved to compunction upon our beds, call to remembrance thy holy Name in the night season: that, enlightened by meditation on thy statutes, we may rise up in joyfulness of soul to glorify thy goodness, offering up prayers and supplications unto thy tender love for our own sins and for those of all thy people: whom do thou visit in mercy, through the intercessions of the holy Birth-giver of God.

For thou art a gracious God, and lovest mankind, and unto thee do we ascribe glory, to the Father, and to the Son, and to the Holy Spirit, now, and ever, and unto ages of ages. Amen.

Secretly.

Then the Priest (or the Deacon, if there be one) shall come out through the North Door, and taking his stand in the usual place, shall recite

THE GREAT LITANY (*Velíkaya Ekténiya*).

In peace let us pray to the Lord.

Choir. Lord, have mercy.

For the peace that is from above, and for the salvation of our souls: ℟

For the peace of the whole world; for the welfare of God's holy Churches, and for the union of all: ℟

For this holy Temple, and for those who with faith, devoutness, and in the fear of God have entered therein: ℟

For our Most Holy Synod (*or* Patriarch); for our Bishop (*or* Archbishop, *or* Metropolitan), N.; for the honourable Presbytery, the Diaconate in Christ; for all the clergy and the laity: ℟

Here follow petitions for the Ruler of the Land and for all the Authorities according to the elements and nationalities of which the Parish is constituted.

That he will aid them and subdue under their feet every foe and adversary: ℟

For this city, for this holy Temple, and for every city and land, and for those who with faith dwell therein: ℟

For healthful seasons; for abundance of the fruits of the earth, and for peaceful times: ℟

For those who travel by sea or by land; for the sick and the suffering; for those who are in captivity, and for their salvation: ℟

That he will deliver us from all tribulation, wrath, and necessity: ℟

Succour us, save us, have mercy upon us, and keep us, O God, by thy grace: ℟

Calling to remembrance our most holy, all-undefiled, most blessed and glorious Lady, the Birth-giver of God and ever-virgin Mary, with all the Saints, let us commend ourselves, and each other, and all our life unto Christ our God.

Choir. To thee, O Lord.

[margin: let us pray to the Lord. Choir. Lord, have mercy.]

Exclamation.

Priest. For unto thee are due all glory, honour and worship, to the Father, and to the Son, and to the Holy Spirit, now, and ever, and unto ages of ages. (5)

Choir. Amen.

Then shall be said or sung several verses from the First Selection of the Psalms (Stik-hoslóvie Kafísmi). (6)

PSALMS I., II.

Blessed is the man that hath not walked in the counsel of the ungodly. Alleluia, alleluia, alleluia.

For the Lord knoweth the way of the righteous, and the way of the ungodly shall perish. Alleluia. (*Thrice.*)

Serve the Lord with fear, and rejoice unto him with reverence. Alleluia. (*Thrice.*)

Blessed are all they that put their trust in him. Alleluia. (*Thrice.*) (7)

Arise. O Lord: Save me, O my God. Alleluia. (*Thrice.*)

Glory to the Father, and to the Son, and to the Holy Spirit, now, and ever, and unto ages of ages. Amen.

Alleluia, alleluia, alleluia. Glory to thee, O Lord. (*Thrice.*)

Then the Deacon saith

THE LITTLE LITANY (*Málaya Ekténiya*).

Again, yet again, in peace let us pray to the Lord.

Choir. Lord, have mercy.

Succour us, save us, have mercy upon us, and keep us, O God, by thy grace.

Choir. Lord, have mercy.

Calling to remembrance our most holy, all-undefiled, most blessed and glorious Lady, the Birth-giver of God and ever-virgin Mary, with all the Saints, let us commend ourselves, and each other, and all our life unto Christ our God.

Choir. To thee, O Lord.

Exclamation.

Priest. For thine is the majesty, and thine are the kingdom and the power and the glory, of the Father, and of the Son, and of the Holy Spirit, now, and ever, and unto ages of ages.

Choir. Amen.

And here shall be sung immediately, Lord, I have cried unto thee, *with its Verses (Stikhi), in the appointed Tone. And in the mean time the Deacon censeth the Sanctuary and all the Temple.*

PSALMS CXLI., CXLII., CXXX., CXVII.

Lord, I have cried unto thee, hear me. Hear me, O Lord. Lord, I have cried unto thee, hear me: receive the voice of my prayer when I call upon thee. Hear me, O Lord. Let my prayer be set forth in thy sight as incense, and let the lifting up of my my hands be an evening sacrifice.

The Canticles (Stikhíri; see Appendix A) are then sung or read in the proper Tone, as appointed, preceded by Verses (Stikhí).

The Priest prayeth, secretly.

In the evening, and in the morning, and at noonday we praise thee, we bless thee, we give thanks unto thee, and we pray unto thee, O Lord of all: Direct thou our prayer before thee as incense, and incline not our hearts unto words or thoughts of wickedness; but deliver us from all who seek after our souls. For unto thee, Lord, O Lord, lift we up our eyes, and in thee have we trusted. Put us not to shame, O our God.

Secretly.

(*On the Lord's Day and the Great Feasts*): Bring my soul out of prison, that I may give thanks unto thy Name.

For unto thee are due all glory, honour and worship, to the Father, and to the Son, and to the Holy Spirit, now, and ever, and unto ages of ages. Amen. *Aloud.*

The righteous await me, until thou shalt requite me.

(*On Feast Days*): Out of the depths have I cried unto thee, O Lord: O Lord, hear my voice.

O let thine ears consider well the voice of my complaint.

(*On Ordinary Days*): If thou, Lord, wilt be extreme to mark what is done amiss, O Lord, who may abide it. But with thee is forgiveness.

For thy Name's sake I have patiently waited for thee, O Lord; my soul hath waited patiently for thy word; my soul hath trusted in the Lord.

(*Or*): Before the morning watch until the evening, before the morning watch, let Israel trust in the Lord.

For with the Lord there is mercy, and with him is plenteous redemption. And he shall redeem Israel from all his sins.

Praise the Lord, all ye heathen; praise him all ye people.

For his mercy hath been established upon us, and the truth of the Lord abideth forever.

Glory to the Father, and to the Son, and to the Holy Spirit, now, and ever, and unto ages of ages. Amen.

Then shall be sung the HYMN TO THE BIRTH-GIVER OF GOD (*Dogmátik*) (8) *in the proper Tone.*

TONE I.* (Example.)

Let us sing the praises of Mary, Virgin, Door of heaven, Glory of all the world, sprung forth from man, who also bare the Lord; the Song of the Bodiless Powers, and the Enriching of the faithful. For she revealed herself as Heaven and the Temple of the Godhead. She destroyed the bulwarks of enmity, and ushered in peace, and threw open the kingdom. Wherefore, in that we possess this confirmation of our faith we have a defender, even the Lord who was born of her. Be bold, therefore, be bold, ye people of God, for he, the All-Powerful, will vanquish your foes.

While the Dogmátik is being sung, the Holy Door is opened, and the Priest and Deacon pass before the High Place, through the Left Door, and stand before the Holy Door. (9)

Then the Deacon, having censed the Holy Pictures (ikóni), shall say in a low voice to the Priest:

Bless, Master, the Holy Entrance.

And the Priest, blessing with the sign of the cross, shall say:

Blessed is the Entrance of thy Holy Ones, now, and ever, and unto ages of ages.

Deacon. Amen.

And when the Dogmátik is finished the Deacon shall lift up the censer, as he standeth in the middle of the Holy Door, and shall say aloud:

Wisdom, O believers!

* For the Dogmátiki, see Appendix A.

Then shall be sung the Hymn (Tropár) composed by Sophronius, Patriarch of Jerusalem.

O gladsome radiance of the holy glory of the Father immortal, heavenly, holy, blessed, Jesus Christ! In that we now are come unto the setting of the sun, and behold the light of even, we hymn thee, Father, Son, and Holy Spirit, God. For meet is it that at all times thou shouldest be magnified by voices propitious, O Son of God, who bestowest life. For which cause all the world doth glorify thee.

The Priest and the Deacon enter the Sanctuary and go to the High Place.

Deacon. Wisdom!

Priest. Peace be unto all.

Reader. And to thy spirit.

Deacon. Wisdom! Let us attend. — The Gradual (*Prokímen*) of the . . . Tone. (10)

On Sunday Evening, Tone VIII.:

Behold now, praise the Lord, all ye servants of the Lord.

Verse (Stikh): Ye that stand in the temple of the Lord, even in the courts of the house of our God.

On Monday Evening, Tone IV.:

When I call upon the Lord, he will hear me.

Verse: Hear me when I call, O God of my righteousness.

On Tuesday Evening, Tone I.:

Thy mercy, O Lord, shall follow me all the days of my life.

Verse: The Lord is my shepherd, therefore can I lack nothing: he hath led me in a green pasture.

On Wednesday Evening, Tone V.:

Save me, O God, for thy Name's sake, and judge me in thy strength.

Verse: Hear my prayer, O God, and hearken unto the words of my mouth.

On Thursday Evening, Tone VI.:

My help cometh even from the Lord, who hath made heaven and earth.

Verse: I will lift up mine eyes unto the hills, from whence cometh my help.

On Friday Evening, Tone VII.:

Thou art my defence, O God, and thy goodness preventeth me.

Verse: Deliver me from mine enemies, O God, and save me from them that rise up against me.

On Saturday Evening (the Lord's Day):

The Lord is King, and hath put on glorious apparel.

Verse: The Lord hath put on his apparel, and hath girded himself with strength.

Verse: For he hath made the round world so sure that it shall not be moved.

Verse: Holiness becometh thy house, O Lord, forever.

Here, on certain Feasts and appointed days only, are read the PARABLES (11) *(Paremii), the Deacon having said before each Parable:* Wisdom! Let us attend! *The Gradual being finished, the Deacon shutteth the Holy Door, and goeth out through the North Door, and saith*

THE AUGMENTED LITANY (*Sugúbaya Ekténiya*).

Let us say, with all our soul and with all our mind let us say,

Choir. Lord, have mercy.

O Lord Almighty, the God of our fathers, we beseech thee, hearken and have mercy.

Choir. Lord, have mercy.

Have mercy upon us, O God, according to thy great mercy, we beseech thee: hearken, and have mercy. ℟

Again we pray for (*the Ruler of the Land, according to the elements and nationalities of which the Parish is constituted*); for his might, victory, maintenance, peace, health, salvation; and that the Lord our God will abundantly aid and prosper him in all things, and subdue under his feet every foe and adversary. ℟

Furthermore we pray for our Most Holy Synod (*or* Patriarch); for our Bishop (*or* Archbishop, *or* Metropolitan), N.; and for all our brethren in Christ.

Furthermore we pray for all his Christ-loving Army and Navy. ℟

Furthermore we pray for the blessed and ever-memorable founders of this holy Temple; and for all our devout fathers and brethren, Orthodox believers, departed this life before us, who here and in all the world lie asleep in the Lord. ℟

Furthermore we pray for mercy, life, peace, health, salvation, visitation, forgiveness and remission of sins for the servants of God, our brethren of this holy Temple. ℟

Furthermore we pray for those who bear fruit and do good works in this holy and all-honourable Temple; for those who labour in its service; for the singers; and for the people here present, who await in firm hope thy great and rich mercies. ℟

Choir. Lord, have mercy. (*Thrice.*)

Exclamation.

Priest. For thou art a merciful God, who lovest mankind, and unto thee we ascribe glory, to the Father, and to the Son, and to the Holy Spirit, now, and ever, and unto ages of ages.

Choir. Amen.

Reader. Vouchsafe, O Lord, to keep us this night without sin. Blessed art thou, O Lord, the God of our fathers, and praised and glorified is thy name forever. Amen.

Let thy mercy be upon us, O Lord, even as we have set our hope on thee. Blessed art thou, O Lord; teach me thy statutes. Blessed **art** thou, O Master; make me to understand thy commandments. Blessed art thou, O Holy One; enlighten me with thy precepts.

Thy mercy, O Lord, endureth forever: O despise not the works of thy hands. To thee belongeth worship, to thee belongeth praise, to thee belongeth glory, to the Father, and to the Son, and to the Holy Spirit, now, and ever, unto ages of ages. Amen.

Deacon. Let us complete our evening prayer unto the Lord.

Choir. Lord, have mercy.

Succour us, save us, be merciful unto us, and keep us, O God, by thy grace.

Choir. Lord, have mercy.

An evening all-perfect, holy, peaceful and sinless, let us beseech of the Lord: ℞

An Angel of Peace, the faithful guide and guardian both of our souls and bodies: ℞

The pardon and remission of our sins and transgressions: ℞

All things which are good and profitable to our souls, and peace to the world: ℞

That we may pass the residue of our life in peace and penitence: ℞

A Christian ending to our life, painless, blameless, peaceful; and a good defence before the dread Judgment Seat of Christ: ℞

let us beseech of the Lord. Choir. Grant it, O Lord.

Calling to remembrance our most holy, all-undefiled, most blessed and glorious Lady, the Birth-giver of God and ever-virgin Mary, with all the Saints, let us commend ourselves, and each other, and all our life unto Christ our God.

Choir. To thee, O Lord.

Exclamation.

Priest. For thou art a gracious God, and lovest mankind, and unto thee we ascribe glory, to the Father, and to the Son, and to the Holy Spirit, now, and ever, and unto ages of ages.

Choir. Amen.

Priest. Peace be with you all.

Choir. And with thy spirit.

Deacon. Let us bow our heads unto the Lord.

Choir. To thee, O Lord.

The Priest, secretly.

O Lord our God, who didst bow the heavens and come down for the salvation of mankind: Look upon thy servants and thine inheritance; for unto thee, the awful Judge, who yet lovest mankind, *Secretly.*

have thy servants bowed their heads, and submissively inclined their necks, awaiting not succour from men, but entreating thy mercy and looking confidently for thy salvation. Guard them at all times, both during this present evening and in the approaching night, from every foe, from all adverse powers of the Devil, and from vain thoughts and from evil imaginations.

Aloud. Blessed and glorified be the majesty of thy kingdom, of the Father, and of the Son, and of the Holy Spirit, now, and ever, and unto ages of ages.

Choir. Amen.

Then the Stikhíry na Stikhóvne (Selected Verses) shall be sung, and the Song of St. Simeon followeth: Lord, now lettest: (*See page* 13.)

THE LITIYÁ. (12)

But sometimes (especially on the Eve of a Great Feast) there followeth the Litiyá, that is, the Petitions of Fervent Devotion.

When there is a Litiyá, the Priest and Deacon, preceded by taper bearers, come together to the end of the Temple opposite the Sanctuary, while the Choir is singing the Canticles (Stikhíry Litíyiny) of the Temple or of the Feast.

Then the Deacon saith, aloud, the following Prayer:

O God, save thy people, and bless thine heritage. Visit thy world with mercy and bounties; exalt the horn of Orthodox Christians, and send down upon us thy rich mercies. Through the prayers of our all-undefiled Lady, the Birth-giver of God and ever-virgin Mary: through the might of the precious and life-giving Cross: through the protection of the honourable Bodiless Powers of heaven; of the honourable, glorious Prophet, Forerunner and Baptist, John; of the holy, glorious and all-laudable Apostles; of our Holy Fathers, great Hierarchs and Œcumenical Teachers, Basil the Great, Gregory the Theologian and John Chrysostom; of our Holy Father Nicholas, Archbishop of Myra in Lycia, the Wonder-worker; of our Holy Fathers Methodius and Kyril, Evangelizers of the Slavs; (of our Holy Fathers of All-Russia, Wonder-workers, Peter, Alexis, Jonah, Philip); of the holy, glorious, right-victorious Martyrs; of our reverend and God-bearing Fathers, the holy and righteous ancestors of God, Joachim and Anna; of Saint N. (*the Patron Saint of the Temple*); and of all thy Saints: We beseech thee, O all-merciful Lord, give ear unto us sinners, who make our supplications unto thee, and have mercy upon us. ℟

Here follow petitions for the Ruler of the Land and for all the Authorities according to the elements and nationalities of which the Parish is constituted.

Furthermore we pray for our Holy Synod (*or* Patriarch); for our Bishop (*or* Archbishop, *or* Metropolitan), N.; and for all our brethren in Christ; and for every Christian soul that is afflicted and weary in well-doing, in need of God's mercies and succour; for the protection of this holy Temple, and for those who abide therein; for the peace and quietness of the whole world; for the welfare of God's holy Churches; for the salvation and assistance of our fathers and brethren who, with diligence and in the fear of God, do labour

(40, usually 12, times.)

Choir. Lord, have mercy.

(8, usually 12, times.)

and serve; for those who are absent and abroad; for the healing of those who lie in sickness; for the repose, refreshment, blessed memory and remission of sins of all our devout fathers and brethren, Orthodox believers, departed this life before us, who here, and in all the world, lie asleep in the Lord; for the deliverance of captives; and for our brethren who are taking part in these ministrations; and for all who minister and have ministered in this holy Temple, let us say: ℞

Furthermore we pray that he will preserve this city and this holy Temple, and every city and land from pestilence, famine, earthquake, flood, fire, the sword, the invasion of enemies, and from civil war; and that our good God, who loveth mankind, will be graciously favourable and easy to be entreated, and will turn away from us all the wrath stirred up against us, and deliver us from all his righteous chastisement which impendeth against us, and have mercy upon us. ℞

Choir. Lord, have mercy. (8, usually 12, times.) (3 times.)

Furthermore we pray that the Lord God will hearken unto the voice of petition of us sinners, and show mercy upon us.

Choir. Lord, have mercy. (*Thrice.*)

Then the Priest maketh mention, secretly, *of whomsoever he will, both of the living and of the dead.*

Priest, aloud. Hear us, O God our Saviour, the hope of all the ends of the earth, and of those who are far off upon the sea; and show mercy, show mercy, O Master, upon us sinners, and be merciful unto us.

For thou art a merciful God and lovest mankind, and unto thee we ascribe glory, to the Father, and to the Son, and to the Holy Spirit, now, and ever, and unto ages of ages.

Choir. Amen.

Priest. Peace be with you all.

Choir. And with thy spirit.

Deacon. Let us bow our heads unto the Lord.

Then, as all bow their heads, the Priest reciteth the following Prayer, so that all may hear:

O most merciful Master, Lord Jesus Christ our God, through the prayers of our all-undefiled Lady, the Birth-giver of God and ever-virgin Mary (*and thence as in the preceding prayer, page* 11, *ending with*): and of all thy Saints: Make our prayer acceptable; grant us remission of our transgressions; hide us under the shadow of thy wings; drive far from us every foe and adversary; make our life peaceful, O Lord. Have mercy upon us and upon thy world; and save our souls: forasmuch as thou art gracious and lovest mankind.

End of Litiyá. *Here are sung the appointed Canticles (Stikhíry) in the proper Tone, or of the Feast; and so singing we return to the centre of the Temple, where in special vessels the bread, wine, oil and wheat are already prepared.*

Choir. Lord, now lettest thou thy servant depart in peace, Great according to thy word. For mine eyes have seen thy salvation, Vespers. which thou hast prepared before the face of all people. To be a light to lighten the Gentiles, and to be the glory of thy people Israel.

Reader.. O Holy God, Holy Mighty, Holy Immortal One, have mercy upon us. (*Thrice.*)

Glory to the Father, and to the Son, and to the Holy Spirit, now, and ever, and unto ages of ages. Amen.

O all-holy Trinity, have mercy upon us. O Lord, wash away our sins. O Master, pardon our transgressions. O Holy One, visit and heal our infirmities, for thy Name's sake.

Lord, have mercy. (*Thrice.*)

Glory to the Father, and to the Son, and to the Holy Spirit, now, and ever, and unto ages of ages. Amen.

Our Father, who art in heaven, Hallowed be thy Name. Thy kingdom come. Thy will be done on earth, As it is in heaven. Give us this day our daily bread. And forgive us our trespasses, As we forgive those who trespass against us. And lead us not into temptation; But deliver us from the Evil One:

Priest. For thine is the kingdom, and the power, and the glory, of the Father, and of the Son, and of the Holy Spirit, now, and ever, and unto ages of ages.

Choir. Amen.

Then shall be sung the Hymn (Tropár) of the Feast. *

Hail, O Virgin Birth-giver of God! Mary full of grace, the Lord is with thee. Blessed art thou among women, and blessed is the fruit of thy womb. For thou hast borne the Saviour of our souls.

After the Deacon hath censed about the table whereon stand the bread, wheat, **Blessing** *wine and oil, (12) the Priest, taking one of the loaves, shall make there-* **of Bread,** *with the sign of the cross over the other loaves, and shall say aloud the fol-* **Wine and** **Oil at** *lowing Prayer, pointing with his right hand to the loaves, wheat, wine* **Great** *and oil, as he uttereth the words,* Do thou, the same Lord, bless: **Feasts.**

O Lord Jesus Christ our God, who didst bless the five loaves and didst therewith feed the five thousand: Do thou, the same Lord, bless these loaves, wheat, wine and oil; and multiply them in this holy habitation, and in all thy world; and sanctify all the faithful who shall partake of them. For it is thou, O Christ our God, who dost bless and sanctify all things; and unto thee we ascribe glory, with thy Father which hath no beginning, and thine all-holy, good, and life-creating Spirit, now, and ever, and unto ages of ages.

Choir. Amen.

* For Hymns of the Twelve Great Feasts, see the Special Services.

And immediately after the Amen:

Great Vespers.   *Choir.* Blessed be the Name of the Lord, henceforth and for-ever. (*Thrice.*)

PSALM XXXIV.

Reader. I will alway give thanks unto the Lord; his praise shall ever be in my mouth. My soul shall make her boast in the Lord; the humble shall hear thereof, and be glad. O praise the Lord with me, and let us magnify his Name together. I sought the Lord, and he heard me; yea, he delivered me out of all my fear. They had an eye unto him, and were lightened, and their faces were not ashamed. Lo, the poor crieth, and the Lord heareth him; yea, and saveth him out of all his troubles. The angel of the Lord tarrieth round about them that fear him, and delivereth them. O taste, and see, how gracious the Lord is: blessed is the man that trusteth in him. O fear the Lord, ye that are his saints; for they that fear him lack nothing. The lions do lack, and suffer hunger; but they who seek the Lord shall want no manner of thing that is good.

And the Priest cometh forth, and standeth before the Holy Door. And when the Psalm is finished, he turneth and saith to the People:

The blessing of the Lord, through his grace and loving-kindness, be upon you always, now, and ever, and unto ages of ages.

Choir. Amen.

And at Eastertide:

Easter-tide.   Christ is risen from the dead, trampling down Death by death, and upon those in the tomb bestowing life.

And if it be the VIGIL OFFICE, *and not* VESPERS *only, the Reader immediately begin-neth the* SIX PSALMS *of the* MATINS *office.* (*See page* 18.)

But if it be GREAT VESPERS *alone:*

Deacon. Wisdom.

Choir. Bless, Master.

Priest. The Existing is blessed, even Christ our God, always, now, and ever, and unto ages of ages.

Choir. Amen. Establish, O God, the Holy Orthodox Faith, and Ortho-dox Christians, unto ages of ages.

Priest. Save us, O most pure Birth-giver of God.

Choir. More honourable than the Cherubim, and beyond compare more glorious than the Seraphim, thou who without defilement barest God the Word, true Birth-giver of God, we magnify thee.

Priest. Glory to thee, O Christ our God, our sure hope; glory to thee.

Choir. Glory to the Father, and to the Son, and to the Holy Spirit, now, and ever, and unto ages of ages. Amen. Lord, have mercy. Bless, Master.

And the Priest, turning from the Holy Door towards the people, pronounceth the
BENEDICTION:

May Christ, our true God, through the prayers of his most-holy Mother; of Saint N. (*the saint of the day*); of Saint N. (*the Saint of the Church*), and of all the Saints, have mercy upon us and save us, forasmuch as he is gracious and loveth mankind.

THE ORDER FOR MATINS *

When the ALL-NIGHT VIGIL *is celebrated consecutively, as is the general custom, on the Eve of the Lord's Day or of a Feast, all that here followeth, down to* Glory to God in the highest (*see page* 18), *shall be omitted. When, however, from necessity or for convenience, Matins are celebrated separately, the Priest shall begin (the Holy Door being closed):*

Blessed is our God always, now, and ever, and unto ages of ages.

Reader. Amen.

O Holy God, Holy Mighty, Holy Immortal One, have mercy upon us. (*Thrice.*)

Glory to the Father, and to the Son, and to the Holy Spirit, now, and ever, and unto ages of ages. Amen.

O all-holy Trinity, have mercy upon us. O Lord, wash away our sins. O Master, pardon our transgressions. O Holy One, visit and heal our infirmities, for thy Name's sake. Glory . . . now, and ever . . .

Lord, have mercy. (*Thrice.*)

Our Father, who art in heaven, Hallowed by thy Name. Thy kingdom come. Thy will be done on earth, As it is in heaven. Give us this day our daily bread. And forgive us our trespasses, As we forgive those who trespass against us, And lead us not into temptation; But deliver us from the Evil One:

Priest. For thine is the kingdom, and the power, and the glory, of the Father, and of the Son, and of the Holy Spirit, now, and ever, and unto ages of ages. Amen.

Reader. Lord, have mercy. (*Twelve times.*)

Glory to the Father, and to the Son, and to the Holy Spirit, now, and ever, and unto ages of ages. Amen.

O come, let us worship God our King. O come, let us worship and fall down before Christ, our King and our God. O come, let us worship and fall down before the Very Christ, our King and our God. O come, let us worship and fall down before him.

While the following Psalms are being read, the Priest censeth the Holy Altar, (1) and coming forth through the North Door, he censeth the Holy Images and the People.

PSALM XX.

The Lord hear thee in the day of trouble; the Name of the God of

* For an explanation of the Symbolism, see Appendix B, II.

Jacob defend thee: send thee help from the sanctuary, and strengthen thee out of Zion: remember all thy offerings, and accept thy burnt-sacrifice: grant thee thy heart's desire, and fulfil all thy mind. We will rejoice in thy salvation, and triumph in the Name of the Lord our God: the Lord perform all thy petitions. Now know I that the Lord helpeth his Anointed, and will hear him from his holy heaven, even with the wholesome strength of his right hand. Some put their trust in chariots, and some in horses; but we will remember the Name of the Lord our God. They are brought down and fallen; but we are risen and stand upright. Save, Lord; and hear us, O King of heaven, when we call upon thee.

Psalm XXI.

The King shall rejoice in thy strength, O Lord; exceeding glad shall he be of thy salvation. Thou hast given him his heart's desire, and hast not denied him the request of his lips. For thou shalt prevent him with the blessings of goodness, and shalt set a crown of pure gold upon his head. He asked life of thee; and thou gavest him a long life, even for ever and ever. His honour is great in thy salvation; glory and great worship shalt thou lay upon him. For thou shalt give him everlasting felicity, and make him glad with the joy of thy countenance. And why? because the King putteth his trust in the Lord; and in the mercy of the Most Highest he shall not miscarry. All thine enemies shall feel thy hand; thy right hand shall find out them that hate thee. Thou shalt make them like a fiery oven in time of thy wrath: the Lord shall destroy them in his displeasure, and the fire shall consume them. Their fruit shalt thou root out of the earth, and their seed from among the children of men. For they intended mischief against thee, and imagined such a device as they are not able to perform. Therefore shalt thou put them to flight, and the strings of thy bow shalt thou make ready against the face of them. Be thou exalted, Lord, in thine own strength; so will we sing, and praise thy power.

Glory to the Father, and to the Son, and to the Holy Spirit, now, and ever, and unto ages of ages. Amen.

O Holy God, Holy Mighty, Holy Immortal One, have mercy upon us. (*Thrice.*)

O all-holy Trinity have mercy upon us. O Lord, wash away our sins. O Master, pardon our transgressions. O Holy One, visit and heal our infirmities, for thy Name's sake.

Lord, have mercy. (*Thrice.*) Glory . . . now, and ever . . .

Our Father, who art in heaven, Hallowed be thy Name. Thy kingdom come. Thy will be done on earth, As it is in heaven. Give us this day our daily bread. And forgive us our trespasses, As we for-

Matins.

give those who trespass against us. And lead us not into temptation; But deliver us from the Evil One:

Priest. For thine is the kingdom, and the power, and the glory, of the Father, and of the Son, and of the Holy Spirit, now, and ever, and unto ages of ages. Amen.

And the following Hymns (Tropari):

O Lord, save thy people, and bless thine inheritance, granting to our God-fearing Ruler, N., victory over all adversaries, and by thy Cross preserving thine Estate.

Glory to the Father, and to the Son, and to the Holy Spirit.

Do thou who, of thine own good will, upon the Cross wast lifted up, bestow thy bounties upon the new State which is called by thy Name, O Christ, God; make glad with thy might our God-fearing Ruler, N., granting victory over his adversaries unto him who hath thine aid, which is a panoply of peace, a trophy invincible.

Now, and ever, and unto ages of ages. Amen.

HYMN TO THE BIRTH-GIVER OF GOD (*Bogoróditchen*).

O Champion dread, who cannot be put to confusion, despise not our petitions. O Good One, all-lauded Birth-giver of our God, stablish thou the State of those who hold the Orthodox faith: save our God-fearing Ruler, N., whom thou hast called to rule over us, and bestow upon him victory from heaven: for thou didst give birth unto God, O only-blessed One.

Then shall the Priest say:

Have mercy upon us, O God, according to thy great mercy, we beseech thee: hearken, and have mercy.

Choir. Lord, have mercy. (*Thrice.*)

Here follow petitions for the Ruler of the Land and for all the Authorities, according to the elements and nationalities of which the Parish is constituted.

Choir. Lord, have mercy. (*Thrice.*)

Furthermore we pray for our Holy Synod (*or* Patriarch); and for our Bishop (*or* Archbishop, *or* Metropolitan), N.

Choir. Lord, have mercy. (*Thrice.*)

Furthermore we pray for all our brethren, and for all Christians.

Choir. Lord, have mercy. (*Thrice.*)

Exclamation.

Priest. For thou art a merciful God, who lovest mankind, and unto thee we ascribe glory, to the Father, and to the Son, and to the Holy Spirit, now, and ever, and unto ages of ages.

Choir. Amen. Bless, Father, in the name of the Lord.

Priest. Glory to the Holy, Consubstantial, Life-giving and Undivided Trinity, always, now, and ever, and unto ages of ages.

Choir. Amen.

Matins.

VIGIL.

When the ALL-NIGHT VIGIL is celebrated in its usual form, all the foregoing shall be omitted; and after the Blessing (see page 15) the Holy Doors shall be closed, and the Reader shall immediately say:

Glory to God in the highest, and on earth peace, good will toward men. (*Thrice.*)

O Lord, open thou my lips, and my mouth shall show forth thy praise. (*Twice.*)

Easter-tide. Christ is risen from the dead, trampling down Death by death, and upon those in the tomb bestowing life. (*Thrice.*)

The Reader then readeth the SIX PSALMS.

PSALM III.

Lord, how are they increased that trouble me! many are they that rise against me. Many one there be that say of my soul, There is no help for him in his God. But thou, O Lord, art my defender; thou art my worship, and the lifter up of my head. I did call upon the Lord with my voice, and he heard me out of his holy hill. I laid me down and slept, and rose up again; for the Lord sustained me. I will not be afraid for ten thousands of the people, that have set themselves against me round about. Up, Lord, and help me, O my God! For thou smitest all mine enemies upon the cheek-bone; thou hast broken the teeth of the ungodly. Salvation belongeth unto the Lord; and thy blessing is upon thy people. I laid me down and slept, and rose up again; for the Lord sustained me.

PSALM XXXVIII.

Put me not to rebuke, O Lord, in thine anger; neither chasten me in thy heavy displeasure. For thine arrows stick fast in me, and thy hand presseth me sore. There is no health in my flesh, because of thy displeasure; neither is there any rest in my bones, by reason of my sin. For my wickednesses are gone over my head, and are like a sore burden, too heavy for me to bear. My wounds stink, and are corrupt, through my foolishness. I am brought into so great trouble and misery, that I go mourning all the day long. For my loins are filled with a sore disease, and there is no whole part in my body. I am feeble and sore smitten; I have roared for the very disquietness of my heart. Lord, thou knowest all my desire; and my groaning is not hid from thee. My heart panteth, my strength hath failed me, and the sight of mine eyes is gone from me. My lovers and my neighbours did stand looking upon my trouble, and my kinsmen stood afar off. They also that sought after my life laid snares for me; and they that went about to do me evil talked of wickedness, and imagined deceit all the day long. As for me, I was like a deaf man, and heard not; and as one that is dumb, who doth not open his mouth. I became even as a man that heareth not, and in whose mouth are no reproofs. For in thee,

O Lord, have I put my trust; thou shalt answer for me, O Lord my God. I have required that they, even mine enemies, should not triumph over me; for when my foot slipt, they rejoiced greatly against me. And I truly am set in the plague, and my heaviness is ever in my sight. For I will confess my wickedness, and be sorry for my sin. But mine enemies live, and are mighty; and they that hate me wrongfully are many in number. They also that reward evil for good are against me; because I follow the thing that good is.

Forsake me not, O Lord my God; be not thou far from me. Haste thee to help me, O Lord God of my salvation. (*Twice.*)

Psalm LXIII.

O God, thou art my God; early will I seek thee. My soul thirsteth for thee; my flesh also longeth after thee, in a barren and dry land where no water is. Thus have I looked for thee in holiness, that I might behold thy power and glory. For thy loving-kindness is better than the life itself: my lips shall praise thee. As long as I live will I magnify thee in this manner, and lift up my hands in thy Name. My soul shall be satisfied, even as it were with marrow and fatness, when my mouth praiseth thee with joyful lips. Have I not remembered thee in my bed, and thought upon thee when I was waking? Because thou hast been my helper; therefore under the shadow of thy wings will I rejoice. My soul hangeth upon thee; thy right hand hath upholden me. These also that seek the hurt of my soul, they shall go under the earth. Let them fall upon the edge of the sword, that they may be a portion for foxes. But the King shall rejoice in God; all they also that swear by him shall be commended; for the mouth of them that speak lies shall be stopped. In the night watches have I trusted in thee: For thou hast been my helper, and under the shadow of thy wings will I rejoice. My soul cleaveth unto thee: and thy right hand shall uphold me.

Glory to the Father, and to the Son, and to the Holy Spirit, now, and ever, and unto ages of ages. Amen.

Alleluia, alleluia, alleluia. Glory to thee, O God. (*Thrice, without reverences.*)

Lord, have mercy. (*Thrice.*)

Glory to the Father, and to the Son, and to the Holy Spirit, now, and ever, and unto ages of ages. Amen.

PSALM LXXXVIII.

O Lord God of my salvation, I have cried day and night before thee: O let my prayer enter into thy presence, incline thine ear unto my calling; for my soul is full of trouble, and my life draweth nigh unto hell. I am counted as one of them that go down into the pit, and I have been even as a man that hath no strength. Free among the dead, like unto them that are wounded, and lie in the grave, who are out of remembrance, and are cut away from thy hand. Thou hast laid me in the lowest pit, in a place of darkness, and in the deep. Thine indignation lieth hard upon me, and thou hast vexed me with all thy storms. Thou hast put away mine acquaintance far from me, and made me to be abhorred of them. I am so fast in prison that I cannot get forth. My sight faileth for very trouble; Lord, I have called daily upon thee, I have stretched forth my hands unto thee. Dost thou show won-

The Priest now saith, secretly, *the* MORNING PRAYERS; *the first three in the Sanctuary.*

I.

We give thanks unto thee, O Lord our God, who hast raised us up from our beds, and hast put into our mouths the word of praise, that we may adore and call upon thy holy Name. And we entreat thee, by thy mercies which thou hast exercised always in our life, send down now also thine aid upon those who stand before the presence of thy holy glory, and await the rich mercy which is from thee. And grant that they may always with fear and love worship thee, praise thee, hymn thee, and adore thine inexpressible goodness.

For unto thee is due all honour, glory and worship, to the Father, and to the Son, and to the Holy Spirit, now, and ever, and unto ages of ages. Amen.

II.

From the night season our soul awaketh early unto thee, O our God; for thy precepts are a light upon the earth. Teach us to perfect righteousness and holiness in thy fear; for we glorify thee, our God, who existest in verity. Incline thine ear and hear us; and call to remembrance by their names, O Lord, all those who are with us and pray with us; and save them by thy might. Bless thy people and sanctify thine inheritance. Grant peace to thy world, to thy Churches, to the priests, to the AUTHORITIES, and to all thy people.

For blessed and glorified is thine all-honourable and majestic Name, of the Father, and of the Son, and of the Holy Spirit, now, and ever, and unto ages of ages. Amen.

III.

In the night season our soul awaketh early unto thee, O God, for thy precepts are light. Teach us thy righteousness, thy commandments and thy statutes, O God. Enlighten

Secretly.

ders among the dead? or shall the dead rise up again, and praise thee? Shall thy loving-kindness be showed in the grave? or thy faithfulness in destruction? Shall thy wondrous works be known in the dark? and thy righteousness in the land where all things are forgotten? Unto thee have I cried, O Lord; and early shall my prayer come before thee. Lord, why abhorrest thou my soul, and hidest thou thy face from me? I am in misery, and like unto him that is at the point to die; even from my youth up thy terrors have I suffered with a troubled mind. Thy wrathful displeasure goeth over me, and the fear of thee hath undone me. They came round about me daily like water, and compassed me together on every side. My lovers and friends hast thou put away from me, and hid mine acquaintance out of my sight. O Lord God of my salvation I have cried day and night before thee: O let my

the eyes of our understanding, lest at any time we sleep unto death in sins. Dispel all darkness from our hearts. Graciously give unto us the Sun of Righteousness, and preserve our life unassailed, by the seal of thy Holy Spirit. Guide our steps into the way of peace. Grant us to behold the dawn and the day with joy, that we may raise our morning prayers unto thee.

For thine is the dominion, and thine are the majesty and the power and the glory, of the Father, and of the Son, and of the Holy Spirit, now, and ever, and unto ages of ages. Amen.

The Priest now cometh forth, and standing with uncovered head before the Holy Door, he saith the remaining Prayers.

IV.

O Lord God, holy and unsearchable, who didst command the light to shine forth from the darkness; who hast refreshed us by the slumber of the night, and hast raised us up to glorify and supplicate thy goodness: Being implored of thine own tender loving-kindness, accept us also now who bow down in adoration before thee, and render thanks unto thee according to the measure of our strength; and grant us all our petitions which are unto salvation. Make us children of the light, and of the day, and heirs of thine everlasting good things. Call to remembrance, O Lord, in the multitude of thy bounties, all thy people here present with us who make their supplications unto thee, and all our brethren on land, on the sea, and in every place of thy dominion, who are in need of thy loving-kindness and of thy succour, and vouchsafe unto them all thy great mercy, that being always preserved in safety of soul and body, we may with boldness magnify thy wondrous and blessed Name, of the Father, and of the Son, and of the Holy Spirit, now, and ever, and unto ages of ages. Amen.

Secretly.

prayer enter into thy presence, incline thine ear unto my calling.

PSALM CIII.

Praise the Lord, O my soul; and all that is within me, praise his holy Name. Praise the Lord, O my soul, and forget not all his benefits: who forgiveth all thy sin, and healeth all thine infirmities; who saveth thy life from destruction, and crowneth thee with mercy and loving-kindness; who satisfieth thy mouth with good things, making thee young and lusty as an eagle. The Lord executeth righteousness and judgment for all them that are oppressed with wrong. He showed his ways unto Moses, his works unto the children of Israel. The Lord is full of compassion and mercy, long-suffering, and of great goodness. He will not alway be chiding; neither keepeth he his anger forever. He hath not dealt with us after our sins; nor rewarded us according to our

For thou art the God of bounties and of loving-kindness, and unto thee we ascribe glory, to the Father, and to the Son, and to the Holy Spirit, now, and ever, and unto ages of ages. Amen.

v.

O Treasury of good things, Fountain eternal, O Father all-holy who workest wonders, all-powerful and almighty: We all adore thee and entreat thee, calling thy mercies and thy compassion to the aid and defence of our lowliness. Call to remembrance thy servants, O Lord; accept the morning prayers of us all as incense before thee; and let none of us be found reprobate, but encompass us with thy bounties. Call to remembrance, O Lord, those who watch and sing praises to thy glory, and to the glory of thine Only-begotten Son who is our God, and of thy Holy Spirit. Be thou their helper and their support. Receive thou their supplications upon thy most heavenly and spiritually discerning altar.

For thou art our God, and unto thee we ascribe glory, to the Father, and to the Son, and to the Holy Spirit, now, and ever, and unto ages of ages. Amen.

vi.

We give thanks unto thee, O Lord God of our salvation; for thou doest all things which are for the welfare of our life, that we may ever look upward unto thee, our Saviour and the Benefactor of our souls. For thou hast refreshed us in that part of the night which is past, and hast raised us up from our beds, and hast led us to stand here in adoration of thy precious Name. Wherefore we entreat thee, O Lord, vouchsafe unto us grace and power, that we may be enabled with understanding to sing praises unto thee, and to pray without ceasing, in fear and trembling working out our own salvation, through the

Secretly.

wickednesses. For look how high the heaven is in comparison of the earth; so great is his mercy also toward them that fear him. Look how wide also the east is from the west: so far hath he set our sins from us. Yea, like as a father pitieth his own children; even so is the Lord merciful unto them that fear him. For he knoweth whereof we are made; he remembereth that we are but dust. The days of man are but as grass; for he flourisheth as a flower of the field. For as soon as the wind goeth over it, it is gone; and the place thereof shall know it no more. But the merciful goodness of the Lord endureth for ever and ever upon them that fear him; and his righteousness upon children's children; even upon such as keep his covenant, and think upon his commandments to do them. The Lord hath prepared his seat in heaven, and his kingdom ruleth over all. O praise the Lord, ye succour of thy Christ. Call to remembrance, O Lord, those who cry aloud unto thee in the night season; hearken unto them and have mercy, and crush under their feet invisible and warring enemies.

For thou art the King of Peace and the Saviour of our souls, and unto thee we ascribe glory, to the Father, and to the Son, and to the Holy Spirit, now, and ever, and unto ages of ages. Amen.

VII.

O God and Father of our Lord Jesus Christ, who hast raised us up from our beds, and hast gathered us together at this hour of prayer: Grant us grace in the opening of our lips, and accept our thanksgivings as we have power to make them; and instruct us in thy statutes. For we know not how to pray as we ought unless thou, O Lord, by thy Holy Spirit, dost guide us. Wherefore we beseech thee: Pardon, remit, forgive whatsoever sins we may have committed unto this present hour, whether by word, or deed, or thought, whether voluntarily or involuntarily; for if thou wilt be extreme to mark iniquity, O Lord, Lord, who shall stand? For with thee is redemption. For thou only art holy, a mighty helper and the defender of our life; and our song shall be ever of thee.

Blessed and glorified be the might of thy kingdom, of the Father, and of the Son, and of the Holy Spirit, now, and ever, and unto ages of ages. Amen.

VIII.

O Lord our God, who hast banished from us the sluggishness of sleep, and hast assembled us together by a holy bidding, that in the night-season also we may lift up our hands, and make unto thee thankful acknowledgment of thy righteous judgments: Accept our prayers, petitions, confessions of thanks and nocturnal worship; and grant unto us,

angels of his, ye that excel in strength; ye that fulfil his commandment and hearken unto the voice of his word, O praise the Lord, all ye his hosts; ye servants of his that do his pleasure. O speak good of the Lord, all ye works of his, in all places of his dominion: praise thou the Lord, O my soul.

In all places of his dominion, praise thou the Lord, O my soul. (*Twice.*)

PSALM CXLIII.

Hear my prayer, O Lord, and consider my desire; hearken unto me for thy truth and righteousness' sake. And enter not into judgment with thy servant; for in thy sight shall no man living be justified. For the enemy hath persecuted my soul; he hath smitten my life down to the ground; he hath laid me in the darkness, as the men that have been long dead. Therefore is my spirit vexed within me, and my heart within me is desolate. Yet do I remember the time past: I muse

O God, faith invincible, love unwavering, hope unfeigned. Bless our goings out and our comings in; our deeds and works, and words and thoughts. And grant that we may come to the beginning of this day praising, singing and blessing the goodness of thine ineffable beneficence.

For blessed is thine all-holy Name, and all-magnified is the kingdom of the Father, and of the Son, and of the Holy Spirit, now, and ever, and unto ages of ages. Amen.

IX.

Illumine our hearts, O Sovereign Master, who lovest man, with the pure light of thy wisdom, and open the eyes of our understanding to the comprehension of the proclamation of thy Gospel. Implant in us, also, the fear of thy blessed commandments; that trampling down all carnal appetites, we may lead a godly life, both thinking and doing always such things as are well pleasing in thy sight.

For thou art the sanctification and the illumination both of our souls and bodies, O Christ our God, and unto thee we ascribe glory, together with thy Father, who hath no beginning, and thine all-holy and blessed and life-giving Spirit, now, and ever, and unto ages of ages. Amen.

X.

O Lord our God, who hast granted unto men pardon through repentance, and hast set us, as an example of the acknowledgment of sin and of the confession which is unto forgiveness, the repentance of the Prophet David: Do thou, the same Lord, have mercy upon us according to thy great mercy, notwithstanding the manifold and great iniquities into which we have fallen; and through the multitude of thy bounties, blot out our transgressions. For unto thee have we sinned, O Lord, who knowest the secret and

Secretly.

upon all thy works; yea, I exercise myself in the works of thy hands. I stretch forth my hands unto thee; my soul gaspeth unto thee as a thirsty land. Hear me, O Lord, and that soon; for my spirit waxeth faint: hide not thy face from me, lest I be like unto them that go down into the pit. O let me hear thy loving-kindness betimes in the morning; for in thee is my trust: show thou me the way that I should walk in; for I lift up my soul unto thee. Deliver me, O Lord, from mine enemies; for I flee unto thee to hide me. Teach me to do the thing that pleaseth thee; for thou art my God: let thy loving Spirit lead me forth into the land of righteousness. Quicken me, O Lord, for thy Name's sake: and for thy righteousness' sake bring my soul out of trouble. And of thy goodness slay mine enemies, and destroy all them that vex my soul; for I am thy servant.

Hearken unto me in thy righteousness,
hidden things of the heart of man, and who alone hast power to remit sins; and as thou hast created a clean heart within us, and established us with thy guiding Spirit, and made known unto us the joy of salvation, cast thou us not away from thy presence. But inasmuch as thou art good and lovest man, graciously vouchsafe unto us that even until our uttermost breath, we may offer unto thee the sacrifice of righteousness, and an offering upon thy holy altars.

Through the mercies and bounties and love toward mankind of thine Only-begotten Son, with whom thou art blessed, together with thine all-holy, and good, and life-giving Spirit, now, and ever, and unto ages of ages. Amen.

XI.

O God, our God, who hast brought into being by thy will all the powers endowed with speech and reason, we beseech thee and supplicate thee: Accept our praises, which together with all thy creatures we offer according to our strength; and reward us with the rich gifts of thy goodness. For unto thee every knee doth bow, whether in heaven or on the earth, or in the regions under the earth, and every breath and created being doth sing thine ineffable glory. For thou only art the true and most merciful God.

For all the powers of heaven magnify thee, and unto thee we ascribe glory, to the Father, and to the Son, and to the Holy Spirit, now, and ever, and unto ages of ages. Amen.

XII.

We praise thee, we hymn thee, we bless thee, we give thanks unto thee, O God of our fathers, that thou hast brought us in safety through the shades of night, and hast shown unto us once again the light of day. And we entreat of thy goodness: Be gracious unto our sins, and accept our prayer in thy great

Secretly.

O Lord, and enter not into judgment with thy servant. (*Twice.*) Thy gracious spirit shall direct my paths upon earth.

Glory to the Father, and to the Son, and to the Holy Spirit, now, and ever, and unto ages of ages. Amen.

tenderness of heart. For we flee unto thee, the merciful and almighty God. Shine in our hearts with the true Sun of thy Righteousness; enlighten our mind and guard all our senses; that walking uprightly as in the day, in the way of thy statutes, we may attain unto life eternal (for with thee is the source of life); and graciously be permitted to come unto the fruition of the light unapproachable.

For thou art our God, and unto thee we ascribe glory, to the Father, and to the Son, and to the Holy Spirit, now, and ever, and unto ages of ages. Amen.

Secretly.

Alleluia, alleluia, alleluia. Glory to thee, O Lord. (*Thrice.*)

Then the Deacon, or if there be none, the Priest, standing in the customary place, in front of the Holy Door, shall recite

THE GREAT LITANY (*Velíkaya Ekténiya*).

In peace let us pray to the Lord.
Choir. Lord, have mercy.

For the peace that is from above, and for the salvation of our souls: ℞

For the peace of the whole world; for the welfare of God's holy churches, and for the union of all: ℞

For this holy Temple, and for those who with faith, devoutness and in the fear of God have entered therein: ℞

For our Most Holy Synod (*or* Patriarch); for our Bishop (*or* Archbishop, *or* Metropolitan), N.; for the honourable Presbytery, the Diaconate in Christ; for all the clergy and the laity: ℞

Here follow petitions for the Ruler of the Land and for all the Authorities according to the elements and nationalities of which the Parish is constituted.

That he will aid them and subdue under their feet every foe and adversary: ℞

For this city, for this holy Temple, and for every city and land, and for those who with faith dwell therein: ℞

For healthful seasons; for abundance of the fruits of the earth, and for peaceful times: ℞

For those who travel by sea or by land; for the sick and the suffering; for those who are in captivity, and for their salvation: ℞

That he will deliver us from all tribulation, wrath, and necessity: ℞

Succour us, save us, have mercy upon us, and keep us, O God, by thy grace: ℞

Calling to remembrance our most holy, all-undefiled, most blessed and glorious Lady, the Birth-giver of God and ever-virgin Mary, with all the

let us pray to the Lord. Choir. Lord, have mercy.

Saints, let us commend ourselves, and each other, and all our life unto Christ our God.

Choir. To thee, O Lord.

Exclamation.

Priest. For unto thee are due all glory, honour and worship, to the Father, and to the Son, and to the Holy Spirit, now, and ever, and unto ages of ages.

Choir. Amen.

Then immediately the Deacon exclaimeth, and the Choir singeth: (3)

God is the Lord, and hath revealed himself unto us. Blessed is he that cometh in the Name of the Lord. (*Four times.*)

And the Deacon, meanwhile, interposeth the following Verses (Stikhí): (4)

Verse 1: O give thanks unto the Lord, for he is gracious; because his mercy endureth forever.

Verse 2: All the nations compassed me about, but in the Name of the Lord have I driven them back.

Verse 3: I shall not die but live, and declare the works of the Lord.

Verse 4: The stone which the builders rejected, the same is become the head of the corner. This is the Lord's doing, and it is marvellous in our eyes.

> *Then shall be sung the Hymn (Tropár) of the Feast. or of the Saint, or of the proper Tone for the Sunday (twice); and the* HYMN TO THE BIRTH-GIVER OF GOD (*Bogoróditchen*) *of the same Tone (Appendix A).*
>
> *Then shall be read the Selection of Psalms appointed (Stikhoslóvie Kafísmi).*
>
> *And after the first portion of the Selection shall be said*

THE LITTLE LITANY (*Málaya Ekténiya*).

Again, yet again, in peace let us pray to the Lord.

Choir. Lord, have mercy.

Succour us, save us, have mercy upon us, and keep us, O God, by thy grace.

Choir. Lord, have mercy.

Calling to remembrance our most holy, all-undefiled, most blessed and glorious Lady, the Birth-giver of God and ever-virgin Mary, with all the Saints, let us commend ourselves, and each other, and all our life unto Christ our God.

Choir. To thee, O Lord.

Exclamation.

Priest. For thine is the majesty, and thine are the kingdom and the power and the glory, of the Father, and of the Son, and of the Holy Spirit, now, and ever, and unto ages of ages.

Choir. Amen.

In some churches omitted.

Then shall be read the second portion of the Selection of Psalms. And when it is finished, there shall be said

THE LITTLE LITANY.

Again, yet again: . . . Succour us, save us: . . . Calling to remembrance: . . .

Exclamation.

Priest. For thou art a good God, who lovest mankind, and unto thee we ascribe glory, to the Father, and to the Son, and to the Holy Spirit, now, and ever, and unto ages of ages.

Choir. Amen.

Then the Holy Door is opened, and the Priest, accompanied by the Deacon (5) *bearing a lighted taper, censeth the Sanctuary, the Holy Images, and the People, and all the Temple (Polieléy).* (6)

And the POLIELÉY *is sung:*

PSALMS CXXXV., CXXXVI.

1. Praise ye the Name of the Lord, O ye servants of the Lord. Alleluia. (*Thrice.*)

2. Praised be the Lord out of Zion, who dwelleth at Jerusalem. Alleluia. (*Thrice.*)

3. O give thanks unto the Lord, for he is gracious, for his mercy endureth forever. Alleluia. (*Thrice.*)

Great Feasts. *And if it be a Great Feast, or other appointed Saint's Day, the proper* EXALTATION * *shall be chanted, first by the Priest and the Deacon, and then by the Choir, before the Holy Image of the Day, as the Priest censeth it where it lieth on the folding-stand.*

Then shall be sung the Hymns (Tropari), with the Refrain; but only on the Lord's Day.

Refrain. Blessed art thou, O Lord: teach me thy statutes.

The company of the Angels was amazed, when they beheld thee numbered among the dead, yet thyself, O Saviour, destroying the power of death, and with thee raising up Adam and releasing all men from Hell. ℟

Wherefore, O Women Disciples, do ye mingle sweet-smelling spices with your tears of pity? the radiant Angel within the sepulchre cried unto the Myrrh-bearing Women: Behold the grave, and understand; for the Saviour is risen from the tomb. ℟

Very early in the morning did the Myrrh-bearing Women run lamenting unto thy tomb; but an Angel came toward them, saying: The time for lamentation is passed; weep not; but announce unto the Apostles the Resurrection. ℟

The Myrrh-bearing Women mourned as, bearing unguents, they drew near thy tomb, O Saviour. But the Angel spake unto them, saying: Why number ye the living among the dead? In that he is God he is risen from the grave. ℟

Glory to the Father, and to the Son, and to the Holy Spirit.

* For Exaltations (or Magnifyings), see the Special Services of the Great Feasts.

In some churches omitted.

Refrain. Blessed art thou, O Lord: teach me thy statutes.

HYMN TO THE TRINITY (*Tróilchny*).

We adore the Father, as also his Son, and the Holy Spirit, the Holy Trinity in One Essence, crying with the Seraphim: Holy, holy, holy art thou, O Lord.

Now, and ever, and unto ages of ages.   Amen.

HYMN TO THE BIRTH-GIVER OF GOD (*Bogoródilchen*).

In that thou didst bear the Giver of Life, O Virgin, thou didst redeem Adam from sin, and didst give to Eve joy in place of sadness; and He who was incarnate of thee, both God and man, hath restored to life those who had fallen therefrom.

Alleluia, alleluia, alleluia.   Glory to thee, O God.   (*Thrice.*)

Then the LITTLE LITANY.

Deacon. Again, yet again, in peace let us pray to the Lord.

Choir. Lord, have mercy.

Succour us, save us, have mercy upon us, and keep us, O God, by thy grace.

Choir. Lord, have mercy.

Calling to remembrance our most holy, all-undefiled, most blessed and glorious Lady, the Birth-giver of God and ever-virgin Mary, with all the Saints, let us commend ourselves, and each other, and all our life unto Christ our God.

Choir. To thee, O Lord.

Exclamation.

Priest. For blessed is thy Name, and glorified is thy kingdom, of the Father, and of the Son, and of the Holy Spirit, now, and ever, and unto ages of ages.

Choir. Amen.

Then the DEGREES OF THE ANTIPHON (*Stepénny Antifóni*) *are sung, according to the Tone of the week.*

Antiphon. Tone IV. From my youth up many passions have warred against me.   But do thou succour and save me, O my Saviour.

Ye who hate Zion shall be put to confusion of the Lord; like grass in the fire shall ye be withered up.

Glory to the Father, and to the Son, and to the Holy Spirit, now, and ever, and unto ages of ages.   Amen.

Through the Holy Spirit is every soul quickened and exalted in purity, and illumined by the Triune Unity in mystic holiness.

Deacon. Let us attend.

Priest. Peace be with you all.

Deacon. Wisdom!   The Gradual (*Prokímen*) in the . . . Tone.

The Graduals (*Prokimená*) in the EIGHT TONES.

Tone I: Now will I arise, saith the Lord: I will set myself for salvation, I will make no tarrying therein.

Verse: The words of the Lord are pure words.

Tone II.: Rise up for me, O Lord, in the judgment that thou hast commanded. And so shall the congregation of the people come about thee.

Verse: O Lord my God, I have put my trust in thee: save me.

Tone III.: Tell it out among the heathen that the Lord is King, and that it is he that hath made the round world so fast that it cannot be moved.

Verse: O sing unto the Lord a new song: Sing unto the Lord all the whole earth.

Tone IV.: Arise, O Lord, and help us, and deliver us, for thy Name's sake.

Verse: O God, we have heard with our ears, and our fathers have told us.

Tone V.: Arise, O Lord my God, and let thy hand be lifted up, for thou reignest forever.

Verse: I will confess unto thee, O Lord: with my whole heart, I will proclaim all thy wondrous works.

Tone VI.: O Lord, stir up thy might, and come and save us.

Verse: Hear, O thou Shepherd of Israel, who leadeth Joseph like a sheep.

Tone VII.: Arise, O Lord, my God, and let thy hand be lifted up: forget not thy poor forever.

Verse: I will confess unto thee, O Lord: with my whole heart, I will proclaim all thy wondrous works.

Tone VIII.: The Lord shall reign forever; thy God, O Zion, from generation to generation.

Verse: Praise the Lord, O my soul: while I live will I praise the Lord.

Deacon. Let us pray to the Lord.

Choir. Lord, have mercy.

The Priest exclaimeth:

For holy art thou, O our God, who restest in the Saints, and unto thee we ascribe glory, to the Father, and to the Son, and to the Holy Spirit, now, and ever, and unto ages of ages.

Choir. Amen.

Glory to the Father, and to the Son, and to the Holy Spirit, now, and ever, and unto ages of ages.

Choir. Amen.

Then the Deacon and the Choir sing:

Let everything that hath breath praise the Lord. (*Four times.*)

Verse: Praise ye God in his Saints. Praise him in the firm foundation of his power.

Then the Deacon proclaimeth:

And that he will graciously vouchsafe unto us to hear his Holy Gospel, let us pray to the Lord God.

Choir. Lord, have mercy. (*Thrice.*)
Deacon. Wisdom, O believers. Let us listen to the Holy Gospel.
Priest. Peace be with you all.
The People. And with thy spirit.

Immediately he addeth:

Priest. The Lesson from the Holy Gospel according to N.* (7)
Choir. Glory to thee, O Lord; glory to thee.
Deacon. Let us attend.

Then the Priest readeth the Holy Gospel.

Choir. Glory to thee, O Lord; glory to thee.

The Choir then singeth, while the book of the Holy Gospels is laid upon the table at the centre of the Temple:

In that we have beheld the Resurrection of Christ, let us bow down before the Holy Lord Jesus, the only sinless One. Thy Cross do we adore, O Christ, and thy holy Resurrection we laud and glorify: for thou art our God, and we know none other beside thee; we call upon thy Name. O come, all ye faithful, let us adore Christ's holy Resurrection. For lo, through the Cross is joy come into all the world. Ever blessing the Lord, let us sing his Resurrection: for in that he endured the Cross he hath destroyed Death by death.

This Hymn is always sung at the Lord's Day Matins, with rare exceptions. It is sung on Lazarus's Saturday, and on all week-days from Easter until Ascension-Day.) (8)

And if it be the Eve of Palm Sunday, Psalm li. is read, and the Priest censeth **Palm**
the Palms. And when it is finished, he blesseth the Palms.† **Sunday.**

But if it be the ordinary VIGIL OFFICE:

Glory to the Father, and to the Son, and to the Holy Spirit.

Through the prayers of the Apostles, O Merciful One, blot out the multitude of our transgressions.

Now, and ever, and unto ages of ages. Amen.

Through the prayers of the Birth-giver of God, O Merciful One, blot out the multitude of our transgressions.

Have mercy upon me, O God, according to thy great goodness; according to the multitude of thy mercies do away mine offences.

On the Lord's Day:

Jesus, having risen from the grave as he foretold, hath given unto us life eternal and great mercy.

On Feast Days, instead of this, the Canticles (Stikhíry) of the Feast. **The Great**
Feasts.

Deacon. O Lord, save thy people, and bless thine heritage. Visit thy world with mercies and bounties. Exalt the horn of Orthodox Christians, and send down upon us thy rich mercies. Through the intercessions of

* See Table of the Gospel Lessons, page xix.
† See the Service for Blessing the Palms, at end of Service for Palm Sunday (Special Services).

our all-undefiled Lady, the Birth-giver of God and ever-virgin Mary, through the might of the precious and life-giving Cross; through the protection of the honourable Bodiless Powers of Heaven; of the honourable, glorious Prophet, Forerunner and Baptist, John; of the holy, glorious and all-laudable Apostles; of our Holy Fathers, great Hierarchs and Œcumenical Teachers, Basil the Great, Gregory the Theologian and John Chrysostom; of our Holy Father Nicholas, Archbishop of Myra in Lycia, the Wonder-worker; (of our Holy Fathers of All-Russia, Wonder-workers, Peter, Alexis, Jonah and Philip); of our Holy Fathers Methodius and Kyril, Evangelizers of the Slavs; of the holy, glorious and right-victorious Martyrs; of our reverend and God-bearing Fathers, the holy and righteous Ancestors of God, Joachim and Anna; of Saint N. (*the holy patron of the Temple*); and of all thy Saints, we beseech thee, O most merciful Lord, give ear unto the petitions of us sinners who make our supplications unto thee, and have mercy upon us.

Choir. Lord, have mercy. (*Twelve times.*)

Priest. Through the mercies and bounties and compassion of thine Only-begotten Son, with whom thou art blessed, together with thine all-holy, and good, and life-giving Spirit, now, and ever, and unto ages of ages.

Choir. Amen.

The Priest, the Deacon and the People now salute the Holy Gospels and the Holy Image of the Feast.

Great Feasts. *And if the bread and wine and oil have been blessed during Vespers, before the Matins, the Priest now anointeth the faithful with the oil, and the bread is distributed.* (9)

The CANON *of the proper Tone,* or of the Feast, is then sung.* (10)

After the Third Theme-Song (Irmós) the LITTLE LITANY (*see page 29*) *followeth.*

Exclamation.

Priest. For thou art our God, and unto thee we ascribe glory, to the Father, and to the Son, and to the Holy Spirit, now, and ever, and unto ages of ages.

Choir. Amen.

After the Sixth Theme-Song of the Canon also the LITTLE LITANY (*see page 29*) *followeth, with the Exclamation at the end:*

For thou art the King of the world, and the Saviour of our souls, and unto thee we ascribe glory, to the Father, and to the Son, and to the Holy Spirit, now, and ever, and unto ages of ages. Amen.

Before the Ninth Ode the Magnificat (or the Refrain appointed for Matins on certain of the Great Feasts) is sung.

The Deacon cometh and standeth before the Holy Image of the Birth-giver of God, and censing it, he saith:

The Birth-giver of God and Mother of the Light let us honour and extol in song.

* See Appendix A.

Choir. My soul doth magnify the Lord, and my spirit hath rejoiced in God my Saviour.

Refrain. More honourable than the Cherubim, and beyond compare more glorious than the Seraphim, thou who without defilement barest God the Word, true Birth-giver of God, we magnify thee.

For he hath regarded the lowliness of his handmaiden; for behold from henceforth all generations shall call me blessed.

More honourable than the Cherubim, . . .

For he that is mighty hath magnified me, and holy is his Name; and his mercy is on them that fear him, throughout all generations. ℞

He hath showed strength with his arm; he hath scattered the proud in the imagination of their hearts. ℞

He hath put down the mighty from their seat, and hath exalted the humble and meek. He hath filled the empty with good things, and the rich hath he sent empty away. ℞

He remembering his mercy hath holpen his servant Israel, as he promised to our forefathers, Abraham and his seed forever. ℞

Also the SONG OF ZACHARIAS (Luke i. 68–79).

Blessed be the Lord God of Israel, for he hath visited and redeemed his people; and hath raised up a mighty salvation for us, in the house of his servant David; as he spake by the mouth of his holy prophets, which have been since the world began; that we should be saved from our enemies, and from the hand of all that hate us. To perform the mercy promised to our forefathers, and to remember his holy covenant; to perform the oath which he sware to our forefather Abraham that he would give us; that we being delivered out of the hand of our enemies, might serve him without fear; in holiness and righteousness before him all the days of our life. And thou, child, shalt be called the prophet of the Highest, for thou shalt go before the face of the Lord to prepare his ways! To give knowledge of salvation unto his people, for the remission of their sins, through the tender mercy of our God, whereby the day-spring from on high hath visited us: to give light to them that sit in darkness and in the shadow of death, and to guide our feet into the way of peace.

The Ninth Ode followeth, and then:

THE LITTLE LITANY.

Deacon. Again, yet again, in peace let us pray to the Lord.

Choir. Lord, have mercy.

Succour us, save us, have mercy upon us, and keep us, O God, by thy grace.

Choir. Lord, have mercy.

Calling to remembrance our most holy, all-undefiled, most blessed and glorious Lady, the Birth-giver of God and ever-virgin Mary, with all the

Saints, let us commend ourselves, and each other, and all our life unto Christ our God.

  Choir. To thee, O Lord.

Exclamation.

Priest. For all the powers of heaven praise thee, and unto thee we ascribe glory, to the Father, and to the Son, and to the Holy Spirit, now, and ever, and unto ages of ages.

Choir. Amen.

The EXAPOSTILÁRION *of the Lord's Day.* (11)

Verse 1: Holy is the Lord our God. (*Thrice.*)

Verse 2: Over all men is our God.

Let everything which hath breath praise the Lord. Praise the Lord of heaven: praise Him in the height.

Refrain. To thee, O God, is due our song.

Praise him all ye Angels of his: praise him all his host.

Refrain. To thee, O God, is due our song.

And here begin the Verses (Stikhíry) of the Tone, or of the Feast. And then:

Glory to the Father, and to the Son, and to the Holy Spirit, now, and ever, and unto ages of ages. Amen.

HYMN TO THE BIRTH-GIVER OF GOD (*Bogoróditchen*). (*On the Lord's Day Evening*):

Most blessed art thou, O Virgin Birth-giver of God: For through him who became incarnate of thee Hell is led captive, Adam is recalled from the dead, the curse is made void, Eve is set free, Death is slain, and we have been endowed with life. Wherefore we cry aloud, extolling in song: Blessed art thou, O Christ our God, in whose sight it is thus well-pleasing. Glory to thee.

Priest. Glory to thee, who hast shown us the light. (12)

Choir. Glory be to God on high, and on earth peace, good will towards men. We praise thee, we bless thee, we worship thee, we glorify thee, we give thanks to thee for thy great glory, O Lord God, heavenly King, God the Father Almighty. O Lord, the only-begotten Son Jesus Christ, and the Holy Spirit; O Lord God, Lamb of God, Son of the Father, that takest away the sins of the world, have mercy upon us. Thou that takest away the sins of the world, receive our prayer. Thou that sittest at the right hand of God the Father, have mercy upon us. For thou only art holy; thou only art the Lord, thou only, O Jesus Christ, art most high in the glory of God the Father. Amen.

Every day will I give thanks unto thee, and praise thy Name forever and ever. Lord, thou hast been our refuge from one generation to another. I said, Lord, be merciful unto me; heal my soul, for I have sinned against thee. I flee unto thee. Teach me to do thy will; for thou art my God. For with thee is the well of life, and in thy light shall we see light. O continue forth thy loving-kindness unto them that know thee.

Vouchsafe, O Lord, to keep us this day without sin. Blessed art thou, O Lord God of our fathers, and praised and glorified be thy holy Name forever. Amen.

Let thy merciful kindness, O Lord, be upon us, as we do put our trust in thee.

Blessed art thou, O Lord: O teach me thy statutes. (*Thrice.*)

Lord, thou hast been our refuge from one generation to another. said: Lord, be merciful unto me; heal my soul, for I have sinned against thee. Lord, I flee unto thee. Teach me to do the thing that pleaseth thee; for thou art my God. For with thee is the well of life, and in thy light shall we see light. O continue forth thy loving-kindness unto those who know thee.

O Holy God, Holy Mighty, Holy Immortal One, have mercy upon us. (*Thrice.*)

Glory to the Father, and to the Son, and to the Holy Spirit, now, and ever, and unto ages of ages. Amen.

O Holy Immortal One, have mercy upon us.

Then in a loud voice:

O Holy God, Holy Mighty, Holy Immortal One, have mercy upon us.

Then shall be sung the appointed Hymn of Dismissal.

The Saturday Evening (Sunday) Hymns:

In Tones I., III., V., VII.:

To-day is salvation come into the world. Let us sing praises unto him who rose again from the grave, the Author of our life: For in that by death he hath destroyed Death, he hath given unto us the victory and great mercy.

In Tones II., IV., VI., VIII.:

When thou hadst risen again from the tomb, and hadst burst the bonds of Hell, thou didst loose the condemnation of death, O Lord, redeeming all men from the snares of the enemy. When thou hadst revealed thyself to thine Apostles, thou didst send them forth to proclaim thee. And through them thou hast granted thy peace unto the universe, O only All-merciful One.

Then the AUGMENTED LITANY (*Sugúbaya Ekténiya*).

Deacon. Have mercy upon us, O God, according to thy great mercy, we beseech thee: hearken, and have mercy.

Choir. Lord, have mercy.

Here follow petitions for the Ruler of the Land and for all the Authorities (according to the elements and nationalities of which the Parish is constituted).

Again we pray for our Holy Synod (*or* Patriarch); for our Bishop (*or* Archbishop, *or* Metropolitan), N.; and for all our brethren in Christ.

Choir. Lord, have mercy. (*Thrice.*)

Furthermore we pray for all their Christ-loving Army and Navy. ℞

Furthermore we pray for the blessed and ever-memorable founders of this holy Temple; and for all our devout fathers and brethren, Orthodox believers, departed this life before us, who here and in all the world lie asleep in the Lord. ℞

Furthermore we pray for mercy, life, health, peace, salvation, forgiveness and remission of sins for the servants of God, our brethren of this holy Temple.

Furthermore we pray for those who bear fruit and do good works in this holy and all-honourable Temple; for those who labour in its service; for the singers; and for the people here present, who await in firm hope thy great and rich mercies. ℞

Choir. Lord, have mercy. *(Thrice.)*

Exclamation.

Priest. For thou art a merciful God, who lovest mankind, and unto thee we ascribe glory, to the Father, and to the Son, and to the Holy Spirit, now, and ever, and unto ages of ages.

Choir. Amen.

Deacon. Let us complete our morning prayer unto the Lord.

Choir. Lord, have mercy.

Succour us, save us, have mercy upon us, and keep us, O God, by thy grace.

Choir. Lord, have mercy.

A day all-perfect, holy, peaceful and sinless, let us beseech of the Lord: ℞

An Angel of Peace, the faithful guide and guardian of our souls: ℞

The pardon and remission of our sins and transgressions: ℞

All things which are good and profitable to our souls, and peace to the world: ℞

That we may pass the residue of our life in peace and penitence: ℞

A Christian ending to our life, painless, blameless, peaceful; and a good defence before the dread Judgment Seat of Christ. ℞

let us beseech of the Lord. Choir. Grant it, O Lord.

Calling to remembrance our most holy, all-undefiled, most blessed and glorious Lady, the Birth-giver of God and ever-virgin Mary, with all the Saints, let us commend ourselves, and each other, and all our life unto Christ our God.

Choir. To thee, O Lord.

Exclamation.

Priest. For thou art the God of mercies and of bounties, and of love toward mankind, and unto thee we ascribe glory, to the Father, and to the Son, and to the Holy Spirit, now, and ever, and unto ages of ages.

Choir. Amen.

Priest. Peace be with you all.

People. And with thy spirit.

Deacon. Let us bow our heads unto the Lord.

Choir. Unto thee, O Lord.

And the Priest saith this Prayer, secretly:

O holy Lord, who dwellest on high, and regardest the humble of heart, and with thine all-seeing eye dost behold all creation, unto Thee have we bowed the neck of our soul and body, and we entreat thee: Stretch forth thine invisible hand from thy holy dwelling-place and bless us all. And if in aught we have sinned, whether voluntarily or involuntarily, forgive, inasmuch as thou art a good God, and lovest mankind; vouchsafing unto us thy earthly and heavenly good things.

Secretly.

Exclamation.

For thine it is to show mercy and to save us, O our God, and unto thee we ascribe glory, to the Father, and to the Son, and to the Holy Spirit, now, and ever, and unto ages of ages.

Choir. Amen.

Deacon. Wisdom!

Choir. Bless.

Priest. He who in verity existeth, even Christ our God, is blessed always, now, and ever, and unto ages of ages.

Choir. Amen.

Establish, O Lord, our most God-fearing Ruler, and the Holy Orthodox faith, and Orthodox Christians, unto ages of ages.

Priest. Save us, O most holy Birth-giver of God.

Choir. More honourable than the Cherubim, and beyond compare more glorious than the Seraphim, thou who without defilement barest God the Word, in very truth the Birth-giver of God, we magnify thee.

Priest. Glory to thee, O Christ our God, our sure hope; glory to thee.

Choir. Glory to the Father, and to the Son, and to the Holy Spirit, now, and ever, and unto ages of ages. Amen.

Lord, have mercy. (*Thrice.*) Bless.

Then the Priest bestoweth the BENEDICTION. *On Saturday Evening:*

May he who rose again from the dead, Christ our true God; through the prayers of his most holy Mother, of the holy, glorious and all-praise-worthy Apostles, of Saint N. (*the Patron of the Church*); of Saint N. (*the Saint of the Day*); and of all the Saints, have mercy upon us and save us; inasmuch as he is good and loveth mankind.

Then the Choir singeth the MANY YEARS:

Preserve, O Lord, our most God-fearing Ruler; our (Patriarch, *or* Holy Synod); our (Metropolitan, Archbishop, *or* Bishop), N.; and all Orthodox Christians, for many years.

———

The Holy Doors or curtain shall be closed, and THE FIRST HOUR *is then read.*

THE FIRST HOUR *

O come, let us worship God our King. O come, let us worship and fall down before Christ our King, and our God. O come, let us worship and fall down before the Very Christ, our King and our God. (*Three reverences.*)

Ponder my words, O Lord, consider my meditation. O hearken thou unto the voice of my calling, my King, and my God: for unto thee will I make my prayer. My voice shalt thou hear betimes, O Lord; early in the morning will I direct my prayer unto thee, and will look up. For thou art the God that hast no pleasure in wickedness; neither shall any evil dwell with thee. Such as be foolish shall not stand in thy sight; for thou hatest all them that work vanity. Thou shalt destroy them that speak lies: the Lord will abhor both the blood-thirsty and deceitful man. But as for me, I will come into thine house, even upon the multitude of thy mercy; and in thy fear will I worship toward thy holy temple. Lead me, O Lord, in thy righteousness, because of mine enemies; make thy way plain before my face. For there is no faithfulness in his mouth; their inward parts are very wickedness. Their throat is an open sepulchre; they flatter with their tongue. Destroy thou them, O God; let them perish through their own imaginations; cast them out in the multitude of their ungodliness; for they have rebelled against thee. And let all them that put their trust in thee rejoice: they shall ever be giving of thanks, because thou defendest them; they that love thy Name shall be joyful in thee; for thou, Lord, wilt give thy blessing unto the righteous, and with thy favourable kindness wilt thou defend him, as with a shield.

PSALM XC.

Lord, thou hast been our refuge, from one generation to another. Before the mountains were brought forth, or ever the earth and the world were made, thou art God from everlasting, and world without end. Thou turnest man to destruction; again thou sayest, Come again, ye children of men. For a thousand years in thy sight are but as yesterday; seeing that is past as a watch in the night. As soon as thou scatterest them they are even as a sleep; and fade away suddenly like the grass. In the morning it is green, and groweth up; but in the evening it is cut down, dried up, and withered. For we consume away in thy displeasure, and are afraid at thy wrathful indignation. Thou hast set our misdeeds before thee; and our secret sins in the light of thy countenance. For when thou

* See Appendix B, III.

art angry all our days are gone: we bring our years to an end, as it were a tale that is told. The days of our age are threescore years and ten; and though men be so strong that they come to fourscore years, yet is their strength then but labour and sorrow; so soon passeth it away, and we are gone. But who regardeth the power of thy wrath? for even thereafter as a man feareth, so is thy displeasure. So teach us to number our days, that we may apply our hearts unto wisdom. Turn thee again, O Lord, at the last, and be gracious unto thy servants. O satisfy us with thy mercy, and that soon: so shall we rejoice and be glad all the days of our life. Comfort us again now after the time that thou hast plagued us; and for the years wherein we have suffered adversity. Show thy servants thy work, and their children thy glory. And the glorious Majesty of the Lord our God be upon us: prosper thou the work of our hands upon us; O prosper thou our handy-work.

PSALM CI.

. My song shall be of mercy and judgment; unto thee, O Lord, will I sing. O let me have understanding in the way of godliness! When wilt thou come unto me? I will walk in my house with a perfect heart. I will take no wicked thing in hand; I hate the sins of unfaithfulness; there shall no such cleave unto me. A froward heart shall depart from me; I will not know a wicked person. Whoso privily slandereth his neighbour, him will I destroy. Whoso hath also a proud look and high stomach, I will not suffer him. Mine eyes look upon such as are faithful in the land, that they may dwell with me. Whoso leadeth a godly life, he shall be my servant. There shall no deceitful person dwell in my house; he that telleth lies shall not tarry in my sight. I shall soon destroy all the ungodly that are in the land; that I may root out all wicked doers from the city of the Lord.

Glory to the Father, and to the Son, and to the Holy Spirit, now, and ever, and unto ages of ages. Amen.

Alleluia, alleluia, alleluia. Glory to thee, O God. (*Thrice; three reverences.*)

Lord, have mercy. (*Thrice.*)

Glory to the Father, and to the Son, and to the Holy Spirit.

*Then the Hymn (Tropár) for the Day, in the proper Tone, is read.**

Now, and ever, and unto ages of ages. Amen.

HYMN TO THE BIRTH-GIVER OF GOD (*Bogoródilchen*).

What shall we call thee, O thou who art full of grace? Heaven, for from thee shone forth the Sun of Righteousness; Paradise, for thou hast budded forth the Flower of Immortality; Virgin, for thou hast remained undefiled: Pure Mother, for thou hast held in thy holy embrace thy Son, who is God of all. Beseech thou him that he will save our souls.

* For the Hymns in the Eight Tones, see Appendix A.

But if it be during Great Fast (Lent), we say the Hymn (Tropár) in Tone VI.

Then: O hearken thou betimes unto the voice of my calling, my King and my God.

Verse (Stikh) 1: Ponder my words, O Lord: consider my meditation.

Verse 2: For unto thee will I make my prayer.

Glory to the Father, and to the Son, and to the Holy Spirit, now, and ever, and unto ages of ages. Amen.

And again the Hymn to the Birth-giver of God: What shall we call thee:

Order my steps in thy word, and so shall no wickedness have dominion over me. O deliver me from the wrongful dealings of men, and so shall I keep thy commandments. Show the light of thy countenance upon thy servant, and teach me thy statutes.

Let my mouth be filled with thy praise, O Lord, that I may sing of thy glory and honour all the day long.

O Holy God, Holy Mighty, Holy Immortal One, have mercy upon us. (*Thrice.*)

Glory to the Father, and to the Son, and to the Holy Spirit, now, and ever, and unto ages of ages. Amen.

O all-holy Trinity, have mercy upon us. O Lord, wash away our sins. O Master, pardon our transgressions. O Holy One, visit and heal our infirmities, for thy Name's sake.

Lord, have mercy. (*Thrice.*) Glory . . . now, and ever . . .

Our Father, who art in heaven, Hallowed be thy Name. Thy kingdom come. Thy will be done on earth, As it is in heaven. Give us this day our daily bread. And forgive us our trespasses, As we forgive those who trespass against us. And lead us not into temptation; But deliver us from the Evil One:

Priest. For thine is the kingdom, and the power, and the glory, of the Father, and of the Son, and of the Holy Spirit, now, and ever, and unto ages of ages.

Amen. Lord, have mercy. (*Twelve times.*) Glory . . . now and ever. . .

*If it be not the Great Fast (Lent), the Collect-Hymn (Kondák) of the Tone, or of the Saint for the Day, or of the approaching Feast, is then read.**

But if it be the Great Fast, or if there be no special Collect-Hymn, on Monday, Tuesday and Thursday, the following HYMN TO THE BIRTH-GIVER OF GOD *(Bogoróditchen) shall be read:*

With heart and lips let us continually magnify the glorious Mother of God, more holy than the Angels, confessing her to be the Birth-giver of God, who did, in very truth, bring forth God incarnate, and who unceasingly doth intercede for our souls.

* For Collect-Hymns for the Twelve Great Feasts, see the Special Services.

But on Wednesday and Friday the following shall be read:

Speedily prevent, ere he lead us into captivity, the enemy which blasphemeth thee and constraineth us, O Christ our God: Overcome by thy Cross those who war against us, that they may know what power hath the faith of Orthodox believers; through the intercessions of the Birth-giver of God, O thou who alone lovest mankind.

On Saturday the following shall be said:

Unto thee, O Lord, the Author of Creation, the universe doth offer the God-bearing martyrs as the first-fruits of nature. By whose prayers, through the Birth-giver of God, do thou preserve in peace profound thy Church, which is thine estate, O most merciful One.

Lord, have mercy. (*Forty times.*)

Thou who, at all times, and at every hour, both in heaven and on earth, art worshipped and glorified, O Christ-God, long-suffering and plenteous in mercy and compassion; who lovest the just and showest mercy to those who are hardened in sin; who callest all men to salvation through the promise of good things to come: Do thou, the same Lord, receive also our supplications at this present time, and direct our lives according to thy commandments. Sanctify our souls; purify our bodies; set aright our minds; cleanse our thoughts; and deliver us from all calamity, wrath and distress. Compass us round about with thy holy Angels; that, guided and guarded by their host, we may attain unto the unity of the faith, and unto the comprehension of thine ineffable glory. For blessed art thou unto ages of ages. Amen.

Glory to the Father, and to the Son, and to the Holy Spirit, now, and ever, and unto ages of ages. Amen. Lord, have mercy. (*Thrice.*)

More honourable than the Cherubim, and beyond compare more glorious than the Seraphim, thou who without defilement barest God the Word, true Birth-giver of God, we magnify thee.

In the Name of the Lord bless, Father.

Priest. God be bountiful unto us, and bless us, and show us the light of his countenance, and be merciful unto us.

And if it be the Great Fast, we make three great reverences to the earth, reciting the prescribed

PRAYER OF ST. EPHRAIM THE SYRIAN.

O Lord and Master of my life, grant not unto me a spirit of slothfulness, of discouragement, of lust of power, of vain babbling. (*Reverence.*)

But vouchsafe unto me thy servant the spirit of continence, of meekness, of patience, and of love. (*Reverence.*)

Yea, O Lord and King, grant that I may perceive my own transgressions, and judge not my brother. For blessed art thou unto ages of ages. Amen. (*Reverence. Then twelve lesser reverences, saying at each:* O God, cleanse thou me, a sinner. *Then the whole Prayer is repeated; with one great reverence in conclusion.*)

O Holy God, Holy Mighty, Holy Immortal One, have mercy upon us. (*Thrice.*)

Glory to the Father, and to the Son, and to the Holy Spirit, now, and ever, and unto ages of ages. Amen.

O all-holy Trinity, have mercy upon us. O Lord, wash away our sins. O Master, pardon our transgressions. O Holy One, visit and heal our infirmities, for thy Name's sake.

Lord, have mercy. (*Thrice.*)

Glory to the Father, and to the Son, and to the Holy Spirit, now, and ever, and unto ages of ages. Amen.

Our Father, who art in heaven, Hallowed be thy Name. Thy kingdom come. Thy will be done on earth, As it is in heaven. Give us this day our daily bread. And forgive us our trespasses, As we forgive those who trespass against us. And lead us not into temptation; But deliver us from the Evil One:

Priest. For thine is the kingdom, and the power, and the glory, of the Father, and of the Son, and of the Holy Spirit, now, and ever, and unto ages of ages.

Reader. Glory . . . now, and ever . . . Amen. Lord, have mercy. (*Twelve times.*)

And this Prayer:

O Christ, the true Light, which illumineth and sanctifieth every man who cometh into the world! Let the light of thy countenance be showed upon us, that in it we may behold the light ineffable; and guide our footsteps aright, to the keeping of thy commandments; through the intercessions of thine all-pure Mother, and of all thy Saints. Amen.

Glory to the Father, and to the Son, and to the Holy Spirit, now, and ever, and unto ages of ages. Amen.

Lord, have mercy. (*Thrice.*) Bless.

Priest. Through the prayers of our holy Fathers, O Lord Jesus Christ, have mercy upon us.

Hymn to the Birth-giver of God (*Bogoróditchen*).

We, thy servants, in that we have been delivered from calamities, do offer unto thee, O Birth-giver of God, who as victorious Chieftain warrest for us, songs of triumph and thanksgiving: Do thou also, in that thou hast might invincible, free us from all assaults, that we may cry unto thee: Hail, O Bride unwedded!

Priest. Glory to thee, O Christ-God, our hope; glory to thee.

Choir. Glory to the Father, and to the Son, and to the Holy Spirit, now, and ever, and unto ages of ages. Amen.

Lord, have mercy. (*Thrice.*) Bless.

BENEDICTION.

Priest. May Christ, our true God, through the prayers of his all-pure Mother; of the holy, glorious and all-laudable Apostles (*and of the Saint to whom the church is dedicated; and of the Saint for the day*); of the holy ancestors of God, Joachim and Anna; and of all the Saints, have mercy upon us, and save us: forasmuch as he is gracious and he alone loveth mankind.

Choir. Lord, have mercy. (*Thrice.*)

THE THIRD HOUR *

After the Priest hath bestowed the blessing, we say:

Amen. Glory to thee, our God; glory to thee.

O heavenly King, the Comforter, Spirit of Truth, who art in all places and fillest all things; Treasury of good things and Giver of life: Come and take up thine abode in us, and cleanse us from every stain; and save our souls, O Good One.

O Holy God, Holy Mighty, Holy Immortal One, have mercy upon us. (*Thrice, and three reverences.*)

Glory to the Father, and to the Son, and to the Holy Spirit, now, and ever, and unto ages of ages. Amen.

O all-holy Trinity, have mercy upon us. O Lord, wash away our sins. O Master, pardon our transgressions. O Holy One, visit and heal our infirmities for thy Name's sake.

Lord, have mercy. (*Thrice.*)

Glory to the Father, and to the Son, and to the Holy Spirit, now, and ever, and unto ages of ages. Amen.

Our Father, who art in heaven, Hallowed be thy Name. Thy kingdom come. Thy will be done on earth, As it is in heaven. Give us this day our daily bread. And forgive us our trespasses, As we forgive those who trespass against us. And lead us not into temptation; But deliver us from the Evil One:

Priest. For thine is the kingdom, and the power, and the glory, of the Father, and of the Son, and of the Holy Spirit, now, and ever, and unto ages of ages.

Reader. Amen.

Lord, have mercy. (*Twelve times.*) Glory . . . now, and ever . . .

O come, let us worship God our King. O come, let us worship and fall down before Christ, our King and our God. O come, let us worship and fall down before the Very Christ, our King and our God. (*Three reverences.*)

PSALM XVII.

Hear the right, O Lord, consider my complaint, and hearken unto my

* See Appendix B, III.

prayer, that goeth not out of feigned lips. Let my sentence come forth from thy presence; and let thine eyes look upon the thing that is equal. Thou hast proved and visited mine heart in the night-season; thou hast tried me, and shalt find no wickedness in me; for I am utterly purposed that my mouth shall not offend. Because of men's works that are done against the words of thy lips, I have kept me from the ways of the destroyer. O hold thou up my goings in thy paths, that my footsteps slip not. I have called upon thee, O God, for thou shalt hear me: incline thine ear to me, and hearken unto my words. Show thy marvellous loving-kindness, thou that art the Saviour of them which put their trust in thee, from such as resist thy right hand. Keep me as the apple of an eye; hide me under the shadow of thy wings, from the ungodly, that trouble me; mine enemies compass me round about, to take away my soul. They are inclosed in their own fat, and their mouth speaketh proud things. They lie waiting in our way on every side, turning their eyes down to the ground; like as a lion that is greedy of his prey, and as it were a lion's whelp lurking in secret places. Up, Lord, disappoint him, and cast him down; deliver my soul from the ungodly, which is a sword of thine; from the men of thy hand, O Lord, from the men, I say, and from the evil world; which have their portion in this life, whose bellies thou fillest with thy hid treasure. They have children at their desire, and leave the rest of their substance for their babes. But as for me, I will behold thy presence in righteousness; and when I awake up after thy likeness, I shall be satisfied with it.

Psalm xxv.

Unto thee, O Lord, will I lift up my soul; my God, I have put my trust in thee: O let me not be confounded, neither let mine enemies triumph over me. For all they that hope in thee shall not be ashamed; but such as transgress without a cause shall be put to confusion. Show me thy ways, O Lord, and teach me thy paths. Lead me forth in thy truth, and learn me: for thou art the God of my salvation; in thee hath been my hope all the day long. Call to remembrance, O Lord, thy tender mercies, and thy loving-kindnesses, which have been ever of old. O remember not the sins and offences of my youth; but according to thy mercy think thou upon me, O Lord, for thy goodness. Gracious and righteous is the Lord; therefore will he teach sinners in the way. Them that are meek shall he guide in judgment; and such as are gentle, them shall he learn his way. All the paths of the Lord are mercy and truth, unto such as keep his covenant, and his testimonies. For thy Name's sake, O Lord, be merciful unto my sin; for it is great. What man is he that feareth the Lord? him shall he teach in the way that he shall choose. His soul shall dwell at ease, and his seed shall inherit the land. The secret of the Lord is among them that fear him; and he will show them his covenant. Mine eyes are ever looking unto the Lord; for he shall pluck my feet out of the net. Turn thee unto me, and have mercy upon me; for I am desolate, and in misery. The sorrows of my heart are enlarged: O bring thou me out of my troubles. Look upon my adversity and misery, and forgive me all my sin. Consider mine enemies, how many they are; and they bear a tyrannous hate against me. O keep my soul, and deliver me: let me not be confounded, for I have put my trust in thee. Let perfectness and righteous dealing wait upon me; for my hope hath been in thee. Deliver Israel, O God, out of all his troubles.

PSALM LI.

Have mercy upon me, O God, after thy great goodness; according to the multitude of thy mercies do away mine offences. Wash me throughly from my wickedness, and cleanse me from my sin. For I acknowledge my faults, and my sin is ever before me. Against thee only have I sinned, and done this evil in thy sight; that thou mightest be justified in thy saying, and clear when thou art judged. Behold, I was shapen in wickedness, and in sin hath my mother conceived me. But lo, thou requirest truth in the inward parts, and shalt make me to understand wisdom secretly. Thou shalt purge me with hyssop, and I shall be clean; thou shalt wash me, and I shall be whiter than snow. Thou shalt make me hear of joy and gladness, that the bones which thou hast broken may rejoice. Turn thy face from my sins, and put out all my misdeeds. Make me a clean heart, O God, and renew a right spirit within me. Cast me not away from thy presence, and take not thy Holy Spirit from me. O give me the comfort of thy help again, and stablish me with thy free Spirit. Then shall I teach thy ways unto the wicked, and sinners shall be converted unto thee. Deliver me from blood-guiltiness, O God, thou that art the God of my health; and my tongue shall sing of thy righteousness. Thou shalt open my lips, O Lord, and my mouth shall show thy praise. For thou desirest no sacrifice, else would I give it thee; but thou delightest not in burnt-offerings. The sacrifice of God is a troubled spirit: a broken and contrite heart, O God, shalt thou not despise. O be favourable and gracious unto Sion; build thou the walls of Jerusalem. Then shalt thou be pleased with the sacrifice of righteousness, with the burnt-offerings and oblations; then shall they offer young bullocks upon thine altar.

Glory to the Father, and to the Son, and to the Holy Spirit, now, and ever, and unto ages of ages. Amen.

Alleluia, alleluia, alleluia. Glory to thee, O God. (*Thrice.*)

Lord, have mercy. (*Thrice.*)

Glory to the Father, and to the Son, and to the Holy Spirit.

Then the Hymn for the Day (Tropár): *

Now, and ever, and unto ages of ages. Amen.

* For Hymns in the Eight Tones, see Appendix A; for the Great Feasts, see the Special Services.

HYMN TO THE BIRTH-GIVER OF GOD (*Bogoróditchen*).

O Birth-giver of God, thou art the true Vine who didst bud forth for us the Fruit of Life: Implore thou him, we beseech thee, O Lady, together with the Apostles and all the Saints, that he will have mercy on our souls.

But if it be the Great Fast (Lent), then this Hymn (Tropár), in Tone VI., is said:

O Lord, who at the Third Hour didst send down upon thine Apostles thy Holy Spirit: Take not the same from us, O Good One, but renew Him in us who make our supplications unto thee.

Verse (Stikh) 1: Make me a clean heart, O God, and renew a right spirit within me.

Verse 2: Cast me not away from thy presence, and take not thy Holy Spirit from me.

And to these we add: O Lord, who at the Third Hour: *and the rest of the Hymn again, to the end, making one reverence for each.*

Glory to the Father, and to the Son, and to the Holy Spirit, now, and ever, and unto ages of ages. Amen.

And again the HYMN TO THE BIRTH-GIVER OF GOD (*Bogoróditchen*): O Birth-giver of God, thou art the true Vine. . . .

Praised be the Lord God, praised be the Lord daily, the God of our salvation: who helpeth us: our God is the God of whom cometh salvation. He is our God, even the God of our salvation.

O Holy God, Holy Mighty, . . . O all-holy Trinity, . . .

Lord, have mercy. (*Thrice.*)

Then (as at the beginning of the Hour):

Glory . . . now, and ever. . . . Our Father, who art in heaven . . .

Then the Collect Hymn (Kondák) of the Day, or of the Saint. *

But if it be a Fast, we say the following Hymns (Tropari), in Tone VIII.:

Blessed art thou, O Christ our God, who hast revealed fishers most wise, sending down upon them the Holy Spirit, and thereby catching the universe as in a net. O thou, who lovest mankind, glory to thee.

Glory to the Father, and to the Son, and to the Holy Spirit.

Grant speedy and steadfast consolation unto thy servants, O Jesus, when our spirit is cast down within us. Depart not from our souls in affliction; be not far from our thoughts in time of trouble; but always defend us. Draw near unto us, draw near unto us, thou who art omnipresent! As thou art ever with thine Apostles, so, also, O Bountiful One, unite thyself unto those who long for thee; that with one accord we may sing praises unto thee, and laud thy most holy Spirit.

Now, and ever, and unto ages of ages. Amen.

The Hope and Chieftain, and Refuge of Christians art thou, the

Lent.

Lent.

---

* For Collect-Hymns in the Eight Tones, see Appendix A: for the Great Feasts, see the Special Services.

Wall Impregnable and the Haven unvexed by storms, O most pure Birth-giver of God; but in that thou dost save the world by thine unceasing intercessions, call thou us also to remembrance, O Virgin, all-lauded.

Lord, have mercy. (*Forty times.*)

Thou who, at all times, and at every hour, both in heaven and on earth art worshipped and glorified, O Christ-God, long-suffering, plenteous in mercy and compassion; who lovest the just and showest mercy to those who are hardened in sin; who callest all men to salvation through the promise of good things to come: Do thou, the same Lord, receive also our supplications at this present time, and direct our lives according to thy commandments; sanctify our souls; purify our bodies; set aright our minds; cleanse our thoughts; and deliver us from all calamity, wrath and distress. Compass us round about with thy holy Angels; that, guided and guarded by their host, we may attain unto the unity of the faith, and unto the comprehension of thine ineffable glory. For blessed art thou unto ages of ages. Amen.

Lord, have mercy. (*Thrice.*)

Glory to the Father, and to the Son, and to the Holy Spirit, now, and ever, and unto ages of ages. Amen.

More honourable than the Cherubim, and more glorious beyond compare than the Seraphim, thou who without defilement barest God the Word, true Birth-giver of God, we magnify thee.

In the Name of the Lord bless, Father.

Priest. Through the prayers of our Holy Fathers, O Lord Jesus Christ, our God, have mercy upon us.

And if it be the Great Fast (Lent), we make three great reverences, reciting the prescribed

PRAYER OF ST. EPHRAIM THE SYRIAN.

O Lord and Master of my life, grant not unto me a spirit of slothfulness, of discouragement, of lust of power, of vain babbling. (*Reverence.*)

But vouchsafe unto me, thy servant, the spirit of continence, of meekness, of patience, and of love. (*Reverence.*)

Yea, O Lord and King, grant that I may perceive my own transgressions, and judge not my brother. For blessed art thou unto ages of ages. Amen. (*Reverence. Then twelve lesser reverences, saying at each:* O God, cleanse thou me, a sinner. *Then the whole Prayer is repeated; with one great reverence in conclusion.*)

And when we have finished the reverences, we say this

PRAYER OF ST. MARDARIUS.

O Lord God, Father almighty, O Lord the Only-begotten Son, Jesus Christ, and O Holy Spirit, one Godhead, one Power, have mercy upon me, a sinner. And by the judgments which thou hast established, save me, thine unworthy servant. For blessed art thou unto ages of ages. Amen. *Lent.*

THE SIXTH HOUR *

O come, let us worship God our King. O come, let us worship and fall down before Christ, our King and our God. O come, let us worship and fall down before the Very Christ, our King and our God. (*Three reverences.*)

PSALM LIV.

Save me, O God, for thy Name's sake, and avenge me in thy strength. Hear my prayer, O God, and hearken unto the words of my mouth. For strangers are risen up against me; and tyrants, which have not God before their eyes, seek after my soul. Behold, God is my helper; the Lord is with them that uphold my soul. He shall reward evil unto mine enemies: destroy thou them in thy truth. An offering of a free heart will I give thee, and praise thy Name, O Lord; because it is so comfortable. For he hath delivered me out of all my trouble, and mine eye hath seen his desire upon mine enemies.

PSALM LV.

Hear my prayer, O God, and hide not thyself from my petition. Take heed unto me, and hear me, how I mourn in my prayer, and am vexed. The enemy crieth so, and the ungodly cometh on so fast; for they are minded to do me some mischief, so maliciously are they set against me. My heart is disquieted within me, and the fear of death is fallen upon me. Fearfulness and trembling are come upon me, and an horrible dread hath overwhelmed me. And I said, Oh that I had wings like a dove! for then would I flee away, and be at rest. Lo, then would I get me away far off, and remain in the wilderness. I would make haste to escape, because of the stormy wind and tempest. Destroy their tongues, O Lord, and divide them, for I have spied unrighteousness and strife in the city. Day and night they go about within the walls thereof: mischief also and sorrow are in the midst of it. Wickedness is therein; deceit and guile go not out of their streets. For it is not an open enemy that hath done me this dishonour; for then I could have borne it: neither was it mine adversary that did magnify himself against me; for then peradventure I would have hid myself from him: but it was even thou, my companion, my guide, and mine own familiar friend. We took sweet counsel together, and walked in the house of God as friends. Let death come hastily upon them, and

* See Appendix B, III.

let them go down quick into hell; for wickedness is in their dwellings, and among them. As for me, I will call upon God, and the Lord shall save me. In the evening, and morning, and at noon-day will I pray, and that instantly; and he shall hear my voice. It is he that hath delivered my soul in peace from the battle that was against me; for there were many with me. Yea, even God, that endureth forever, shall hear me, and bring them down; for they will not turn, nor fear God. He laid his hands upon such as be at peace with him, and he brake his covenant. The words of his mouth were softer than butter, having war in his heart; his words were smoother than oil, and yet be they very swords. O cast thy burden upon the Lord, and he shall nourish thee, and shall not suffer the righteous to fall forever. And as for them, thou, O God, shalt bring them into the pit of destruction. The blood-thirsty and deceitful men shall not live out half their days: nevertheless, my trust shall be in thee, O Lord.

PSALM XCI.

Whoso dwelleth under the defence of the Most High, shall abide under the shadow of the Almighty. I will say unto the Lord, Thou art my hope, and my strong hold; my God, in him will I trust. For he shall deliver thee from the snare of the hunter, and from the noisome pestilence. He shall defend thee under his wings, and thou shalt be safe under his feathers; his faithfulness and truth shall be thy shield and buckler. Thou shalt not be afraid for any terror by night, nor for the arrow that flieth by day; for the pestilence that walketh in darkness, nor for the sickness that destroyeth in the noon-day. A thousand shall fall beside thee, and ten thousand at thy right hand; but it shall not come nigh thee. Yea, with thine eyes shalt thou behold, and see the reward of the ungodly. For thou, Lord, art my hope; thou hast set thine house of defence very high. There shall no evil happen unto thee, neither shall any plague come nigh thy dwelling. For he shall give his angels charge over thee, to keep thee in all thy ways. They shall bear thee in their hands, that thou hurt not thy foot against a stone. Thou shalt go upon the lion and adder: the young lion and the dragon shalt thou tread under thy feet. Because he hath set his love upon me, therefore will I deliver him; I will set him up, because he hath known my Name. He shall call upon me, and I will hear him; yea, I am with him in trouble; I will deliver him, and bring him to honour. With long life will I satisfy him, and show him my salvation.

Glory to the Father, and to the Son, and to the Holy Spirit, now, and ever, and unto ages of ages. Amen.

Alleluia, alleluia, alleluia; glory to thee, O God. (*Thrice.*)

Glory to the Father, and to the Son, and to the Holy Spirit.

*And the Hymn for the Day (Tropár).**

* For Hymns in the Eight Tones, see Appendix A; for the Great Feasts, see the Special Services.

But if it be the Great Fast (Lent), we recite the following Hymn, in Tone III.:

O thou who, on the sixth day and Hour didst nail to the Cross the sin which Adam, through presumption, committed in Paradise: Tear asunder also the handwriting of our iniquities, O Christ-God, and save us.

Verse (Stikh) 1: Hear my prayer, O God, and hide not thyself from my petition.

Verse 2: As for me, I will call upon God, and the Lord shall save me. Now, and ever, and unto ages of ages. Amen.

Hymn to the Birth-giver of God *(Bogoróditchen)*.

Seeing that we have no boldness, because of the multitude of our sins, do thou, O Virgin Birth-giver of God, fervently entreat Him who was born of thee: for the prayer of a Mother availeth much to the good will of the Lord. Despise not the supplications of sinners, O all-pure One; for merciful and mighty to save is He who graciously deigned to suffer for us.

With thy bounties speedily prevent us, O Lord, for we have grievously sinned; help us, O God our Saviour, for the glory of thy Name. O Lord, deliver us, and purge away our sins, for thy Name's sake.

O Holy God, Holy Mighty, Holy Immortal One, have mercy upon us. *(Thrice.)*

Glory to the Father, and to the Son, and to the Holy Spirit, now, and ever, and unto ages of ages. Amen.

O all-holy Trinity, have mercy upon us. O Lord, wash away our sins. O Master, pardon our transgressions. O Holy One, visit and heal our infirmities, for thy Name's sake.

Lord, have mercy. *(Thrice.)* Glory . . . now, and ever . . .

Our Father, who art in heaven, Hallowed be thy Name. Thy kingdom come. Thy will be done on earth, As it is in heaven. Give us this day our daily bread. And forgive us our trepasses, As we forgive those who trespass against us. And lead us not into temptation; But deliver us from the Evil One:

Priest. For thine is the kingdom, and the power, and the glory, of the Father, and of the Son, and of the Holy Spirit, now, and ever, and unto ages of ages. Amen.

Then the Collect-Hymn (Kondák) of the Day or of the Tone.*

But if it be the Great Fast, we say these Hymns (Troparf), in Tone II.:

Thou hast wrought salvation in the midst of the earth, O Christ-God. Thou didst stretch out thine all-pure hands upon the Cross; thou hast gathered together all the nations, who cry aloud unto thee: Glory to thee, O Lord.

Glory to the Father, and to the Son, and to the Holy Spirit.

* For Collect-Hymns in the Eight Tones, see Appendix A; for the Great Feasts, see the Special Services.

We bow down in reverence before thy holy Image, O Good One, entreating forgiveness for our transgressions, O Christ-God; for of thine own good will thou didst graciously deign to ascend the Cross in the flesh, that thou mightest deliver from the works of the enemy those whom thou hadst fashioned. Wherefore we cry aloud unto thee in thanksgiving: With joy thou didst fill all things, O our Saviour, when thou didst come to save the world.

And then immediately, on Monday, Tuesday and Thursday:

Now, and ever, and unto ages of ages. Amen.

HYMN TO THE BIRTH-GIVER OF GOD (*Bogoróditchen*).

Vouchsafe unto us thy mercy, O Birth-giver of God, thou who art a Fount of tender compassion. Look upon the people who have sinned; manifest, as always, thy power. For trusting in thee we cry unto thee: Hail! as did aforetime Gabriel, Chief of the Bodiless Powers.

On Wednesday and Friday:

Now, and ever, and unto ages of ages. Amen.

CROSS-HYMN TO THE BIRTH-GIVER OF GOD (*Krestobogoróditchen*).

Exceedingly blessed art thou, O Virgin Birth-giver of God, and we sing thy praise: for by the Cross of thy Son was Hell overthrown and Death was slain; and we who were dead have risen again, and have mercifully been deemed worthy of life, and have received Paradise, which was our delight of old. For which cause, with thanksgiving we magnify Christ our God, in that he is mighty and in that he alone loveth mankind.

Lord, have mercy. (*Forty times.*)

Thou who, at all times and at every hour, both in heaven and on earth, art worshipped and glorified, O Christ our God, long-suffering, plenteous in mercy and compassion; who lovest the just and showest mercy to those who are hardened in sin; who callest all men to salvation through the promise of good things to come: Do thou, the same Lord, receive also our supplications at this present time, and direct our lives according to thy commandments. Sanctify our souls; purify our bodies; set aright our minds; cleanse our thoughts; and deliver us from all calamity, wrath, and distress. Compass us round about with thy holy Angels; that, guided and guarded by their host, we may attain unto the unity of the faith, and unto the comprehension of thine ineffable glory. For blessed art thou unto ages of ages. Amen.

Lord, have mercy. (*Thrice.*)

Glory to the Father, and to the Son, and to the Holy Spirit, now, and ever, and unto ages of ages. Amen.

More honourable than the Cherubim, and beyond compare more glorious than the Seraphim, thou who without defilement barest God the Word, true Birth-giver of God, we magnify thee.

Lent.

In the Name of the Lord bless, Father.

Priest. Through the prayers of our holy Fathers, O Lord Jesus Christ our God, have mercy upon us.

And if it be a Fast, we make three great reverences to the very earth and say the prescribed

PRAYER OF ST. EPHRAIM THE SYRIAN.

O Lord and Master of my life, grant not unto me a spirit of slothfulness, of discouragement, of lust of power, of vain babbling. (*Reverence.*)

But vouchsafe unto me, thy servant the spirit of continence, of meekness, of patience, and of love. (*Reverence.*)

Yea, O Lord and King, grant that I may perceive my own transgressions, and judge not my brother. For blessed art thou unto ages of ages. Amen. (*Reverence. Then twelve lesser reverences, saying at each:* O God, cleanse thou me, a sinner. *Then the whole Prayer is repeated; with one great reverence in conclusion.*)

Then this PRAYER OF ST. BASIL THE GREAT.

O God and Lord of hosts, and Maker of all things created, who through the tender-hearted compassion of thine incomparable mercy didst send down thine Only-begotten Son, our Lord Jesus Christ, for the redemption of our race, and by his precious Cross didst destroy the handwriting of our sins, and didst thereby triumph over the Origin and Powers of darkness: Do thou, the same Lord, who lovest mankind, accept also these thanksgivings and fervent prayers of us sinners. And deliver us from every harmful and gloomy transgression, and from all enemies, both visible and invisible, who seek after us to destroy us. Nail our flesh to the fear of thee, and incline not our hearts to words or thoughts of guile: but wound our souls with the love of thee; that looking ever unto thee, and guided by thee in the light, beholding thee, the Light Ineffable and Everlasting, we may ascribe unto thee ceaseless praise and thanksgiving: unto the Father who hath no beginning, together with thine Only-begotten Son, and thine all-holy, and good, and life-giving Spirit, now, and ever, and unto ages of ages. Amen.

Generally the DIVINE LITURGY *beginneth here. But if it be the Great Fast (Lent), after this is read the* NINTH HOUR; *and the* NINTH HOUR, *when it followeth the* SIXTH HOUR, *beginneth thus:*

O Holy God, Holy Mighty, Holy Immortal One, have mercy upon us. (*Thrice.*) Glory . . . now, and ever . . .

O all-holy Trinity, . . .

Lent.

THE NINTH HOUR *

Priest. Blessed is our God always, now, and ever, and unto ages of ages.

And We. Amen.

Glory to thee, O our God; glory to thee.

O heavenly King, the Comforter, Spirit of Truth, who art in all places, and fillest all things; Treasury of good things and Giver of life: Come, and take up thine abode in us, and cleanse us from every stain; and save our souls, O Good One.

O Holy God, Holy Mighty, Holy Immortal One, have mercy upon us. (*Thrice.*)

Glory to the Father, and to the Son, and to the Holy Spirit, now, and ever, and unto ages of ages.   Amen.

O all-holy Trinity, have mercy upon us.   O Lord, wash away our sins. O Master, pardon our transgressions.   O Holy One, visit and heal our infirmities, for thy Name's sake.

Lord, have mercy.   (*Thrice.*)

Glory to the Father, and to the Son, and to the Holy Spirit, now, and ever, and unto ages of ages.   Amen.

Our Father, who art in heaven, Hallowed be thy Name.   Thy kingdom come.   Thy will be done on earth, As it is in heaven.   Give us this day our daily bread.   And forgive us our trespasses, As we forgive those who trespass against us.   And lead us not into temptation; But deliver us from the Evil One:

Priest. For thine is the kingdom, and the power, and the glory, of the Father, and of the Son, and of the Holy Spirit, now, and ever, and unto ages of ages.

Reader. Amen.

Lord, have mercy.   (*Twelve times.*)

Glory to the Father, and to the Son, and to the Holy Spirit, now, and ever, and unto ages of ages.   Amen.

O come, let us worship God our King.   O come, let us worship and fall down before Christ, our King and our God.   O come, let us worship and fall down before the Very Christ, our King and our God.   (*Three reverences.*)

PSALM LXXXIV.

O how amiable are thy dwellings, thou Lord of hosts!   My soul hath a desire and longing to enter into the courts of the Lord; my heart and my flesh rejoice in the living God.   Yea, the sparrow hath found her an house, and the swallow a nest, where she may lay her young; even thy altars,

* See Appendix B, III.

O Lord of hosts, my King and my God. Blessed are they that dwell in thy house; they will be alway praising thee. Blessed is the man whose strength is in thee; in whose heart are thy ways. Who going through the vale of misery use it for a well; and the pools are filled with water. They will go from strength to strength, and unto the God of gods appeareth every one of them in Sion. O Lord God of hosts, hear my prayer; hearken, O God of Jacob. Behold, O God our defender, and look upon the face of thine Anointed. For one day in thy courts is better than a thousand. I had rather be a door-keeper in the house of my God, than to dwell in the tents of ungodliness. For the Lord God is a light and defence; the Lord will give grace and worship; and no good thing shall he withhold from them that live a godly life. O Lord God of hosts, blessed is the man that putteth his trust in thee.

Psalm lxxxv.

Lord, thou art become gracious unto thy land; thou hast turned away the captivity of Jacob. Thou hast forgiven the offence of thy people, and covered all their sins. Thou hast taken away all thy displeasure, and turned thyself from thy wrathful indignation. Turn us then, O God our Saviour, and let thine anger cease from us. Wilt thou be displeased at us for ever? and wilt thou stretch out thy wrath from one generation to another? Wilt thou not turn again and quicken us, that thy people may rejoice in thee? Show us thy mercy, O Lord, and grant us thy salvation. I will hearken what the Lord God will say concerning me; for he shall speak peace unto his people, and to his saints, that they turn not again. For his salvation is nigh them that fear him; that glory may dwell in our land. Mercy and truth are met together; righteousness and peace have kissed each other. Truth shall flourish out of the earth, and righteousness hath looked down from heaven. Yea, the Lord shall show loving-kindness; and our land shall give her increase. Righteousness shall go before him; and he shall direct his going in the way.

Psalm lxxxvi.

Bow down thine ear, O Lord, and hear me; for I am poor, and in misery. Preserve thou my soul, for I am holy: my God, save thy servant that putteth his trust in thee. Be merciful unto me, O Lord; for I will call daily upon thee. Comfort the soul of thy servant; for unto thee, O Lord, do I lift up my soul. For thou, Lord, art good and gracious, and of great mercy unto all them that call upon thee. Give ear, Lord, unto my prayer, and ponder the voice of my humble desires. In the time of my trouble I will call upon thee; for thou hearest me. Among the gods there is none like unto thee, O Lord; there is not one that can do as thou doest. All nations whom thou hast made shall come and worship thee, O Lord; and shall glorify thy Name. For thou art great and doest wondrous things; thou art God alone. Teach me thy way, O Lord, and I will walk in thy truth: O knit my heart unto thee, that I may fear thy Name. I will thank thee, O Lord my God, with all my heart; and will praise thy Name for evermore. For great is thy mercy toward me; and thou hast delivered my soul from the nethermost hell. O God, the proud are risen against me: and the congregations of naughty men have sought after my soul, and have not set thee before their eyes. But thou, O Lord God, art full of compassion and mercy, long-suffering, plenteous in goodness and truth. O turn thee then unto me, and have mercy upon me: give thy strength unto thy servant, and help the son of thine handmaid. Show some token upon me for good; that they who hate me may see it, and be ashamed, because thou, Lord, hast holpen me, and comforted me. *And again:* Show some token upon me for good; that they who hate me may see it, and be ashamed, because thou, Lord, hast holpen me, and comforted me.

Glory to the Father, and to the Son, and to the Holy Spirit, now, and ever, and unto ages of ages. Amen.

Alleluia, alleluia, alleluia; glory to thee, O God. (*Thrice.*)

Lord, have mercy. (*Thrice.*)

Glory . . . now, and ever.

And we read the Hymn for the Day (Tropár).*

But if it be the Great Fast (Lent), this Hymn, in Tone VIII., is used:

O thou who, at the Ninth Hour, for our sake didst taste of death in the flesh: Mortify thou the presumption of our flesh, and save us, O Christ-God.

Verse (Stikh) 1: Let my complaint come before thee, O Lord: give me understanding, according to thy word.

Verse 2: Let my supplication come before thee, O Lord: deliver me according to thy word.

Glory . . . now, and ever. Amen.

Lent.

HYMN TO THE BIRTH-GIVER OF GOD.

Thou who for our sake wast born of a Virgin, and didst suffer crucifixion, O Good One, and didst despoil Death through death, and as God didst reveal Resurrection: Despise not those whom thou hast created with thine own hand; show forth thy love for mankind, O Merciful One; accept the Birth-giver of God who bare thee, and who entreateth thee for us; and save thy despairing people, O our Saviour.

Forsake us not utterly, for thy Name's sake, and destroy not thy covenant; and take not thy mercies from us, for the sake of Abraham whom thou lovedst, and for the sake of Isaac thy servant, and of Israel, thy Holy One.

O Holy God, Holy Mighty, . . . (*as at the beginning of the Hour*) . . . Glory . . . now, and ever . . . O all-holy Trinity, . . . Lord, have mercy.

* For Hymns in the Eight Tones, see Appendix A; for the Great Feasts, see the Special Services.

(*Thrice.*) . . . Glory . . . now, and ever . . . Our Father, who art in heaven, . . . Lord, have mercy . . . Glory . . . now, and ever . . .

*And if it be a Feast, we say the Collect-Hymn (Kondák) thereof.**
But if not, these Hymns in Tone VIII.:

When the thief beheld the Author of life hanging upon the Cross, he said: If thou wert not God incarnate, who art here crucified with us, then had the Sun not veiled its rays, neither would the earth have shaken with trembling. But do thou, who sufferest for all men, remember me, O Lord, when thou comest into thy kingdom.

Glory to the Father, and to the Son, and to the Holy Spirit.

In the midst, between two thieves, was thy Cross found the balance-beam of righteousness; for while the one was led down to hell by the burden of his blaspheming, the other was lightened of his sins, unto the knowledge of things divine. O Christ-God, glory to thee.

Now, and ever, and unto ages of ages. Amen.

When she who bare thee beheld upon the Cross thee, the Lamb, and Shepherd, and Saviour of the world, she weeping said: The world rejoiceth, in that it hath received redemption, but my heart kindleth with yearning as I look upon thy crucifixion, which thou sufferest for all men, O my Son and my God.

Lord, have mercy. (*Forty times.*)

Thou who, at all times and at every hour, both in heaven and on earth art worshipped and glorified, O Christ-God, long-suffering, plenteous in mercy and compassion; who lovest the just and showest mercy to those who are hardened in sin; who callest all men to salvation through the promise of good things to come: Do thou, the same Lord, receive also our supplications at this present time, and direct our lives according to thy commandments. Sanctify our souls; purify our bodies; set aright our minds; cleanse our thoughts; and deliver us from all calamity, wrath and distress. Compass us round about with thy holy Angels; that, guided and guarded by their host, we may attain unto the unity of the faith, and unto the comprehension of thine ineffable glory. For blessed art thou unto ages of ages. Amen.

Lord, have mercy. (*Thrice.*)

Glory to the Father, and to the Son, and to the Holy Spirit, now, and ever, and unto ages of ages. Amen.

More honourable than the Cherubim, and beyond compare more glorious than the Seraphim, thou who without defilement barest God the Word, true Birth-giver of God, we magnify thee.

In the name of the Lord bless, Father.

Priest. God be merciful unto us, and bless us, and show us the light of his countenance, and be merciful unto us.

* For Collect-Hymns in the Eight Tones, see Appendix A; for the Great Feasts, see the Special Services.

Then the INTERHOUR.

In the holy Great Fast (Lent), three great reverences shall be made, and the Prayer of St. Ephraim shall be recited once. (See page 52.)

But otherwise, after the Exclamation, God be merciful unto us, *there shall be said this*

PRAYER OF ST. BASIL THE GREAT.

O Master, Lord Jesus Christ our God, who art long-suffering toward our sins, and who hast led us even to the present hour, in the which, as thou didst hang upon the life-giving Tree thou didst make a way into Paradise for the penitent thief, and by death didst destroy Death: Cleanse us sinners and thine unworthy servants; for we have sinned and have dealt iniquitously, and we are not worthy to lift up our eyes and look upon the heights of heaven, inasmuch as we have departed from the path of thy righteousness, and have walked after the desires of our own hearts. But we implore of thy boundless goodness: Spare us, O Lord, according to the multitude of thy mercies, and save us, for thy holy Name's sake; for our days have passed away in vanity. Wrest us out of the hand of the adversary, and forgive our sins, and mortify in us carnal imagination; that putting off the old man we may be clothed upon with the new man, and may live unto thee, our Master and our Benefactor; and that so following after thy commandments, we may attain unto rest eternal, where is the abode of all those who rejoice. For thou art, in verity, the true joy and exultation of those who love thee, O Christ our God, and unto thee we ascribe glory, together with the Father, who is without beginning, and thine all-holy, and good, and life-giving Spirit, now, and ever, and unto ages of ages. Amen.

When the NINTH HOUR *is read separately from the* TYPICAL PSALMS:

Glory to the Father, and to the Son, and to the Holy Spirit, now, and ever, and unto ages of ages. Amen.

Lord, have mercy. (*Thrice.*) Bless.

Then the BENEDICTION.

Priest. May Christ, our true God, through the prayers of his most holy Mother (of the holy, glorious and all-laudable Apostles); of Saint N. (*the Saint of the day*); of Saint N. (*the Saint of the Church*); and of all the Saints, have mercy upon us and save us: forasmuch as he is gracious and loveth mankind.

But if it be the Great Fast (Lent), then the TYPICAL PSALMS *immediately follow, and Psalms ciii. and cxvi. are omitted.*

THE TYPICAL PSALMS *

The beginning of the TYPICAL PSALMS *shall be said thus:*
Bless the Lord, O my soul: blessed art thou, O Lord.

PSALM CIII.

Bless the Lord, O my soul; and all that is within me, bless his holy name.
Bless the Lord, O my soul, and forget not all his benefits: who forgiveth
all thine iniquities, and healeth all thy diseases; who redeemeth thy life
from destruction; who crowneth thee with loving-kindness and tender
mercies; who satisfieth thy mouth with good things; so that thy youth is
renewed like the eagle's. The Lord executeth righteousness and judgment for all that are oppressed. He made known his ways unto Moses,
his acts unto the children of Israel. The Lord is merciful and gracious,
slow to anger, and plenteous in mercy. He will not always chide; neither
will he keep his anger forever. He hath not dealt with us after our sins,
nor rewarded us according to our iniquities. For as the heaven is high
above the earth, so great is his mercy toward them that fear him. As far
as the east is from the west, so far hath he removed our transgressions
from us. Like as a father pitieth his children, so the Lord pitieth them
that fear him. For he knoweth our frame; he remembereth that we are
dust. As for man, his days are as grass; as a flower of the field, so he
flourisheth. For the wind passeth over it, and it is gone; and the place
thereof shall know it no more. But the mercy of the Lord is from everlasting to everlasting, upon them that fear him, and his righteousness
unto children's children; to such as keep his covenant, and to those that
remember his commandments to do them. The Lord hath prepared his
throne in the heavens; and his kingdom ruleth over all. Bless the Lord,
ye his angels, that excel in strength, that do his commandments, hearken-
ing unto the voice of his word. Bless the Lord, all ye his hosts; ye ministers of his that do his pleasure. Bless the Lord all works of his, in all
places of his dominion: bless the Lord, O my soul.

Glory to the Father, and to the Son, and to the Holy Spirit: *The first
Choir, with heightened voices.* Now, and ever, and unto ages of ages: *The
second Choir.*

The First Choir.

Bless the Lord, O my soul, and all that is within me, bless his holy
name. Blessed art thou, O Lord.

Glory to the Father, and to the Son, and to the Holy Spirit.

* See Appendix B, III.

Psalm CXLVI.

Praise the Lord, O my soul. While I live will I praise the Lord: I will sing praises unto my God while I have any being. Put not your trust in princes, nor in the son of man, in whom there is no help. His breath goeth forth, he returneth to his earth; in that very day his thoughts perish. Happy is he that hath the God of Jacob for his help, whose hope is in the Lord his God: which made heaven and earth, the sea, and all that therein is; which keepeth truth forever: which executeth judgment for the oppressed: which giveth food to the hungry. The Lord looseth the prisoners: the Lord openeth the eyes of the blind: the Lord raiseth them that are bowed down: the Lord loveth the righteous: the Lord preserveth the strangers; he relieveth the fatherless and widow: but the way of the wicked he turneth upside down. The Lord shall reign forever, even thy God, O Zion, unto all generations.

Now, and ever, and unto ages of ages. Amen.

O Only-begotten Son, and Word of God! Thou who art immortal yet didst deign for our salvation to become incarnate of the Holy Birth-giver of God and ever-virgin Mary: and without change of essence wast made man; who also wast crucified for us, O Christ-God, trampling down Death by death; who art one of the Holy Trinity and art glorified together with the Father and the Holy Spirit: Save us.

In the Great Fast, after the Ninth Hour, *and the Prayer,* O Master, Lord Jesus Christ our God *(page* 57), *we sing, in Tone VIII.:*

The Beatitudes.

In thy kingdom remember us, O Lord, when thou comest into thy kingdom.

Blessed are the poor in spirit: for theirs is the kingdom of heaven.

And if it be the Great Fast, to every verse is added the Refrain: Remember us, O Lord, when thou comest into thy kingdom.

Blessed are they that mourn: for they shall be comforted. ℟

Blessed are the meek: for they shall inherit the earth. ℟

Blessed are they that do hunger and thirst after righteousness: for they shall be filled. ℟

Blessed are the merciful: for they shall obtain mercy. ℟

Blessed are the pure in heart: for they shall see God. ℟

Blessed are the peacemakers: for they shall be called the children of God. ℟

Blessed are they which are persecuted for righteousness' sake: for theirs is the kingdom of heaven. ℟

Blessed are ye when men shall revile you, and persecute you, and shall say all manner of evil against you falsely, for my sake. ℟

Rejoice, and be exceeding glad, for great is your reward in heaven. ℟

Remember us, O Lord, when thou comest into thy kingdom.

Glory to the Father, and to the Son, and to the Holy Spirit, now, and ever, and unto ages of ages.   Amen.

Remember us, O Lord, when thou comest into thy kingdom.

Remember us, O Master, when thou comest into thy kingdom.

Remember us, O Holy One, when thou comest into thy kingdom.

(And one reverence at each.)

The heavenly choir doth hymn thee, and doth cry, Holy, holy, holy, Lord God of Hosts: heaven and earth are full of thy glory.

Verse: Come unto him and be enlightened, and your faces shall not be ashamed.

The heavenly choir doth hymn thee, and doth cry: Holy, holy, holy, Lord God of Hosts: heaven and earth are full of thy glory.

Glory to the Father, and to the Son, and to the Holy Spirit.

The Choir of holy Angels and Archangels, with all the Powers of heaven, sing thy praises and do cry, Holy, holy, holy, Lord God of Hosts: heaven and earth are full of thy glory.

Now, and ever, and unto ages of ages.   Amen.

I believe in one God the Father Almighty, Maker of heaven and earth, And of all things visible and invisible.

And in one Lord Jesus Christ, the only-begotten Son of God, Begotten of his Father before all worlds; Light of Light, Very God of very God, Begotten, not made; Being of one Essence with the Father; By whom all things were made; Who, for us men, and for our salvation, came down from heaven, And was incarnate by the Holy Ghost of the Virgin Mary, And was made man.   And was crucified also for us under Pontius Pilate, and suffered and was buried.   And the third day he rose again, according to the Scriptures.   And ascended into heaven, And sitteth on the right hand of the Father, And he shall come again with glory to judge both the quick and the dead; Whose kingdom shall have no end.

And in the Holy Ghost, the Lord and Giver of Life, Who proceedeth from the Father, Who with the Father and the Son together is worshipped and glorified, Who spake by the Prophets.   In one Holy Catholic and Apostolic Church.   I acknowledge one Baptism for the remission of sins. I look for the Resurrection of the dead, And the Life of the world to come. Amen.

Loose, remit, pardon, O God, our transgressions, voluntary and involuntary; whether of word or of deed; whether of knowledge or of ignorance; whether of the day or of the night; whether of the mind, or of the intention: Forgive us all, for thou art good and lovest mankind.

Our Father, who art in heaven, Hallowed be thy Name.   Thy kingdom come.   Thy will be done on earth, As it is in heaven.   Give us this day our daily bread.   And forgive us our trespasses, As we forgive those who trespass against us.   And lead us not into temptation; But deliver us from the Evil One:

Priest. For thine is the kingdom, and the power, and the glory, of the Father, and of the Son, and of the Holy Spirit, now, and ever, and unto ages of ages. Amen.

If it be Saturday:

Unto thee, O Lord, the Author of Creation, the universe doth offer the God-bearing Martyrs as the first-fruits of nature: By whose prayers, through the Birth-giver of God, do thou preserve in peace profound thy Church, which is thine estate, O most merciful One.

COLLECT-HYMN (*Kondák*) OF THE TRANSFIGURATION.

Thou wast transfigured on the Mount, and in so far as they were able to receive it, thy disciples, with wonder, beheld thy glory, O Christ-God. And when they beheld thee crucified, they understood thy voluntary Passion, and proclaimed unto the world that thou art, of a truth, the Radiance of the Father.

COLLECT-HYMNS FOR:

Monday: Hymn of the Bodiless Powers, Tone II.:

O ye Chieftains of God, servitors of the divine glory, Captains of the Angels and Guides of men: Entreat that which is profitable for us, and great mercy; in that ye are the Chieftains of the Bodiless Powers.

Tuesday: Hymn of the Forerunner, Tone II.:

O Prophet of God, and Forerunner of Grace, in that we have found thy holy head as a most sacred rose budding forth from the earth, we receive always thy healing. For still, as aforetime in the world, thou dost preach repentance.

Wednesday and Friday: Tone III.:

Do thou who, of thine own good will, upon the cross wast lifted up, bestow thy bounties upon the new State which is called by thy Name, O Christ-God; make glad with thy might our God-fearing Ruler, granting victory over his adversaries unto him who hath thine aid, which is a panoply of peace, a trophy invincible.

Thursday: the Holy Apostles, Tone II.:

Thou hast received thy steadfast Preachers, God-inspired in speech, the Crown of thy Disciples, O Lord, into the delights and the repose of thy blessed ones; for thou hast accepted their sufferings and their death as greater than any whole burnt-offerings, O thou who alone knowest the secrets of the heart.

The same day: the Collect-Hymn (Kondák) of St. Nicholas, Tone III.:

In Myra, O Saint, wast thou shown forth a sacrificing priest; for fulfilling the Gospel of Christ, O Holy One, thou didst lay down thy life for thy people, and didst save the innocent from death. For which cause thou wert proclaimed a Saint, as one deeply initiated into the mysteries of the goodness of God.

Then, on every day:

Glory to the Father, and to the Son, and to the Holy Spirit.

To the souls of thy servants, O Lord, give rest with thy Saints, where there is neither sickness, nor sorrow, nor sighing, but life everlasting.

Then immediately, on every day except Saturday, is said:

Now, and ever, and unto ages of ages. Amen.

O Protection of Christians that maketh not ashamed, O Mediatrix never-failing with the Creator: Despise not the sinners' voice of supplication; but in that thou art good, come speedily to the aid of us who faithfully call upon thee; make haste to our petition and further our prayer, O Birth-giver of God, who ever protectest them that do thee honour.

And if it be the Great Fast:

Lord, have mercy. (*Forty times.*)

Glory to the Father, and to the Son, and to the Holy Spirit, now, and ever, and unto ages of ages. Amen.

More honourable than the Cherubim, and beyond compare more glorious than the Seraphim, thou who without defilement barest God the Word, true Birth-giver of God, we magnify thee.

In the Name of the Lord, bless, Father.

Priest. God be merciful to us, and bless us, and show us the light of his countenance, and be merciful unto us.

Then the PRAYER OF ST. EPHRAIM THE SYRIAN.

O Lord and Master of my life, grant not unto me a spirit of slothfulness, of discouragement, of lust of power, of vain babbling. (*A great reverence to the earth.*)

But vouchsafe unto me, thy servant the spirit of continence, of meekness, of patience, and of love. (*Reverence.*)

Yea, O Lord and King, grant that I may perceive my own transgressions, and judge not my brother. For blessed art thou unto ages of ages. Amen. (*Reverence. Then twelve lesser reverences, saying at each reverence:* O God, cleanse thou me, a sinner. *Then the whole prayer is repeated, with one great reverence in conclusion.*)

If it be not the Great Fast:

Lord, have mercy. (*Twelve times.*)

And the Prayer:

O all-holy Trinity, Might one in Essence, Kingdom undivided, Origin of all good things, be graciously inclined also unto me, a sinner. Establish thou me; give understanding unto my heart, and purge away all my vileness. Enlighten my mind, that I may glorify, sing praises, and adore thee, and say: Thou only art holy, thou only art the Lord, O Jesus Christ, in the glory of the Father.   Amen.

Meet is it in very truth to bless thee, O Birth-giver of God, ever-blessed and all-undefiled One, and the Mother of our God.

Priest. Wisdom!

O most holy Birth-giver of God, save us.

Choir. More honourable than the Cherubim, and beyond compare more glorious than the Seraphim, thou who without corruption barest God the Word, true Birth-giver of God, we magnify thee.

Priest. Glory to thee, O Christ-God our hope; glory to thee.

Choir. Glory to the Father, and to the Son, and to the Holy Spirit, now, and ever, and unto ages of ages.   Amen.

Lord, have mercy.   (*Thrice.*)   Bless.

Then the BENEDICTION.

Priest. May Christ, our true God, through the prayers of his most holy Mother, and of all the Saints, have mercy upon us and save us; for he is gracious and loveth mankind.

THE DIVINE LITURGY

PREFATORY NOTE AND DIRECTIONS

The word LITURGY, which in the Greek means "A public work" or "Ministry," is particularly applied (heightened by the adjective "Divine") to the chief service of the day, in which the Holy Eucharist, or Service of Thanksgiving, is celebrated.

Three Liturgies are used in the Holy Orthodox Catholic Apostolic Church of the East:

That of St. John Chrysostom; that of St. Basil the Great; and that of the Presanctified Gifts.

The Divine Liturgy of St. John Chrysostom and that of St. Basil the Great are divided into three parts. In the first part, the clergy prepare the bread and wine, and it is called *The Office of Oblation*. The second part consists of prayers, reading and singing, with which the faithful prepare themselves for the Holy Sacrament, and at which alone Catechumens (or learners) were allowed, in former times, to be present: it is called *The Liturgy of the Catechumens*. The third part, called *The Liturgy of the Faithful*, is the celebration of the Sacrament of the Holy Eucharist; and in the early Church only the Faithful — that is to say, members of the Christian Church — were permitted to be present at it.

The Liturgy of St. Basil the Great differs from that of St. John Chrysostom only in certain of the Secret Prayers, one Hymn, and three phrases in the Consecration of the Holy Gifts (as duly indicated at the proper places), the Liturgy of St. John Chrysostom being a later and abbreviated form of St. Basil's Liturgy, as the latter, in turn, was a later and abbreviated form of a still earlier Liturgy.

It is appointed to be used on the Sundays of the Great Fast (Lent), except on Palm Sunday; on Holy Thursday and Holy Saturday; and on Christmas Day and the Epiphany, when those feasts fall upon Sunday or Monday; otherwise, on the days preceding those feasts. Also, on St. Basil's Day, January 1; in all, ten times in the course of the year.

The Liturgy of the Presanctified Gifts, so called because the Holy Gifts which have previously been consecrated are used for the Holy Communion, has existed from ancient times, although, in its present form, it is ascribed to St. Gregory Homiliastes of Rome (sixth century). The Orthodox Church decrees that this Liturgy shall be celebrated during the Great Fast (but at no other time), since the triumphantly joyous feelings associated with the complete Liturgy and the consecration of the Holy Gifts are incompatible with the strictness of the Fast. Hence it is ordained that the complete Liturgy shall be celebrated only on Saturdays and Sundays during the weeks of the Great Fast (Lent). The customary days for the celebration of the Liturgy of the Presanctified Gifts are Wednesday and Friday of every week, and on Monday, Tuesday and Wednesday of Passion Week.

The Liturgy of the Presanctified Gifts consists of Vespers (and therefore is appointed for a late hour in the day), and of a portion of the ordinary Liturgy, omitting the most essential part of the latter, namely, the consecration of the Gifts. The Liturgy of the Presanctified Gifts is usually preceded by the reading of the Third, Sixth and Ninth Hours, and of the Typical Psalms. Under certain circumstances an earlier celebration is admissible.

The usual hour for celebrating the ordinary Liturgy is, not earlier than dawn, and not later than noon.

For the celebration of the Mystery of the Eucharist the following are indispensable: A Priest or a Bishop regularly ordained, and having a steadfast will and intention to fulfil the Mystery of the Lord's Body and Blood. Of material things: five Altar-breads, made of pure wheaten flour, and leavened; wine of the grape. The accomplishment of the Mystery through prayer and words, with the blessing of the Priest's hand: "And make this bread the precious Body of thy Christ, and also that which is in this cup the precious Blood of thy Christ, transmuting them by thy Holy Spirit."

In addition to the above, the following things are indispensable for the Liturgy: A Corporal (*Antimíns*),* consecrated by a Bishop; vestments for the Priest, consisting of a cassock (*stikhár*), a stole (*epitrakhíl*), gauntlets (*pórutchi*), girdle (*póyas*), and chasuble (*felón*); vessels, — a chalice, a paten, a star-cover, a spear, a spoon; veils, a censer, a service book; lights burning on the altar; and an acolyte.

Only one Liturgy may be celebrated on any Altar in the course of one day; and no Bishop or Priest may celebrate more than one Liturgy in the course of one and the same day.

The Priest who enters upon the celebration of the Liturgy must be free from inhibition, and from mortal sin, and must prepare himself, — spiritually, by reconciling himself with all men, by penitence, and the appointed devotions; bodily, by abstinence from food and drink (from midnight at the least), and from fleshly desires, and by cleanliness of body and garments.

The appointed devotions consist of the celebration or the hearing of the Evening and Morning Services and Prayers; and there must also be read: On Monday: The Canon to the Lord Jesus, the Invocation to the Birth-giver of God, the Canon to the Archangels; and, if he so desire, to his Guardian Angel. On Tuesday: The Canon to the Lord Jesus, the Invocation to the Birth-giver of God, to John the Forerunner, and to his Guardian Angel. On Wednesday: The Canon to the Lord Jesus, the Canon to the Birth-giver of God, and to his Guardian Angel. On Thursday: The Canon to the Lord Jesus, the Invocation to the Birth-giver of God, to his Guardian Angel, to the Holy Apostles; and, if he so desire, to St. Nicholas. On Friday, the Canon to the Life-giving Cross, the Invocation to the Birth-giver of God, and to his Guardian Angel. On Saturday: The Canon to the Lord Jesus, the Chant of Prayer and Praise (*Akáfist*) to the Birth-giver of God, to his Guardian Angel, and to all the Saints. On Sunday: The Canon to the Lord Jesus, the Invocation to the Birth-giver of God, and to his Guardian Angel.

In addition to these, on every occasion, the Canon of the Communion, and the Prayers before the Communion. (*See Index.*)

THE CURTAIN AND THE HOLY DOOR. *At Divine Service the curtain is drawn aside before the beginning of the Liturgy, when the benediction is given at the end of the Oblation. The Holy Door is opened before the Lesser Entrance, and closed before the Litany of the Catechumens. It is opened again before the Cherubimic Hymn, and closed after the Great Entrance, at which time the curtain also is drawn. The curtain is drawn aside at the words:* The Doors! The Doors! . . . *It is drawn again at the Exclamation:* Holy Things to the Holy. *The curtain is drawn aside and the Holy Door is opened before:* In the fear of God . . .; *and is finally closed after the Dismissal.*

AT A PONTIFICAL SERVICE: *The Holy Door is opened at the beginning of the service, and so remains until the Exclamation:* Let us attend! Holy Things to the Holy. *After that it is opened and closed as usual.*

THE BISHOP'S PALL AND MITRE. *At a Pontifical Service, the pall (omofór) is removed before the Epistle; is put on while the particles are being taken from the sacred breads before the Great Entrance, and is immediately laid aside again. After the prayer:* With them also . . . (*and the Hymn:* Holy, holy, holy . . .), *it is put on; and it is removed when the Holy Spirit is invoked. At the Exclamation:* Let us attend! Holy

---

* For explanation, see introductory chapter on The Symbolism of the Church, page xxiv.

things to the holy: *it is put on, and is then worn until the Dismissal. In addition to the above, the Bishop puts on his pall when he ordains a Deacon or a Priest.*

THE MITRE *is removed while the particles are being taken from the holy breads, and at the Commemoration of Persons at the Great Entrance; while:* Let us love one another . . .: *is being said, and while the Creed is being chanted; also, from:* Take, eat . . .; *and until:* More especially for the Most Holy . . . (*and during the reception of the Holy Communion by the Bishop*).

THE LITURGY OF ST. JOHN CHRYSOSTOM

AND

THE LITURGY OF ST. BASIL THE GREAT (1)*

1. THE OFFICE OF OBLATION

When the time is come to celebrate the Divine Liturgy, the Priest entereth the Temple, and, in company with the Deacon, maketh three lowly reverences before the Holy Door.

Then the Deacon saith:

Bless, Master.

Priest. Blessed is our God always, now, and ever, and unto ages of ages. Amen.

Deacon. O heavenly King, the Comforter, Spirit of Truth, who art in all places and fillest all things; Treasury of good things and Giver of life: Come, and take up thine abode in us, and cleanse us from every stain; and save our souls, O Good One.

O Holy God, Holy Mighty, Holy Immortal One, have mercy upon us. (*Thrice.*)

Glory to the Father, and to the Son, and to the Holy Spirit, now, and ever, and unto ages of ages. Amen.

O all-holy Trinity, have mercy upon us. O Lord, wash away our sins. O Master, pardon our transgressions. O Holy One, visit and heal our infirmities, for thy Name's sake.

Lord, have mercy. (*Thrice.*)

Our Father, who art in heaven, Hallowed be thy Name. Thy kingdom come. Thy will be done on earth, As it is in heaven. Give us this day our daily bread. And forgive us our trespasses, As we forgive those who trespass against us. And lead us not into temptation; But deliver us from the Evil One:

Priest. For thine is the kingdom, and the power, and the glory, of the Father, and of the Son, and of the Holy Spirit, now, and ever, and unto ages of ages. Amen.

And then shall they say:

Have mercy upon us, O Lord, have mercy upon us. For we sinners devoid of all defence, do offer unto thee, as to our Master, this supplication: Have mercy upon us.

Glory to the Father, and to the Son, and to the Holy Spirit.

Have mercy upon us, O Lord, for in thee have we trusted, and be not very wroth with us, neither call thou to remembrance our iniqui-

Secretly.

* See Appendix B, IV.

ties; but look down even now upon us, inasmuch as thou art of tender compassion, and deliver us from our enemies: for thou art our God, and we are thy people, we are all the work of thy hand, and we call upon thy Name.

Now, and ever, and unto ages of ages. Amen.

HYMN TO THE BIRTH-GIVER OF GOD (*Bogoródilchen*).

Open unto us the door of thy loving-kindness, O blessed Birth-giver of God. In that we set our hope on thee may we not fail, but through thee may we be delivered from adversities; for thou art the salvation of all Christian people.

Then shall they approach the holy picture (ikóna) of Christ, and shall kiss it, saying:

We do homage to thy most pure image, O Good One, entreating forgiveness of our transgressions, O Christ-God; for of thine own good will thou wast graciously pleased to ascend the Cross in the flesh, that thou mightest deliver from bondage to the enemy those whom thou hadst fashioned; for which cause we cry aloud unto thee with thanksgiving: With joy hast thou filled all things, O our Saviour, in that thou didst come to save the world.

In like manner they shall kiss also the holy picture of the Birth-giver of God, reciting the while this Hymn, secretly:

O Birth-giver of God, in that thou art a well-spring of loving-kindness, vouchsafe unto us thy compassion. Look upon the people who have sinned. Manifest thy power as ever; for trusting in thee we cry aloud unto thee: Hail! as aforetime did Gabriel, Chief Captain of the Bodiless Powers.

Secretly.

Then, with bowed heads, they say the following Prayer:

Stretch forth thy hand, O Lord, from thy holy dwelling-place on high, and strengthen me for this, thine appointed service; that standing uncondemned before thy dread Altar, I may fulfil the sacred, unbloody rite. For thine is the power unto ages of ages. Amen.

Then they make one reverence to the People, (2) and enter the Sanctuary saying, secretly:

I will enter into thy house, I will worship toward thy holy Temple in thy fear. Guide me, O Lord, with thy righteousness; make straight my path before thee, because of mine enemies. For there is no truth in their mouth; their heart is vanity; their throat is an open sepulchre; with their tongues have they dealt deceitfully. Judge them, O God. Let them fall through their own counsels: according to the multitude of their iniquities cast thou them out, for they have provoked thee exceedingly, O Lord. And let all those who trust in thee be joyful; and so shall they rejoice evermore; and thou shalt dwell in them forever. And those who love thy Name shall make

their boast of thee.   For thou, O Lord, wilt bless the upright man.
As with the panoply of thine approval hast thou crowned us.

When they enter the Sanctuary, they make three lowly reverences of adoration be-
fore the Holy Altar, and kiss the book of the Holy Gospels, and the Holy Altar,
saying:

O God, cleanse thou me, a sinner, and have mercy upon me.

Then the Deacon approacheth the Priest, holding in his right hand his dalmatic *
(stikhár), his stole (orár), and his gauntlets (pórutchi); and bowing his head
before the Priest, he saith: (3)

Bless, Master, the dalmatic and the stole.

Priest. Blessed is our God always, now, and ever, and unto ages of
ages.   Amen.

The Deacon then retireth, kisseth the cross on his dalmatic, and putteth it on,
praying thus:

My soul shall exult in the Lord.   For he hath endued me with the
robe of salvation, and with the garment of joy hath he clothed me.
He hath set a crown upon my head, like unto a bridegroom, and as a
bride hath he adorned me with comeliness.

Then, having kissed his stole, he layeth it on his right shoulder.   And when he
putteth the cuffs on his wrists, he saith, as he putteth that on the right:

Thy right hand, O Lord, is glorified in strength.   Thy right hand,
O Lord, hath shattered the enemy, and through the multitude of thy
glory hast thou crushed the adversaries.

And with the left he saith:

Thy hands have made me and fashioned me.   Enlighten my mind,
and I shall learn thy commandments.

(The clergy usually kiss each vestment before putting it on.)

Then, going to the Table of Oblation, he prepareth the Holy Things.   The holy
paten he setteth on the left side; the holy chalice, which is the holy cup, on the
right; and with them the other holy utensils.

And the Priest vesteth himself in this wise: Taking his cassock (podríznik) in his
left hand, and making three lowly reverences toward the east, as aforesaid, he
signeth it with the sign of the cross, saying:

Blessed is our God always, now, and ever, and unto ages of ages.
Amen.

Then he putteth it on, saying:

My soul shall exult in the Lord: . . . *as the Deacon hath said.*

Then taking his priestly stole (epitrakhíl), and signing it with the sign of the
cross, he putteth it on, saying:

Blessed is God, who poureth out upon his priests his grace, like
unto the precious ointment on the head, which ran down upon the

* For explanation, see introductory chapter on The Symbolism of the Church, p. xxiv.

Secretly.

beard, even upon the beard of Aaron; which ran down to the skirts of his garment.

Then, taking the girdle, and girding himself, he saith:

Blessed is God, who girdeth me with strength, and hath made my path blameless, and hath given me feet like unto those of a hart, and hath set me on high.

Then he putteth on the cuffs as already described for the Deacon. And taking his epigonátion, if he hath that dignity, he blesseth it, saying:

Gird thy sword upon thy thigh, O Mighty One, in thy vigour, and in thy beauty: and go forth, and prosper, and reign, because of truth, and meekness, and righteousness; and thy right hand shall guide thee wondrously always, now, and ever, and unto ages of ages. Amen.

Then, taking his chasuble (felón), he blesseth it, and, kissing it, he putteth it on, saying:

Thy priests, O Lord, shall clothe themselves with righteousness, and thy Holy Ones shall rejoice with exultation always, now, and ever, and unto ages of ages. Amen.

Then they shall wash their hands, saying:

I will wash my hands among the innocent, and so will I compass thine Altar, O Lord; that I may hear the voice of thy praise, and tell of all thy wondrous works. Lord, I have loved the beauty of thy house, and the place where thy glory dwelleth. Destroy not my soul with the ungodly, nor my life with the men of blood, in whose hands is iniquity, and their right hand is full of gifts. But I have walked in mine innocency: Deliver me, O Lord, and have mercy upon me. My foot hath been set on righteousness. In the churches will I bless thee, O Lord.

And thus they go forth to the Chapel of Oblation, making three lowly reverences before the Table of Oblation. And each saith within himself:

O God, cleanse thou me, a sinner, and have mercy upon me.

And: By thy precious Blood hast thou redeemed us from the curse of the Law: in that thou wast nailed to the Cross, and wast pierced with a spear, thou hast poured forth immortality upon mankind, as from a fountain. O our Saviour, Glory to thee.

If it be not a Pontifical Service, the HOURS *are now read, while the Holy Gifts are prepared for the Holy Sacrament.*

Hours. *But if it be a Pontifical Service, then the* HOURS *are read later, as indicated.*

Deacon. Bless, Master *(aloud, if it be not a Pontifical Service).*

Priest. Blessed is our God always, now, and ever, and unto ages of ages.

Deacon. Amen.

Then the Priest taketh in his left hand one of the altar-breads, and in his right hand the holy spear; and making therewith the sign of the cross, thrice, above the seal of the bread, he saith:

In remembrance of our Lord, and God, and Saviour, Jesus Christ. (*Thrice.*)

And immediately he thrusteth the spear into the right side of the seal and as he cutteth it, he saith:

He was led as a sheep to the slaughter.

And as he cutteth the left side:

And as a spotless lamb before his shearers is dumb, so opened he not his mouth.

And at the top of the seal:

In his humiliation his judgment was taken away.

And at the bottom:

For his generation, who shall declare it?

And the Deacon, gazing reverently at the Holy Mystic Rite, as each incision is made saith, holding his stole in his hand the while:

Let us pray to the Lord.

And when the Priest, having thrust the spear, obliquely, from below, into the right side of the bread, taketh away the whole part with the seal, thus cut, the Deacon saith:

Master, take away.

And the Priest saith:

For his life is taken away from the earth.

And having laid it, inverted, on the holy paten, and the Deacon having said:

Sacrifice, Master.

He sacrificeth, cutting it crosswise, but leaving the seal intact, and saying:

Sacrificed is the Lamb of God who taketh away the sins of the world, for the life of the world, and for its salvation.

He then turneth upward the other side, which hath upon it the emblem of the Cross. And as he pierceth the right side with the spear, the Deacon saith:

Pierce, Master.

And the Priest: One of the soldiers did pierce his side with a spear, and straightway there came forth blood and water. And he that saw it bare witness, and his witness is true.

Secretly.

Then the Deacon poureth into the holy chalice the mingled wine and water, in amount according to the number of communicants, having first said to the Priest:

Bless, Master, the holy union.

And the Priest blesseth it, saying:

Blessed be the union of thy Holy Things always, now, and ever, and unto ages of ages.   Amen.

Then, taking in his hand another altar-bread, the Priest shall say:

In honour and commemoration of our most blessed Lady, the Birth-giver of God and ever-virgin Mary; through whose intercessions accept, O Lord, this sacrifice upon thy most heavenly Altar.

And with the spear taking out a portion, he layeth it on the right side of the Holy Bread, near the centre thereof, saying:

On thy right hand stood the Queen, clothed in a vesture wrought with gold and divers colours.

Then taking the third altar-bread, he saith:

In commemoration of the most honourable and glorious prophet, Forerunner and Baptist, John.

And taking out the first particle, he placeth it on the left hand of the Holy Bread, making the beginning of the first row.   Then he saith:

Of the holy, glorious Prophets, Moses and Aaron; Elijah and Elisha; David and Jesse; of the Three Holy Children, also of Daniel the Prophet; and of all the holy prophets.

And taking out another particle, he placeth it below the first, in due order.   Then he saith:

Of the holy, glorious and all-laudable Apostles, Peter and Paul; and of all the other holy Apostles.

Secretly.

In the same manner, he placeth a third particle below the second, thus completing the first rank. And he saith:

Of our holy Fathers and Saints, the Prelates Basil the Great, Gregory the Theologian and John Chrysostom; Athanasius and Kyril, Nicholas of Myra in Lycia; (Peter, Alexis, Jonah and Philip of Moscow;) Nikíta, Bishop of Novgorod, Leónty, Bishop of Rostóff; and of all thy holy Prelates.

And taking out a fourth particle, he placeth it beside the first particle, making a second beginning. And he saith:

Of the holy Apostle and First Martyr and Archdeacon, Stephen; of the holy Great Martyrs Demetrius, George, Theodore of Tyre, Theodore the Strategist; and of all holy Martyrs, both men and women; of Thekla, Barbara, Kyriaka, Euphemia, Paraskeva, Katherine; and of all other holy martyred women.

And taking out a fifth particle, he placeth it below the first, which is in the second row. And he saith:

Of our devout and God-bearing Fathers, Anthony, Euthymius, Sabba, Onuphrius, Athanasius of Mount Athos, Anthony and Theodosius of the Catacombs, Sergius of Radónezh, Barlaam of Khútinsk; and of all our devout fathers; and of our devout mothers in God, Pelagia, Theodosia, Anastasia, Eupraxia, Fevronia, Theodulia, Euphrosyne, Mary of Egypt; and of all our holy and devout mothers.

And in like manner, taking out a sixth particle, he placeth it below the second, completing the second row. After which he saith:

Of the holy and wonder-working Unmercenaries Cosmas and Damian, Cyrus and John, Panteleimon, Hermolaus; and of all the Holy Unmercenaries.

And taking out a seventh particle, he placeth it above, making the beginning of the third row. Then he saith:

Of the holy and righteous Ancestors of God, Joachim and Anna. And of Saint N. (*the Saint of the Church*) and of Saint N. (*the Saint of the day*); and of Saint Methodius and Saint Kyril, the Equals of the Apostles the Evangelizers of the Slavonians, and of all the Saints; through whose supplications do thou visit us, O Lord.

Then he layeth the eighth particle below the former, in due order. And thereafter he saith:

Of our Father in the Saints, John Chrysostom, Bishop of Constantinople (*if his Liturgy is to be celebrated. But if the Liturgy of St. Basil the Great is to be celebrated, then shall he be commemorated instead*).

Then taking out the ninth particle, he placeth it at the end of the third row, completing it. And taking the fourth altar-bread, he saith:

Remember, O Lord, Lover of mankind, every Bishopric over Or-

Secretly.

thodox Christians; the Most Holy Governing Synod, and Orthodox Patriarchs; and our Bishop, N.; the honourable Priesthood, the Diaconate in Christ, and every Sacerdotal Order; our brethren and fellow-ministers, the priests, the deacons, and all our brethren whom thou hast called into thy communion, through thy tenderness of heart, O all-good Lord.

And taking out a portion, he layeth it below the Holy Bread. Then he commemorateth the Ruler, saying:

Call to remembrance, O Lord, our most God-fearing Ruler, N. (4)

Then he maketh mention, by name, of the living who are to be prayed for, if any such there be; and at each name he taketh out a particle, saying:

Call to remembrance, O Lord, N.

Having thus taken out the particles, the Priest placeth them below the Holy Bread. Then taking the fifth altar-bread, he saith:

In memory, and for the remission of sins, of the most holy Patriarchs; of Orthodox and God-fearing Rulers; and of the blessed founders of this holy Temple.

Then shall he make mention of the Bishop who ordained him; and of whatsoever persons he may desire, who have departed this life, by name. And at each name, he shall take out a particle, saying:

Call to remembrance, O Lord, N.

And, in conclusion, he shall say as followeth:

And of all our Orthodox fathers and brethren who have fallen asleep in the hope of resurrection, of life eternal, and of communion with thee, O Lord, who lovest mankind.

And he taketh out a particle. Thereafter he saith:

Call to remembrance, O Lord, my unworthy self, and pardon me every transgression, whether voluntary or involuntary.

And he taketh out of the fourth prosforá a particle. Then, taking the sponge, he gathereth together the particles taken from the fourth and fifth prosforí on the paten, below the Holy Bread, so that they may be in safety, and that none of them may fall. Then the Deacon taketh the censer, and having placed incense therein, he saith to the Priest:

Bless, Master, the censer.

And straightway he saith:

Let us pray to the Lord.

Then the Priest saith the PRAYER OF THE CENSER.

Unto thee, O Christ-God, do we offer incense for an odour of spiritual fragrance: which do thou accept upon thy most heavenly Altar, and pour forth upon us in return the grace of thine all-holy Spirit.

Deacon. Let us pray to the Lord.

Secretly.

Then the Priest, having censed the star-cover, placeth it over the Holy Bread, saying:

And the Star came and stood over the place where the young Child was.

Deacon. Let us pray to the Lord.

[he Priest, having censed the first veil, covereth therewith the Holy Bread, saying:

The Lord is King, and hath put on glorious apparel; the Lord hath put on his apparel, and girded himself with strength. He hath made the round world so sure, that it cannot be moved. Ever since the world began hath thy seat been prepared: thou art from everlasting. The floods are risen, O Lord, the floods have lift up their voice; the floods lift up their waves. The waves of the sea are mighty, and rage horribly; but yet the Lord, who dwelleth on high, is mightier. Thy testimonies, O Lord, are very sure: holiness becometh thine house forever.

Deacon. Let us pray to the Lord.

Cover, Master.

The Priest, having censed the second veil, covereth therewith the holy chalice, saying:

Thy virtue, O Christ, hath covered the heavens, and the earth also is full of thy praise.

Deacon. Let us pray to the Lord.

Cover, Master.

The Priest, having censed the veil, that is to say, the air (vózdukh), covereth therewith the paten and chalice, saying:

Cover us with the shelter of thy wings, and drive away from us every foe and adversary. Order our lives in peace, O Lord; have mercy upon us, and upon thy world, and save our souls; forasmuch as thou art good and lovest mankind.

Then, taking the censer, the Priest censeth the Table of Oblation, saying thrice:

Blessed art thou, O our God, who herein art well pleased. Glory to thee.

And each time the Deacon shall respond:

Always, now, and ever, and unto ages of ages. Amen.

Then both make three devout reverences. And the Deacon, taking the censer, saith:

For the Precious Gifts now offered up, let us pray to the Lord.

Then the Priest maketh the PRAYER OF OBLATION:

O God our God, who didst send forth the Heavenly Bread, the Nourishment of the whole world, our Lord and God, Jesus Christ, to be our Saviour and Redeemer and Benefactor, blessing and sanctifying us: Do thou, the same Lord, bless also this oblation, and accept it

Secretly.

on thy most heavenly Altar. Call to remembrance those who offer it, and those for whom it is offered, inasmuch as thou art good and lovest mankind; and preserve us blameless in the holy ministry of thy Divine Mysteries.

For sanctified and glorified be thy most honourable and majestic Name, of the Father, and of the Son, and of the Holy Spirit, now, and ever, and unto ages of ages. Amen.

Then the Priest pronounceth the DISMISSAL, *saying:*

Glory to thee, O Christ-God our hope; glory to thee.

Deacon. Glory to the Father, and to the Son, and to the Holy Spirit, now, and ever, and unto ages of ages. Amen.

Lord, have mercy. (*Thrice.*)

Master, bless.

Then the Priest pronounceth the BENEDICTION. *If it be Sunday:*

May he who rose again from the dead, Christ our true God, . . .

But if it be not Sunday:

May Christ, our true God, through the intercessions of his all-undefiled Mother; of our Father among the Saints, John Chrysostom, Bishop of Constantinople (*or, if the Liturgy of St. Basil be used:* of Basil the Great, of Cæsarea in Cappadocia); and of all the Saints, have mercy upon us, and save us: for he is good and loveth mankind.

Deacon. Amen.

After the Benediction, the Deacon censeth the Holy Oblation. Then (if the Pontifical Service is to follow, see page 78. If not:) he goeth and censeth the Holy Altar round about, in the form of a cross, saying, secretly: (5)

In the grave with the body, but in Hell with the soul, in that thou art God; in Paradise with the thief, and on the throne with the Father and the Spirit, wast thou, O Christ, filling all things, in that thou art infinite.

Then he shall recite Psalm li.: Have mercy upon me, O God, after thy great goodness; . . . (*See page* 45).

Meanwhile, he censeth the Sanctuary and all the Temple, and returneth again to the Holy Altar; and having again censed it and the Priest, he putteth the censer aside in its place, and approacheth the Priest. And standing together before the Holy Altar, they make three lowly reverences, praying secretly, and saying:

O heavenly King, the Comforter, Spirit of Truth, who art in all places and fillest all things; Treasury of good things, and Giver of life: Come, and take up thine abode in us, and cleanse us from every stain; and save our souls, O Good One.

Glory to God in the highest, and on earth peace, good will towards men. (*Twice.*) O Lord, open thou my lips, and my mouth shall show forth thy praise.

Secretly.

Then the Priest kisseth the book of the Holy Gospels, and the Deacon kisseth the Holy Altar. Then the Deacon, bowing his head before the Priest, and holding his stole with three fingers, saith:

It is time to sacrifice unto the Lord. Bless, Master.

And the (Bishop or the) Priest, signing him with the sign of the cross, saith:

Blessed is our God always, now, and ever, and unto ages of ages.

Deacon. Pray for me, holy Master.

(Bishop or) Priest. May the Lord direct thy steps.

Deacon. Remember me, holy Master.

(Bishop or) Priest. May the Lord God remember thee in his kingdom always, now, and ever, and unto ages of ages.

Deacon. Amen.

And having made a humble reverence, he goeth out through the north door, and standing in his accustomed place before the Holy Door, he thrice boweth his head reverently, and saith, secretly:

O Lord, open thou my lips, and my mouth shall show forth thy praise.

Thereafter he beginneth, aloud:

Bless, Master. *(See page 80.)*

If the Priest celebrate without a Deacon, the words assigned to the Deacon in the OFFICE OF OBLATION *and in the* LITURGY, *before the Gospel are read; and in response:* Bless, Master; *and:* Pierce, Master; *and:* It is time to sacrifice: *shall not be said. As, likewise, the litany and oblation of ranks. But if many Priests serve, as in a Cathedral, only one Priest shall perform the Office of Oblation, and shall say what is herein set forth; but no other of the Priests shall say that Office separately. They are allowed only to take out the particles for the living and the dead.*

If a Pontifical Service is to follow, then, after the Benediction of the Office of Oblation, the Priest who hath celebrated the Office of Oblation (and the other Priests, in their cassocks), bearing a cross upon a salver, accompanied by the Proto-Deacon or Deacon with the censer and taper, the crozier-bearer with the Bishop's crozier, and the Sub-Deacons with the mantle and the eagle-rugs, go forth to meet the Bishop at the western door. As the Bishop entereth the Temple, the Deacon exclaimeth: Wisdom! *And the Bishop saith, secretly:* I will enter into thy house . . . *(see page 68). He is then vested in his mantle, and kisseth the cross, and giveth it to be kissed by all the Priests who are preparing to celebrate the Liturgy; and then, while the Choir singeth:* Meet is it: . . . More honourable . . . *and, while he saluteth the holy pictures of our Lord and of His Mother, and of the Patron Saint of the Church, he reciteth the prescribed hymns (see page 107), supporting himself on his crozier, he approacheth the Holy Door, and there giveth the blessing for the* PRAYER OF ENTRANCE, *as shown above. (See page 68.)*

After the Prayer: Stretch forth thy hand, O Lord . . . *(see page 68), the Bishop turneth his face towards the People, and blesseth the worshippers, while the Choir singeth:*

Ton Despótin kai Arkhieréa imón, Kýrie fýlatte. Eis pollá éti, Déspota. (Preserve, O Lord, our Master and Bishop. For many years, O Master.)

The Bishop then goeth to his dais; the Clergy ask his blessing, and withdraw into the Sanctuary to vest themselves. The Priest who hath celebrated the Office of Oblation blesseth the beginning of the Hours:

Blessed is our God always, now, and ever, and unto ages of ages.
Reader. Amen.

And he readeth the THIRD HOUR *and the* SIXTH HOUR.

Choir. The prophets proclaimed thee from on high, O Virgin, the Jar, the Staff, the Tables of the Law, the Ark, the Candlestick, the Table, the Mount Uncloven, the Golden Censer, and the Tabernacle, the Gate Impassable, the Palace and Ladder, and the Throne of Kings.

Meanwhile the Sub-Deacons begin to vest the Bishop, having first removed his mantle, cowl, pectoral holy image, and outer cassock. While the Bishop's vestments are being put upon him, the Proto-Deacon, censer in hand, reciteth the same Verses which the Priests recite as they vest themselves. (See above.) Or, sometimes, they are chanted by the Choir, the Proto-Deacon exclaiming before each: Let us pray to the Lord; and using the second person, and substituting for "Priests" the word "Bishops," and so forth.

When the pall (omofór) is put on, the Deacon saith:

When thou hadst taken upon thy shoulders human nature which had gone astray, O Christ, thou didst bear it to heaven, unto thy God and Father, always, now, and ever, and unto ages of ages. Amen.

And with the pectoral holy image he saith:

May God create in thee a clean heart, and renew a right spirit within thee, always, now, and ever, and unto ages of ages. Amen.

At the second pectoral image (if there be one), he saith:

Thy heart is inditing of a good matter; thou shalt speak of thy deeds unto the King, always, now, and ever, and unto ages of ages. Amen.

And with the cross he saith:

If any man will come after me, let him deny himself, saith the Lord, and take up his cross and follow me, always, now, and ever, and unto ages of ages. Amen.

And with the mitre he saith:

The Lord hath set upon thy head a crown of precious stones. Thou askedst life of him, and he shall give thee length of days, always, now, and ever, and unto ages of ages. Amen.

Then the Proto-Deacon standeth aside, and the Sub-Deacons enter the Sanctuary, and taking from the Clergy the dikíri and the trikíri, they bear them to the Bishop. And the Proto-Deacon saith:

May thy light so shine before men that they may see thy good works and glorify our Father which is in heaven, always, now, and ever, and unto ages of ages. Amen.

Bishop.

And the Bishop bestoweth the blessing, in cross-form, with the dikíri and the trikíri, to the east, and the west, and the south, and the north, while the Choir singeth slowly:

Ton Despótin kai Arkhieréa imón, Kýrie fýlatte. Eis pollá éti, Déspota. (Preserve, O Lord, our Master and Bishop. For many years, O Master.) (6)

Then the ewer and basin are brought by the Proto-Deacon and the Deacon, and the Bishop washeth his hands, if there be no Setting-apart of a Reader or Chanter, or the Ordination of a Sub-Deacon. But if there be a Setting-apart or an Ordination, then he who is to be set apart or ordained bringeth the ewer and basin, after he hath been vested in his dalmatic, in the manner set forth in the Order for the Laying-on of Hands: and the Bishop saith, secretly:

Setting-
apart of
Readers
and
Chanters;
Ordina-
tion of
Sub-
Deacons.

O Lord our God, who didst sanctify the streams of Jordan by thy saving manifestation: Do thou now, also, send down the grace of thy Holy Spirit, and bless this water, to the sanctification of all thy people for blessed art thou unto ages of ages.

When the SIXTH HOUR *approacheth its close, all the Clergy, having vested themselves, come forth from the Sanctuary through the north door, and taking their stand beside the Bishop, begin to pray:*

O God, cleanse thou me, a sinner. (*Thrice.*)

Bishop. O Heavenly King . . . (*See page* 67), *with hands uplifted.*

Glory to God in the highest, . . . (*Twice.*)

O Lord, open thou my lips, . . .

Proto-Deacon. It is time to sacrifice unto the Lord. Bless, Right Reverend Master. (*See page* 77.)

The First Priest and the Proto-Deacon kiss the Bishop's hand, and the Priest goeth into the Sanctuary, and openeth the Holy Door, while the Proto-Deacon remaineth standing outside, in front of the holy picture of the Saviour.

The Bishop remaineth on his dais (káthedra), until the Little Entrance. The other Clergy enter the Sanctuary after the Exclamations at the Great and Little Litanies.

THE DIVINE LITURGY

II. THE LITURGY OF THE CATECHUMENS

Deacon. Bless, Master.

Priest (bestowing the blessing, in cross-form, with the book of the Gospels from the Altar). Blessed is the kingdom of the Father, and of the Son, and of the Holy Spirit, now, and ever, and unto ages of ages.

Choir. Amen.

And if it be at Eastertide:

Easter-tide. Christ is risen from the dead, trampling down Death by death, and upon those in the tomb bestowing life.

THE GREAT LITANY (*Velíkaya Ekténiya*).

Deacon. In peace let us pray to the Lord.

Choir. Lord, have mercy.

For the peace that is from above, and for the salvation of our souls, let us pray to the Lord. ℞

For the peace of the whole world; for the welfare of God's holy Churches, and for the union of all: ℞

For this holy Temple, and for those who with faith, devoutness, and in the fear of God have entered therein: ℞

For our Most Holy Synod (*or* Patriarch); for our Bishop (*or* Archbishop, *or* Metropolitan), N.; for the honourable Presbytery, the Diaconate in Christ; for all the clergy and the laity: ℞

Here follow petitions for the Ruler of the Land and for all the Authorities according to the elements and nationalities of which the Parish is constituted.

let us pray to the Lord. Choir. Lord, have mercy.

If a Bishop be the celebrant, he **Bishop.** *saith here,* secretly, *the* PRAYER OF OBLATION.

O God our God, who didst send forth the Heavenly Bread, the Nourishment of the whole world, our Lord and God, Jesus Christ, to be our Saviour and Redeemer and Benefactor, blessing and sanctifying us: Do thou, the same Lord, bless also this oblation, and accept it on thy most heavenly Altar. Call to remembrance those who offer it, and those for whom it is offered, inasmuch as thou art good and lovest mankind; and preserve us blameless in the holy ministry of thy Divine Mysteries.

For sanctified and glorified be thy most honourable and majestic Name, of the Father, and of the Son, and of the Holy Spirit, now, and ever, and unto ages of ages. Amen.

Secretly.

That he will aid them and subdue under their feet every foe and adversary: ℞

For this city, for this holy Temple, and for every city and land, and for those who with faith dwell therein: ℞

For healthful seasons; for abundance of the fruits of the earth, and for peaceful times: ℞

For those who travel by sea or by land; for the sick and the suffering; for those who are in captivity, and for their salvation: ℞

That he will deliver us from all tribulation, wrath, and necessity: ℞

let us pray to the Lord.
Choir. Lord, have mercy.

Succour us, save us, have mercy upon us, and keep us, O God, by thy grace.

Choir. Lord, have mercy.

Calling to remembrance our most holy, all-undefiled, most blessed and glorious Lady, the Birth-giver of God and ever-virgin Mary, with all the Saints, let us commend ourselves, and each other, and all our life unto Christ our God.

Choir. To thee, O Lord.

Exclamation.

Priest. For unto thee are due all glory, honour and worship, to the Father, and to the Son, and to the Holy Spirit, now, and ever, and unto ages of ages.

Choir. Amen.

And the Deacon, having made a reverence, shall leave his place, and shall go and stand before the holy picture (ikóna) of Christ, holding his stole with three fingers of his right hand.

Here shall be sung the FIRST ANTI-PHON, *Psalm* ciii. (*or on the Great Feasts its appointed substitute*).*

Bless the Lord, O my soul: Blessed art thou, O Lord. Bless the Lord, O my soul; and all that is within me bless his holy Name. Bless the Lord, O my soul, and forget not all his benefits. Who forgiveth all thy sin, and healeth all thine infirmities. The Lord is full of compassion and mercy, long-suffering and of great goodness. He will not alway be chiding, neither keepeth he his

And the Priest saith, secretly, *the* PRAYER OF THE FIRST ANTIPHON.

O Lord our God, whose might is ineffable, whose glory is inconceivable, whose mercy is infinite, and whose love toward mankind is unutterable: Look down, O Master, in thy tender compassion, upon us and upon this holy Temple; and deal with us and with those people who here pray with us, according to the riches of thy mercies and thy bounties.

Secretly.

wrath forever. He hath not dealt with us after our sins, nor rewarded
* See the Special Services for the Great Feasts.

us according to our iniquities. Bless the Lord, O my soul, and all that is within me bless his holy Name. Blessed art thou, O Lord.

And at the conclusion of the Antiphon, the Deacon shall come and stand again in his accustomed place, and shall say:

THE LITTLE LITANY (*Málaya Ekténiya*).

Again, yet again, in peace let us pray to the Lord.

Choir. Lord, have mercy.

Succour us, save us, have mercy upon us, and keep us, O God, by thy grace.

Choir. Lord, have mercy.

While the Priest (likewise the Bishop) saith, secretly, *the* PRAYER OF THE SECOND ANTIPHON.

O Lord our God, save thy people, and bless thine heritage. Preserve the fulness of thy Church: sanctify those who love the beauty of thy house: glorify them by thy divine might in recompense; and forsake not us who put our trust in thee.

Secretly.

Calling to remembrance our most holy, all-undefiled, most blessed and glorious Lady, the Birth-giver of God and ever-virgin Mary, with all the Saints, let us commend ourselves, and each other, and all our life, unto Christ our God.

Choir. To thee, O Lord.

Exclamation.

Priest. For thine is the majesty, and thine are the kingdom and the power and the glory, of the Father, and of the Son. and of the Holy Spirit, now, and ever, and unto ages of ages.

Choir. Amen.

The Deacon shall do as he hath done at the First Antiphon.
Here shall be sung the SECOND ANTIPHON, *Psalm cxlvi. (or on the Great Feasts its appointed substitute).*

Praise the Lord, O my soul: while I live, will I praise the Lord; yea, as long as I have any being, I will sing praises unto my God. Blessed is he that hath the God of Jacob for his help, and whose hope is in the Lord his God; who made the sea, and all that therein is; who keepeth his promise forever. Who helpeth them to right that suffer wrong; who feedeth the hungry. The Lord looseth men out of prison; the Lord giveth sight to the blind. The Lord helpeth them that are fallen; the Lord careth for the righteous. The Lord careth for the strangers; he defendeth the fatherless and widow: as for the way of the ungodly, he turneth it upside down. The Lord thy God, O Sion, shall be King forevermore.

Glory to the Father, and to the Son, and to the Holy Spirit, now, and ever, and unto ages of ages. Amen.

Here shall be sung the Anthem.

O Only-begotten Son and Word of God! Thou who art immortal yet didst deign for our salvation to become incarnate of the Holy Birth-giver of God and ever-virgin Mary; and without change of essence wast made

* See the Special Services for the Great Feasts.

man; who also wast crucified for us, O Christ-God, trampling down Death by death; who art one of the Holy Trinity, and art glorified together with the Father and the Holy Spirit: Save us.

Deacon. Again, yet again, in peace let us pray to the Lord.

Choir. Lord, have mercy.

Succour us, save us, have mercy upon us, and keep us, O God, by thy grace.

Choir. Lord, have mercy.

Calling to remembrance our most holy, all-undefiled, most blessed and glorious Lady, the Birth-giver of God and ever-virgin Mary, with all the Saints, let us commend ourselves, and each other, and all our life unto Christ our God.

Choir. To thee, O Lord.

Then by (the Bishop and) the Priest is said, secretly, the PRAYER OF THE THIRD ANTIPHON.

O thou, who hast given us grace at this time, with one accord, to make our common supplications unto thee; and dost promise that when two or three are gathered together in thy Name thou wilt grant their requests. Fulfil now, O Lord, the desires and petitions of thy servants as may be most expedient for them; granting them in this world knowledge of thy truth, and in the world to come, life everlasting. *Secretly.*

Exclamation.

Priest. For thou art a good God, and lovest mankind, and unto thee we ascribe glory, to the Father, and to the Son, and to the Holy Spirit, now, and ever, and unto ages of ages.

Choir. Amen.

The Deacon then entereth the Sanctuary, and the Choir chanteth the THIRD ANTIPHON.

In thy Kingdom remember us, O Lord, when thou comest into thy Kingdom. Blessed are the poor in spirit: for theirs is the kingdom of heaven. Blessed are they that mourn: for they shall be comforted. Blessed are the meek: for they shall inherit the earth. Blessed are they that do hunger and thirst after righteousness: for they shall be filled. Blessed are the merciful: for they shall obtain mercy. Blessed are the pure in heart: for they shall see God. Blessed are the peacemakers: for they shall be called the children of God. Blessed are they which are perse-

The Priest saith the PRAYER OF THE LITTLE ENTRANCE *while the last portion of the Beatitudes is being sung.*

O Master, Lord our God, who hast appointed in heaven ranks and hosts of Angels and Archangels for the ministry of thy glory: Cause that with our entrance may enter also the holy Angels with us serving thee, and with us glorifying thy goodness. *Secretly.*

For unto thee are due all glory, honour and worship, to the Father, and to the Son, and to the Holy Spirit, now, and ever, and unto ages of ages. Amen.

If it be a Pontifical Service, the head Priest giveth the book of the Holy Gospels to the Proto-Deacon, who *Bishop.*

cuted for righteousness' sake: for theirs is the kingdom of heaven. Blessed are ye when men shall revile you, and persecute you, and shall say all manner of evil against you falsely, for my sake.

Then the Priest, taking the book of the Holy Gospels from the Altar, giveth it to the Deacon; and preceded by a light, they both make the Lesser Entrance.

Deacon. Let us pray to the Lord.

Choir. Lord, have mercy.

Rejoice, and be exceeding glad; for great is your reward in heaven.

The Deacon, taking his stand before the Holy Door, saith:

Deacon. Bless, Master, the Holy Entrance.

Priest. Blessed is the Entrance of thy Holy Ones always, now, and ever, and unto ages of ages.

Choir. Amen.

Then the Deacon shall go to the Priest, and the Priest shall kiss the book of the Holy Gospels; and the Deacon shall come to the centre of the Holy Door, and there standing in front of the Priest, he shall elevate the Holy Gospels, and shall say, so that all may hear:

Wisdom, O believers! (8)

Then shall they go to the Holy Altar; and the Deacon shall lay the Gospels on the Altar, and the Choir shall sing:

O come, let us worship and fall down before Christ. Save, O Son of God, who didst rise again from the dead,* us who sing unto thee: Alleluia. (*Thrice.*)

beareth it, preceded by the Sub-Deacons with the dikíri and trikíri and the sacramental fans (rípidi).

The Priests follow, in the order of their rank; and the whole procession, while the Beatitudes are being sung, maketh the circuit of the Altar, and coming forth, through the north door, goeth to the Bishop's dais. And there the Proto-Deacon standeth in front of the Bishop.

Proto-Deacon. Let us pray to the Lord.

Choir. Lord, have mercy.

Proto-Deacon. Bless, Right Reverend Master, the Holy Entrance.

Bishop. Blessed is the Entrance of thy Holy Ones, always, now, and ever, and unto ages of ages.

Choir. Amen.

The Bishop kisseth the Holy Gospels.

Proto-Deacon. Wisdom, O Believers!

The Clergy who are taking part in the service sing:

O come, let us worship and fall down before Christ. Save, O Son of God, who didst rise again from the dead,* us who sing unto thee: Alleluia.

The Bishop bestoweth the blessing with the dikíri and trikíri, on all four sides, as after his vesting. And all proceed to the Sanctuary, where the Bishop, bearing the dikíri and censer, accompanied by the Proto-Deacon bearing the trikíri, censeth the Holy Altar, the image-screen, and the People, while the Choir chanteth.

Eis pollá éti, Déspota. (*Thrice.*)

Then shall be sung the proper Hymn (Tropár) and Collect-Hymn (Kondák) for the Day. (See Appendix A.)

---

* *If it be a week day: . . . who art wonderful in the Saints. Or, at Feasts, the proper Refrain, from the Antiphon of the Feast.*

(Margin notes: Bishop. — Ordination of Proto-Deacons and Arch-Priests. — Bishop.)

THE PRAYER OF THE THRICE-HOLY.

The Priest, secretly.

O holy God, who restest in the Saints; who art hymned by the Seraphim with a thrice-holy cry, and glorified by the Cherubim, and adored by every heavenly Power; who out of nothingness hast brought all things into being; who hast created man after thine own image and likeness, and hast adorned him with every gift of thine; who givest unto those that ask of thee wisdom and understanding; who despisest not the sinner, but hast appointed repentance unto salvation; and hast vouchsafed unto us, thy humble and unworthy servants here, at this hour, to stand before the glory of thy holy Altar, and to render unto thee that adoration and praise which are thy due: Do thou, the same Lord, accept from the mouths of us sinners, the Thrice-Holy song, and visit us with thy beneficence. Pardon us every transgression, whether voluntary or involuntary. Sanctify both our souls and bodies, and grant that we may serve thee in uprightness all the days of our life: through the intercessions of the holy Birth-giver of God, and of all the Saints of all the ages who have been well-pleasing unto thee.

Secretly.

If it be at a Pontifical Service, the last Collect-Hymn is omitted, and the Proto-Deacon, coming forth from the Sanctuary, saith:

O Lord, save the God-fearing.

And the Choir singeth the same.

Proto-Deacon. And hear us.
Choir. And hear us.

Then (in Russian Churches) the Proto-Deacon saith the GREAT EULOGY.

To His Holiness, the Patriarch of All-Russia, N., many years!

And the Clergy and the Choir repeat the same.

Proto-Deacon. To our Most God-fearing Ruler, N., and to all the Authorities (*and to the Ruler of the Land, if it be in a foreign country, mentioning his name and title*), many years!

And the Choir singeth the same.

Proto-Deacon. To our Lord, the Right (*or:* Most) Reverend, N., of N., many years!

And the Clergy and the Choir repeat the same.

Proto-Deacon. To the Right Reverend Patriarchs, Metropolitans, Archbishops and Bishops, many years!

And the Clergy and the Choir sing the same.

To the Orthodox Governing Council, and Commanders of the Army and the Navy; to Governors of Towns, and the Christ-loving Army; and to all Orthodox Christians, many years!

The Choir repeat the same, and the Bishop, after each "many years!" blesseth all, and then reciteth, secretly, the PRAYER OF THE THRICE-HOLY.

Bishop.

And when the Choir come to the last Hymn, the Deacon shall say to the Priest, as both bow their heads, and he holdeth his stole with three fingers:

Bless, Master, the time of the Thrice-Holy.

And the Priest shall bless him, with the sign of the cross, and shall say, aloud:

For holy art thou, O our God, and unto thee we ascribe glory, to the Father, and to the Son, and to the Holy Spirit, now, and ever;

Priest. Let us pray to the Lord.

Choir. Lord, have mercy.

And when the Hymn is finished, the Deacon shall come close to the Holy Door, and pointing with his stole, first to the holy picture of Christ, he shall say:

O Lord, save the God-fearing, and hear us.

Then shall he point, in like manner, to those who stand without, and shall say:

Even unto ages of ages.

Choir. Amen.

And then the Choir:

O Holy God, Holy Mighty, Holy Immortal One, have mercy upon us. (*Five times.*)* (9)

The Clergy in the Sanctuary:

Glory to the Father, and to the Son, and to the Holy Spirit, now, and ever, and unto ages of ages. Amen.

We, thy servants, in that we have been delivered from calamity, do offer unto thee, O Birth-giver of God, who as a victorious Chieftain warrest for us, songs of triumph and thanksgiving. Do thou also, in that thou hast might invincible, free us from all assaults, that we may cry unto thee: Hail, O Bride Unwedded!

Proto-Deacon. Bless, Right Reverend Master, the time of the Thrice-Holy.

And standing in front of the Holy Door, he shall say:

Let us pray to the Lord.

Choir. Lord, have mercy.

Bishop. For holy art thou, O our God, and unto thee we ascribe glory, to the Father, and to the Son, and to the Holy Spirit, now, and ever;

And the Proto-Deacon, standing near the Holy Door, and holding his stole with three fingers, and pointing therewith to the People, saith:

Even unto ages of ages.

Choir. Amen. O Holy God, Holy Mighty, Holy Immortal One, have mercy upon us. (*Once.*)

*The Priests repeat the same once.**

The Choir repeateth the same once.

After the third repetition, the Bishop, holding the cross and the dikiri, saith, with his face towards the People:

Look down from heaven, O God,

Bishop.

---

* *At Christmas, the Epiphany, on the Eve of Palm Sunday, on Holy Saturday, during Easter-tide and at Pentecost, in place of the Thrice-Holy shall be sung:*

As many as have been baptized into Christ have put on Christ. Alleluia. (10)

At the Feast of the Setting-up (Exaltation) of the Holy Cross; and at the third week of the Great Fast (Lent), when is the Feast of the Adoration of the Cross, in place of the Thrice-Holy there shall be sung:

Thy Cross do we worship, O Master, and we glorify thy Resurrection.

And the Deacon shall say to the Priest:

Command, Master.

Then shall they approach the Holy Throne, and as he approacheth, the Priest shall say:

Blessed is he that cometh in the Name of the Lord.

Deacon. Bless,. Master, the seat on high.

Priest. Blessed art thou on the throne of glory of thy kingdom, who sittest on the Cherubim, always, now, and ever, and unto ages of ages.

The Priest doth not ascend the High Place, nor sit upon it, but taketh his seat beside it, to the south.

Secretly.

and behold and visit this vine which thou hast planted with thy right hand, and establish it.

Deacon. Command, Most Reverend Master.

Bishop. Blessed is he that cometh in the Name of the Lord.

And while the Choir singeth the Thrice-Holy for the fourth time, the Bishop bestoweth the blessing with the cross and the dikíri. Then the Clergy and the Choir each repeat the Thrice-Holy once more.

Here Bishops are ordained. **Ordination of Bishops.**

Proto-Deacon. Bless, Right Reverend Master, the seat on high.

Bishop. Blessed art thou on the throne of glory of thy kingdom, who sittest on the Cherubim all-hymned and exalted forever. (11)

The Bishop then ascendeth the High Place, and standeth there, looking towards the People. And he giveth the dikíri to the Deacon. And the Proto-Deacon giveth the trikíri to the Bishop, reciting the Hymn.

Bishop.

Bishop.

In Jordan was the Trinity made manifest; for the Most-Divine Person of the Father Himself proclaimed: He that is baptized, the same is my beloved Son. And the Spirit descended upon Him that was like unto Himself. For which cause men shall bless Him and exalt Him forever.

The Bishop taketh the trikíri, and blesseth thrice with the trikíri, as usual. When the Bishop giveth the trikíri to the Deacon:

Choir. Glory . . . now, and ever . . . Amen. O Holy Immortal One, have mercy upon us. O Holy God . . . (*See page 86.*)

After the Thrice-Holy, the Deacon shall say:

Let us attend.

(*Bishop* or) *Priest.* Peace be with you all.

Reader. And with thy spirit.

Deacon. Wisdom!

Reader. The Gradual (*Prokímen*), in the . . . Tone. (12)

Tone I.: Let thy mercy, O Lord, be upon us, as we have set our hope on thee.

Verse: Rejoice in the Lord, O ye righteous: for it becometh the just to be thankful.

Tone II.: The Lord is my strength and my song, and is become my salvation.

Verse: The Lord hath chastened and corrected me; but he hath not given me over unto death.

Tone III.: O sing praises, sing praises unto our God: O sing praises, sing praises unto our King.

Verse: O clap your hands together, all ye people: O sing unto God with the voice of melody.

Tone IV.: O Lord, how manifold are thy works: in wisdom hast thou made them all.

Verse: Bless the Lord, O my soul: O Lord my God, thou art become exceeding glorious.

Tone V.: Thou shalt keep us, O Lord: thou shalt preserve us from this generation henceforth forever.

Verse: Save me, O Lord, for there is not one godly man left.

Tone VI.: O Lord, save thy people, and bless thine inheritance.

Verse: Unto thee will I cry, O Lord my strength: keep thou not silence towards me.

Tone VII.: The Lord shall give strength unto his people: the Lord shall give his people the blessing of peace.

Verse: Bring unto the Lord, O ye sons of God, bring young rams unto the Lord.

Tone VIII.: Pray ye unto the Lord our God, and render thanks.

Verse: In Jewry is God known, his Name is great in Israel.

Deacon: Wisdom!

Reader. The Lesson from the Epistle of the Holy Apostle (N. to the N.).

Deacon. Let us attend.

The Reader then readeth the Epistle: * Brethren . . .

And while the Epistle is being read, the Deacon shall take the censer, and approaching the Priest shall receive his blessing, and shall cense the Holy Altar round about, and all the Sanctuary, and the Priest, and the People. (13)	*If a Bishop be the celebrant, the Proto-Deacon taketh the censer, and a Deacon the incense, and they approach the Bishop. And the Bishop, putting incense into the censer, reciteth the while* the PRAYER OF THE CENSER. We offer unto thee the censer, O Christ our God, for the savour of a sweet spiritual odour; which do thou accept upon thy most heavenly Altar, requiting us with the grace of thy Holy Spirit.	*Bishop.*

And when the Epistle is finished, the Priest shall say:

Peace be with thee. *Reader.* And with thy spirit. *Deacon.* Wisdom! *Reader.* Alleluia.	THE PRAYER BEFORE THE GOSPEL *The Priest,* secretly. Illumine our hearts, O God who lovest mankind, with the pure light of thy divine knowledge, and open the eyes of our under-	*Secretly.*

* *While the Epistle is being read the Bishop sitteth on the High Place, and the Priests sit beside it. And while the Gospel is being read, they stand at their places.*

standing to the comprehension of the proclamation of thy Gospel. Implant in us, likewise, the fear of thy blessed commandments; that, trampling down all carnal desires, we may pursue a godly life, both thinking and performing such things as are well-pleasing unto thee. For thou art the light of our souls, and of our bodies, O Christ-God, and unto thee do we ascribe glory, together with thy Father who is from everlasting, and thy holy, and blessed, and life-giving Spirit, now, and ever, and unto ages of ages. Amen.

Secretly.

Then the Deacon, having set the censer in its proper place, shall come to the Priest, and bowing his head, and holding his stole and the book of the Holy Gospels with the tips of his fingers, at the Holy Altar, shall say:

Bless, Master, him who proclaimeth the good tidings of the holy Apostle and Evangelist, N.

(For a Bishop: Bless, Right Reverend Master, him who proclaimeth . . .)
And the Bishop or the Priest, blessing him with the sign of the cross, shall say:

May God, through the intercessions of the holy, glorious and all-laudable Apostle and Evangelist, N., grant utterance with great power unto thee, who proclaimest the good tidings; unto the fulfilment of the Gospel of his beloved Son, our Lord Jesus Christ.

Deacon. Amen.

All this is omitted, if the Priest serve without a Deacon.

Then the Deacon doeth reverence to the book of the Holy Gospels, and taketh it, and goeth out through the Holy Door, preceded by a taper, and standeth on the tribune, or on the place prepared. And the Priest, standing before the Holy Altar, with his face to the west, proclaimeth:

Wisdom, O believers! Let us listen to the Holy Gospel.

The Bishop. Peace be with you all.

Choir. And with thy spirit.

Deacon. The Lesson from the Holy Gospel according to N.

Choir. Glory to thee, O Lord; glory to thee.

Priest. Let us attend.

And the Deacon, or the Priest, if there be no Deacon, readeth the Gospel; and when he hath finished, the Priest shall say: (14)

Peace be unto thee, who hast announced the good tidings.

Choir. Glory to thee, O Lord; glory to thee.

And if it be a Pontifical Service, the Choir singeth: **Bishop.**

Eis pollá éti, Déspota. (Many years, O Lord.)

While the Bishop blesseth the People with the trikíri and the dikíri.

Then the Deacon shall go to the Holy Door, and shall give the book of the Gospels to the Priest, who placeth it on the Altar, behind the corporal (antimíns).

And the Deacon, standing in his accustomed place, shall say:

Let us all say, with all our soul and with all our mind let us say: (15)

Choir. Lord, have mercy.

O Lord Almighty, the God of our fathers, we beseech thee, hearken, and have mercy.

Choir. Lord, have mercy.

Have mercy upon us, O God, according to thy great mercy, we beseech thee: hearken, and have mercy.

Choir. Lord, have mercy. *(Thrice.)*

Here follow petitions for the Ruler of the Land and for all the Authorities, according to the elements and nationalities of which the Parish is constituted.

For our Most Holy Governing Synod (*or* Patriarch); for our Bishop (*or* Archbishop, *or* Metropolitan), N.; and for all our brethren in Christ. ℟ (*the ℟ is sung by the clergy also, when a Bishop serves.*)

Furthermore

THE PRAYER OF THE LITANY OF FERVENT SUPPLICATION.

The Priest, secretly.

O Lord our God, accept this, the fervent supplication of thy servants, and be gracious unto us, according to the multitude of thy mercy; and send down thy bounties upon us, and upon all thy people, who here await the rich mercy which is from thee.

Secretly.

The corporal (antimíns) is now unfolded, except the upper edge.

we pray for all their Christ-loving Army and Navy. ℟

Furthermore we pray for our brethren the Priests; for ordained Monks, and for all our brotherhood in Christ. ℟

Furthermore we pray for the blessed and ever-memorable most holy Orthodox Patriarchs, and God-fearing Rulers; and for the founders of this holy Temple; and for all our devout fathers and brethren, Orthodox believers, departed this life before us, who here and in all the world lie asleep in the Lord. ℟

Furthermore we pray for those who bear fruit and do good works in this holy, and all-honourable Temple; for those who labour in its service; for the singers; and for the people here present, who await in firm hope thy great and rich mercies. ℟

Choir. Lord, have mercy. (Thrice.)

Exclamation.

Priest. For thou art a merciful God, who lovest mankind, and unto thee we ascribe glory, to the Father, and to the Son, and to the Holy Spirit, now, and ever, and unto ages of ages.

Choir. Amen.

[*And the Priest saith this Prayer:*

O Lord our God, who art great

Deacon. Let us pray to the Lord.
Choir. Lord, have mercy.

and full of compassion, in meekness of heart we make our humble supplication unto thee: Preserve beneath the shelter of thy loving-kindness from every calamity our most God-fearing Ruler. Guard him in his ways by thy holy Angels, and let no enemy by any means prevail against him, nor any son of iniquity aim to offend him. Satisfy him with length of days and plenitude of strength; and enable him to accomplish all things to thy glory, and to the welfare of his people. So we, rejoicing in thy abounding grace toward him every day and every hour, shall bless and glorify thy most holy Name, of the Father, and of the Son, and of the Holy Spirit, now, and ever, and unto ages of ages.

Choir. Amen.]

And if there be offerings on behalf of the dead, the Deacon or the Priest shall say the following LITANY:

Have mercy upon us, O God, according to thy great mercy, we beseech thee: hearken, and have mercy.

Choir. Lord, have mercy. (*Thrice.*)

Furthermore we pray for the repose of the souls of the servants of God departed this life, NN.; and that thou wilt pardon all their sins, both voluntary and involuntary. ℞

That the Lord God will establish their souls where the just repose. ℞

The mercies of God, the kingdom of heaven, and the remission of their sins we entreat of Christ, our King Immortal and our God.

Choir. Grant it, O Lord.

Let us pray to the Lord.

Choir. Lord, have mercy.

The PRIEST, aloud or secretly.

O God of spirits, and of all flesh, who hast trampled down death, and overthrown the Devil, and given life unto thy world: Do thou, the same Lord, give rest to the souls of thy departed servants, NN., in a place of brightness, a place of verdure, a place of repose, whence all sickness, sorrow and sighing have fled away. Pardon every transgression which they have committed, whether by word, or deed, or thought. For thou art a good God, and lovest mankind; because there is no man who liveth and sinneth not; for thou only art without sin, and thy righteousness is to all eternity, and thy word is true.

Sometimes omitted.

Secretly.

Exclamation.

Priest. For thou art the Resurrection, and the Life, and the Repose of thy departed servants, NN., O Christ our God, and unto thee we ascribe glory, together with thy Father, who is from everlasting, and thine all-holy, and good, and life-giving Spirit, now, and ever, and unto ages of ages. — *Choir.* Amen.

THE LITANY OF THE CATE-
CHUMENS.

Deacon. Pray ye unto the Lord, ye Catechumens.

Choir. Lord, have mercy.

Ye faithful, pray ye unto the Lord for the Catechumens; that the Lord will have mercy upon them.

Choir. Lord, have mercy.

That he will teach them the word of truth.

Choir. Lord, have mercy.

That he will reveal to them the gospel of righteousness.

Choir. Lord, have mercy.

That he will unite them unto his Holy Catholic and Apostolic Church.

Choir. Lord, have mercy.

Save them, have mercy upon them, succour them, and keep them, O God, by thy grace.

Choir. Lord, have mercy.

Bow your heads unto the Lord, ye Catechumens.

Choir. To thee, O Lord.

THE PRAYER FOR THE CATECHUMENS.
The Priest, secretly.

O Lord our God, who dwellest on high, and dost regard the humble of heart; who hast sent forth as the salvation of the race of men thine Only-begotten Son and God, our Lord Jesus Christ: Look down upon thy servants the Catechumens, who have bowed their necks before thee. Grant unto them in due season the laver of regeneration, remission of sins, and the robe of incorruption. Unite them unto thy Holy Catholic and Apostolic Church, and number them with thy chosen flock.

Here the last edge of the corporal is spread out.

[*Or, if it be at the* LITURGY OF ST. BASIL THE GREAT:

O Lord our God, who dwellest in the heavens, and lookest down upon all thy works: Look upon thy servants, the Catechumens, who have bowed their necks before thee, and grant them the light yoke. Make them honourable members of thy holy Church; and vouchsafe unto them the laver of regeneration, the remission of sins, and the robe of incorruption, unto the knowledge of thee, our true God.]

Secretly.

Exclamation.

Priest. That with us they may magnify thine all-honourable and majestic Name, of the Father, and of the Son, and of the Holy Spirit, now, and ever, and unto ages of ages.

Choir. Amen.

The Priest maketh the sign of the cross over the corporal with the sponge, which he then kisseth, and layeth on one side.

Deacon. Depart, all ye Catechumens, depart. Depart, all ye Catechumens: let no Catechumen remain: but let us who are in the faith again, yet again, in peace pray unto the Lord. (16)

Choir. Lord, have mercy.

III. THE LITURGY OF THE FAITHFUL

Succour us, save us, have mercy upon us, and keep us, O God, by thy grace.

Choir. Lord, have mercy.

THE FIRST PRAYER OF THE FAITHFUL.

The Priest, secretly.

We give thanks unto thee, O Lord God of the Powers, who hast graciously vouchsafed unto us to stand now before thy holy Altar, and fall down in adoration before thy compassion toward our sins, and the errors of the people. Accept our supplications, O God; make us worthy to offer unto thee prayers and supplications, and unbloody sacrifices for all thy people. And enable us, whom thou hast appointed to this thy ministry, by the power of thy Holy Spirit, at all times, and in every place, blamelessly, without offence, and in the witness of a pure conscience, to call upon thee; that hearing us thou mayest show mercy upon us, according to the plenitude of thy goodness.

Secretly.

[Or, *if the* LITURGY OF ST. BASIL THE GREAT *be used:*

Thou, O Lord, hast shown us this great mystery of salvation. Thou hast graciously permitted us, thy humble and unworthy servants, to be the ministrants of thy holy Altar. Do thou enable us with the power of thy Holy Spirit for this ministry; that, standing uncondemned before thy holy glory, we may offer unto thee an oblation of praise. For thou art he who worketh all things in all men. Grant, therefore, O Lord, that our sacrifice for our own sins, and for the errors of thy people, may be acceptable and well-pleasing in thy sight.] *Deacon.* Wisdom!

Exclamation.

Priest. For unto thee are due all honour, glory and worship, to the Father, and to the Son, and to the Holy Spirit, now, and ever and unto, ages of ages.

Choir. Amen.

Deacon. Again, yet again, in peace let us pray to the Lord.

Choir. Lord, have mercy.

When the Priest serveth without a Deacon, the following part of this Litany is omitted as indicated.

For the peace that is from above, and for the salvation of our souls, let us pray to the Lord.

Choir. Lord, have mercy.

Sometimes omitted.

THE SECOND PRAYER OF THE FAITHFUL.

The Priest, secretly.

Again and oftentimes we fall down before thee, and beseech thee, O Good One who lovest mankind, that, looking down upon our petition, thou wilt purify both our souls and bodies from all defilement of the flesh and of the spirit; and grant that in blamelessness and without condemnation we

Secretly.

For the peace of the whole world; for the welfare of God's holy Churches, and for the union of all, let us pray to the Lord.

. *Choir.* Lord, have mercy.

For this holy Temple, and for those who with faith, devoutness, and in the fear of God have entered therein, let us pray to the Lord.

Choir. Lord, have mercy.

That he will deliver us from all tribulation, wrath, and necessity, let us pray to the Lord.

Choir. Lord, have mercy.

Succour us, save us, have mercy upon us, and keep us, O God, by thy grace.

Choir. Lord, have mercy.

Sometimes omitted.

may stand here before thy holy Altar. Grant also, O God, unto us and unto those who here with us make their supplications unto thee, prosperity of life and increase of faith, and of spiritual understanding. Grant that they may serve thee continually with love and fear, and that they may partake of thy Holy Mysteries in blamelessness of heart and without condemnation, and be deemed worthy of thy heavenly kingdom.

[*Or. if the* LITURGY OF ST. BASIL THE GREAT *be used:*

O God, who in mercy and bounties hast visited our lowliness; who hast set us, thy humble, and sinful, and unworthy servants before thy holy glory, to serve thy holy Altar: Strengthen us by the power of thy Holy Spirit for this ministry, and grant us utterance, in the opening of our lips, to invoke the grace of thy Holy Spirit upon the Gifts which we are about to set forth.]

Secretly.

Deacon. Wisdom!

Then shall the Deacon enter through the north door.
Exclamation.

Priest. That being kept always by thy might, we may ascribe glory to the Father, and to the Son, and to the Holy Spirit, now, and ever, and unto ages of ages.

Choir. Amen.

THE CHERUBIMIC HYMN.

Choir. Let us, the Cherubim mystically representing, and unto the Life-giving Trinity the thrice-holy chant intoning, all cares terrestrial now lay aside. (17)

(*Here the Great Entrance, with the Holy Gifts, is made. And after it the Hymn is finished:*)

That we may raise on high the King of all, like conqueror on shield and spears, by the Angelic Hosts invisibly up-borne. Alleluia. (*Thrice.*)

THE PRAYER OF THE CHERUBIMIC HYMN.

The Priest, secretly.

No one who is in bondage unto carnal desires and sensual pleasures is worthy to approach, or to come near, or to serve thee, O King of Glory: For to serve thee is a great and terrible thing even to the Heavenly Powers. Nevertheless, through thine unutterable and boundless love toward mankind thou didst become man, yet without change, and without transmutation,

Secretly.

and art become our High Priest, and hast committed unto us the ministry of this unbloody Sacrifice, in that thou art Lord over all. For thou alone, O Lord our God, rulest over those in heaven and on earth; who art borne on the throne of the Cherubim; who art Lord of the Seraphim and King over Israel; who alone art holy and restest in the Saints.   Therefore do I now make my entreaty unto thee, who alone art good and art ready to listen: Look down upon me, a sinner, and thine unprofitable servant, and cleanse my soul and my heart from an evil conscience; and by the might of thy Holy Spirit enable me, who am endued with the grace of the priesthood, to stand before this thy holy Altar, and perform the sacred Mystery of thy Holy and Pure Body and Precious Blood.   For unto thee do I draw near, and bowing my neck I implore thee: turn not thy face from me, neither cast me out from among thy children; but graciously vouchsafe that I, a sinner and thine unworthy servant, may offer unto thee these Holy Gifts.   For it is thou who offerest and art offered, who receivest and art thyself received, O Christ our God: and unto thee we ascribe glory, together with thy Father, who is from everlasting, and thine all-holy, and good, and life-giving Spirit, now, and ever, and unto ages of ages.

Secretly.

(At a Pontifical Service the Bishop washeth his hands, saying the prayer: **Bishop.** O Lord our God . . . *see page* 79.)   *Then the Deacon taketh the censer, and having received the Priest's blessing, he censeth the Holy Altar round about, and the Sanctuary, saying,* secretly, *to himself, Psalm li.:* Have mercy upon me, O God, according to thy great goodness.   *Then the Priest and Deacon stand before the Altar, and make three reverences, saying:*

O God, cleanse thou me, a sinner.

The Priest, elevating his hands, saith in a low voice: Let us. the Cherubim mystically representing . . . now lay aside.   *(Thrice.)   (See page* 94.)   *Then each finisheth the Hymn:* That we may raise on high . . . *And they kiss the Altar, and go to the Chapel of Oblation, which the Priest censeth.*

Secretly.

If it be a Pontifical Service, the Bishop taketh out the particles at the Table **Bishop.** *of Oblation, making mention of the living, and the dead, and his fellow-clergy, saying:* Remember, O Lord, thy servant, N., *at each name, and ending:* Remember also, O Lord, me, thine unworthy servant, N.

Then shall the Deacon say to the Priest:

Take up, Master.

And the Priest, taking the air (vózdukh), *shall lay it on the Deacon's left shoulder, and shall say:*

Lift up your hands unto the Holy Things in peace, and bless the Lord.

Secretly.

Then taking the holy paten (dískos), in like manner, he shall set it on the head of the Deacon, with all reverence, the Deacon holding the censer the while on one of his fingers.   But the Priest himself shall take in his hand the holy chalice (potír), and they shall go forth through the north door, preceded by a taper, and shall stand facing the People.   (But the Bishop remaineth in the Sanctuary.)

THE GREAT ENTRANCE (*following the Russian Service Book*).

Deacon. Our most God-fearing Ruler, may the Lord God remember in his kingdom always, now, and ever, and unto ages of ages.

Priest. And all the Authorities may the Lord God remember in his kingdom always, now, and ever, and unto ages of ages.

Deacon. The most Holy Synod (*or* Patriarch), and our Archbishop, N., may the Lord God remember in his kingdom always, now, and ever, and unto ages of ages.

Priest. All you Orthodox Christians, may the Lord God remember in his kingdom always, now, and ever, and unto ages of ages.

Choir. Amen.

Then the Choir finisheth the Cherubimic Hymn:

That we may raise on high the King of all, like conqueror on shield and spears, by the Angelic Hosts invisibly upborne. Alleluia. (*Thrice.*)

Then the Deacon shall enter in through the Holy Door, and shall take his stand on the right, and shall say to the Priest, as the latter entereth:

May the Lord God remember thy priesthood in his kingdom.

And the Priest shall say to him:

May the Lord God remember thy diaconate in his kingdom always, now, and ever, and unto ages of ages.

Then the Priest shall set the holy chalice

Secretly:

If it be a Pontifical Service, the Bishop now cometh forward in the Sanctuary, to the Holy Door, and taketh the holy paten from the Deacon. **Bishop.**

(*Deacon.* Thy Bishopric may the Lord God remember in his kingdom always, now, and ever, and unto ages of ages.)

And exclaimeth:

Our most God-fearing Ruler, N., and all the Authorities, may the Lord God remember in his kingdom always, now, and ever, and unto ages of ages.

Choir. Amen.

The Bishop, having placed the paten on the Altar, censeth the chalice, and taketh it from the Priest.

(*Priest.* Thy Bishopric may the Lord God remember in his kingdom always, now, and ever, and unto ages of ages. — *Bishop.* Thy priesthood may the Lord God remember in his kingdom always, now, and ever, and unto ages of ages.)

Bishop. The Most Holy Synod may the Lord God remember in his kingdom always, now, and ever, and unto ages of ages.

The right Reverend Patriarchs, Metropolitans, Archbishops, Bishops, and all orders of the clergy and of monks may the Lord God remember in his kingdom always, now, and ever, and unto ages of ages.

The Devout Governing Councils, and Commanders of the Army, Chiefs of Cities, and the Christ-loving Army and the Navy (*and the Ruler of the land, if in a foreign country, N.*), and all you Orthodox Chris-

Bishop.

upon the Holy Altar, to the right; taking the holy paten from the head of the Deacon, he shall place it also upon the Holy Altar, to the left, saying:

Secretly.

tians, may the Lord God remember in his kingdom always, now, and ever, and unto ages of ages.

Choir. Amen.

Choir. That we may raise on high . . . (*Page 96.*)

And all Clergy enter the Sanctuary.

The Bishop shall set the holy chalice upon the Holy Altar, saying:

Bishop.

Noble Joseph, when he had taken thy pure Body from the tree did wrap it in fine linen and spices, and sorrowing did lay it in a new sepulchre.

In the Grave with the body, but in Hell with the soul, in that thou art God; in Paradise with the thief, and on the throne with the Father and the Spirit, wast thou, O Christ, filling all things, in that thou art infinite.

How life-giving, how than Paradise more fair and, of a truth, more splendid than any king's chamber, O Christ, is shown forth thy tomb, the fountain of our resurrection.

Then shall he take the veils from the holy paten and the holy chalice, and shall lay them on one side of the Holy Altar; and having taken the air from the Deacon's shoulder, and censed it, he shall cover therewith the Holy Gifts, and shall say:

Secretly.

Noble Joseph, when he had taken thy pure Body from the tree, did wrap it in fine linen and spices, and sorrowing did lay it in a new sepulchre.

Then taking the censer from the hands of the Deacon, he shall thrice cense the Holy Gifts, saying:

Exalt thou Zion by thy favour, O Lord, and let the walls of Jerusalem be built. Then shalt thou be pleased with the sacrifice of righteousness, with sacrifices and burnt-offerings; then shall they offer young bullocks upon thine altar.

Then he shall give the censer to the Deacon, and shall bow his head, saying:

Remember me, O brother, and fellow-minister.

And the Deacon shall say to him:

May the Lord God remember thy priesthood in his kingdom.

The Deacon also, bowing his head. and holding his stole with three fingers of his right hand, shall say to the Priest:

Pray for me, holy Master.

If a Bishop be the celebrant, he saith to those who serve with him:

Bishop

Brethren, fellow-servitors, Abbots and Priests, pray for me.

And they all answer:

Secretly.

The Priest (or all the Clergy). May the Holy Spirit come upon thee, and the power of the Most High overshadow thee.

Deacon. May the Holy Spirit himself minister together with us, all the days of our life.

And again: Remember me, holy Master. | *Bishop.* May the Lord direct your steps.
| *Clergy.* Remember us, holy Master.

Bishop or Priest. May the Lord God remember you (thee) in his kingdom always, now, and ever, and unto ages of ages.

Choir. Amen.

Choir. Eis pollá éti, Déspota!

Deacon. Let us complete our prayer unto the Lord.

Choir. Lord, have mercy.

For these Holy Elements now spread forth, let us pray to the Lord.

Choir. Lord, have mercy.

For this holy Temple, and for all those who with faith, devoutness, and in the fear of God have entered therein, let us pray to the Lord.

Choir. Lord, have mercy.

That he will deliver us from all tribulation, wrath, and necessity, let us pray to the Lord.

Choir. Lord, have mercy.

Succour us, save us, have mercy upon us, and keep us, O God, by thy grace.

Choir. Lord, have mercy.

A day all-perfect, holy, peaceful and

Secretly.

Here Priests are Ordained.

The Bishop blesseth with the dikíri and trikíri, while the Choir chanteth: Eis pollá éti, Déspota.
The Bishop, or Priest, secretly.

O Lord God Almighty, who alone art holy; who acceptest the sacrifice of praise from those who call upon thee with their whole heart: Accept also the prayer of us sinners, and bear it to thy holy Altar; and enable us to offer unto thee gifts and spiritual sacrifices for our sins and for the errors which thy people have committed through ignorance. And graciously grant us to obtain grace in thy sight, that our sacrifice may be acceptable unto thee; and that the good spirit of thy grace may rest upon us, and upon these Holy Gifts, now offered up unto thee, and upon all thy people.

[Or, if the LITURGY OF ST. BASIL THE GREAT be used:

O Lord our God, who hast created us, and hast brought us into this life; who hast shown us the way of salvation, graciously bestowing upon us the revelation of heavenly Mysteries: Thou art he who hath appointed us to this ministry in the power of thy Holy Spirit. Graciously grant us, therefore, O Lord, to be servitors of thy new Covenant, ministers of thy Holy Mysteries. Accept us who draw near to thy holy Altar, according to the plenitude of thy mercy, that we may be worthy to offer unto thee this reasonable and unbloody sacrifice for our own sins, and for the errors of thy people: which do thou accept upon thy holy, and heavenly, and super-

Secretly.

sinless, let us beseech of the Lord.

Choir. Grant it, O Lord.

An Angel of Peace, the faithful guide and guardian both of our souls and bodies, let us beseech of the Lord.

Choir. Grant it, O Lord.

The pardon and remission of our sins and transgressions, let us beseech of the Lord.

sensual Altar for the savour of a sweet odour. Send down upon us the grace of thy Holy Spirit. Look upon us, O God, and behold this our service, and accept it as thou didst accept the gifts of Abel, the sacrifices of Noah, the burnt-offerings of Abraham, the priestly offices of Moses and Aaron, the peace-offerings of Samuel. Even as thou didst accept at the hands of the holy Apostles this true ministry, so also do thou in thy beneficence, O Lord, accept from the hands of us sinners these gifts; that having been accounted worthy blamelessly to minister at thy holy Altar, we may receive the recompense of wise and faithful stewards, in the terrible day of thy just requiting.]

Secretly.

Choir. Grant it, O Lord.

All things which are good and profitable to our souls, and peace to the world, let us beseech of the Lord.

Choir. Grant it, O Lord.

That we may pass the residue of our life in peace and penitence, let us beseech of the Lord.

Choir. Grant it, O Lord.

A Christian ending to our life, painless, blameless, peaceful; and a good defence before the dread Judgment Seat of Christ, let us beseech of the Lord.

Choir. Grant it, O Lord.

Calling to remembrance our most holy all-undefiled, most blessed and glorious Lady, the Birth-giver of God and ever-virgin Mary, with all the Saints, let us commend ourselves, and each other, and all our life unto Christ our God.

Choir. To thee, O Lord.

Exclamation.

Through the bounties of thine Only-begotten Son, with whom thou art glorified, together with the most holy, and good, and life-giving Spirit, now, and ever, and unto ages of ages.

Choir. Amen.

Priest. Peace be with you all.

Choir. And with thy spirit.

Deacon. Let us love one another, that with one accord we may confess:

Choir: Father, Son, and Holy Spirit, the Trinity, one in Essence and undivided.

Deacon. The Doors! The Doors! In wisdom, let us attend! (18)

The Symbol of the Faith.

Choir. I believe in one God the Father Almighty, Maker of heaven and earth, And of all things visible and invisible:

And in one Lord Jesus Christ, Son of God, the only-begotten. Begotten of his Father before all worlds; Light of Light, Very God of very God, Begotten, not made; Being of one Essence with the Father; By whom all things were made; Who, for us men, and for our salvation, came down from heaven, And was incarnate by the Holy Ghost of the Virgin Mary, And was made man. And was crucified also for us under Pontius Pilate, and suffered and was buried. And the third day he rose again, according to the Scriptures. And ascended into heaven, And sitteth on the right hand of the Father. And he shall come again with glory to judge both the quick and the dead; Whose kingdom shall have no end.

And in the Holy Ghost, the Lord, Giver of Life, Who proceedeth from the Father, Who with the Father and the Son together is worshipped and glorified, Who spake by the Prophets. In one Holy Catholic and Apostolic Church. I acknowledge one Baptism for the remission of sins. I look for the Resurrection of the dead, And the Life of the world to come. Amen.

Deacon (or Priest). Let us stand aright, let us stand with fear, let us attend, that we may offer in peace the Holy Oblation.

Choir. A mercy of peace, a sacrifice of praise.

The Priest shall do reverence, and shall say privately, within himself:

I will love thee, O Lord my strength; the Lord is my firm foundation, and my deliverer. (*Thrice.*)

And he shall kiss the Holy Gifts, they being still covered; first the top of the holy paten, and likewise the top of the holy chalice, and the edge of the Holy Altar before him. If there be several Priests, they shall both kiss all the Holy Things, and each other on the shoulder.

And if a Bishop be the celebrant, he saith, secretly, *as he kisseth the paten:* O Holy God; *and the holy chalice:* O Holy Mighty; *and the Holy Altar:* O Holy Immortal One, have mercy upon us.

Then the Bishop or Priest shall say:

Christ is in the midst of us.

And having been kissed on the shoulder and on the hand, he is answered:

He is and shall be.

The Priest shall fan the Holy Elements with the air. If several Priests take part in the service, they shall all fan the Holy Elements with the air, in like manner, and shall repeat, as do the People also, the Symbol of the Faith.

Then the Priest shall take the air from the Holy Elements, and having kissed it, he shall lay it aside.

Secretly.

Priest. The grace of our Lord Jesus Christ, and the love of God, and the fellowship of the Holy Spirit, be with you all.

Choir. And with thy spirit.

Priest (pointing upward). Lift up your hearts.

Choir. We lift them up unto the Lord.

Priest. Let us give thanks unto the Lord.

Choir. Meet and right is it that we should adore the Father, the Son, and the Holy Spirit, the Trinity, one in Essence and undivided.

If a Bishop celebrateth, as he saith this he turneth to the People, and blesseth with the dikíri and the trikíri. **Bishop.**

The (Bishop) Priest shall offer this Prayer, secretly.

It is meet and right that we should laud thee, bless thee, praise thee, give thanks unto thee, and adore thee in all places of thy dominion: for thou art God ineffable, incomprehensible, invisible, inconceivable; thou art from everlasting and art changeless, thou, and thine Only-begotten Son, and thy Holy Spirit. Thou from nothingness hast called us into being; and when we had fallen away from thee, thou didst raise us up again; and thou hast not ceased to do all things until thou hadst brought us back to heaven, and hadst endowed us with thy kingdom which is to come. For all which things we give thanks unto thee, and thine Only-begotten Son, and thy Holy Spirit; for all the things whereof we know, and whereof we know not; for all thy benefits bestowed upon us, both manifest and unseen. And we render thanks unto thee for this ministry which thou dost deign to accept at our hands, although before thee stand thousands of Archangels and myriads of Angels, with the Cherubim, and Seraphim, six-winged, many-eyed, who soar aloft, borne on their pinions.

Secretly.

[*Or, if the* LITURGY OF ST. BASIL THE GREAT *be used, this Prayer:*

O thou who in verity existest, Master, Lord God, Father Almighty adorable: Meet is it, in truth, and just and befitting the majesty of thy holiness, that we should magnify thee, praise thee, bless thee, adore thee, give thanks unto thee and glorify thee, the only God which verily existeth, and offer unto thee, with contrite heart and humbleness of spirit, this our reasonable service: for it is thou who hast graciously bestowed upon us the knowledge of thy truth. And who hath power enough to express thy mighty acts, to make all thy praises to be heard, or to utter forth all thy wonders at all times? O Master, O Sovereign Master of all things, Lord of heaven and earth, and of all created beings both visible and invisible; who sittest on the throne of glory and beholdest the depths; who art from everlasting, invisible, inscrutable, ineffable, immutable, the Father of our Lord Jesus Christ, our great God and the Saviour, our hope, who is the image of thy goodness, the seal of equal type, in himself showing forth thee, the Father, the living Word, the true God, the Wisdom before all the ages, the Life, the Sanctification, the Might, and the true Light, through whom, also, the Holy Spirit was manifested; the Spirit of Truth, the Gift of Adoption, the Earnest of an inheritance to come, the First-fruits of eternal good things, the life-giving Power, the Fountain of holiness; by whom enabled every creature endowed with reason and intelligence doth serve thee, and evermore doth send up unto thee an everlasting tribute of praise; for all things are thy servants. For Angels and Archangels, Thrones, Dominions, Principalities, Authorities, Powers, and the many-eyed Cherubim do laud thee. Before thee, round about, stand the Seraphim, having each six wings; for with twain do they cover their faces, and with twain their feet, and with twain do they fly, crying one to another continually, with never-ceasing praises.]

Exclamation.

Priest. Singing the triumphant song, crying, calling aloud, and saying:

Choir. Holy, holy, holy, Lord of Sabaoth; heaven and earth are full of thy glory: Hosanna in the highest: Blessed is he that cometh in the Name of the Lord. Hosanna in the highest.

The Deacon now taking the holy star-cover from the holy paten, shall make the sign of the cross above it, and shall kiss it, and lay it on one side. He shall then go and stand on the right of the Holy Altar.

The Priest prayeth, secretly.

And we also, O Lord who lovest mankind, in company with these blessed Powers do cry aloud and say: Holy art thou, and all-holy thou, and thine Only-begotten Son, and thy Holy Spirit; holy and all-holy; and majestic is thy glory. Who hast so loved thy world that thou gavest thine Only-begotten Son, that whosoever believeth on him should not perish, but should have everlasting life; who, when he had come and had performed all the dispensation for us, in the night in which he was given up, — in the

Secretly.

which, rather, he did give himself for the life of the world, — took bread in his holy and pure and sinless hands; and when he had given thanks, and blessed it, and so sanctified it, he gave it to his holy disciples and apostles, saying:

[*Or, if the* LITURGY OF ST. BASIL THE GREAT *be used, this Prayer:*

With these blessed Powers, O Master who lovest mankind, we sinners also do cry aloud and say: Holy art thou, of a truth, and all-holy, and there are no bounds to the majesty of thy holiness, and just art thou in all thy works; for in righteousness and true judgment hast thou ordered all things for us. When thou hadst created man, and hadst fashioned him from the dust of the earth, and hadst honoured him with thine own image, O God, thou didst set him in the midst of a Paradise of plenty, promising him life eternal and the enjoyment of everlasting good things in keeping thy commandments.

But when he disobeyed thee, the true God, who had created him, and was led astray by the guile of the serpent, and rendered subject to death through his own transgressions, thou didst banish him, in thy righteous judgment, O God, from Paradise into this present world, and didst turn him again to the earth from which he was taken, providing for him the salvation of regeneration, which is in thy Christ himself. For thou didst not turn thyself away forever from thy creature, whom thou hadst made, O Good One, neither didst thou forget the work of thy hands; but thou didst visit him in divers manners, through the tender compassion of thy mercy. Thou didst send forth Prophets; thou didst perform mighty works by the Saints who, in every generation, were well-pleasing unto thee; thou didst speak to us by the mouths of thy servants the Prophets, who foretold unto us the salvation which was to come; thou didst give us the Law to aid us; thou didst appoint guardian Angels. And when the fulness of time was come, thou didst speak unto us by thy Son himself, by whom also thou madest the ages; who, being the Brightness of thy glory, and the Express Image of thy Person, and upholding all things by the word of his power, thought it no robbery to be equal to thee, the God and Father. But albeit he was God before all the ages, yet he appeared upon earth and dwelt among men; and was incarnate of a Holy Virgin, and did empty himself, taking on the form of a servant, and becoming conformed to the fashion of our lowliness, that he might make us conformable to the image of his glory. For as by man sin entered into the world, and by sin death, so it seemed good unto thine Only-begotten Son, who is in thy bosom, our God and Father, to be born of a woman, the holy Birth-giver of God and ever-virgin Mary; to be born under the Law, that he might condemn sin in his flesh; that they who were dead in Adam might be made alive in thy Christ. And becoming a dweller in this world, and giving commandments of salvation, he released us from the delusions of idols, and brought us unto a knowledge of thee, the true God and Father, having won us unto himself for a peculiar people, a royal priesthood, a holy nation; and being purified with water, and sanctified with the Holy Spirit, he gave himself a ransom to Death, whereby we were held, sold into bondage under sin. And having descended into Hell through the Cross, that he might fill all things with himself, he loosed the pains of death, and rose again from the dead on the third day, making a way for all flesh through the Resurrection from the dead — for it was not possible that the Author of Life should be holden of corruption — that he might be the first-fruits of those who have fallen asleep, the first-born from the dead; and he shall be all things, the first in all things. And ascending into heaven, he sat down at the right hand of thy Majesty on high; and he shall come again to render

Secretly.

unto every man according to his works. And he hath left with us, as memorials of his saving Passion, these Things which we have spread forth according to his commandment. For when he was about to go forth to his voluntary, and ever-memorable, and life-creating death, in the night in which he gave himself for the life of the world, he took bread in his holy and stainless hands, and when he had shown it unto thee, his God and Father, he gave thanks, blessing it, sanctifying it, and breaking it, he gave it to his holy disciples and apostles, saying:] *Secretly.*

Exclamation.

Priest. Take, eat, this is my Body which is broken for you, for the remission of sins.

Choir. Amen.

As he saith this, the Deacon shall point out the holy paten to the Priest, holding his stole with three fingers of his right hand.

Priest. And in like manner, after supper he took the cup, saying:

As he saith this, the Deacon pointeth to the holy chalice.

[*At the* LITURGY OF ST. BASIL THE GREAT:

The Priest, secretly.

In like manner, having taken the cup of the fruit of the vine, and mingled it, given thanks, blessed it, and sanctified it, *Secretly.*

Exclamation.

He gave it to his holy disciples and apostles, saying:]

Exclamation.

Priest. Drink ye all of this: for this is my Blood of the New Testament, which is shed for you, and for many, for the remission of sins.

Choir. Amen.

The Priest, secretly.

Bearing in remembrance, therefore, this commandment of salvation, and all those things which came to pass for us; the Cross, the Grave, the Resurrection on the third day, the Ascension into Heaven, the Sitting on the right hand, the Second and glorious Coming-again:

[*Or, if the* LITURGY OF ST. BASIL THE GREAT *be used:*

This do, in remembrance of me: for as often as ye shall eat this Bread and drink of this Cup ye do proclaim my death and confess my Resurrection. *Secretly.*

Wherefore, we also, O Master, having in remembrance his redeeming Passion and life-giving Cross, his three days' Burial, and his Resurrection from the dead, his Ascension into Heaven, and his Sitting on the right hand of thee, the God and Father, and his glorious and terrible Coming-again:]

Exclamation.

Priest. Thine own, of thine own, we offer unto thee, in behalf of all, and for all.

Here the Deacon, crossing his hands, shall lift up the holy paten and the holy chalice, and making with them the sign of the cross, he shall himself make a humble reverence.

Choir. We praise thee, we bless thee, we give thanks unto thee, O Lord, and we pray unto thee, O our God.

The Priest prayeth, secretly.

Again we offer unto thee this reasonable and unbloody service. And we beseech and implore thee, and offer our supplications unto thee, that thou wilt send thy Holy Spirit upon us, and upon these Gifts here spread forth.

[*Or, if the* LITURGY OF ST. BASIL THE GREAT *be used:*

Wherefore, O all-holy Master, we also, thy sinful and unworthy servants, whom thou hast graciously permitted to minister at thy holy Altar, not through our own righteousness (for we have done no good deed on earth), but because of thy mercies and bounties, which thou hast richly poured out upon us, now have boldness to draw near unto this, thy holy Altar; and presenting unto thee the holy emblems of the sacred Body and Blood of thy Christ, we pray thee and implore thee, O Holy of Holies, by the favour of thy goodness, that thy Holy Spirit may descend upon us, and upon these Gifts here spread forth before thee, and bless them, and sanctify and manifest them.]

Then the Deacon shall approach the Priest; and standing side by side, they shall both make three lowly reverences before the Holy Altar, praying silently thus:

Priest. O Lord, who at the Third Hour didst send down upon thine Apostles thy Holy Spirit: Take not the same from us, O Good One, but renew Him in us who make our supplications unto thee.

Deacon. Make me a clean heart, O God, and renew a right spirit within me.

Priest. O Lord, who at the Third Hour . . .

Deacon. Cast me not away from thy presence, and take not thy Holy Spirit from me.

Priest. O Lord, who at the Third Hour . . .

Then the Deacon, bowing his head and pointing with his stole to the Holy Bread, shall say:

Bless, Master, the Holy Bread.

And the Priest, standing erect, shall sign the Holy Bread with the sign of the cross, and shall say:

And make this bread the precious Body of thy Christ.

Secretly.

[*Or, if the* LITURGY OF ST. BASIL THE GREAT *be used:*

For this bread is in very truth the precious Body of our Lord, and God, and Saviour, Jesus Christ.]

Deacon. Amen.   Bless, Master, the holy chalice.

And the Priest shall bless it, and shall say:

And make that which is in this chalice the precious Blood of thy Christ.

[*Or, if the* LITURGY OF ST. BASIL THE GREAT *be used:*

For this chalice is, in very truth the precious Blood of our Lord, and God, and Saviour, Jesus Christ (*Deacon.* Amen), which was poured out for the life of the world.]

Deacon. Amen.

And again, the Deacon, pointing to both the Holy Elements, shall say:

Master, bless both.

And the Priest, blessing both, shall say:

Transmuting them by thy Holy Spirit.

Deacon. Amen, amen, amen.

Secretly.

And bowing his head to the Priest, the Deacon shall say:	*If a Bishop be the celebrant, the Proto-Deacon saith:*
Bear me in remembrance, holy Master.	Bear us in remembrance, holy Master.
And the Priest shall say:	*Bishop.* May the Lord God remember you in his kingdom always, now, and ever, and unto ages of ages.
May the Lord God remember thee in his kingdom always, now and ever, and unto ages of ages.	
Deacon. Amen.	*Priest and Deacon.* Amen.

Bishop.

And if a Priest hath been ordained at this same Liturgy, the Bishop now biddeth him to draw near, and taking the Holy Bread, and breaking the portion XC from the top thereof, where the cross is, he giveth it to him, saying:

Receive thou this pledge, and preserve it whole and unharmed until thy last breath, because thou shalt be held to an accounting therefor in the second and terrible Coming of our great Lord, God, and Saviour, Jesus Christ.

And taking it, the Priest kisseth the Bishop's hand, and withdrawing he standeth behind the Holy Altar; and placing his hand on the Holy Altar, he prayeth, saying:

Have mercy upon me, O God. . . . (*Psalm li.*).

And when: Holy things to the holy: *is to be said, he who hath received Ordination restoreth the Bread, and the Bishop layeth it on the holy paten; and the newly ordained Priest is communicated before the other Priests.*

The Priest prayeth.

That to those who shall partake thereof they may be unto soberness of soul, unto the remission of sins, unto the fellowship of thy Holy Spirit, unto the fulfilling of the kingdom of Heaven, and unto boldness toward thee; and not unto judgment or unto condemnation.

And again we offer unto thee this our reasonable service, for all thy servants departed this life before us in the faith; for our ancestors, fathers, the Patriarchs, Prophets, Apostles, Preachers, Evangelists, Martyrs, Confessors, Ascetics; and for every righteous soul who hath died in the faith:

[*Or, if the* LITURGY OF ST. BASIL THE GREAT *be used:*

And unite all us who partake of the one Bread and the one Cup, one to another in the communion of the Holy Spirit: and grant that no one of us may partake of that holy Body and Blood of thy Christ unto judgment or unto condemnation; but that we may find mercy and grace, together with all the Saints who, in all the ages, have been acceptable unto thee, our ancestors, fathers, the Patriarchs, Prophets, Apostles, Preachers, Evangelists, Martyrs, Confessors, Teachers; and with all righteous souls who have died in the faith:]

Secretly.

And the Deacon shall cense the Holy Altar round about, and shall make mention of the living and of the dead.

(*For the Living:* For the salvation, visitation, and remission of sins of the servants of God N. N.)

(*For the Dead*): For the repose and remission of sins of thy servants, N. N: Give them rest, O God, in a place of brightness, whence sorrow and sighing have fled away. And give them rest where the light of thy countenance shall visit them.

Then the Priest shall say, aloud:

Especially our most holy, all-undefiled, most blessed and glorious Lady, the Birth-giver of God and ever-virgin Mary:

And Saint John, the Prophet, Forerunner and Baptist; the holy, glorious and all-laudable Apostles; Saint N. (*the Saint of the day*), whose memory we commemorate; and all thy Saints: through whose prayers visit thou us, O God. And call to remembrance all those who have fallen asleep before us in the hope of Resurrection unto life eternal. And give them rest where the light of thy countenance shall visit them.

Secretly.

(*Here he maketh mention of the Names, in the order of their rank.*)

If it be at the LITURGY OF ST. JOHN CHRYSOSTOM:

Choir. Meet is it, in truth, to bless thee, the Birth-giver of

Furthermore we beseech thee, O Lord, that thou wilt call to remembrance all Bishops of Orthodox Christians, who rightly dispense

God, ever-blessed, and all-undefiled, and the Mother of our God. More honourable than the Cherubim, and beyond compare more glorious than the Seraphim, thou who without defilement barest God the Word, true Birth-giver of God, we magnify thee.

the word of thy truth; all the Priesthood, the Diaconate in Christ, and every order of the Clergy.

` Furthermore we offer unto thee this our reasonable worship on behalf of the whole universe; of the Holy Catholic and Apostolic Church; of those who continue in chastity and soberness of life; of our most God-fearing Ruler, N.; and all the Authorities, and all their Council and Army and Navy. Grant unto them, O Lord, a peaceful reign, and that we, through their tranquillity, may pass our time in rest and quietness, in all godliness and soberness of life.

[But if the LITURGY OF ST. BASIL THE GREAT *be used:*

Choir. In thee rejoiceth, O thou who art full of Grace, every created being, the Hierarchy of the Angels, and all mankind, O Consecrated Temple and supersensual Paradise, Glory of Virgins, of whom God, who is our God before all the ages, was incarnate and became a little child. For he made of thy womb a throne, and thy belly did he make more spacious than the heavens. In thee doth all Creation rejoice, O thou who art full of Glory: Glory to thee.

Or, at the different Feasts, there shall be sung the appointed Hymn to the Birthgiver of God.

And give them rest where the light of thy countenance shall visit them.

Have in remembrance, also, O Lord, we beseech thee, thy Holy Catholic and Apostolic Church, which is from end to end of the Universe; and give peace unto Her whom thou hast purchased with the precious Blood of thy Christ: and establish thou firmly this holy Temple, even unto the end of the world. Remember, O Lord, those who have offered unto thee these Gifts; and those for whom, and by whom, and in behalf of whom they have offered them.

Have in remembrance, O Lord, those who bear fruit and do good works in thy holy churches, and those who are mindful of the poor. Requite them with thy rich and heavenly gifts. Give them things heavenly for things earthly; things eternal for things temporal; things incorruptible for things corruptible.

Have in remembrance, O Lord, those who are in the deserts, and mountains, and caverns, and in the subterranean pits of the earth.

Have in remembrance, O Lord, all those who continue in virginity and godliness, and in asceticism and devoutness of life.

Secretly.

Have in remembrance, O Lord, our most God-fearing and Christ-loving Ruler, N., to whom thou hast given the right to reign in the earth. Crown him with the armour of truth, with the panoply of contentment. Overshadow his head in the day of battle. Strengthen his arm, exalt his right hand; make mighty his kingdom; subdue under him all barbarous nations which seek wars; grant unto him peace profound and inviolate; inspire his heart with good deeds toward thy Church, and toward all thy people; that through his serenity we may lead a quiet and tranquil life, in all godliness and soberness.

Have in remembrance, O Lord, all Rulers and Authorities, as also our brethren who are in their Council; and all their Army and Navy. In their goodness, preserve thou the good, and through thine own goodness make thou the evil good.

Have in remembrance, O Lord, this congregation here present, and those who are absent for reasonable cause; and have mercy upon them and upon us, according to the multitude of thy mercies. Fill their treasuries with every good thing; maintain their marriage-bond in peace and concord; rear the infants; guide the young; support the aged; encourage the faint-hearted. Collect the scattered, and turn them from their wandering astray, and unite them to thy Holy Catholic and Apostolic Church. Set at liberty those who are vexed by unclean spirits; voyage with those who voyage, journey with those who journey; defend the widows; protect the orphans; free the captives; heal the sick. Have in remembrance, O God, those who are under trial, and in the mines, and in prison, and in bitter labors, and in all affliction, distress and tribulation.

Have in remembrance, O God, all those who invoke thy great loving-kindness; those also who love us, and those who hate us, and those who have enjoined us, unworthy though we are, that we should pray for them; and all thy people, O Lord our God: And upon them all pour out thy rich mercy, granting unto all such of their petitions as are unto salvation. And those whom we, through ignorance, or forgetfulness, or the multitude of names, have not remembered, do thou thyself call to mind, O God, who knowest the age and the name of each, and knowest every man even from his mother's womb. For thou, O Lord, art the Helper of the helpless, the Hope of the hopeless, the Saviour of the storm-tossed, the Haven of the voyager, the Healer of the sick. Be thyself all things unto all men, O thou who knowest every man, his petition, his abode, and his need. Deliver, O Lord, this city, and every city and land from famine, plague, earthquake, flood, fire, sword, the invasion of enemies, and from civil war.]

Secretly.

And when the Hymn is finished, the Priest shall say, aloud:

Among the first have in remembrance, O Lord, the Most Holy Synod (*or* Patriarch); and grant that they (*or* he) may rightly administer unto thy Churches the word of thy truth, in peace, safety, health, honour and length of days.

And the Choir singeth:

And all the people.

If a Bishop be the celebrant, the Proto-Deacon, Bishop. standing at the Holy Door, and looking on the People, saith:

And all the people.

Choir. And all the people

And the Bishop reciteth the Prayer for the Synod: Among the first . . .

The Senior Priest then saith:

Have in remembrance, O Lord, our Right Reverend Bishop, N., granting that in peace, safety, honour, health and length of days he may guide thy holy Churches, rightly administering the word of thy truth.

He kisseth the Bishop's mitre, and the Bishop, blessing him, saith:

May the Lord have in remembrance thy priesthood.

The Senior Deacon, turning to the People:

The Most Holy Synod (or Patriarch) and the Right Reverend N., who offereth these Holy Elements unto the Lord our God.

For the salvation of our most God-fearing Ruler; and for all the Authorities; and for all their Council and Army and Navy.

Choir. And for all the people.

The Deacon then commemorateth the living, while the Priest prayeth, secretly.

Have in remembrance, O Lord, this city in which we dwell; and every city and country, and all those who with faith dwell therein. Have in remembrance, O Lord, all those who journey by sea or by land, all sick persons and sufferers and captives, and their salvation. Have in remembrance, O Lord, those who bear fruit and do good works in thy holy Churches, and those who are mindful of the poor; and send down thy grace upon us all.

[*If the* LITURGY OF ST. BASIL THE GREAT *be used, this Prayer is said*, secretly:

Priest. Have in remembrance, O Lord, every Bishop of the Orthodox who rightly administereth the word of thy truth.

Have in remembrance, also, O Lord, my unworthiness, according to the multitude of thy bounties; pardon me every transgression, whether voluntary or involuntary, and withhold not, because of my sins, the grace of thy Holy Spirit from the Gifts now spread forth unto thee.

Have in remembrance, O Lord, the Priesthood, as also the Diaconate in Christ, and all sacerdotal orders, and put not to confusion any one of us who stand about thy holy Altar. Visit us with thy loving-

Bishop.

Secretly.

kindness, O Lord; manifest thyself unto us in thy rich bounties. Vouchsafe unto us temperate and healthful seasons. Give gentle showers upon the earth, unto fruitfulness. Bless the crown of the year of thy beneficence. Make schisms to cease in the Church. Quench the ragings of the nations; speedily destroy, by the might of thy Holy Spirit, all uprisings of heresies. Receive us all into thy kingdom, making us children of the light and of the day; and grant unto us thy peace, and thy love, O Lord our God; for all things hast thou given unto us.] *Secretly.*

Exclamation.

Priest. And grant that with one mouth and one heart we may glorify and praise thine all-honourable and majestic Name, of the Father, and of the Son, and of the Holy Spirit, now, and ever, and unto ages of ages.

Choir. Amen.

And turning to the People and blessing them, the Priest saith:

And may the mercy of the great God, and of our Saviour Jesus Christ, be with you all.

Choir. And with thy spirit.

And the Deacon shall stand at his accustomed place, and shall say: **Here Deacons are Ordained.**

Calling to remembrance all the Saints, again, yet again, in peace let us pray to the Lord. ℞

For the Precious Gifts which have been offered and sanctified, let us pray to the Lord. ℞

That our God, who loveth mankind, will accept them upon his holy, and most heavenly, and supersensual Altar, for an odour of spiritual fragrance; and will send down upon us in return his divine grace and the gift of his Holy Spirit, let us pray to the Lord. ℞

That he will deliver us from all tribulation, wrath, and necessity, let us pray to the Lord. ℞

Choir. Lord have mercy.

Succour us, save us, have mercy upon us, and keep us, O God, by thy grace.

Choir. Lord, have mercy.

A day all-perfect, holy, peaceful and sinless, let us beseech of the Lord.

Choir. Grant it, O Lord.

An Angel of Peace, the faithful

Choir. Grant it, O Lord.

The Priest prayeth, secretly.

Unto thee do we commit our whole life and hope, O Lord, who lovest mankind. And we entreat thee, and beseech thee, and implore thee: Vouchsafe that we may partake of thy heavenly and terrible Mysteries, of this sacred and spiritual food, with a pure conscience, unto the remission of our sins, unto the pardon of our transgressions, unto the communion of the Holy Spirit, unto inheritance of the kingdom of Heaven, and unto boldness toward thee; not unto judgment or condemnation.

Secretly.

guide and guardian both of our souls and bodies, let us beseech of the Lord. ℞

The pardon and remission of our sins and transgressions, let us beseech of the Lord. ℞

All things which are good and profitable to our souls, and peace to the world, let us beseech of the Lord. ℞

That we may pass the residue of our life in peace and penitence, let us beseech of the Lord. ℞

A Christian ending to our life, painless, blameless, peaceful; and a good defence before the dread Judgment Seat of Christ, let us beseech of the Lord. ℞

Having made our petition for the unity of the faith, and the communion of the Holy Spirit, let us commend ourselves, and each other, and all our life unto Christ our God.

Choir. To thee, O Lord.

Choir. Grant it, O Lord.

[*Or, if the* LITURGY OF ST. BASIL THE GREAT *be used:*

O our God, the God of salvation, do thou teach us how we may worthily give thanks unto thee for thy benefits, which thou hast ever bestowed and yet dost bestow upon us. Do thou, O our God, who acceptest these Gifts, purify us from every defilement of flesh and spirit, and teach us to perfect holiness in thy fear; that we, receiving a portion of thy Holy Things in the witness of a pure conscience toward thee, may be made one with the holy Body and Blood of thy Christ; and that having received them worthily, we may have Christ abiding in our hearts, and may become a Temple of thy Holy Spirit.

Yea, O our God, cause also that none of us may be guilty of these thy terrible and heavenly Mysteries, or sick in soul or in body through an unworthy partaking of the same: but enable us, even unto our last breath, worthily to receive a portion of thy Holy Things, which is a support upon the road to life eternal, an acceptable defence at the dread Judgment Seat of thy Christ. That we also, together with all the Saints who, in all the ages, have been acceptable unto thee, may be made partakers of thine everlasting good things, which thou hast prepared for those who love thee, O Lord.]

Secretly.

Exclamation.

Priest. And vouchsafe, O Lord, that boldly and without condemnation we may dare to call upon thee, God the heavenly Father, and to say:

Here the Deacon bindeth his stole about him in the form of a cross. (19)

The People:

Our Father, who art in heaven, Hallowed be thy Name. Thy kingdom come. Thy will be done on earth, As it is in heaven. Give us this day our daily bread. And forgive us our trespasses, As we forgive those who trespass against us. And lead us not into temptation; But deliver us from the Evil One:

Exclamation.

Priest. For thine is the kingdom, and the power, and the glory, of the Father, and of the Son, and of the Holy Spirit, now, and ever, and unto ages of ages.

Choir. Amen.

Priest. Peace be with you all.

Choir. And with thy spirit.

Deacon. Let us bow our heads unto the Lord.

Choir. To thee, O Lord.

The Priest prayeth, secretly.

We give thanks unto thee, O King invisible, who by thine illimitable power hast made all things, and by the plenitude of thy mercy hast called into being all things from nothingness. Do thou, the same Lord, look down from heaven upon those who have bowed their heads before thee; for they have not bowed down unto flesh and blood, but unto thee, the terrible God. Do thou, therefore, O Lord, render this oblation efficacious to us all, according to the individual need of each. Voyage with those who sail upon the seas; journey with those who travel on dry land. Heal the sick, O thou who art the healer of our souls and bodies.

[*Or, if the* LITURGY OF ST. BASIL THE GREAT *be used, the following Prayer:*

O Master, Lord, the Father of bounties, and the God of all comfort, bless, sanctify, guard, strengthen, fortify those who have bowed their heads unto thee; withdraw them from every evil work; unite them to every good work; and graciously grant that, without condemnation, they may partake of these, thy pure and life-giving Mysteries, unto the remission of their sins, and unto the communion of the Holy Spirit.]

Exclamation.

Priest. Through the grace, and bounties, and love toward mankind of thine Only-begotten Son, with whom thou art blessed, together with thine all-holy, good and life-giving Spirit, now, and ever, and unto ages of ages.

Choir. Amen.

The Priest prayeth, secretly:

Hear us, O Lord Jesus Christ our God, from thy holy dwelling-place, and from the throne of glory of thy kingdom; and come and cleanse us, O thou who sittest on high with the Father, and art here invisibly present with us: and graciously vouchsafe, by thy mighty hand, to impart unto us thy most holy Body, and thy most precious Blood, and by us to all thy people.

Secretly.

Secretly.

Then the Priest shall do homage, and the Deacon, standing before the Holy Door, shall repeat, secretly, thrice: *Secretly.*

O God, cleanse thou me, a sinner.

When the Deacon seeth the Priest stretch out his hand and touch the Holy Bread in the act of making the Holy Oblation, he shall say,
loudly:

Here the Holy Door is closed, and the curtain is drawn.

Let us attend.

And the Priest, as he elevateth the Holy Bread, shall say:

Holy things unto the Holy.

Choir. One only is holy, one only is the Lord, Jesus Christ, in the glory of God the Father.   Amen.

Then shall the Choir chant the Anthem for the Day (or of the Saint, or of the Feast):	*And the Deacon shall enter the Sanctuary, and standing at the right hand of the Priest, who holdeth the Holy Bread, he shall say:*
Praise ye the Lord from heaven: praise him in the height. Alleluia.	Break, Master, the Holy Bread.
	And the Priest, breaking it in four pieces, with all heedfulness and awe, shall say:
	Broken and divided is the Lamb of God, which is broken, yet not disunited; which is ever eaten, yet never consumed, but sanctifieth those who partake thereof.

CONCERNING THE PARTITION OF THE HOLY LAMB.

After dividing the Holy Lamb, the Priest must place the portions in the form of a cross upon the holy paten, with a profound reverence, such as he hath made before when censing. He shall lay the IHC at the upper part of the holy paten, which lieth towards the east. The XC shall he place in a line beneath it, on that side of the paten which lieth to the west; and the NI upon the north side, while the KA shall be opposite, upon the south side, as is here set forth. (20) *Secretly.*

When the portion IHC hath been removed, it shall be placed in the holy chalice.
The portion XC shall be partaken of by the Clergy who take part in the Lit-
urgy. The two other portions, namely, the NI and the KA, are broken for the
communion of the laity. And from the portion which representeth the Holy
Birth-giver of God, or from the particles representing the nine ranks of the
Heavenly Hierarchy, which are upon the holy paten, shall no one be communi-
cated: but only from the two portions of the Holy Lamb which remain shall the
laity be communicated.

Then the Deacon, pointing with his stole to the holy chalice, shall exclaim:

Fill, Master, the holy chalice.

And the Priest, taking the portion IHC from the place where it lieth, shall make
therewith the sign of the cross above the holy chalice, saying:

The fulness of the Holy Spirit: (*and shall place it in the holy chalice*).
Deacon. Amen. (21)

And taking the warm water, he shall say to the Priest:

Bless, Master, the warm water.

And the Priest shall bless it, saying:

Blessed is the fervour of thy Saints always, now, and ever, and unto
ages of ages. Amen.

Then the Deacon shall pour into the holy chalice, in the form of a cross, what is
required, saying:

The warmth of faith, full of the Holy Spirit. Amen.

When the divine Blood of the Lord is mingled with the holy warm water, it must
be done with heed, and in amount according to the number of those who desire to
receive the Holy Sacrament.

The Priest breaketh the portion XC
into a number of pieces, correspond-
ing to the number of Clergy who take
part in the Liturgy.
Then the Priest saith:

Deacon, draw near.

And the Deacon shall approach, and
shall make a devout reverence, en-
treating forgiveness; and having
kissed the Altar, he shall say:

Lo, I draw near unto the King
Immortal and our God.

Impart unto me, Master, the
precious and holy Body of our
Lord, and God, and Saviour,
Jesus Christ.

And the Priest shall give him a por-
tion of the Holy Body, and shall say:

To N., Deacon, is imparted the

When a Bishop is the celebrant, he
divideth the portion XC, and hav-
ing prayed: I believe, O Lord, and
I confess, that thou art, in very
truth, the Christ, the ·Son of the
living God: . . . *he consumeth part*
of the portion XC, saying:

The precious, and all-holy, and
most pure Body of our Lord, and
God, and Saviour, Jesus Christ,
is imparted to me, the unworthy,
N., Bishop, unto the remission
of my sins, and unto life eternal.
(In the Name of the Father, and
of the Son, and of the Holy
Spirit. Amen.)

Secretly.

(Bishop.)

precious, and holy, and all-pure Body of our Lord, and God, and Saviour, Jesus Christ, unto the remission of his sins, and unto life everlasting.

And the Deacon shall kiss the Priest's hand as he taketh the Holy Body, and shall withdraw behind the Holy Altar; and bowing his head over the Holy Altar, he shall pray like the Priest:

I believe, O Lord, and I confess, that thou art, in very truth, the Christ, the Son of the living God: . . .

All the Priests, in the order of their seniority, first make an obeisance to each other, and to the People; and having besought forgiveness: Forgive me, fathers and brethren: *and kissed the side of the Altar, they say:*

· Lo, I draw near unto the King Immortal, and to God.

The precious and all-holy Body of our Lord, and God, and Saviour, Jesus Christ, is imparted to me, N., Priest, unto the remission of my sins, and unto life everlasting.

Then each taketh a piece of the Holy Body, and bowing low over the Holy Altar, and gazing devoutly upon the Holy Body of Christ, they say privately, each to himself:

I believe, O Lord, and I confess, that thou art, in very truth, the Christ, the Son of the living God, who didst come into the world to save sinners, of whom I am chief. And I believe that this is, of a truth, thine all-pure Body, and that this is thine own precious Blood. Wherefore, I beseech thee, have mercy upon me, and forgive my transgressions,

Then, taking the sponge, he wipeth his hand; and having kissed the sponge, he layeth it aside. Then, taking the holy veil and the chalice with both hands, he communicateth himself therefrom thrice, saying:

The precious, and holy, and life-giving Blood of our Lord, and God, and Saviour, Jesus Christ, is imparted to me, the unworthy, N., Bishop, unto the remission of my sins, and unto life everlasting. (In the Name of the Father, and of the Son, and of the Holy Spirit. Amen.)

Then he wipeth his lips and the chalice with the veil which is in his hand, saying:

Lo, this hath touched my lips, and shall take away mine iniquities, and shall purge away my sins.

Then kissing the holy chalice, he saith:

Glory to thee, O God. (*Thrice.*) *Proto-Deacon.* Archimandrites, Archpriests, Priests, Deacons, draw near.

Then the other Clergy approach the Bishop in the order of their seniority and kiss the edge of the Altar, and having said:

Lo, I draw near unto the King Immortal and our God.

Impart to me, Right Reverend Master, the precious and holy Body of our Lord, and God, and Saviour Jesus Christ:

Each receiveth from him a portion of the Holy Body, the Bishop saying to each:

To thee, Priest (*or* Deacon, *or as his rank may be*), is imparted the precious, and all-pure, and

(Bishop.)

Secretly.

whether voluntary or involuntary; whether of word or of deed; whether committed with knowledge or in ignorance. And vouchsafe that I may partake without condemnation of thine all-pure Mysteries, unto the remission of my sins, and unto life eternal. Amen.

Of thy Mystical Supper, O Son of God, accept me to-day as a communicant: for I will not speak of thy Mystery to thine enemies, neither, like Judas, will I give thee a kiss; but like the thief will I confess thee: Remember me, O Lord, in thy kingdom.

And let not this participation in thy Holy Mysteries be unto judgment upon me, or unto condemnation, O Lord, but unto the healing of soul and body.

(Bishop.)

immortal Body of our Lord, and God, and Saviour Jesus Christ, unto the remission of thy sins, and unto life everlasting. (In the name of the Father, and of the Son, and of the Holy Spirit. Amen.)

And they kiss the hand and the shoulder of the Bishop; and to his greeting:

Christ is in the midst of us,

They reply:

He is, and shall be.

Then he giveth to each of them thrice the holy chalice, saying:

Lo, this hath touched thy lips, and shall take away thine iniquities, and shall purge away thy sins.

And he saith the Prayer of Thanksgiving. (See page 118.)

Secretly.

And so shall they partake of the Holy Body which they hold in their hands, with awe, and all godly fear.

And when they have partaken thereof, the Priests partake, in due order, of the Holy Blood from the chalice, thrice, saying:

The precious and holy Blood of our Lord, and God, and Saviour, Jesus Christ, is imparted to me, the servant of God, Priest, N., unto the remission of my sins, and unto life everlasting.

In the Name of the Father, and of the Son, and of the Holy Spirit. Amen.

Sometimes: O Holy God, Holy Mighty, Holy Immortal One, have mercy upon us.

Then having wiped his mouth and the holy chalice with the veil, which he holdeth in his hand, the Priest shall say:

Lo, this hath touched my lips, and shall take away mine iniquities, and shall purge away my sins.

Then the Senior Priest saith again:

Deacon, draw near.

And the Deacon shall approach, and shall make one reverence, saying:

Lo, I draw near unto the King Immortal, and our God.

Impart unto me, Master, the precious and holy Blood of our Lord and God, and Saviour, Jesus Christ.

And the Priest, giving him the chalice, shall say:

The servant of God, N., Deacon, partaketh of the precious and all-holy Blood of our Lord, and God, and Saviour, Jesus Christ, unto the remission of his sins, and unto life everlasting.

And having communicated the Deacon, the Priest shall say:

Lo, this hath touched thy lips, and shall take away thine iniquities, and shall purge away thy sins.

If there be any who desire to partake of the Holy Mysteries, the Priest shall divide the remaining portions, the NI and the KA, into small particles, sufficient for all, and place them in the chalice.

Then the Deacon, setting the holy paten above the holy chalice, saith these Hymns of the Resurrection:

In that we have beheld the Resurrection of Christ, let us bow down before the holy Lord Jesus, the only sinless One. Thy Cross do we adore, O Christ, and thy holy Resurrection we laud and glorify: for thou art our God, and we know none other beside thee; we call upon thy Name. O come, all ye faithful, let us adore Christ's holy Resurrection. For lo, through the Cross is joy come into all the world. Ever blessing the Lord, let us sing his Resurrection: for in that he endured the Cross he hath destroyed Death by death.

Shine, shine, O new Jerusalem, for the glory of the Lord is risen upon thee! Shout now and be glad, O Zion! And do thou, O Pure One, Birth-giver of God, rejoice in the Rising-again of him whom thou didst bear.

O Christ, Passover great and most Holy! O Wisdom, Word, and Power of God! Vouchsafe that we may more perfectly partake of thee in the days which know no evening of thy kingdom.

While with the sponge he wipeth all the particles into the chalice with all care and reverence, he saith:

Wash away, O Lord, the sins of all who are here commemorated, by thy precious Blood, through the prayers of thy Saints.

And he shall cover the holy chalice with the veil; and in like manner he shall cover the holy paten with the star-cover and the veil. Then the Priest shall recite the

PRAYER OF THANKSGIVING, secretly.

We give thanks unto thee, O Lord, who lovest mankind, Benefactor of our souls and bodies, for that thou hast vouchsafed this day to feed us with thy heavenly and immortal Mysteries. Guide our path aright; stablish us all in thy fear; guard our life; make sure our steps: through the prayers and supplications of the glorious Birth-giver of God and ever-virgin Mary, and of all thy Saints.

[*Or, if the* LITURGY OF ST. BASIL THE GREAT *be used, this Prayer:*

We give thanks unto thee, O Lord our God, for the participation

Secretly.

in thy holy, pure, immortal and heavenly Mysteries, which thou hast given unto us for the welfare and sanctification and healing of our souls and bodies. Do thou, the same Lord of all, grant that the communion of the holy Body and Blood of thy Christ may be for us unto faith which cannot be put to confusion, unto love unfeigned, unto increase of wisdom, unto the healing of soul and body, unto the turning aside of every adversary, unto the fulfilment of thy commandments, unto an acceptable defence at the dread Judgment Seat of thy Christ.]

Secretly.

Then the Holy Door is opened, and the Deacon, making a reverence, shall approach the Holy Door; and he taketh from the Bishop or the Priest the holy chalice, and elevating it, he saith:

In the fear of God and with faith draw near.

Choir. Blessed is he that cometh in the Name of the Lord; God is the Lord and hath revealed himself unto us.

Christ is risen from the dead, trampling down Death by death, and upon those in the tomb bestowing life.

Easter-tide

Those who desire to communicate shall then approach. They shall come singly, and shall do reverence, with all devoutness and awe, with their hands crossed on their breasts: and in this manner shall they receive the Holy Mysteries, after the Priest hath said aloud the Prayer:

I believe, O Lord, and I confess, . . . (*See page* 116.)

And as he communicateth each one, the Priest shall say:

The servant of God, N., partaketh of the precious and holy Body and Blood of our Lord, and God, and Saviour, Jesus Christ, unto the remission of his (*or* her) sins, and unto life everlasting. (22)

And as each person is communicated, the Choir singeth:

Receive ye the Body of Christ; taste ye of the Fountain of Life.

Then the communicant's mouth shall be wiped with the holy veil, and he shall kiss the holy chalice, and making a reverence, he shall go aside where he is given the antidóron and the holy warm water.

And when all have finished, the Choir singeth:

Alleluia, alleluia, alleluia.

If there are communicants.

And the Priest shall set the chalice on the Altar, and shall bless the People, saying:

O God, save thy people, and bless thine inheritance. ·

Eis pollá éti, Déspota.

Bishop.

(The Bishop blesseth with the dikíri and the trikíri.)

Choir. We have beheld the true Light; we have received the heavenly Spirit; we have found the true faith. Let us bow down in worship to the Trinity Undivided, for He hath saved us.

Or, at Eastertide:

Christ is risen from the dead, trampling down Death by death, and upon those in the tomb bestowing life.

Then the Priest and the Deacon shall turn to the Holy Altar; and the Priest shall cense it, saying thrice, to himself: **Bishop.**

Be thou exalted in heaven, O God, and thy glory above all the earth.

The Priest, taking the holy paten, shall then set it upon the head of the Deacon; and the Deacon, holding it reverently, shall go to the Table of Oblation, and set it down there. *Secretly.*

The Priest, having done reverence also, shall take the holy chalice (from the Bishop, if it be a Pontifical Service); and turning to face the Holy Door, he shall look upon the People, while he saith, secretly: (23)

Blessed is our God!

Then, aloud: Always, now, and ever, and unto ages of ages.

Choir. Amen.

Let our mouths be filled with thy praise, O Lord, that we may extol thy glory, for that thou hast deigned to make us partakers of thy holy, divine, immortal and life-giving Mysteries. Establish us in thy Sanctification, that all the day long we may meditate upon thy righteousness. Alleluia, alleluia, alleluia.

Eastertide. Christ is risen from the dead, trampling down Death by death, and upon those in the tomb bestowing life.

And the Deacon, coming forth through the north door, and standing in his accustomed place, saith:

Having received the divine, holy, pure, immortal, heavenly, life-giving and terrible Mysteries of Christ, O believers, let us worthily give thanks unto the Lord.

Choir. Lord, have mercy.

Succour us, save us, have mercy upon us, and keep us, O God, by thy grace.

Choir. Lord, have mercy.

Beseeching that this whole day may be perfect, holy, peaceful and sinless, let us commend ourselves, and each other, and all our life unto Christ our God.

Choir. To thee, O Lord.

Then the Priest, folding the corporal (antimíns), shall make over it, with the book of the Holy Gospels, the sign of the cross.

Exclamation.

Priest. For thou art our sanctification, and unto thee we ascribe glory, to the Father, and to the Son, and to the Holy Spirit, now, and ever, and unto ages of ages.

Choir. Amen.

Priest. Let us depart in peace.

Choir. In the Name of the Lord.

Deacon. Let us pray to the Lord.

Choir. Lord, have mercy.

Then the Junior Priest cometh forth, and, standing at the foot of the Tribune, readeth the PRAYER BEFORE THE TRIBUNE.

O Lord, who blessest those who bless thee, and sanctifiest those who put their trust in thee: Save thy people and bless thine inheritance. Preserve the fulness of thy Church; sanctify those who love the beauty of thy house; glorify them in recompense with thy divine might, and forsake not us who set our hope on thee. Give peace to thy world, and to thy Churches, and to thy Priests: and to our most God-fearing Ruler N., to the Army and Navy, and to all thy people. For every good gift and every perfect gift is from above, and cometh from thee, the Father of Lights. And unto thee we ascribe glory, and thanksgiving, and worship, to the Father, and to the Son, and to the Holy Spirit, now, and ever, and unto ages of ages.

Choir. Amen. —— Blessed be the Name of the Lord henceforth and forever. (*Thrice.*)

Reader: Psalm xxxiv. I will alway give thanks unto the Lord: Come, ye children, and hearken unto me: I will teach you the fear of the Lord. What man is he that lusteth to live, and would fain see good days? Keep thy tongue from evil, and do good: seek peace, and ensue it. The eyes of the Lord are over the righteous, and his ears are open unto their prayers. The countenance of the Lord is against them that do evil, to root out the remembrance of them from the earth. The righteous cry, and the Lord heareth them, and delivereth them out of all their troubles. The Lord is nigh unto them that are of a contrite heart, and will save such as be of an humble spirit. Great are the troubles of the righteous, but the Lord delivereth him out of all. He keepeth all his bones, so that not one of them is broken. But misfortune

The Deacon shall stand at the right side of the image-screen (ikonostás), before the holy picture (ikóna) of our Lord Christ, holding his stole in his hand, and with bowed head, until the conclusion of the PRAYER BEFORE THE TRIBUNE. *And when this hath been said, the Priest shall enter through the Holy Door, and going to the Table of Oblation, he shall say, secretly, the following Prayer:*

Thou who art the fulfilling of the Law and the Prophets, O Christ our God, and hast accomplished all the dispensation of the Father: Fill thou our hearts with joy and gladness always, now, and ever, and unto ages of ages.

And the Deacon, entering through the north door, shall consume the Holy Gifts, with all reverence and awe.

Secretly.

shall slay the ungodly, and they that hate the righteous shall be desolate. The Lord delivereth the souls of his servants, and all they that put their trust in him shall not be destitute.

Easter-tide. Christ is risen from the dead, trampling down Death by death, and upon those in the tomb bestowing life.

When the Deacon hath consumed the Holy Elements, so that no smallest morsel of the broken Bread is allowed to fall or remain; and hath poured into the holy chalice of the water and the wine, and hath wiped away with the sponge all the moisture, he shall lay the holy vessels together, and set them in their accustomed place, saying: Lord, now lettest thou thy servant depart: . . .

Secretly.

And when the Psalm hath been read, the Priest shall say:

The blessing of the Lord, through his grace and love towards mankind, be upon you always, now, and ever, and unto ages of ages.

Choir. Amen.

Priest. Glory to thee, O Christ-God, our sure hope; glory to thee.

Choir. Glory to the Father, and to the Son, and to the Holy Spirit, now, and ever, and unto ages of ages.

Lord, have mercy. (*Thrice.*)   Master, bless.

Easter-tide. Christ is risen from the dead, trampling down Death by death, and upon those in the tomb bestowing life.

(The Bishop or) the Priest saith the BENEDICTION.*

May (*Sunday:* he who rose from the dead) Christ, our true God, through the prayers of his all-holy Mother (*Wednesday and Friday:* through the might of the precious and life-giving Cross), (*Monday:* through the intercessions of the honourable Bodiless Powers of Heaven), (*Tuesday:* of the honourable and glorious Prophet and Forerunner and Baptist, John), of the holy, glorious and all-laudable Apostles (*Saturday:* of the holy, glorious and right victorious Martyrs; of our reverend and God-bearing Fathers); (*according to the Liturgy used:* of our Father among the Saints, Basil the Great *or* John Chrysostom), (*Thursday:* of our Father among the Saints, Nicholas, Archbishop of Myra in Lycia, the Wonder-worker), of Saint N. (*of the Temple*), of Saint N. (*of the day*), of the holy and righteous Ancestors of God, Joachim and Anna, and of all the Saints, have mercy upon us and save us, forasmuch as he is good and loveth mankind.

Bishop. *At a Pontifical Service: Choir.* Eis pollá éti, Déspota.

Choir. Preserve, O Lord, our most God-fearing Ruler, N., and all the Authorities; the Most Holy Synod (*or* Patriarch), our Master, the Right Reverend N., Bishop of N., and all Orthodox Christians, for many years.

* For Benedictions at the Feasts, see Special Services of the Feasts.

The Priest holdeth the cross for the People to kiss, and distributeth the antidóron (24), *after which he withdraweth to the Sanctuary, and the Holy Door is closed. And (if he have celebrated without a Deacon) the Priest consumeth the Holy Gifts; after which he reciteth the* POST-COMMUNION PRAYERS.

Glory to thee, O God. (*Thrice.*)

I thank thee, O Lord my God, that thou hast not rejected me, a sinner, but hast deemed me worthy to become a partaker of thy Holy Things. I thank thee that thou hast graciously granted unto me, though unworthy, to receive thy pure and heavenly Gifts. But, O Master who lovest mankind, who for our sake didst die, and didst rise again, and hast graciously bestowed upon us these terrible and life-giving Mysteries, for the benefit and sanctification of our souls and bodies: Vouchsafe that they may be efficacious for me also unto the healing of my soul and body, unto the averting of everything contrary thereto; unto the enlightenment of the eyes of my heart; unto the peace of my spiritual powers; unto faith invincible; unto love unfeigned; unto the fulfilling of wisdom; unto the keeping of thy commandments; unto the increase of thy divine grace and the attainment of thy kingdom: that by them preserved in thy holiness I may ever bear in mind thy grace, and live henceforth not unto myself, but unto thee, our Master and Benefactor. And so, this life ended in the hope of life everlasting, I may come unto that rest eternal, where the voice of those who keep high festival ceaseth never, and where endless is the sweetness of those who behold the beauty inexpressible of thy countenance. For thou art the true desire and the happiness unutterable of those who love thee, O Christ our God, and every created being shall laud thee unto ages of ages. Amen.

A Prayer of St. Basil the Great.

O Lord Christ-God, King of the Ages, and Maker of all men, I thank thee for all the good things which thou hast bestowed upon me, and for this Communion of thy most pure and life-giving Mysteries. Therefore I entreat thee, O Good One who lovest mankind: Keep me in thy tabernacle and under the shadow of thy wings; and grant that, with a pure conscience, even unto my uttermost breath, I may worthily partake of thy Holy Things, unto the remission of my sins, and unto life eternal. For thou art the Bread of Life, the Fountain of all holiness, the Giver of good things; and unto thee we ascribe glory, to the Father, and to the Son, and to the Holy Spirit, now, and ever, and unto ages of ages. Amen.

A Prayer of St. Simeon Metaphrastis.

O thou who, of thine own good will, dost give me thy body as my food; thou who art a Fire consuming the unworthy: Consume me not, O my Creator. But enter thou rather into my members, into my whole being, all my joints, my reins, my heart. Consume thou the thorns of all mine iniquities. Cleanse my soul. Sanctify my thoughts. Make stable my knees, and my bones likewise. Enlighten my five simple senses. Knit me wholly to the fear of thee. Ever cover me, guard me and keep me from every word and deed which may hurt the soul. Purify me and wash me clean, and bring me into concord. Adorn me, give me understanding and enlighten me. Manifest me as the dwelling of thy one Spirit, and in nowise as the dwelling of sin. That being made thy tabernacle through the reception of thy holy Communion every evil thing, every carnal passion may flee away from me as from fire. I offer unto thee as intercessors all the Saints, the Chieftains of the Bodiless Powers, thy Forerunner, the wise Apostles, and joined with them thy Mother pure and undefiled; whose prayers do thou accept, in thy tender loving-kindness, O my Christ, and make thy servant to be a child of the light. For thou alone art the sanctification and splendour of our souls, O Good One, and unto thee, as God and Lord over all, do we, as it behooveth us, every day ascribe all glory.

Another Prayer.

May thy holy Body, O Lord Jesus Christ our God, profit me unto life eternal, and thy precious Blood unto the remission of my sins. May this Eucharist be unto me for joy, and health, and gladness, and render me, a sinner, worthy to stand at the right hand of thy glory in thy terrible and second Coming-again; through the intercessions of thine all-pure Mother, and all of the Saints.

Another Prayer, to the Most Holy Birth-giver of God.

O all-holy Lady, Birth-giver of our God, of my darkened soul the light, hope, shelter, refuge, the consolation and the joy: I thank thee that thou hast deemed me, all unworthy as I am, worthy to be a partaker of the pure Body and precious Blood of thy Son. O thou who didst bring forth the true Light, enlighten the intellectually-discerning eyes of my heart; O thou who didst bear the Fountain of Immortality, quicken thou me, who lie dead in sin. O compassionately loving Mother of the merciful God, have mercy upon me, and grant unto me humility and contrition of heart, and humbleness of mind, and deliverance from bondage to evil thoughts. And vouchsafe that even unto my last breath I may, without condemnation, receive the sanctification of these Holy Mysteries, unto the healing of both soul and body. And grant me tears of penitence and of confession, that I may laud and glorify thee all the days of my life. For blessed art thou and all-glorified unto all the ages. Amen.

Lord, now lettest thou thy servant depart in peace, according to thy word. For mine eyes have seen thy salvation, which thou hast prepared before the face of all people. To be a light to lighten the Gentiles, and to be the glory of thy people Israel.

O Holy God, Holy Mighty, Holy Immortal One, have mercy upon us.

Glory to the Father, and to the Son, and to the Holy Spirit, now, and ever, and unto ages of ages. Amen.

O all-holy Trinity, have mercy upon us. O Lord, wash away our sins. O Master, pardon our transgressions. O Holy One, visit and heal our infirmities, for thy Name's sake.

Our Father, who art in heaven, Hallowed be thy Name. Thy kingdom come. Thy will be done on earth, As it is in heaven. Give us this day our daily bread. And forgive us our trespasses, As we forgive those who trespass against us. And lead us not into temptation; But deliver us from the Evil One:

For thine is the kingdom, and the power, and the glory, of the Father, and of the Son, and of the Holy Spirit, now, and ever, and unto ages of ages. Amen.

The Hymn (Tropár) of Dismissal, in Tone V.:

The grace of thy lips, shining forth like a beacon-fire, hath illumined the universe, and hath bestowed upon the world the treasure of non-avariciousness, and hath shown us the height of humility. But as thou instructest us with thy words, O Father John Chrysostom, so also intercede thou with Christ God, the Word, that our souls may be saved.

Glory to the Father, and to the Son, and to the Holy Spirit.

Collect-Hymn (Kondák), in Tone VI.:

From heaven hast thou received grace divine, and with thy lips dost thou teach all men to adore the One God in• three Persons. O John Chrysostom, all-blessed Saint, we rightly praise thee: for thou art our Teacher, in that thou dost reveal things divine.

Now, and ever, and unto ages of ages. Amen.

[But if the LITURGY OF ST. BASIL THE GREAT hath been used, this Hymn (Tropár), in Tone I.:

Thy voice is gone out into all the world, in that it hath received thy word, wherewith thou hast taught in manner well pleasing unto God, hast expounded the nature of existing things, and hast adorned the customs of mankind. O Royal Priesthood, Sainted Father, pray thou unto Christ our God that our souls may be saved.

Collect-Hymn (Kondák), in Tone IV.:

Thou hast shown thyself a foundation immovable of the Church, dispensing unto all men the dominion inviolate, sealing it with thy decrees, O Saint Basil, who wast manifested from heaven.]

HYMN TO THE HOLY BIRTH-GIVER OF GOD (Bogoróditchen).

O Protection of Christians that maketh not ashamed, O Mediatrix never-failing with the Creator: Despise not the sinners' voice of supplication; but in that thou art good, come speedily to the aid of us who faithfully call upon thee; make haste to our petition and further our prayer, O Birth-giver of God, who ever protectest them that do thee honour.

Secretly.

The Priest and Deacon wash their hands at the appointed place; and having done reverence together, the Priest shall pronounce the Dismissal. And giving thanks unto God for all things, they shall say, also, the proper Hymn for the Day. Then: Lord, have mercy. (*Twelve times.*)

More honourable than the Cherubim, and beyond compare more glorious than the Seraphim, thou who without defilement barest God the Word, true Birth-giver of God, we magnify thee.

Glory to the Father, and to the Son, and to the Holy Spirit, now, and ever, and unto ages of ages. Amen.

THE OFFICE OF THE DIVINE LITURGY OF THE PRESANCTIFIED (GIFTS) *

PREFATORY NOTE

During the Holy and Great Fast, when the Priest is to celebrate the LITURGY OF THE PRESANCTIFIED, *at the Office of Oblation on the Sunday preceding, (1) after he hath cut the first altar-bread, and sacrificed and pierced it (as indicated in the Ritual of the preceding Liturgy), he cutteth the extra breads, saying over each one of them these words following:*

In commemoration of our Lord, and God, and Saviour, Jesus Christ.

He was led as a lamb to the slaughter. And as a spotless lamb before its shearers is dumb, so opened he not his mouth.

Sacrificed is the Lamb of God, who taketh away the sins of the world, for the life of the world, and for its salvation.

One of the soldiers did pierce his side with a spear, and straightway there came forth blood and water. And he that saw it bare witness, and his witness is true.

Then he poureth the wine and water into the holy chalice, saying the customary words; and covereth them with the holy veil, and censeth them, repeating the Prayer of Oblation. And then he beginneth the Divine Liturgy and celebrateth as usual.

And when he is to sign the breads, at the invocation of the Holy Spirit, he saith: Make this bread the precious Body of thy Christ, *in the singular, and he doth not speak of the breads in the plural. And when he maketh the oblation, he offereth them all together. And he breaketh only the first bread, and layeth the portion in the holy chalice, and poureth in the warm water as usual.*

Then, taking the holy spoon in his right hand, he dippeth it in the Holy Blood. With his left hand he taketh one of the breads, and toucheth it with the holy spoon, which hath been wetted with the Holy Blood, in the form of a cross, on the side whereon is depicted the cross, under the soft portion, and placeth it in the tabernacle.

Then he doth the same with the other breads, and placeth them all in the tabernacle. Thereafter the Priest prayeth as usual, and communicateth as usual, and performeth the Divine Liturgy as usual.

When a Priest is to celebrate the Liturgy of the Presanctified, after he hath read the Entrance Prayer, as in the ordinary Liturgy (except: Stretch forth thy hand, O Lord: *at the end of the Hours and the Typical Psalms, and what is generally read before the Liturgy†) he entereth the Chapel of Oblation, and vesteth himself, signing with the cross and kissing each vestment, but saying nothing as he doth so, except:* Lord, have

At a Pontifical Service the Bishop is met in the usual manner, and the usual Entrance Prayers are read, with the exception of: Stretch forth thy hand, O Lord. *He is vested, as usual, in the centre of the Temple, but without the Verses, and only with the exclamations:* Let us pray to the Lord.

Before Vespers is begun, the Bishop standeth in his place, in the centre of the Temple, and bestoweth his blessing on the Rector and the Deacon

Secretly.

* For Explanation of the Symbolism, see Appendix B, V.
† See the ordinary Liturgy.

mercy: over each of them. And the Deacon, taking the time from him, goeth and taketh his stand at his appointed place, and (the Holy Door being closed, and the curtain drawn aside), exclaimeth:

to begin Vespers, he himself remaining on his dais until the Little Entrance. The Priest readeth the Prayers of Light in the Sanctuary. The Holy Door is opened at the Exclamations, and during the Litanies, but remaineth closed the rest of the time until the Entrance.

Secretly.

Deacon. Bless, Master.

Priest. Blessed is the kingdom of the Father, and of the Son, and of the Holy Spirit, now, and ever, and unto ages of ages.

Choir. Amen.

Reader. O come, let us worship God our King. O come, let us worship and fall down before Christ, our King and our God. O come, let us worship and fall down before the Very Christ, our King and our God.

Then the Preliminary Psalm, civ., is read. And in the mean while the Priest reciteth in front of the Holy Door the Prayers of Light (see Vespers); that is to say, the Vesper Prayers, beginning with the fourth Prayer; the first three being said later on, after the Litanies. (The Priest entereth the Sanctuary.) And when the Psalm is finished, the Deacon saith the

GREAT LITANY.

Deacon. In peace let us pray to the Lord.

Choir. Lord, have mercy.

For the peace that is from above, and for the salvation of our souls: ℞

For the peace of the whole world; for the welfare of God's holy Churches, and for the union of all: ℞

For this holy Temple, and for all those who with faith, devoutness, and in the fear of God have entered therein: ℞

For our Most Holy Synod (*or* Patriarch); for our Bishop (*or* Archbishop, *or* Metropolitan), N., for the honourable Presbytery, the Diaconate in Christ; for all the clergy and the laity: ℞

Here follow petitions for the Ruler of the Land and for all the Authorities, according to the elements and nationalities of which the Parish is constituted.

That he will aid them, and subdue under their feet every foe and adversary: ℞

For this city, for this holy Temple, and

let us pray to the Lord. Choir. Lord, have mercy.

And the Priest reciteth, secretly, the PRAYER OF THE FIRST ANTIPHON (*The first of the Vesper Prayers*).

O Lord, bountiful and compassionate, long-suffering and plenteous in mercy, give ear unto our prayer, and attend to the voice of our supplication. Work upon us a sign for good. Lead us in thy way, that we may walk in thy truth. Make glad our hearts, that we may fear thy holy Name. For thou art great, and doest wonders. Thou alone art

Secretly.

for every city and land, and for those who with faith dwell therein: ℞

For healthful seasons; for abundance of the fruits of the earth, and for peaceful times: ℞

For those who travel by sea or by land; for the sick and the suffering; for those who are in captivity, and for their salvation: ℞

That he will deliver us from all tribulation, wrath, and necessity: ℞

Succour us, save us, have mercy upon us, and keep us, O God, by thy grace.

Choir. Lord, have mercy.

Calling to remembrance our most holy, all-undefiled, most blessed and glorious Lady, the Birth-giver of God and ever-virgin Mary, with all the Saints, let us commend ourselves, and each other, and all our life unto Christ our God.

Choir. To thee, O Lord.

Exclamation.

Priest. For unto thee are due all glory, honour and worship, to the Father, and to the Son, and to the Holy Spirit, now, and ever, and unto ages of ages.

Choir. Amen.

Choir. let us pray to the Lord. Lord, have mercy.

God, and among all the gods there is none like unto thee, O Lord, mighty in mercy, gracious in strength, to aid, and to comfort and save all those who put their trust in thy holy Name.

Secretly.

The Reader then readeth the Eighteenth Selection of Psalms (Kafisma): FIRST ANTIPHON *(Psalms cxx., cxxiii.).*

PSALM CXX.

When I was in trouble, I called upon the Lord, and he heard me. Deliver my soul, O Lord, from lying lips, and from a deceitful tongue. What reward shall be given or done unto thee, thou false tongue? even mighty and sharp arrows, with hot burning coals. Woe is me, that I am constrained to dwell with Mesech, and to have my habitation among the tents of Kedar! My soul hath long dwelt among them that are en-

The Priest unfoldeth the corporal (which lieth upon the Altar), and setteth the holy paten thereon. Then he openeth the tabernacle, and placeth the Presanctified Lamb upon the paten, making a lowly reverence.

And the Priest reciteth, secretly, *the* PRAYER OF THE SECOND ANTIPHON *(the second Vesper Prayer).*

O Lord, rebuke us not in thy displeasure, neither chasten us in thy wrath: but deal with us according to thy mercy, O Physician and Healer of our souls. Guide us unto the haven of thy will. Enlighten the eyes of our hearts to the knowledge of thy truth, and vouchsafe that the residue of this day and our whole life may be peaceful and without

Secretly.

emies unto peace. I labour for peace; but when I speak unto them thereof, they make them ready to battle.

sin; through the intercessions of the holy Birth-giver of God, and of all the Saints.

Secretly.

PSALM CXXIII.

Unto thee lift I up mine eyes, O thou that dwellest in the heavens. Behold, even as the eyes of servants look unto the hand of their masters, and as the eyes of a maiden unto the hand of her mistress, even so our eyes wait upon the Lord our God, until he have mercy upon us. Have mercy upon us, O Lord, have mercy upon us; for we are utterly despised. Our soul is filled with the scornful reproof of the wealthy; and with the despitefulness of the proud.

Deacon. Again, yet again, in peace let us pray to the Lord.

Choir. Lord, have mercy.

Succour us, save us, have mercy upon us, and keep us, O God, by thy grace.

Choir. Lord, have mercy.

Calling to remembrance our most holy, all-undefiled, most blessed and glorious Lady, the Birth-giver of God and ever-virgin Mary, with all the Saints, let us commend ourselves, and each other, and all our life unto Christ our God.

Choir. To thee, O Lord.

Exclamation.

For thine is the majesty, and thine are the kingdom and the power and the glory, of the Father, and of the Son, and of the Holy Spirit, now, and ever, and unto ages of ages.

Choir. Amen.

The Reader continueth the Selection of Psalms: THE SECOND ANTIPHON (*Psalms cxxiv., cxxix.*).

PSALM CXXIV.

If the Lord himself had not been on our side, now may Israel say; if the Lord himself had not been on our side, when men rose up against us; they had swallowed us up quick; when they were so wrathfully displeased at us. Yea, the waters had drowned us, and the stream had gone over our soul. The deep waters of the proud had gone even over our soul. But praised be the Lord, who hath not given us over for a prey unto their teeth. Our soul is escaped even as a bird out of the snare of the fowler; the snare is broken, and we are delivered.

The Priest, accompanied by the Deacon holding a taper, or alone, censeth the Altar.

Then he saith, secretly, *the* PRAYER OF THE THIRD ANTIPHON (*the third Vesper Prayer*).

O Lord our God, remember us sinners and thine unprofitable servants, when we call upon thy holy Name, and put us not to shame in our expectation of thy

Secretly.

Our help standeth in the Name of the Lord; who hath made heaven and earth.

PSALM CXXIX.

Many a time have they fought against me from my youth up, may Israel now say: yea, many a time have they vexed me from my youth up; but they have not prevailed against me. The plowers plowed upon my back, and made long furrows. But the righteous Lord hath hewn the snares of the ungodly in pieces. Let them be confounded and turned backward, as many as have evil will at Zion. Let them be even as the grass growing upon the house-tops, which withereth afore it be plucked up; whereof the mower filleth not his hand, neither he that bindeth up the sheaves his bosom. So that they who go by say not so much as, The Lord prosper you; we wish you good luck in the Name of the Lord.

THE LITTLE LITANY.

Deacon. Again, yet again, in peace . . .

Choir. Lord, have mercy.

Succour us, save us . . .

Choir. Lord, have mercy.

Calling to remembrance our most holy, all-undefiled . . . (*page* 130).

Choir. To thee, O Lord.

Priest. For thou art our God, the God of mercy and salvation, and unto thee do we ascribe glory, to the Father, and to the Son, and to the Holy Spirit, now, and ever, and unto ages of ages. Amen.

The THIRD ANTIPHON (*Psalms cxli., cxlii., cxxx., cxvii.*).

Choir. Lord, I have cried unto thee, hear me. Hear me, O Lord. Lord, I have cried unto thee, hear me. Receive the voice of my prayer, when I call upon thee. Hear me, O Lord. Let my prayer be set forth in thy sight as the incense, and let the lifting up of my hands be an evening sacrifice.

Reader. Set a watch, O Lord, before my mouth, and keep the door of my lips. O let

mercy: but grant us, O Lord, all our petitions which are unto salvation, and vouchsafe that we may love and fear thee with all our hearts, and do thy will in all things.

Priest. For thou art a good God, and lovest mankind, and unto thee do we ascribe glory, to the Father, and to the Son, and to the Holy Spirit, now, and ever, and unto ages of ages. Amen.

The Priest maketh three lowly reverences to the Holy Gifts, setteth the paten on his head, and beareth it to the Table of Oblation, preceded by the Deacon with the taper and censer. Then, on the Table of Oblation he poureth wine and water into the chalice, censeth the starcover and the veil, and covereth therewith the paten and the chalice, saying the while:

Through the prayers of our holy Fathers, O Lord Jesus Christ our God, have mercy upon us.

Then he goeth to the Altar, foldeth the corporal, and setteth the Gospels thereon.

The Priest saith, secretly, the PRAYER OF THE ENTRANCE.

In the evening, and

not mine heart be inclined to any evil thing; let me not be occupied in ungodly works with the men that work wickedness, lest I eat of such things as please them. Let the righteous rather smite me friendly, and reprove me. But let not their precious balms break my head; yea, I will pray yet against their wickedness. Let their judges be overthrown in stony places, that they may hear my words; for they are sweet. Our bones lie scattered before the pit, like as when one breaketh and heweth wood upon the earth. But mine eyes look unto thee, O Lord God; in thee is my trust; O cast not out my soul. Keep me from the snare that they have laid for me, and from the traps of the wicked doers. Let the ungodly fall into their own nets together, and let me ever escape them.

Psalm CXLII.

I cried unto the Lord with my voice; yea, even unto the Lord did I make my supplication. I poured out my complaints before him, and showed him of my trouble. When my spirit was in heaviness, thou knewest my path; in the way wherein I walked, have they privily laid a snare for me. I looked also upon my right hand, and saw there was no man that would know me. I had no place to flee unto, and no man cared for my soul.

Secretly. in the morning, and at noon-day we praise thee, we bless thee, we give thanks unto thee, and we pray unto thee, O Lord of all: Direct thou our prayer before thee as incense, and incline not our hearts unto words or thoughts of wickedness: but deliver us from all who seek after our souls. For unto thee, Lord, O Lord, lift we up our eyes, and in thee have we trusted. Put us not to shame, O our God.

For unto thee are due all glory, honour and worship, to the Father, and to the Son, and to the Holy Spirit, now, and ever, and unto ages of ages. Amen.

I cried unto thee, O Lord, and said, Thou art my hope, and my portion in the land of the living. Consider my complaint, for I am brought very low. O deliver me from my persecutors; for they are too strong for me. Bring my soul out of prison, that I may give thanks unto thy Name; which thing if thou wilt grant me, then shall the righteous resort unto my company.

Then shall be sung Hymns to the Martyrs, and Hymns from the Triódion (the Hymns for the Great Fast), and from the Miníya. (2)

Glory to the Father, and to the Son, and to the Holy Spirit, now, and ever, and unto ages of ages. Amen.

Then the Hymn to the Birth-giver of God (Bogoróditchen or Dogmátik), in the proper Tone.*

* For these Hymns, in the Eight Tones, see Appendix A.

The Holy Door is now opened, and the Entrance is made with the Censer. But when the Gospel is to be read (at the Feast Day of the Temple, or of a Saint), the Entrance is made with the Holy Gospels.	*At a Pontifical Service the Entrance is always made with the book of the Gospels, and in precisely the same manner as the Entrance at the Liturgy; except that the Evening Prayer of the Entrance is read, and that in place of:* O come, let us worship: *there is sung:* O gladsome radiance:

When the Hymn to the Birth-giver of God is finished, the Deacon shall make with the censer the sign of the cross, as he standeth in the middle of the Holy Door, and shall enter the Sanctuary, and shall say, aloud:

Wisdom, O believers!

Choir. O gladsome radiance of the holy glory of the Father immortal, heavenly, holy, blessed, Jesus Christ! In that we now are come unto the setting of the sun, and behold the light of even, we hymn thee, Father, Son, and Holy Spirit, God. For meet is it that at all times thou shouldest be magnified by voices propitious, O Son of God, who bestowest life. For which cause all the world doth glorify thee.

The Priest and the Deacon now go to the High Place.

Deacon. Wisdom!

Priest. Peace be unto all.

Reader. And to thy spirit.

Deacon. Wisdom! Let us attend. The Gradual, in the . . . Tone.

The Choir then singeth the Gradual (Prokímen) for the Day, thrice.

Deacon. Wisdom!

Reader. The Lesson from Genesis.

Deacon. Let us attend!

The Reader then readeth the Lesson, as appointed. (The Holy Door is closed.)

When the Lesson from Genesis is finished, the Holy Door is opened. And the Reader saith, and the Choir repeateth, in the usual manner, the Second Gradual (Prokímen).

The Deacon exclaimeth: Command!

And the Priest taketh the candlestick with its taper, and the censer, in his hands,	*If it be a Pontifical Service, the Bishop taketh the trikíri and the censer,*

and standing before the Holy Altar, and making therewith the sign of the cross, he exclaimeth:

Wisdom, O believers!

Then, turning to the People, he saith:

The light of Christ illumineth all men. (3)

And the People kneel.

Deacon. Wisdom! *(The Holy Door is closed.)*

Reader. The Lesson from the Proverbs.

Deacon. Let us attend!

Then the Reader readeth the appointed Lesson. And when he hath finished, the Priest saith:

Peace be unto thee.

Reader. And to thy spirit.

Deacon. Wisdom! (*The Holy Door is opened.*)

The Reader then chanteth, and the Choir repeateth:

1: Let my prayer be set forth in thy sight as the incense, and let the lifting up of my hands be an evening sacrifice.

Choir. Let my prayer . . .

2: O Lord, I have cried unto thee, hear me; give ear unto the voice of my petition, when I cry unto thee. ℞

3: Set a watch, O Lord, before my mouth, and a door of enclosure about my lips. ℞

4: Incline not my heart to the words of wickedness, to contrive excuses for sins. ℞

5: Let my prayer be set forth in thy sight as the incense. And let the lifting up of my hands be an evening sacrifice. ℞

When the Choir chanteth: Let my prayer (1–5), all who are present in the Temple, and they who are in the Sanctuary, kneel and pray. And the Priest taketh the censer and censeth before the Holy Altar (verses 1–3); and before the Table of Oblation (verse 4). And during verse 5 he putteth aside the censer, and kneeleth and prayeth.

Priest: THE PRAYER OF ST. EPHRAIM THE SYRIAN.

O Lord and Master of my life, grant not unto me a spirit of slothfulness, of discouragement, of lust of power, of vain babbling. (*Reverence.*)

But vouchsafe unto me, thy servant, the spirit of continence, of meekness, of patience, and of love. (*Reverence.*)

Yea, O Lord and King, grant that I may perceive my own transgressions, and judge not my brother. For blessed art thou unto ages of ages. Amen. (*Reverence.*)

If it be the Feast of a Saint, or of the Temple, then the Priest or the Deacon saith:

Feast Days.

Let us attend!

Priest. Peace be with you all.

Choir. And with thy spirit.

Deacon. Wisdom!

Reader. The Gradual, in the . . . Tone.

Then the Reader readeth the appointed Gradual (Prokímen), and the Choir singeth it, in the usual manner.

Deacon. Wisdom!

Reader. The Lesson from the holy Apostle, N. (to the Romans; *or* to the Corinthians; *or* otherwise, as appointed).

Deacon. Let us attend!

And when it is finished, the Priest saith:

Peace be unto thee.

Reader. And to thy spirit.

Feast Days.

And the Priest saith, secretly, *the* PRAYER BEFORE THE GOSPEL.

Deacon. Wisdom! | Illumine our hearts, O God who lovest
Choir. Alleluia. | mankind, with the pure light of thy divine
knowledge, and open the eyes of our understanding to the comprehension of the proclamation of thy Gospel. Implant in us, likewise, the fear of thy blessed commandments; that, trampling down all carnal desires, we may pursue a godly life, both thinking and performing such things as are well pleasing unto thee. For thou art the light of our souls and of our bodies, O Christ-God, and unto thee do we ascribe glory, together with thy Father, who is from everlasting, and thy holy, and blessed, and life-giving Spirit, now, and ever, and unto ages of ages. Amen.

Deacon. Wisdom, O believers! Let us listen to the Holy Gospel. Peace be with you all.

People. And with thy spirit.

Deacon. The Lesson from the Holy Gospel according to N.

Choir. Glory to thee, O Lord; glory to thee.

The Deacon then readeth the Gospel. And when it is finished:

Priest. Peace be with thee, who hast announced the good tidings.

Choir. Glory to thee, O Lord; glory to thee.

The LITANY OF FERVENT PETITION.

Deacon. Let us all say, with all our soul and with all our mind, let us say,

Choir. Lord, have mercy.

O Lord Almighty, the God of our fathers, we beseech thee; hearken, and have mercy.

Choir. Lord, have mercy.

And the Priest saith, secretly, *the* PRAYER OF THE LITANY OF FERVENT PETITION.

O Lord our God, accept this, the fervent supplication of thy servants, and be gracious unto us, according to the multitude of thy mercy. And send down thy bounties upon us, and upon all thy people, who here await the rich mercy which is from thee.

Have mercy upon us, O God, according to thy great mercy, we beseech thee, hearken and have mercy. ℞ (*Thrice.*)

Again we pray for (*the Ruler of the Land, according to the elements and nationalities of which the Parish is constituted*); for his might, victory, maintenance, peace, health, salvation; and that the Lord our God will abundantly aid and prosper him in all things, and subdue under his feet every foe and adversary. ℞ | *Here the Priest unfoldeth the corporal, except the upper edge.*

Again we pray for our Most Holy Synod(*or* Patriarch); for our Bishop (*or* Archbishop, *or* Metropolitan), N., and for all our brethren in Christ. ℞

Furthermore we pray for all their Christ-loving Army and Navy. ℞

Secretly. (Feast Days.)

Secretly.

Choir. Lord, have mercy. (Thrice.)

Furthermore we pray for our brethren the Priests; for ordained Monks; and for all our brotherhood in Christ. ℟

Furthermore we pray for the blessed and ever-memorable most holy Orthodox Patriarchs, and God-fearing Rulers; and for the founders of this holy Temple; and for all our devout fathers and brethren, Orthodox believers, departed this life before us, who here and in all the world lie asleep in the Lord. ℟

Furthermore we pray for those who bear fruit and do good works in this holy and all-honourable Temple; for those who labour in its service; for the singers; and for the people here present who await in firm hope thy great and rich mercies. ℟

Choir. Lord, have mercy. (Thrice.)

Exclamation.

Priest. For thou art a merciful God, who lovest mankind, and unto thee do we ascribe glory, to the Father, and to the Son, and to the Holy Spirit, now, and ever, and unto ages of ages.

Choir. Amen.

The LITANY OF THE CATECHUMENS.

Deacon. Pray ye unto the Lord, ye Catechumens.

Choir. Lord, have mercy.

Ye faithful, pray ye unto the Lord for the Catechumens, that the Lord will have mercy upon them. ℟

That he will teach them the word of truth. ℟

That he will reveal to them the Gospel of righteousness. ℟

(Here the Priest unfoldeth the last edge of the corporal.)

That he will unite them unto his Holy Catholic and Apostolic Church. ℟

Save them, have mercy upon them, succour them, and keep them, O God, by thy grace. ℟

Choir. Lord, have mercy.

The Priest saith, secretly, *the* PRAYER FOR THE CATE-CHUMENS.

O God, our God, the Creator and Maker of all things; who willest that all men should be saved, and should come unto the knowledge of the truth: Look upon thy servants the Catechumens, and deliver them from their ancient errors, and from the wiles of the adversary. And call them unto life eternal, illumining their souls and bodies, and numbering them with thy reason-endowed flock, which is called by thy holy Name. Amen.

Secretly.

Bow your heads unto the Lord, ye Catechumens.

Choir. To thee, O Lord.

Exclamation.

Priest. That with us they may magnify thine all-honourable and majestic Name, of the Father, and of the Son, and of the Holy Spirit, now, and ever, and unto ages of ages. — *Choir.* Amen.

(The Priest maketh the sign of the cross over the corporal with the sponge, which he then kisseth and layeth on one side.)

Then the following EXHORTATION TO THE CATECHUMENS *is said; but only from Wednesday of the Fourth Week of the Great Fast until the end of the Fast.* (4)

Deacon. As many as are Catechumens, depart. Catechumens, depart. Ye who are ready for Illumination, depart. Pray, ye who are preparing for Illumination.*

Choir. Lord, have mercy.

Ye faithful, for these brethren who are preparing for holy Illumination, and for their salvation, let us pray to the Lord.

Choir. Lord, have mercy.

That the Lord our God will stablish and strengthen them. ℟

That he will illumine them with the light of wisdom and of piety. ℟

That he will vouchsafe unto them, in his own good time, the laver of regeneration, the remission of sins, and the garment of incorruption. ℟

The Priest saith, secretly, the PRAYER FOR THOSE WHO ARE PREPARING FOR ILLUMINATION.

Show the light of thy countenance, O God, upon those who are preparing for holy Illumination, and who desire to put away the defilement of sin. Enlighten their understanding. Establish them in the faith. Strengthen them in hope. Perfect them in love. Make them honourable members of thy Christ, who gave himself a ransom for our souls.

That he will beget them with water and the Spirit. ℟

That he will grant unto them the perfection of the faith. ℟

That he will number them with his holy and chosen flock. ℟

Save them, have mercy upon them, succour them, and keep them, O God, by thy grace. ℟

Ye who are ready for Illumination, bow your heads unto the Lord.

Choir. To thee, O Lord.

Exclamation.

For thou art our illumination, and unto thee do we ascribe glory, to the Father, and to the Son, and to the Holy Spirit, now, and ever, and unto ages of ages.

Choir. Amen.

Deacon. As many as are preparing for Illumination, depart. Depart, ye who are preparing for Illumination.

* Baptism.

(Last half of the Fast.)   *Secretly.*   *(Last half of Fast.)*

Catechumens, depart. Let none of the Catechumens remain; but let us who are in the faith again, yet again, in peace pray unto the Lord.

Choir. Lord, have mercy.

Deacon. Succour us, save us, have mercy upon us, and keep us, O God, by thy grace.

Choir. Lord, have mercy.

The Priest saith, secretly, *the* FIRST PRAYER OF THE FAITHFUL.

O God, great and worthy to be praised, who through the life-giving death of thy Christ hast translated us from corruption to incorruption: Deliver thou all our senses from death-dealing carnal desires, setting over them as a good ruler the understanding that is in us. Let our eye have no part in any evil sight; let our hearing be inaccessible to all idle words; and let our tongue be purged from unseemly speech. Purify our lips which praise thee, O Lord. Make our hands to abstain from evil deeds, and to work only such things as are acceptable unto thee, establishing all our members and our minds by thy grace.

Deacon. Wisdom!

Secretly.

Exclamation.

Priest. For unto thee are due all glory, honour and worship, to the Father, and to the Son. and to the Holy Spirit, now, and ever, and unto ages of ages.

Choir. Amen.

Deacon. Again, yet again, in peace let us pray to the Lord. ℞

If there be no Deacon, the following LITANY *is omitted.*

For the peace that is from above, and for the salvation of our souls: ℞

For the peace of the whole world; for the welfare of God's holy Churches, and for the union of all: ℞

For this holy Temple, and for those who with faith, devoutness, and in the fear of God have entered therein: ℞

That he will deliver us from all tribulation, wrath, and necessity: ℞

let us pray to the Lord. Choir. Lord, have mercy.

The Priest saith, secretly, *the* SECOND PRAYER OF THE FAITHFUL.

O Master, holy and exceeding good, we beseech thee, who art rich in mercy, that thou wilt show compassion on us sinners, and render us worthy to receive thine Only-begotten Son and our God, the King of glory. For behold, his most pure Body and his life-giving Blood, entering at this present hour, are about to be spread forth upon this mystical Altar, invisibly escorted by a great multitude of the Heavenly Host. Enable us to partake of them in blamelessness; that, the eyes of our understanding being enlightened thereby, we may become children of the light and of the day.

Secretly.

Succour us, save us, have mercy upon us, and keep us, O God, by thy grace.

Choir. Lord, have mercy.

Deacon. Wisdom!   *Exclamation.*

Priest. Through the gift of thy Christ, with whom thou art blessed, together with thy most holy, and good, and life-giving Spirit, now, and ever, and unto ages of ages.

Choir. Amen.

(Here the Holy Door is opened.)

In place of the Cherubimic Hymn there shall now be sung:

Now the Powers of Heaven with us invisibly do minister. For lo! the King of Glory entereth now. Behold the Mystical Sacrifice, all accomplished, is ushered in.

(Here the Great Entrance is made.)

Let us with faith and love draw near, that we may become partakers of life everlasting. Alleluia, alleluia, alleluia.

At a Pontifical Service the Bishop washeth his hands in front of the Holy Door. (See p. 79.) Then his pall (omofór) is put on him, and he maketh three lowly reverences before the Holy Altar, saying: Now the Powers of Heaven. . . . Then he goeth to the Table of Oblation, and maketh three reverences, saying: O God, cleanse thou me, a sinner: removeth his mitre, giveth his pall to the Deacon, and censeth the Table of Oblation thrice, after which he giveth the censer to the Proto-Deacon; and taking the air in both hands, he layeth it on the shoulder of the Proto-Deacon.

Bishop.

And while this is being sung the Deacon entereth the Sanctuary through the north door, and censeth the Holy Altar and the holy oblation and the Priest. And they stand there, saying thrice: Now the Powers of Heaven. . . . And having made three lowly reverences, they go to the Chapel of Oblation; and the Priest bringeth the Holy Gifts, as usual, after he hath made three lowly reverences before the Table of Oblation, saying: O God, cleanse thou me, a sinner. While the Divine Mysteries are being borne in solemn silence from the Chapel of Oblation to the Altar, all the People and the Singers, kneeling humbly, render divine reverence to Christ our God, who is in the Holy Mysteries; for they are presanctified. After the Holy Gifts have been brought to the Altar, all stand, and the Singers finish the Hymn, as indicated: Let us with faith and love draw near:

After the Holy Gifts have been placed on the Altar, the Priest taketh the veil from the Holy Gifts and the air from the shoulder of the Deacon, approacheth the air to the censer, and covereth therewith with fragrance the Holy Gifts.

Secretly.

The Bishop then taketh the holy paten with both hands, and having kissed it, he setteth it on the head of the senior Priest, but saith nothing. The Priest kisseth the Bishop's hand. Another Priest, after making a reverence to the Bishop, taketh from him the holy chalice, and kisseth his hand. The other Priests who take part in the celebration carry the cross, the spoon, the spear, and the rest of the holy utensils, and kiss the Bishop's hand. And all come forth in the same order as at the Great Entrance in the Liturgy of St. John Chrysostom or St. Basil the Great.

(Bishop.)

When the Bishop cometh to the Holy Door, the Proto-Deacon taketh his stand opposite him and censeth him. The Bishop, taking the censer, censeth the Holy Gifts thrice, and having made a reverence, he receiveth the holy paten from the head of the Senior Priest, kisseth it, and showeth it to the People, without saying anything. And the Priest bearing the chalice entereth the Sanctuary, saying nothing. But the Bishop setteth the holy chalice upon the Altar. The other Priests enter the Sanctuary without saying anything.

The Bishop removeth the air from the shoulder of the Proto-Deacon, holdeth it over the censer, and covereth the paten and the chalice with fragrance, saying nothing. Then he putteth on his mitre, and censeth the Holy Gifts only, and maketh three reverences, and giveth the censer to the Deacon, without censing, any one.

And he bestoweth his blessing on the People, as usual, with the dikíri and the trikíri while the Choir singeth: Eis pollá éti, Déspota.

(Bishop.) Secretly.

Then the Priest saith, aloud, the PRAYER OF ST. EPHRAIM THE SYRIAN; *and maketh the prescribed reverences, the People kneeling with him.*

O Lord and Master of my life, grant not unto me a spirit of slothfulness, of discouragement, of lust of power, of vain babbling. (*Reverence.*)

But vouchsafe unto me, thy servant, the spirit of continence, of meekness, of patience, and of love. (*Reverence.*)

Yea, O Lord and King, grant that I may perceive my own transgressions, and judge not my brother. For blessed art thou unto ages of ages. Amen. (*Reverence.*)

Here the Holy Door is closed, and the curtain is drawn halfway. (5)

Then the Deacon goeth to his accustomed place, and saith:

Let us complete our evening prayer unto the Lord.

Choir. Lord, have mercy.

For the Precious Gifts spread forth and presanctified: ℟

That our God, who loveth mankind, accepting them upon his holy and most heavenly and supersensual Altar, in the odour of a spiritual sweet savour, will send down upon us in return his divine grace and the gift of the Holy Spirit: ℟

That he will deliver us from all tribulation, wrath and necessity: ℟

Succour us, save us, have mercy upon us, and keep us, O God, by thy grace.

Choir. Lord, have mercy.

let us pray to the Lord. Choir. Lord, have mercy.

The Priest prayeth, secretly.

O God of ineffable and invisible Mysteries, with whom are the hidden treasures of wisdom and knowledge, who hast revealed unto us the service of this Ministry, and hast appointed unto us sinners, through thy great love towards mankind, to offer unto thee gifts and sacrifices for our sins, and for the errors of thy people: Do thou, the same Invisible King, who doest things great and inscrutable, glorious and marvellous, which cannot be numbered, look upon us, thine unworthy servants who stand at this Holy

Secretly.

An evening all perfect, holy, peaceful and sinless: ℞

An Angel of Peace, the faithful guide and guardian both of our souls and bodies: ℞

The pardon and remission of our sins and transgressions: ℞

All things which are good and profitable to our souls, and peace to the world: ℞

That we may pass the residue of our life in peace and penitence: ℞

A Christian ending to our life; painless, blameless, peaceful; and a good defence before the dread Judgment Seat of Christ: ℞

Calling to remembrance our most holy, all-undefiled, most blessed and glorious Lady, the Birth-giver of God and ever-virgin Mary, with all the Saints, let us commend ourselves, and each other, and all our life unto Christ our God.

Choir. To thee, O Lord.

let us beseech of the Lord. Choir. Grant it, O Lord.

Altar as at thy Cherubimic throne, upon which lieth thine Only-begotten Son and our God, in the dread Mysteries spread forth thereon; and having delivered us and all thy faithful people from every impurity, hallow all our souls and bodies with the sanctification which cannot be taken away. That partaking with a pure conscience, with faces unashamed, with hearts illumined, of these divine, consecrated Gifts, and being quickened through them, we may be united unto thy Christ himself, our true God, who hath said: Whoso eateth my flesh and drinketh my blood abideth in me and I in him; that thy Word, O Lord, making its abode in us and accompanying our path, we may become the temple of thine all-holy and adorable Spirit, redeemed from every wile of the Devil, wrought either by deed or word or thought; and may ob-

Secretly.

tain the good things promised unto us, with all thy Saints, who in all the ages have been acceptable in thy sight.

Exclamation.

And vouchsafe, O Lord, that with boldness, and without condemnation, we may dare to call upon thee, the God of heaven and our Father, and to say:

Our Father, who art in heaven, Hallowed be thy Name. Thy kingdom come. Thy will be done on earth, As it is in heaven. Give us this day our daily bread. And forgive us our trespasses, As we forgive those who trespass against us. And lead us not into temptation; But deliver us from the Evil One:

Priest. For thine is the kingdom, and the power, and the glory, of the Father, and of the Son, and of the Holy Spirit, now, and ever, and unto ages of ages.

Choir. Amen.

Priest. Peace be with you.

Choir. And with thy spirit.

Priest. Bow your heads unto the Lord.

Choir. To thee, O Lord.

The Priest, bowing his head, prayeth secretly.

O God, who alone art good and of tender compassion; who dwellest on high and regardest the humble of heart: Look with the eye of thy tender loving-kindness upon all thy people, and preserve them.   And graciously enable us all to partake without condemnation of these thy life-giving Mysteries: for unto thee have we bowed our heads, in the hope of thy rich mercies. *Secretly.*

Exclamation.

Priest. Through the grace, and bounties, and love towards mankind of thine Only-begotten Son, with whom thou art blessed, together with thine all-holy, and good, and life-giving Spirit, now, and ever, and unto ages of ages.

Choir. Amen.

The Priest, secretly.

Hear us, O Lord Jesus Christ our God, from thy holy dwelling-place, and from the throne of glory of thy kingdom; and come and cleanse us, O thou who sittest on high with the Father, and art here invisibly present with us: and graciously vouchsafe, by thy mighty hand, to impart unto us thy most holy Body, and thy most precious Blood, and by us to all thy people. *Secretly.*

And after the Prayer, the Priest and Deacon make three reverences, saying:

O God, cleanse thou me, a sinner.

Then the Priest, the Holy Gifts being still covered, laying on his hand doth (6) *touch the life-giving Bread with great reverence and fear.   And the Deacon saith:*

Let us attend.

The Priest exclaimeth:

The Presanctified Holy Things to the holy.

Choir. One only is holy, one only is the Lord, Jesus Christ, in the glory of God the Father.   Amen.

(The rest of the curtain is now drawn.)

And when the Priest hath said: The Presanctified Holy Things to the holy: *he layeth aside the holy veil, and the Deacon entereth the holy Sanctuary; and standing near the Priest, he saith:*

Break, Master, the holy Bread. *Secretly.*

And the Priest, with great heedfulness, breaketh it into four pieces, saying:

Broken and divided is the Lamb of God, which is broken, yet not disunited; ever eaten, yet never consumed, but sanctifieth those who partake thereof.

And he layeth a portion on the paten, saying nothing: and the Deacon poureth the warm water into the chalice, saying nothing. And he standeth a little apart. Then the Priest saith:

Deacon, draw near.

And the Deacon, approaching, maketh a devout reverence, asking forgiveness, and saith:

Lo, I draw near unto the King immortal, and to God.

Impart unto me, Master, the precious and holy Body and Blood of our Lord, and God, and Saviour, Jesus Christ.

And the Priest, taking a portion of the Holy Mysteries, giveth it to the Deacon, saying:

To N., Deacon, is imparted the precious, and holy, and all-pure Body and Blood of our Lord, and God, and Saviour, Jesus Christ, unto the remission of his sins, and unto life everlasting.

And the Deacon, having kissed the Priest's hand, shall withdraw, and stand behind the Holy Altar; and bowing his head, he shall pray, like the Priest, I believe, O Lord, and I confess. . . . And the Priest also, taking in the same manner a portion of the Holy Mysteries, saith:

The precious and all-holy Body and Blood of our Lord, and God, and Saviour, Jesus Christ, is imparted to me, N., Priest, unto the remission of my sins, and unto life everlasting.

And bowing his head, he prayeth, saying:

I believe, O Lord, and I confess, that thou art, in very truth, the Christ the Son of the living God, who didst come into the world to save sinners, of whom I am chief. And I believe that this is, of a truth, thine all-pure Body, and that this is thine own precious Blood. Wherefore I beseech thee, have mercy upon me, and forgive my transgressions, whether voluntary or involuntary; whether of word or of deed; whether committed with knowledge or in ignorance. And vouchsafe that I may partake without condemnation of thine all-pure Mysteries, unto the remission of my sins, and unto life eternal.

Of thy Mystical Supper, O Son of God, accept me to-day as a communicant: for I will not speak of thy Mystery to thine enemies, neither like Judas will I give thee a kiss; but like the thief will I confess thee: Remember me, O Lord, in thy kingdom. And let not this participation in thy Holy Mysteries be unto judgment upon me, or unto condemnation, O Lord, but unto the healing of soul and body.

Choir. THE SHORT CANON.

O taste, and see how good the Lord is. Alleluia, alleluia, alleluia.

Secretly.

And in this manner they partake of the Holy Mysteries, with awe and all godly fear.

Then he taketh the holy chalice with the veil in both hands, and drinketh from it, saying nothing; and wipeth his mouth and the holy chalice with the veil which is in his hands, setteth it on the Holy Altar, and saith, secretly, the PRAYER OF THANKSGIVING:

We give thanks unto thee, O God, the Saviour of all men, for all the good things which thou hast vouchsafed unto us, and for the Communion of the holy Body and Blood of thy Christ. And we beseech thee, O Lord, who lovest mankind, to keep us under the shelter of thy wings. And grant that, even to our last breath, we may worthily partake of thy Holy Things, unto the illumination of soul and body, and unto the inheritance of the kingdom of heaven.

Secretly.

The Deacon doth not drink from the chalice at this time, but after the Prayer before the Tribune, and after the remaining particles of the Holy Mysteries have been consumed. (But if the Priest celebrate alone, without a Deacon, he, also, doth not drink from the chalice after his Communion, but after the Liturgy is finished, and after the Holy Mysteries have been consumed. For if the wine be sanctified by placing in it the particles, yet hath it not been transmuted into the Divine Blood, seeing that the words of consecration are not recited over it in this service, as they are in the Liturgies of Basil the Great and John Chrysostom.) And the Deacon, taking the holy paten, approacheth it to the holy chalice, and putteth in the Holy Gifts, saying nothing. And having made three reverences, he draweth aside the curtain, and openeth the Holy Door.

But if there be Communicants from the People, the Deacon, having covered the Holy Things as usual, and drawn aside the curtain, and opened the Holy Door, taketh the sacred chalice from the hands of the Priest or the Bishop, and saith:

In the fear of God, and with faith, draw near.

And the Communion is administered as usual. (As a rule, infants are not admitted to this Communion.)

Exclamation.

Priest. O God, save thy people, and bless thine heritage.

Choir. I will bless the Lord at all times. His praise shall continually be in my mouth. Taste ye the heavenly Bread and the Cup of Life, and see how good the Lord is. Alleluia, alleluia, alleluia.

And when he hath censed the Holy Things, he giveth the censer to the Deacon. And taking the holy paten, he setteth it on the head of the Deacon. And the Deacon, taking it with all reverence, gazeth out through the Holy Door, but doth not say anything; and he goeth to the Chapel of Oblation, and there setteth it down. Then the Priest taketh the holy chalice, and turning towards the Holy Door, he looketh forth upon the People, saying, secretly:

Blessed is our God.

And aloud:

Always, now, and ever, and unto ages of ages.

And he beareth the Holy Things to the Chapel of Oblation.

Choir. Amen.

Let our mouths be filled with thy praise, O Lord, that we may extol thy glory: for that thou hast deigned to make us partakers of thy holy, divine, immortal and life-giving Mysteries. Establish us in thy Sanctification, that all the day long we may meditate upon thy righteousness.   Alleluia, alleluia, alleluia.

Deacon. Having received the divine, holy, pure, immortal, heavenly, life-giving and terrible Mysteries of Christ, O believers, let us worthily give thanks unto the Lord.

Choir. Lord, have mercy.

Succour us, save us, have mercy upon us, and keep us, O God, by thy grace.

Choir. Lord, have mercy.

Having besought an evening all-perfect, holy, peaceful and sinless, let us commend ourselves, and each other, and all our life unto Christ our God.

Choir. To thee, O Lord.

(*Here the corporal is folded, and the book of the Holy Gospel is set upon it.*)

Exclamation.

Priest. For thou art our sanctification, and unto thee we ascribe glory, to the Father, and to the Son, and to the Holy Spirit, now, and ever, and unto ages of ages.

Choir. Amen.

Priest. Let us depart in peace.

Choir. In the Name of the Lord.

Deacon. Let us pray to the Lord.

Choir. Lord, have mercy.

The PRAYER BEFORE THE TRIBUNE *is then said,* aloud:

O Almighty Lord, who hast made all created things in wisdom, and by thine inexpressible Providence and great goodness hast brought us to these all-holy days, for the purification of body and soul, for the controlling of carnal passions, and for the hope of the Resurrection; who, during the forty days didst give into the hand of thy servant Moses the Tables of the Law, in characters divinely traced by thee: Enable us also, O Good One, to fight the good fight; to accomplish the course of the Fast; to preserve inviolate the faith; to crush under foot the heads of invisible serpents; to be accounted victors over sin; and uncondemned to attain unto and adore the holy Resurrection.   For blessed and glorified is thine all-honourable and majestic Name, of the Father, and of the Son, and of the Holy Spirit, now, and ever, and unto ages of ages.

Choir. Amen.

Blessed be the Name of the Lord henceforth and for ever. (*Thrice.*)

And Psalm xxxiv.: I will alway give thanks. . . . (*See page* 121.)

The Priest, secretly:

O Lord our God, who hast brought us to these all-holy days, and hast made us partakers of thy terrible Mysteries: Unite us to thy rational flock, and make us heirs of thy kingdom, now, and ever, and unto ages of ages.   Amen.

Secretly.

Then the Priest cometh forth, and standing in his accustomed place, he saith:

The blessing of the Lord, through his grace and love towards mankind, be upon you always, now, and ever, and unto ages of ages.

Choir. Amen.

Priest. Glory to thee, Christ-God, our sure hope; glory to thee.

Choir. Glory . . . now and ever . . . Lord, have mercy. (*Thrice.*) Master, bless.

Then he bestoweth the BENEDICTION.

May Christ our true God, through the prayers of his all-holy Mother; of the holy, glorious and all-laudable Apostles; and of Saint N. (*the Saint of the day*); and of our father in the Saints, Gregory Homiliastes, and of all the Saints, have mercy upon us and save us, forasmuch as he is good and loveth mankind.

After this Final Benediction, the rest of the ceremony followeth as at the ordinary Liturgy; except that instead of the Hymns there used, the Hymn here following is read:

Hymn in Tone IV.

That which constituteth the verity of things revealed thee as a Rule of the faith, a Pattern of meekness and a Preceptor of continence to thy flock: wherefore thou, through humility, didst win exaltation, and by poverty didst win wealth. O Father Gregory, pray thou unto Christ our God, that he will save our souls.

Glory to the Father, and to the Son, and to the Holy Spirit, now, and ever, and unto ages of ages. Amen.

HYMN TO THE HOLY BIRTH-GIVER OF GOD.

O Protection of Christians that maketh not ashamed, O Mediatrix never-failing with the Creator: Despise not the sinners' voice of supplication; but in that thou art good, come speedily to the aid of us who faithfully call upon thee; make haste to our petition and further our prayer, O Birth-giver of God, who ever protectest them that do thee honour.

END.

(GENERAL NOTE. — *If a Bishop be the celebrant, he communicateth himself and the Clergy as indicated in the Liturgy of St. John Chrysostom and St. Basil; and the Choir chanteth at the usual places:* Eis pollá éti, Déspota.)

THE OFFICE OF GRAND COMPLINE *

The Priest saith: Blessed is our God always, now, and ever, and unto ages of ages.

Reader. Amen. Glory to thee, our God; glory to thee.

O heavenly King, the Comforter, Spirit of Truth, who art in all places and fillest all things; Treasury of good things and Giver of life: Come and take up thine abode in us, and cleanse us from every stain; and save our souls, O Good One.

O Holy God, Holy Mighty, Holy Immortal One, have mercy upon us. (*Thrice, and three reverences.*)

Glory to the Father, and to the Son, and to the Holy Spirit, now, and ever, and unto ages of ages. Amen.

O all-holy Trinity, have mercy upon us. O Lord, wash away our sins. O Master, pardon our transgressions. O Holy One, visit and heal our infirmities, for thy Name's sake.

Lord, have mercy. (*Thrice.*)

Glory to the Father, and to the Son, and to the Holy Spirit, now, and ever, and unto ages of ages. Amen.

Our Father, who art in heaven, Hallowed be thy Name. Thy kingdom come. Thy will be done on earth, As it is in heaven. Give us this day our daily bread. And forgive us our trespasses, As we forgive those who trespass against us. And lead us not into temptation; But deliver us from the Evil One:

Priest. For thine is the kingdom, and the power, and the glory of the Father, and of the Son, and of the Holy Spirit, now, and ever, and unto ages of ages.

Reader. Amen.—— Lord, have mercy. (*Twelve times.*)

O come, let us worship God our King. O come, let us worship and fall down before Christ, our King and our God. O come, let us worship and fall down before the Very Christ, our King and our God. (*Three reverences.*)

And if it be during the first week of the Great Fast (Lent), we begin:
PSALM LXX.

Haste thee, O God, to deliver me; make haste to help me, O Lord. Let them be ashamed and confounded that seek after my soul; let them be turned backward and put to confusion that wish me evil. Let them for their reward be soon brought to shame, that

Lent.

* Grand Compline is said not only alone, but also in conjunction with Matins (Vespers being said separately) to form the All-Night Vigil Service on the Eves of Christmas and the Epiphany; and sometimes on the Eve of the Annunciation.

cry over me, There! there! But let all those that seek thee be joyful and glad in thee: and let all such as delight in thy salvation say
alway, The Lord be praised. As for me, I am poor and in misery:
haste thee unto me, O God. Thou art my helper and my redeemer:
O Lord, make no long tarrying.

And when this is finished, the Great Canon of St. Andrew of Crete is chanted.

But otherwise, the beginning is as followeth:

PSALM IV.

Hear me, when I call, O God of my righteousness: thou hast set me at
liberty, when I was in trouble; have mercy upon me, and hearken unto
my prayer. O ye sons of men, how long will ye blaspheme mine honour,
and have such pleasure in vanity, and seek after falsehood? Know this
also, that the Lord hath chosen to himself the man that is godly; when I
call upon the Lord he will hear me. Stand in awe, and sin not; commune
with your own heart, and in your chamber, and be still. Offer the sacrifice of righteousness, and put your trust in the Lord. There be many
that say, Who will show us any good? Lord, lift thou up the light of thy
countenance upon us. Thou hast put gladness in my heart, since the time
that their corn, and wine, and oil increased. I will lay me down in peace,
and take my rest; for it is thou, Lord, only, that makest me dwell in safety.

PSALM VI.

O Lord, rebuke me not in thine indignation, neither chasten me in thy
displeasure. Have mercy upon me, O Lord, for I am weak; O Lord, heal
me, for my bones are vexed. My soul also is sore troubled: but, Lord,
how long wilt thou punish me? Turn thee, O Lord, and deliver my soul;
O save me, for thy mercy's sake. For in death no man remembereth thee;
and who will give thee thanks in the pit? I am weary of my groaning:
every night wash I my bed, and water my couch with my tears. My
beauty is gone for very trouble, and worn away because of all mine
enemies. Away from me, all ye that work vanity; for the Lord hath
heard the voice of my weeping. The Lord hath heard my petition; the
Lord will receive my prayer. All mine enemies shall be confounded, and
sore vexed; they shall be turned back, and put to shame suddenly.

PSALM XIII.

How long wilt thou forget me, O Lord; for ever? how long wilt thou
hide thy face from me? How long shall I seek counsel in my soul, and be
so vexed in my heart? how long shall mine enemies triumph over me?
Consider, and hear me, O Lord my God: lighten mine eyes, that I sleep
not in death; lest mine enemy say, I have prevailed against him: for if I be
cast down, they that trouble me will rejoice at it. But my trust is in thy
mercy, and my heart is joyful in thy salvation. I will sing of the Lord,
because he hath dealt so lovingly with me; yea, I will praise the Name of
the Lord most Highest. Consider, and hear me, O Lord my God: lighten

mine eyes, that I sleep not in death; lest mine enemy say, I have prevailed against him.

Glory to the Father, and to the Son, and to the Holy Spirit, now, and ever, and unto ages of ages. Amen.

Alleluia, alleluia, alleluia. Glory to thee, O God. (*Thrice, and three reverences.*)

Lord, have mercy. (*Thrice.*)

Glory . . . now, and ever, . . .

PSALM XXV.

Unto thee, O Lord, will I lift up my soul; my God, I have put my trust in thee: O let me not be confounded, neither let mine enemies triumph over me. For all they that hope in thee shall not be ashamed; but such as transgress without a cause shall be put to confusion. Show me thy ways, O Lord, and teach me thy paths. Lead me forth in thy truth, and learn me: for thou art the God of my salvation; in thee hath been my hope all the day long. Call to remembrance, O Lord, thy tender mercies, and thy loving-kindnesses, which have been ever of old. O remember not the sins and offences of my youth; but according to thy mercy think thou upon me, O Lord, for thy goodness. Gracious and righteous is the Lord; therefore will he teach sinners in the way. Them that are meek shall he guide in judgment: and such are as gentle, them shall he learn his way. All the paths of the Lord are mercy and truth, unto such as keep his covenant and his testimonies. For thy Name's sake, O Lord, be merciful unto my sin; for it is great. What man is he that feareth the Lord? him shall he teach in the way that he shall choose. His soul shall dwell at ease, and his seed shall inherit the land. The secret of the Lord is among them that fear him; and he will show them his covenant. Mine eyes are ever looking unto the Lord; for he shall pluck my feet out of the net. Turn thee unto me, and have mercy upon me; for I am desolate, and in misery. The sorrows of my heart are enlarged: O bring thou me out of my troubles. Look upon my adversity and misery, and forgive me all my sin. Consider mine enemies, how many they are; and they bear a tyrannous hate against me. O keep my soul, and deliver me; let me not be confounded, for I have put my trust in thee. Let perfectness and righteous dealing wait upon me; for my hope hath been in thee. Deliver Israel, O God, out of all his troubles.

PSALM XXXI.

In thee, O Lord, have I put my trust; let me never be put to confusion; deliver me in thy righteousness. Bow down thine ear to me; make haste to deliver me. And be thou my strong rock, and house of defence, that thou mayest save me. For thou art my strong rock, and my castle: be thou also my guide, and lead me for thy Name's sake. Draw me out of the net that they have laid privily for me: for thou art my strength. Into thy hands I commend my spirit; for thou hast redeemed me, O Lord, thou God of truth. I have hated them that hold of superstitious vanities, and my trust hath been in the Lord. I will be glad, and rejoice in thy mercy; for thou hast considered my trouble, and hast known my soul in adversities. Thou hast not shut me up into the hand of the enemy; but hast set my feet in a large room. Have mercy upon me, O Lord, for I am in trouble, and mine eye is consumed for very heaviness; yea my soul and my body. For my life is waxen old with heaviness, and my years with mourning. My strength faileth me, because of mine iniquity, and my bones are consumed. I became a reproof among all mine enemies, but especially among my neighbours, and they of mine acquaintance were afraid of me; and they that did see me without, conveyed themselves from me. I am clean forgotten as a dead man out of mind; I am become like a broken vessel. For I have heard the blasphemy of the multitude, and fear is on every side; while they conspire together against me, and take their counsel to take away my life. But my hope hath been in thee, O Lord; I have said, Thou art my God. My time is in thy hand; deliver me from the hand of mine enemies, and from them that persecute me. Show thy servant the light of thy countenance, and save me for thy mercy's sake. Let me not be confounded, O Lord, for I have called upon thee; let the ungodly be put to confusion, and be put to silence in the grave. Let the lying lips be put to silence, which cruelly, disdainfully, and despitefully speak against the righteous. O how plentiful is thy goodness, which thou hast laid up for them that fear thee, and that thou hast prepared for them that put their trust in thee, even before the sons of men! Thou shalt hide them privily by thine own presence from the provoking of all men: thou shalt keep them secretly in thy tabernacle from the strife of tongues. Thanks be to the Lord; for he hath showed me marvellous great kindness in a strong city. And when I made haste, I said, I am cast out of the sight of thine eyes. Nevertheless, thou heardest the voice of my prayer, when I cried unto thee. O love the Lord, all ye his saints; for the Lord preserveth them that are faithful, and plenteously rewardeth the proud doer. Be strong, and he shall establish your heart, all ye that put your trust in the Lord.

Psalm xci.

Whoso dwelleth under the defence of the Most High, shall abide under the shadow of the Almighty. I will say unto the Lord, Thou art my hope, and my stronghold; my God, in him will I trust. For he shall deliver thee from the snare of the hunter, and from the noisome pestilence. He shall defend thee under his wings, and thou shalt be safe under his feathers; his faithfulness and truth shall be thy shield and buckler. Thou shalt not be afraid for any terror by night, nor for the arrow that flieth by day; for the pestilence that walketh in darkness, nor for the sickness that destroyeth in the noonday. A thousand shall fall beside thee, and ten thousand at thy right hand; but it shall not come nigh thee.   Yea, with thine eyes shalt thou behold, and see the reward of the ungodly.   For thou, Lord, art my hope; thou hast set thine house of defence very high.   There shall no evil happen unto thee, neither shall any plague come nigh thy dwelling. For he shall give his angels charge over thee, to keep thee in all thy ways. They shall bear thee in their hands, that thou hurt not thy foot against a stone.   Thou shalt go upon the lion and adder: the young lion and the dragon shalt thou tread under thy feet.   Because he hath set his love upon me, therefore will I deliver him; I will set him up, because he hath known my Name.   He shall call upon me, and I will hear him; yea, I am with him in trouble; I will deliver him and bring him to honour.   With long life will I satisfy him, and show him my salvation.

Glory to the Father, and to the Son, and to the Holy Spirit, now, and ever, and unto ages of ages.   Amen.

Alleluia, alleluia, alleluia: glory to thee, O God.   (*Thrice, and three reverences.*)   Lord, have mercy. · (*Thrice.*)   Glory . . . now, and ever, . . .

Then the Choir chanteth the Verses, singing them with sweet melody, slowly and loudly.

God is with us: understand, ye nations, and submit yourselves: for God is with us.

And the second Choir repeateth the same.

Then each Choir singeth a Verse in turn.   And to each Verse the Refrain is sung:
For God is with us.

Hear ye, even unto the uttermost ends of the earth: ℞
Submit yourselves, ye mighty ones:
If again ye shall rise up in your might, again shall ye be overthrown: ℞
If any take counsel together, them shall the Lord destroy: ℞
And the word which ye shall speak shall not abide in you: ℞
For we fear not your terror, neither are we troubled: ℞
But the Lord our God, he it is to whom we will ascribe holiness, and him will we fear: ℞
And if I put my trust in him, he shall be my sanctification: ℞
I will set my hope on him, and through him shall I be saved: ℞
Lo, I and the children whom God hath given me: ℞
The people that walked in darkness have seen a great light: ℞
And they that dwelt in the land of the shadow of death, on them hath the light shined: ℞
For unto us a son is born, unto us a child is given: ℞ ·
And the government shall be upon his shoulder: ℞
And of his peace there shall be no end: ℞
And his Name shall be called the great Council of the Angels: ℞
Wonderful, Counsellor: ℞

Refrain. For God is with us.

The Mighty God, the Everlasting Father, the Prince of Peace: ℞

The Father of the world to come: ℞

And when the Verses have been sung by the Choirs alternately, as ordered, there is sung:

God is with us: understand, ye nations, and submit yourselves: for God is with us.

Then both Choirs sing, once: Glory . . . *First Choir.* For God is with us. Now, and ever, . . . *Second Choir*, For God is with us.

Then both Choirs. For God is with us.

And immediately, the following Hymns:

The day is past; I thank thee, O Lord: Grant me, I entreat thee, that this evening and this night I fall into no sin; and save me, O Saviour.

Second Choir. Glory . . . The day is past; I sing praises unto thee, O Master. Grant, I entreat thee, that this evening and this night I may be without guile; and save me, O Saviour:

Both Choirs. Now, and ever, . . . The day is past: I hymn thee, O Holy One. Grant, I entreat thee, that this evening and this night I may be assailed by no temptation; and save me, O Saviour.

The Choirs, in unison: With songs unceasing the Bodiless Powers of the Cherubim glorify thee; the six-winged beings, the Seraphim, with voices perpetual, extol thee exceedingly. With thrice-holy songs, all the Host of the Angels laud thee. For thou art the Father before all worlds, and hast with thee thy Son, who also is from everlasting; and hast also the Spirit of Life, coequal in honour, and showest forth the Trinity Undivided. O most holy Virgin, Mother of God, and ye eye-witnesses and servants of the Word, with all the company of the Prophets and the Martyrs, who have attained unto life immortal: Pray ye zealously for us all, for all we are in dire distress; that, being delivered from the wiles of the Evil One, we may loudly sing the Angelic Song: Holy, Holy, Holy Thrice-Holy Lord, have mercy upon us, and save us. Amen.

And immediately, in a lower voice:

I believe in one God the Father Almighty, Maker of heaven and earth, And of all things visible and invisible:

And in one Lord Jesus Christ, Son of God, the only-begotten, Begotten of his Father before all worlds; Light of Light, Very God of very God, Begotten, not made, Being of one Essence with the Father; By whom all things were made; Who, for us men, and for our salvation, came down from heaven, And was incarnate by the Holy Ghost of the Virgin Mary, And was made man. And was crucified also for us under Pontius Pilate; and suffered and was buried. And the third day he rose again, according to the Scriptures. And ascended into heaven, And sitteth on the right hand of the Father. And he shall come again with glory to judge both the quick and the dead; Whose kingdom shall have no end.

And in the Holy Ghost, the Lord and Giver of Life, Who proceedeth from the Father, Who with the Father and the Son together is worshipped and glorified, Who spake by the Prophets.   In one Holy Catholic and Apostolic Church.   I acknowledge one Baptism for the remission of sins. I look for the Resurrection of the dead, And the Life of the world to come. Amen.

Then straightway the ALL-HOLY:

O all-holy Sovereign Lady, Birth-giver of God, pray for us sinners. (*Thrice.*)

O all ye heavenly Host of Angels and Archangels, pray for us sinners. (*Twice.*)

O holy John, Prophet, and Forerunner, and Baptist of our Lord Jesus Christ, pray for us sinners.   (*Twice.*)

O holy, glorious Apostles, Prophets and Martyrs, and all Saints, pray for us sinners.   (*Twice.*)

O ye, our reverend and God-fearing Fathers, Pastors and Œcumenical Teachers, pray for us sinners.   (*Twice.*)

Then the Patron Saint of the Church is invoked:

O invincible, and ineffable, and divine power of the Honourable and Life-giving Cross, forsake not us sinners.   (*Twice.*)

O God, cleanse us sinners.   (*Twice.*)

O God, cleanse us sinners, and have mercy upon us.

O Holy God, Holy Mighty, . . . Glory . . . now, and ever, . . . O all-holy Trinity, . . . Lord, have mercy.   (*Thrice.*)   Glory . . . now, and ever, . . . Our Father, . . . Lord, have mercy.   (*Twelve times.*)   Glory . . . now, and ever, . . . (*See page* 147.)

And if a Feast be impending, then the Hymns for that Feast are sung.   Otherwise, the following Hymns are used:

On Monday and Wednesday Evenings, Tone II.:

Lighten mine eyes, O Christ-God, that I sleep not unto death; lest mine enemy say: I have prevailed against him.

Glory to the Father, and to the Son, and to the Holy Spirit.

Be thou the defender of my soul, O God, for I walk amid a multitude of snares.   Deliver me from them and save me, O Good One: for thou lovest mankind.

Now, and ever, and unto ages of ages.   Amen.

And since, through our manifold iniquities, we have no boldness, do thou, O Virgin Birth-giver of God, make fervent entreaty unto him who was born of thee: for the prayer of a mother availeth much unto the benignity of the Master.   Despise not the petitions of sinners, O All-Pure One; for gracious and mighty to save is he who deigned to suffer for us. (*A Hymn to the Birth-giver of God.*)

On Tuesday and Thursday Evenings the following Hymns shall be sung, Tone VIII.:

Thou knowest, O Lord my Creator, the sleepless vigilance of mine invisible enemies, and the frailty of my miserable flesh. Into thy hands, therefore, will I commit my spirit. Cover me with the wings of thy goodness, that I sleep not unto death; and enlighten the eyes of my spiritual understanding, that I may delight in thy divine words: and make me, in a time acceptable unto thee, to glorify thee in praise, as the only Good One who loveth mankind.

Verse: Look upon me, and give ear unto me, O Lord my God.

How terrible is thy Judgment, O Lord, when the angels stand round about, and men are led before thee; and the books are opened, and deeds are tried; and all thoughts are searched out. What judgment shall then be awarded unto me, who was conceived in sins? Who shall quench the flame for me? Who shall enlighten my darkness, if not thou, O Lord, who showest mercy upon me because of thy love towards mankind?

Glory to the Father, and to the Son, and to the Holy Spirit.

Grant me tears, O God, as once to the sinning woman of old: And graciously vouchsafe that I may wash thy feet which delivered me from the path of straying, and that I may offer unto thee an incense of sweet savour, even a pure life, fashioned by my repentance. And so shall I, also, hear thy voice which I long for, saying: Thy faith hath saved thee: go in peace.

Now, and ever, and unto ages of ages. Amen.

HYMN TO THE BIRTH-GIVER OF GOD.

In that I have in thee, O Birth-giver of God, that hope which maketh not ashamed, I shall be saved; in that I possess thy intercession, O All-Pure One, I will not fear. I will follow hard after mine enemies, and put them to flight, invested only, as it were in a cuirass, with thy protection and all-powerful aid, and fervently imploring I cry unto thee: O Lady, save me by thy prayers, and raise me up again from gloomy sleep to glorify thee in song, by the might of the Son of God, who through thee was made flesh.

Lord, have mercy. (*Forty times.*)

Glory . . . now, and ever . . .

More honourable than the Cherubim, and beyond compare more glorious than the Seraphim, thou who without defilement barest God the Word, true Birth-giver of God, we magnify thee.

Bless, Father, in the Name of the Lord.

Priest. Through the prayers of our holy Fathers, O Lord Jesus Christ our God, have mercy upon us. Amen.

Then shall this PRAYER OF ST. BASIL THE GREAT *be said:*

O Lord, Lord, who deliverest us from all the arrows that fly by day, deliver thou us, also, from all the things that infest the darkness. Accept our evening sacrifice, even the lifting-up of our hands. Grant that we may pass through the course of the night without sin, untempted of evil things; and deliver us from every alarm and cowardice that cometh to us from the Devil. Grant unto our souls contrition, and unto our minds anxiety concerning that strict searching out of the thoughts which shall come in thy dread and just Day of Judgment. Nail our flesh to the fear of thee, and mortify our earthly members: that, in the quietness of sleep, we may be illuminated by the vision of thy judgments. Remove from us, also, every unseemly imagination and hurtful carnal passion. Raise us up again at the hour of prayer fortified in the faith, and advancing in thy commandments; through the favour and goodness of thine Only-begotten Son, with whom thou art blessed together with thine all-holy, and good, and life-giving Spirit, now, and ever, and unto ages of ages. Amen.

Then immediately the Priest shall exclaim:

O come, let us worship God our King. O come, let us worship and fall down before Christ, our King and our God. O come, let us worship and fall down before the Very Christ, our King and our God. (*Three reverences.*)

Psalm LI.

Have mercy upon me, O God, after thy great goodness; according to the multitude of thy mercies do away mine offences. Wash me throughly from my wickedness, and cleanse me from my sin. For I acknowledge my faults, and my sin is ever before me. Against thee only have I sinned, and done this evil in thy sight; that thou mightest be justified in thy saying, and clear when thou art judged. Behold, I was shapen in wickedness, and in sin hath my mother conceived me. But lo, thou requirest truth in the inward parts, and shalt make me to understand wisdom secretly. Thou shalt purge me with hyssop, and I shall be clean; thou shalt wash me, and I shall be whiter than snow. Thou shalt make me hear of joy and gladness, that the bones which thou hast broken may rejoice. Turn thy face from my sins, and put out all my misdeeds. Make me a clean heart, O God, and renew a right spirit within me. Cast me not away from thy presence, and take not thy holy spirit from me. O give me the comfort of thy help again, and stablish me with thy free Spirit. Then shall I teach thy ways unto the wicked, and sinners shall be converted unto thee. Deliver me from blood-guiltiness, O God, thou that art the God of my health, and my tongue shall sing of thy righteousness. Thou shalt open my lips, O Lord, and my mouth shall show thy praise. For thou desirest no sacrifice, else would I give it thee; but thou delightest not in burnt-offerings. The sacrifice of God is a troubled spirit: a broken and contrite heart, O God, shalt thou not despise. O be favourable and gracious unto Sion: build thou the walls of Jerusalem. Then shalt thou be pleased with the sacrifice of righteousness, with the burnt-offerings and oblations: then shall they offer young bullocks upon thine altar.

Psalm CII.

Hear my prayer, O Lord, and let my crying come unto thee. Hide not thy face from me in the time of my trouble; incline thine ear unto me when I call; O hear me, and that right soon. For my days are consumed away like smoke, and my bones are burnt up as it were a firebrand. My heart is smitten down, and withered like grass; so that I forget to eat my bread. For the voice of my groaning, my bones will scarce cleave to my flesh. I am become like a pelican in the wilderness, and like an owl that is in the desert. I have watched, and am even as it were a sparrow, that sitteth alone upon the house-top. Mine enemies revile me all the day long; and they that are mad upon me are sworn together against me. For I have eaten ashes as it were bread, and mingled my drink with weeping; and that, because of thine indignation and wrath; for thou hast taken me up, and cast me down. My days are gone like a shadow, and I am withered like grass. But thou, O Lord, shalt endure forever, and thy remembrance throughout all generations. Thou shalt arise, and have mercy upon Sion; for it is time that thou have mercy upon her, yea, the time is come. And why? thy servants think upon her stones, and it pitieth them to see her in the dust. The heathen shall fear thy Name, O Lord: and all the kings of the earth thy majesty; when the Lord shall build up Sion, and when his glory shall appear; when he turneth him unto the prayer of the poor destitute, and despiseth not their desire. This shall be written for those that come after, and the people which shall be born shall praise the Lord. For he hath looked down from his sanctuary: out of the heaven did the Lord behold the earth; that he might hear the mournings of such as are in captivity, and deliver the children appointed unto death; that they may declare the Name of the Lord in Sion, and his worship at Jerusalem; when the people are gathered together, and the kingdoms also, to serve the Lord. He brought down my strength in my journey, and shortened my days. But I said, O my God, take me not away in the midst of mine age; as for thy years, they endure throughout all generations. Thou, Lord, in the beginning hast laid the foundation of the earth, and the heavens are the work of thy hands. They shall perish, but thou shalt endure: they all shall wax old as doth a garment; and as a vesture shalt thou change them, and they shall be changed; but thou art the same, and thy years shall not fail. The children of thy servants shall continue, and their seed shall stand fast in thy sight.

The Prayer of Manasses, *King of Judah.*

O Lord Almighty, thou God of our fathers, of Abraham, of Isaac, and of Jacob, and of their righteous seed; who hast made heaven and earth, with all the firmament thereof; who hast bound the sea with the word of thy commandment; who hast shut up the deep and sealed it with thy terrible and glorious Name: All creatures fear thee, yea, they do tremble before the presence of thy power; for the majesty of thy glory cannot be borne, and not to be resisted is the anger of thy threatening toward sinners; but thy merciful promise is unmeasurable and unsearchable. For thou art the Lord most high, of tender compassion, long-suffering, rich in mercy, and grievest over the evils of men. Thou, O Lord, according to the multitude of thy loving-kindness, hast promised repentance and forgiveness to those who have sinned against thee, and in the plenitude of thy compassions hast appointed repentance unto sinners, that they may be saved. Thou, therefore, the Lord God of Hosts, hast not appointed repentance to the just, to Abraham, and to Isaac, and to Jacob, who have not sinned against thee; but thou hast appointed repentance to me a sinner: for my sins are more in number than the sands of the sea. My transgressions are multiplied, O Lord, my transgressions are multiplied, and I am not worthy to behold and see the height of heaven because of the multitude of mine iniquities. I am bowed down with many iron bands, so that I cannot lift up my head by reason of my sins, neither have I any respite: for I have provoked thy wrath, and have done that which is evil in thy sight: I have not done thy will, neither have I kept thy commandments. Now, therefore, I bow the knees of my heart, supplicating grace of thee. I have sinned, O Lord, I have sinned, and I acknowledge mine iniquities: but I humbly beseech thee, forgive me, O Lord, forgive me, and destroy me not together with mine iniquities, neither preserve thou thy divine wrath against my evil deeds forever; neither condemn me to the lower parts of the earth. For thou, O God, art the God of those who are penitent; and in me wilt thou manifest all thy goodness; for thou wilt save me, unworthy though I be, because of thy great mercy, and I will praise thee henceforth, all the days of my life. For all the Host of heaven doth sing thy praise, and thine is the glory, unto ages of ages. Amen.

O Holy God, Holy Mighty, . . . (*See page* 147.) (*Thrice, with three reverences.*) Glory . . . now, and ever, . . . O all-holy Trinity, . . . Lord, have mercy. (*Thrice.*) Our Father, . . . Lord, have mercy. (*Twelve times.*) Glory . . . now, and ever . . .

Then shall be sung, in Tone VI., the following Hymns:

Have mercy upon us, O Lord, have mercy upon us. For we sinners, void of all defence, do offer unto thee this petition, as unto our Master: Have mercy upon us.

Glory to the Father, and to the Son, and to the Holy Spirit.

Have mercy upon us, O Lord, for we have put our trust in thee. Be not exceeding wroth with us, neither call to mind our iniquities; but look down upon us now, also, in thy loving-kindness, and deliver us from our enemies. For thou art our God, and we are thy people, we are all the work of thy hands, and we call upon thy Name.

Now, and ever, and unto ages of ages. Amen.

HYMN TO THE BIRTH-GIVER OF GOD (*Bogoróditchen*).

Open unto us the door of thy loving-kindness, O blessed Birth-giver of God. In that we have set our hope on thee, may we not fail; but through thee may we be delivered from adversities; for thou art the salvation of the race of all Christian people.

Lord, have mercy. (*Forty times.*) . . . Glory . . . now, and ever . . .

More honourable than the Cherubim, . . . (*See page* 154.)

In the Name of the Lord bless, Father.

Priest. Through the prayers of our holy fathers, O Lord Jesus Christ our God, have mercy upon us.

Amen.

And the Prayer:

O Sovereign Master, God, O Father Almighty, O Lord, the Only-begotten Son, Jesus Christ, and the Holy Spirit, one Godhead, one Power, have mercy upon me, a sinner; and by means which are known unto thee, save me, thine unworthy servant: for blessed art thou unto ages of ages. Amen.

Then: O come, let us worship . . . (*See page* 147.)

And then shall be read (except when the Great Canon is used):

PSALM LXX.

Haste thee, O God, to deliver me; make haste to help me, O Lord. Let them be ashamed and confounded that seek after my soul; let them be turned backward and put to confusion that wish me evil. Let them for their reward be soon brought to shame, that cry over me, There! there! But let all those that seek thee be joyful and glad in thee: and let all such as delight in thy salvation say alway, The Lord be praised. As for me, I am poor and in misery: haste thee unto me, O God. Thou art my helper, and my redeemer: O Lord, make no long tarrying.

PSALM CXLIII.

Hear my prayer, O Lord, and consider my desire; hearken unto me for thy truth and righteousness' sake. And enter not into judgment with thy servant; for in thy sight shall no man living be justified. For the enemy hath persecuted my soul; he hath smitten my life down to the ground; he hath laid me in the darkness, as the men that have been long dead. Therefore is my spirit vexed within me, and my heart within me is desolate. Yet do I remember the time past: I muse upon all thy works; yea, I exercise myself in the works of thy hands. I stretch forth my hands unto thee; my soul gaspeth unto thee as a thirsty land. Hear me, O Lord, and that soon; for my spirit waxeth faint: hide not thy face from me, lest I be like unto them that go down into the pit. O let me hear thy loving-kindness betimes in the morning; for in thee is my trust: show thou me the way that I should walk in; for I lift up my soul unto thee. Deliver me, O Lord, from mine enemies; for I flee unto thee to hide me.

Teach me to do the thing that pleaseth thee; for thou art my God: let thy loving Spirit lead me forth into the land of righteousness. Quicken me, O Lord, for thy Name's sake; and for thy righteousness' sake bring my soul out of trouble. And of thy goodness slay mine enemies, and destroy all them that vex my soul; for I am thy servant.

Glory be to God on high, and on earth peace, good will towards men. We praise thee, we bless thee, we worship thee, we glorify thee, we give thanks to thee for thy great glory, O Lord, heavenly King, God the Father Almighty. O Lord, the Only-begotten Son, Jesus Christ, and the Holy Spirit, O Lord God, Lamb of God, Son of the Father, that takest away the sins of the world, have mercy upon us. Thou that takest away the sins of the world, receive our prayer. Thou that sittest at the right hand of God, the Father, have mercy upon us. For thou only art holy; thou only art the Lord, O Jesus Christ, with the Holy Ghost, in the glory of God the Father. Amen.

Every night will I give thanks unto thee: and praise thy Name for ever and ever.

Lord, thou hast been our refuge, from one generation to another. I said, Lord, be merciful unto me: heal my soul, for I have sinned against thee. I flee unto thee. Teach me to do thy will; for thou art my God. For with thee is the well of life, and in thy light shall we see light. O continue forth thy loving-kindness unto them that know thee.

Vouchsafe, O Lord, to keep us this night without sin. Blessed art thou, O Lord, the God of our fathers, and praised and glorified is thy Name forever. Amen.

Let thy mercy be upon us, O Lord, even as we have set our hope on thee. Blessed art thou, O Lord; teach me thy statutes. Blessed art thou, O Master; make me to understand thy commandments. Blessed art thou, O Holy One; enlighten me with thy precepts.

Thy mercy, O Lord, endureth forever: O despise not the works of thy hands. To thee belongeth worship, to thee belongeth praise, to thee belongeth glory, to the Father, and to the Son, and to the Holy Spirit, now, and ever, unto ages of ages. Amen.

If it be the Eve of Christmas, the Epiphany, or the Annunciation, then shall be sung the Canon of the Saint of the day, or of the Birth-giver of God.

And at the conclusion of the Canon and the Hymns:

O Holy.God, Holy Mighty, . . . (*Thrice, with three reverences.*) Glory . . . now, and ever, . . . O all-holy Trinity, . . . Lord, have mercy. (*Thrice.*) Our Father, . . . For thine is the kingdom, . . . Lord, have mercy. (*Twelve times.*) Glory . . . now, and ever, . . . (*See page* 147.)

Then shall be sung, in Tone VI.:

O Lord of Hosts, be with us, for beside thee we have no other helper in adversity. Have mercy upon us, O Lord of Hosts.

PSALM CL.

First Choir, Verse 1: O praise God in his holiness: praise him in the firmament of his power.

Refrain: O Lord of Hosts, be with us; for beside thee we have no other helper in adversity. Have mercy upon us, O Lord of Hosts.

Second Choir, Verse 2: Praise him in his noble acts: praise him according to his excellent greatness.

And the Refrain after every Verse.

Praise him in the sound of the trumpet: praise him upon the lute and harp.

Praise him in the cymbals and dances: praise him upon the strings and pipe.

Praise him upon the well-tuned cymbals: praise him upon the loud cymbals. Let everything that hath breath praise the Lord.

O praise God in his holiness: praise him in the firmament of his power.

Glory to the Father, and to the Son, and to the Holy Spirit.

O Lord, if we had not thy Saints as our intercessors, and thy gracious loving-kindness which showeth mercy upon us, how should we presume, O Saviour, to sing unto thee, whom the Angels unceasingly do glorify in song? O thou who knowest hearts, spare thou our souls.

Now, and ever, and unto ages of ages. Amen.

Exceeding great, O Birth-giver of God, is the multitude of my transgressions; I have fled unto thee, O Pure One, entreating salvation. Visit thou my feeble soul, and pray to thy Son and our God that he will grant me remission of the terrible deeds which I have wrought, O Only-Blessed One.

O all-holy Birth-giver of God, forsake me not all the days of my life: Give me not over to the protection of men, but do thou thyself defend me and have mercy on me.

In thee put I my whole trust, O Mother of God: Keep me under thy protection. —— Lord, have mercy. (*Forty times.*)

Thou who, at all times and at every hour, . . . (*See page* 51.) Lord, have mercy. (*Thrice.*) Glory . . . now, and ever, . . .

More honourable than the Cherubim, . . . (*See page* 154.)

Bless, Father, in the Name of the Lord.

Priest. God, be merciful unto us, and bless us, and show us the light of his countenance, and be merciful unto us.

Then we make three great reverences, and recite the Prayer of St. Ephraim the Syrian. (See page 41.)

Then: O Holy God, Holy Mighty, . . . (*Thrice, with three reverences.*) Glory . . . now, and ever, . . . O all-holy Trinity, . . . Lord, have mercy. (*Thrice.*) Our Father, . . . For thine is the kingdom, . . . Lord, have mercy. (*Twelve times.*) Glory . . . now, and ever, . . . (*See page* 147.)

And the PRAYER OF SUPPLICATION TO THE MOST HOLY BIRTH-GIVER OF GOD, *of Paul, a Monk of the Monastery of the Benefactress.*

O Virgin, pure, spotless, incorrupt, undefiled, all-pure; thou Bride of God and Sovereign Lady, who didst unite the Word of God with men through thy most glorious birth-giving, and hast yoked the apostate nature of our race with the heavenly; who art the sole hope of the hopeless, and the helper of the assailed, a speedy defender of those who flee unto thee, and the refuge of all Christians: Hold not in loathing me, a sinner and polluted, who have made myself of no worth through my shameful thoughts, and words, and deeds, and who, through slothfulness of mind have been a slave to the carnal lusts of life. But, in that thou art the Mother of the God who loveth mankind, mercifully have compassion upon me, a sinner and a prodigal, and accept my prayer which is offered unto thee with lips impure; and exercising thy maternal boldness, importune thou thy Son, who is also our Master and our Lord, that he will open unto me also the compassionate loving-kindness of his goodness, and disregarding my countless wickednesses, will turn me again unto repentance, and show me forth a well-skilled doer of his commandments. And be thou ever present with me, in that thou art gracious, and pitiful, and full of loving-kindness: For thou art a fervent Mediatrix and Helper who, in this present life, repellest the assaults of adversaries, and guidest me unto salvation, and at the hour of death carest diligently for my wretched soul, driving far from it the dark forms of evil spirits; and in the dread Judgment Day thou shalt deliver me from torment eternal, and shalt manifest me an heir of the glory ineffable of thy Son and our God: All which I shall obtain, O Lady and most holy Birth-giver of God, by thy mediation and intercession, through the mercy and love toward mankind of thine Only-begotten Son, our Lord, and God, and Saviour, Jesus Christ, to whom are due all glory, honour and worship, together with his Father, who is from everlasting, and his all-holy, and good, and life-giving Spirit, now, and ever, and unto ages of ages. Amen.

Another Prayer, TO OUR LORD JESUS CHRIST, *by Antiochus, a Monk of the Monastery of the Pandect.*

And grant unto us, O Master, as we lay us down to sleep, repose both of body and of soul, and preserve us from the gloomy slumber of sin, and from every dark and nocturnal sensuality. Calm thou the impulses of carnal desires: quench the fiery darts of the Evil One which are craftily directed against us. Assuage the rebellions of our flesh. Still our every earthly and material anxiety; and vouchsafe unto us, O God, a watchful mind, a chaste reason, a sober heart, sleep gentle and free from every vision of the Devil; and raise us up again at the hour of prayer, strengthened in thy precepts, and holding steadfastly within us the memory of thy commandments. Grant that all the night long we may sing praises unto thee, and that we may hymn, and bless, and glorify thine all-honourable and majestic Name, of the Father, and of the Son, and of the Holy Spirit, now, and ever, and unto ages of ages.   Amen.

O exceeding glorious, ever-virgin Mother of Christ-God, bear thou our petitions unto thy Son and our God, and implore thou him that, through thee, he will save our souls.

Another Prayer, by St. Ioannikius.

The Father is my hope; the Son is my refuge; the Holy Spirit is my protector.   O Holy Trinity, glory to thee.

Glory to the Father, and to the Son, and to the Holy Spirit, now, and ever, and unto ages of ages.   Amen.

Lord, have mercy.   (*Thrice.*)   Bless.

And immediately the Priest saith, aloud, while we kneel humbly:

O Master, great in mercy, Lord Jesus Christ our God: through the prayers of our all-pure Lady, the Birth-giver of God and ever-virgin Mary; through the might of the precious and life-giving Cross; through the prayers of the honourable Bodiless Powers of Heaven; of the honourable, glorious Prophet, Forerunner and Baptist, John; of the holy, glorious and all-laudable Apostles; of the holy, glorious and gloriously triumphant Martyrs; of our venerable and God-bearing Fathers; of the holy, righteous Ancestors of God, Joachim and Anna; and of all thy Saints: Make our prayer acceptable.   Grant unto us remission of our iniquities. Hide us under the shadow of thy wings.   Drive far from us every foe and adversary.   Give peace to our life.   Have mercy upon us and upon thy world, O Lord, and save our souls, forasmuch as thou art merciful and lovest mankind.

Then the Superior maketh a reverence to the earth (if it be in a monastery), and saith to the Brethren:

Bless me, holy Fathers.   Pardon me, a sinner.

And the Brethren:

May God pardon thee, holy Father.

Let us pray for our most Holy Synod (*or* Patriarch); for our Bishop (*or* Archbishop, *or* Metropolitan), N., for the honourable Presbytery, the Diaconate in Christ, and for all the clergy and the laity:

Choir: Lord, have mercy.

Here follow petitions for the Ruler of the Land and for all the Authorities, according to the elements and nationalities of which the Parish is constituted.

For the welfare and strengthening of the Christ-loving Army and Navy: ℞

For our Father (N)., and for all our brethren in Christ: ℞

For those who hate us and who love us: ℞

Choir. Lord, have mercy.

For those who are kind to us and who serve us: ℞

For those who have enjoined us to pray for them, unworthy though we be: ℞   For the release of prisoners: ℞

For our departed fathers and brethren: ℞

For those who sail upon the sea: ℞

For those who lie sick: ℞

Let us pray, also, for abundance of the fruits of the earth: ℞

And for every soul of Orthodox Christians: ℞

Let us intercede for our God-fearing Rulers: ℞

For Orthodox Bishops, and for the wardens of this holy Temple (*or* habitation): ℞

For our parents and brethren, and for all Orthodox believers, departed this life before us, who here, and in all the world, lie asleep in the Lord: ℞

Superior. ·Let us say also for ourselves,

We. Lord, have mercy. (*Thrice.*)

Through the prayers of our holy Fathers, O Lord Jesus Christ our God, have mercy upon us.

Choir. Lord, have mercy.

And we go forth after we have said this Prayer:

Forgive, O Lord who lovest man, those who hate us, and those who have wronged us.   Do well unto those who do well.   Grant unto our brethren and our kin those petitions which are unto salvation and life eternal. Visit the sick, and grant them healing.   Guide thou those who sail upon the sea.   Journey with those who journey.   Succour thou our Ruler. Unto those who have served us and have been kind to us, grant forgiveness of their sins.   Upon those who have enjoined us, unworthy though we be, to pray for them, have mercy, according to thy great goodness. Have in remembrance, O Lord, our fathers and brethren who have fallen asleep before us, and give them rest where the light of thy countenance shall visit them.   Remember, O Lord, our brethren who are in captivity, and release them from all the difficulties which beset them.   Remember, O Lord, those who bring gifts, and the benefactors of thy holy churches, and grant them those petitions which are unto salvation and life eternal. Remember, also, O Lord, us, thy humble, and sinful, and unworthy servants, and illumine our minds with the light of thy wisdom, and guide us in the way of thy commandments.   Through the prayers of our all-pure Lady, the Birth-giver of God and ever-virgin Mary, and of all thy saints: For blessed art thou unto ages of ages.   Amen.

SPECIAL SERVICES

VARIABLE PORTIONS OF THE SERVICES ON THE GREAT FEASTS
IN THE REGULAR COURSE OF THE CHURCH YEAR

THE NATIVITY OF THE MOST HOLY BIRTH–GIVER OF GOD

(SEPTEMBER 8 — 21 N.S.)

At the All-Night Vigil.

The Stanza (Stikhíra) for: Lord, I have cried: *In Tone VI.* To-day hath God who sitteth on supersensual thrones prepared for himself upon earth a holy throne. He who in wisdom established the heavens hath, in his love toward mankind, made a living heaven; for from a barren root hath he made to bourgeon forth to us a life-bearing garden, even his Mother. Thou who art the God of wonders, and the hope of the hopeless, O Lord, glory to thee.

Glory to the Father, and to the Son, and to the Holy Spirit, now, and ever, and unto ages of ages. Amen.

And again the Stanza: To-day hath God who sitteth . . .

The Gradual (Prokímen) for the Day.

The Parables (Paremíí). Genesis xxviii. 10–17; Ezek. xliii. 27, xliv. 1–4; Prov. ix. 1–11.

The Stanza at the Litiyá, in Tone VIII. (by Patriarch Sergius). On this blessed illustrious day of our Feast, let us sound the spiritual trumpets: for she who is of the seed of David is born this day as the Mother of Life, dispersing darkness; who also is the renewal of Adam and the recall of Eve, the fountain of incorruption, and the annihilation of corruption; through whom, also, we have become godlike, and have been delivered from death. And unto her, with Gabriel, let us cry, O ye faithful: Hail, thou that art full of grace! The Lord is with thee, for thy sake giving unto us great mercy.

The Hymn for the Day (Tropár), in Tone IV. Thy holy Nativity, O virgin Birth-giver of God, hath proclaimed joy unto all the universe; for from thee is risen the Sun of Righteousness, even Christ our God. And having destroyed the curse, he hath bestowed a blessing; and having brought Death to naught, he hath given unto us life eternal.

The Exaltation (Velitchánie). We magnify thee, O most holy Virgin, and do homage to thy holy Parents, and exalt thy glorious Nativity.

The Gradual (Prokímen), in the Fourth Tone. I will call to remembrance thy name from generation to generation.

Verse (*Stikh*): My heart is inditing of a good matter.
Verse: Praise ye God in his Saints.
The Gospel. Luke i. 39–49, 56.

THE CANON.

The First Canon.   Tone II.   (St. John of Damascus.)

Theme-Songs (*Irmosí*).   I. Come, O ye people, let us sing a song unto Christ-God, who parted asunder the Sea, and guided through it the nation which he had brought forth from the bondage of Egypt: for gloriously hath he been glorified.

III. Establish us in thee, O Lord, who through the Tree didst annihilate sin, and implant the fear of thee in the hearts of us who sing praises unto thee.

IV. I have heard, O Lord, the fame of thy dispensation, and have glorified thee, who alone lovest mankind.

V. O thou who didst dispel the dim obscurity of the dark sayings in the Scriptures, and didst illumine the hearts of the faithful by the advent of truth through the God-Maiden: Guide thou us, also, by thy light, O Christ.

VI. From within the whale Jonah cried unto the Lord: Lead me forth I beseech thee, from the depths of Hell; and unto thee, as the deliverer, with the voice of praise, and in the spirit of truth, I will offer sacrifice.

VII. The bush which upon the mount burned with fire, and the Chaldæan furnace which dropped dew, clearly foreshadowed thee, the Bride of God: for, unconsumed by the flame, thou didst receive the immaterial Fire Divine in thy material womb. For which cause we cry unto him who was born of thee: Blessed be thou, O God of our fathers.

VIII. In the furnace of the Children thou didst, of old, foreshadow thy Mother, O Lord, and this foreshadowing saved from the fire those who walked in the midst thereof unconsumed. Her who, through thee, is manifested unto the ends of the world, to-day we hymn and magnify exceedingly.

IX. Thee, who from thy Virgin womb ineffably didst incarnate God, the Light which shone forth before the Sun was made, and came down to us in the flesh, O blessed, all-pure Birth-giver of God, we magnify.

In place of: My soul doth magnify the Lord: *the Refrains:*

Magnify, O my soul, the most glorious Nativity of the Mother of God.
Magnify, O my soul, Mary the Virgin, who of the barren one was born.

At the Liturgy.

The Introit: The Hymn for the Day.   (See page 164.)

The Collect-Hymn (*Kondák*).   Joachim and Anna were delivered from the reproach of childlessness, and Adam and Eve from the corruption of death, in thy holy Nativity, O All-pure One. This do thy people celebrate, being redeemed from the guilt of transgressions, when they cry unto thee: The barren giveth birth to the Birth-giver of God and the Nourisher of our Life.

The Gradual (Prokímen), in the Fourth Tone. My soul doth magnify the Lord, and my spirit hath rejoiced in God my Saviour.

Verse (Stikh): For he hath regarded the lowliness of his handmaiden. For behold, from henceforth all generations shall call me blessed.

The Epistle. Phil. ii. 5–11.

Alleluia. (*Tone VIII.*)   Hearken, O Daughter, and behold, and incline thine ear.

Verse: A rich nation shall worship before thy presence.

The Gospel. Luke x. 38–42, xi. 27, 28.

The Hymn in place of: Meet is it: *The Ninth Theme-Song of the Second Canon.*   Alien to mothers is virginity, and strange unto virgins is childbirth; in thee, O Birth-giver of God, were both achieved.   Wherefore all we nations of the earth unceasingly do magnify thee.

The Communion Hymn. I will take the cup of salvation, and call upon the Name of the Lord.

THE ELEVATION OF THE PRECIOUS CROSS OF THE LORD

(SEPTEMBER 14 — 27 N.S.   A STRICT FAST.)

At the All-Night Vigil.

The Stanza (*Stikhíra*) *for:* Lord, I have cried: *In Tone VI.* The Cross being set up, doth command every created being to sing the most pure Passion of him who was lifted up thereon.   For having upon the same slain him who had slain us, he endowed with life those who were slain, and adorned them, and vouchsafed that they might dwell in heaven, forasmuch as he is compassionate, through the rich abundance of his goodness. Wherefore, rejoicing, let us exalt his Name, and magnify his exceeding condescension. (*Thrice.*)

Glory to the Father, and to the Son, and to the Holy Spirit, now, and ever, and unto ages of ages.   Amen.

O come, all ye nations, let us adore the blessed Tree, through which the righteousness eternal hath come to pass: for he who beguiled our fore-father Adam with the tree is himself beguiled by the Cross, and he who, like a tyrant, did lord it over that which the King had fashioned, falleth, being overthrown by a downfall strange.   The poison of the serpent is washed away by the blood of God, and the curse of just condemnation is abolished, in that the Righteous One hath been condemned by unright-eous judgment: for it was meet that the tree should be healed by the Tree, and that by the passion of the Passionless One upon the Tree, the passions of the condemned one should be destroyed.   But glory, O Christ our King, unto thy wise providence to usward, whereby thou hast saved all men, forasmuch as thou art good and lovest mankind.

The Gradual (*Prokímen*) *for the Day.*

The Parables (*Paremíí*).   Exodus xv. 22–27, xvi. 1; Prov. iii. 11–18; Isaiah lx. 11–16.

The Stanza at the Litiyá, in Tone I. To-day, of a truth, hath the sa-credly prophetic saying of David received its fulfilment; for lo! we visibly bow down before the footstool of thine all-spotless feet, and putting our trust under the shadow of thy wings, O all-bountiful One, we cry aloud unto thee: Let the light of thy countenance be showed upon us.   Exalt thou the horn of thine Orthodox people through the Elevation of thy precious Cross, O greatly merciful Christ.

The Hymn (*Tropár*), *in Tone I.*   O Lord, save thy people, and bless thine inheritance, granting victory over enemies unto our Ruler, N., and through thy Cross preserving thine Estate. (*Thrice.*)

The Exaltation (*Velitchánie*).   We magnify thee, O life-giving Christ, and do homage to thy holy Cross, whereby thou hast saved us from the works of the enemy.

The Gradual (*Prokímen*), *in the Fourth Tone.*   All the ends of the earth have seen the salvation of our God.

Verse (*Stikh*): Sing unto the Lord a new song, for the Lord hath done marvellous things.

Verse: Praise ye God in his Saints.   Let everything that hath breath praise the Lord.

The Gospel. John xii. 28–36.

THE CANON.

The First Canon.   Tone VIII.   (St. Cosmas of Maium.)

Theme-Songs (*Irmosí*).   I. Moses, having with his rod made a long line, divided the Red Sea for Israel journeying on foot; and having again struck the same with a transverse blow, thus tracing the Cross which is the weapon invincible, he united it against the armies of Pharaoh. Wherefore we sing unto Christ our God, for he hath been glorified.

III. The Rod is accepted as the symbol of a mystery; for by its budding-forth it designated the Priest; and in the Church, which before was barren, there now hath budded forth the Tree of the Cross for her power and strengthening.

IV. I have given heed to the mystery of thy dispensation, O Lord, I have understood thy works, and have glorified thy divinity.

V. O Tree thrice blessed, whereon was crucified Christ our King and our Lord!   Through thee he is fallen who by a tree did beguile, having himself been beguiled by Him who was nailed upon thee in the flesh, even God, who granteth peace unto our souls.

VI. Jonah, when he stretched forth his arms in the form of a cross within the belly of the sea-monster, did clearly typify the Redeeming Suffering; and when he came forth thence after three days, he imaged forth by anticipation the supernatural Resurrection of Christ-God, who was crucified in the flesh, and hath illumined the world by his rising on the third day.

VII. The mad behest of the impious tyrant breathing forth threats and godless blasphemies troubled the people: yet neither the brutal rage nor the devouring fire terrified the Three Children; but when, as they stood amid the flames, a dew-bearing breath was wafted against it, they sang: Blessed be thou, O God of our fathers, exceedingly praised, and our God!

VIII. O Children, in number equal to the Trinity!   Bless ye God the Father, the Creator; sing ye the Word who came down and turned the fire into dew; and magnify ye the Spirit all-holy, who giveth life unto all men, unto all the ages.

In place of: My soul doth magnify the Lord: *the Refrains:*

Magnify, O my soul, the all-precious Cross of the Lord.

Magnify, O my soul, the Elevation of the life-giving Cross of the Lord.

IX. Thou art the mystical Paradise, O Birth-giver of God, who though untilled didst bud forth Christ, by whom the life-bearing Tree of the Cross was planted upon earth. For which cause, now, at its Elevation. adoring it, we magnify thee.

> *While the Canon is being sung, the Senior Priest putteth on all his vestments, and after the Great Glory* (Glory be to God on high) *hath been sung slowly and melodiously, and he hath censed all about the Altar whereon lieth the precious Cross, while:* O Holy God, Holy Mighty: *is being chanted: he placeth the Cross on his head, and making the circuit of the Altar therewith, preceded by a Taper-bearer, he halteth in front of the Holy Door, and having proclaimed:* Wisdom, O believers! *he goeth to the folding-stand, which is in the middle of the Temple, while the Choir chanteth the Hymn:* O Lord, save thy people: *After this, the Priest censeth round about the Cross, and having made the customary reverences, he beginneth:* Thy Cross do we adore, O Master, and thy holy Resurrection do we glorify. (*Thrice.*) *The Choir also singeth this thrice; and the Stanza, in Tone VIII.:*

To-day is the Master of creation and the Lord of glory nailed upon the Cross, and is pierced in the side, and of gall and vinegar doth the Sweetness of the Church partake. With a crown of thorns is he invested who covereth the heavens with clouds, and with the robe of scorn is he endued; and he who with his hand did fashion man is smitten by a human hand. He who clotheth the heavens with clouds is beaten upon his shoulders, and receiveth spitting and wounds, indignities and buffetings in the face; and he, my Redeemer and my Saviour, doth endure all these things for the sake of me, the accursed, that He may save the world from guile, forasmuch as he is compassionate.

Then the Litanies; and the Benediction: May Christ, our true God, through the prayers of his most pure Mother; through the might of the precious and life-giving Cross: *and so forth, as usual.*

At the Liturgy.

In place of: Bless the Lord, O my soul:

Antiphon I., Tone II.

Verse 1: O God, my God, hear me: why hast thou forsaken me?

Refrain. Through the prayers of the Birth-giver of God, O Saviour, save us.

Verse 2: Far from my salvation are the words of my transgression: ℟

Verse 5: O my God, I cry in the daytime and thou hearest not, and in the night-season also I take no rest: ℟

Verse 4: And thou continuest holy, O thou Worship of Israel: ℟

Glory to the Father, and to the Son, and to the Holy Spirit, now, and ever, and unto ages of ages. Amen: ℟

Antiphon II., Tone II.

Verse 1: O God, wherefore art thou absent from us so long?

Refrain. Save, O Son of God, who wast crucified in the flesh, us who sing unto thee, Alleluia.

Verse 2: O think upon thy congregation, whom thou hast purchased and redeemed of old: ℞

Verse 3: And Mount Zion, wherein thou hast dwelt: ℞

Verse 4: For God is our King before the ages: he hath wrought salvation upon earth: ℞

Glory . . . now, and ever.

O Only-begotten Son and Word of God! Thou who art immortal yet didst deign for our salvation to become incarnate of the Holy Birth-giver of God and ever-virgin Mary; and without change of essence wast made man; who also wast crucified for us, O Christ our God, trampling down Death by death; who art one of the Holy Trinity, and art glorified together with the Father and the Holy Spirit: Save us.

Antiphon III., Tone I.

Verse 1: The Lord is King, be the people never so impatient.

Refrain: The Hymn for the Day (Tropár). O Lord, save thy people and bless thine inheritance, granting victory over enemies unto our Ruler, N., and through thy Cross preserving thine Estate.

Verse 2: The Lord is King, be the people never so impatient: he sitteth between the Cherubim, be the earth never so unquiet: ℞

Verse 3: The Lord is great in Zion, and high above all people: ℞

Verse 4: Worship ye the Lord in the courts of His Saints.

In place of: O Holy God, Holy Mighty:

The Introit. O magnify the Lord our God, and fall down before his footstool, for he is holy.

Thy Cross do we adore, O Master, and thy holy Resurrection do we glorify.

The Collect-Hymn (Kondák). Do thou who, of thine own good will, . . . *(See page* 61.)

The Gradual (Prokímen), in the Seventh Tone (the same as the Introit).

Verse: The Lord is King, be the people never so impatient.   Alleluia. *(Tone I.)*

Verse: O think upon thy congregation, whom thou hast purchased and redeemed of old.

Verse: God is our King before the ages: he hath wrought salvation upon earth.

The Epistle. 1 Cor. i. 18–24.

The Gospel. John xix. 6–11, 13–20, 25–28, 30–35.

The Communion Hymn. The light of thy countenance hath been showed upon us, O Lord.

THE ENTRANCE INTO (PRESENTATION IN) THE TEMPLE OF OUR MOST HOLY LADY, THE BIRTH-GIVER OF GOD AND EVER-VIRGIN MARY

(NOVEMBER 21 — DECEMBER 4 N.S.)

At the All-Night Vigil Service.

The Stanza (Stikhíra) for: Lord, I have cried: *In Tone I.* To-day let us faithful exult, singing unto the Lord in psalms and songs, and doing honour unto his holy Tabernacle, the Ark imbued with life, which containeth the uncontainable Word: for in wise supernatural is she brought unto the Lord, being still of tender age in the flesh, and Zacharias, the High Priest, doth with joy receive her, as the abode of God. (*Twice.*)

Glory to the Father, and to the Son, and to the Holy Spirit, now, and ever, and unto ages of ages. Amen.

After thy nativity, O Lady, Bride of God, thou didst come into the temple of the Lord, as one consecrated, to be reared in the Holy of Holies. Then, also, was Gabriel sent unto thee, O all-undefiled One, bearing nourishment unto thee. All the powers of Heaven were amazed when they beheld the Holy Spirit take up its abode in thee. Wherefore, O most pure and undefiled Mother of God, who art glorified in heaven and on earth, save thou our race.

The Gradual (Prokímen) for the Day.

The Parables (Paremíí). Exodus xl. 1–5, 9, 10, 16, 34, 35; I Kings viii. 1, 3–7, 9–11; Ezek. xliii. 27, xliv. 1–4.

The Stanza at the Litiyá, in Tone IV. To-day is the Tabernacle which containeth God, even the Birth-giver of God, brought into the temple of the Lord, and Zacharias receiveth the same: To-day doth the Holy of Holies rejoice, and the Angelic Choir doth mystically triumph. With them also keeping festival to-day, let us cry aloud with Gabriel: Hail, thou that art full of grace! The Lord most merciful is with thee.

The Hymn for the Day (Tropár). To-day is the foreshadowing of the beneficence of God which is to come, and the heralding of man's salvation. The Virgin is clearly manifested in the temple of God, and in anticipation announceth Christ unto all men. Unto her let us, also, cry aloud: Hail, thou who art the fulfilment of the Creator's providence! (*Thrice.*)

The Exaltation (Velitchánie). We magnify thee, O all-holy Virgin, Maiden chosen by the Lord, and do homage to thy Presentation in the temple of the Lord.

The Gradual (Prokímen), in the Fourth Tone. Hearken, O daughter, and behold, and incline thine ear.

Verse (Stikh): My heart is inditing of a good matter.
The Gospel. Luke i. 39–49, 56.

THE CANON.

The First Canon.   Tone IV.   (The Blessed George.)

Theme-Songs (Irmosí).   I. I will open my mouth, and it shall be filled with the Spirit, and will utter a saying to the Queen-Mother; I will reveal myself, as one keeping high festival, and with joy will I sihg her Presentation.

III. O Birth-giver of God, Fountain living and inexhaustible! Spiritually establish thou those who hymn thee, convoked in a festival choir, and vouchsafe unto them crowns of glory for the sake of thine august Presentation.

IV. As he contemplated the unfathomable counsel of God concerning the incarnation by a Virgin, of thee, the Most High, Habakkuk the Prophet cried aloud: Glory to thy power, O Lord!

V. All creation marvelled at thine august Presentation; for thou, O Virgin who knewest not wedlock, didst enter into the temple of God as the Temple most pure, giving peace unto all those who sing thy praises.

VI. In celebration of this divine and all-honourable feast of the Mother of God, come, O ye godly-minded, let us clap our hands and glorify God, who was born of her.

VII. The godly-minded ones obeyed not the creature rather than the Creator, but valiantly trampling under foot the threatened fire, they rejoiced in song, saying: Blessed be thou, O Lord and God of our fathers, exceedingly praised.

VIII. Hearken, O Maiden, Virgin pure! Let Gabriel announce the true will of the Most High, which was from of old. Make thou ready to receive God; for through thee the Uncontainable hath dwelt among men: For which cause I cry aloud with joy: O all ye works of the Lord, bless ye the Lord!

IX. Let no hand profane in any wise touch the living Ark of God; but let the lips of the faithful unceasingly chanting the Salutation of the Angel to the Birth-giver of God, cry aloud with rejoicing: Thou art, in very truth, higher than all men, O Virgin pure!

In place of: My soul doth magnify the Lord: *the Refrains:*

The Angels marvelled when they beheld the Presentation of the All-pure One: how that with glory she entered into the Holy of Holies.

The Angels marvelled when they beheld the Presentation of the Virgin: how that with glory she entered into the Holy of Holies.

O ye Angels and men, let us do homage to the Presentation of the Virgin: for with glory hath she entered into the Holy of Holies.

The Angels marvelled when they beheld the Presentation of the Virgin: how she who was well-pleasing unto God did enter into the Holy of Holies.

Ye Angels, with the Saints, leap for joy! Ye Virgins, sing together with exultation! For the God-Maiden hath entered into the Holy of Holies.

O ye Angels and men, let us magnify the Virgin in Hymns: for in god-like wise hath she entered into the Holy of Holies.

At the Liturgy.

The Introit: The Hymn for the Day. (*See page* 171.)

The Collect-Hymn (*Kondák*). The all-pure Temple of the Saviour, the most precious Bridal-chamber and Virgin, the Treasure-house of the glory of God, to-day is led into the temple of the Lord, bringing with her the grace which is in the Spirit Divine; whom also the Angels of God do celebrate in song: This is the Abode of Heaven.

The Gradual (*Prokímen*), *in the Fourth Tone.* My soul doth magnify the Lord, and my spirit hath rejoiced in God my Saviour.

Verse (*Stikh*): For he hath regarded the lowliness of his handmaiden: for, behold, from henceforth all generations shall call me blessed.

The Epistle. Heb. ix. 1-7.

Alleluia. (*Tone VIII.*) Hearken, O daughter, and behold, and incline thine ear.

Verse: A rich nation shall worship before thy presence.

The Gospel. Luke x. 38–42, xi. 27, 28.

The Hymn in place of: Meet is it: *The Ninth Theme-Song of the Canon:* Let no hand profane . . . (*See above.*)

The Communion Hymn. I will take the cup of salvation, and call upon the Name of the Lord.

THE NATIVITY OF CHRIST (CHRISTMAS)

(DECEMBER 25 — JANUARY 7 N.S.)

The faithful prepare themselves for this great Feast by a prolonged Fast, which beginneth on November 15, and is called the Christmas Fast, or the Fast of St. Philip. The Eve of the Feast (Sotchélnik) is dedicated to a specially strict abstinence.

On Christmas Eve the customary festival Compline service is celebrated. If the Eve falleth on any day except Saturday or Sunday, then on the morning of that day the IMPERIAL HOURS *are read, and, later on, the Liturgy of St. Basil the Great is celebrated, preceded by Vespers. But if the day before the Feast be Saturday or Sunday, then the Imperial Hours are read on Friday, while the Liturgy of St. John Chrysostom is celebrated on the preceding day (Sotchélnik). If the Liturgy of St. Basil the Great be used on the preceding day (Sotchélnik) then on the Feast of the Nativity itself the Liturgy of St. John Chrysostom is used; and contrariwise.*

The other general differences of this festival service are as followeth: Matins are preceded, not by Vespers, but by GRAND COMPLINE: *and after the Liturgy, on the day of the Feast, a service of thanksgiving is celebrated.*

THE IMPERIAL HOURS,* to precede Christmas.

In addition to many of the Prayers and so forth which are used in the daily Hours, and the Christmas Hymns, the following are read:

FIRST HOUR. Psalms v., xlv., xlvi. *The Parable (Paremiyá).* Micah v. 2-4. *The Epistle.* Heb. i. 1-12. *The Gospel.* Matt. i. 18-25.

THIRD HOUR. Psalms lxvii., lxxxvii., li. *The Parable (Paremiyá).* Jer. (Baruch iii. 36-38, iv. 1-4). *The Epistle.* Gal. iii. 23-29. *The Gospel.* Luke ii. 1-20.

SIXTH HOUR. Psalms lxxii., cxxxii., xci. *The Parable (Paremiyá).* Isaiah vii. 10-16, viii. 1-4, 9, 10. *The Epistle.* Heb. i. 10-14, ii. 1-3. *The Gospel.* Matt. ii. 1-12.

NINTH HOUR. Psalms cx., cxi., lxxxvi.

Then Many Years are proclaimed for the Ruler, the Patriarch, the Holy Synod, the Bishop, the Orthodox Patriarchs of Constantinople, Alexandria, Antioch and Jerusalem, and others; and the Choir respondeth: Many years!

ON THE DAY BEFORE CHRISTMAS

At the Vespers which immediately precede the Liturgy. the Stanza (Stikhíra) for: Lord, I have cried: *In Tone II.*

O come, let us rejoice in the Lord, as we declare this present mystery: The partition wall of disunion hath been destroyed, the flaming sword is turned back, and the Cherubim withdraw from the Tree of Life, and I partake of the food of Paradise, whence, because of disobedience, I was expelled. For the Image Immutable of the Father, the Image of his Eternity, taketh the form of a servant, having come forth from a Mother

* The Emperors of Byzantium were wont to attend the Hours on certain of the great Feasts of the Church, which received their name of "the Imperial Hours" from that circumstance, as well as from their extraordinary splendour and importance.

unwedded, yet having suffered no change: for that which he was that he remaineth, being very God; and that which he was not he hath assumed, becoming very man because of his love toward mankind. Unto him let us cry aloud: O God, who wast born of a Virgin, have mercy upon us. (*Twice.*)

When Augustus reigned alone upon the earth, the polygarchy of men came to an end: and when thou didst become incarnate of the Pure One, the polytheism of idols was annulled. Under one earthly sway were the cities, and in one dominion of the Godhead did the Gentiles believe. By the command of Cæsar were the people inscribed; and we faithful have been inscribed with the name of the Godhead, of thee our God, who hast become man. Great is thy mercy. O Lord, glory to thee.

The Entrance is made with the book of the Holy Gospels, and the Hymn: O gladsome radiance! . . .

The Gradual (Prokímen) for the Day.

The Parables (Paremíî). Gen. i. 1–13. Num. xxiv. 2, 3, 5–9, 17, 18; Micah iv. 6, 7, v. 2–4; Isaiah xi. 1–10; Jer. (Baruch iii. 36–38, iv. 1–4); Dan. ii. 31–36, 44–46; Isaiah ix. 6, 7, vii. 10–15, viii. 1–4, 9–11.

The Little Litany: Again, yet again, in peace . . . : *with the Exclamation:* For holy art thou, O our God, and unto thee do we ascribe glory, to the Father, and to the Son, and to the Holy Spirit, now, and ever, and unto ages of ages. Amen.

The Gradual (Prokímen), in the First Tone. The Lord said unto me, Thou art my Son, this day have I begotten thee.

Verse (Stikh): Ask of me, and I will give the heathen for thine inheritance, and the uttermost parts of the earth for thy possession.

The Epistle. Heb. i. 1–12.

The Gospel. Luke ii. 1–20.

CHRISTMAS EVE.

Compline and Matins.

Compline is read in the usual order, with the Hymns and Collect-Hymn of the Feast in place of the ordinary ones. After: Glory be to God on high: *hath been read, the Clergy come forth to the centre of the Temple, and perform the Litiyá, with the Blessing of the Loaves.*

The Stanzas (Stikhíri) of the Litiyá, in Tone I. Let heaven and earth to-day prophetically exult, and let Angels and men spiritually rejoice: for God hath revealed himself in the flesh unto those who were in darkness and sat in the shadow, and hath been born of a Virgin. The cavern and the manger have received him; Shepherds proclaim the marvel, and Magi from the Orient bring gifts unto Bethlehem. And we, also, with lips unworthy, do bring unto him praise in Angelic wise: Glory be to God on high, and on earth peace: for the Hope of the nations is come, and having come hath saved us from bondage to the enemy.

The Hymn at the Blessing of the Loaves, and: God is the Lord: *Tone IV.* Thy Nativity, O Christ our God, hath arisen upon the world as the light of wisdom. / For at it, they who worshipped the stars were, by a Star,׳ taught to adore thee, the Sun of Righteousness,/and to know thee, the Orient from on high. / O Lord, glory to thee.

The Exaltation of the Feast. We magnify thee, O Life-giving Christ, who for our sakes now art born in the flesh of the Virgin Mary, unwedded and most pure.

The Gradual (Prokímen), in the Fourth Tone. Out of the womb, before the morning star, have I begotten thee. The Lord sweareth and will not repent.

Verse (Stikh): The Lord said unto my Lord: Sit thou at my right hand until I make thine enemies thy footstool.

The Gospel. Matt. i. 18–25.

THE CANON.

In Tone I. (Composed by St. Cosmas of Maium, about 760.)

Canticle I.

Theme-Song (Irmós). Christ is born: extol him! Christ from heaven: go to meet him! Christ on earth: be ye lifted up! Sing unto the Lord, all the whole earth, and praise him in song with joy, O ye people: For he hath glorified himself.

℟ Glory to thee, O our God; glory to thee.

Hymns (Tropari). Man who, being made in the image of God, had become corrupt through sin, and was full of vileness, and had fallen away from the better life divine, doth the wise Creator restore anew: For he hath glorified himself.

When the Creator beheld man, whom he had made with his hands, about to perish, he bowed the heavens and came down; and was endued with man's nature in very truth, becoming incarnate of a Virgin divinely pure: For he hath glorified himself.

The Wisdom, Word, and Might, the Son and Effulgence of the Father, Christ our God, without the knowledge of the supra-mundane Powers and the Powers of the earth, is become incarnate and hath renewed us: For he hath glorified himself.

Canticle III.

Theme-Song (Irmós). Unto the Son, who, in wise immortal, was born of the Father before all the ages, and in these latter days is become incarnate without seed of a Virgin, Christ our God, let us cry aloud: O Lord, who hast exalted our horn, holy art thou!

Hymns (Tropari). Adam, mortal, made of clay, yet a participant of the divine inspiration, who had become subject to corruption through a woman's seduction, when he beheld Christ sprung from a woman, exclaimed: Holy art thou, O Lord, who for my sake hast made thyself like unto me.

O Christ, who hast conformed thyself unto our base, mortal mould, and by that participation in our lowly flesh hast imparted unto us a share of the nature divine; who, though thou didst become earthborn, yet didst remain still God, and hast exalted our horn: Holy art thou, O Lord.

Rejoice, O Bethlehem, which art King over the princes of Judah; for he who feedeth Israel and is borne on the shoulders of the Cherubim is visibly come forth from thee; and he who exalteth our horn is enthroned over all.

Canticle IV.

Theme-Song (Irmós). The Rod of the Root of Jesse and its Flower, from a Virgin didst thou bud forth, O most-lauded Christ. From the Mount covered with dense shadow art thou come, being incarnate of a Maid who knew not man, O thou Immaterial One and God: Glory to thy might, O Lord.

Hymns (Tropari). Thou, O Christ, the Expectation of the nations, whom Jacob did foretell of old, art risen from the tribe of Judah, and art come to annihilate the power of Damascus, and the spoils of Samaria, replacing error with truth acceptable to God: Glory to thy might, O Lord.

By thy rising as a Star from Jacob, O Lord, thou didst fill with joy the wise initiates in the word of Balaam the Prophet of old, the Watchers of the Stars, who were led unto thee as the first-fruits of the Gentiles, and didst manifestly receive them: Glory to thy might, O Lord.

Like the rain upon the fleece, and like drops of dew falling upon the earth, O Christ, didst thou descend into the Virgin's womb. Ethiopia and Tarshish, the Isles of Araby, and Sheba of the Midians, the Rulers of all the earth, fell down in adoration before thee, O Saviour: Glory to thy might, O Lord.

Canticle V.

Theme-Song (Irmós). O God of peace, the Father of mercies, thou hast sent unto us the Angel of thy Great Council, who giveth peace: wherefore we, in that we have been led unto the light of godly wisdom, waking right early from the night, do sing praises unto thee, O thou who lovest mankind.

Hymns (Tropari). In obedience to the command of Cæsar, O Christ, thou didst enroll thyself among the slaves, and didst set free us who were slaves of the enemy and of sin; and didst make thyself a beggar, in every way like unto us; and through that same union and community didst render the mortal divine.

Lo, a Virgin, as it was foretold of old, having conceived in her womb, hath brought forth God incarnate, yet remaineth Virgin still. Let us sinners, in that we have become reconciled unto God through her, magnify her in song as the true Birth-giver of the Lord.

Canticle VI.

Theme-Song (Irmós). The sea-monster cast forth Jonah like an infant from its belly unharmed as it had swallowed him.   And when the Word took up his abode in a Virgin, and was made flesh, He came forth preserving her undefiled.   For in that He Himself suffered not corruption, He preserved unharmed her who bare Him.

Hymns (Tropari). Christ our God, whom the Father begat of his own loins before the morning star, is come in the flesh.   He who ruleth the most pure Powers lieth in a manger of dumb beasts, and is wrapped in swaddling-bands; yet doth he loose the thick-entangled bonds of transgression.

Born of Adam's nature and given unto the faithful as a little child is the Son: yet he is also the Father and the Ruler of the world to come, and is called the Angel of the Great Council.   He is the mighty God who ruleth the Universe by his power.

Collect-Hymn (Kondák).

To-day a Virgin bringeth forth the Super-substantial, and earth offereth a cavern to the Unapproachable; Angels together with the Shepherds sing praises; the Wise Men journey on with the Star.   For, for our sakes, God, who is before all the ages, is born a little Child.

Ikos.

Bethlehem hath opened Eden: O come, let us gaze!   We have found nourishment in a secret place: O come, let us receive the things of Paradise within the cavern!   There hath appeared the Root Unwatered which buddeth forth remission.   There hath been found the Well Undigged, from which David of old longed that he might drink.   There a Virgin hath brought forth a Child; and straightway the thirst of Adam and of David hath been assuaged.   Wherefore let us go unto him where He is born a little Child, yet is God before the ages.

Canticle VII.

Theme-Song (Irmós). The youths reared together in godliness, despising the unrighteous command, were not terrified by the threatened fire, but standing in the midst of the flames did sing: O God of our fathers, blessed art thou.

Hymns (Tropari). The shepherds skilled upon the tuneful pipes beheld a revelation marvellous of light; for the glory of the Lord shone round about them, and the Angel proclaimed: Sing praises, for Christ is born. O God of our fathers, blessed art thou.

Suddenly, at the word of the Angel, the Heavenly Hosts began to cry aloud: Glory to God in the highest, and on earth peace, good will toward men; Christ hath shone forth: O God of our fathers, blessed art thou!

What meaneth this saying? spake the shepherds: Let us go, let us gaze upon that which is come to pass, upon Christ divine.   And when they were come unto Bethlehem, they fell down in worship before him, together with her who had given him birth, singing: O God of our fathers, blessed art thou.

Canticle VIII.

Theme-Song (Irmós). The dew-shedding, fiery furnace imaged forth the type of a marvellous wonder: for its flames scorched not the Holy Children whom it had received, even as the fire of the Godhead scorched not the Virgin when it entered into her womb. Therefore let us raise the song: Let all creation bless the Lord, and magnify him unto all the ages.

Hymns (Tropari). The Daughter of Babylon doth bear away unto herself the children of David as captives, out of Zion: but she sendeth her children, the Magi, bearing gifts, to do homage unto the Daughter of David, who had received within her God: wherefore, chanting songs of praise, let us sing: Let all creation bless the Lord, and magnify him unto all the ages.

Grief put aside the instruments of song; for the children of Zion sang not in alien lands. But Christ, in that he hath shone forth in Bethlehem, setteth free every error, and the musical harmony of Babylon. Wherefore let us sing the song: Let all creation bless the Lord, and magnify him unto all the ages.

Babylon carried the spoil and the spear-won wealth of the kingdom of Zion into captivity. But Christ draweth unto Zion the treasures of the same and its Kings, the Watchers of the Stars, guiding them by a Star. Wherefore, let us sing the song: Let all creation bless the Lord, and magnify him unto all the ages.

Canticle IX.

With the Ninth Theme-Song, instead of: More honourable than the Cherubim: *the* REFRAINS *of the Feast qre sung:*

Refrain 1. Magnify, O my soul, the Virgin, the all-pure Birth-giver of God, more honourable and more glorious than the hosts on high.

Theme-Song (Irmós). A mystery strange and most glorious I behold: The cavern, Heaven: the Cherubimic Throne, a Virgin; the manger, the receptacle wherein lieth Christ our God, whom nothing may contain. Him, therefore, do we magnify, praising him in song.

Refrain 2. Magnify, O my soul, God born in the flesh of a Virgin.

Refrain 3. Magnify, O my soul, the King born in a cavern.

Hymn (Tropár). When the Wise Men beheld the unwonted course of the wondrous, newly revealed Star, exceeding the heavenly bodies in brightness, they divined that Christ the King was born on earth in Bethlehem, for our salvation.

Refrain 4. Magnify, O my soul, God who was worshipped by the Magi.

Refrain 5. Magnify, O my soul, him who was announced unto the Wise Men by a Star.

Hymn. When the Wise Men said: Where is the new-born Infant King whom the Star hath revealed? For we are come to worship him. Then the wrathful Herod was troubled, and, raging against the Lord, that impious man sought to slay Christ.

Refrain 6. Magnify, O my soul, the pure Virgin and only Birth-giver of God, who gave birth unto Christ the King.

Refrain 7. The Wise Men and the shepherds came to worship Christ who was born in the town of Bethlehem.

Hymn. Herod inquired the time of the Star, through whose guiding the Wise Men were come to Bethlehem to worship Christ with gifts. But being by it led again unto their own country, they left confounded behind them the cruel slayer of the children.

The Benediction. (*See page* 181.)

At the Liturgy.

Antiphon I., Tone II.

Verse 1: I will give thanks unto the Lord with my whole heart.

Refrain. Through the prayers of the Birth-giver of God, O Saviour, save us.

Verse 2: In the council of the faithful and in the congregation, the great works of the Lord. ℞

Verse 3: Sought out of all them that have pleasure therein. ℞

Verse 4: His work is honour and majesty, and his righteousness endureth forever. ℞

Antiphon II., Tone II.

Verse 1: Blessed is the man that feareth the Lord, that hath great delight in his commandments.

Refrain. O Son of God, who wast born of a Virgin, save us who sing unto thee: Alleluia.

Verse 2: His seed shall be mighty upon earth, the generation of the faithful shall be blessed. ℞

Verse 3: Riches and plenteousness shall be in his house, and his righteousness endureth forever. ℞

Verse 4: Unto the godly there ariseth up light in the darkness: he is merciful, loving and righteous. ℞

Glory to the Father, and to the Son, and to the Holy Spirit, now, and ever, and unto ages of ages. Amen.

O Only-begotten Son and Word of God! . . . (*See page* 170.)

Antiphon III., Tone II.

Verse 1: The Lord said unto my Lord: Sit thou on my right hand.

Hymn. Thy Nativity, O Christ our God, . . . (*See page* 176.)

Verse 2: Until I make thine enemies thy footstool. ℞ (*Hymn.*)

Verse 3: The Lord shall send thee the rod of thy power out of Zion: be thou ruler, even in the midst among thine enemies. ℞ (*Hymn.*)

Verse 4: In the day of thy power with an holy worship.

.

Introit. Out of the womb, before the morning star have I begotten thee: the Lord hath sworn and will not repent: thou art a Priest forever, after the order of Melchizidech.

Instead of: O Holy God, Holy Mighty: *is sung:* As many as are baptized into Christ have put on Christ. Alleluia.

The Gradual (Prokímen), in the Eighth Tóne. Let all the earth worship thee, and hymn thee, yea, let it hymn thy Name, O Most Highest.

Verse: Shout unto the Lord, all ye lands, sing unto his Name, give glory to his praise.

Verse: The heavens declare the glory of God, and the dry land proclaimeth the work of thy hands.

Verse: Day unto day uttereth speech, and night unto night proclaimeth knowledge.

The Epistle. Gal. iv. 4–7.

The Gospel. Matt. ii. 1–12.

Instead of: Meet is it: *The Ninth Theme-Song of the Canon:* A mystery strange . . . (*See page* 179.)

The Communion Hymn. The Lord hath sent deliverance unto his people.

The Benediction. May he who was born in a cavern, and lay in a manger, for the sake of our salvation, Christ our true God, through the prayers of his most pure Mother; of the holy, glorious and all-laudable Apostles; of our holy and God-bearing Fathers; of the holy and righteous Ancestors of God, Joachim and Anna; and of all the Saints, have mercy upon us and save us, forasmuch as he is good, and loveth mankind.

THE EPIPHANY

(JANUARY 6—19 N.S.)

On the Eve of the Epiphany the same strict fast is observed, and the same services are celebrated as on the Eve of Christ's Nativity (Christmas). That is to say: The IMPERIAL HOURS are read, and the Liturgy of St. Basil the Great is celebrated (if the Eve doth not fall upon Saturday or Sunday), preceded by Vespers; while in the evening the service consisteth of Grand Compline joined to Matins. The differences between these services and those of Christmas lie in the festival hymns and the consecration of the water.

At this Feast there are two Blessings of the Waters: the first, on the Eve, in Church; the second, after the Divine Liturgy, on the day of the Feast, under the open sky, of rivers, lakes, pools and wells. In ancient times the former was intended for the Catechumens who were prepared to receive baptism, and were then baptized. The second was instituted later, in imitation of the custom among the Christians of Jerusalem, who were wont to go forth to the Jordan to celebrate the festival, and to pray: also in memory of the consecration of the waters of the Jordan at the time our Lord Jesus Christ was baptized therein. This Blessing of the Waters is often called "The Jordan Festival" for that reason.

THE IMPERIAL HOURS, *to precede the Epiphany.*

FIRST HOUR. Psalms v., xxiii., xxvii.; Isaiah xxxv. 1–10. *The Epistle.* Acts xiii. 25–33. *The Gospel.* Matt. iii. 1–12.

THIRD HOUR. Psalms xxix., xlii., li.; Isaiah i. 16–20. *The Epistle.* Acts. xix 1–8. *The Gospel.* Mark i. 1–8.

SIXTH HOUR. Psalms lxxiv., lxxvii., xci.; Isaiah xii. 3–6. *The Epistle.* Rom. vi. 3–11. *The Gospel.* Mark i. 9–15.

NINTH HOUR. Psalms xciii., cxiv., lxxxvi.; Isaiah xlix. 8–15. *The Epistle.* Titus ii. 11–14, iii. 4–7. *The Gospel.* Matt. iii. 13–17.

Then the TYPICAL PSALMS.

Vespers: and the Liturgy, on January 6th.—19 N.S.

The Stanzas (Stikíri) for: Lord, I have cried: *In Tone II.* The Forerunner, beholding our Illuminator who illumineth every man, coming to be baptized, rejoiceth in his soul; and he trembleth, and with his hand doth he point Him out to the people, saying: Lo, this is he who redeemeth Israel, setting us free from corruption. O Christ our God, the Sinless One, glory to thee! (*Twice.*)

Glory to the Father, and to the Son, and to the Holy Spirit, now, and ever, and unto ages of ages. Amen.

Thou didst bow thy head unto the Forerunner, and thereby didst crush the heads of the serpents. And having entered into the stream thou didst illumine all things, that they might glorify thee, O Saviour, even the Illuminator of our souls.

The Entrance is made with the book of the Gospels.

The Gradual (Prokímen) for the Day.

The Parables (Paremíí). Genesis i. 1–13; Exodus xiv. 15–18, 21–25, 27 –29, xv. 22–27, xvi. 1; Joshua iii. 7, 8, 15–17; 2 Kings ii. 6–14, v. 9–14; Isaiah i. 16–20; Genesis xxxii. 1–10; Exodus ii. 5–10; Judges vi. 36–40; 1 Kings xviii. 30–39; 2 Kings ii. 19–22; Isaiah xlix. 8–15.

The Little Litany. Again, yet again, . . .

Exclamation. For holy art thou, O our God, and unto thee do we ascribe glory, to the Father, and to the Son, and to the Holy Spirit, now, and ever, and unto ages of ages. Amen.

The Gradual (Prokímen), in the Third Tone. The Lord is my light and my salvation: whom shall I fear?

Verse (Stikh): The Lord is the strength of my life: of whom shall I be afraid?

The Epistle. 1 Cor. ix. 19–27, x. 1–4.

The Gospel. Luke iii. 1–18.

After the Prayer before the Tribune the Blessing of the Water taketh place.

Grand Compline and Matins.

Compline is celebrated in its usual order, the Hymn for the Day and the Collect-Hymn being substituted for the ordinary ones.

After: Glory be to God on high: *the procession from the Sanctuary for the Litiyá taketh place.* (*See the* ALL-NIGHT VIGIL OFFICE, *page* 11.)

The Stanza for the Litiyá, in Tone VIII. To-day is creation illumined, to-day do all things both heavenly and earthly rejoice. Angels and men are intermingled; for whithersoever the King cometh, there also cometh orderliness. Let us make haste then unto Jordan, and we shall all behold John, as he baptizeth the head not made with hands and sinless. Wherefore, singing the song of the Apostles, let us cry with one accord: The grace of God, which is saving unto all men, hath manifested itself, illumining the faithful and bestowing upon the same great mercy.

The Hymn (Tropár) at the Blessing of the Loaves: The Hymn of the Feast. When in Jordan thou wast baptized, O Lord, the worship of the Trinity was made manifest. For the voice of the Father bare witness unto thee, calling thee his beloved Son, and the Spirit, in the form of a Dove, confirmed the steadfastness of that word: O Christ our God, who didst manifest thyself, and dost enlighten the world, glory to thee.

The Exaltation (Velitchánie). We magnify thee, O life-giving Christ, for our sakes now baptized of John in the waters of the Jordan.

The Gradual (Prokímen), in the Fourth Tone. The sea saw that and fled: Jordan was driven back.

Verse (Stikh): What aileth thee, O thou sea, that thou fleddest, and Jordan that thou wast driven back?

The Gospel. Matt. i. 9–11.

THE CANON.

In Tone II. (*St. Cosmas of Maium.*)

Canticle I.

Theme-Song (*Irmós*). The Lord mighty in battle hath laid bare the depths of the sea, and hath led forth his people on dry ground, after having overwhelmed therein their adversaries: For he hath glorified himself.

Hymns (*Tropari*). The Lord, the King of the ages, reneweth corrupt Adam by the waters of Jordan, and crusheth the heads of the dragons which lurked therein: For he hath glorified himself.

The Lord having become incarnate of a Virgin and clothed the immaterial fire of the Godhead in material flesh, is encompassed by the waters of Jordan: For he hath glorified himself.

The Lord, who, through his own cleansing in Jordan, washeth away the vileness of men, to whom he was graciously pleased to conform himself, remaining still as he was before, giveth light unto those who are in darkness: For he hath glorified himself.

Canticle III.

Theme-Song (*Irmós*). The Lord, who giveth strength unto our Kings and exalteth the horn of his Anointed, is born of a Virgin, and cometh unto Baptism. Unto him will we faithful cry aloud: There is none holy like unto our God.

Hymns (*Tropari*). Rejoice thou to-day, O Church of Christ, which aforetime wast sterile and barren of children; for through water and the Spirit have sons been born unto thee, who with faith do cry aloud: There is none holy like unto our God.

With a loud voice crieth the Forerunner in the wilderness: Prepare ye the way for Christ, and make straight the paths for our God, crying aloud with faith: There is none holy like unto our God.

Canticle IV.

Theme-Song (*Irmós*). I have heard, O Lord, thy voice which thou didst call the voice of one crying in the wilderness, which, when thou didst thunder over many waters, bearing witness to thy Son, being filled with the Spirit which had revealed itself, did cry aloud: Thou art Christ, the Wisdom and the Power of God.

Hymns (*Tropari*). Hath any one — crieth the Messenger — beheld the Sun, which is by nature radiant, cleansed? Shall I then wash clean with the waters thee who art the Brightness of Glory, the Express Image of the Father who is from everlasting? And shall I, who am but grass, touch the fire of thy divinity? For thou art Christ, the Wisdom and the Power of God.

Moses, when he drew near to thee, manifested the God-inspired awe wherewith he was seized. When he understood that it was thou speaking from the bush, he straightway turned aside his face. How then shall I gaze openly upon thee, and how shall I lay my hand upon thee? For thou art Christ, the Wisdom, and the Power of God.

In that I have a rational soul, and am honoured with the gift of speech, I stand in fear of things without a soul. For if I baptize thee, the mountain which smoked with fire, the sea which was parted in twain, and that Jordan which rolleth back its waves shall be my accusers: For thou art Christ, the Wisdom and the Power of God.

Canticle V.

Theme-Song (Irmós). Jesus, the Chieftain of Life, cometh to abolish the condemnation of Adam the first-created; and though, in that he is God, he hath no need of cleansing, yet for the fallen is he cleansed in Jordan, where, having slain enmity, he bestoweth the peace which passeth understanding.

Hymns. When a multitude innumerable of people had gathered together to be baptized of John, he stood in their midst and cried aloud unto those who were present: Who hath warned you, ye disobedient, to flee from the wrath to come? Bring ye worthy fruits unto Christ; for now revealing himself he bestoweth peace.

The Husbandman and Creator, standing in the midst as one of the throng, searcheth hearts; and having taken in his hand the winnowing fan, with exceeding wisdom doth he purge the threshing-floor of the universe, burning up the chaff, but granting unto the fruitful grain life eternal.

Canticle VI.

Theme-Song (Irmós). The Voice of the Word, the Candlestick of the Light, the Morning Star, the Forerunner of the Sun, crieth aloud in the wilderness unto all men: Repent ye, and be ye cleansed in preparation. For lo! Christ cometh, who redeemeth the world from corruption.

Hymns. Christ, whose latchet —when the Word had taken our form upon Him — it is impossible to unloose, as the Forerunner teacheth, in that he was born without corruption of God the Father, is without defilement made flesh of a Virgin: For he redeemeth the earth-born from their guile.

With extirpating fire doth Christ baptize the froward and those who acknowledge him not as God. But with the Spirit, by means of water, doth he graciously renew those who confess his divinity, freeing them from their sins.

Canticle VII.

Theme-Song (Irmós). A rushing mighty wind bearing dew, and the descent of the Angel of God preserved unscathed the Children who held converse together in the fiery furnace. When, therefore, they were bedewed amid the flames, with gratitude did they sing aloud: Blessed be thou, O exceeding glorious God of our fathers and our God!

Hymns. With trembling and amazement, as over heaven itself, did the

Angelic Host stand over Jordan, gazing down upon such condescension of God; beholding how he who ruleth the firmament of the waters on high, the God of our fathers, bearing bodily form, stood in the water.

The marvel of the baptism divine was foreshadowed of old by the cloud and the sea, wherein as they journeyed onward the ancient people were baptized into the Giver of the Law. The sea was the symbol of the water, and the cloud of the Spirit; being made perfect in which, let us cry: Blessed be thou, O Lord God forever!

Let all us faithful, speaking devoutly of Him from whom we have received sanctification, in company with the Angels perpetually glorify the Father, Son and Holy Spirit: for He is a Trinity in Persons, but one in Essence, one God; to whom, also, let us sing: Blessed be thou, O Lord God forever!

Canticle VIII.

Theme-Song (Irmós). The Babylonian furnace, dew-dropping, foreshadowed the image of the wondrous mystery that Jordan was to receive into its waters the Fire Immaterial, and contain the Creator when he should be baptized in the flesh: whom also all men do bless and exalt unto all the ages.

Hymns. Put away all fear, said the Redeemer to the Forerunner; obey me, come unto me, as unto the Gracious One, for that am I in my Essence. Submit thyself to my command, and baptize me, who have come down hither; whom also all men do bless and exalt unto all the ages.

The Baptist, when he heard the words of the Lord, stretched forth his hand with trembling; but when he had touched the crown of his Creator's head, he cried unto him who was receiving baptism: Sanctify thou me, for thou art my God; whom also all men do bless and exalt unto all the ages.

In Jordan was the Trinity made manifest; for the Most Divine Person of the Father Himself proclaimed: He that is baptized, the same is my beloved Son. And the Spirit descended upon him that was like unto Himself. Him do men bless and exalt unto all the ages.

Canticle IX.

Before the Ninth Theme-Song: More honourable than the Cherubim: *is not sung, but instead thereof the Refrain of the Feast:*

Magnify, O my soul, her who is more honourable than the hosts on high, even the most pure Virgin Birth-giver of God.

Theme-Song (Irmós). No tongue hath power worthily to praise thee, and even the supra-mundane mind is perplexed how to hymn thee, O Birth-giver of God. But inasmuch as thou art gracious, accept thou our faith; for our God-inspired love thou knowest. For thou art the Intercessor of Christians. We magnify thee.

And the remaining six Refrains are sung once with each Hymn.

Refrain 2. Magnify, O my soul, him who asketh baptism of the Fore-runner.

Refrain 3. Magnify, O my soul, him who is come unto the Jordan to be baptized.

Hymn. Come thou in spirit, O David, unto those who are being illumined by the Spirit, and sing, saying: Draw near now unto God and be ye illumined by faith. That poor man, Adam, cried in his fall, and the Lord heard him as he came, and in the waters of Jordan did he renew that corrupted one.

Refrain 4. Magnify, O my soul, him to whom the voice of the Father bare witness.

Refrain 5. Magnify, O my soul, One of the Trinity who hath bowed his neck and accepted baptism.

Hymn. Wash you, make you clean, saith Isaiah; put away the evil of your doings before the Lord. Ye who thirst, come ye unto the Living Water; for Christ sprinkleth with water which giveth new life those who make supplication unto him in faith, and baptizeth them with the Spirit unto the life which waxeth not old.

Refrain 6. O Prophet, come thou unto me; stretch forth thy hand, and baptize me quickly.

Refrain 7. O Prophet, lay aside now all other things, and baptize me who desire it; for I am come to fulfil all righteousness.

Hymn. May the grace and seal (of the Spirit) preserve us, O faithful! For as the Hebrews of old were delivered from destruction when their door-posts were smeared with blood, even so also shall this divine bath of regeneration be made a deliverance for us, and even so also shall we behold the light of the Trinity which knoweth no setting.

At the Liturgy.

Antiphon I., Tone I.

Verse 1: When Israel came out of Egypt, and the house of Jacob from among the strange people:

Refrain. Through the prayers of the Birth-giver of God, O Saviour, save us.

Verse 2: Judah was his sanctuary, and Israel his dominion: ℞

Verse 3: The sea saw it and fled: Jordan was driven back: ℞

Verse 4: Why hast thou fled, O sea: and why art thou driven back, O Jordan? ℞

Antiphon II., Tone II.

Verse 1: I am well pleased that the Lord hath heard the voice of my prayer.

Refrain. O Son of God, who wast baptized in Jordan, save us who sing unto thee, Alleluia.

Verse 2: Because he hath inclined his ear unto me: therefore will I call upon him as long as I live: ℞

Verse 3: The snares of death compassed me round about, and the pains of hell gat hold upon me. I found trouble and heaviness, and I called upon the Name of the Lord: O Lord, I beseech thee, deliver my soul: ℞

Verse 4: Gracious is the Lord, and righteous: yea, our God is merciful: ℞

Glory to the Father, and to the Son, and to the Holy Spirit, now, and ever, and unto ages of ages. Amen.

O Only-begotten Son and Word of God! . . . (*See page* 170.)

Antiphon III., Tone I.

Verse 1: O give thanks unto the Lord, for he is gracious: his mercy endureth forever.

Refrain: The Hymn for the Day (Tropár). When in Jordan thou wast baptized, O Lord, the worship of the Trinity was made manifest. For the voice of the Father bare witness unto thee, calling thee his beloved Son, and the Spirit, in the form of a dove, confirmed the steadfastness of that word. O Christ our God, who didst manifest thyself, and dost enlighten the world, glory to thee.

Verse 2: Let Israel now confess that he is gracious, and that his mercy endureth forever: ℞

Verse 3: Let the house of Aaron now confess that he is gracious, and that his mercy endureth forever: ℞

Verse 4: Yea, let them that fear the Lord now confess that his mercy endureth forever: ℞

The Introit. Blessed is he that cometh in the Name of the Lord. We have blessed you from the house of the Lord: God is the Lord, and hath revealed himself unto us.

The Collect-Hymn (Kondák). To-day hast thou revealed thyself unto the universe, and thy Light, O Lord, hath showed a sign unto us, who with understanding sing unto thee: Thou art come, and hast revealed thyself, O Light Unapproachable.

In place of: O Holy God: As many as have been baptized into Christ have put on Christ.

The Gradual (Prokímen), in the Fourth Tone. Blessed is he that cometh in the Name of the Lord. God is the Lord, and hath revealed himself unto us.

Verse (Stikh): Confess unto the Lord that he is gracious, that his mercy endureth forever.

The Epistle. Titus ii. 11–14, iii. 4–7.

Alleluia. (*Tone IV.*) Offer thanks unto the Lord, ye sons of God.

Verse: The voice of the Lord upon the waters.

The Gospel. Matt. iii. 13–17.

The Communion Hymn (Pritchásten). The saving grace of God hath manifested itself unto all men.

For the BENEDICTION, *see page* 197, *Epiphany (end of Great Blessing of Waters).*

THE OFFICE AT THE GREAT BLESSING OF WATERS AT THE HOLY EPIPHANY

At the end of the Divine Liturgy, after the Prayer before the Tribune: O Lord, who blessest those who bless thee: *hath been said by the Priest, we all go forth to the Baptismal Font, preceded by the taper-bearers, after whom go the Deacon and the Priest bearing the book of the Holy Gospels and the censer, and the Brethren, singing the following Hymn, in Tone VIII.:*

The voice of the Lord crieth out over the waters, saying: Come, receive ye all the spirit of wisdom, the spirit of understanding, the spirit of the fear of God, even Christ who is made manifest. (*Thrice.*)

To-day is the nature of water sanctified, and Jordan is cloven asunder, and rolleth back the current of its flood, as it beholdeth the Lord baptized. (*Twice.*)

As a man didst thou come unto that river, O Christ our King, and didst earnestly desire to receive the baptism of a servant, O Good One, at the hands of the Forerunner, because of our sins, O thou who lovest mankind. (*Twice.*)

Glory to the Father, and to the Son, and to the Holy Spirit, now, and ever, and unto ages of ages. Amen.

In the same Tone:

Unto the voice of him crying in the wilderness: Prepare ye the way of the Lord: thou didst come forth, O Lord, having taken on the form of a servant, and asking baptism, though thou knewest not sin. The waters beheld thee and were affrighted. The Baptist became all trembling, and cried aloud, saying: How shall the candlestick illumine the light? How shall a slave lay hands upon his Lord? Sanctify thou me and these waters, O Saviour, who takest away the sins of the world.

And taking his stand beside the Font, the Deacon immediately saith:

Wisdom!

The Reader. The Parable from the Prophecy of Isaiah.

Deacon. Let us attend.

Thus saith the Lord (*ch. xxxv.*): The wilderness and the solitary place shall be glad for them; and the desert shall rejoice, and blossom as the rose. It shall blossom abundantly, and rejoice, even with joy and singing: the glory of Lebanon shall be given unto it, the excellency of Carmel and Sharon, they shall see the glory of the Lord, and the excellency of our God. Strengthen ye the weak hands, and confirm the feeble knees. Say to them that are of a fearful heart, Be strong, fear not: behold, your God will come with vengeance, even God with a recompense; he will come and save you.   Then the eyes of the blind shall be opened, and the ears of the deaf shall be unstopped.   Then shall the lame man leap as an hart, and the tongue of the dumb sing: for in the wilderness shall waters break out, and streams in the desert.   And the parched ground shall become a pool, and the thirsty land springs of water: in the habitation of dragons, where each lay, shall be grass with reeds and rushes.   And an highway shall be there, and a way, and it shall be called, The way of holiness, the unclean shall not pass over it; but it shall be for those: the wayfaring men, though fools, shall not err therein.   No lion shall be there, nor any ravenous beast shall go up thereon, it shall not be found there; but the redeemed shall walk there: and the ransomed of the Lord shall return, and come to Zion with songs and everlasting joy upon their heads: they shall obtain joy and gladness, and sorrow and sighing shall flee away.

Deacon. Wisdom!

Reader. The Parable from the Prophecy of Isaiah.

Deacon. Let us attend.

Thus saith the Lord (*ch. lv.*): Ho, every one that thirsteth, come ye to the waters, and he that hath no money; come ye, buy, and eat; yea, come, buy wine and milk without money and without price.   Wherefore do ye spend money for that which is not bread? and your labour for that which satisfieth not? hearken diligently unto me, and eat ye that which is good, and let your soul delight itself in fatness.   Incline your ear, and come unto me: hear, and your soul shall live; and I will make an everlasting covenant with you, even the sure mercies of David.   Behold, I have given him for a witness to the people, a leader and commander to the people.   Behold, thou shalt call a nation that thou knowest not, and nations that knew not these shall run unto thee, because of the Lord thy God, and for the Holy One of Israel; for he hath glorified thee.   Seek ye the Lord while he may be found, call ye upon him while he is near: let the wicked forsake his way, and the unrighteous man his thoughts: and let him return unto the Lord, and he will have mercy upon him; and to our God, for he will abundantly pardon.   For my thoughts are not your thoughts, neither are your ways my ways, saith the Lord.   For as the heavens are higher than the earth, so are my ways higher than your ways, and my thoughts than your thoughts.   For as the rain cometh down, and the snow from heaven, and returneth not thither, but watereth the earth, and maketh it bring forth and bud, that it may give seed to the sower, and bread to the eater: so shall my word be that goeth forth out of my mouth: it shall not return unto me void, but it shall accomplish that which I please, and it shall prosper in the thing whereto I sent it.   For ye shall go out with joy, and be led forth with peace: the mountains and the hills shall break forth before you into singing, and all the trees of the field shall clap their hands.   Instead of the thorn shall come up the fir-tree, and instead of the brier shall come up the myrtle-tree: and it shall be to the Lord for a name, for an everlasting sign that shall not be cut off.

Deacon. Wisdom!

Reader. The Parable from the Prophecy of Isaiah.

Deacon. Let us attend.

Thus saith the Lord (*ch. xii. 3–6*): Therefore with joy shall ye draw water out of the wells of salvation. And in that day shall ye say, Praise the Lord, call upon his name, declare his doings among the people, make mention that his name is exalted. Sing unto the Lord; for he hath done excellent things: this is known in all the earth. Cry out and shout, thou inhabitant of Zion: for great is the Holy One of Israel in the midst of thee.

Deacon. Let us attend.

Priest. Peace be with you all.

Reader. And with thy spirit.

Deacon. Wisdom!

Reader. The Gradual (*Prokímen*), in the Third Tone. The Lord is my light and my salvation, whom shall I fear?

Verse: The Lord is the strength of my life; of whom shall I be afraid?

Deacon. Wisdom!

Reader. The Lesson from the Epistle of the holy Apostle Paul to the Corinthians.

Deacon. Let us attend.

Brethren (*1 Cor. x. 1–4*): I would not that ye should be ignorant how that all our fathers were under the cloud, and all passed through the sea; and were all baptized unto Moses in the cloud and in the sea; and did all eat the same spiritual meat; and did all drink the same spiritual drink (for they drank of that spiritual Rock that followed them; and that Rock was Christ).

Priest. Peace be with thee.

Reader. And with thy spirit.

Deacon. Wisdom!

Alleluia. (*Tone IV.*)

Verse: The voice of the Lord upon the waters, the God of glory hath thundered: the Lord upon many waters.

Deacon. Wisdom, O believers! Let us listen to the Holy Gospel.

Priest. Peace be with you all.

People. And with thy spirit.

Priest. The Lesson from the holy Gospel of Mark.

Choir. Glory to thee, O Lord; glory to thee.

Deacon. Let us attend.

(*Ch. i. 9–11.*) *Priest.* And it came to pass in those days, that Jesus came from Nazareth of Galilee, and was baptized of John in Jordan. And straightway coming up out of the water, he saw the heavens opened, and the Spirit like a dove descending upon him   And there came a voice from heaven, saying, Thou art my beloved Son, in whom I am well pleased.

Choir. Glory to thee, O Lord; glory to thee.

Then the Deacon reciteth the LITANY.

In peace let us pray to the Lord.

Choir. Lord, have mercy.

For the peace that is from above, and for the salvation of our souls: ℞

For the peace of the whole world; for the welfare of God's holy Churches, and for the union of all: ℞

For this holy temple, and for those who with faith, devoutness, and in the fear of God have entered therein: ℞

For our Most Holy Synod (*or* Patriarch); for our Bishop (*or* Archbishop, *or* Metropolitan), N.; for the honourable Presbytery, the Diaconate in Christ, and for all the clergy and the laity: ℞

For our most God-fearing Ruler, and for all the Authorities; and for all their Council and Army and Navy: ℞

That he will aid them and subdue under their feet every foe and adversary: ℞

For this city (*if in a monastery,* for this holy habitation), and for those who in the faith dwell therein: ℞

For healthful seasons; for abundance of the fruits of the earth; and for peaceful times: ℞

For those who travel by sea or by land; for the sick and the suffering; for those who are in captivity, and for their salvation: ℞

That these waters may be sanctified by the power, and effectual operation, and descent of the Holy Spirit: ℞

That there may descend upon these waters the cleansing operation of the super-substantial Trinity: ℞

That he will endue them with the grace of redemption, the blessing of Jordan, the might, and operation, and descent of the Holy Spirit: ℞

let us pray to the Lord. Choir. Lord, have mercy.

And while this is being said, the Priest saith, secretly, the following Prayer:

O Lord Jesus Christ, the Only-begotten Son, who art in the bosom of the Father, the true God, Source of Life and of Immortality; Light of Light, who art come into the world to illuminate it: Enlighten our minds with thy Holy Spirit, and accept us who offer unto thee majesty and thanksgiving for thy marvellous mighty works, which are from all eternity; as, also, for thy saving providence in these latter ages, in which thou hast clothed thyself in our frail and lowly substance, and hast condescended to the stature of a servant; who yet art King of all; who also didst receive baptism in Jordan at the hands of a servant: that thou, O Sinless One, having sanctified the nature of water, mightest make for us a way which

Secretly.

That Satan may speedily be crushed under our feet, and that every evil council directed against us may be brought to nought: ℟

That the Lord our God will free us from every attack and temptation of the enemy, and make us worthy of the good things which he hath promised: ℟

That he will illumine us with the light of understanding and of piety, and with the descent of the Holy Spirit: ℟

That the Lord our God will send down the blessing of Jordan and sanctify these waters: ℟

That this water may be unto the bestowing of sanctification; unto the remission of sins; unto the healing of soul and body: and unto every expedient service: ℟

That this water may be a fountain welling forth unto life eternal: ℟

That it may manifest itself effectual unto the averting of every machination of our foes, whether visible or invisible: ℟

For those who shall draw of it and take of it unto the sanctification of their homes: ℟

That it may be for the purification of the souls and bodies of all those who, with faith, shall draw and partake of it: ℟

That he will graciously enable us to perfect sanctification by participation in these waters, through the invisible manifestation of the Holy Spirit: ℟

That the Lord God will hearken unto the voice of petition of us sinners, and will have mercy upon us: ℟

That he will deliver us from all tribulation, wrath, and necessity: ℟

let us pray to the Lord. Choir. Lord, have mercy.

Secretly.

should be unto a new birth, through water and the Spirit, and unto the deliverance then first instituted for us. Celebrating the memory of which divine mystery, we beseech thee, O Lord who lovest mankind, sprinkle us, thine unworthy servants, according to thy divine promise, with pure water, the gift of thy tenderness of heart. And may the supplications of us sinners over this holy water be well pleasing unto thy goodness: and may thy blessing through it be vouchsafed unto us, and unto all thy faithful people, to the glory of thy holy and adorable Name.

For unto thee belongeth all glory, honour and worship, together with thy Father who is from everlasting, and thine all-holy, and good, and life-giving Spirit, now, and ever, and unto ages of ages.

And he saith within himself: Amen.

Succour us, save us, have mercy upon us, and keep us, O God, by thy grace.

Choir. Lord, have mercy.

Calling to remembrance our most holy, all-undefiled, most blessed and glorious Lady, the Birth-giver of God and ever-virgin Mary, with all the Saints, let us commend ourselves, and each other, and all our life unto Christ our God.

Choir. To thee, O Lord.

And when the Deacon hath finished the Litany, the Priest reciteth, aloud, the following Prayer:

Great art thou, O Lord, and marvellous are thy works, and speech sufficeth not to sing the praises of thy wonders. (*Thrice.*)

·For thou, by thy will, from nothingness hast brought all things into being; by thy majesty thou dost uphold all creation, and by thy providence thou dost direct the world. When thou hadst framed the universe out of four elements, thou didst crown the circle of the year with four seasons. All the reason-endowed powers tremble before thee. The Sun singeth thy praises, and the Moon glorifieth thee; the Stars, also, stand before thy presence. The Light obeyeth thee. The deeps shudder with awe before thee; the water-springs do thy bidding. Thou hast spread out the heavens like a curtain. Thou hast established the earth upon the waters. With sand hast thou walled in the sea. Thou hast shed abroad the air for breathing. The Angelic Powers serve thee. The Archangelic hosts adore thee. The many-eyed Cherubim and the six-winged Seraphim, as they stand round about and do fly, veil their faces with awe before thine unapproachable glory. For thou, the God which cannot be circumscribed, who art from everlasting and ineffable, didst come down upon earth, taking on the form of a servant, and being made in the likeness of men. For thou couldst not endure, O Master, because of thy tender-hearted mercy, to behold the children of men tormented by the devil; but thou didst come, and didst save us. We confess thy grace; we proclaim thy mercy; we conceal not thy gracious deeds. Thou hast set at liberty the generations of our race; by thy birth thou hast sanctified a Virgin's womb. All creation singeth praises unto thee, who didst reveal thyself; for thou, our God, didst manifest thyself upon earth, and didst dwell among men. Thou didst hallow, also, the streams of Jordan, in that thou didst send down from heaven thy Holy Spirit, and didst crush the heads of the serpents which lurked there.

Then the Priest repeateth, thrice, the following, and blesseth the water with his hand at each repetition.

Wherefore do thou, O King who lovest mankind, come down now also through the descent of thy Holy Spirit, and sanctify this water. (*Thrice.*)

And impart unto it the grace of redemption, the blessing of Jordan. Make it a fountain of immortality, a gift of sanctification, a remission of sins, a healing of infirmities, a destruction of demons; unapproachable by hostile powers, filled with angelic might. And may it be unto all those who shall draw it, and shall partake of it unto the purification of their souls and bodies, unto the healing of their passions, unto the sanctification of their houses, and unto every expedient service. For thou art our God, who through water and the Spirit dost renew our nature, which had fallen into decay through sin. For thou art our God, who with water didst drown sin in the days of Noah. For thou art our God, who by the sea, through Moses, didst set free from slavery to Pharaoh the Hebrew race. For thou art our God, who didst cleave the rock in the wilderness, so that water gushed forth, and who madest the floods to well forth abundantly; and didst satisfy thy thirsty people. For thou art our God, who by fire and water, through Elijah, didst set Israel free from the errors of Baal.

Do thou, the same Master, sanctify now also this water by thy Holy Spirit. (*Thrice.*)

Grant also unto all who shall be sprinkled therewith, and shall partake thereof, and shall anoint themselves therewith, sanctification, blessing, purification and bodily health.

And save, O Lord, thy servant, our most God-fearing Ruler, N., and all the Authorities.

Save, O Lord, and show mercy upon the Most Holy Synod, and keep them in peace beneath thy shelter. Subdue under them every foe and adversary; grant all their petitions which are unto salvation and life eternal; that with the elements, and men, and Angels, and with all things visible and invisible, they may magnify thy most holy Name, together with the Father, and the Holy Spirit, now, and ever, and unto ages of ages. Amen.

Priest. Peace be with you.

Choir. And with thy spirit.

Deacon. Bow your heads unto the Lord.

Choir. To thee, O Lord.

And the Priest, bowing his head, prayeth:

Incline thine ear, O Lord, and hear us, O thou who wast graciously pleased to receive baptism in Jordan, and didst sanctify the waters. Bless all us who, by the bowing of our necks, do outwardly signify our humility of mind: and graciously grant that we may be filled with thy sanctification, through our partaking of this water, and through sprinkling therewith. And may be it unto us, O Lord, for the health of our souls and bodies.

Exclamation.

Priest. For thou art the sanctification of our souls and bodies, and unto thee we ascribe glory, and thanksgiving and worship, together with thy Father, who is from everlasting, and thine all-holy, and good, and life-giving Spirit, now, and ever, and unto ages of ages. Amen.

And again blessing the water in cross-form with the holy cross, he dippeth it therein, upright, elevating and lowering it, holding it with both hands, and singing the following Hymn in Tone I.:

When in Jordan thou wast baptized, O Lord, the worship of the Trinity was made manifest.   For the voice of the Father bare witness unto thee, calling thee his beloved Son, and the Spirit, in the form of a dove, confirmed the steadfastness of that word.   O Christ, who didst manifest thyself, and dost enlighten the world, glory to thee.

And the Choir singeth the same.

Then he blesseth the waters a second time, in like manner.   And the Singers repeat.

And likewise, a third time.

Then the Priest taketh of the holy water in a vessel, and turneth his face toward the People, holding the cross in his left hand, and in his right the aspergillus.   And the People approach, and kiss the precious cross; and the Priest blesseth them, and signeth them, on the face, with the sign of the cross, with the holy water on the aspergillus.

Then they enter the Church again, singing, in Tone VI.:

Let us praise in song, ye faithful, the greatness of God's favour to us-ward.   For, having become man because of our transgressions, by our purification is he purified in Jordan, he, the only pure and spotless One, who sanctifieth me and the waters, and crusheth the heads of the serpents in the water.   Wherefore, O brethren, let us draw of that water with joy; for the grace of the Spirit is invisibly imparted unto him who, with faith, doth draw thereof, by Christ our God, who also is the Saviour of our souls.

Choir. Blessed be the Name of the Lord, henceforth, and forever. (*Thrice.*)

PSALM XXXIV.

I will alway give thanks unto the Lord: his praise shall ever be in my mouth.   My soul shall make her boast in the Lord; the humble shall hear thereof, and be glad.   O praise the Lord with me, and let us magnify his Name together.   I sought the Lord, and he heard me; yea, he delivered me out of all my fear.   They had an eye unto him, and were lightened; and their faces were not ashamed.   Lo, the poor crieth, and the Lord heareth him; yea, and saveth him out of all his troubles.   The angel of the Lord tarrieth round about them that fear him, and delivereth them.   O taste, and see, how gracious the Lord is: blessed is the man that trusteth in him.   O fear the Lord, ye that are his saints; for they that fear him lack nothing.   The lions do lack, and suffer hunger; but they who seek the Lord shall want no manner of thing that is good.   Come, ye children, and hearken unto me; I will teach you the fear of the Lord.   What man is he that lusteth to live, and would fain see good days?   Keep thy tongue from evil, and thy lips, that they speak no guile.   Eschew evil, and do good; seek peace, and ensue it.   The eyes of the Lord are over the right-eous, and his ears are open unto their prayers.   The countenance of the Lord is against them that do evil; to root out the remembrance of them from the earth.   The righteous cry, and the Lord heareth them, and de-livereth them out of all their troubles.   The Lord is nigh unto them that are of a contrite heart, and will save such as be of an humble spirit. Great are the troubles of the righteous; but the Lord delivereth him out of all.   He keepeth all his bones, so that not one of them is broken.   But misfortune shall slay the ungodly; and they that hate the righteous shall be desolate.   The Lord delivereth the souls of his servants; and all they that put their trust in him shall not be destitute.

And having first drunk of the holy water, the People take the ANTIDÓRON, *that is, the blessed bread, from the Priest.*

Then the BENEDICTION *is pronounced:*

May he who was graciously pleased to accept baptism from John, in Jordan, for the sake of our salvation, Christ our true God, through the prayers of his most pure Mother, and of all the Saints, have mercy upon us and save us; forasmuch as he is gracious and loveth mankind.

THE MEETING OF THE LORD

THE PURIFICATION OF THE HOLY BIRTH–GIVER OF GOD

(FEBRUARY 2—15 N.S.)

The Stanza (Stikhíra) for: Lord, I have cried: *In Tone I.* Let us also come: with hymns divine let us meet Christ and receive him whose salvation Simeon beheld. For this is he of whom David prophesied: This is he who spake by the prophets; who for our sakes became incarnate, and proclaimed the law. Him let us worship. (*Twice.*)

Glory to the Father, and to the Son, and to the Holy Spirit, now, and ever, and unto ages of ages. Amen.

Tone VI. To-day let the door of heaven be opened: for the Father's Word, which is from everlasting, having taken his beginning in time from a Virgin, without renouncing his Godhead, is of her own free will brought by his mother, as a babe of forty days, into the temple under the law: and an aged man receiveth him in his arms, crying: Let thy servant depart, O Lord; for mine eyes have seen thy salvation, which is come into the world to save the race of men. Glory to thee, O Lord.

The Parables (Paremíi). Exodus xii. 51, xiii. 1–3, 11–12, 14–16; Lev. xii. 2–4, 6, 8; Isaiah vi. 1–13, xix. 1, 3–5, 12, 19–21.

The Stanza at the Litiyá, in Tone I. (by Anatolius). The Ancient of Days, who of old gave the Law unto Moses, on Sinai, to-day is seen as a little Child; and in accordance with the Law, as the creator of the Law, fulfilling the Law, is brought into the temple, and given to an aged man. And Simeon the Righteous, having received him, and perceived the fulfilment of the promises accomplished, cried aloud with joy: Mine eyes have seen the mystery hidden from eternity in these latter days revealed, the light which destroyeth the darkness of unbelieving heathen, and giveth glory unto newly chosen Israel. Wherefore, release thou thy servant from the bonds of this flesh unto the life which waxeth not old, marvellous and unending; granting unto the world great mercy.

The Hymn for the Day (Tropár), in Tone I. Hail, O Virgin Birth-giver of God: for from thee hath shone forth the Sun of Righteousness, Christ our God, who giveth light to those who are in darkness. And rejoice, thou aged, righteous man, that didst receive in thine arms the Redeemer of our souls, who giveth unto us resurrection.

The Exaltation (Velitchánie). We magnify thee, O life-giving Christ, and we do homage to thy Mother most pure, by whom thou hast now been brought into the Temple of the Lord, according to the Law.

The Gradual (Prokímen), in the Fourth Tone. I will call to remembrance thy Name from generation to generation.

Verse (Stikh): My heart is inditing of a good matter.

The Gospel. Luke ii. 25–32.

The Benediction. May he who, for the sake of our salvation, deigned to be held in the arms of the righteous Simeon, Christ our true God: *and the rest.* (*See page* 122.)

THE CANON.

The First Canon. Tone III. (St. Cosmas of Maium.)

Theme-Songs (Irmosi). I. The sun once, of old, rose over the dry land born of the deep: for the water was hardened into walls upon either side, and the people passed on foot over the sea, and sang, in manner well-pleasing unto God: Let us sing unto the Lord, for gloriously hath he been glorified.

III. O Lord, the Confirmation of those who set their hope on thee, confirm thou thy Church, which thou hast bought with thy precious blood.

IV. Thine excellence, O Christ, hath covered the heavens; for when thou hadst come forth from the ark of thy Holy Place, even thy Mother undefiled, thou didst appear in the temple of thy glory as a little Child borne in arms: and all things were filled with thy praise.

V. When Isaiah symbolically beheld God borne on high upon the throne, attended by a body-guard of Angels of glory, he exclaimed: O miserable man that I am, I have foreseen God Incarnate, who hath dominion over the Light which knoweth no setting, and the Peace which reigneth forever.

VI. The Aged Man, when with his eyes he beheld the salvation which was come from God unto the nations, cried aloud unto thee: Thou art my God, O Christ!

VII. Thee, O God the Word, who didst shed dew upon the Children which sang praises unto God in the fire, and who didst take up thine abode in a Virgin undefiled, do we hymn, devoutly singing: Blessed is the God of our fathers!

VIII. The Youths supreme in godliness, when they were thrust into the fire insupportable yet suffered no hurt from the flame, sang aloud the song divine: O all ye works of the Lord, bless ye the Lord, and magnify him unto all the ages!

In place of: My soul doth magnify the Lord: *the Refrains:*

O Virgin Birth-giver of God, the Hope of Christians, protect, guard and save thou those who put their trust in thee.

O Virgin Birth-giver of God, gracious Helper of the world, protect and keep us from all need and distress.

O God-bearing Simeon, come and take in thine arms Christ, to whom Mary the Virgin Pure hath given birth.

Simeon the aged encompasseth in his embrace the Creator of the Law, and the Lord of all.

The Aged Man holdeth not Me, but I hold him: for he entreateth of Me that he may depart in peace.

Ye Pincers mystical, how shall ye bear the coal of fire?　How shall ye nourish the Nourisher of all?

O Daughter of Phanuel, come and abide with us, and bless Christ the Saviour, the Son of God.

Anna the Chaste foretelleth terrible things, confessing Christ to be the Maker of heaven and earth.

Incomprehensible unto Angels and unto men is that which is wrought with thee, O Virgin Mother Pure.

A pure dove, a spotless lamb bringeth into the Church the Lamb and the Shepherd.

O Christ, King of all!　Grant me burning tears, and I will weep for my soul which is all ruined.

IX. In the Law — in the shadow and in the Scriptures — do we, the faithful, behold the symbol.　Every male child which first opened the womb was consecrated to God: wherefore, also, the first-born Word of the Father, who is from everlasting, the first-born Son of his Mother who knew not man, do we magnify.

At the Liturgy.

The Introit. The Lord hath declared his salvation, he hath revealed his righteousness in the presence of the nations.

The Collect-Hymn (Kondák). Thou who by thy birth didst sanctify the Virgin's womb, and didst bless the arms of Simeon, as it was meet, having preserved us in anticipation from condemnation, hast now also saved us, O Christ-God.　But grant tranquillity amid the alarms of war unto our Ruler, and keep him, whom thou hast adopted into thy love, O thou who alone lovest mankind.

The Gradual (Prokímen), in the Fourth Tone. My soul doth magnify the Lord, and my spirit hath rejoiced in God my Saviour.

Verse: For he hath regarded the lowliness of his handmaiden: for behold, from henceforth, all generations shall call me blessed.

The Epistle. Heb. vii. 7–17.

Alleluia.　(*Tone VIII.*)　Lord, now lettest thou thy servant depart in peace, according to thy word.

Verse: A light to lighten the Gentiles, and the glory of thy people Israel.

The Gospel. Luke ii. 22–40.

The Communion Hymn. I will take the cup of salvation, and call upon the Name of the Lord.

The Benediction. (*See page* 199.)

THE ANNUNCIATION OF THE MOST HOLY VIRGIN

(MARCH 25—APRIL 7 N.S.)

This Feast almost always falleth in the Great Fast (Lent).
If the Feast of the Annunciation fall upon any day upon the eve whereof Vespers
  hath been celebrated alone, or in conjunction with the Liturgy of the Presanctified
  Gifts, then the Vigil Service beginneth with Great Compline.
If it fall upon Sunday or Monday, the Vigil Service beginneth with Great Vespers.
  But if it fall upon Great (Good) Friday, or Great (Holy) Saturday, the Vigil
  Service beginneth directly with Matins.

The Stanza (Stikhíra) for: Lord, I have cried: *In Tone VI.* Gabriel,
when he revealed unto thee, O Maiden, the counsel of God which was
from everlasting, did stand before thee, saluting thee, and proclaiming:
Hail, O Earth Unsown! Hail, O Bush which Burned, yet was not consumed! Hail, O Abyss Unfathomable! Hail, O Bridge which leadeth
unto heaven, and Ladder lofty, which Jacob saw! Hail, O Pot Divine of
Manna! Hail, O Abrogation of the curse! Hail, O Recall of Adam!
The Lord is with thee.

Glory to the Father, and to the Son, and to the Holy Spirit, now, and
ever, and unto ages of ages. Amen.

Gabriel the Archangel was sent from heaven to announce the glad
tidings of conception unto a Virgin; and when he was come to Nazareth,
he mused within himself, being astonished at the marvel: O, how can he
who on high is beyond comprehension be born of a Virgin! He who hath
heaven for his throne, and earth for his footstool, taketh up his abode in
the womb of a Virgin! He upon whom the Six-winged and the Many-
eyed are unable to gaze deigneth, by his word alone, to become incarnate
of her, and he is the true Word of God. Wherefore then stand I thus,
and say not unto the Virign: Hail, O pure Virgin! Hail, O Bride unwedded, the Lord is with thee! Hail, O Mother of the Life, blessed is the
fruit of thy womb!

The Parables (Paremíí) are the same as at the Feast of the Nativity of the
Virgin (see page 164), and Exodus iii. 1–8; Prov. viii. 22–30.

At Great Compline.

There is a procession from the Sanctuary, for the Litiyá (see page 11), after: Glory to
  God in the highest: *hath been read.*

The Stanza for the Litiyá, in Tone I. In the sixth month was the
Chieftain of the Archangels sent unto thee, a Virgin undefiled, to announce unto thee the word of salvation and to proclaim unto thee: Hail,
thou who art made glad, the Lord is with thee! Thou shalt bear the Son
of the Father who was before the ages, and he shall save his people from
their sins.

The Hymn for the Day (Tropár), in Tone IV. To-day is the crown of our salvation, and the manifestation of that mystery which is from everlasting: The Son of God becometh the son of a Virgin, and Gabriel announceth the glad tidings of grace. Wherefore let us also cry aloud with him unto the Birth-giver of God: Hail, thou that art full of grace, the Lord is with thee!

The Exaltation (Velitchánie). The song of the Archangel sing we unto thee, O Pure One: Hail, thou that art full of grace, the Lord is with thee!

The Gradual (Prokímen), in the Fourth Tone. Proclaim ye, from day unto day, the glad tidings of the salvation of our God.

Verse (Stikh): Sing unto the Lord a new song, sing unto the Lord, all the whole earth.

The Gospel. Luke i. 39–49, 56.

THE CANON.

The First Canon. In Tone IV. (The Blessed Theophanius and St. John of Damascus.)

Theme-Songs (Irmosí). I. I will open my mouth, and it shall be filled with the Spirit, and I will utter a saying to the Queen-Mother. I will reveal myself radiantly keeping high festival, and with rejoicing will I sing her marvels.

III. O Birth-giver of God, Fountain living and inexhaustible! Spiritually establish thou those who hymn thee, convoked in a choir, and vouchsafe unto them crowns of glory in thy glory divine.

IV. Jesus, the Most Divine, who sitteth in glory upon the throne of the Godhead, is come, upon a light cloud borne by a palm undefiled, and hath saved those who cry: Glory to thy power, O Christ!

V. All things marvelled at thy glory divine; for thou, O Virgin, though thou knewest not wedlock, didst have in thy womb God who is over all, and didst give birth to the timeless Son, who granteth peace unto all that sing praises unto thee.

VI. Jonah the Prophet, typifying the three days' burial, exclaimed, as he prayed within the whale: Deliver me from corruption, O Jesus, King of the Powers!

VII. The godly-minded ones worshipped not the creature rather than the Creator, but valiantly trampling under foot the threatened fire, they rejoiced in song, saying: Blessed art thou, O Lord and God of our fathers, exceedingly praised!

VIII. Hearken, O Maiden, Virgin Pure, and let Gabriel announce the true will of the Most High, which was from of old: Make thou ready to receive God; for through thee the Uncontainable shall dwell among men. For which cause, also, I cry aloud with joy: O all ye works of the Lord, bless ye the Lord!

In place of: My soul doth magnify the Lord: *The Refrain:* O Earth, proclaim the great gladness! and ye Heavens, praise ye the glory of God!

IX. Let no hand profane in anywise touch the living Ark of God; but let the lips of the faithful unceasingly singing the Salutation of the Angel to the Birth-giver of God, cry aloud with rejoicing: Hail, thou that art full of grace, the Lord is with thee!

The Liturgy at the Feast of the Annunciation beginneth with Vespers on those days when the HOURS OF THE GREAT FAST *are celebrated; but on the Saturdays and Sundays of the third, fourth, fifth and sixth weeks of the Fast Vespers is celebrated after the Liturgy. The Liturgy used is either that of St. John Chrysostom or of St. Basil the Great; never that of the Presanctified Gifts.*

The Stanza (Stikhíra) for: Lord, I have cried: *In Tone IV.* In the sixth month was an Archangel sent unto a Virgin pure; and when he had said unto her, Hail! he announced unto her the glad tidings that from her should come forth the Redeemer. Wherefore, having received the salutation, she conceived thee, the God who is before the ages, who in wise unutterable didst deign to become man for the salvation of our souls.

The Entrance is made with the book of the Holy Gospels. O gladsome radiance . . .

The Gradual (Prokímen) for the Day. (See Vespers, page 8.)

The Parables (Paremíí). The same as on the Eve. (See page 164.)

The Little Litany. Again, yet again, . . .

The Exclamation. For holy art thou, O our God; and unto thee do we ascribe glory, to the Father, and to the Son, and to the Holy Spirit, now, and ever, and unto ages of ages. Amen.

Choir. O Holy God, Holy Mighty, Holy Immortal One, have mercy upon us. *(Thrice.)*

At the Liturgy.

The Collect-Hymn (Kondák). We, thy servants, . . . *(See page 42.)*

The Gradual (Prokímen), in the Fourth Tone: Proclaim ye, from day unto day, the glad tidings of the salvation of our God.

Verse (Stikh): Sing unto the Lord a new song, sing unto the Lord all the whole earth. Alleluia. *(Tone I.)*

The Epistle. Heb. ii. 11–18.

He shall descend like dew upon the fleece, and like drops of rain dropping upon the earth.

Verse: His Name shall be blessed forevermore: his Name endureth before the sun.

Alleluia. *(Tone VI.)*

The Gospel. Luke i. 24–38.

The Hymn in place of: Meet is it: *The Ninth Theme-Song of the Canon:* Let no hand profane . . . *(See above.)*

The Communion Hymn (Pritchásten). For the Lord hath chosen Zion: he hath desired it for his habitation.

THE ENTRANCE OF THE LORD INTO JERUSALEM
(PALM SUNDAY)

At Vespers, on the Eve.

The Stanzas (Stikhíry) for: Lord, I have cried: *In Tone VI.* To-day hath the grace of the Holy Spirit assembled us together, and taking up thy cross let us all say: Blessed is he that cometh in the Name of the Lord. Hosanna in the highest!

He who hath the heavens for his throne, and the earth for his footstool, the coeternal Word and Son of God the Father, to-day is come to Bethany, and humbled himself on the dumb foal of an ass. For which cause the Hebrew children, bearing branches of trees in their hands, exalted him with the shout: Hosanna in the highest! Blessed is he that cometh in the Name of the Lord.

Glory to the Father, and to the Son, and to the Holy Spirit, now, and ever, and unto ages of ages. Amen.

To-day hath the grace of the Holy Spirit . . . (*See above.*)

The Parables (Paremíí). Genesis xlix. 1–12; Zeph. iii. 14–19; Zech. ix. 9–15.

At the Litiyá, in Tone I. The all-holy Spirit, which taught the Apostles to speak in other and strange tongues, the same commandeth the Hebrew children devoid of guile to cry aloud: Hosanna in the highest! Blessed is the King of Israel who cometh.

The Hymn for the Day (Tropár). Thou didst raise Lazarus from the dead, O Christ-God, making certain the universal resurrection, before thy Passion. For which cause we also, like unto the children, bearing the emblems of victory, cry aloud unto thee, the Conqueror of Death: Hosanna in the highest! Blessed is he that cometh in the Name of the Lord.

Another. Having been buried with thee in baptism, O Christ our God, we have been vouchsafed life immortal through thy Resurrection, and singing praises unto thee, we cry: Hosanna in the highest! Blessed is he that cometh in the Name of the Lord.

The Exaltation. We magnify thee, O Life-giving Christ! Hosanna in the highest! And we cry aloud unto thee: Blessed is he that cometh in the Name of the Lord.

The Gradual (Prokímen), in Tone IV. Out of the mouth of babes and sucklings hast thou ordained praise.

Verse: O Lord, the Lord our God, how wonderful is thy Name in all the earth.

The Gospel. Matt. xxi. 1–11, 15–17.

After the Gospel, Psalm li., and the PRAYER AT THE BLESSING OF THE PALMS.

Priest. O Lord our God, who sittest upon the Cherubim, who didst restore the might of thy Son, our Lord Jesus Christ, that through his Cross and Grave and Resurrection he might save the world; whom, also, when to-day he was come into Jerusalem, unto his voluntary Passion, the people who sat in darkness and in the shadow of death, taking the symbols of victory, even boughs of trees and branches of palms, emblematical of the Resurrection, did go forth to meet: Do thou, the same Lord, preserve · and keep us also who on this eve of the feast in imitation of them do bear in our hands palms and branches of trees.   And like unto those multitudes and children who offered unto thee Hosanna! may we also in hymns and spiritual songs, attain unto the life-giving Resurrection on the third day, through the same Christ Jesus our Lord; with whom thou art blessed, together with thine all-holy, and good, and life-giving Spirit, now, and ever, and unto ages of ages.   Amen.

The Priest distributeth the palms to the People, after they have saluted the Gospels and received his benediction.   The people then light their tapers and so stand until the end of the service, holding their palms.

PALM SUNDAY.
The First Canon.   In Tone IV.   (St. Cosmas of Maium.)

Theme-Songs (Irmosi).   I. The springs of the deep were seen to be bereft of water, and the foundations of the sea surging with a tempest were laid bare.   For thou, by a sign, didst lay thine interdiction upon it, and didst save thy chosen people, who sang a song of victory unto thee, O Lord.

III. The Children of Israel drank from the solid rock which, when its edge was cleft at thy command, poured forth water abundantly.   But that rock and that life art thou, O Christ, upon whom is founded the Church which crieth: Hosanna!   Blessed art thou who comest.

IV. Christ our God, who cometh visibly, shall come and shall not tarry, from the Mount grove-shadowed, born of a Maiden without husband, saith the Prophet of old: wherefore, let us all cry aloud: Glory to thy might, O Lord!

V. O thou who announcest the good tidings, get thee up into the Mount Zion, and lift up thy voice with strength, thou who proclaimest unto Jerusalem: Glorious things are spoken of thee, O city of God; peace upon Israel, and salvation unto the nations.

VI. The spirits of the righteous have cried aloud with joy: Now is a new covenant appointed unto the world, and all people shall be renewed through sprinkling with the blood divine.

VII. Thou who didst save thy children of Abraham in the fire, and didst annihilate the Chaldæans, who were overtaken by that righteous judgment: O Lord and God of our fathers, exceedingly praised, blessed art thou!

VIII. Rejoice, O Jerusalem! Keep high festival, O ye who love Zion! For the Lord of Hosts is come, who reigneth throughout the ages. Let all the earth fall down in adoration before his presence, and cry aloud: O all ye works of the Lord, bless ye the Lord!

IX. God is the Lord, and hath revealed himself unto us. O come, let us make ready a feast, let us magnify Christ with gladness and with palms and branches of trees, crying aloud unto him in hymns: Blessed is he that cometh in the Name of the Lord our Saviour.

The Benediction. May he who, for the sake of our salvation, did deign to sit upon the foal of an ass, Christ our true God: *and the rest, as usual.* (*See page* 122.)

At the Liturgy.
Antiphon I., Tone II.

Verse 1: I am well pleased that the Lord hath heard the voice of my prayer.

Refrain. Through the prayers of the Birth-giver of God, O Saviour, save us.

2: He hath inclined his ear unto me: therefore will I call upon him as long as I live. ℟

3: The snares of death compassed me round about, and the pains of hell gat hold upon me. ℟

4: I found trouble and heaviness, and I called upon the Name of the Lord. ℟

Glory to the Father, and to the Son, and to the Holy Spirit, now, and ever, and unto ages of ages. Amen. ℟

Antiphon II., Tone II.

Verse 1: I believed, and therefore have I spoken: but I was sore troubled.

Refrain. Save, O Son of God, who didst sit upon the foal of an ass, us who sing unto thee: Alleluia.

2: What reward shall I give unto the Lord, for all the benefits he hath done unto me? ℟

3: I will receive the cup of salvation, and call upon the Name of the Lord. ℟

4: I will pay my vows unto the Lord now, in the presence of all his people. ℟

Glory . . . now, and ever, . . . ℟

O Only-begotten Son and Word of God! . . . (*See page* 170.)

Antiphon III., Tone I.

Verse 1: O give thanks unto the Lord, for he is gracious, because his mercy endureth forever.

Refrain: The Hymn for the Day (Tropár). Thou didst raise Lazarus . . . (*See page* 204.)

2: Let the house of Israel now confess that he is gracious, and that his mercy endureth forever. ℟

3: Let the house of Aaron now confess that his mercy endureth forever. ℟

4: Yea, let all that fear the Lord confess that his mercy endureth forever. ℟

The Introit. Blessed is he that cometh in the Name of the Lord: we have blessed ye from the house of the Lord.   God is the Lord, and hath revealed himself unto us.

Glory to the Father, and to the Son, and to the Holy Spirit.   (*Tone IV.*)

Having been buried with thee in baptism, . . . (*See page* 204.)

Now, and ever, and unto ages of ages.   Amen.

The Collect-Hymn (*Kondák*). O Christ-God, who in heaven art borne upon the throne, and on earth upon the foal of an ass, thou didst accept the praises of the Angels, and the hymns of the children that cried unto thee: Blessed art thou who art come to recall Adam from the dead!

The Epistle. Phil. iv. 4–9.

The Gospel. John xii. 1–18.

In place of: Meet is it: *The Ninth Theme-Song of the Canon.*

The Communion Hymn. Blessed is he that cometh in the Name of the Lord.   God is the Lord, and hath revealed himself unto us.

GREAT THURSDAY

On Great Thursday the Church commemorateth the Lord's humbling of himself for our sakes: his washing the feet of his disciples, and the institution of the dread Mystery of the Body and Blood of Christ; his prayer in the garden, and his betrayal by Judas.

On this day, in some cathedral churches, the ceremony of the Washing of Feet is performed, as a lesson to us that we should serve one another.

In the Cathedral of the Falling-asleep of the Birth-giver of God (the Assumption), in Moscow; and in the Monastery of the Catacombs, in Kieff, at the conclusion of the Divine Liturgy on Holy Thursday is consecrated the Holy Chrism, which is used in all Russian churches, in the Sacrament of Chrismation, after Baptism. The Consecration of the Chrism taketh place at the Altar, after the Great Entrance.

MATINS.

Priest. Blessed is our God always, now, and ever, and unto ages of ages.

Then as usual (see MATINS) *until:* God is the Lord: *in place of which* Alleluia, *in the Fifth Tone, is sung.*

The Deacon readeth the Verses (Stikhí).

I. With my soul have I desired thee in the night, O God, before the dawn: thy judgments are in the earth.

Choir. Alleluia. (*Thrice.*)

II. The inhabitants of the earth will learn righteousness. ℟

III. Envy shall seize the people who have not been chastised. ℟

IV. Thou hast increased evil, O Lord, thou hast increased evil to the high ones of the earth. ℟

Hymn for the Day (Tropár). When the glorious disciples were illumined by the Washing at the Supper, then was the impious Judas, ailing with covetousness, darkened. And to the unjust judges doth he betray thee, the just Judge. Behold his money beloved, for the sake of which he hanged himself. Flee the insatiate soul which dared such things against the Master. O Lord who art good above all men, glory to thee. (*Tone VIII.*)

Glory to the Father, and to the Son, and to the Holy Spirit.

When the glorious disciples . . .

Now, and ever, and unto ages of ages. Amen.

When the glorious disciples . . .

Then the Deacon exclaimeth:

And that he will vouchsafe us grace to hear the Holy Gospel, let us pray to the Lord.

Choir. Lord, have mercy. (*Thrice.*)

Deacon. Wisdom, O believers! Let us listen to the Holy Gospel.

Priest. Peace be with you all.

Choir. And with thy spirit.

Priest. The Lesson from the holy Gospel of Luke.

Choir. Glory to thee, O Lord; glory to thee.

Deacon. Let us attend!

The Priest readeth the Gospel: Luke xx. 1–39.

Choir. Glory to thee, O Lord; glory to thee.

Then Psalm li. is read: Have mercy upon me, O God, according to thy great mercy. . . . *(See page 45.)*

The Prayer: O God, save thy people: *is not read but the Singers immediately begin*

THE CANON.

In Tone V. (St. Cosmas of Maium.)

The Theme-Songs (Irmosi). I. The Red Sea by a stroke is parted in twain, and the depth which feedeth the waves is dried up, the same being trodden by the unarmed, and becoming a grave to those fully armed. And a song well-pleasing unto God is sung: Gloriously hath Christ our God been glorified!

III. He who is the Lord of all, and God the Creator, the Passionless One, united the creature with himself, in that he did humble himself; and himself becoming the Passover, did offer himself in anticipation unto those on behalf of whom it was his will to die, crying: Eat ye my body, and ye shall be strengthened in faith.

IV. The Prophet, when he beheld in a vision thine ineffable Mystery, O Christ, cried out in anticipation: Thou, O bountiful Father, didst appoint the firm love of thy might: for thou didst give thine Only-begotten Son to the world as an Atonement, O Good One.

V. The Apostles, united in the bond of love, having dedicated themselves unto Christ who reigneth over all, made beautiful their feet to go and proclaim the glad tidings of peace unto all the world.

VI. The nethermost abyss of sins hath compassed me about, and unable longer to endure the billows thereof, like Jonah I cry aloud unto thee, O Master: Lead me forth from corruption.

The Collect-Hymn (Kondák), Tone II. The Traitor, having taken bread in his hand, privily stretched forth the same, and taketh a price for him who with his hands had made man; and Judas, the slave and the deceiver, remaineth reprobate.

VII. The Children in Babylon felt no fear of the furnace's flames; but when they were cast into the midst of the fire, being besprinkled with dew, they cried aloud in song: Blessed art thou, O God of our fathers!

VIII. The blessed Youths in Babylon, braving danger for the laws of their fathers, despised the mad behest of the potentate; and when they were encompassed by the fire in which they were not consumed, they sang a worthy song unto the Almighty: O all ye works of the Lord, bless ye the Lord, and magnify him unto all the ages.

Let us praise, bless and worship the Lord, hymning and magnifying him unto all the ages.

IX. Come, O ye faithful, let us enjoy the hospitality and the banquet immortal of the Lord, in the upper chamber, with minds uplifted, in that we have learned the Word from the Word who hath gone up on high: Whom also we do magnify.

Then the Choir: Exapostilárion.

I behold thy richly adorned dwelling-place, O my Saviour, and I have no festal raiment, that I may enter in.　Illumine thou the raiment of my soul, O Light-giver, and save me.

Glory to the Father, and to the Son, and to the Holy Spirit.

I behold . . .

Now, and ever, and unto ages of ages.　Amen.

I behold . . .

Then the Reader readeth the three customary Psalms: O praise the Lord of heaven (*Psalm cxlviii.*); O sing unto the Lord a new song (*Psalm cxlix.*); O praise God in his holiness (*Psalm cl.*).

Glory to thee who hast shown us the light.

Glory be to God on high, and on earth peace, good will toward men: We praise thee: *and the rest, as usual, to the end, as shown in the Office for Matins, when celebrated separately.*

THE FIRST HOUR.

The Order for the First Hour is as usual (see FIRST HOUR, *page 38), with the Hymn for the Day (Tropár).*

When the glorious disciples . . . (*See page 208.*)

And then: What shall we call thee, . . . (*See page 39.*)

The Reader readeth the HYMN OF PROPHECY, *in Tone IV.*

O Lord, who wast buffeted in the face for the sake of the human race, and yet waxed not wroth, deliver thou our life from corruption, and save us.　(*Twice.*)

Priest. Let us attend.

Reader. The Gradual (*Prokímen*), in the First Tone.　Let the heathen understand that thy Name is the Lord.　*The Choir repeateth.*

Verse (Stikh): Who is like unto thee, O God.

Priest. Wisdom!

Reader. The Parable (*Paremiyá*) from the Prophecy of Jeremiah.

Priest. Let us attend.

The Reader then readeth the Parable: Jer. xi. 18–23, xii. 1–5, 9–11 (*selected*), 14–15

Priest. Let us attend.　Wisdom!

Reader. The Gradual (*Prokimen*), in the Eighth Tone. Pray and return thanks unto the Lord our God.

Verse: We have seen God in Judah; great is his Name in Israel.

Reader. Order my steps in thy word, and so shall no wickedness . . . (*See* FIRST HOUR, *page* 40.)

The BENEDICTION.

May the Lord who, for the sake of our salvation, cometh to his voluntary Passion, Christ, our true God; through the prayers . . . (*See page* 122.)

And the MANY YEARS.

THE LITURGY.

The Liturgy, which is always that of St. Basil the Great, beginneth with Vespers. Vespers is celebrated as usual, with the following exceptions:

The Verses (Stikhíri) for: Lord, I have cried: *In Tone I.* Bring my soul out of prison, that I may give thanks unto thy Name.

The whole multitude of the Jews assembleth together, and delivereth over unto Pilate the Maker and Creator of all men. O iniquitous! O faithless! They prepare for judgment him who shall come to judge both the quick and the dead; him who healeth passions they prepare for his Passion. O Lord long-suffering, great is thy mercy: glory to thee.

Out of the depths have I cried unto thee, O Lord: O Lord, hear my voice.

Judas the impious, when at supper he had dipped his hand in the salt with thee, O Lord, stretched forth to the impious his hand to receive the pieces of silver; and having meditated upon the price of the ointment, was not afraid to betray thee, the Priceless One: For he stretched forth his foot to be washed, he deceitfully kissed the Master, that he might betray him to the impious ones; he was cast out from the company of the Apostles, and flung down the thirty pieces of silver, and beheld not thy rising on the third day: Through which show thou mercy upon us.

If thou, Lord, wilt be extreme to mark what is done amiss, O Lord, who may abide it?

Judas the traitor, being deceitful, with a deceitful kiss did betray the Saviour, and Lord and Master of all men, in that he sold him like a slave to the Jews; like a sheep to the slaughter even so went the Lamb of God, the Son of the Father, the only All-Merciful One.

My soul doth wait upon the Lord, before the morning watch, I say, before the morning watch.

Judas showed himself a slave and deceiver, a disciple and a calumniator, a friend and a devil in his deeds; for having followed the Teacher and learned the doctrine from him, he said within himself: I will betray him, and acquire the possessions which he hath accumulated; for he sought to sell the ointment, and to take Jesus by guile. He gave a kiss, he betrayed Christ. And like a sheep to the slaughter, even so went the Lamb of God, the only Compassionate One who loveth mankind.

O praise the Lord, all ye heathen: praise him, all ye nations.

The Lamb which was prophesied by Isaiah cometh to his voluntary slaughter, and giveth his back to the smiters and his cheeks to buffeting, and his face hath he not turned away from the ignominy of the spitting, and he is condemned to a shameful death. The Sinless One of his own will accepteth all things, and unto all men giveth he resurrection from the dead.

Glory . . . now, and ever, . . .

Tone VI.

Judas was, of a truth, the descendant of the vipers who ate manna in the wilderness, and murmured against Him who fed them: for while the food was still in their mouths, the ingrates spake evil against God. And this godless man, while he bare in his mouth the heavenly bread, committed treachery against the Saviour. O nature insatiable, and audacity inhuman! He selleth the One who feedeth him, and betrayeth unto death the Master who loveth him. Of a truth is he the son of the impious, and with them hath he inherited perdition. But spare thou our souls, O Lord, from such inhumanity, O thou who alone art of ineffable long-suffering.

The Entrance is then made with the Gospels.

Deacon. Wisdom, O believers!

Choir. O gladsome radiance . . . (*See page* 8.)

Deacon. Let us attend.

Priest. Peace be with you all.

Deacon. Wisdom! Let us attend.

Reader. The Gradual (*Prokímen*), in the First Tone. Deliver me from the deceitful and wicked man, O Lord.

Verse (Stikh): Who hath imagined evil in his heart all the day long.

Deacon. Wisdom!

Reader. The Parable (*Paremiyá*) from Exodus.

Deacon. Let us attend.

The Reader then readeth the Parable (Paremiyá): Exodus xix. 10–19.

Reader. The Gradual (*Prokímen*), in the Seventh Tone. Remove me from mine enemies, O God, and deliver me from them that rise up against me.

Verse (Stikh): Deliver me from them that work wickedness.

Deacon. Wisdom!

Reader. The Parable (*Paremiyá*) from Job.

Deacon. Let us attend.

The Reader then readeth the Parable: Job xxxviii. 1–22, xlii. 1–5.

Deacon. Wisdom!

Reader. The Parable (*Paremiyá*) from the Prophecy of Isaiah.

Deacon. Let us attend.

The Reader then readeth: Isaiah l. 4–11.

Then the Little Litany, with the Exclamation:

For holy art thou, O our God, and unto thee do we ascribe glory, to the Father, and to the Son, and to the Holy Spirit, now, and ever, and unto ages of ages.

Choir. Amen.   O Holy God, Holy Mighty: *and the rest, as usual.*   (*See page* 86.)

Reader. The Gradual (*Prokímen*), in the Seventh Tone.   The princes of the people are assembled together against the Lord, and against his Anointed.

Verse (*Stikh*): Why do the heathen rage, and the people imagine a vain thing?

Reader. The Lesson from the First Epistle of St. Paul to the Corinthians.

And the Reader readeth the Epistle: 1 Cor. xi. 23–32.

Deacon. The Lesson from the holy Gospel of Matthew.

And the Deacon readeth the Gospel: Matt. xxvi. 1–20; John xiii. 3–17; Matt. xxvi. 21–39; Luke xxii. 43–45; Matt. xxvi. 40, xxvii. 1–2.

In place of the Cherubimic Hymn, the Choir singeth, in Tone VI.:

Of thy Mystical Supper, O Son of God, accept me to-day as a communicant; for I will not speak of thy Mystery to thine enemies, neither like Judas will I give thee a kiss; but like the thief will I confess thee: Remember me, O Lord, in thy kingdom.

And in place of: Meet is it:

Come, O ye faithful, let us enjoy the hospitality and the banquet immortal of the Lord, in the upper chamber, with minds uplifted, in that we have learned the Word from the Word who hath gone up on high: Whom we do magnify.

And in place of the Communion Hymn:

Of thy Mystical Supper, . . . (*See above.*)

Also, in place of: Let our mouths be filled:

Of thy Mystical Supper, . . .

The BENEDICTION.

Priest. May he who, because of his surpassing graciousness, showed unto us the most excellent way of humility, when he washed the disciples' feet, and condescended even unto the Cross, and burial, Christ our true God: *and the rest, as usual.*   (*See page* 122.)

GREAT (GOOD) FRIDAY

*On Great Friday we commemorate the redeeming sufferings of our Lord Jesus Christ,
who for our sakes voluntarily endured being spat upon, beaten, buffeted in the face,
jeered at, pierced with the nails and the spear, and, in conclusion, — death upon
the Cross. Wherefore, the Service for Matins is entitled:* THE OFFICE OF THE
HOLY AND REDEEMING SUFFERINGS OF OUR LORD JESUS CHRIST; *and its charac-
teristic feature consisteth in the reading of the Twelve Gospels, which narrate the
same.*

Matins beginneth in the same manner as on Thursday. While: Alleluia, *and:* When
the glorious disciples . . . (*see* GREAT THURSDAY) *are being sung, the Clergy
come forth from the Sanctuary with the book of the Gospels to the centre of the Temple, place the book on the lectern, light tapers (as do the People also), and cense the
Temple and those present.*

Then the Little Litany: Again, yet again, . . . *with the Exclamation:* For thine are
the kingdom and the power . . .

That he will graciously vouchsafe unto us: *and the rest.* (*See page* 30.)

Glory to thy Passion, O Lord. (*Before each Gospel.*)

Then the Gospels. (1) John xiii. 31–xviii. 1. (2) John xviii. 1–28. (3) Matt. xxvi.
57–75. (4) John xviii. 28–xix. 16. (5) Matt. xxvii. 3–32. (6) Mark xv. 16–32.
(7) Matt. xxvii. 33–54. (8) Luke xxiii. 32–49. (9) John xix. 25–37. (10) Mark
xv. 43–47. (11) John xix. 38–42. (12) Matt. xxvii. 62–66.

Glory to thy long-suffering, O Lord. (*After each Gospel.*)

After the first Gospel, the Antiphon, in Tone VIII.

The Princes of the people are assembled against the Lord, and against
his Christ.

Thou hast laid upon me the word of transgression, O Lord: Lord,
forsake me not.

Let us offer unto Christ our pure affections, and as his friends let us
sacrifice our souls for his sake; and let us not be oppressed, like unto
Judas, with the cares of life, but in our closets let us cry aloud: Our
Father, who art in heaven, from the Evil One deliver thou us.

After the second Gospel, the Antiphon, in Tone V.

To-day doth Judas abandon the Master, and accept the devil: he is
blinded by the passion of cupidity; being darkened, he falleth away from
the light. For how can he see who, for thirty pieces of silver, hath sold the
Light? But he who hath suffered for the world hath shone upon us.
Unto him let us cry aloud: O Lord, who hast suffered, and who hast compassion upon men, glory to thee.

After the third Gospel, the Antiphon, in Tone VIII.

Unto those who unlawfully did seize thee, having suffered much, thus
didst thou cry, O Lord: If ye smite the Shepherd, and scatter abroad the

twelve sheep, my disciples, I might summon more than twelve legions of Angels.   But I will forbear, that the obscure and secret things, which I have revealed unto you through my prophets, may be fulfilled.   Glory, O Lord, to thee.

After the fourth Gospel, the Antiphon, in Tone VI.

He who decketh himself with light as it were with a garment, stood naked at the judgment seat, and received buffetings upon the cheek from the hands of those whom he had created.   The iniquitous people, also, did nail to the Cross the Lord of glory.   Then was the veil of the Temple rent in twain, and the sun was darkened, for it could not endure to behold affronted God, before whom all things do quake.   Unto him let us bow down.

After the fifth Gospel, the Antiphon, in Tone VI.

The assembly of the Jews besought Pilate to crucify thee, O Lord.   For though they found no fault in thee, they liberated the guilty Barabbas, and condemned thee, the Just One, and became guilty of the sin of foul murder.   But grant, O Lord, their reward unto those who vainly wrought evil against thee.

But besides the above Antiphons, between the reading of the second, third, fourth, fifth and sixth Gospels, are sung three more Antiphons.   The Little Litany and a Sitting-Hymn (Syedálen) are said and sung; and the customary censing of the Temple is performed.

After the sixth Gospel, the Beatitudes, with their Hymns (Tropari), are chanted, and the Gradual (Prokímen):

They parted my garments among them, and upon my vesture did they cast lots.

Verse. O God, my God, hear me.   Why hast thou forsaken me?

After the seventh Gospel, Psalm li. is read.

After the eighth Gospel, is sung the THREE-SONG CANON, *in Tone VI.*

Theme-Song V. (Irmós). My soul awaketh early unto thee, who through tenderness of heart didst empty thyself, yet without change of Essence; and being thyself without passion, didst condescend unto thy Passion, O Word of God.   Grant peace unto me who have fallen, O thou who lovest mankind.   (*Twice.*)

Refrain. Glory to thee, O our God; glory to thee.

And its two Hymns, each six times, with the Refrain: Glory . . . now, and ever, . . .; *the Theme-Song; the Little Litany; the Collect-Hymn (Kondák) (see page 217); and the Ikos.   Then,*

Theme-Song VIII. (Irmós). The divine Children put to shame the Champion of blasphemous wrath.   And the unlawful Council of the impious, raging against Christ, took counsel in vain, when they sought to slay him who holdeth life in the hollow of his hand; whom, also, let all creation bless, magnifying him unto all the ages.   ℞

And its four Hymns, with the Refrain.

Theme-Song IX. (*Irmós*). More honourable than the Cherubim, and beyond compare more glorious than the Seraphim, thou who without defilement barest God the Word, true Birth-giver of God, we magnify thee.

And its four Hymns, with the Refrain.

The Exapostilárion. In one moment thou didst graciously vouchsafe Paradise unto the wise thief, O Lord: Illumine thou me, also, by the tree of the Cross, and save me.

After the ninth Gospel: Let everything that hath breath praise the Lord: *with its Stanzas* (*Stikhíri*). *As:*

Two treacherous things hath my first-born son, Israel, done: He hath abandoned my fountain of living water, and hath digged for himself a well of wretchedness; he hath crucified me on the Cross, and hath asked for himself and hath released Barabbas. Heaven was affrighted thereat, and the sun hid its rays, but thou, O Israel, hast not been ashamed, but hast delivered me over unto death. Forgive them, Father; for they know not what they have done.

After the tenth Gospel: Glory be to God on high, . . . (*see page* 34) *is read; then the Litany:* Let us complete our morning prayer . . .

After the eleventh Gospel, the Canticles of the Psalms. *As:*

All creation was confounded with terror when it beheld thee suspended on the Cross, O Christ. The sun was darkened, and the foundations of the earth were shaken: all things suffered in sympathy with him who had created all things. O Lord, who of thine own good will didst suffer for us, glory to thee.

Then the final censing.

After the twelfth Gospel, the ending of Matins.

It is a good thing to give thanks unto the Lord, . . . O Holy God, Holy Mighty, . . . Our Father, . . .

The Hymn (*Tropár*), *in Tone IV.* Thou hast ransomed us from the curse of the law by thy precious blood; when thou wast nailed to the Cross and pierced with a spear, thou didst pour forth immortality for men, O our Saviour: glory to thee.

The Augmented Litany, and the Benediction. May he who, for the sake of us men, and for our salvation, deigned to endure terrible sufferings, and the life-giving Cross, and voluntary burial, Christ, our true God: *and the rest, as usual.* (*See page* 122.)

The First Hour is not joined to Matins, but is read separately, together with the Third, Sixth and Ninth Hours.

THE IMPERIAL HOURS. (*Composed by Kyril of Alexandria.*)

FIRST HOUR. Psalms v., ii., xxii.

Hymn (Tropár). When thou wast crucified, O Christ, the tormentor was overcome, the power of the enemy was shattered; for neither Angel nor man, but the Lord himself hath saved us: Glory to thee.

The Parable (Paremiyá). Zech. xix. 10–13.

The Epistle. Gal. vi. 14–18.

The Gospel. Matt. xxvii. 1–56.

The Collect-Hymn (Kondák), in Tone VIII. Come, all ye, let us sing him who was crucified for us. For him did Mary behold on the Tree, and say: Even though thou sufferest crucifixion, yet art thou my Son and my God.

THIRD HOUR. Psalms xxxv., cix., li.

The Hymn, in Tone VI. The Jews who had passed through the Red Sea by the rod, condemned to death and crucified on the Cross thee, O Lord, the life of all men; and they who had sucked honey from the rock brought gall unto thee; but of thine own good will didst thou suffer, and free us from the works of the enemy. O Christ-God, glory to thee.

The Parable (Paremiyá). Isaiah l. 4–11.

The Epistle. Rom. v. 6–10.

The Gospel. Mark xv. 1–41.

The Collect-Hymn. Come, all ye, . . . *(See First Hour, above.)*

SIXTH HOUR. Psalms liv., cxl., xci.

The Hymn, in Tone II. Thou hast effected salvation on earth, O Christ-God, thou hast stretched out thy most pure hands on the Cross, collecting together all the Nations, who cried: Glory to thee, O Lord.

The Parable (Paremiyá). Isaiah lii. 13–15, liii. 1–12, liv. 1.

The Epistle. Heb. ii. 11–18.

The Gospel. Luke xxiii. 32–49.

The Collect-Hymn (Kondák). Come, all ye, . . . *(See above.)*

NINTH HOUR. Psalms lxix., lxx., lxxxvi.

The Hymn (Tropár). When the thief beheld the Author of Life hanging upon the Cross, he said: If thou, who art crucified with us, wast not God incarnate, the sun would not have hidden its rays, neither would the earth have quaked with trembling. But do thou, who sufferest all things, remember me in thy kingdom, O Lord.

The Parable (Paremiyá). Jer. xii. 18–23, xii. 1–15.

The Epistle. Heb. x. 19–31.

The Gospel. John xviii. 28–, xix. 1–37.

The Collect-Hymn. *(See above.)*

The Typical Psalms are as usual.

In order that the fast which the Holy Church imposeth upon the faithful in her great affliction at the removal of her Bridegroom may not be broken, the Liturgy is not celebrated on Great Friday. *The sacrifice, on that day, is offered on Golgotha. (Only in case the Feast of the Annunciation falleth on that day the Liturgy of St. John Chrysostom is celebrated.)*

VESPERS.

Especially affecting is Vespers, which is celebrated on Great Friday at four o'clock, when the winding-sheet (plashtschantíza) is brought into the centre of the Temple.

Before the beginning of the service the winding-sheet is laid on the Altar. The Senior Priest vesteth himself in all the ecclesiastical vestments pertaining to his rank. The beginning of the service is as usual. The Stanzas (Stikhíri) of: Lord, I have cried:

I. *Tone I.* All creation was confounded with terror when it beheld thee suspended on the Cross, O Christ. The sun was darkened, and the foundations of the earth were shaken: all things suffered in sympathy with him who had created all things. O Lord, who of thine own good will didst suffer for us, glory to thee.

II. *Tone II.* To-day the Virgin undefiled, beholding thee, the Word, uplifted upon the Cross, weeping with the tender love of a mother, was sore wounded in heart, and moaned grievously from the depths of her soul, wiping her face with her hair. Wherefore also beating her hands, she cried piteously: Woe is me, O my Son divine! Woe is me, O Light of the World! Why hast thou departed from mine eyes, O Lamb of God? For which cause also the host of the Bodiless Powers were seized with trembling, and said: O Lord Ineffable, glory to thee!

Glory to the Father, and to the Son, and to the Holy Spirit, now, and ever, and unto ages of ages. Amen.

III. *Tone VI.* A mystery dread and most glorious to-day is seen to be accomplished: he who is intangible is held fast; he who loosed Adam from the curse is bound; he who trieth the heart and reins unlawfully is tried; he is confined in darkness who confined the abyss; before Pilate standeth he before whom, with trembling, stand the Powers of Heaven; the Creator is buffeted in the face by the hand of the creature; to the Tree he is adjudged who judgeth the living and the dead; the Destroyer of Hell is confined in the tomb. O Benignant Lord, who compassionately endurest all things, and savest all men from the curse, glory to thee.

The Entrance with the Gospels. O gladsome radiance . . . (*Page* 8.)

The Gradual (Prokímen). They parted my garments among them, and upon my vesture did they cast lots.

O God, my God, why hast thou forsaken me.

The Parables (Paremíí). Exodus xxxiii. 11–23; Job xlii. 12–17; Isaiah lii. 13–15, liii. 1–12, liv. 1.

The Epistle. 1 Cor. i. 18–, ii. 1, 2.

The Gospel. Matt. xxvii. 1–38; Luke xxiii, 39–43; Matt. xxvii. 39–54; John xix. 31–37; Matt. xxvii. 55–61.

The Augmented Litany. Let us all say, . . . ; *The Litany of Supplication.* Let us complete . . . (*See page* 35.)

When Joseph, together with Nicodemus, had taken from the Tree thee, who clothest thyself in light as in a garment, and beheld thee dead, naked and unburied. that compassionate man was seized with weeping, and with lamentation said: Woe is me, O sweetest Jesus, beholding whom so little while ago hanging on the Cross, the sun shrouded itself in darkness, while the earth did quake and the veil of the Temple was rent in twain! But lo, now I behold thee, who for my sake, of thine own good will, hast endured death. How shall I bury thee, O my God? Or with what winding-sheet shall I enshroud thee? With what hands shall I touch thy body incorruptible? Or what songs shall I sing at thy forthgoing, O Bountiful One? I exalt thy sufferings, and in song will I glorify thy burial, with Resurrection, crying: O Lord, glory to thee!

During this time, the Senior Priest, accompanied by the Deacon with a taper, censeth round about the Altar, thrice.

Lord, now lettest thou thy servant depart in peace, . . . O Holy God, Holy Mighty, . . . Our Father, . . . For thine is the kingdom, . . . (*See page* 13.)

And the Choir singeth:

Noble Joseph, when he had taken thy pure Body from the Tree, did wrap it in fine linen and spices, and sorrowing did lay it in a new sepulchre.

An Angel stood before the Myrrh-bearing Women at the tomb, crying: Spices are meet for the dead, but Christ hath revealed himself as a stranger to corruption.

While these Hymns are being sung, the Clergy lift the winding-sheet from the Altar, and preceded by assistants bearing tapers, they make the circuit of the Altar, bearing the winding-sheet on their heads. And they go to the centre of the Temple and lay it on the tomb there prepared. Then followeth a triple censing of the winding-sheet, and of the whole Temple, and of those present.

An address appropriate to the day is generally made here. Then the

BENEDICTION.

May he who for the sake of us men, and for our salvation, deigned to endure terrible sufferings, and the life-giving Cross, and voluntary burial, Christ, our true God: *and the rest, as usual.* (*See page* 122.)

The faithful, following the example of the Priest, approach the tomb of the Lord, kneeling and kissing it.

GREAT SATURDAY

On Great Saturday the Church commemorateth the Burial of the body of our Lord Jesus Christ, and his descent into Hell. As a watch was set over the tomb of the Saviour, in like manner, during the whole course of the Matins service the Clergy hardly depart from the tomb of the winding-sheet; while during the Hours and the Liturgy, all the exits from the sanctuary are performed around the winding-sheet; as, for example, the Little and Great Entrances.

The beginning of Matins is as usual. While: God is the Lord: *is being sung, the Holy Door is opened, and the Clergy come forth to the centre of the Temple. The winding-sheet and the Temple are censed.*

The Hymns (Tropari), in Tone II. I. Noble Joseph, when he had taken thy pure Body from the Tree, did wrap it in fine linen and spices, and sorrowing did lay it in a new sepulchre.

II. When thou didst descend into death, O Life Immortal, then didst thou annihilate Hell with the radiance of thy divinity. And when thou hadst raised up the dead from the nethermost regions, all the Powers of heaven cried aloud: O Life-giver, Christ our God, glory to thee!

III. An Angel stood before the Myrrh-bearing Women at the tomb, crying: Spices are meet for the dead, but Christ hath revealed himself as a stranger to corruption.

Then, directly in front of the winding-sheet, the Seventeenth Selection of Psalms is read (Psalm cxix. See page 370), each verse being followed by Eulogies of the dead and buried Lord. This selection of Psalms is divided into three parts, separated by the Little Litany, and an Exclamation.

Examples of the Eulogies. Tone V. Part I.

I. Thou didst lay down thy life in the grave, O Christ, and the Angelic Host was affrighted, glorifying thy condescension.

II. O Life, how shalt thou die? How shalt thou dwell in the grave? But thou shalt annihilate the kingdom of Death, and shalt raise up the dead out of Hell.

III. We magnify thee, O Jesus the King, and we reverence thy burial and thy sufferings, whereby thou hast saved us from corruption.

Exclamation. (After the Litany.) For blessed is thy Name, and glorified is thy kingdom, of the Father, and of the Son, and of the Holy Spirit, now, and ever, and unto ages of ages.

Choir. Amen.

Part II.

Eulogies. I. Meet is it that we should magnify thee, the Life-giver, who hast stretched out thy hands upon the Cross, and hast shattered the dominion of the enemy.

Thy hands have made me, and fashioned me; give me understanding, that I may learn thy commandments.

II. Meet is it that we should magnify thee, the Creator of all men: for by thy sufferings we have passionlessness, O thou who deliverest us from corruption.

III. The earth was affrighted, and the sun hid itself, O Saviour, when it beheld thee, the light which knoweth no setting, O Christ, entering into the grave in the flesh.

IV. Thou didst fall asleep in the grave, O Christ, with sleep which is natural to creatures, and from the heavy sleep of sin didst raise up the human race.

Exclamation. (After the Litany.) For holy art thou, O our God, who restest on the cherubimic throne of glory, and unto thee do we ascribe glory, together with thy Father who is from everlasting, and thine all-holy, good and life-giving Spirit, now, and ever, and unto ages of ages.

Choir. Amen.

Part III. Tone III.

Eulogies. I. All nations bring a song to thy burial, O my Christ.

O look thou upon me, and be merciful unto me, as thou usest to do unto those that love thy Name.

II. He of Arimathea, having taken thee from the Tree, and wrapped thee in a winding-sheet, interreth thee in the tomb.

III. The Myrrh-bearing Women came, most wisely bringing spices unto thee, O my Christ.

IV. O come, all creation, let us offer the parting songs to the Creator.

Exclamation. For thou art the King of Peace, O Christ our God, and unto thee do we ascribe glory, together with thy Father who is from everlasting, and thine all-holy, good and life-giving Spirit, now, and ever, and unto ages of ages.

Choir. Amen.

The Eulogies are followed by the Hymns, The company of the Angels . . . *(See Sunday Matins, page 28), Then Psalm li., and*

THE CANON. *Tone VI.*

Theme-Songs (Irmosi). I. The children of those that were saved, hid under the earth Him who of old drowned in the waves of the sea the tormentor pursuing. But let us like the virgins sing unto the Lord, for gloriously hath he glorified himself.

III. When Creation beheld thee, who didst suspend the whole earth immovably upon the waters, hanging upon Calvary, it quaked with great amaze, and cried: There is none holy, save thou, O Lord.

IV. When Habakkuk by anticipation beheld thy exhaustion divine upon the Cross, he cried in amaze: Thou hast destroyed the dominion of the mighty, O Good One, in that hast joined thyself unto the company of those who were in Hell: for thou art almighty.

V. When Isaiah beheld the light which knoweth no setting of thy divine manifestation, that was graciously made unto us, O Christ, his soul longed for thee in the night-season, and he cried: The dead shall rise, and those who lie in the grave shall arise, and all the earth-born shall rejoice.

VI. Jonah was seized but was not held in the belly of the whale, in that he represented the type of thee, who didst suffer and give thyself over unto burial; and he came forth from the monster as from a chamber of repose, and spake unto the guards: Ye that watch vainly and without avail have forsaken mercy incarnate.

The Collect-Hymn (Kondák). The Immortal One who imprisoned the deep is beheld dead, and, wrapped with spices and a winding-sheet, is laid in the tomb as he were mortal: and the women have come to anoint him with spices, weeping bitterly and crying: This is the blessed Saturday whereon Christ, having fallen asleep, shall rise again on the third day.

VII. O marvel unutterable! He who delivered the Holy Children in the fiery furnace from the flames, is laid dead, bereft of breath, in the grave, for the salvation of us who sing: O God our Redeemer! Blessed art thou.

VIII. Fear with trembling, O ye heavens, and let the foundations of the earth be shaken! For lo, he who dwelleth on high is numbered among the dead and is lodged in the narrow grave. Ye Children, bless; ye Priests, sing praises; ye People, magnify him unto all the ages!

IX. Lament not for me, O Mother, when thou beholdest in the tomb the Son whom, without seed, thou didst conceive in thy womb, for I shall rise again, and glorify myself; and in that I am God, I will raise in glory that hath no ending those who, with faith and love, do magnify thee.

(While the Canon is being sung, the Senior Priest arrayeth himself in his full vestments.)

Holy is the Lord our God. . . . Let everything which hath breath praise the Lord. . . . *(Tone II.)* Most blessed art thou, O Virgin Birthgiver . . . *(See page 34.)*

Priest. Glory to thee, who hast shown us the light.

Choir. Glory be to God on high, . . .

When the Gloria in Excelsis hath been finished, and while the affecting Thrice-Holy (O Holy God, Holy Mighty, . . .) *is being sung, and all the bells are rung, the Senior Priest taketh from the winding-sheet the book of the Holy Gospels which lieth thereon, and with it, beneath the winding-sheet, which is upheld by the Priests, while the Deacons cense, he performeth the procession of bearing the winding-sheet around the Church. When the circuit hath been completed, they carry the winding-sheet back into the Church, and the procession halteth in front of the Holy Door. Here the Exclamation: Wisdom! is made, and the Hymn: Noble Joseph, . . . (see page 220) is sung. The winding-sheet is then replaced on the tomb, and upon the winding-sheet is laid the book of the Holy Gospels.*

*Then follow: The Parables (Paremií), Ezek. xxxvii. 1–14; the Epistle, 1 Cor. v.
6–8; the Gospel, Matt. xxvii. 62–66; the Augmented Litany, Let us say, . . .; and
the Litany of Supplication, Let us complete . . . (See page 36.)*

The Benediction. May he who, for the sake of us men, and for our salvation, endured dire sufferings, and the life-giving Cross, and voluntary
burial in the flesh, Christ our true God: *and the rest. (See page 122.)*

The Choir then singeth the Stanza (Stikhíra), in Tone V.

O come, let us bless Joseph ever-memorable, who came by night unto
Pilate, and begged the Life of all men: Give me this stranger, who hath
not where to lay his head; give me this stranger, whom a crafty disciple
hath betrayed unto death; give me this stranger, whose Mother, when she
beheld him hanging on the Cross, cried with weeping, and with maternal
feeling exclaimed: Woe is me, my child! Woe is me, my Light, and the
beloved of my bosom! that which was foretold in the church by Simeon
to-day hath come to pass! A weapon shall pierce my heart, but into the
joy of the Resurrection shall lament be changed. We worship thy sufferings, O Christ; we worship thy sufferings, O Christ; we worship thy sufferings, O Christ, and thy holy Resurrection.

Then the First Hour is read.

*On Great Saturday, the Third, Sixth and Ninth Hours, as usual; the Hymn: Noble
Joseph, . . . (see page 220); the Collect-Hymn (Kondák): The Immortal One
who imprisoned the deep . . . (See page 222.) The Liturgy of St. Basil the
Great is used, and is celebrated after Vespers. But as the Vespers refer to the fol-
lowing day, in it the joyous songs of the Resurrection are united with the songs of
Great Saturday.*

*Vespers beginneth: Blessed is the kingdom; the Sunday Verses (Stikhíri) of the
First Tone, to: Lord, I have called; the Hymn to the Birth-giver of God (Bogoróditchen):*

Let us sing the praises of Mary, Virgin, Door of heaven, Glory of all the
world, sprung forth from man, who also bare the Lord; the Song of the
Bodiless Powers, and the Enriching of the faithful. For she revealed
herself as Heaven and the Temple of the Godhead. She destroyed the
bulwarks of enmity, and ushered in peace, and threw open the kingdom.
Wherefore, in that we possess this confirmation of our faith, we have a
defender, even the Lord who was born of her. Be bold, therefore, be bold,
ye people of God, for he, the All-Powerful, shall vanquish your foes.

*The Entrance is made with the Gospels. After: O gladsome radiance . . . (page 8);
the Parables (Paremií), Genesis i. 1–13; Isaiah lx. 1–16; Exodus xii. 1–11; Jonah
i. 1–16, ii. 1–11, iii. 1–10, iv. 1–11; Joshua v. 10–15; Exodus xiii. 20–22, xiv., xv.
1–19.*

After the reading of the concluding verses of the sixth Parable (Paremiyá), and

Reader. Let us sing unto the Lord.

The Choir singeth: For gloriously hath he glorified himself.

The Parables (Paremii). Zeph. iii. 8–15; 1 Kings xvii. 8–24; Isaiah lxi. 10, 11, lxii. 1–5; Genesis xxii. 1–18; Isaiah lxi. 1–9; 2 Kings iv. 8–37; Isaiah lxiii. 11–19, xliv. 1–5; Jer. xxxi. 31–34; Dan. iii. 1–23 (*and the* Song of the Holy Children, Apocrypha). *During the reading of the concluding verses of the Fifteenth Lesson, the Choir singeth:* Praise ye the Lord, and exalt him forever.

The Little Litany, Exclamation: For holy art thou . . .: *In place of the Thrice-holy:* Ye who have been baptized into Christ have put on Christ. *The Gradual, in the Fifth Tone:* Let all the earth worship thee, and sing thee, yea, let it sing unto thy Name, O Most Highest. *The Epistle.* Romans vi. 3–11. *Instead of:* Alleluia: Arise, O God, judge the earth; for thou shalt inherit all nations: *with its Verses (Stikhí)*; (Psalm lxxxii.).

While these are being sung, the Clergy change their sombre vestments for light vestments, in preparation for the reading of the Gospel concerning Christ's Resurrection: Matt. xxviii. 1–20.

In place of the Cherubimic Hymn:

Let all mortal flesh hold its peace, and stand with fear and trembling, and meditate nothing earthly within itself: for the King of Kings and the Lord of Lords cometh to be slain, and to give himself to be the food of the faithful. And before him also come the Angelic Hosts with all dominion and power, the many-eyed Cherubim, and the six-winged Seraphim, covering their faces, and crying aloud the song: Alleluia, alleluia, alleluia.

The Communion Hymn.

The Lord is risen, as though he slept, and he who saveth us is risen from the dead.

In place of: Meet is it:

Lament not for me, O Mother, when thou beholdest in the tomb the Son whom, without seed, thou didst conceive in thy womb: for I shall rise again and glorify myself; and in that I am God, I will raise in glory that hath no ending those who with faith and love do magnify thee.

After the Liturgy it is customary to have the Blessing of the Loaves and the Wine, wherewith the faithful may strengthen themselves before they listen to the reading of the Acts of the Apostles.

In the evening the reading of the Acts of the Apostles taketh place. The Priest bestoweth the blessing: Through the prayers of our holy fathers, O Lord Jesus Christ our God, have mercy upon us.

Then followeth the reading of the Acts. It is the custom to have a number of readers, who succeed one another, and read the Acts until the very beginning of the Easter Midnight Service (Polunótchnitza), which precedeth the Easter Matins.

The Easter Midnight Service generally beginneth in such a way that it shall be finished at midnight, as the beginning of the Easter Refrain is always made to coincide with the midnight stroke of the bells. The order of the Midnight Service is as followeth:

Priest. Blessed is our God . . . *Reader.* O Holy God, Holy Mighty, . . .; Our Father, . . .; O come, let us worship . . .; *the Canon of Great Saturday:* The children of those . . . (*See page 221.*)

While: Lament not for me, O Mother, . . . (*the Ninth Theme-Song*) *is being sung, the Priest reverently beareth the winding-sheet from the centre of the Temple to the Sanctuary, and layeth it on the Altar.   Then the doors are closed.   The Litany:* Have mercy upon us, O God, . . .; O Holy God, Holy Mighty, . . .; Our Father, . . .; *the Hymn* (*Tropár*) *in Tone II.,* When thou didst descend into Hell, . . . (*see page* 220) *for Sunday; the Little Benediction.*

EASTER

Easter, the Feast of Feasts, is celebrated by the Church with special solemnity. The Temple is filled with the fragrance of incense and myriads of lights; the Clergy are arrayed in their choicest light-hued vestments. All the People hold lighted tapers in their hands. All these things denote the flood of joy and grace which proceeded from the Resurrection of the Saviour.

At midnight the Holy Door is opened; and it remaineth open for the whole of Easter week. The Rector, with the censer and the triple candlestick and cross, censeth the Altar; then, accompanied by his fellow-clergy, who bear the book of the Holy Gospels and the holy images, and the Deacons who cense, and preceded by a procession of the cross with the church banners and lights, he goeth forth from the church, all singing with him the chant of joy: The Angels in heaven, O Christ our Saviour, sing thy Resurrection. *This chant is taken up and continued by the Choir and the People thus:* And do thou enable us on earth to glorify thee with a pure heart.

They triumphantly make the circuit of the church, the bells pealing the while, and then all enter the porch, the doors leading therefrom into the Temple remaining closed. Across this western door the procession rangeth itself with the Gospels, and images; and the Priest, holding the censer in his right hand, and the triple candlestick with the cross in his left, censeth the Holy Things, and the Brethren, and all the People, and also the closed door, in the form of a cross. After this he beginneth:

Glory to the Holy, Consubstantial, Life-giving and Undivided Trinity, now, and ever, and unto ages of ages.

Choir. Amen.

Priest. Christ is risen from the dead, trampling down Death by death, and upon those in the tomb bestowing life. (*Thrice.*)

And the Choirs sing this thrice also. Then the Priest intoneth the Verses:

1: Let God arise, and let his enemies be scattered, and let them also that hate him flee before him.

And after each Verse the Choirs respond:

Christ is risen from the dead, trampling down Death by death, and upon those in the tomb bestowing life.

2: Like as the smoke vanisheth, so shall they vanish, and like as wax melteth at the fire. ℟

3: Even so let the ungodly perish at the presence of God, but let the righteous rejoice. ℟

4: This is the day which the Lord hath made: we will rejoice and be glad in it. ℟

Glory to the Father, and to the Son, and to the Holy Spirit. ℟

Now, and ever, and unto ages of ages. Amen. ℟

Then the Priest chanteth, in a louder voice:

Christ is risen from the dead, trampling down Death by death.

Then the closed doors are opened, and the Priest entereth with the honourable cross, preceded by the tapers, and by the Brethren singing:

And upon those in the tomb bestowing life.

And thereupon the Priests go to the holy Sanctuary.*

Then the Deacon saith the Litany of Peace (page 26).

Exclamation.

For unto thee are due all glory, honour and worship, to the Father, and to the Son, and to the Holy Spirit, now, and ever, and unto ages of ages. Amen.

Then the principal Priest beginneth the Canon, composed by St. John of Damascus. And at the beginning of the Canon the Priest censeth the holy pictures, and the Choirs, and the Brethren, according to their rank.

And if the Feast of the Annunciation chance to fall on Easter Day (in which case the Feast is called Kiriopaskha), the Hymns for the Annunciation are added to those for Easter.

THE CANON.

(During each Theme-Song the Priest censeth.)

Canticle I., Tone I.

Theme-Song (Irmós). The Day of Resurrection! Let us be illumined, O ye people! The Passover, the Passover of the Lord! From death unto life, and from earth unto heaven hath Christ our God brought us over, singing a song of victory!

Refrain. Christ is risen from the dead!

Hymn (Tropár). Let us purify our senses and we shall behold Christ, radiant with the light ineffable of the Resurrection, and shall hear him say, in accents clear: Rejoice! as we sing the song of victory.

Refrain. Christ is risen from the dead!

Hymn. For meet is it that the heavens should rejoice, and that the earth should be glad, and that the whole world, both visible and invisible, should keep the Feast. For Christ is risen, the everlasting joy!

The Choirs. The Day of Resurrection! . . .

Christ is risen from the dead, trampling down Death by death, and upon those in the tomb bestowing life. *(Thrice.)*

The Little Litany.

Deacon. Again, yet again, in peace let us pray to the Lord.

Choir. Lord, have mercy.

Succour us, save us, have mercy upon us, and keep us, O God, by thy grace.

---

* It is customary to make the circuit of the church outside, to typify the women who came, very early in the morning, bearing spices, to anoint the body of our Lord. The Easter Matins are thus begun outside the church, in memory of the Myrrh-bearing Women and the disciples having first received tidings of Christ's resurrection before the entrance to his tomb.

Choir. Lord, have mercy.

Calling to remembrance our most holy, all-undefiled, most blessed and glorious Lady, the Birth-giver of God and ever-virgin Mary, with all the Saints, let us commend ourselves, and each other, and all our life unto Christ our God.

Choir. To thee, O Lord.

Exclamation.

Priest. For thine is the majesty, and thine are the kingdom and the power and the glory, of the Father, and of the Son, and of the Holy Spirit, now, and ever, and unto ages of ages.

Choir. Amen.

Canticle III.

Theme-Song (Irmós). O come, let us quaff a beverage new, not from a barren rock miraculously called forth; but the Fountain of Immortality springing from the tomb of Christ: on whom also we are founded.

Refrain. Christ is risen from the dead!

Hymn (Tropár). Now are all things filled with light; heaven, and earth, and the places under the earth. All Creation doth celebrate the Resurrection of Christ, on whom also it is founded. ℟

Hymn. Yesterday, O Christ, was I buried with thee, and to-day I rise again with thy rising. Yesterday was I crucified with thee: Do thou thyself glorify me, O Saviour, in thy kingdom. ℟

Then the Choirs repeat, thrice, the Theme-Song: O come, let us quaff . . . *and:* . Christ is risen . . . trampling down Death . . . (*Thrice*).

The Little Litany (see page 227).

Exclamation.

Priest. For thou art our God, and unto thee do we ascribe glory, to the Father, and to the Son, and to the Holy Spirit, now, and ever, and unto ages of ages.

Choir. Amen.

Ipakóï, Tone III.

When they who from Mary came, forestalling the dawn, and found the stone rolled away from the sepulchre, they heard from the Angel: Why seek ye among the dead, as he were mortal, him who abideth in everlasting light? Behold the grave-clothes. Go quickly, and proclaim to the world that the Lord is risen, and hath slain Death. For he is the Son of God who saveth mankind.

Canticle IV.

Theme-Song (Irmós). May Habakkuk, divinely speaking, now stand with us in watch divine, and show the radiant Angel crying early: To-day is salvation come into the world: For Christ is risen, in that he is almighty.

Refrain. Christ is risen from the dead!

Hymn (Tropár). Christ revealed himself as of the male sex when he opened the Virgin's womb, and as mortal was called the Lamb. Without blemish, also, is our Passover, in that he tasted not corruption; and as very God perfect was proclaimed. ℞

Hymn. Christ, our blessed Crown, like unto a yearling Lamb, of his own good will did sacrifice himself for all, a Passover of purification: and from the grave did he, the glorious Sun of Righteousness, shine forth again upon us. ℞

Hymn. David, the ancestor of our God, danced with leaping before the symbolical Ark of the Covenant. Let us also, the holy people of God, beholding the fulfilment of the symbols, rejoice in godly wise: For Christ is risen, in that he is almighty. ℞

Then the Choirs sing the Theme-Song: May Habakkuk . . . *and:* Christ is risen . . . trampling down Death . . . (*Thrice.*)

The Little Litany (see page 227).

Exclamation.

Priest. For thou art a gracious God, and lovest mankind, and unto thee do we ascribe glory, to the Father, and to the Son, and to the Holy Spirit, now, and ever, and unto ages of ages.

Choir. Amen.

Canticle V.

Theme-Song (Irmós). Right early let us wake, and unto the Lord bring a song instead of myrrh, and we shall behold Christ, the Sun of Righteousness, who lighteth the life of all mankind.

Refrain. Christ is risen from the dead!

Hymn (Tropár). When they who were led captive in the bonds of Hell beheld thy loving-kindness infinite, O Christ, they hastened to the light with joyful feet, exalting the Passover Everlasting. ℞

Hymn. Bearing lights, let us go forth to meet Christ, who cometh forth from the grave like a bridegroom. And with the hierarchy of Angels who love and praise, let us celebrate the ransoming Passover of God. ℞

Then the Choir repeat the Theme-Song: Right early let us wake . . . *and:* Christ is risen . . . trampling down Death . . . (*Thrice.*)

The Little Litany (see page 227).

Exclamation.

Priest. For sanctified and glorified be thine all-honourable and majestic Name, of the Father, and of the Son, and of the Holy Spirit, now, and ever, and unto ages of ages.

Choir. Amen.

Canticle VI.

Theme-Song (Irmós). Thou didst descend into the nethermost parts of the earth, O Christ, and didst shatter the bonds eternal which held the prisoners in captivity: and after three days thou didst rise again from the grave, like Jonah from the whale.

Refrain. Christ is risen from the dead!

Hymn (Tropár). O Christ, who didst not break the Virgin's gate by thy birth, thou didst rise again from the dead, having kept intact the seals; and thou hast opened unto us the gates of Paradise. ℞

Hymn. O my Saviour, the sacrifice living and unslain! When, as God, thou, of thine own will, hadst offered up thyself unto the Father, thou didst raise up with thee also, in that thou thyself didst rise from the grave, Adam, the father of our race. ℞

Then the Choirs sing the Theme-Song: Thou didst descend . . . *and:* Christ is risen . . . trampling down Death . . . (*Thrice.*)

The Little Litany (see page 227).

Exclamation.

Priest. For thou art the King of Peace and the Saviour of our souls, and unto thee do we ascribe glory, to the Father, and to the Son, and to the Holy Spirit, now, and ever, and unto ages of ages.

Choir. Amen.

The Collect-Hymn (Kondák).

Though thou didst descend into the grave, O Deathless One, yet didst thou annihilate the power of Hell, and didst rise again as conqueror, O Christ-God, announcing unto the Myrrh-bearing Women: Rejoice! and giving peace unto thine Apostles, and bestowing Resurrection upon the fallen.

The Ikos.

The Myrrh-bearing Women forestalled the dawn, ere the rising of the sun, seeking, as it were day, the Sun which had once set in the tomb, and crying one to another: O friends! Come, let us anoint with sweet-smelling spices the life-bringing and buried body of him who raiseth again in the flesh fallen Adam, which lieth in the grave. Let us go, let us seek, like the Wise Men, and let us fall down in worship before him, and bring unto him an offering of myrrh; not unto him in swaddling-clothes, but in his winding-sheet. And let us weep and cry aloud: Arise, O Master, who givest Resurrection unto the fallen!

In that we have beheld the Resurrection of Christ, let us bow down before the holy Lord Jesus, the only sinless One. Thy Cross do we adore, O Christ, and thy holy Resurrection we laud and glorify: for thou art our God, and we know none other beside thee, we call upon thy Name. O come, all ye faithful, let us adore Christ's holy Resurrection: for lo, through the Cross is joy come into all the world. Ever blessing the Lord, let us sing his Resurrection: for in that he endured the Cross, he hath destroyed Death by death.

Hymn. Jesus having risen from the grave, as he foretold, hath given unto us life eternal, and great mercy. (*Thrice.*)

Canticle VII.

Theme-Song (Irmós). He who delivered the Holy Children from the fiery furnace, when he was made man did suffer like unto a mortal; and through his Passion he doth clothe the mortal in the dignity of immortality, he, the only God of our fathers, blessed and exceedingly glorified.

Refrain. Christ is risen from the dead!

Hymn (Tropár). The godly-wise women followed after thee in haste with sweet-smelling spices. But him whom they sought with tears as dead, they joyfully adored as the living God, and announced unto thy disciples, O Christ, the glad tidings of the mystical Passover. ℞

Hymn. We celebrate the death of Death, the annihilation of Hell, the beginning of a life new and everlasting. And in ecstasy we sing praises unto the author thereof, the only God of our fathers, blessed and exceeding glorious. ℞

Hymn. For holy, in very truth, and worthy of all solemn triumph, is this redeeming and radiantly effulgent night, the harbinger of the bright-beaming Day of the Resurrection, on which the Light Eternal that hath no bounds shone forth in the flesh from the grave for all mankind.

Then the Choir sing the Theme-Song: He who delivered the Holy Children . . . *and:* Christ is risen . . . trampling down Death . . . (*Thrice.*)

The Little Litany (*see page* 227).

Exclamation.

Priest. For blessed and all-glorified be the majesty of thy kingdom, of the Father, and of the Son, and of the Holy Spirit, now, and ever, and unto ages of ages.

Choir. Amen.

Canticle VIII.

Theme-Song (Irmós). This is the chosen and holy Day, the one King and Lord of Sabbaths, the Feast of Feasts, and the Triumph of Triumphs: Wherein let us bless Christ forevermore!

Refrain. Christ is risen from the dead!

Hymn (Tropár). O come, on this auspicious day of the Resurrection, let us partake of the fruit from the new vine of divine gladness of the kingdom of Christ, in song magnifying him as God forevermore. ℞

Hymn. Cast thine eyes about thee, O Zion, and behold! For lo! from the West and from the North, and from the Sea and from the East, as to a light by God illumined, have thy children assembled unto thee, blessing Christ forevermore.

Refrain. O most Holy Trinity, our God, glory to thee!

Hymn. O Father Almighty, the Word and the Spirit, one Essence in Three Persons united, exceeding high and most divine! Into thee have we been baptized, and thee will we bless unto all the ages.

Then the Theme-Song: This is the chosen and holy Day, . . . *and:* Christ is risen . . . trampling down Death . . . (*Thrice.*)

The Little Litany (see page 227).

Exclamation.

Priest. For blessed be thy Name, and glorified be thy Kingdom, of the Father, and of the Son, and of the Holy Spirit, now, and ever, and unto ages of ages.

Choir. Amen.

Canticle IX.

Refrain 1. My soul doth magnify Christ the Life-giver, who rose again from the grave on the third day.

Theme-Song (Irmós). Shine, shine, O New Jerusalem for the glory of the Lord is risen upon thee.   Keep high holiday now and be glad, O Zion! And rejoice thou, O pure Birth-giver of God, in the rising again of him whom thou didst bear!

Refrain 2. My soul doth magnify Christ the Life-giver who, of his own good will, suffered and was buried, and rose again on the third day.   -

Choir. Shine, shine, . . . ℞

Refrain 3. Christ the New Passover, the living Sacrifice, the Lamb of God, taketh away the sins of the world.

Hymn (Tropár). O how divine!   O how loving-kind!   O how most sweet is thy word! For thou, O Christ! hast faithfully promised to be with us, even unto the end of the world.   Having, therefore, this firm foundation of hope, we faithful do rejoice.   (*Twice.*)

Annun-   *And if it be also the Feast of the Annunciation, then the Verses for that*
ciation.   *Feast shall be sung with the Verses for Easter.*

Refrain 4. The Angel cried unto her who is full of grace: Hail, O Pure Virgin! And again, I say: Hail! Thy Son is risen from his three days' sojourn in the grave, and hath raised up the dead: Rejoice, O ye people!

Refrain 5. In that thou thyself didst sleep in death, thou hast raised up again the dead of all the ages, roaring royally, like unto the Lion of Judah.

Refrain 6. Mary Magdalen ran to the sepulchre, and when she beheld Christ, she questioned him, as he had been the gardener.

Hymn (Tropár). O Christ, the Passover great and most holy!   O Wisdom, Word and Power of God!   Grant that we may more perfectly partake of thee in the day which knoweth no night of thy kingdom.

Refrain. The Angel, dazzling the Women, cried: Desist from tears, for Christ is risen.

Refrain. Christ is risen, trampling down Death and raising again the dead: Rejoice, O ye people!

Refrain. To-day doth every creature rejoice and shout for joy.   For Christ is risen, and Hell is led in captivity.

Refrain. To-day hath the Lord led Hell in captivity, raising up the prisoners which from eternity it had held in bitter bondage.

Refrain. My soul doth magnify the majesty of the Godhead, of Three Persons and undivided.

Refrain. Rejoice, O Virgin! Rejoice, O Blessed One! Rejoice, O greatly glorified One! For thy Son is risen from his three days' sojourn in the grave.

Then the Choirs repeat the first Refrain, and the Theme-Song: Shine, shine, O New Jerusalem! . . . *and:* Christ is risen . . . trampling down Death . . . (*Thrice.*)

The Little Litany (see page 227).

Exclamation.

Priest. For all the Powers of heaven magnify thee, the Father, the Son, and the Holy Spirit, and ascribe unto thee glory, now, and ever, and unto ages of ages. Amen.

Exapostilárion.

After that thou hadst fallen asleep, as thou wert mortal, O King and Lord, thou didst rise again on the third day, and didst raise up Adam from corruption, and abolish Death: O Passover of incorruption! O Salvation of the world! (*Thrice.*)

Let everything that hath breath praise the Lord. O praise the Lord of heaven: praise him in the height. To thee, O God, is due our song. (*Tone I.*)

Verse (Stikh): Praise him in his noble acts: praise him according to his excellent greatness.

We sing thy redeeming Passion, O Christ, and glorify thy Resurrection.

Verse: Praise him in the sound of the trumpet: praise him upon the lute and harp.

Hymn (Tropár). O thou who didst endure the Cross, and abolish Death, and didst rise again from the dead, give peace to our life, O Lord: For thou alone art almighty.

Verse: Praise him in the cymbals and dances, praise him upon the strings and lute.

Hymn (Tropár). O thou who didst lead Hell captive, and raise man again from the dead by thy Resurrection, O Christ, grant that with a pure heart we may hymn and glorify thee.

Verse: O praise him upon the well-tuned cymbals: praise him upon the loud cymbals.

Hymn. Lauding thy condescension divine, we sing thy praises, O Christ! For thou wast born of a Virgin, yet didst thou remain unseparated from the Father. Thou didst suffer as a man, and of thine own good pleasure didst thou endure the Cross; and thou didst rise again from the tomb, as thou hadst come forth from a lordly chamber, that thou mightest save the world: O Lord, glory to thee!

The Easter Canticles (Stikhíri), in Tone V.

Verse (Stikh): Let God arise, and let his enemies be scattered.

Hymn (Tropár). To-day is the holy Passover revealed unto us: the

Passover new and holy: the Passover mystical, the Passover all-august, Christ, the Passover and the Atonement. The spotless Passover, the great Passover, the Passover of the faithful, the Passover which openeth unto us the gates of Paradise; the Passover which sanctifieth all the faithful.

Verse: Like as the smoke vanisheth, so shalt thou drive them away.

Hymn. O come from the vision, ye Women, heralds of good tidings, and say ye unto Zion: Receive from us the glad tidings of joy of the Resurrection of Christ. Adorn thyself! Leap for joy and rejoice, O Jerusalem, in that thou beholdest Christ the King, like a Bridegroom come forth from the grave.

Verse: Let the ungodly perish at the presence of God. But let the righteous rejoice.

Hymn. When the Myrrh-bearing Women stood, very early in the morning, before the sepulchre of the Life-giver, they found an Angel sitting upon the stone. And he proclaimed unto them, saying: Why seek ye the living among the dead? Why mourn ye the Incorruptible amid corruption? Go, proclaim the glad tidings to his disciples.

Verse: This is the day which the Lord hath made: we will rejoice and be glad in it.

Hymn. The Passover joyful, the Passover, the Passover of the Lord, the Passover all-majestic hath shone forth upon us! The Passover! With joy let us embrace one another! O Passover, release from sorrow! For to-day from the tomb, as from a chamber of repose, hath Christ shone forth, and hath filled the Women with joy, saying: Proclaim the glad tidings to the Apostles.

Glory to the Father, and to the Son, and to the Holy Spirit, now, and ever, and unto ages of ages. Amen.

Hymn. The Day of Resurrection! Let us be illumined with the solemn Feast! Let us embrace one another. Let us say: Brethren! And because of the Resurrection let us forgive all things to those who hate us, and in this wise exclaim:

Christ is risen from the dead, trampling down Death by death, and upon those in the tomb bestowing life. (*Thrice.*)

And this is sung many times, while the People exchange the Easter kiss. The manner of the Clergy's saluting one another within the holy Sanctuary is as followeth: He who cometh to kiss the Senior Priest saith: Christ is risen! *And he receiveth the reply:* He is risen indeed! *Then the Senior Priest, taking the holy cross, standeth outside, in front of the Holy Door. And all the Priests, whatever may be their number, and the Deacons, each holding one of the Holy Things (the book of the Holy Gospels, and the holy pictures (ikóni), according to their several ranks), take their places in line, on the right hand of the Senior Priest. The People then approach, one by one; and bowing slightly to the Priest, they kiss the holy cross, the Gospels and the holy pictures which the Clergy hold. Then they kiss the Priest himself, saying:* Christ is risen! *And he replieth:* He is risen indeed! *And in the same manner they kiss the other Clergy, and one another.*

And after the salutation is finished, the Senior Priest readeth the Catechetical Address of St. John Chrysostom. And the People shall not sit while it is being read, but shall listen to it standing.

If any man be devout and loveth God, let him enjoy this fair and radiant triumphal feast. If any man be a wise servant, let him rejoicing enter into the joy of his Lord. If any have laboured long in fasting, let him now receive his recompense. If any have wrought from the first hour, let him to-day receive his just reward. If any have come at the third hour, let him with thankfulness keep the feast. If any have arrived at the sixth hour, let him have no misgivings; because he shall in nowise be deprived therefor. If any have delayed until the ninth hour, let him draw near, fearing nothing. If any have tarried even until the eleventh hour let him, also, be not alarmed at his tardiness; for the Lord, who is jealous of his honour, will accept the last even as the first; he giveth rest unto him who cometh at the eleventh hour, even as unto him who hath wrought from the first hour. And he showeth mercy upon the last, and careth for the first; and to the one he giveth, and upon the other he bestoweth gifts. And he both accepteth the deeds, and welcometh the intention, and honoureth the acts and praiseth the offering. Wherefore, enter ye all into the joy of your Lord; and receive ye your reward, both the first, and likewise the second. Ye rich and poor together, hold ye high festival. Ye sober and ye heedless, honour ye the day. Rejoice to-day, both ye who have fasted and ye who have disregarded the fast. The table is full-laden; feast ye all sumptuously. The calf is fatted; let no one go hungry away. Enjoy ye all the feast of faith: Receive ye all the riches of loving-kindness. Let no one bewail his poverty, for the universal kingdom hath been revealed. Let no one weep for his iniquities, for pardon hath shone forth from the grave. Let no one fear death, for the Saviour's death hath set us free. He that was held prisoner of it, hath annihilated it. By descending into Hell, he made Hell captive. He angered it when it tasted of his flesh. And Isaiah, foretelling this, did cry: Hell, said he, was angered, when it encountered thee in the lower regions. It was angered, for it was abolished. It was angered, for it was mocked. It was angered, for it was slain. It was angered, for it was overthrown. It was angered, for it was fettered in chains. It took a body, and met God face to face. It took earth, and encountered Heaven. It took that which was seen, and fell upon the unseen. O Death, where is thy sting? O Hell, where is thy victory? Christ is risen, and thou art overthrown. Christ is risen, and the demons are fallen. Christ is risen, and the Angels rejoice. Christ is risen, and life reigneth. Christ is risen, and not one dead remaineth in the grave. For Christ, being risen from the dead, is become the first-fruits of those who have fallen asleep. To him be glory and dominion unto ages of ages. Amen.

Then is sung the Hymn of St. John Chrysostom.

The grace of thy lips, shining forth like a beacon-fire, . . . (*See the Liturgy, page* 125.)

Then the Deacon saith the Augmented Litany.

Have mercy upon us, O God, according to thy great mercy, . . . (*See Matins, page* 35) *and:* Let us complete our morning prayer unto the Lord. . . . (*See Matins, page* 36.)

And after the Exclamation, the Deacon saith:

Wisdom!

Choir. Bless!

Priest. Blessed is Christ our God always, now, and ever, and unto ages of ages.

Choir. Amen.

Preserve, O Lord, our most God-fearing . . . (*See page* 37.)

Then the Priest, holding the cross, chanteth:

Christ is risen from the dead, trampling down Death by death.

The People. And upon those in the tomb bestowing life.

And straightway the Priest pronounceth the BENEDICTION.

May Christ who is risen from the dead, trampling down Death by death, and upon those in the tomb bestowing life, our true God, through the prayers of his most pure Mother, and of all the Saints, have mercy upon us and bless us, forasmuch as he is good and loveth mankind.

Then elevating the cross, he saith: Christ is risen! (*Thrice.*) *And the People reply:* He is risen indeed! (*Thrice.*)

Then the closing Hymn is sung.

Christ is risen from the dead, trampling down Death by death, and upon those in the tomb bestowing life. And unto us hath he given life eternal. Wherefore, let us adore his Resurrection on the third day.

And the Many Years.

THE HOURS AT EASTER.

During Easter week, until Saturday, the Hours are read in the following order:

Priest. Blessed is our God always, now, and ever, and unto ages of ages. Amen.

Christ is risen from the dead, trampling down Death by death, and upon those in the tomb bestowing life. (*Thrice.*)

The Choir also singeth the Hymn: Christ is risen . . . (*Thrice.*)

In that we have beheld the Resurrection of Christ, let us bow down before the holy Lord Jesus, the only sinless One. Thy Cross do we adore, O Christ, and thy holy Resurrection we laud and glorify. For thou art our God, and we know none other beside thee, we call upon thy Name. O come, all ye faithful, let us adore Christ's holy Resurrection: for lo, through the Cross is joy come into all the world. Ever blessing the Lord, let us sing his Resurrection. For in that he endured the Cross, he hath destroyed Death by death. (*Thrice.*)

Ipakói.

When they who with Mary came, forestalling the dawn, and found the stone rolled away from the sepulchre, they heard from the Angel: Why seek ye among the dead, as he were mortal, him who abideth in ever-lasting light? Behold the grave-clothes. Go quickly, and proclaim to the world that the Lord is risen, and hath slain Death. For he is the Son of God who saveth mankind.

Collect-Hymn (Kondák).

Though thou didst descend into the grave, O Deathless One, yet didst thou annihilate the power of Hell, and didst rise again as conqueror, O Christ-God, announcing unto the Myrrh-bearing Women: Rejoice! and giving grace unto thine Apostles, and bestowing Resurrection upon the fallen.

And the Hymns (Tropari).

In the Grave with the body, and in Hell with the soul, in that thou art God; in Paradise with the thief, and on the throne with the Father and the Spirit, wast thou, O Christ, filling all things, in that thou art infinite.

Glory to the Father, and to the Son, and to the Holy Spirit.

As life-bearing, as of a truth than Paradise more fair, and than every royal palace more bright hath been revealed thy tomb, the source of our Resurrection, O Christ.

Now, and ever, and unto ages of ages. Amen.

HYMN TO THE BIRTH-GIVER OF GOD (*Bogoróditchen*).

Hail, O thou hallowed, divine abode of the Most High! For through thee, O Birth-giver of God, was joy given unto those who cry aloud to thee: Blessed art thou among women, O Lady all-undefiled!

Lord, have mercy. (*Forty times.*) Glory . . . now, and ever, . . .

More honourable than the Cherubim, and beyond compare more glorious than the Seraphim, thou who without defilement barest God the Word, true Birth-giver of God, we magnify thee.

In the Name of the Lord bless, Father.

Priest. Verse (Stikh): Through the prayers of our holy fathers, O Lord Jesus Christ our God, have mercy upon us.

Choir. Amen.

Christ is risen . . . and upon those in the tomb . . . (*Thrice.*)

Glory . . . now, and ever, . . . Lord, have mercy. (*Thrice.*) Bless.

And the BENEDICTION.

May Christ who is risen from the dead, trampling down Death by death, and upon those in the tomb bestowing life, our true God, through the prayers of his most pure Mother, and of all the Saints, have mercy upon us, and bless us, forasmuch as he is good and loveth mankind.

And in like manner the Third, the Sixth, and the Ninth Hours are read; also Compline.

Then the Divine Liturgy of St. John Chrysostom is celebrated.

After: Blessed is the kingdom . . . *the Priest and Deacon chant* (*thrice*): Christ is risen . . . trampling down Death . . . *The Choir repeateth this thrice.*

The Priest. The Verses: Let God arise . . . *and the rest.* (*Page* 226.)

The Choir. Christ is risen . . . trampling down Death . . . (*See the beginning of the Easter Matins.*)

Meanwhile the Priest, with the triple candlestick in his hand, censeth the Altar and the Temple.

In place of: Bless the Lord, O my soul . . . *the Antiphons are sung in full.*

Antiphon I., Tone II.

Verse 1: O be joyful in the Lord, all ye lands.

Refrain. Through the prayers of the Birth-giver of God, O Saviour, save us.

Verse 2: O be joyful in the Lord, all ye lands: sing praises unto his Name; make his praise to be glorious. ℟

Verse 3: Say unto God: How wonderful art thou in thy works: through the greatness of thy power shall thine enemies be found liars unto thee. ℟

Verse 4: For all the world shall worship thee, sing of thee, and praise thy Name, O Most High. ℟

Glory . . . now, and ever, . . . ℟

Antiphon II., Tone II.

Verse 1: O God, be merciful unto us, and bless us; and show us the light of thy countenance, and be merciful unto us.

Refrain. O Son of God, who rose again from the dead on the third day, save us who sing unto thee, Alleluia.

Verse 2: That thy way may be known upon earth: thy saving health among all nations. ℟

Verse 3: Let the people prai e thee, O God: yea, let all the people praise thee. ℟

Glory . . . now, and ever, . . . ℟ O Only-begotten Son . . . (*See page* 82.)

Antiphon III., Tone V.

Verse 1: Let God arise, and let his enemies be scattered: let them also that hate him flee before him.

Refrain. Christ is risen . . . and upon those in the tomb . . .

Verse 2: Like as smoke vanisheth, so shall they vanish, and like as wax melteth at the fire. ℟

Verse 3: Even so let the ungodly perish at the presence of God. But let the righteous rejoice and be glad, yea, let them rejoice before God. ℟

The Introit. Bless the Lord in his temples, the Lord from the sources of Israel.

See Ipakóï (page 228). Glory . . . now, and ever . . . *and the Kondák (page* 230).

In place of: O Holy God, Holy Mighty, . . . *is used:* As many as have been aptized into Christ have put on Christ.

The Gradual (Prokímen), in the Eighth Tone. This is the day which the Lord hath made: we will rejoice and be glad in it.

Verse: Praise ye the Lord, for he is gracious: for his mercy endureth forever.

The Lesson from the Apostle: Acts i. 1–12.

Alleluia. (*Tone IV.*) Thou, O Lord, art risen, and hast been bountiful to Zion.

Verse: The Lord looked down from heaven upon the earth.

The Gospel is: John i. 1–19: *which setteth forth the divinity of our Lord Jesus Christ. And, as our Lord gave command that his Gospel should be preached throughout the world, to every creature, it is customary, on Easter Day, to read it in as many languages as possible; especially in Hebrew, Greek and Latin, the tongues in which was written the superscription on the cross.*

In place of: Meet is it: . . . The Angel cried: (*See Refrain* 4, *page* 232); *and the Theme-Song of the Ninth Canticle:* Shine, shine, O New Jerusalem! . . .; *The Communion Hymn:* Receive ye the Body of Christ; taste ye of the Fountain of Life.

After the Exclamations: In the fear of God . . .; O God, save thy people . . .; Always, now, and ever, . . .; *and in place of:* Blessed be the Name of the Lord: *is sung the Hymn:* Christ is risen . . .

In place of: Glory to thee, O Christ our God, . . . *is sung:* Christ is risen from the dead, trampling down Death by death. *Choir.* And upon those in the tomb bestowing life.

The Benediction is the same as at the end of Matins.

After the Prayer before the Tribune, at the end of the Divine Liturgy, the Ártos is brought to the Priest in the Sanctuary. The Ártos, or universal altar-bread, beareth the image of the cross, and, sometimes, a representation of Christ's Resurrection. As the Paschal Lamb, by God's command, commemorated in the Old Testament the deliverance of his people from bondage to Pharaoh, and, also, the Lamb which taketh away the sins of the world; so, in commemoration of the Resurrection in the New Testament of the Lord Jesus Christ, whereby we are freed from eternal bondage to the enemy, the Ártos is offered, symbolizing the angelic bread, the Bread of Eternal Life, which came down from heaven; even our Lord Jesus Christ. During the whole of Easter week the Ártos lieth on the Altar, or on the lectern, with the holy picture (ikóna) of the Lord's Resurrection. On Saturday, after the Liturgy, the Ártos is broken up and distributed.

THE PRAYER AT THE BLESSING OF THE ÁRTOS.

O God Omnipotent and Lord Almighty, who by thy servant Moses, at the exodus of Israel from Egypt, and the liberation of thy people from the bitter bondage of Pharaoh, didst command that a Lamb be slain, foreshadowing the Lamb which, because of our deeds, of his own good will, was slain on the cross, and taketh away the sins of the whole world, thy beloved Son, our Lord Jesus Christ: Do thou now, also, we humbly entreat thee, look upon this bread, and bless and sanctify it.   For we thy servants, in honour, and glory, and commemoration of the glorious Resurrection of the same, thy Son, our Lord Jesus Christ, through whom, also, we have received freedom and release from the eternal works of the enemy and the indissoluble bonds of Hell, now before thy majesty, on this exceeding bright, and all-glorious, and saving day of Easter, do offer this. Vouchsafe that we who offer it, and those who shall kiss it and shall taste of it, may be partakers of thy heavenly benediction; and by thy might root out from us all sickness and infirmity, granting health unto all.   For thou art the source of blessing, and the bestower of health, and unto thee do we ascribe glory, to the Father who is from everlasting, together with thine Only-begotten Son, and thine all-holy, and good, and life-giving Spirit, now, and ever, and unto ages of ages.   Amen.

And immediately the Priest sprinkleth the Ártos with holy water, saying:

This Ártos is blessed and hallowed by the sprinkling of this holy water, in the Name of the Father, and of the Son, and of the Holy Spirit.   Amen. (*Thrice.*)

Then he cometh forth, and layeth it on the folding stand; and the People, as they receive the Antidóron, kiss the Ártos.

The PRAYER AT THE BREAKING OF THE ÁRTOS *on Saturday of the Bright Week.*

After the Divine Liturgy, when, in front of the stand upon which the Ártos lieth, Christ is risen from the dead, trampling down Death by death, and upon those in the tomb bestowing life: *hath been sung thrice; and after:* Our Father, who art in heaven: *hath been read, with a reverence, the Deacon saith:*

Let us pray to the Lord.   *The Brethren.*   Lord, have mercy.

Then the Priest saith this Prayer over the Ártos:

O Lord Jesus Christ our God, the Angelic Bread, the Bread of life eternal, who came down from heaven, and hast fed us on these mostbright days with the spiritual food of thy divine benefits, for the sake of thy three days' burial and redeeming Resurrection: Look now also, we humbly entreat thee, upon our prayers and thanksgivings; and as thou didst bless the five loaves in the wilderness, so now also do thou bless this bread, that all who shall partake of it may be vouchsafed bodily and spiritual health and blessing, through the grace and bounties of thy love toward mankind.   For thou art our sanctification, and unto thee do we ascribe glory, together with thy Father who is from everlasting, and thine all-holy, and good, and life-giving Spirit, now, and ever, and unto ages of ages.

The Brethren. Amen.

And having broken the Ártos in the usual manner, he distributeth it to all, before their meal. He may also break it during the Liturgy, after the Prayer before the Tribune, and distribute it to the faithful, instead of the Antidóron.

The PRAYER AT THE BLESSING OF FLESH-MEAT *in the Holy and Great Week of Easter.*

Priest. Blessed is our God always, now, and ever, and unto ages of ages. Amen.

Christ is risen from the dead, trampling down Death by death, and upon those in the tomb bestowing life. (*Thrice.*)

Let us pray to the Lord.

Lord, have mercy.

Look down, O Lord Jesus Christ our God, upon these flesh-meats, and sanctify them, as thou didst sanctify the ram which faithful Abraham offered unto thee, and the lamb which Abel brought unto thee as a burnt-offering; likewise the fatted calf which thou didst command to be slain for thy son who had gone astray, and had returned again to thee; that even as he was accounted worthy to enjoy thy good things, so may we, also, enjoy these things which are sanctified and blessed by thee, to the nourishment of us all. For thou art our true nourishment, and the Giver of all good things, and unto thee do we ascribe glory, together with thy Father, who is from everlasting, and thine all-Holy, good and life-giving Spirit, now, and ever, and unto ages of ages. Amen.

The PRAYER AT THE BLESSING OF CHEESE AND EGGS.

O Master, Lord our God, the Creator and Maker of all things: Bless thou this curdled milk, and likewise these eggs; and preserve us in thy loving-kindness. That as we partake of them, even so, also, we may be filled with thy gifts, which ungrudgingly thou bestowest, and with thine unspeakable goodness. For thine are the kingdom and the power and the glory, of the Father, and of the Son, and of the Holy Spirit, now, and ever, and unto ages of ages. Amen.

SPECIAL FEATURES OF THE EASTER VESPERS.

The Vesper service is celebrated in full vestments.

At the beginning, the Verses (as at the beginning of Matins), accompanied by censing.

Entrance with the book of the Holy Gospels.

The Grand Gradual (Prokímen): What God is so great as our God; thou art the God which doest wonders.

After the Gradual the Gospel: John xx. 19–26.

After the Litany, the Easter Verses: Let God arise, . . . (See Matins, page 226.)

THE ASCENSION OF OUR LORD JESUS CHRIST

(THE FORTIETH DAY AFTER EASTER)

The Stanza (Stikhíra) for: Lord, I have cried: *In Tone VI.* The Lord hath ascended into heaven, that he may send the Comforter unto the world. The heavens have prepared his throne, the clouds his ascension. The Angels marvel, beholding a man exalted over them. The Father awaiteth him whom, as coeternal, he hath in his bosom; and the Holy Spirit commandeth all his Angels: Lift up your gates, ye Princes; clap your hands, all ye nations, for Christ is ascended up to the place where he was before. (*Twice.*)

Glory to the Father, and to the Son, and to the Holy Spirit, now, and ever, and unto ages of ages. Amen.

Tone VI. O sweetest Jesus, who, without leaving the bosom of the Father, hast, as a man, dwelt among the earth-born, to-day art thou ascended in glory from the Mount of Olives, and graciously hast borne on high our fallen nature, and hast sat down with the Father. For which cause the Bodiless Powers of heaven, amazed at the marvel, were affrighted with dread, and seized with trembling, they magnified thy love toward mankind. With them also, we earth-born, glorifying thy condescension toward us, and thine Ascension from us, pray, saying: Do thou, who, at thine Ascension, didst fill with joy unutterable thy disciples and the Birth-giver of God who bare thee, vouchsafe unto us, thine elect, joy also, through their prayers, because of thy great mercy.

The Gradual (Prokímen) for the Day.

The Parables (Paremíi). Isaiah ii. 2–3, lxii. 10–12, lxiii. 1–3, 7–10; Zech. xiv. 1, 4, 8–11.

The Stanza for the Litiyá, in Tone I. Being ascended up into heaven, whence also thou hadst come down, leave us not comfortless, O Lord. But let thy Spirit come, bearing peace unto the world, and show the works of thy might upon the sons of men, O Lord who lovest mankind.

The Hymn for the Day (Tropár), in Tone I. Thou art ascended up into glory, O Christ our God, having made joyful thy disciples by the promise of thy Holy Spirit, the blessing which was announced unto them. For thou art the Son of God, the Redeemer of the world.

The Collect-Hymn (Kondák). When thou hadst accomplished thy dispensation to usward, and hadst united things earthly with things heavenly, thou didst ascend into glory, O Christ our God, yet in nowise departing but abiding uninterruptedly with us, and crying unto those who love thee: I am with you, and none shall prevail against you.

The Exaltation (Velitchánie). We magnify thee, O life-giving Christ, and do homage to thy divine Ascension into heaven in thy holy flesh.

The Gradual (Prokimen), in the Fourth Tone. God is gone up with a merry noise, and the Lord with the sound of the trump.

Verse (Stikh): O clap your hands together, all ye people: cry aloud unto God with the voice of gladness.

The Gospel. Mark xvi. 9–20.

THE CANON.

The First Canon.   In Tone V. (St. John of Damascus.)

Theme-Songs (Irmosí). I. Unto God the Saviour, who led his people through the sea with foot unwet, and drowned Pharaoh with all his host,— unto him alone will we sing: For he hath glorified himself.

III. By the might of thy Cross, O Christ, establish thou my mind, that I may sing and glorify thy redeeming Ascension.

IV. I heard the fame of the might of thy Cross, how that through it Paradise was opened; and I cried: Glory to thy might, O Lord!

V. In the morning, waking early, we cry aloud unto thee, O Lord, Save us! For thou art our God: we know none other beside thee.

VI. The abyss compassed me round about, the whale became unto me a tomb: but I cried unto thee who lovest mankind, and thy right hand saved me, O Lord.

VII. Blessed is the God of our fathers, who saved the Youths which sang in the fiery furnace.

VIII. The Son of God, who was born of the Father before the ages, and in these latter days became incarnate of a Virgin-Mother, sing, O ye Priests; and ye people, magnify him unto all the ages.

In place of: My soul doth magnify the Lord: *the Refrains:*

Magnify, O my soul, the Life-giver, who hath ascended up from earth into heaven.

The Angels, when they beheld the Ascension of the Lord, were amazed with awe to see how that he, with glory, was taken up from earth on high.

IX. Thee, who above understanding and speech didst become the Mother of God, and ineffably didst bring forth in time him who knoweth not time, we faithful, with one accord, do magnify.

The Benediction. May he who is ascended up in glory from us into heaven, and sitteth at the right hand of God, Christ our true God: *and the rest.*   (See page 122.)

At the Liturgy.

Antiphon I., Tone II.

Verse 1: O clap your hands together, all ye people: cry aloud unto God with the voice of gladness.

. *Refrain.* Through the prayers of the Birth-giver of God, O Saviour, save us.

Verse 2: For the Lord is high and to be feared: he is the great King upon all the earth. ℞

Verse 3: He shall subdue the people under us, and the nations under our feet. ℞

Verse 4: God is gone up with a merry noise, and the Lord with the sound of the trump. ℞

Antiphon II., Tone II.

Verse 1: Great is the Lord, and highly to be praised, in the city of our God, even upon his holy hill.

Refrain. Save, O son of God who art ascended up in glory, those who sing unto thee: Alleluia.

Verse 2: Upon the north side of the hill of Zion lieth the city of the great King. ℞

Verse 3: God is well known in her palaces as a sure refuge. ℞

Verse 4: For lo, the kings of the earth are gathered and gone by together. ℞

Glory to the Father, and to the Son, and to the Holy Spirit, now, and ever, and unto ages of ages. Amen.

O Only-begotten Son and Word of God! . . . (*See page* 170.)

Antiphon III., Tone IV.

Verse 1: O hear ye this, all ye people; ponder it with your ears, all ye that dwell in the world.

Refrain: The Hymn for the Day (Tropár). Thou art ascended up into glory, O Christ our God, having made joyful thy disciples by the promise of thy Holy Spirit, the blessing which was announced unto them. For thou art the Son of God, the Redeemer of the world.

Verse 2: Ye earth-born and sons of men: rich and poor, one with another.

Verse 3: My mouth shall speak of wisdom, and my heart shall muse of understanding. ℞

Verse 4: I will incline mine ear to the parable, and show my dark speech upon the harp. ℞

The Introit. God is gone up with a merry noise, and the Lord with the sound of the trump. ℞

The Gradual (Prokímen), in the Seventh Tone. Be thou exalted in heaven, O God, and thy glory above all the earth.

Verse (Stikh): My heart is fixed, O God, my heart is fixed; I will sing and give thanks.

The Epistle. Acts i. 1–11.

The Gospel. Luke xxiv. 36–53.

In place of: Meet is it: *The Ninth Theme-Song of the Canon:* Thee, who above understanding . . . (*See page* 243.)

The Communion Hymn. God is gone up with a merry noise, and the Lord with the sound of the trump.

PENTECOST (WHITSUNDAY)

The date of Pentecost is regulated by the date of Easter. But that Sunday is called The Day of the Holy Trinity. The Feast of the Holy Spirit (in that He is separate, yet equal in essence, honour and glory with the Father and the Son) is celebrated on the following day, Monday, and is called the Day of the Spirit.

It is customary to decorate churches and houses at this Feast with freshly cut trees and flowers, and to stand at the Divine Liturgy holding flowers. This custom is founded upon that of the Old Testament Church (Lev. xxiii. 10–17; Num. xxviii. 16). The trees and flowers, the tokens of the renewal of Nature in the Spring, typify also the renewal of mankind through the indwelling o' the Holy Spirit.

The special features in the celebration of this Feast consist of certain petitions in the Litany; and of Prayers recited kneeling at Vespers, which, as a rule, immediately followeth the Liturgy.

At the All-Night Vigil.

The Stanza (Stikhíra) for: Lord, I have cried: *In Tone I.* Let us celebrate Pentecost, and the coming of the Spirit, and the appointed day of promise, and the fulfilment of hope, and the mystery which is as great as it is precious. Wherefore unto thee, O Lord, the Maker of all things, do we cry: Glory to thee.

Glory to the Father, and to the Son, and to the Holy Spirit, now, and ever, and unto ages of ages. Amen.

Come, O ye people, let us worship the Godhead in three Persons, the Son in the Father with the Holy Spirit. For the Father before time was begat the Son, who is coeternal and is equally enthroned, and the Holy Spirit who was in the Father, and was glorified together with the Son; one Might, one Essence, one Godhead. Adoring the same let us all say: O Holy God, who by the Son didst make all things through the coöperation of the Holy Spirit: O Holy Mighty One, through whom we have known the Father, and through whom the Holy Spirit came into the world: O Holy Immortal One, the Spirit of comfort, who proceedest from the Father, and restest in the Son: O Holy Trinity, glory to thee.

The Gradual (Prokímen) for the Day.

The Parables (Paremií). Num. xi. 16, 17, 24–29; Joel ii. 23–32; Ezek. xxxvi. 24–28.

The Stanza at the Litiyá, in Tone VIII. When thou didst send thy Spirit, O Lord, while the Apostles sat together, then were the Hebrew children affrighted with dread as they gazed; for they heard them speak one to another in strange tongues, as the Spirit gave them utterance. For though unlearned they were made wise, and bringing the Gentiles unto the faith, proclaimed things divine. Wherefore, we also do cry unto thee, O Lord, who hast revealed thyself upon earth, and hast saved us from guile: Glory to thee.

The Hymn for the Day (Tropár), in Tone VIII. Blessed art thou, O Christ-God, who hast revealed fishers most wise, sending down upon them the Holy Spirit, and thereby catching the universe as in a net. O Christ-God, who lovest mankind, glory to thee.

The Collect-Hymn (Kondák). When the Most High confounded the tongues, he dispersed the nations: but when he distributed the tongues of fire, he called all men unto unity. Wherefore, with one accord, we glorify the All-holy Spirit.

The Exaltation (Velitchánie). We magnify thee, O life-giving Christ, and do homage to thine all-holy Spirit, whom thou didst send from the Father upon thy disciples divine.

The Gradual (Prokímen), in the Fourth Tone. Thy good spirit shall lead me into the land of righteousness.

Verse (Stikh): O Lord, hear my prayer, give ear to my petition.

The Gospel. John xx. 19–23.

THE CANON.
Tone IV. (St. Cosmas of Maium.)

Theme-Songs (Irmosí). I. He who shattereth the enemies with his lofty arm overwhelmed with the sea Pharaoh and his chariots: To him let us sing, for gloriously hath he been glorified.

III. Tarry ye in Jerusalem until ye shall be endued with power from on high, thou didst say unto thy disciples, O Christ; for I will send another, like unto myself, even the Comforter, my Spirit and the Father's, in whom ye shall be established.

IV. When he foresaw thy coming in the latter days, O Christ, the Prophet exclaimed: I have heard of thy power, O Lord, that thou art come to save all thine anointed.

V. The Spirit of salvation, through thy fear, O Lord, conceived in the womb of the Prophets, and born upon earth maketh pure the hearts of the Apostles, and in that it is righteous, is renewed in the faithful. For thy statutes are light and peace.

VI. Sailing on the stormy sea of earthly cares, drowning in the billows of the sins which compass me round about, and cast forth unto the soul-destroying monster, like Jonah I cry unto thee, O Christ: Lead thou me forth from the death-dealing abyss.

VII. When they were cast into the fiery furnace, the God-fearing Children transmuted the fire into dew, crying aloud, after this manner, in song: Blessed art thou, O Lord God of our Fathers.

VIII. The bush which could not be consumed, though surrounded by fire, on Sinai revealed God unto Moses, slow of tongue and halting of speech: and the zeal toward God of the Three Children showed the singers untouched of the fire. O all ye works of the Lord bless ye the Lord, and magnify him unto all the ages.

IX. O Maiden Birth-giver of God, who in birth-giving suffered not defilement, and didst lend flesh unto the All-creating Word; Mother Unwedded, Receptacle of Him who cannot be contained, Abode of thy Maker illimitable, we magnify thee.

Benediction. May he who sent down the Most Holy Spirit, in the form of fiery tongues, upon his holy disciples and apostles, Christ, our true God: *and so forth, as usual.* (*See page* 122.)

At the Liturgy.

Antiphon I., Tone II.

Verse 1: The heavens declare the glory of God, and the firmament showeth his handiwork.

Refrain. Through the prayers of the Birth-giver of God, O Saviour, save us.

Verse 2: Day unto day uttereth speech, and night unto night showeth knowledge. ℞

Verse 3: Their voice is gone out into all the earth, and their words unto the end of the world. ℞

Antiphon II., Tone II.

Verse 1: The Lord hear thee in the day of trouble: the Name of the God of Jacob defend thee.

Refrain. Save, O blessed Comforter, us who sing unto thee, Alleluia.

Verse 2: Send thee help from the sanctuary, and strengthen thee out of Zion. ℞

Verse 3: Grant thee thy heart's desire, and fulfil all thy mind. ℞

Glory to the Father, and to the Son, and to the Holy Spirit, now, and ever, and unto ages of ages. Amen.

O Only-begotten Son and Word of God! . . . (*See page* 170.)

Antiphon III., Tone VIII.

Verse 1: The King shall rejoice in thy strength, O Lord: exceeding glad shall he be of thy salvation.

Refrain: The Hymn for the Day (Tropár). Blessed art thou, O Christ our God, who hast revealed fishers most wise, sending down upon them thy Holy Spirit, and thereby catching the universe as in a net. Glory to thee, O thou who lovest mankind.

Verse 2: Thou hast given him his heart's desire, and hast not denied him the request of his lips. ℞

Verse 3: Thou shalt prevent him with the blessings of goodness, and shalt set a crown of pure gold upon his head. ℞

The Introit. Exalted be thou, O Lord, in thy power. We will praise and sing thy mighty acts. ℞

In place of: O Holy God, Holy Mighty, . . . As many as have been baptized into Christ have put on Christ.

The Gradual (Prokimen), in the Eighth Tone. Their voice is gone out into all the earth, and their words to the end of the world.

Verse: The heavens declare the glory of God, and the firmament showeth his handiwork.

The Epistle. Acts ii. 1–12.

· Alleluia. *(Tone I.)* By the word of the Lord were the heavens made, and all the host of them by the word of his mouth.

Verse (Stikh): The Lord looked down from heaven, and beheld all the children of men.

The Gospel. John vii. 37–52, viii. 12.

In place of: Meet is it: *The Ninth Theme-Song of the Second Canon.* Hail, O Queen, thou glory of motherhood and maidenhood! For every mouth, however eloquent and sweet of speech, is incapable of worthily singing thy praise; and every mind reeleth when it would fain understand thy birth-giving. For which cause, with one accord, we glorify thee.

The Communion Hymn. Thy good Spirit shall guide me into the land of righteousness.

Vespers.

(Which followeth immediately after the Liturgy.)

After the customary beginning, and the Prefatory Psalm, the Litany:

In peace let us pray to the Lord.   *(Page 5.)*

Choir. Lord, have mercy.

And the rest.   After the Petition:

For those who travel by sea or by land: ℞

For the people here present who await the grace of the Holy Spirit: ℞

For those who have bowed their knees and their hearts before the Lord: ℞

That he will strengthen us in the performance of those things which are well pleasing in his sight: ℞

That he will send down upon us the riches of his grace: ℞

That he will accept this, the bending of our knees, as incense before him: ℞

For those who entreat from him his aid: ℞

That he will deliver us from all tribulation, wrath, and necessity: ℞

let us pray to the Lord. Choir. Lord, have mercy.

Succour us, save us, have mercy upon us, and keep us, O God, by thy grace.

Calling to remembrance our most holy, all-undefiled, most blessed and glorious Lady, the Birth-giver of God and ever-virgin Mary, with all the Saints, let us commend ourselves, and each other, and all our life unto Christ our God.

Choir. To thee, O Lord.

Exclamation. For unto thee are due all glory, honour and worship, to the Father, and to the Son, and to the Holy Spirit, now, and ever, and unto ages of ages. Amen.

The Stanza (Stikhíra) for: Lord, I have cried: *In Tone IV.* Marvellous things have all the nations beheld this day in the city of David, when the Holy Spirit descended in tongues of fire, as Luke, preaching the word of God, doth relate; for he saith: The disciples of Christ being assembled in one place, there came a sound as of a rushing mighty wind, and it filled all the house where they were sitting. And they all began to speak in strange tongues with strange doctrines, by the strange commands of the Holy Trinity.

Glory to the Father, and to the Son, and to the Holy Spirit, now, and ever, and unto ages of ages. Amen.

O heavenly King, the Comforter, Spirit of Truth, who art in all places and fillest all things; Treasury of good things and Giver of life: Come, and take up thine abode in us, and cleanse us from every stain; and save our souls, O Good One.

The Entrance is made with the censer.

O gladsome radiance . . .

The Great Gradual (Prokímen), in the Seventh Tone. Who is so great a God as our God? Thou art God who doest wonders.

Verse (Stikh) 1: Thou hast declared thy power unto the nations.

Verse 2: And I said: Now have I made a beginning; these are the charges of the right hand of the Most High.

Verse 3: I have remembered the works of the Lord, as I have remembered thy marvels from the beginning.

Then the Priest exclaimeth (or the Deacon):

Again, yet again, on bended knees let us pray to the Lord.

Choir. Lord, have mercy. (*Thrice.*)

The First Prayer.

Priest. O Lord most pure, spotless, who art from everlasting, invisible, ineffable, unsearchable, unchanging, unsurpassable, immeasurable, long-suffering; who alone hast immortality; who dwellest in light unapproachable, who hast made heaven and earth and the sea, and all that therein is; who grantest unto all men their petitions before they ask: We pray thee, and beseech thee, O Master who lovest mankind, the Father of our Lord, and God, and Saviour Jesus Christ, who for us men and for our salvation came down from heaven, and was incarnate by the Holy Spirit of Mary the ever-virgin and exceeding-glorious Birth-giver of God; who first did teach in words and afterwards did manifest himself in deeds, when he had suffered his redeeming Passion; who hast given unto us, thy humble, and sinful, and unworthy servants, a command that we should offer supplications unto thee with bending of the neck and of the knees, both for our own iniquities and for the ignorances of the people: Do thou, the same all-merciful God who lovest mankind, hear us in that day when we shall call upon thee, and more especially upon this day of Pentecost, whereon, after that our Lord Jesus Christ had ascended up into heaven, and had sat down at the right hand of thee, who art both his God and his Father, he did send down the Holy Spirit upon his holy disciples and apostles: which also did rest upon each one of them, so that they were all filled with its inexhaustible grace, and did declare thy majesty in divers unknown tongues, and did prophesy. Wherefore hearken now to us who pray unto thee, and remember us, humble and condemned as we are, and turn again the captivity of our souls, exercising thy loving-kindness toward us who now offer up our petitions unto thee. Accept us who fall down before thee, and who cry aloud unto thee, We have sinned! We have cloven unto thee even from our mother's womb: thou art our God. But because we have passed our days in vanity, we have stripped ourselves of thine aid, we have deprived ourselves of every valid defence. But confidently trusting in thy bounties, we call unto thee: Remember not the sins of our youth and our ignorances; and cleanse thou us from our secret sins; and forsake us not in the days of our old age, when our strength faileth us. Even until we return again into the earth, abandon us not, vouchsafe us grace to have recourse unto thee; and receive us, because of thy favour and graciousness. Measure our wickedness according to the measure of thy bounties. Set over against the multitude of our transgressions the abyss of thy compassions. Look down from thy holiness on high, O Lord, upon thy people now present before thee, who await thy rich mercies. Visit us with thy loving-kindness: deliver us from the assaults of the Devil. Establish our life in thy holy and sacred commandments. Commit thy people unto an Angel, a faithful guardian. Gather us all into thy kingdom. Grant pardon unto those who put their trust in thee. Put away from them and from us all sins. Purify us by the operation of thy Holy Spirit; bring to naught the machinations of the enemy against us.

And thereto is added the following Prayer:

Blessed art thou, O Lord, Master Almighty, who hast illumined the day with the light of the sun, and hast made bright the night with the brilliant flashes of the lightning; who hast graciously enabled us to pass through the long day, and to draw near to the beginning of the night. Hear our petitions, and the petitions of all thy people, and granting pardon unto us for all our sins, both voluntary and involuntary, accept our evening prayers, and send down the multitude of thy mercy and thy bounties upon thine inheritance. Guard us with thy holy Angels. Arm us with the armour of thy righteousness. Encompass us round about with the ramparts of thy truth. Guard us by thy might. Deliver us from every assault, and from every treacherous plot of the adversary.

And grant unto us that this present evening and the approaching night, and all the days of our life, may be perfect, holy, peaceful, sinless, without stumbling, untroubled of dreams; through the prayers of the holy Birth-giver of God, and of all the Saints, who, in all the ages, have been acceptable in thy sight.

Then the Little Litany.

Deacon. Again, yet again, in peace let us pray to the Lord.

Choir. Lord, have mercy.

Succour us, save us, have mercy upon us, and keep us, O God, by thy grace.

Choir. Lord, have mercy.

Calling to remembrance our most holy, all-undefiled, most blessed and glorious Lady, the Birth-giver of God and ever-virgin Mary, with all the Saints, let us commend ourselves, and each other, and all our life unto Christ our God.

Choir. To thee, O Lord.

Then the Priest maketh the Exclamation:

For thine it is to show mercy upon us and to save us, O Lord our God, and unto thee do we ascribe glory, to the Father, and to the Son, and to the Holy Spirit, now, and ever, and unto ages of ages.

Choir. Amen.

Then the Priest, or the Deacon, saith this Litany:

Let us all say, with all our soul and with all our mind let us say:

Choir. Lord, have mercy.

Deacon. O Almighty Lord, the God of our fathers, we beseech thee: hearken, and have mercy.

Choir. Lord, have mercy.

Have mercy upon us, O God, according to thy great mercy we beseech thee: hearken, and have mercy.

Here follow petitions for the Ruler of the Land and for all the Authorities (according to the elements and nationalities of which the Parish is constituted).

For our Most Holy Synod (*or* Patriarch); for our Bishop (*or* Archbishop, *or* Metropolitan) N., for the honourable Presbytery, the Diaconate in Christ; for all the clergy and the laity: ℟

Furthermore we pray for all their Christ-loving Army and Navy: ℟

Furthermore we pray for the blessed and ever-memorable founders of this holy Temple: ℟

Furthermore we pray for mercy, life, peace, health, salvation, visitation, forgiveness and remission of the sins of the servants of God, the brethren of this holy Temple (*or* habitation: *if it be a monastery*): ℟

Furthermore we pray for those who bear fruit and do good works in this holy and all-honourable Temple; for those who labour in its service; for the singers; and for the people here present, who await the great and rich mercies which are from thee: ℟

Choir. Lord, have mercy. (Thrice.)

For thou art a merciful God, who lovest mankind, and unto thee do we ascribe glory, to the Father, and to the Son, and to the Holy Spirit, now, and ever, and unto ages of ages.

Choir. Amen. Amen.

And immediately the Deacon saith:

Again, yet again, on bended knees let us pray to the Lord.

Choir. Lord, have mercy. (*Thrice.*)

The Second Prayer.

O Lord Jesus Christ our God, who hast bestowed upon men thy peace and the gift of thy Holy Spirit; who, while thou wast yet with us in this present life, didst give unto thy faithful people an inheritance which shall not be taken away from them forever; who this day didst send down thy grace upon thy disciples and apostles, in manner most clear, and didst furnish their lips with fiery tongues; by whom now, we also, together with all mankind, having received, through the hearing of our own ears divine knowledge in our own tongues, have been illumined with the light of the Spirit, and have put away the delusion of darkness by the distribution of the material and visible tongues of fire, as also by the marvellous operation of the same, whereby we have been inspired with faith toward thee, and to glorify thee, together with the Father and the Holy Spirit in one Godhead and might; and have been enlightened with power: Do thou, who art the Brightness of the Father, of his Essence and his Nature the Express and Immutable Image, the Fountain of Wisdom and of Grace, open the lips of me, a sinner, and teach me in what manner and for what needs I ought to pray; for thou knowest the great multitude of my sins, but thy loving-kindness shall overcome the enormity thereof. For lo! I stand in awe before thee, and have cast into the great deep of thy mercy the despair of my soul. Govern my life, O thou who governest all creation by a word, with the unutterable might of thy wisdom, O tranquil Haven of the storm-tossed; and make known unto me the way in which I should walk. Grant unto my understanding the spirit of thy wisdom, bestowing upon my ignorance the spirit of thy understanding. Overshadow my deeds with the spirit of thy fear, and renew a right spirit within me; and by thy sovereign Spirit make stable the instability of my thoughts. That being daily guided by thy good Spirit in that which is profitable for me, I may be enabled to keep thy statutes, and ever bear in mind thy glorious Coming-again, and those things worthy of torment which I have committed. And give me not over to be led astray by the corrupt pleasures of this present world, but strengthen in me the desire to strive for the treasures to come. For thou hast said, O Master: whatsoever a man shall ask in thy Name, that shall he freely receive from thy God and Father, who is from everlasting. Wherefore, I, also, a sinner, at this descent of thy Holy Spirit, do entreat thy goodness, that thou wilt grant me whatsoever things I have asked which are unto salvation. Yea, O Lord, the bounteous Giver of every benefit, and the Distributor of blessings,— for it is thou who givest most bountifully unto those who ask of thee,— thou art pitiful and gracious, and also wast made a partaker of our flesh, yet without sin, and dost incline thine ear with infinite loving-kindness unto those who bow the knee before thee; who, also, wast made the Propitiation for our sins. Wherefore, O Lord, grant thy bounties unto thy people. Hearken unto us from thy holy heaven. Sanctify us by the saving might of thy right hand. Cover us with the shelter of thy wings; and despise thou not the work of thy hands. Unto thee alone have we sinned, but thee alone do we serve. We know not to adore a strange god, neither have we stretched out our hands, O Lord, unto any other god. Pardon our iniquities, and accept this our prayer, which we make unto thee on bended knees. Extend unto us all the hand of thine aid. Receive the petitions of all men, as it were incense well-pleasing, acceptable before thine all-blessed kingdom.

And thereto is added the following Prayer:

O Lord, Lord, who deliverest us from all the arrows that fly by day, deliver thou us, also, from all things that infest the darkness. Accept our evening sacrifice, even the lifting-up of our hands. Grant that we may pass through the course of the night without sin, untempted of evil things; and deliver us from every alarm and cowardice that cometh to us from the Devil. Grant unto our souls contrition, and unto our minds anxiety concerning that strict searching out of the thoughts which shall come in the dread and just Day of Judgment. Nail our flesh to the fear of thee, and mortify our earthly members: that, in the quietness of sleep, we may be illuminated by the vision of thy judgments. Remove from us, also, every unseemly imagination and hurtful carnal passion. Raise us up again at the hour of prayer, fortified in the faith, and advancing in thy commandments.

And the Deacon saith:

Succour us, save us, have mercy upon us, and keep us, O God, by thy grace.

Choir. Lord, have mercy.

Calling to remembrance our most holy, all-undefiled, most blessed and glorious Lady, the Birth-giver of God and ever-virgin Mary, with all the Saints, let us commend ourselves, and each other, and all our life unto Christ our God.

Choir. To thee, O Lord.

And the Priest maketh the Exclamation:

Through the loving-kindness and goodness of thine Only-begotten Son, with whom thou art blessed, together with thine all-holy, and good, and life-giving Spirit, now, and ever, and unto ages of ages.

Choir. Amen.

Then: Vouchsafe, O Lord, to keep us this night without sin. . . . (*Page 9.*)

Then the Deacon saith:

Again, yet again, on bended knees let us pray to the Lord.

Choir. Lord, have mercy. (*Thrice.*)

And the Priest readeth the Third Prayer.

O Fountain, ever-flowing, living, illumining; Power creative, coeternal with the Father, O Christ our God, who hast most excellently fulfilled all the plan for the salvation of mankind; who didst shatter the bonds indestructible of Death, and the bolts of Hell, and didst trample under foot a host of evil spirits; who didst offer thyself a blameless victim for us, giving thine all-holy body for a sacrifice inviolate, and unassailed of every sin, and who, through that terrible and ineffable act of sacrifice, didst bestow upon us life eternal; who didst descend into Hell, and break the everlasting bars, and show a way up unto those who abode in the lower world; and having enticed, by divinely wise allurements, the origin of mischief and the serpent of the abyss, and bound him with cords of nethermost gloom and fire unquenchable in Tartarus, and confined him in outer darkness, by thine infinite and fettering might, O Wisdom greatly glorified of the Father, thou didst manifest thyself as a mighty helper of the assailed; and didst enlighten those who sat in darkness and in the shadow of death, Do thou, O Lord of the everlasting glory and Son beloved of the Father most high, Light Eternal of Light Eternal, the Sun of Righteousness, hear us, who now make our fervent supplications unto thee, and give rest to the souls of thy servants our fathers and brethren, and our other kinsmen after the flesh, and of all who are of the household of faith, who have fallen asleep, and whom we now call to remembrance. For thou hast power over all things, and in thy hand thou upholdest all the ends of the earth. O Master Almighty, the God of our fathers and Lord of mercy, Creator of the race of mortals and immortals, and of every nature of man; of that which is brought together and is again put asunder; of life and of death; of sojourn in the world that now is, and of translation to the world which is to come: thou metest out the years of life, and appointest the time of death; thou bringest down to Hell, and again raisest up; thou bindest unto impotency and loosest unto power, ordering things present according to their necessity, and appointing things to come as is expedient, quickening with the hope of Resurrection those who were smitten with the sting of death. For thou art, of a truth, the Master of all men, O God our Saviour, the hope of all the ends of the earth, and of those who are afar off upon the sea; Who, on this last, and great, and redeeming day of the Pentecostal feast, didst reveal unto us the mystery of the Holy

Trinity, one in Essence, coeternal, undivided and unmingled; and didst pour out the indwelling and descent of thy holy and life-giving Spirit, in the form of tongues of fire, upon thy holy apostles; and didst appoint the same to be the heralds of the glad tidings of our holy faith; and didst make them confessors and teachers of the true divine knowledge; who, also, on this all-perfect and saving Feast, art graciously pleased to accept propitiatory prayers for those who are imprisoned in Hell, promising unto us who are held in bondage great hope of release from the vileness that doth hinder us and did hinder them; and that thou wilt send down thy consolation. Hear us, thy humble ones, who make our supplications unto thee, and give rest to the souls of thy servants who have fallen asleep, in a place of light, a place of verdure, a place of refreshment whence all sickness, sorrow and sighing have fled away: And establish thou their souls in the mansions of the Just; and graciously vouchsafe unto them peace and pardon; for the dead shall not praise thee, O Lord, neither shall they who are in Hell make bold to offer unto thee confession. But we who are living will bless thee, and will pray, and offer unto thee propitiatory prayers and sacrifices for their souls.

And thereto is added the following Prayer:

O God great and eternal, who art holy and lovest mankind; who hast vouchsafed unto us at this present hour to stand before thine ineffable glory, and to sing and to praise thy wonders: Purify us, thine unworthy servants, and grant us grace that, with a contrite heart, and . without presumption, we may offer unto thee the Thrice-Holy hymn of praise and thanksgiving for thy great gifts, which thou hast bestowed and always dost bestow upon us. Remember, O Lord, our weakness, and destroy us not in our iniquity, but show great mercy upon our humility; that, fleeing from the darkness of sin, we may walk in the daylight of righteousness; and that, putting on the armour of light, we may remain unassailed by any despiteful attack of the Evil One, and with boldness may glorify in all things thee, the only true God, who also lovest mankind. For thine, O Lord and Creator of all men, is that great and veritable mystery, the dissolution of thy creatures for a season, and thereafter their redintegration and their rest forever. We acknowledge thy grace in all things; for our coming into this world and our going out of it; for our hopes of resurrection and of the life immortal faithfully pledged unto us through thine unfailing promises, the which we shall receive hereafter in thy Second Coming. For thou art the Chieftain of our Resurrection, and the Judge impartial and benignant of the dead, and the Master and Lord of recompense, who didst become a partaker, on equal terms, of our flesh and blood, because of thine exceeding great condescension; and when, of thine own will, that thou mightest place thyself under temptation, thou didst accept our congenital passions, because of thy compassion, and didst suffer through them, being thyself tempted thereby, thou didst become for us who are tempted the helper which thou thyself hadst promised; and thereby hast thou led us to thy passionlessness. Wherefore, O Master, receive thou our prayers and supplications, and give rest unto the fathers, mothers, children, brothers, and sisters, blood-relations and kinsfolk of each and all of us, and unto all souls which have fallen asleep before us; and establish their spirits in the hope of Resurrection unto life eternal, and inscribe their names in the Book of Life, in the bosom of Abraham, and of Isaac, and of Jacob, and in the land of the living, in the kingdom of heaven, in the Paradise of sweetness; by thy radiant Angels guiding all into thy holy mansions; raising up with thee, also, our bodies, in that day which thou hast appointed by thy holy and faithful promise. Because there is no death, O Lord, for thy servants when we depart from the body and come unto thee, our God, but a change from things very sorrowful unto things most benignant and most sweet, and unto repose and gladness. If, therefore, we have in aught transgressed against thee, be merciful unto us and unto them; because there is no one pure from stain in thy sight, even for a single day of his life, save thou alone, who didst manifest thyself sinless upon earth, O our Lord Jesus Christ; through whom also we all trust to receive mercy and the remission of our sins. Wherefore, in that thou art a gracious God and lovest mankind, do thou, both to them and to us, pardon, remit, forgive our sins, both voluntary and involuntary, which we have committed whether wilfully or through ignorance; whether those which are manifest or those which have escaped our notice; whether of deed, or of thought, or of word, whatsoever they may be, in all our acts and lives. And unto the departed also grant thou release and pardon; and bless us who are here present, granting unto us, and to all thy people, a good and peaceful ending, and opening unto us the tenderness of thy mercy and love toward mankind at thy dread and terrible Coming-again; and make us worthy of thy kingdom.

And thereto is added the Seventh Evening Prayer. (See Vespers, Prayer G, page 4.)

Then the Deacon saith:

Succour us, save us, have mercy upon us, and keep us, O God, by thy grace.

Choir. Lord, have mercy.

Calling to remembrance our most holy, all-undefiled, most blessed and glorious Lady, the Birth-giver of God and ever-virgin Mary, with all the Saints, let us commend ourselves, and each other, and all our life unto Christ our God.

Choir. To thee, O Lord.

Priest. For thou art the repose of our souls and bodies, and unto thee do we ascribe glory, to the Father, and to the Son, and to the Holy Spirit, now, and ever, and unto ages of ages.

Choir. Amen.

Deacon. Let us complete our evening prayer unto the Lord.

Choir. Lord, have mercy. *And the rest, as usual.* (*See page* 10.)

The Priest then saith, secretly, *the customary Prayer.*

O Lord our God, who didst bow the heavens and come down . . . (*See page* 10.)

Exclamation.

For thou art a gracious God, who lovest mankind, and unto thee do we ascribe glory, to the Father, and to the Son, and to the Holy Spirit, now, and ever, and unto ages of ages.

Choir. Amen.

Lord, now lettest thou thy servant depart in peace, according to thy word. For mine eyes have seen thy salvation, which thou hast prepared before the face of all nations; a light to lighten the Gentiles, and the glory of thy people Israel.

O heavenly King . . . O Holy God . . . O all-holy Trinity . . . Our Father . . . For thine is the kingdom . . . (*See page* 43.)

The Hymn for the Day (*Tropár*). Blessed art thou, O Christ our God, who hast revealed fishers most wise, sending down upon them thy Holy Spirit, and thereby catching the universe as in a net. Glory to thee, O thou who lovest mankind.

Deacon. Wisdom!

Then the Priest pronounceth the BENEDICTION.

May he who emptied himself from the bosom of God and the Father, and descended from heaven upon the earth, and took upon himself all our nature, and rendered it divine; and after that ascended again into heaven, and sitteth at the right hand of God and the Father; who also sent down upon his holy disciples and apostles the divine and holy Spirit, which is of one Essence, equal in power, and equal in glory with himself, and thereby enlightened them, and through them the whole universe — even Christ our true God; through the prayers of his most pure and all-undefiled Mother, of the holy, glorious and all-laudable preachers of God and Spirit-bearing apostles, and of all the Saints, have mercy upon us, and save us, forasmuch as he is good and loveth mankind.

THE TRANSFIGURATION OF THE LORD

At Vespers, on the Eve.

The Stanzas (Stikhíri) for: Lord, I have cried: *In Tone IV.* Before thy Crucifixion, O Christ, the Mount became like unto the heavens, and a cloud was outspread like a canopy, while thou wast transfigured, and while the Father bare witness unto thee. There was Peter, together with James and John, inasmuch as they desired to be with thee at the time of thy betrayal also; that, having beheld thy marvels, they might not be affrighted at thy sufferings. Make us also worthy to adore the same in peace, for the sake of thy great mercy.

Before thy Crucifixion, O Lord, having taken thy disciples into a high mountain, thou wast transfigured before them, dazzling them with rays of might; being desirous to show unto them the radiance of the Resurrection; both because of thy love toward mankind and for the sake of thy power. Vouchsafe the same unto us in peace, O God, inasmuch as thou art merciful and lovest mankind.

The mountain that of old was gloomy and smoking is now honourable and holy, for thereon thy feet have stood, O Lord; for the mystery which was hidden from eternity, even thy dread Transfiguration, was made manifest in these last days unto Peter and John and James, who, unable to endure such splendour of thy countenance and radiance of thy garments, fell with their faces to the earth, and covered themselves: and overcome with dread, they were amazed when they beheld Moses and Elijah talking with thee, touching those things which should happen unto thee. And a voice also from the Father, bare witness unto thee, saying: This is my beloved Son, in whom I am well pleased: hear ye him, who also giveth unto the world great mercy.

When the Saviour was transfigured on the high mountain, having with him the chief disciples, he became most gloriously radiant, showing that inasmuch as he was radiant with the height of virtues, they also would be vouchsafed divine glory. Moses and Elijah, who talked with Christ, made manifest that he ruleth both the quick and the dead, and that he is the God who spake of old through the Law and the Prophets. And unto him also did the voice of the Father from the cloud bear witness, saying: Hear ye him, who hath taken Hell captive by his Cross, and giveth life everlasting unto the dead.

Glory to the Father, and to the Son, and to the Holy Spirit, now, and ever, and unto ages of ages. Amen.

(By Anatolius.) Tone VI. Thou didst prefigure thy Resurrection, O

Christ-God, when thou didst take three of thy disciples, Peter and James and John, and didst ascend Mount Tabor. And when thou wast transfigured, O Saviour, Mount Tabor was covered with light, and thy disciples, O Word, did throw themselves prone upon the earth, being unable to bear the sight of that which may not be looked upon. Angels ministered with fear and trembling; the heavens were affrighted, and the earth did quake, when they beheld on earth the Lord of glory.

The Gradual (Prokímen) for the Day.

The Parables (Paremíí). Exodus xxiv. 12–18, xxxiii. 11–23, xxxiv. 4–6, 8; 1 Kings xix. 3–9, 11–13, 15–16.

The Stanza at the Litiyá, in Tone II. Thou who didst illumine the whole universe with thy light, wast transfigured on a high mountain, O Good One, manifesting unto thy disciples thy power, inasmuch as thou deliverest the world from transgression: For which cause we cry aloud unto thee: O merciful Lord, save thou our souls.

The Hymn (Tropár), in Tone VII. Thou wast transfigured upon the Mount, O Christ-God, revealing unto thy disciples thy glory in so far as they were able to bear it. Let thy light everlasting illumine us sinners also; through the prayers of the Birth-giver of God. O Light-giver, glory to thee!

The Collect-Hymn (Kondák), in Tone VII. Upon the Mount wast thou transfigured, and thy disciples, in so far as they were qualified, beheld thy glory, O Christ-God; that when they should see thee crucified they might comprehend that thy suffering was voluntary, and proclaim it unto the world: For thou art, of a truth, the effulgence of the Father.

The Exaltation. We magnify thee, O life-giving Christ, and we do homage to the exceedingly glorious Transfiguration of thy Body most pure.

The Gradual (Prokímen), in the Fourth Tone. Tabor and Hermon shall rejoice in thy Name.

Verse (Stikh): Thine are the heavens, and the earth is thine.

The Gospel. Luke ix. 28–36.

THE CANON.

The First Canon. Tone IV. (St. Cosmas of Maium.)

Theme-Songs (Irmosí). I. The hosts of Israel, when they had passed with foot unwet through the watery abyss of the Red Sea, and beheld the warriors and the horsemen of the enemy drowned therein, sang aloud with joy: Let us sing praises unto our God, for gloriously hath he been glorified!

III. The bow of the mighty is become feeble, and those who had no strength have girded themselves with might. For which cause my heart is become steadfast in the Lord.

IV. I have given heed to thy glorious providence, O Christ-God, how that thou wast born of a Virgin, to the end that thou mightest deliver from error all those who cry unto thee: Glory to thy might, O Lord.

V. O thou who didst disseminate the primeval radiance of the light, that thy works might sing thee in the light, O Christ their Creator: Guide thou our paths in thy light.

VI. I cried unto the Lord in my trouble, and the God of my salvation heard me.

VII. The Children of Abraham in Babylon of old trampled upon the flame of the furnace, and raised the song of praise: Blessed be thou, O God of our fathers!

VIII. The Children in Babylon, flaming with zeal divine, valiantly trampled under foot the threat of their tormentor, and the flame; and when they were cast into the midst of the fire, being watered with dew, they cried: O all ye works of the Lord bless ye the Lord!

In place of: My soul doth magnify the Lord: *The Refrain:*

Magnify, O my soul, the Lord who was transfigured on Tabor.

IX. Thy birth-giving was shown to be without defilement; God came forth from thy loins, manifested himself as a bearer of the flesh upon earth, and dwelt among men: Wherefore we all do magnify thee, O Birth-giver of God.

The Benediction. May he who on Mount Tabor was transfigured in glory in the presence of his holy disciples and apostles, Christ, our true God, through the prayers of his most holy Mother: *and the rest, as usual.* (*See page* 122.)

At the Liturgy.

Antiphon I., Tone II.

Verse 1: O be joyful in the Lord all ye lands: sing praises unto the honour of his Name; make his praise to be glorious.

Refrain. Through the prayers of the Birth-giver of God, O Saviour, save us.

Verse 2: The voice of thy thunder was heard round about, thy lightnings illumined the universe; the earth was moved and shook withal. ℞

Verse 3: Thou art clothed with majesty and confession: thou deckest thyself with light as it were a garment. ℞

Antiphon II., Tone II.

Verse 1: On the north side of Mount Zion lieth the city of the great King.

Refrain. O Son of God who wast transfigured upon the Mount, save us who sing unto thee, Alleluia.

Verse 2: And he brought them unto the mount of his sanctuary, even the mountain which he had purchased with his right hand. ℞

Verse 3: The hill of Zion which he loved, and built there like the unicorn his sanctuary. ℞

Glory to the Father, and to the Son, and to the Holy Spirit, now, and ever, and unto ages of ages.   Amen.

O Only-begotten Son and Word of God! . . . (*See page* 170.)

Antiphon III., Tone VII.

Verse 1: They that put their trust in the Lord shall be even as the Mount Zion, which may not be removed forever.

Refrain: The Hymn (*Tropár*), *in Tone II.* Thou wast transfigured upon the Mount, O Christ-God, revealing unto thy disciples thy glory in so far as they were able to bear it.   Let thy light everlasting illumine us sinners also; through the prayers of the Birth-giver of God.   O Light-giver, glory to thee!

Verse 2: The hills stand about it, and the Lord about his people, forevermore.   ℞

Verse 3: Lord, who shall dwell in thy tabernacle, or who shall rejoice upon thy holy hill?   ℞

Verse 4: Who shall ascend into the hill of the Lord, or who shall rise up in his holy place?   ℞

The Introit. O Lord, send forth thy light and thy truth, and they shall instruct me and shall lead me unto thy holy hill.

The Gradual (*Prokímen*), *in the Fourth Tone.* O Lord, how marvellous are thy works: in wisdom hast thou made them all.

Verse: Bless the Lord, O my soul: O Lord my God, thou art greatly exalted.

The Epistle. 2 Peter i. 10–19.

Alleluia. (*Tone VIII.*) The heavens are thine, and the earth is thine.

Verse: Blessed are the people who understand the shout of joy.

The Gospel. Matt. xvii. 1–9.

In place of: Meet is it: *The Ninth Theme-Song of the Canon.* Thy birth-giving was shown to be without defilement; . . . (*See page* 260.)

The Communion Hymn (*Pritchásten*). O Lord, in the light of thy countenance will we walk, and in thy Name will we rejoice forevermore.

After the Liturgy on this day it is customary to bless the fruits.

The Prayer at the Partaking of Grapes, on August 6th.

Let us pray to the Lord.

Lord, have mercy.

Bless, O Lord, this new fruit of the vine, which thou hast graciously been pleased to permit to come to maturity, through salubrious seasons, and drops of rain, and propitious weather: and let it be unto joy for those of us who shall partake of this offspring of the vine; and may we offer it as a gift to thee unto the purification of our sins, through the sacred and holy Body of thy Christ: with whom thou art blessed, together with thine all-holy, and good, and life-giving Spirit, now, and ever, and unto ages of ages.   Amen.

This Prayer is said over grapes which are brought into the Temple to be blessed on the sixth day of August, at places where there are vineyards. But in Great Russia, where there are no vineyards, apples are brought into the Temple on that day, and the Prayer for those who bring the first-fruits of vegetables is said.

Each vegetable is brought to the Temple in its season, and the Prayer is said over it also.

The Prayer for those who bring the first-fruits of vegetables.

O Master, Lord our God, who hast commanded that we should bring unto thee an offering of each of thine own things, and who requitest the same with the gift of thine eternal good things; who didst graciously accept the offering of the widow, according to her ability: Accept thou now also these things which are offered unto thee by thy servant, N., and vouchsafe to place the same among thine eternal treasures; granting unto him (*her*) an abundant harvest of thy worldly benefits, together with all things profitable unto him (*her*).

For blessed is thy Name, and glorified is thy kingdom, of the Father, and of the Son, and of the Holy Spirit, now, and ever, and unto ages of ages. Amen.

THE FALLING–ASLEEP (ASSUMPTION) OF THE MOST HOLY BIRTH–GIVER OF GOD

(AUGUST 15.)

(This Feast is preceded by a Fast of two weeks' duration.)

At Vespers.

The Stanza (Stikhíra) for: Lord, I have cried: *In Tone I.* O marvel wonderful! The Source of life is laid in the grave, and the tomb becometh the ladder unto heaven. Rejoice, O Gethsemane, thou holy abode of the Birth-giver of God! In that we have Gabriel for our chieftain, let us cry aloud, ye faithful: Hail, thou that art full of grace! The Lord is with thee, through thee granting unto the world great mercy. (*Twice.*)

Glory to the Father, and to the Son, and to the Holy Spirit, now, and ever, and unto ages of ages. Amen.

At the sovereign command of God were the God-bearing apostles caught up on high in the clouds from every place; and when they were come to thine all-holy and life-originating body, they kissed the same with love. The heavenly powers most high also, when they were come with their Master, were seized with dread as they escorted the body all-pure and well-pleasing unto God, which had received God; with stately mien, also, they went before, and invisibly cried aloud unto the Powers most high: Lo, the Queen over all, and the Maiden of God cometh. Be ye lifted up, O gates, and lift ye up Her who in more than earthly wise is the Mother of the Everlasting Light. For through her was salvation universal brought to pass for men: and we cannot gaze upon her, and it is not possible to render unto her the honour that is meet: for her surpassing merit exceedeth all understanding. Wherefore, O Birth-giver of God most pure, who abidest ever with the life-bearing King, who also is thy Son, entreat thou him that he will ever preserve thy new people, and save them from every hostile assault; for we have acquired thine intercession, forever blessing thee who art revealed in light.

The Gradual (Prokímen) for the Day.

The Parables (Paremíí), the same as for the NATIVITY OF THE BIRTH-GIVER OF GOD.

The Stanza at the Litiyá, in Tone V. Sing, O ye people, sing the Mother of our God; for to-day she doth yield up her all-radiant soul into the hands most pure of Him who, without seed, was incarnate of her: Whom, also, she doth unceasingly entreat that he will give unto the world peace and great mercy.

The Hymn for the Day (Tropár), in Tone I. In Birth-giving thou didst preserve thy virginity; in thy Falling-asleep thou hast not forsaken the world, O Birth-giver of God. Thou hast passed over into life, thou who art the Mother of Life, and through thine intercessions dost deliver our souls from death. (*Kondák.*) Collect-Hymn. (*Page 265.*)

The Exaltation (*Velitchánie*). We magnify thee, O Mother all-undefiled of Christ our God, and we glorify thine all-glorious Falling-asleep.

The Gradual (*Prokímen*), *in the Fourth Tone.* I will call to mind thy name from generation to generation.

Verse (*Stikh*): Hearken, O daughter, and behold, and incline thine ear.

The Gospel. Luke i. 39–49, 56.

THE CANON.

The First Canon. Tone I. (*St. Cosmas of Maium.*)

Theme-Songs (*Irmosí*). I. Adorned with glory divine thy holy and illustrious memory, O Virgin, hath gathered together all the faithful unto joy; that after the manner of Miriam, with choirs and cymbals, they may sing thine Only-born: For gloriously hath he been glorified.

III. O Christ, the Wisdom and the Power of God, who createth and maintaineth all things, establish thou the Church steadfast and immovable. For thou only art holy who restest in the Saints.

IV. The predictions and dark sayings of the Prophets proclaimed beforehand thine incarnation of a Virgin, O Christ: The splendour of thy shining forth (said they) shall come for the enlightenment of the nations; and the deep with joy shall cry unto thee: Glory to thy might, O thou who lovest mankind.

V. The beauty divine and ineffable of thy perfection will I declare, O Christ; for thou who didst shine forth from the Glory eternal, as an effulgence coeternal and one in Essence, when thou didst become incarnate of a Virgin's womb, didst shine as the sun upon those who sat in darkness and the shadow.

VI. The fire (of pain) within the whale of the sea, the denizen of the deep, in which the Prophet Jonah was found, was the prototype of thy three days' burial; for remaining unscathed, as before the swallowing, he cried aloud: With the voice of praise will I sacrifice unto thee, O Lord.

VII. Love divine, resisting the wrath audacious and the fire, did sprinkle the fire with dew, but laughed to scorn the wrath, proclaiming above the instruments of music upon the God-inspired, supersensual and triple-stringed lyre of the Righteous Ones amid the flame: Blessed art thou, O God of our fathers, and our God, exceeding glorious!

VIII. As dew-dropping for the Godly Ones, but as consuming to the impious, did the all-powerful Angel of God manifest forth the flame to the Children. And the Birth-giver of God did he make a life-originating Pountain, pouring forth destruction to Death and life to those who sing:

The only Creator do we, who have been delivered, praise in song and magnify unto all the ages.

In place of: My soul doth magnify the Lord: *The Refrain:* We, even all the nations, do bless thee, the only Birth-giver of God. *Or:* When the all-holy Angels beheld thine Assumption they marvelled how a Virgin should ascend from earth into heaven.

IX. The laws of Nature were conquered in thee, O Virgin pure; for in birth-giving was virginity preserved, and with death is life conjoined. Thou who, after birth-giving, a Virgin didst remain, though dead, art yet alive, O Birth-giver of God, and savest always thine inheritance.

At the Liturgy.

The Collect-Hymn (Kondák). The tomb and death have not been able to hold the Birth-giver of God, who is constant in supplications, in intercession an unfailing hope: for the Mother of the Life is come into the presence of the Life, who took up his abode in her ever-Virgin womb.

The Gradual (Prokimen), in the Third Tone. My soul doth magnify the Lord, and my spirit hath rejoiced in God my Saviour.

Verse: For he hath regarded the lowliness of his handmaiden; for behold, from henceforth all generations shall call me blessed.

The Epistle. Phil. ii. 5–11.

Alleluia. (*Tone II.*) Arise, O Lord, in thy rest, thou, and the tabernacle of thy holiness.

Verse: The Lord sware truth unto David, and he shall not abjure it.

The Gospel. Luke x. 38–42, xi. 27, 28.

The Hymn in place of: Meet is it: *The Ninth Theme-Song of the Canon:* The laws of Nature were conquered in thee, . . . (*See above.*)

The Communion Hymn. I will take the cup of salvation, and call upon the Name of the Lord.

PRERS

ON THE FIRST DAY AFTER A WOMAN HATH GIVEN BIRTH TO A CHILD

Priest. Let us pray to the Lord.

O Master, Lord Almighty, who healest every infirmity and every weakness: Heal thou also this thy servant, N., who this day hath given birth to a child, and raise her up from the bed whereon she lieth. For, according to the words of the Prophet David, in sin are we conceived, and we are all vile in thy sight. Preserve her and this child which she hath borne. Cover her with the shadow of thy wings, from the day that now is even unto her last end; through the prayers of the all-pure Birth-giver of God, and of all the Saints. For blessed art thou unto ages of ages. Amen.

Let us pray to the Lord.

O Master, Lord our God, who wast born of our all-pure Lady, the Birth-giver of God, and ever-virgin Mary, and as a babe didst lie in a manger, and as a little child wast held in arms: Show mercy also upon this thy servant, who to-day hath borne this child; and forgive her sins, both voluntary and involuntary; and preserve her from every oppression of the Devil; and preserve the child which hath been born of her from every spell and perplexity, from every storm of adversity, and from evil spirits, whether of the day or of the night. Keep her under thy mighty hand, and grant that she may speedily arise, and purify her from uncleanness, and heal her sickness; and vouchsafe unto her health and strength both of soul and body; and hedge her round about with bright and shining Angels; and preserve her from every invasion of invisible spirits. Yea, Lord, and from infirmity and weakness, from jealousy and envy, and from the evil eye; and have mercy upon her and upon the child, according to thy great mercy; and purify her from bodily uncleanness, and from the divers inward troubles which assail her. And lead her forth by thy speedy mercy, in submissiveness of her body, unto recovery. And grant that the child that hath been born of her may do reverence to the earthly temple which thou hast prepared to glorify thy holy Name.

For unto thee are due all glory, honour and worship, to the Father, and to the Son, and to the Holy Spirit, now, and ever, and unto ages of ages. Amen.

Let us pray to the Lord.

O Lord our God, who wast graciously pleased to come down from heaven, and to be born of the holy Birth-giver of God and ever-virgin Mary, for the salvation of us sinners, and who knowest the frailty of man's nature: Forgive thy servant, N., who to-day hath given birth, according to the multitude of thy bounties. For thou hast said, O Lord: Increase, and multiply, and fill the earth, and possess it. For which cause also do we, thy servants, pray, and emboldened by thy long-suffering love towards mankind, with awe do cry aloud to the kingdom of thy holy Name: Look down from heaven and behold the weakness of us who are condemned; and pardon this thy servant, N., and all the house wherein the child hath been born, and those who have touched her, and all those who are here present; inasmuch as thou art a good God and lovest mankind; for thou only hast power to remit sins. Through the prayers of the all-holy Birth-giver of God and of all the Saints.

AT THE NAMING OF A CHILD, WHEN HE RECEIVETH HIS NAME, ON THE EIGHTH DAY AFTER HIS BIRTH

Priest: Blessed is our God always, now, and ever, and unto ages of ages. Amen. O heavenly King: *and the rest ending:* For thine is the Kingdom. . . (*See page* 43.) *Then the final* Hymn *for the Day, or for the Patron Saint of the Church.*

The Priest maketh the sign of the cross upon the forehead, lips and breast of the Infant and saith this Prayer:

Let us pray to the Lord.

O Lord our God, we pray unto thee, and we beseech thee, that the light of thy countenance may be shown upon this thy servant, N.; and that the cross of thine Only-begotten Son may be graven in his (*her*) heart, and in his (*her*) thoughts: that he (*she*) may flee from the vanity of the world and from every evil snare of the enemy, and may follow after thy commandments. And grant, O Lord, that thy holy Name may remain unrejected, by him (*her*); and that he (*she*) may be united, in due time, to thy holy Church; and that the dread Sacraments of thy Christ may be administered unto him (*her*): That, having lived according to thy commandments, and preserved without flaw the seal, he (*she*) may receive the bliss of the elect in thy kingdom; through the grace and love towards mankind of thine Only-begotten Son, with whom also thou art blessed, together with thine all-holy, and good, and life-giving Spirit, now, and ever, and unto ages of ages. Amen.

Then, taking the Infant in his arms, he standeth before the door of the Temple, or before the holy image of the most holy Birth-giver of God, and maketh the sign of the cross, saying:

Hail, O Virgin Birth-giver of God, thou who art full of grace! For from thee hath shone forth the Sun of Righteousness, Christ our God, who giveth light to them that are in darkness. And rejoice, thou aged, righteous man, that didst receive in thine arms the Redeemer of our souls, who giveth unto us resurrection!

Then the BENEDICTION.

FOR A WOMAN ON THE FORTIETH DAY AFTER CHILD BIRTH

The beginning is the same as in the preceding service.

On the fortieth day the Infant is brought to the Temple to be churched; that is, to make a beginning of being taken into the Church. And it is brought by the Mother, who, being already cleansed and washed, standeth there at the Entrance, and desireth to receive the Rite, after the Baptism.

Bending down his head to the Mother, as she standeth with the Infant, the Priest maketh the sign of the cross over the Infant; and touching its head, he saith the Prayer:

Glory to thee, Our God . . . *and ending with the* Lord's Prayer *and the* Benediction. (*Page* 286.)

Let us pray to the Lord.

O Lord God Almighty, the Father of our Lord Jesus Christ, who by thy word hast created all things, both men endowed with speech and dumb animals, and hast brought all things from nothingness into being, we pray and implore thee: Thou hast saved this thy servant, N., by thy will. Purify her, therefore, from all sin and from every uncleanness, as she now draweth near unto thy holy Church; and make her worthy to partake, uncondemned, of thy Holy Mysteries.

(*And if the Child be not living, the Prayer is read only thus far. Then the Exclamation.*

For thou art a good God, who lovest mankind, and unto thee do we ascribe glory, to the Father, and to the Son, and to the Holy Spirit, now, and ever, and unto ages of ages. Amen.

But if the Child be alive, the following is added, to the end:)

And bless thou the child which hath been born of her. Increase him (*her*); sanctify him (*her*); enlighten him (*her*); render him (*her*) chaste, and endow him (*her*) with good understanding. For thou hast brought him (*her*) into being, and hast shown him (*her*) the physical light, and hast appointed him (*her*) to be vouchsafed in due time spiritual light, and that he (*she*) may be numbered among thy chosen flock, through thine Only-begotten Son: with whom, also, thou art blessed, together with thine all-holy, and good, and life-giving Spirit, now, and ever, and unto ages of ages. Amen.

Peace be unto all.

Bow your heads unto the Lord.

The Prayer for the Mother of the Child.

O Lord our God, who didst come for the redemption of the human race, come thou also upon thy servant, N., and grant unto her, through the prayers of thine honourable Priest, entrance into the temple of thy glory. Wash away her bodily uncleanness, and the stains of her soul, in the fulfilling of the forty days.   Make her worthy of the communion of thy holy Body and of thy Blood.

For sanctified and glorified is thine all-honourable and majestic Name, of the Father, and of the Son, and of the Holy Spirit, now, and ever, and unto ages of ages.   Amen.

The Prayer for the Child.   The Priest, making over the Child the sign of the cross, prayeth:

Let us pray to the Lord.

O Lord our God, who wast brought, on the fortieth day, as an infant into the Temple according to the Law, by Mary the Bride Unwedded, who also was thy holy Mother; and wast borne in the arms of Simeon the Just: Do thou, O Master all-powerful, bless also unto every good deed this infant which hath been brought hither, that he (*she*) may present himself (*herself*) unto thee, the Creator of all men, and rear him (*her*) well-pleasing unto thee in all things; and drive far from him (*her*) every adverse power, through sealing with the sign of thy cross; for thou art he who preserveth infants, O Lord.   And grant that having been vouchsafed holy Baptism, he (*she*) may receive the portion of the elect ones of thy kingdom, and be preserved, together with us, through the grace of the holy, and consubstantial, and undivided Trinity.

For unto thee are due all glory, thanksgiving and worship, together with thy Father who is from everlasting, and thine all-holy, and good, and life-giving Spirit, now, and ever, and unto ages of ages.   Amen.

Peace be with you all.

Bow your heads unto the Lord.

O God the Father Almighty, who by thy trumpet-voiced Prophet Isaiah didst foretell unto us the incarnation through a Virgin of thine Only-begotten Son and our God; who in these latter days, by thy good pleasure and the coöperation of the Holy Spirit, for the salvation of us men, and because of thy boundless compassion, didst graciously deign to become a babe by her; and according to the custom of thy holy Law didst suffer thyself to be brought into thy holy Sanctuary, after that the days of purification were fulfilled, being thyself the true law-giver; and didst condescend to be borne in the arms of the righteous Simeon, of which mystery we have recognized the prototype, revealed by the coal in the tongs, foretold by the prophet; which thing, also, we faithful, by grace do imitate: Do thou now also, O Lord, who preservest children, bless this Infant, together with his (*her*) parents and his (*her*) sponsors; and grant that, in due season, he (*she*) may be united, through water and the Spirit of the new birth, unto thy holy flock of reason-endowed sheep, which is called by the name of thy Christ.   For thou art he who dwelleth on high, and looketh down upon the humble of heart; and unto thee do we ascribe glory, to the Father, and to the Son, and to the Holy Spirit, now, and ever, and unto ages of ages.   Amen.   .

And if the Child be already baptized, the Priest performeth the churching. But if not, he doth this after the Baptism. And the Benediction to the Prayers is made here.

May Christ our true God, through the prayers of his most pure Mother, of the holy, glorious and all-laudable Apostles (*and of the Patron Saint of the Temple; and of the Saint of the day*); of the holy and righteous Ancestors of God, Joachim and Anna, and of all the Saints, have mercy upon us, and save us, in that he is good and loveth mankind.

Then the Priest taketh the Infant, and maketh with it the sign of the cross in front of the door of the Temple, saying:

The servant of God, N., is churched: In the Name of the Father, and of the Son, and of the Holy Spirit.   Amen.

Then he beareth him into the Temple, saying:

He (*she*) entereth into thy house, to worship towards thy holy Temple.

And going to the middle of the Temple, he saith:

The servant of God is churched: In the Name of the Father, and of the Son, and of the Holy Spirit.   Amen.

Then he saith:

In the midst of the church shall he (*she*) sing praises unto thee.

Then he beareth him before the door of the Sanctuary, saying:

The servant of God is churched: In the Name of the Father, and of the Son, and of the Holy Spirit.

And he beareth it into the holy Sanctuary, if it be a male child; but if it be a female child, to the Holy Door only, saying:

Lord now lettest thou thy servant depart in peace, according to thy word.

For mine eyes have seen thy salvation,

Which thou hast prepared: before the face of all people;

To be a light to lighten the Gentiles, and to be the glory of thy people Israel.

And after this, at the door of the Sanctuary, he giveth the Child to the Sponsor, who maketh three lowly reverences, and taketh the Child.

And the Priest pronounceth the customary Benediction.   (See above.)

THE OFFICE OF HOLY BAPTISM *

THE PRAYERS AT THE RECEPTION OF CATECHUMENS

The Priest looseth the girdle of the Person who desireth Illumination, and removeth it, and putteth it off from him; and placeth him with his face towards the east, clothed in one garment only, unshod, and with head uncovered, and with his arms hanging by his sides; and he breatheth thrice in his face; and signeth his brow and his breast thrice with the sign of the cross; and layeth his hand upon his head, saying:

Let us pray to the Lord. (1)

Choir. Lord, have mercy.

In thy Name, O Lord God of truth, and in the Name of thine Only-begotten Son, and of thy Holy Spirit, I lay my hand upon thy servant, N., who hath been found worthy to flee unto thy holy Name, and to take refuge under the shelter of thy wings. Remove far from him (*her*) his (*her*) former delusion, and fill him (*her*) with the faith, hope and love which are in thee; that he (*she*) may know that thou art the only true God, with thine Only-begotten Son, our Lord Jesus Christ, and thy Holy Spirit. Enable him (*her*) to walk in all thy commandments, and to fulfil those things which are well-pleasing unto thee; for if a man do those things, he shall find life in them. Inscribe him (*her*) in thy Book of Life, and unite him (*her*) to the flock of thine inheritance. And may thy holy Name be glorified in him (*her*), together with that of thy beloved Son, our Lord Jesus Christ, and of thy life-giving Spirit. Let thine eyes ever regard him (*her*) with mercy, and let thine ears attend unto the voice of his (*her*) supplication. Make him (*her*) to rejoice in the works of his (*her*) hands, and in all his (*her*) generation; that he (*she*) may render praise unto thee, may sing, worship and glorify thy great and exalted Name always, all the days of his (*her*) life.

Exclamation.

For all the Powers of Heaven sing praises unto thee, and thine is the glory, of the Father, and of the Son, and of the Holy Spirit, now, and ever, and unto ages of ages. Amen.

The First Exorcism

Let us pray to the Lord. —— *Choir.* Lord, have mercy.

The Lord layeth thee under ban, O Devil: He who came into the world, and made his abode among men, that he might overthrow thy tyranny and deliver men; who also upon the Tree did triumph over the adverse powers, when the sun was darkened, and the earth did quake, and the graves were opened, and the bodies of the Saints arose; who also by death

* For explanations, indicated by numbers in text, see Appendix B, VI.

annihilated Death, and overthrew him who exercised the dominion of Death, that is thee, the Devil. I adjure thee by God, who hath revealed the Tree of Life, and hath arrayed in ranks the Cherubim and the flaming sword which turneth all ways to guard it: Be thou under ban. For I adjure thee by him who walketh upon the surface of the sea as it were dry land, and layeth under his ban the tempests of the winds; whose glance drieth up the deep, and whose interdict maketh the mountains to melt away. The same now, through us, doth lay thee under ban. Fear, begone and depart from this creature, and return not again, neither hide thyself in him (*her*), neither seek thou to meet him (*her*), nor to influence him (*her*), either by night or by day; either in the morning, or at noonday: but depart hence to thine own Tartarus, until the great Day of Judgment which is ordained. Fear thou God who sitteth upon the Cherubim and looketh upon the deeps; before whom tremble Angels and Archangels, Thrones, Dominions, Principalities, Authorities, Powers, the many-eyed Cherubim and the six-winged Seraphim; before whom, likewise, heaven and earth do quake, the sea and all that therein is. Begone, and depart from this sealed, newly-enlisted warrior of Christ our God. For I adjure thee by him who rideth upon the wings of the wind, and maketh his Angels spirits, and his ministers a flaming fire: Begone, and depart from this creature, with all thy powers and thine angels.

Exclamation.

For glorified is the Name of the Father, and of the Son, and of the Holy Spirit, now, and ever, and unto ages of ages. Amen.

The Second Exorcism.

Let us pray to the Lord.

God, holy, terrible and glorious, who is unsearchable and inscrutable in all his works and might, hath foreordained for thee the penalty of eternal punishment, O Devil: the same, through us, his unworthy servant, doth command thee, with all thy confederate hosts, to depart hence, from him (*her*) who hath been newly sealed in the Name of our Lord Jesus Christ, our true God. Wherefore I adjure thee, O most crafty, impure, vile, loathsome and alien spirit, by the might of Jesus Christ, who hath all power, both in heaven and on earth, and who said unto the deaf and dumb demon, Come out of the man, and in nowise enter thou a second time into him: Depart! Acknowledge the vainness of thy might, which hath not power even over swine. Call to mind him who, at thy request, commanded thee to enter into the herd of swine. Fear God, by whŏse decree the earth is established upon the waters; who hath made the heavens, and hath set the mountains with a line, and the valleys with a measure; and hath fixed bounds to the sands of the sea, and a firm path upon the stormy waters; who toucheth the mountains and they smoke; who clotheth himself with light as with a garment; who spreadeth out the heavens as it were a curtain; who covereth his exceeding high places with the waters; who hath made fast the earth upon its foundations, so that it shall not be removed unto ages of ages; who collecteth the water of the sea and poureth it out upon the face of the whole earth: Begone, and depart from him (*her*) who hath made himself (*herself*) ready for holy Illumination.   I adjure thee by the redeeming Passion of our Lord Jesus Christ, and by his precious Body and Blood, and by his terrible Coming-again; for he shall come, and shall not tarry, to judge the whole earth; and he shall chastise thee and thy confederate host with burning Gehenna, committing thee to outer darkness, where the worm ceaseth not, and the fire is not quenched. For of Christ our God is the dominion, with the Father and the Holy Spirit, now, and ever, and unto ages of ages.   Amen.

The Third Exorcism.

Let us pray to the Lord.

O Lord of Sabaoth, the God of Israel, who healest every malady and every infirmity: Look upon thy servant; prove him (*her*) and search him (*her*), and root out of him (*her*) every operation of the Devil.   Rebuke the unclean spirits and expel them, and purify the works of thy hands; and exerting thy trenchant might, speedily crush down Satan under his (*her*) feet; and give him (*her*) victory over the same, and over his foul spirits; that, having obtained mercy from thee, he (*she*) may be made worthy to partake of thy heavenly Mysteries; and may ascribe unto thee glory, to the Father, and to the Son, and to the Holy Spirit, now, and ever, and unto ages of ages.   Amen.

A Fourth Prayer.

Let us pray to the Lord.

Thou who in verity existest, O Lord the Master; who hast created man in thine own likeness, and hast bestowed upon him the power of life eternal; who also despisest not those who have fallen away through sin, but hast provided salvation for the world through the incarnation of thy Christ: Do thou, the same Lord, delivering also this thy creature from the bondage of the enemy, receive him (*her*) into thy heavenly kingdom. Open the eyes of his (*her*) understanding, that the light of thy Gospel may shine brightly in him (*her*).   Yoke unto his (*her*) life a radiant Angel, who shall deliver him (*her*) from every snare of the adversary, from encounter with evil, from the demon of the noonday, and from evil visions.

Then the Priest breatheth upon his mouth, his brow, and his breast, saying:

Expel from him (*her*) every evil and impure spirit which hideth and maketh its lair in his (*her*) heart.   (*And this he saith thrice.*)

The spirit of error, the spirit of guile, the spirit of idolatry and of every concupiscence; the spirit of deceit and of every uncleanness which operateth through the prompting of the Devil.   And make him (*her*) a reason-endowed sheep (2) in the holy flock of thy Christ, an honourable member of thy Church, a consecrated vessel, a child of the light, and an heir of thy kingdom; that having lived in accordance with thy commandments, and preserved inviolate the seal, and kept his (*her*) garment undefiled, he (*she*) may receive the blessedness of the Saints in thy kingdom.

In a loud voice.

Through the grace, and bounties, and love towards mankind of thine Only-begotten Son, with whom thou art blessed, together with thy most holy, and good, and life-giving Spirit, now, and ever, and unto ages of ages. Amen.

Then the Priest turneth the person who is come to Baptism to face the west, (3) unclad, unshod, and having his hands uplifted. And he saith:

Dost thou renounce Satan, and all his Angels, and all his works, and all his service, and all his pride?

And the Catechumen maketh answer, or his Sponsor for him, and saith:

I do. (*And this question and answer are thrice repeated.*)

Again the Priest questioneth the Catechumen.

Hast thou renounced Satan?

And the Catechumen, or his Sponsor for him, maketh answer:

I have. (*And this question and answer, likewise, are thrice repeated.*)

Then saith the Priest:

Breathe and spit upon him.

And when he hath done this, the Priest turneth him to the east, (4) with his hands lowered, and saith:

Dost thou unite thyself unto Christ?

And the Catechumen, or his Sponsor for him, maketh answer:

I do. (*And this question and answer are thrice repeated.*)

Then the Priest saith to him:

Hast thou united thyself unto Christ?

And he replieth:

I have.
Dost thou believe in him?
I believe in him as King and as God.

And he reciteth THE HOLY SYMBOL OF THE FAITH.

I believe in one God the Father Almighty, Maker of heaven and earth, And of all things visible and invisible:

And in one Lord Jesus Christ, the only-begotten Son of God. Begotten of his Father before all worlds; Light of Light, Very God of very God, Begotten, not made; Being of one Essence with the Father; By whom all things were made; Who, for us men, and for our salvation, came down from heaven, And was incarnate by the Holy Ghost of the Virgin Mary, And was made man. And was crucified also for us under Pontius Pilate, and suffered and was buried, And the third day he rose again, according to the Scriptures. And ascended into heaven, And sitteth on the right hand of the Father. And he shall come again with glory to judge both the quick and the dead; Whose kingdom shall have no end.

And in the Holy Ghost, the Lord, Giver of Life, Who proceedeth from the Father, Who with the Father and the Son together is worshipped and glorified, Who spake by the Prophets. In one Holy Catholic and Apostolic Church. I acknowledge one Baptism for the remission of sins. I look for the Resurrection of the dead, And the Life of the world to come. Amen.

And when he hath finished the Holy Symbol of the Faith the Priest inquireth of him:

Hast thou united thyself unto Christ?

I have. (*This question and answer are thrice repeated.*)

Bow down also before him.

And the Catechumen boweth himself, saying:

I bow down before the Father, and the Son, and the Holy Spirit, the Trinity, one in Essence and undivided.

Priest. Blessed is God, who willeth that all men should be saved, and should come to the knowledge of the truth, now, and ever, and unto ages of ages. Amen.

Then he reciteth this Prayer.

Let us pray to the Lord.

O Master, Lord our God, call thy servant, N., to thy holy Illumination, and grant unto him (*her*) that great grace of thy holy Baptism. Put off from him (*her*) the old man, and renew him (*her*) unto life everlasting; and fill him (*her*) with the power of thy Holy Spirit, in the unity of thy Christ: that he (*she*) may be no more a child of the body, but a child of thy kingdom. Through the good will and grace of thine Only-begotten Son, with whom thou art blessed, together with thy most holy, and good, and life-giving Spirit, now, and ever, and unto ages of ages. Amen.

THE OFFICE OF HOLY BAPTISM

The Priest entereth the Sanctuary and putteth on white vestments, and his gauntlets. And when he hath lighted all the tapers, (5) he taketh the censer, and goeth to the Font, and censeth round about it; and having given the censer to be held, he maketh a reverence.

Then the Deacon saith:

Bless, Master.

And the Priest saith, aloud:

Blessed is the kingdom of the Father, and of the Son, and of the Holy Spirit, now, and ever, and unto ages of ages.

Choir. Amen!

And straightway the Deacon saith the LITANY.

In peace let us pray to the Lord.

Choir. Lord, have mercy.

For the peace that is from above: *and the rest, ending with the petition:* That he will aid them. (*See pages* 80, 81.)

That this water may be sanctified with the power, and effectual operation, and descent of the Holy Spirit: ℟

That there may be sent down into it the grace of redemption, the blessing of Jordan: ℟

That there may come upon this water the purifying operation of the super-substantial Trinity: ℟

That we may be illumined by the light of understanding and piety, and by the descent of the Holy Spirit: ℟

That this water may prove effectual unto the averting of every snare of enemies, both visible and invisible: ℟

That he (*she*) who is baptized therein may be made worthy of the kingdom incorruptible: ℟

For him (*her*) who is now come unto holy Baptism, and for his (*her*) salvation: ℟

That he (*she*) may prove

let us pray to the Lord. Choir. Lord, have mercy.

And the Priest prayeth, secretly.

O compassionate and merciful God, who triest the heart and the reins, and who alone knowest the secret thoughts of men (for no deeds are hidden before thee, but all things are naked and manifest before thine eyes); Thou who knowest all things concerning me, regard me not with loathing, neither turn thou thy face from me; but consider not mine iniquities at this present hour, O thou who disregardest man's sins unto his repentance. And wash away the vileness of my body, and the pollution of my soul. And sanctify me wholly by thine all-perfect, invisible might, and by thy spiritual right hand; lest, while I proclaim liberty unto others, and administer this rite with perfect faith in thine unutterable love toward mankind, I myself may become the base slave of sin. Yea, O Master, who alone art good and full of love toward mankind, let not thy humble servant be led astray; but send thou down upon me power from on high, and strengthen thou me in the administration

Secretly.

himself (*herself*) a child of the light, and an heir of eternal good things: ℞

That he (*she*) may be a member and partaker of the death and resurrection of Christ our God: ℞

That he (*she*) may preserve his baptismal garment and the earnest of the Spirit pure and undefiled unto the dread Day of Christ our God: ℞

That this water may be to him (*her*) a laver of regeneration, unto the remission of sins, and a garment of incorruption: ℞

That the Lord God will hearken unto the voice of our petition: ℞

That he will deliver him (*her*) and us from all tribulation, wrath, and necessity: ℞

let us pray to the Lord. Choir. Lord, have mercy.

of thine impending Mystery, which is both great and most heavenly: and create the image of thy Christ in him (*her*) who now desireth to be born again through my unworthy ministry. And build him (*her*) up upon the foundation of thine Apostles and Prophets, that he (*she*) may not be overthrown; but implant him (*her*) firmly as a plant of truth, in thy Holy Catholic and Apostolic Church, that he (*she*) be not plucked out. That, as he (*she*) increaseth in godliness, through him (*her*) may be glorified thine all-holy Name, of the Father, and of the Son, and of the Holy Spirit, now, and ever, and unto ages of ages. Amen.

Secretly.

Succour us, save us, have mercy upon us, and keep us, O God, by thy grace.

Choir. Lord, have mercy.

Calling to remembrance our most holy, all-undefiled, most blessed and glorious Lady, the Birth-giver of God and ever-virgin Mary, with all the Saints, let us commend ourselves, and each other, and all our life unto Christ our God.

Choir. To thee, O Lord.

The Priest saith also the following Prayer, but aloud:

Great art thou, O Lord, and marvellous are thy works, and there is no word which sufficeth to hymn thy wonders. (*Thrice.*)

For thou, of thine own good will, hast brought into being all things which before were not, and by thy might thou upholdest creation, and by thy providence thou orderest the world. When thou hadst joined together the universe out of four elements, thou didst crown the circle of the year with four seasons. Before thee tremble all the Powers endowed with intelligence. The sun singeth unto thee. The moon glorifieth thee. The stars meet together before thy presence. The light obeyeth thee. The deeps tremble before thee. The water-springs are subject unto thee. Thou hast spread out the heavens as it were a curtain. Thou hast established the earth upon the waters. Thou hast set round about the sea barriers of sand. Thou hast shed abroad the air for breathing. The

Angelic Powers serve thee. The Choirs of the Archangels fall down in adoration before thee. The many-eyed Cherubim and the six-winged Seraphim, as they stand round about and fly, veil their faces in awe before thine ineffable glory. For thou, who art God inexpressible, existing uncreated before the ages, and ineffable, didst descend upon earth, and didst take on the semblance of a servant, and wast made in the likeness of man: for, because of the tender compassion of thy mercy, O Master, thou couldest not endure to behold mankind oppressed by the Devil; but thou didst come, and didst save us. We confess thy grace. We proclaim thy mercy. We conceal not thy gracious acts. Thou hast delivered the generation of our mortal nature. By thy birth thou didst sanctify a Virgin's womb. All creation magnifieth thee, who hast manifested thyself. For thou, O our God, hast revealed thyself upon earth, and hast dwelt among men. Thou didst hallow the streams of Jordan, sending down upon them from heaven thy Holy Spirit, and didst crush the heads of the dragons who lurked there.

Wherefore, O King who lovest mankind, come thou now and sanctify this water, by the indwelling of thy Holy Spirit. (*Thrice.*)

And grant unto it the grace of redemption, the blessing of Jordan. Make it the fountain of incorruption, the gift of sanctification, the remission of sins, the remedy of infirmities; the final destruction of demons, unassailable by hostile powers, filled with angelic might. Let those who would ensnare thy creature flee far from it. For we have called upon thy Name, O Lord, and it is wonderful, and glorious, and terrible unto adversaries.

Then he signeth the water thrice with the sign of the cross, dipping his fingers therein. And breathing upon it, he saith:

Let all adverse powers be crushed beneath the sign of the image of thy cross. (*Thrice.*)

We pray thee, O God, that every aerial and obscure phantom may withdraw itself from us; and that no demon of darkness may conceal himself in this water; and that no evil spirit which instilleth darkening of intentions and rebelliousness of thought may descend into it with him (*her*) who is about to be baptized.

But do thou, O Master of all, show this water to be the water of redemption, the water of sanctification, the purification of flesh and spirit, the loosing of bonds, the remission of sins, the illumination of the soul, the laver of regeneration, the renewal of the Spirit, the gift of adoption to sonship, the garment of incorruption, the fountain of life. For thou hast said, O Lord: Wash ye, be ye clean; put away evil things from your souls. Thou hast bestowed upon us from on high a new birth through water and the Spirit. Wherefore, O Lord, manifest thyself in this water, and grant that he (*she*) who is baptized therein may be transformed; that he (*she*) may put away from him (*her*) the old man, which is corrupt through the lusts of the flesh, and that he (*she*) may be clothed upon with the new man, and renewed after the image of him who created him (*her*): that being buried, after the pattern of thy death, in baptism, he (*she*) may, in like manner, be a partaker of thy Resurrection; and having preserved the gift of thy Holy Spirit, and increased the measure of grace committed unto him (*her*), he (*she*) may receive the prize of his (*her*) high calling, and be numbered with the first-born whose names are written in heaven, in thee, our God and Lord, Jesus Christ. For unto thee are due glory, dominion, honour and worship, together with thy Father, who is from everlasting, and thine all-holy, and good, and life-giving Spirit, now, and ever, and unto ages of ages. Amen.

Peace be with you all.

Bow your heads unto the Lord.

And he breatheth thrice upon the vessel containing the oil, and maketh thrice over it the sign of the cross, as it is held by the Deacon. And when the Deacon hath said:

Let us pray to the Lord.

The Priest saith the following Prayer:

O Lord and Master, the God of our fathers, who didst send unto them that were in the ark of Noah thy dove, bearing in its beak a twig of olive, the token of reconciliation and of salvation from the flood, the foreshadowing of the mystery of grace; and didst provide the fruit of the olive for the fulfilling of thy Holy Mysteries; who thereby fillest them that were under the Law with thy Holy Spirit, and perfectest them that are under grace: Bless also this holy oil with the power, and operation and indwelling of thy Holy Spirit, that it may be an anointing unto incorruption, an armour of righteousness, to the renewing of soul and body, to the averting of every assault of the devil, to deliverance from all evil of those who shall be anointed therewith in faith, or who are partakers thereof; unto thy glory and the glory of thine Only-begotten Son, and of thine all-holy, and good, and life-giving Spirit, now, and ever, and unto ages of ages.

Choir. Amen.

Deacon. Let us attend.

Then the Priest, singing Alleluia (*thrice*), *with the People, maketh three signs of the cross in the water with the oil. And he saith:*

Blessed is God, who illumineth and sanctifieth every man that cometh into the world, now, and ever, and unto ages of ages.

Choir. Amen.

Then the Person who is to be baptized is presented. The Priest taketh of the oil with two fingers, and maketh the sign of the cross upon his brow, his breast, and between his shoulders, saying:

The servant of God, N., is anointed with the oil of gladness; (5) in the Name of the Father, and of the Son, and of the Holy Spirit. Amen.

And he anointeth his breast and shoulders.   On the breast, saying:

Unto the healing of soul and body.

On the ears.

Unto the hearing of faith.

On the hands.

Thy hands have made me and fashioned me.

On the feet.

That he may walk in the way of thy commandments.

And when his whole body is thus anointed, the Priest baptizeth him, holding him upright, and looking toward the east, as he saith:

The servant of God, N., is baptized, in the name of the Father, Amen. And of the Son, Amen.   And of the Holy Spirit, Amen.

At each invocation he immerseth him, and raiseth him again.   And after the Baptism the Priest washeth his hands, singing with the People Psalm xxxii.

Blessed is he whose unrighteousness is forgiven, and whose sin is covered.   Blessed is the man unto whom the Lord imputeth no sin, and in whose spirit there is no guile.   For whilst I held my tongue, my bones consumed away through my daily complaining.   For thy hand is heavy upon me day and night, and my moisture is like the drought in summer. I will acknowledge my sin unto thee; and mine unrighteousness have I not hid.   I said, I will confess my sins unto the Lord; and so thou forgavest the wickedness of my sin.   For this shall every one that is godly make his prayer unto thee, in a time when thou mayest be found; but in the great water-floods they shall not come nigh him.   Thou art a place to hide me in; thou shalt preserve me from trouble; thou shalt compass me about with songs of deliverance.   I will inform thee, and teach thee in the way wherein thou shalt go; and I will guide thee with mine eye.   Be ye not like to horse and mule, which have no understanding; whose mouths must be held with bit and bridle, lest they fall upon thee.   Great plagues remain for the ungodly; but whoso putteth his trust in the Lord, mercy embraceth him on every side.   Be glad, O ye righteous, and rejoice in the Lord; and be joyful, all ye that are true of heart.

Then, as he putteth his garment upon him, the Priest saith:

The servant of God, N., is clothed with the robe of righteousness; in the Name of the Father, and of the Son, and of the Holy Spirit.   Amen.

Then shall be sung the following Hymn (Tropár), in Tone VIII.

Vouchsafe unto me the robe of light, O thou who clothest thyself with light as with a garment, Christ our God, plenteous in mercy.

THE OFFICE OF HOLY CHRISMATION

And when he hath put the garment on him the Priest prayeth thus:

Blessed art thou, O Lord God Almighty, Source of all good things, Sun of Righteousness, who sheddest forth upon them that were in darkness the light of salvation, through the manifestation of thine Only-begotten Son and our God; and who hast given unto us, unworthy though we be, blessed purification through hallowed water, and divine sanctification through life-giving Chrismation; who now, also, hast been graciously pleased to regenerate thy servant that hath newly received Illumination, by water and the Spirit, and grantest unto him (*her*) remission of sins, whether voluntary or involuntary. Do thou, the same Master, compassionate King of kings, grant also unto him (*her*) the seal of the gift of thy holy, and almighty, and adorable Spirit, and participation in the holy Body and the precious Blood of thy Christ. Keep him (*her*) in thy sanctification; confirm him (*her*), in the Orthodox faith; deliver him (*her*) from the Evil One, and from all the machinations of the same. And preserve his (*her*) soul in purity and uprightness, through the saving fear of thee; that he (*she*) may please thee in every deed and word, and may be a child and heir of thy heavenly kingdom.

Exclamation.

For thou art our God, the God who showeth mercy and saveth; and unto thee do we ascribe glory, to the Father, and to the Son, and to the Holy Spirit, now, and ever, and unto ages of ages. Amen.

And after this Prayer he anointeth with the holy Chrism (6) the person who hath been baptized, making the sign of the cross: On the brow, and on the eyes, and the nostrils, and the lips, and on both ears, and the breast, and the hands, and the feet, saying, each time:

The seal of the gift of the Holy Spirit. Amen.

Then the Priest, accompanied by the Sponsors, bearing the Infant, maketh the circuit of the Font. (7) And all sing:

As many as have been baptized into Christ have put on Christ. Alleluia. (*Thrice.*)

Deacon. Let us attend.

Priest. Peace be with you all.

Reader. And with thy spirit.

Deacon. Wisdom!

Reader. The Gradual (*Prokimen*), in the Third Tone. The Lord is my light and my salvation: whom then shall I fear?

Verse: The Lord is the strength of my life: of whom then shall I be afraid?

Deacon. Wisdom!

Reader. The Lesson from the Epistle of the holy Apostle Paul to the Romans.

Deacon. Let us attend.

Reader. (*Rom. vi. 3–11.*) Brethren: Know ye not that so many of us as were baptized into Jesus Christ, were baptized into his death? Therefore we are buried with him by baptism into death: that like as Christ was raised up from the dead by the glory of the Father, even so we also should walk in newness of life. For if we have been planted together in the likeness of his death, we shall be also in the likeness of his resurrection: knowing this, that our old man is crucified with him, that the body of sin might be destroyed, that henceforth we should not serve sin. For he that is dead is freed from sin. Now, if we be dead with Christ, we believe that we shall also live with him: knowing that Christ, being raised from the dead, dieth no more; death hath no more dominion over him. For in that he died, he died unto sin once: but in that he liveth, he liveth unto God. Likewise reckon ye also yourselves to be dead indeed unto sin, but alive unto God through Jesus Christ our Lord.

Priest. Peace be unto thee.

Reader. And to' thy spirit.

Deacon. Wisdom, let us attend!

Reader. Alleluia.

Deacon. Wisdom, O believers! Let us listen to the Holy Gospel.

Priest. Peace be with you all.

Choir. And with thy spirit.

Priest. The Lesson from the holy Gospel according to Matthew.

Choir. Glory to thee, O Lord; glory to thee.

Deacon. Let us attend.

Priest. (*Matt. xxviii. 16–20.*) Then the eleven disciples went away nto Galilee, into a mountain where Jesus had appointed them. And when they saw him, they worshipped him: but some doubted. And Jesus came, and spake unto them, saying, All power is given unto me in heaven and in earth. Go ye therefore and teach all nations, baptizing them in the name of the Father, and of the Son, and of the Holy Ghost; teaching them to observe all things whatsoever I have commanded you: and lo, I am with you always, even unto the end of the world. Amen.

Choir. Glory to thee, O Lord; glory to thee.

Then shall be said the LITANY (*usually omitted*).

Have mercy upon us, O God, according to thy great mercy, we beseech thee: hearken, and have mercy.

Choir. Lord, have mercy. (*Thrice.*)

Furthermore we pray for mercy, life, peace, health, salvation and remission of sins of the servant of God, N., the Sponsor.

Choir. Lord, have mercy.

Furthermore we pray for the newly-illumined servant of God, N.

Choir. Lord, have mercy.

That he may be kept in the faith of a pure confession, in all godliness, and in the fulfilling of the commandments of Christ all the days of his life.

Choir. Lord, have mercy.

For thou art a merciful God, who lovest mankind, and unto thee do we ascribe glory, to the Father, and to the Son, and to the Holy Spirit, now, and ever, and unto ages of ages.

Choir. Amen.

Priest. Glory to thee, O Christ-God our hope; glory to thee.

Choir. Glory to the Father, and to the Son, and to the Holy Spirit, now, and ever, and unto ages of ages. Amen.

Lord, have mercy. (*Thrice.*) —— Bless.

And the Priest bestoweth the BENEDICTION (*usually omitted*).

May Christ, our true God, through the prayers of his all-pure Mother; of the holy, glorious and all-laudable Apostles; of Saint N. (*the Patron Saint of the Temple*); of Saint N. (*the Saint of the day*); of the holy and righteous Ancestors of God, Joachim and Anna; and of all the Saints, have mercy upon us and save us, forasmuch as he is good and loveth mankind.

And on the eighth day the Baptized Person is brought again to the church for Ablution.
(8) *And the Priest looseth his girdle and his garment, saying this Prayer which followeth:*

Let us pray to the Lord.

Choir. Lord, have mercy.

O thou who, through holy Baptism, hast given unto thy servant remission of sins, and hast bestowed upon him (*her*) a life of regeneration: Do thou, the same Lord and Master, ever graciously illumine his (*her*) heart with the light of thy countenance. Maintain the shield of his (*her*) faith unassailed by the enemy. Preserve pure and unpolluted the garment of incorruption wherewith thou hast endued him (*her*), upholding inviolate in him (*her*), by thy grace, the seal of the Spirit, and showing mercy unto him (*her*) and unto us, through the multitude of thy mercies.

For blessed and glorified is thine all-honourable and majestic Name, of the Father, and of the Son, and of the Holy Spirit, now, and ever, and unto ages of ages.

Choir. Amen.

A Second Prayer.

Let us pray to the Lord.

Choir. Lord, have mercy.

O Master, Lord our God, who through the Font bestowest heavenly Illumination upon them that are baptized; who hast regenerated thy newly-baptized servant by water and the Spirit, and hast granted unto him (*her*) remission of his (*her*) sins, whether voluntary or involuntary:

Lay thine almighty hand upon him (*her*) and preserve him (*her*) by the power of thy goodness.   Maintain unassailed the earnest of the Spirit, and make him (*her*) worthy of life everlasting, and of thy favour.

For thou art our sanctification, and unto thee do we ascribe glory, to the Father, and to the Son, and to the Holy Spirit, now, and ever, and unto ages of ages.

Choir. Amen.

Priest. Peace be with you all.

Choir. And with thy spirit.

Priest. Bow your heads unto the Lord.

Choir. To thee, O Lord.

Priest. He (*she*) who hath put on thee, O Christ our God, boweth also his (*her*) head with us, unto thee.   Keep him (*her*) ever a warrior invincible in every attack of those who assail him (*her*) and us; and make us all victors, even unto the end, through thy crown incorruptible.   For thine it is to show mercy and to save us, and unto thee do we ascribe glory, together with thy Father who is from everlasting, and thine all-holy, and good, and life-giving Spirit, now, and ever, and unto ages of ages.

Choir. Amen.

Then the Priest dippeth the sponge in pure water, and sprinkleth the child, saying:

Thou art justified.   Thou art illumined.   Thou art sanctified.   Thou art washed: (9) in the Name of our Lord Jesus Christ, and by the Spirit of our God.

And with the sponge he washeth the face and head of the child, and his breast, and the rest, saying:

Thou art baptized.   Thou art illumined.   Thou hast received anointment with the holy Chrism.   Thou art sanctified.   Thou art washed: in the Name of the Father, and of the Son, and of the Holy Spirit.   Amen.

Prayer at the cutting of the hair.   (10)

Deacon. Let us pray to the Lord. —— *Choir.* Lord, have mercy.

O Master, Lord our God, who hast honoured man with thine own image, thou hast fashioned him from a speech-endowed (2) soul and a comely body (inasmuch as the body serveth the speech-endowed soul): for thou didst set the head on high, and endow it with the chiefest portion of the senses, which, nevertheless, impede not one another: and thou hast covered the head with hair, that it be not injured with the changes of the weather, and hast fitly joined together all his members, that with them all he may give thanks unto thee, the Great Artificer.   Thou, the same Master, through thy chosen vessel, the Apostle Paul, hast given us a commandment that we should do all things to thy glory: Bless, now, thy servant, N., who is come to make a first offering shorn from the hair of his head, and likewise his Sponsor; and grant that they may all exercise themselves in thy law, and do those things which are well pleasing in thy sight.

For thou art a merciful God, who lovest mankind, and unto thee do we ascribe glory, to the Father, and to the Son, and to the Holy Spirit, now, and ever, and unto ages of ages.

Choir. Amen.

Priest. Peace be with you all.

Choir. And with thy spirit.

Deacon. Bow your heads unto the Lord.

Choir. To thee, O Lord.

Then the Priest shall recite this Prayer.

O Lord our God, who, through the fulfilling of the baptismal font, by thy goodness dost sanctify them that believe on thee: Bless this child here present, and let thy blessing descend upon his (*her*) head. And as thou didst bless David the King by the hand of thy Prophet Samuel, bless also the head of thy servant, N., by the hand of me, a sinner, inspiring him (*her*) with thy Holy Spirit; that as he (*she*) increaseth in stature, and even unto hoary old age, he (*she*) may ascribe glory unto thee, and behold the good things of Jerusalem all the days of his (*her*) life.

For unto thee are due all glory, honour and worship, to the Father, and to the Son, and to the Holy Spirit, now, and ever, and unto ages of ages.

Choir. Amen.

Then he sheareth the hair in the form of a cross, saying:

N., the servant of God, is shorn: In the Name of the Father, and of the Son, and of the Holy Spirit.

Choir. Amen.

Deacon. Have mercy upon us, O God, according to thy great mercy, we beseech thee: hearken, and have mercy.

Choir. Lord, have mercy.

And the rest of the Litany, page 90, ending with the petition:

Furthermore we pray for all their Christ-loving Army.

Furthermore we pray for mercy, life, peace, health, salvation and remission of sins of the servant of God, N., the Sponsor, and for the newly-illumined servant of God, N. ℞

That he (*she*) may be kept in the faith of a pure confession, in all godliness, and the fulfilling of the commandments of Christ, all the days of his (*her*) life. ℞

For thou art a merciful God, who lovest mankind, and unto thee do we ascribe glory, to the Father, and to the Son, and to the Holy Spirit, now, and ever, and unto ages of ages.

Choir. Amen.

And he maketh the customary Benediction. (*See page 283.*)

THE RITE OF CONFESSION

The Spiritual Father leadeth the Person who desireth to confess before the holy image (ikóna) of our Lord Jesus Christ-Not-made-with-Hands. And he saith:

O Holy God, Holy Mighty, Holy Immortal One, have mercy upon us. (*Thrice.*)

Glory to the Father, and to the Son, and to the Holy Spirit, now, and ever, and unto ages of ages. Amen.

O all-holy Trinity, have mercy upon us. O Lord, wash away our sins. O Master, pardon our transgressions. O Holy One, visit and heal our infirmities, for thy Name's sake.

Lord, have mercy. (*Thrice.*)

Glory . . . now, and ever, . . .

Our Father, who art in heaven, Hallowed be thy Name. Thy kingdom come. Thy will be done on earth, As it is in heaven. Give us this day our daily bread. And forgive us our trespasses, As we forgive those who trespass against us. And lead us not into temptation; But deliver us from the Evil One:

For thine is the kingdom, and the power, and the glory, of the Father, and of the Son, and of the Holy Spirit, now, and ever, and unto ages of ages. Amen.

Lord, have mercy. (*Twelve times.*) Glory . . . now, and ever . . .

O come, let us worship God our King. O come, let us worship and fall down before Christ, our King and our God. O come, let us worship and fall down before the Very Christ, our King and our God. (*Three reverences.*)

Psalm li.

Have mercy upon me, O God, after thy great goodness; according to the multitude of thy mercies do away mine offences. Wash me throughly from my wickedness; and cleanse me from my sin. For I acknowledge my faults, and my sin is ever before me. Against thee only have I sinned, and done this evil in thy sight; that thou mightest be justified in thy saying, and clear when thou art judged. Behold, I was shapen in wickedness; and in sin hath my mother conceived me. But lo, thou requirest truth in the inward parts; and shalt make me to understand wisdom secretly. Thou shalt purge me with hyssop, and I shall be clean: thou shalt wash me, and I shall be whiter than snow. Thou shalt make me hear of joy and gladness; that the bones which thou hast broken may rejoice. Turn thy face from my sins, and put out all my misdeeds. Make me a clean heart, O God; and renew a right spirit within me. Cast me not away from thy presence; and take not thy holy Spirit from me. O give me the comfort of thy help again; and stablish me with thy free

Spirit. Then shall I teach thy ways unto the wicked; and sinners shall be converted unto thee. Deliver me from blood-guiltiness, O God, thou that art the God of my health; and my tongue shall sing of thy righteousness. Thou shalt open my lips, O Lord; and my mouth shall show thy praise. For thou desirest no sacrifice, else would I give it thee: but thou delightest not in burnt-offerings. The sacrifice of God is a troubled spirit: a broken and contrite heart, O God, shalt thou not despise. O be favourable and gracious unto Zion: build thou the walls of Jerusalem. Then shalt thou be pleased with the sacrifice of righteousness, with the burnt-offerings and oblations: then shall they offer young bullocks upon thine altar.

And the following Hymns (Tropari), in Tone VI.

Have mercy upon us, O Lord, have mercy upon us. For we sinners void of all defence, do offer unto thee, as to our Master, this supplication: Have mercy upon us.

Glory to the Father, and to the Son, and to the Holy Spirit.

Have mercy upon us, O Lord, for in thee have we trusted, and be not very wroth with us, neither call thou to remembrance, our iniquities; but look down even now upon us, inasmuch as thou art of tender compassion, and deliver us from our enemies; for thou art our God, and we are thy people, we are all the works of thy hands, and we call upon thy Name.

Now, and ever, and unto ages of ages. Amen.

Open unto us the door of thy loving-kindness, O blessed Birth-giver of God. In that we set our hope on thee may we not fail, but through thee may we be delivered from all adversities; for thou art the salvation of all Christian people.

Lord, have mercy. (*Forty times.*)

Then the Priest saith:

Let us pray to the Lord.

O God our Saviour, who by thy Prophet Nathan didst grant unto repentant David pardon of his transgressions, and didst accept Manasses' prayer of penitence: Do thou, with thy wonted love towards mankind, accept also thy servant, N., who repenteth him (*her*) of the sins which he (*she*) hath committed; overlooking all that he (*she*) hath done, pardoning his (*her*) offences, and passing by his (*her*) iniquities. For thou hast said, O Lord: With desire have I desired not the death of a sinner, but rather that he should turn from the wickedness which he hath committed, and live; and that even unto seventy times seven, sins ought to be forgiven. For thy majesty is incomparable, and thy mercy is illimitable; and if thou shouldest regard iniquity, who should stand? For thou art the God of the penitent, and unto thee do we ascribe glory, to the Father, and to the Son, and to the Holy Spirit, now, and ever, and unto ages of ages. Amen.

Then another Prayer:

Let us pray to the Lord.

O Lord Jesus Christ, Son of the living God, both Shepherd and Lamb, who takest away the sins of the world; who didst remit the loan unto the two debtors, and didst vouchsafe to the woman who was a sinner the remission of her sins: Do thou, the same Lord, loose, remit, forgive the sins, transgressions and iniquities, whether voluntary or involuntary, whether of wilfulness or of ignorance, which have been committed unto guilt and disobedience by these thy servants. And if they, bearing flesh and dwelling in the world, in that they are men, have in any way been beguiled of the devil; if in word or deed, whether wittingly or unwittingly, they have sinned, either contemning the word of a priest, or falling under his anathema, or have broken their oath: Do thou, the same Master, in that thou art good and cherishest not ill-will, graciously grant unto these thy servants the word of absolution, remitting unto them their anathema and curse, according to thy great mercy. Yea, O Lord and Master, who lovest mankind, hear thou us who make our petitions unto thy goodness on behalf of these thy servants, and disregard thou all their errors, inasmuch as thou art exceedingly merciful; and loose them from punishment eternal. For thou hast said, O Master: Whatsoever ye shall bind on earth shall be bound in heaven, and whatsoever ye shall loose on earth shall be loosed in heaven.

For thou alone art without sin, and unto thee do we ascribe glory, to the Father, and to the Son, and to the Holy Spirit, now, and ever, and unto ages of ages. Amen.

Then shall the Priest say to the Penitent:

Behold, my child, Christ standeth here invisibly, and receiveth thy confession: wherefore, be not ashamed, neither be afraid, and conceal thou nothing from me: but tell me, doubting not, all things which thou hast done; and so shalt thou have pardon from our Lord Jesus Christ. Lo, his holy image is before us: and I am but a witness, bearing testimony before him of all things which thou dost say to me. But if thou shalt conceal anything from me, thou shalt have the greater sin. Take heed, therefore, lest, having come to the physician, thou depart unhealed.

And then shall he question him diligently, point by point, and shall await his reply to every question. And first of all he shall inquire concerning his faith:

Tell me, my child, dost thou believe that which hath been transmitted and is taught by the Catholic, Apostolic Church, which was planted and nurtured in the East, and hath spread from the East throughout the world, and which abideth even unto this day, immovable and unchangeable? And dost thou doubt any of her doctrines?

And if he believeth rightly and undoubtingly he shall repeat THE SYMBOL OF THE
FAITH:

I believe in one God the Father Almighty, Maker of heaven and earth,
And of all things visible and invisible:

And in one Lord Jesus Christ, the only-begotten Son of God, Begotten
of his Father before all worlds; Light of Light, Very God of very God,
Begotten, not made; Being of one Essence with the Father; By whom all
things were made; Who, for us men, and for our salvation, came down
from heaven, And was incarnate by the Holy Ghost of the Virgin Mary,
And was made man.   And was crucified also for us under Pontius Pilate,
and suffered and was buried.   And the third day he rose again, according
to the Scriptures.   And ascended into heaven, And sitteth on the right
hand of the Father.   And he shall come again with glory to judge both
the quick and the dead; Whose kingdom shall have no end.

And in the Holy Ghost, the Lord, Giver of Life, Who proceedeth
from the Father, Who with the Father and the Son together is worshipped
and glorified, Who spake by the Prophets.   In one Holy Catholic and
Apostolic Church.   I acknowledge one Baptism for the remission of sins.
I look for the Resurrection of the dead, And the Life of the world to come.
Amen.

And when he hath finished, the Priest shall interrogate him in detail.

NOTE.   *The Priest doth not use the questions of olden days, which are still retained in
the Ritual, but interrogateth the Penitent discreetly: and at the last, when he hath
questioned him concerning the seven deadly sins, he saith the following* EXHORTA-
TION:

In all these points thou must henceforth be upon thy guard.   For
thou hast received a second Baptism, according to the Christian Mystery.   And thou must see to it that, God helping, thou make a good beginning.   But, above all, thou must not bear thyself lightly towards these
things, lest thou become a cause of scorn to men; for these things do not
befit a Christian.   But may God, by his grace, aid thee to live honourably,
uprightly and devoutly.

*And when the Priest hath said all these things unto him; and when he hath revealed all
things concerning himself. concealing nothing, the Priest shall say to him:*

Bow thy head.

*Then the Person who hath made his Confession boweth his head, and the Confessor
reciteth this Prayer:*

Let us pray to the Lord.

O Lord God of the salvation of thy servants, gracious, bountiful and
long-suffering, who repentest thee concerning our evil deeds, and desirest
not the death of a sinner, but rather that he should turn from his wickedness and live: Show thy mercy now upon thy servant, N., and grant unto
him (*her*) an image of repentance, forgiveness of sins, and deliverance,

pardoning his (*her*) every transgression, whether voluntary or involuntary. Reconcile and unite him (*her*) unto thy holy Church, through Jesus Christ our Lord, with whom also are due unto thee dominion and majesty, now, and ever, and unto ages of ages. Amen.

After this Prayer the Priest pronounceth the Absolution over the Penitent, who kneeleth humbly, saying as follows, in completion of the Holy Sacrament of Confession:

May our Lord and God Jesus Christ, through the grace and bounties of his love towards mankind, forgive thee, my child, N., all thy transgressions. And I, his unworthy Priest, through the power given unto me by him, do forgive and absolve thee from all thy sins, in the Name of the Father, and of the Son, and of the Holy Spirit. Amen.

And having finished the Absolution, the Priest maketh with his hand over the Penitent the sign of the cross.

Then: Meet is it: *page* (107.) Glory . . . now and ever . . . *And the*

BENEDICTION.

May Christ, our true God, through the prayers of his most holy Mother, and of all the Saints, have mercy upon us and save us: for he is gracious and loveth mankind.

THE RITE OF HOLY MATRIMONY *

THE BETROTHAL SERVICE

After the Divine Liturgy, the Priest being in the Temple, those who desire to be joined together take their stand before the Holy Door. The two rings lie on the right-hand side of the Holy Altar. The Priest maketh, thrice, the sign of the cross over the heads of the bridal pair; and giveth them lighted tapers. (1) *And the Deacon saith:*

Bless, Master.

Priest. Blessed is our God always, now, and ever, and unto ages of ages.

Choir. Amen.

Deacon. In peace let us pray to the Lord.

Choir. Lord, have mercy.

For the peace of the whole world: *and the rest, ending:* That he will aid them: (*page 82.*)

For the servant of God, N., and for the handmaid of God, N., who now plight each other their troth, and for their salvation: ℞

That there may be granted unto them children for the continuation of their race, and all their petitions which are unto salvation: ℞

That he will send down upon them perfect and peaceful love, and succour: ℞

That he will preserve them in oneness of mind, and in steadfastness of faith: ℞

That he will bless them with a blameless life: ℞

That the Lord our God will grant unto them an honourable marriage, and a bed undefiled: ℞

That he will deliver us from all tribulation, wrath, and necessity: ℞

Choir. Lord, have mercy. } *let us pray to the Lord.*

Succour us, save us, have mercy upon us, and keep us, O God, by thy grace.

Choir. Lord, have mercy.

Calling to remembrance our most holy, all-undefiled, most blessed and glorious Lady, the Birth-giver of God and ever-virgin Mary, with all the Saints, let us commend ourselves, and each other, and all our life unto Christ our God.

Choir. To thee, O Lord.

Priest. For unto thee are due all glory, honour and worship, to the Father, and to the Son, and to the Holy Spirit, now, and ever, and unto ages of ages.

Choir. Amen.

* Appendix B, VII.

Priest. O eternal God, who hast brought into unity those who were sundered, and hast ordained for them an indissoluble bond of love; who didst bless Isaac and Rebecca, and didst make them heirs of thy promise: Bless also these thy servants, N. and N., guiding them unto every good work.   For thou art a merciful God, who lovest mankind, and unto thee do we ascribe glory, to the Father, and to the Son, and to the Holy Spirit, now, and ever, and unto ages of ages.

Choir. Amen.

Priest. Peace be with you all.

Choir. And with thy spirit.

Deacon. Bow your heads unto the Lord.

Choir. To thee, O Lord.

Priest. .O Lord our God, who hast espoused the Church as a pure Virgin from among the Gentiles: Bless this Betrothal, and unite and maintain these thy servants in peace and oneness of mind.

For unto thee are due all glory, honour and worship, to the Father, and to the Son, and to the Holy Spirit, now, and ever, and unto ages of ages.

Choir. Amen.

Then taking the rings, the Priest blesseth the bridal pair therewith, making the sign of the cross with the ring of the Bride over the Bridegroom, and with that of the Bridegroom over the Bride, saying to the Man: (2)

The servant of God, N., is betrothed to the handmaid of God, N.: In the Name of the Father, and of the Son, and of the Holy Spirit.   Amen.

And to the Woman:

The handmaid of God, N., is betrothed to the servant of God, N.: In the Name of the Father, and of the Son, and of the Holy Spirit.   Amen.

And when he hath spoken thus to each one thrice, he placeth the rings on their right hands.   Then the bridal pair exchange the rings, and the Priest saith the following Prayer:

Let us pray to the Lord. ——*Choir.* Lord, have mercy.

O Lord our God, who didst accompany the servant of the patriarch, Abraham into Mesopotamia, when he was sent to espouse a wife for his lord Isaac; and who, by means of the drawing of water, didst reveal unto him that he should betroth Rebecca: Do thou, the same Lord, bless also the betrothal of these thy servants, N. and N., and confirm the word which they have spoken.   Establish them in the holy union which is from thee.   For thou, in the beginning, didst make them male and female, and by thee is the woman joined unto the man as a helpmeet, and for the procreation of the human race.   Wherefore, O Lord our God, who hast sent forth thy truth upon thine inheritance, and thy covenant unto thy servants our fathers, even thine elect, from generation to generation: Look thou upon thy servant, N., and upon thy handmaid, N., and establish and make stable their betrothal in faith, and in oneness of mind, in truth and in love. For thou, O Lord, hast declared that a pledge should be given and confirmed in all things. By a ring was power given unto Joseph in Egypt; by a ring was Daniel glorified in the land of Babylon; by a ring was the uprightness of Tamar revealed; by a ring did our heavenly Father show forth his bounty upon his Son; for he saith: Put a ring on his hand, and bring hither the fatted calf, and kill it, and eat, and make merry. By thine own right hand, O Lord, didst thou arm Moses in the Red Sea; by the word of thy truth were the heavens established, and the foundations of the earth were made firm; and the right hands of thy servants shall be blessed also by thy mighty word, and by thine upraised arm. Wherefore, O Lord, do thou now bless this putting-on of rings with thy heavenly benediction: and let thine Angel go before them all the days of their life.

For thou art he who blesseth and sanctifieth all things, and unto thee do we ascribe glory, to the Father, and to the Son, and to the Holy Spirit, now, and ever, and unto ages of ages.

Choir. Amen.

THE ORDER OF MARRIAGE, OR OF CROWNING (3)

Priest and Choir. Refrain. Glory to thee, our God; glory to thee.
Blessed are all they that fear the Lord. ℟
All they who walk in his paths. ℟
Thou shalt eat of the fruit of thy labours. ℟
O blessed art thou, and happy shalt thou be. ℟
Thy wife shall be as the fruitful vine upon the walls of thine house. ℟
Thy children like a newly-planted olive-orchard round about thy table. ℟
Lo, thus shall the man be blessed that feareth the Lord. ℟
The Lord in Zion shall so bless thee, that thou shalt see the good things of Jerusalem all thy life long. ℟
Yea, that thou shalt see thy children's children, and peace upon Israel. ℟

Then the Priest shall make them an exhortation, telling them wherein the Sacrament of Marriage consisteth, and how they ought to live godly and uprightly in the wedded state. And when his exhortation is finished, the Priest shall inquire of the Bridegroom, saying:

Hast thou, N., a good, free and unconstrained will and a firm intention to take unto thyself to wife this woman, N., whom thou seest here before thee?

And the Bridegroom maketh answer:

I have, reverend Father.
Priest. Thou hast not promised thyself to any other bride?
The Bridegroom. I have not promised myself, reverend Father.

And straightway the Priest, looking at the Bride, shall inquire of her, saying:

Hast thou, N., a good, free and unconstrained will and a firm intention to take unto thyself to husband this man, N., whom thou seest here before thee?

And the Bride maketh answer, saying:

I have, reverend Father.

Priest. Thou hast not promised thyself to any other man?

The Bride. I have not promised myself, reverend Father.

Then the Deacon saith:

Bless, Master.

Priest. Blessed is the kingdom of the Father, and of the Son, and of the Holy Spirit always, now, and ever, and unto ages of ages.

Choir. Amen.

Deacon. In peace let us pray to the Lord.

Choir. Lord, have mercy.

For the peace that is from above: *and the rest, ending:* That he will aid them . . . (*See page* 80.)

For the servants of God, N. and N., who are now being united to each other in the community of marriage, and for their salvation: ℟

That he will bless this marriage, as he blessed that in Cana of Galilee: ℟

That he will grant unto them chastity, and of the fruit of the womb as is expedient for them: ℟

That he will make them glad with the sight of sons and daughters: ℟

That he will grant unto them the procreation of virtuous offspring, and an upright life: ℟

That he will grant to them and to us all our petitions which **are** unto salvation: ℟

That he will deliver them and us from all tribulation, wrath, and necessity. ℟

Choir. let us pray to the Lord. *Choir.* Lord, have mercy.

Succour us, save us, have mercy upon us, and keep us, O God, by thy grace.

Choir. Lord, have mercy.

Calling to remembrance our most holy, all-undefiled, most blessed and glorious Lady, the Birth-giver of God and ever-virgin Mary, with all the Saints, let us commend ourselves, and each other, and all our life unto Christ our God.

Choir. To thee, O Lord.

Priest. For unto thee are due all glory, honour and worship, to the Father, and to the Son, and to the Holy Spirit, now, and ever, and unto ages of ages.

Choir. Amen.

Deacon. Let us pray to the Lord. —— *Choir.* Lord, have mercy.

Then the Priest reciteth, aloud, *the following Prayer:*

O God most pure, the Creator of every living thing, who didst transform the rib of our forefather Adam into a wife, because of thy love towards mankind, and didst bless them, and say unto them: Increase, and multiply, and have dominion over the earth; and didst make of the twain one flesh: for which cause a man shall leave his father and mother and cleave unto his wife, and the two shall be one flesh: and what God hath joined together, that let no man put asunder: Thou who didst bless thy servant Abraham, and opening the womb of Sarah didst make him to be the father of many nations; who didst give Isaac to Rebecca, and didst bless her in child-bearing; who didst join Jacob unto Rachel, and from that union didst generate the twelve Patriarchs; who didst unite Joseph and Asenath, giving unto them as the fruit of their procreation Ephraim and Manasses; who didst accept Zacharias and Elizabeth, and didst make their offspring to be the Forerunner; who, from the Root of Jesse according to the flesh, didst bud forth the ever-Virgin One, and wast incarnate of her; and wast born of her for the redemption of the human race; who, through thine unutterable gift and manifold goodness didst come to Cana of Galilee, and didst bless the marriage there, that thou mightest make manifest that it is thy will that there should be lawful marriage and the begetting of children: Do thou, the same all-holy Master, accept the prayer of us thy servants. As thou wert present there, so likewise be thou present here, with thine invisible protection. Bless this marriage, and vouchsafe unto these thy servants, N. and N., a peaceful life, length of days, chastity, mutual love in the bond of peace, long-lived seed, gratitude from their posterity, a crown of glory which fadeth not away. Graciously grant that they may behold their children's children. Preserve their bed unassailed, and give them of the dew of heaven from on high, and of the fatness of the earth. Fill their houses with wheat, and wine, and oil, and with every beneficence, that they may bestow in turn upon the needy; granting also unto those who are here present with them all those petitions which are for their salvation.

For thou art the God of mercies, and bounties, and love towards mankind, and unto thee do we ascribe glory, to the Father, and to the Son, and to the Holy Spirit, now, and ever, and unto ages of ages.

Choir. Amen.

Deacon. Let us pray to the Lord.

Choir. Lord, have mercy.

Then the Priest reciteth, aloud, *the following Prayer:*

Blessed art thou, O Lord our God, the Priest of mystical and pure marriage, and the Ordainer of the law of the marriage of the body, the Preserver of immortality, and the Provider of good things; do thou, the same Master, who in the beginning didst make man and set him to be, as it were, a King over thy creation, and didst say: It is not good for man to be alone on the earth; let us make a helpmeet for him; and taking one of his ribs didst fashion Woman, which when Adam beheld, he said: This is now bone of my bone, and flesh of my flesh; she shall be called Woman, for she was taken out of man; for this cause shall a man leave father and mother, and shall cleave unto his wife, and the twain shall be one flesh; and those whom God hath joined together let no man put asunder: — Do thou now also, O Master, our Lord and our God, send down thy heavenly grace upon these thy servants, N. and N.; and grant that this thy hand-maid may, in all things, be subject unto her husband; and that this thy servant may be the head of his wife, that they may live according to thy will.   Bless them, O Lord our God, as thou didst bless Abraham and Sarah: Bless them, O Lord our God, as thou didst bless Isaac and Re-becca: Bless them, O Lord our God, as thou didst bless Jacob and all the patriarchs: Bless them, O Lord our God, as thou didst bless Joseph and Asenath: Bless them, O Lord our God, as thou didst bless Moses and Sepphora: Bless them, O Lord our God, as thou didst bless Joachim and Anna: Bless them, O Lord our God, as thou didst bless Zacharias and Elizabeth: Preserve them, O Lord our God, as thou didst preserve Noah in the ark: Preserve them, O Lord our God, as thou didst preserve Jonah in the belly of the whale: Preserve them, O Lord our God, as thou didst preserve the three Holy Children from the fire, sending down upon them dew from heaven; and let that gladness come upon them which the blessed Helena had when she found the precious Cross.   Remember them, O Lord our God, as thou didst remember Enoch, Shem, Elijah: Remember them, O Lord our God, as thou didst remember thy Forty Holy Martyrs, sending down upon them crowns from heaven: Remember them, O Lord our God, and the parents who have nurtured them; for the prayers of parents make firm the foundations of houses.   Remember, O Lord our God, thy servants the groomsman and the bridesmaid of the bridal pair, who are come together in this joy.   Remember, O Lord our God, thy servant, N., and thy handmaid, N., and bless them.   Grant them of the fruit of their bodies, fair children, concord of soul and of body: Exalt them like the cedars of Lebanon, like a luxuriant vine.   Give them seed in num-ber like unto the full ears of grain; that, having sufficiency in all things, they may abound in every work that is good and acceptable unto thee. And let them behold their children's children, like a newly-planted olive-orchard, round about their table; that, obtaining favour in thy sight, they may shine like the stars of heaven, in thee, our God.   For unto thee are due all glory, honour and worship, to the Father, who is from everlasting, and to the Son, and to thy Life-giving Spirit, now, and ever, and unto ages of ages. —— *Choir*. Amen.

Deacon. Let us pray to the Lord.

Choir. Lord, have mercy.

And again the Priest prayeth, aloud, *as followeth:*

O holy God, who didst create man out of the dust, and didst fashion his wife out of his rib, and didst join her unto him as a helpmeet; for it seemed good to thy majesty that man should not be alone upon earth: Do thou, the same Lord, stretch out now also thy hand from thy holy dwelling-place, and conjoin this thy servant, N., and this thy handmaid, N.; for by thee is the husband united unto the wife. Unite them in one mind: wed them into one flesh, granting unto them of the fruit of the body and the procreation of fair children.

For thine is the majesty, and thine are the kingdom and the power and the glory, of the Father, and of the Son, and of the Holy Spirit, now, and ever, and unto ages of ages. —— *Choir.* Amen.

And after the Amen, *the Priest taketh the crowns* (4), *and crowneth first the Bridegroom, saying:*

The servant of God, N., is crowned unto the handmaid of God, N.: In the Name of the Father, and of the Son, and of the Holy Spirit.
Choir. Amen.

In like manner he then crowneth the Bride, saying:

The handmaid of God, N., is crowned unto the servant of God, N.: In the Name of the Father, and of the Son, and of the Holy Spirit.
Choir. Amen.

Then he blesseth them thrice, saying, thrice:

O Lord our God, crown them with glory and honour.
Deacon. Let us attend.
Priest. Peace be with you all.
Reader. And with thy spirit.
Deacon. Wisdom!
Reader. The Gradual (*Prokímen*), in Tone VIII. Thou hast set upon their heads crowns of precious stones; they asked life of thee, and thou gavest it them.
Verse: For thou wilt give them thy blessing forever and ever: thou wilt make them to rejoice with gladness through thy presence.
Deacon. Wisdom!
Reader. The Lesson from the Epistle of the holy Apostle Paul to the Ephesians.
Deacon. Let us attend.
Reader. (*Eph. v. 20–33.*) Brethren: Give thanks always for all things unto God and the Father, in the name of our Lord Jesus Christ; submitting yourselves one to another in the fear of God. Wives, submit yourselves unto your own husbands, as unto the Lord. For the husband is the head of the wife, even as Christ is the head of the church: and he is the Saviour of the body. Therefore as the church is subject unto Christ, so let the wives be to their own husbands in everything. Husbands, love

your wives, even as Christ also loved the church, and gave himself for it; that he might sanctify and cleanse it with the washing of water by the word, that he might present it to himself a glorious church, not having spot or wrinkle, or any such thing; but that it should be holy and without blemish. So ought men to love their wives, as their own bodies. He that loveth his wife loveth himself. For no man ever yet hated his own flesh; but nourisheth and cherisheth it, even as the Lord the church: we are members of his body, of his flesh, and of his bones. For this cause shall a man leave his father and mother, and shall be joined unto his wife, and they two shall be one flesh. This is a great mystery: but I speak concerning Christ and the church. Nevertheless, let every one of you in particular so love his wife even as himself: and the wife see that she reverence her husband.

Priest. Peace be unto thee.

Reader. And to thy spirit.

Deacon. Wisdom!

Reader. Alleluia.

Deacon. Wisdom, O believers! Let us listen to the Holy Gospel.

Priest. Peace be with you all.

Choir. And with thy spirit.

Priest. The Lesson from the holy Gospel according to John.

Choir. Glory to thee, O Lord; glory to thee.

Deacon. Let us attend.

(*John ii. 1–12.*) And the third day there was a marriage in Cana of Galilee; and the mother of Jesus was there. And both Jesus was called, and his disciples, to the marriage. And when they wanted wine, the mother of Jesus saith unto him, They have no wine. Jesus saith unto her, Woman, what have I to do with thee? mine hour is not yet come. His mother saith unto the servants, Whatsoever he saith unto you, do it. And there were set there six water-pots of stone, after the manner of the purifying of the Jews, containing two or three firkins apiece. Jesus saith unto them, Fill the water-pots with water. And they filled them up to the brim. And he saith unto them, Draw out now, and bear unto the governor of the feast. And they bare it. When the ruler of the feast had tasted the water that was made wine, and knew not whence it was (but the servants which drew the water knew), the governor of the feast called the bridegroom, and saith unto him, Every man at the beginning doth set forth good wine; and when men have well drunk, then that which is worse: but thou hast kept the good wine until now. This beginning of miracles did Jesus in Cana of Galilee, and manifested forth his glory; and his disciples believed on him.

Choir. Glory to thee, O Lord; glory to thee.

Deacon. Let us all say, with all our soul and with all our mind let us say: ℟

O Lord Almighty, the God of our fathers, we beseech thee: hearken, and have mercy: ℞

Have mercy upon us according to thy great mercy, we beseech thee: hearken, and have mercy: ℞

Furthermore we pray for mercy, life, peace, health, salvation and visitation for the servants of God, N. and N. (*and he also maketh mention of whomsoever else he will*): ℞

Choir. Lord, have mercy.

Priest. For thou art a merciful God, who lovest mankind, and unto thee do we ascribe glory, to the Father, and to the Son, and to the Holy Spirit, now, and ever, and unto ages of ages. —— *Choir.* Amen.

Deacon. Let us pray to the Lord. —— *Choir.* Lord, have mercy.

And the Priest reciteth this Prayer.

O Lord our God, who in thy saving providence didst vouchsafe by thy presence in Cana of Galilee to declare marriage honourable: Do thou, the same Lord, now also maintain in peace and concord thy servants, N. and N., whom it hath pleased thee to join together. Cause their marriage to be honourable. Preserve their bed blameless. Mercifully grant that they may live together in purity; and enable them to attain to a ripe old age, walking in thy commandments with a pure heart.

For thou art our God, the God whose property it is to show mercy and to save, and unto thee do we ascribe glory, to the Father, and to the Son, and to the Holy Spirit, now, and ever, and unto ages of ages.

Choir. Amen.

Deacon. Succour us, save us, have mercy upon us, and keep us, O God, by thy grace. —— *Choir.* Lord, have mercy.

Deacon. A day all-perfect, holy, peaceful and sinless: ℞

An Angel of Peace, the faithful guide and guardian both of our souls and bodies: ℞

The forgiveness and remission of our sins and transgressions: ℞

All things which are good and profitable to our souls, and peace to the world: ℞

That we may pass the residue of our life in peace and penitence: ℞

A Christian ending to our life, painless, blameless, peaceful; and a good defence before the dread Judgment Seat of Christ: ℞

The unity of the faith, and the communion of the Holy Spirit let us beseech of the Lord: and let us commend ourselves, and each other, and all our life unto Christ our God.

Choir. To thee, O Lord.

And the Priest maketh the Exclamation:

And vouchsafe, O Lord, that boldly and without condemnation, we may dare to call upon thee, God, the heavenly Father, and to say:

And the People recite the Lord's Prayer to the end.

Our Father, who art in heaven, Hallowed be thy Name. Thy kingdom come. Thy will be done on earth, As it is in heaven. Give us this day our daily bread. And forgive us our trespasses, As we forgive those who trespass against us. And lead us not into temptation; But deliver us from the Evil One:

Priest. For thine is the kingdom, and the power, and the glory, of the Father, and of the Son, and of the Holy Spirit, now, and ever, and unto ages of ages.

Choir. Amen.

Priest. Peace be with you all.

Choir. And with thy spirit.

Priest. Bow your heads unto the Lord.

Choir. To thee, O Lord.

Then the Common Cup (5) is brought, and the Priest blesseth it, and reciteth this Prayer:

Deacon. Let us pray to the Lord.

Choir. Lord, have mercy.

O God, who hast created all things by thy might, and hast made fast the round world, and adornest the crown of all things which thou hast made: Bless now, with thy spiritual blessing, this common cup, which thou dost give to those who are now united for a community of marriage. *Secretly.*

Aloud: For blessed is thy Name, and glorified is thy kingdom, of the Father, and of the Son, and of the Holy Spirit, now, and ever, and unto ages of ages.

Choir. Amen.

Then, taking the Cup in his hand, the Priest giveth it thrice to them: first to the Man, and then to the Woman. Then immediately the Priest taketh them, the groomsmen behind them holding their crowns, and leadeth them in a circle (6) round about the lectern. And the Priest, or the People, sing the following Hymn, in Tone V.:

Rejoice, O Isaiah! A Virgin is with child, and shall bear a Son, Emmanuel, both God and man: and Orient is his name; whom magnifying we call the Virgin blessed.

Another, in Tone VII.

O Holy Martyrs, who fought the good fight and have received your crowns: Entreat ye the Lord that he will have mercy on our souls. Glory to thee, O Christ-God, the Apostles' boast, the Martyrs' joy, whose preaching was the consubstantial Trinity.

Then, taking the crown of the Bridegroom, he saith:

Be thou exalted, O Bridegroom, like unto Abraham; and be thou blessed, like unto Isaac; and do thou multiply like unto Jacob, walking in peace, and keeping the commandments of God in righteousness.

Then, taking the crown of the Bride, he saith:

And thou, O Bride: Be thou exalted like unto Sarah; and exult thou, like unto Rebecca; and do thou multiply, like unto Rachel: and rejoice thou in thy husband, fulfilling the conditions of the law: for so is it well-pleasing unto God.

Deacon. Let us pray to the Lord.

Choir. Lord, have mercy.

The Priest prayeth:

O God, our God, who didst come to Cana of Galilee, and didst bless there the marriage feast: Bless, also, these thy servants, who through thy good providence are now united together in wedlock. Bless their goings out and their comings in: replenish their life with good things: receive their crowns into thy kingdom, preserving them spotless, blameless, and without reproach, unto ages of ages.

Choir. Amen. ―― *Priest.* Peace be with you all. ―― *Choir.* And with thy spirit. ―― *Deacon.* Bow your heads unto the Lord. ―― *Choir.* To thee, O Lord.

And the Priest prayeth:

May the Father, and the Son, and the Holy Spirit, the all-holy, consubstantial and life-giving Trinity, one Godhead, and one Kingdom, bless you; and grant unto you length of days, fair children, prosperity of life, and faith: and fill you with abundance of all earthly good things, and make you worthy to obtain the blessings of the promise: through the prayers of the holy Birth-giver of God, and of all the Saints. Amen.

And the Deacon saith:

Wisdom!

Choir. More honourable than the Cherubim, . . . (*See page* 302.)

Priest. Glory to thee, Christ-God, our hope, glory to thee.

Choir. Glory . . . now, and ever . . . Lord, have mercy. (*Thrice.*) Bless.

Then the Priest bestoweth the final BENEDICTION.

May he who by his presence at the marriage feast in Cana of Galilee did declare marriage to be an honourable estate, Christ our true God; through the prayers of his all-holy Mother; of the holy, glorious and all-laudable Apostles; of the holy, God-crowned Kings and Saints-equal-to-the-Apostles Constantine and Helena: of the holy Great Martyr, Procopius; (7) and of all the Saints, have mercy upon you and save you: forasmuch as he is good, and loveth mankind.

Then the Priest maketh an exhortation to the newly-married pair.

And the People come and congratulate them; and they kiss each other.

PRAYER AT THE REMOVAL OF THE CROWNS ON THE EIGHTH DAY (8)

O Lord our God, who hast blessed the crown of the year, and permittest these crowns to be laid upon those who are united to one another by the law of marriage, and thus grantest unto them, as it were a reward of chastity; for they are pure who are united in the marriage which thou hast made lawful: Do thou bless also in the removal of these crowns those who have been united to one another, and preserve their union indissoluble; that they may evermore give thanks unto thine all-holy Name, of the Father, and of the Son, and of the Holy Spirit, now, and ever, and unto ages of ages.   Amen.

Priest. Peace be with you all.

Choir. And with thy spirit.

Deacon. Bow your heads unto the Lord.

Choir. To thee, O Lord.

Priest. These thy servants having come together in concord, O Lord, and having accomplished the compact of marriage, as at Cana of Galilee, and contracted the pledges thereof, ascribe glory unto thee, to the Father, and to the Son, and to the Holy Spirit, now, and ever, and unto ages of ages.   Amen.

And the Dismissal.

Wisdom!

Choir. O most holy Birth-giver of God, save us.

More honourable than the Cherubim, and beyond compare more glorious than the Seraphim, thou who without defilement barest God the Word, true Birth-giver of God, we magnify thee.

Glory to the Father, and to the Son, and to the Holy Spirit, now, and ever, and unto ages of ages.   Amen.

Lord, have mercy.   (*Thrice.*)   Bless.

And the Priest bestoweth the BENEDICTION.   (*See page 301.*)

THE ORDER OF SECOND MARRIAGE (9)

The Priest beginneth:

Blessed is our God always, now and ever, and unto ages of ages.

Choir. Amen.

O heavenly King . . . (*See page 43.*)

O Holy God, Holy Mighty, Holy Immortal One, have mercy upon us.   (*Thrice.*)

Glory to the Father, and to the Son, and to the Holy Spirit, now, and ever, and unto ages of ages.   Amen.

O all-holy Trinity, have mercy upon us.   O Lord, wash away our sins.

O Master, pardon our transgressions. O Holy One, visit and heal our infirmities, for thy Name's sake.

Lord, have mercy. (*Thrice.*) Glory . . . now, and ever, . . .

Our Father, who art in heaven, Hallowed be thy Name. Thy kingdom come. Thy will be done on earth, As it is in heaven. Give us this day our daily bread. And forgive us our trespasses, As we forgive those who trespass against us. And lead us not into temptation; But deliver us from the Evil One:

Priest. For thine is the kingdom, and the power, and the glory, of the Father, and of the Son, and of the Holy Spirit, now, and ever, and unto ages of ages.

Choir. Amen. —— *Choir.* Lord, have mercy. (*Twelve Times.*)

The Hymn for the Day.

Deacon. In peace let us pray to the Lord. —— *Choir.* Lord, have mercy.

For the peace of the whole world: *and the rest, ending:* That he will aid them . . . (*See page* 80.)

For the servants of God, N. and N., and for the protection which is from God; and for their life together: let us pray to the Lord.

Choir. Lord, have mercy.

That they may dwell together uprightly and in oneness of mind: let us pray to the Lord.

Choir. Lord, have mercy.

Succour us, save us, have mercy upon us, and keep us, O God, by thy grace.

Choir. Lord, have mercy.

Calling to remembrance our most holy, all-undefiled, most blessed and glorious Lady, the Birth-giver of God and ever-virgin Mary, with all the Saints, let us commend ourselves, and each other, and all our life unto Christ our God.

Choir. To thee, O Lord.

Priest. For unto thee are due all glory, honour and worship, to the Father, and to the Son, and to the Holy Spirit, now, and ever, and unto ages of ages. —— *Choir.* Amen. —— *Deacon.* Let us pray to the Lord.

Choir. Lord, have mercy.

The Priest saith this Prayer:

O eternal God, who hast brought into unity those who were sundered, and hast ordained for them an indissoluble bond of love; who didst bless Isaac and Rebecca, and didst make them heirs of thy promise: Bless also these thy servants, N. and N., directing them unto every good work.

For thou art a merciful God, who lovest mankind, and unto thee do we ascribe glory, to the Father, and to the Son, and to the Holy Spirit, now, and ever, and unto ages of ages.

Choir. Amen. —— *Priest.* Peace be with you all. —— *Choir.* And with thy spirit. —— *Deacon.* Bow your heads unto the Lord. —— *Choir.* To thee, O Lord.

The Priest prayeth:

O Lord our God, who hast espoused the Church as a pure Virgin from among the Gentiles: Bless this Betrothal, and unite and maintain these thy servants in peace and oneness of mind.

For unto thee are due all honour, glory and worship, to the Father, and to the Son, and to the Holy Spirit, now, and ever, and unto ages of ages.

Choir. Amen.

Then the Priest, taking the rings, giveth one first to the Man, and to the Woman another, and saith to the Man:

The servant of God, N., is betrothed to the handmaid of God, N.: In the Name of the Father, and of the Son, and of the Holy Spirit. Amen.

And in like manner to the Woman:

The handmaid of God, N., is betrothed to the servant of God, N.: In the Name of the Father, and of the Son, and of the Holy Spirit. Amen.   '

Then he maketh with the rings the sign of the cross over their heads, and putteth the rings on the fingers of their right hands. The Sponsor of the bridal pair exchangeth them. Then the Deacon:

Let us pray to the Lord.

Choir. Lord, have mercy.

Priest. O Master, Lord our God, who showest pity upon all men, and whose providence is over all thy works; who knowest the secrets of man, and understandest all men: Purge away our sins, and forgive the transgressions of thy servants, calling them to repentance, granting them remission of their iniquities, purification from their sins, and pardon of their errors, whether voluntary or involuntary. O thou who knowest the frailty of man's nature, in that thou art his Maker and Creator; who didst pardon Rahab the harlot, and accept the contrition of the Publican: remember not the sins of our ignorance from our youth up. For if thou wilt consider iniquity, O Lord, Lord, who shall stand before thee? Or what flesh shall be justified in thy sight? For thou only art righteous, sinless, holy, plenteous in mercy, of great compassion, and repentest thee of the evils of men. Do thou, O Master, who hast brought together in wedlock thy servants, N. and N., unite them to one another in love: vouchsafe unto them the contrition of the Publican, the tears of the Harlot, the confession of the Thief; that, repenting with their whole heart, and doing thy commandments in peace and oneness of mind, they may be deemed worthy also of thy heavenly kingdom.

For thou art he who ordereth all things, and unto thee do we ascribe glory, to the Father, and to the Son, and to the Holy Spirit, now, and ever, and unto ages of ages.

Choir. Amen.
Priest. Peace be with you all.
Choir. And with thy spirit.
Priest. Bow your heads unto the Lord.
Choir. To thee, O Lord.

The Priest saith this Prayer:

O Lord Jesus Christ, the Word of God, who wast lifted up on the precious and life-giving cross, and didst thereby destroy the handwriting against us, and deliver us from the dominion of the Devil: Cleanse thou the iniquities of thy servants; because they, being unable to bear the heat and burden of the day and the hot desires of the flesh, are now entering into the bond of a second marriage, as thou didst render lawful by thy chosen vessel, the Apostle Paul, saying, for the sake of us humble sinners, It is better to marry in the Lord than to burn. Wherefore, inasmuch as thou art good and lovest mankind, do thou show mercy and forgive. Cleanse, put away, pardon our transgressions; for thou art he who didst take our infirmities on thy shoulders; for there is none sinless, or without uncleanness for so much as a single day of his life, save only Thou, who without sin didst endure the flesh, and bestowest on us passionlessness eternal.

For thou art God, the God of the contrite in heart, and unto thee do we ascribe glory, to the Father, and to the Son, and to the Holy Spirit, now, and ever, and unto ages of ages.

People. Amen.
Deacon. Let us pray to the Lord.
Choir. Lord, have mercy.

Then the Priest saith the Prayer:

O holy God, who didst create man out of the dust, . . .

And the rest, as in the First Rite of Marriage, page 297.

THE OFFICE OF SETTING APART READERS AND CHANTERS*

He who is to be made a Taper-bearer is led by the Sub-Deacon into the centre of the Church, before the beginning of the Divine Liturgy (see page 79), and there maketh three reverences: and turning, he saluteth the Bishop, thrice. Then, drawing near to the Bishop, he boweth his head; and the Bishop signeth him, in crosswise form, on the head with his hand. Then, laying his hand upon the candidate's head, the Bishop saith the following Prayer:

O Lord, who enlightenest all created beings with the light of thy marvels, and knowest the intent of every man before it is formed, and strengthenest those who are desirous of serving thee: Do thou, the same Lord, array in thy fair and spotless vesture this thy servant who desireth to become a Taper-bearer (*these thy servants who desire to become Taper-bearers*) before thy Holy Mysteries; that he (*they*) may be illumined; and that attaining unto the world to come he (*they*) may receive the incorruptible crown of life, and rejoice with thine elect in bliss everlasting.

For hallowed is thy Name, and glorified is thy kingdom, of the Father, and of the Son, and of the Holy Spirit, now, and ever, and unto ages of ages. Amen.

But when there is no Liturgy the Bishop beginneth as follows:

Blessed is our God always, now, and ever, and unto ages of ages. Amen.

Then shall be sung:

O heavenly King, the Comforter, Spirit of Truth, who art in all places and fillest all things; Treasury of good things and Giver of life: Come, and take up thine abode in us, and cleanse us from every stain; and save our souls, O Good One.

O Holy God, Holy Mighty, Holy Immortal One, have mercy upon us. (*Thrice.*)

Glory to the Father, and to the Son, and to the Holy Spirit, now, and ever, and unto ages of ages. Amen.

O all-holy Trinity, have mercy upon us. O Lord, wash away our sins. O Master, pardon our transgressions. O Holy One, visit and heal our infirmities, for thy Name's sake.

Lord, have mercy. (*Thrice.*) Glory . . . now, and ever, . . .

Our Father, who art in heaven, Hallowed be thy Name. Thy kingdom come. Thy will be done on earth, As it is in heaven. Give us this day our daily bread. And forgive us our trespasses, As we forgive those who trespass against us. And lead us not into temptation; But deliver us from the Evil One:

* See page xxxii.

For thine is the kingdom, and the power, and the glory, of the Father, and of the Son, and of the Holy Spirit, now, and ever, and unto ages of ages.

Choir. Amen. —— Lord, have mercy. (*Twelve times.*)

Glory to the Father, and to the Son, and to the Holy Spirit, now, and ever, and unto ages of ages. Amen.

Then the Hymn (Tropár) for the Day shall be read.

But if there be a Liturgy, then O Heavenly King, *and* O Holy God, *and* Our Father *shall be omitted, and only the following Hymns shall be read:*

O holy Apostles, entreat the merciful God that he will grant our souls remission of their sins.

The grace of thy lips, shining forth like a beacon-fire, hath illumined the universe, and hath bestowed upon the world the treasure of non-avariciousness, and hath shown us the height of humility. But as thou instructest us with thy words, O Father John Chrysostum, so also intercede thou with Christ-God, the Word, that our souls may be saved.

Thy voice is gone out into all the world, in that it hath received thy word, wherewith thou hast taught in manner well-pleasing unto God, hast expounded the nature of existing things, and hast adorned the customs of mankind. O Royal Priesthood, Sainted Father, pray thou unto Christ our God, that our souls may be saved.

The shepherd's reed of thy divine theology hath confounded the trumpets of the rhetoricians, the same being bestowed upon thee as upon one who hath searched out the deep things of the spirit, and grace of proclamation. Wherefore, O Father Gregory, entreat thou Christ-God that our souls may be saved.

Glory . . . now, and ever, . . .

Through the prayers of all the Saints, and of the Birth-giver of God, O Lord, grant us thy peace, and have mercy upon us: for thou only art bountiful.

Then the Bishop sheareth the candidate's head in the form of a cross, saying:

In the Name of the Father.

Then the Proto-Deacon, and the Reader, or a Chanter, shall say:

Amen.

Bishop. And of the Son.

Proto-Deacon. Amen.

Bishop. And of the Holy Spirit.

Proto-Deacon. Amen.

Then the Bishop putteth upon him the short chasuble, and again maketh, thrice, with his hand, the sign of the cross upon his head, and reciteth this Prayer:

O Lord God Almighty, elect this thy servant (*these thy servants*), and sanctify him (*them*); and enable him (*them*), with all wisdom and understanding, to exercise the study and reading of thy divine words, preserving him (*them*) in blamelessness of life.

Through the mercies and bounties and love towards mankind of thine Only-begotten Son, with whom also thou art blessed, together with thine all-holy, and good, and life-giving Spirit, now, and ever, and unto ages of ages.

Choir. Amen.

And after the Prayer, the Bishop openeth the book of the Epistles upon the head of the Reader. And the Sub-Deacons lead him from the Bishop, and place him in the middle of the Church, with his face to the east; and the book of the Epistles is given to him, and he readeth, a little, wheresoever it may chance to befall, and turning, he boweth to the Bishop thrice, according to the rubric, and the Sub-Deacons divest him of the short chasuble. Then the tunic is brought to the Bishop, and he signeth it with his hand, over the cross. And he who hath been set apart (or ordained), having signed himself with the cross, kisseth the cross upon the tunic, and the hand of the Bishop: And the Sub-Deacons vest him in the tunic; and the Bishop exhorteth him thus:

My son(*s*), the first degree in the Priesthood is that of Reader. It behooveth thee (*you*) therefore, to peruse the divine Scriptures daily, to the end that the hearers, regarding thee (*you*) may receive edification; that thou (*ye*) in nowise shaming thine (*your*) election, mayest prepare thyself (*may prepare yourselves*) for a higher degree. For by a chaste, holy and upright life thou shalt (*ye shall*) gain the favour of the God of loving-kindness, and shalt render thyself (*shall render yourselves*) worthy of a greater ministry, through Jesus Christ our Lord; to whom be glory unto ages of ages. Amen.

Then shall the Bishop say:

Blessed is the Lord. Lo, the servant(*s*) of God, N. (*NN.*), is (*are*) become a Reader (*Readers*) of the most holy Church of N.: In the Name of the Father, and of the Son, and of the Holy Spirit.

Then the Bishop giveth him (or them) *a shrine-lamp, and he standeth* (they stand) *before the Bishop with the lamp, in the appointed place.*

THE MANNER OF ORDAINING SUB-DEACONS*

If the Candidate is to receive the Laying-on of Hands to the Sub-Diaconate (see page 79) on the same day, after he hath been invested with the tunic, the Sub-Deacons bring the dalmatic and the dalmatic-girdle (that is the stole) to the Bishop. And when the Bishop hath signed the girdle with the cross, and he who is to receive Ordination hath kissed it, and the hand of the Bishop, they gird him therewith. And the Bishop signeth him with his hand, in the form of a cross; after which the Archpriest saith:

Let us pray to the Lord.

And the Bishop laying his hand on the Candidate's head, reciteth the following Prayer:

O Lord our God, who, through one and the same Holy Spirit distributing gifts of grace to each one of those whom thou hast chosen, hast given to thy Church divers Orders; who, through thine inscrutable providence hast appointed degrees of ministry therein, for the service of thy holy, spotless Mysteries; and who, through thine ineffable foreknowledge, hast ordained this thy servant to be worthy to serve in thy Holy Church: Do thou, the same Lord, preserve him uncondemned in all things. And grant that he may love the beauty of thy house, stand before the doors of thy holy Temple, and kindle the lamps in the tabernacle of thy glory. And plant him in thy holy Church like a fruitful olive-tree, which bringeth forth the fruits of righteousness. And make him thy perfect servant in the time of thine advent, that he may receive the recompense of those who are well-pleasing in thy sight. For thine are the kingdom and the power and the glory, of the Father, and of the Son, and of the Holy Spirit, now, and ever, and unto ages of ages. Amen.

And after the Prayer, the Sub-Deacons give the ewer and basin to him who is to receive the Laying-on of Hands, and lay a towel on his shoulders. And the Bishop washeth his hands. And he who is to be ordained Sub-Deacon poureth water over the hands of the Bishop. Then he and the Sub-Deacons kiss the hand of the Bishop and depart to their appointed place. And he who is to be ordained Sub-Deacon standeth, holding the ewer and basin, with the towel, until the Cherubimic Hymn. And he saith, secretly:

O Holy God, Holy Mighty, . . . (*Thrice*). Glory . . . now, and ever, . . . O all-holy Trinity, . . . Lord, have mercy. (*Thrice.*) Our Father, who art in heaven, . . . For thine is the kingdom, . . . Lord, have mercy. (*Thrice.*) I believe in one God, . . .
Pardon, remit, forgive, O God, our transgressions, both vol-

Secretly.

* For explanation, see Introductory Chapter on the Symbolism of the Church. Also, Appendix B, VIII (1).

untary and involuntary, whether of word or of deed, whether of knowl-edge or of ignorance, whether of the day or of the night, whether of the mind or of the intentions: forgive us all, forasmuch as thou art good and lovest mankind.

Secretly.

And if he desireth to say anything further, he doth so secretly.

At the time of the Cherubimic Hymn, he is led in front of the Holy Doors, to the Bishop: and the Bishop washeth his hands, according to the rite, and saith the Prayer. Then he signeth the water with his hand, in the form of a cross, thrice. And the Bishop, with this holy water, wetteth his eyes and ears, nostrils, and lips. And at the Great Entrance, the Candidate for Holy Orders walketh behind all the clergy. Then the Bishop saith:

And may the mercy of the great God, and of our Saviour Jesus Christ, be with you all. (*See Liturgy, page* 79.)

And after the Exclamation he is led into the Sanctuary by the Sub-Deacons, according to the rubric, and having received the Bishop's blessing, he taketh his stand with the Sub-Deacons. (2)

THE FORM WHICH IS USED AT THE ORDINATION OF A DEACON *

After the Bishop hath said: (See the Liturgy, page 111.)

And may the mercy of the great God, and of our Saviour Jesus Christ, be with you all:

The Sub-Deacons bring the Bishop's pontifical seat and place it in front, and some-what toward the left side of the Holy Altar, that he may not turn his back upon the Holy Things. And the Bishop seateth himself thereon; and two Sub-Deacons take him who is to receive the Laying-on of Hands from the middle of the Church, having him between them, and each laying one hand upon his neck, and holding him by the hands with the other: and they bow him down as low as possible. And one Deacon in the Sanctuary saith:

Command.

And leading him forward a little, they bow him down again. And another Deacon saith:

Command (3).

And thereupon they draw near to the Holy Door, bowing him down before the Bishop. Then the Proto-Deacon saith:

Command, Most Reverend Master.

Then the Sub-Deacons leave him who is to receive Ordination at the Holy Door: whereupon two others, a Proto-Deacon and a Deacon, take him, the one by the right hand, the other by the left; and he boweth before the Bishop. Then the Bishop signeth him with his hand in the form of a cross, and they walk round the Holy Altar, (4) they that lead him and the rest, singing:

O holy Martyrs, who fought the good fight and have received your crowns: Entreat ye the Lord that our souls may be saved.

Then those who are without the Sanctuary sing the same, once. And he who is to receive the Laying-on of Hands kisseth the four corners of the Holy Altar, and the hand and knee of the Bishop. (5)

Then they compass about the Altar again, singing:

Glory to thee, O Christ-God, the Apostles' boast, the Martyrs' joy, whose preaching was the consubstantial Trinity.

And the Choir without singeth the same, once. And again he who is to receive Ordination kisseth the Holy Altar, and the epigonation and hand of the Bishop. Then they compass about the Altar again, singing:

Rejoice, O Isaiah! A Virgin is with child, and shall bear a Son, Emmanuel, both God and man; and Orient is his name; whom magnifying we call the Virgin blessed.

* See Appendix B, VIII (2).

And they do according to the Ritual.   And those without sing the same.

Then the Bishop riseth, and the pontifical chair is removed; and he who is to receive the laying-on of hands goeth to the right side of the Bishop, and boweth down before the Holy Altar, thrice, saying:

O God, have mercy upon me, a sinner.

And bending the right knee (6) he layeth his palms upon the Holy Altar, in the form of a cross, and placeth his brow between his hands on the Holy Altar.   Then the Bishop layeth the end of his stole upon his head, and (7) blesseth him, thrice, upon the head, and when the Proto-Deacon, or the Deacon, hath said:

Let us attend:

The Bishop, laying his hand on the Candidate's head, saith, aloud, in the hearing of all those who are in the Church:

The grace divine, which always healeth that which is infirm, and completeth that which is wanting, elevateth, through the laying-on of hands, N., the most devout Sub-Deacon, to be a Deacon: Wherefore, let us pray for him, that the grace of the all-holy Spirit may come upon him.

Then the Priests in the Sanctuary, on the right side, chant: Lord, have mercy. *(Thrice.) Likewise, those on the left:* Lord, have mercy. *(Thrice.) And the singers without in the right and left Choirs:* Kyrie eleison *(thrice, slowly), while the Bishop reciteth this*

The Proto-Deacon having said, in a low voice:

Let us pray to the Lord.

And the Bishop blesseth, thrice, the head of him that is receiving Ordination.

Prayer.

O Lord our God, who by thy foreknowledge dost send down the fulness of the Holy Spirit upon whose who are ordained by thine inscrutable power to be thy servitors, and to administer thy spotless Sacraments: ·Do thou, the same Sovereign Master, preserve also this man, whom thou hast been pleased to ordain, through me, by the Laying-on of Hands, to the service of the Diaconate, in all soberness of life, holding the mystery of the faith in a pure conscience.   Vouchsafe unto him the grace which thou didst grant unto Stephen, thy first Martyr, whom, also, thou didst call to be the first in the work of thy ministry; and make him worthy to administer after thy pleasure the degree which it hath seemed good to thee to confer upon him.   For they who minister well prepare for themselves a good degree.   And manifest him as wholly thy servant.

Secretly.

For thine are the kingdom and the power and the glory, of the Father, and of the Son, and of the Holy Spirit, now, and ever, and unto ages of ages.   Amen.

Then the Proto-Deacon saith softly, in a low voice:

In peace let us pray to the Lord.

Choir. Lord, have mercy.

For the peace that is from above, and for the salvation of our souls: ℟

For the peace of the whole world; for the welfare of God's holy Churches, and for the union of all: ℟

For our Bishop N., of N., and for his priesthood, succour, maintenance, peace, health and salvation; and for the work of his hands: ℟

For the servant of God, N., who hath now received the Laying-on of Hands to be a Deacon, and for his salvation: ℟

That the God who loveth mankind will vouchsafe unto him a pure and blameless Diaconate: ℟

For our most God-fearing Ruler, N., and for all his Council and his Army: ℟

For this city, and for every city and land; and for those who with faith dwell therein: ℟

That he will deliver us from all tribulation, wrath, and necessity: ℟

let us pray to the Lord.

Choir. Lord, have mercy.

And the Bishop, keeping his hand on the head of him who is receiving Holy Orders, prayeth the while:

O God our Saviour, who by thine incorruptible voice didst appoint unto thine Apostles the law of the Diaconate, and didst manifest the first Martyr, Stephen, to be of the same; and didst proclaim him the first who should exercise the office of a Deacon, as it is written in thy Holy Gospel: Whosoever desireth to be first among you, let him be your servant: Do thou, O Master of all men, fill also this thy servant, whom thou hast graciously permitted to enter upon the ministry of a Deacon, with all faith, and love, and power, and holiness, through the inspiration of thy holy and life-giving Spirit; for not through the Laying-on of my hands, but through the visitation of thy rich bounties, is grace bestowed upon thy worthy ones: That he, being devoid of all sin, may stand blameless before thee in the terrible Day of thy Judgment, and receive the unfailing reward of thy promise.

Secretly.

Succour us, save us, have mercy upon us, and keep us, O God, by thy grace.

Choir. Lord, have mercy.

Calling to remembrance our most holy, all-undefiled, most blessed and glorious Lady, the Birth-giver of God and ever-virgin Mary, with all the Saints, let us commend ourselves, and each other, and all our life unto Christ our God.

Choir. To thee, O God.

Exclamation.

The Bishop. For thou art our God, and unto thee do we ascribe glory, to the Father, and to the Son, and to the Holy Spirit, now, and ever, and unto ages of ages.

Choir. Amen.

Then they raise the Candidate, and loose his stole, which is bound cross-wise.   And taking the stole, the Bishop layeth it on his left shoulder, saying in a loud voice:

Axios! (Worthy!) (8)

And they within the Sanctuary sing, thrice:

Axios.

And likewise they without, in both Choirs, sing, thrice:

Axios.

Then the gauntlets are given to him, and the Bishop saith:

Axios.

And they within the Sanctuary, and they without, sing the same, as before.

Then the sacramental fan is given to him, and the Bishop saith:

Axios.

And they who are within, and without, the Sanctuary, sing, as before.   And he kisseth the Bishop on the shoulder, and placeth himself at the Altar, and fanneth the Holy Gifts.

THE OFFICE USED AT THE ELEVATION OF AN ARCHDEACON, OR A PROTO–DEACON

He that is to be raised to the Archdiaconate is led, by a Proto-Deacon and a Deacon, to the Reverend Bishop, in the middle of the Church, where the Bishop standeth, at the time when the Lesser Entrance with the book of the Holy Gospels is made. (See page 84.) And he boweth, thrice, before the Bishop, even to his girdle, and bendeth his head. Then the Bishop, sitting, maketh the sign of the cross, thrice, with his hand, upon his head; and rising, layeth his hand upon his head. And when the Deacon hath said:

Let us pray to the Lord:

The Bishop reciteth the following Prayer:

O Master, Lord our God, who hast bestowed upon our race the Archdeaconship, granting, through thine unspeakable providence, that they who are endued therewith may order and serve thy Divine Mysteries as lesser ministers: Do thou, the same Lord, endue with this grace of the Archdeaconship this thy servant, N., and adorn him with thine integrity, to stand at the head of the Deacons of thy people, and to be an example of good to those who are under him. Cause him to attain unto a ripe old age, that he may magnify thy glorious Name, of the Father, and of the Son, and of the Holy Spirit, now, and ever, and unto ages of ages. Amen.

Then the Bishop maketh the sign of the cross upon his head, saying:

Blessed is the Lord. Lo, the servant of God, N., becometh an Archdeacon (*or* a Proto-Deacon): In the Name of the Father, and of the Son, and of the Holy Spirit.

And laying his hand upon the head of him that is elevated, the Bishop exclaimeth:
Axios! (*Thrice.*) *

And the Choir singeth, thrice:

Axios.

And then they enter the Sanctuary, according to the Ritual.

* See Appendix B, VIII (8).

THE FORM AND MANNER OF ORDAINING A PRIEST *

After the Cherubimic Hymn hath been finished (see page 98), he who is to be ordained Priest is led by an Archdeacon, or another Deacon, in the same manner, and after the same exclamations of Command and Command, as at the ordination of a Deacon, through the Holy Door, to the Holy Altar, before the Bishop, at the right hand side thereof. The Bishop signeth him with his hand, in the form of a cross: and he is led thrice round the Altar, as is described in the OFFICE FOR MAKING A DEACON, *(see page 312) while all within the Sanctuary sing the following Hymns:*

O holy Martyrs, who fought the good fight and have received your crowns: Entreat ye the Lord that our souls may be saved.

Glory to thee, O Christ-God, the Apostles' boast, the Martyrs' joy, whose preaching was the consubstantial Trinity.

Rejoice, O Isaiah! A Virgin is with child, and shall bear a Son, Emmanuel, both God and man: and Orient is his name; whom magnifying we call the Virgin blessed.

Then he who is to be ordained bendeth both knees, and placeth his brow between his palms crossed upon the Holy Altar, and the Bishop layeth the end of his stole upon the head of him who is to receive the Laying-on of Hands, and blesseth him, thrice, upon the head. And when the principal Priest hath said:

Let us attend.

The Bishop, laying his hand upon his head, pronounceth, aloud, in the hearing of all those who stand in the Church:

The grace divine, which always healeth that which is infirm, and completeth (1) that which is wanting, elevateth through the laying-on of hands, N., the most devout Deacon, to be a Priest. Wherefore, let us pray for him, that the grace of the all-holy Spirit may come upon him.

Then the Proto-Deacon saith in a low voice:

Let us pray to the Lord.

And the Priests within the Sanctuary sing: Lord, have mercy, thrice on the right side, and again thrice on the left side.

And the Singers without, in the right and left Choirs, sing: Kyrie eleison (*thrice, slowly*), *while the Bishop reciteth the Prayer.*

And the Bishop, again blessing him thrice, reciteth, secretly, *the following Prayer:*

O God, who hast no beginning and no ending; who art older than every created thing; who crownest with the name of Presbyter those whom thou deemest worthy to serve the word of thy truth in the divine ministry of this degree: Do thou, the same Lord of all men, deign to preserve in pureness of life and in unswerv-

Secretly.

* Appendix B, VIII (10).

ing faith this man also, upon whom, through me, thou hast graciously been pleased to lay hands.   Be favourably pleased to grant unto him the great grace of thy Holy Spirit, and make him wholly thy servant, in all things acceptable unto thee, and worthily exercising the great honours of the priesthood which thou hast conferred upon him by thy prescient power.

Secretly.

Exclamation.

For thine is the majesty, and thine are the kingdom and the power and the glory, of the Father, and of the Son, and of the Holy Spirit, now, and ever, and unto ages of ages.

Choir. Amen.

And the Proto-Deacon saith, in a low voice:

Let us pray to the Lord.

Then the Priest, in a low voice, reciteth the LITANY OF PEACE.

In peace let us pray to the Lord.

Choir. Lord, have mercy.

For the peace that is from above, and for the salvation of our souls: R̶

For the peace of the whole world; for the welfare of God's holy Churches, and for the union of all: R̶

For our Bishop, N. of N., his priesthood, succour, maintenance, peace, health and salvation; and for the works of his hands: R̶

For the servant of God, N., who now hath received the Laying-on of Hands to the Priesthood, and for his salvation: R̶

That the God who loveth mankind will vouchsafe unto him a pure and blameless ministry: R̶

... let us pray to the Lord. Choir. Lord, have mercy.

And the Bishop, blessing, thrice, him who is receiving Ordination, keepeth his hand on the Candidate's head, and prayeth, secretly:

O God great in might and inscrutable in wisdom, marvellous in counsel above the sons of men: Do thou, the same Lord, fill with the gift of thy Holy Spirit this man whom it hath pleased thee to advance to the degree of Priest; that he may be worthy to stand in innocency before thine Altar; to proclaim the Gospel of thy kingdom; to minister the word of thy truth; to offer unto thee spiritual gifts and sacrifices; to renew thy people through the laver of regeneration.   That when he shall go to meet thee, at the Second Coming of our great God and Saviour, Jesus Christ, thine Only-begotten Son, he may receive the reward of a good steward in the degree committed unto him, through the plenitude of thy goodness.

Secretly.

For our most God-fearing Ruler, N., and for all his Council and his Army, R̶

For this city; and for every city and land; and for those who with faith dwell therein: R̶

Succour us, save us, have mercy upon us, and keep us, O God, by thy grace.

Choir. Lord, have mercy.

Calling to remembrance our most holy, all-undefiled, most blessed and glorious Lady, the Birth-giver of God and ever-virgin Mary, with all the Saints, let us commend ourselves, and each other, and all our life unto Christ our God.

Choir. To thee, O Lord.

Exclamation.

Bishop. For blessed and glorified is thine all-holy and majestic Name, of the Father, and of the Son, and of the Holy Spirit, now, and ever, and unto ages of ages.

Choir. Amen.

Then they raise up the Candidate, and bring the Priest's stole; and taking the Deacon's stole from him that hath received the Laying-on of Hands, the Bishop endueth him with the priestly stole, after he hath blessed it; and he that receiveth it kisseth it, and the hand of the Bishop. And the Bishop layeth it about his neck, saying, loudly:

Axios! (Worthy!)

And they within the Sanctuary sing the same:

Axios. (*Thrice.*)

And the Singers without, in both Choirs, sing also:

Axios. (*Thrice.*)

The Bishop then, in like manner, endueth him with the zone, and he kisseth it, and the hand of the Bishop, and girdeth himself. And the Bishop saith:

Axios. (8)

And they within the Sanctuary and they without do the same.

Thus they do also with the chasuble: and with the Service-Book, which is given to him as his guide in the holy ministry; for he saith not from memory the Prayers, but readeth them.

Then they sing as usual, and the Priest who hath received the Laying-on of Hands goeth forth, after he hath kissed the Bishop's stole and his hand, and kisseth the Archimandrites, and all his fellow-clergy, on the shoulder; and taketh his place among the Priests.

THE FORM AND MANNER OF MAKING AN ARCHPRIEST

He who is to be advanced to the rank of Archpriest is conducted by a Proto-Deacon, or by two Deacons, to the Right Reverend Bishop, in the middle of the Church, at the time when the Little Entrance with the book of the Holy Gospels is made. He boweth before the Bishop, even to the girdle, thrice, and bendeth his head. And the Bishop, as he sitteth, signeth him, thrice, upon the head, in cross-form, with his hand. Then, rising, he layeth his hand upon the Priest's head. And after the Proto-Deacon hath said:

Let us pray to the Lord:

The Bishop saith the following Prayer:

O Master, Lord Jesus Christ, our God, who hast bestowed the priesthood upon our race, and hast endued us with the grace of this gift and honour, and hast appointed us who are duly devout to exercise command over the members of the Priesthood, and the other servitors in lesser degree of thy Mysteries: Endue thou now, also, with thy grace, our brother N., and adorn him with integrity; that he may stand at the head of the Priests of thy people. And enable him to set a good example to those who are with him; and graciously grant that he may attain, in piety and veneration, unto a good old age; and have mercy upon us all, inasmuch as thou art a good God. For thou art the bestower of wisdom; and unto thee doth all creation sing praises unto ages of ages.

Then the Bishop signeth him upon the head with the sign of the cross, saying:

Blessed is the Lord. Lo, the servant of God, N., is made an Archpriest of God's holy Church, N.: In the Name of the Father, and of the Son, and of the Holy Spirit.

Then, laying his hand upon the Priest's head, the Bishop exclaimeth:

Axios! *(Thrice.)** —— *Choir.* Axios! *(Thrice.)*

Then they place the Archpriest with the other clergy, according to their rank, and enter the Sanctuary through the Holy Door, and minister with the Clergy.

* Appendix B, VIII (8).

THE OFFICE THAT IS USED AT THE INSTITU-
TION OF AN ABBOT

He who is to be elevated to the rank of Abbot is led by a Proto-Deacon, or by two Dea-
cons, to the Bishop, in the middle of the Church, where the Bishop standeth, at the
time of the Lesser Entrance with the book of the Holy Gospels (see page 84), if so be
that the Bishop himself officiate at the Liturgy. But if not, then they bring to the
Bishop his priestly stole, gauntlets and omofór and he vesteth himself where he
standeth. He who is to be advanced to the rank of Abbot is brought to his appointed
place, and boweth low to the Bishop, even to his girdle, thrice, and bendeth his head.
And the Bishop, sitting, signeth his head, thrice, with his hand, in the form of a
cross. And rising, he layeth his hand upon his head; and when the Proto-Deacon
hath said:

Let us pray to the Lord:

The Bishop reciteth the following Prayer:

O God, who ever exercisest divine foresight concerning the salvation
of men, and hast gathered into one this reason-endowed flock: Do thou,
O Master of all, through thy boundless love for mankind, preserve the
same spotless, ever keeping thy commandments, that not one sheep perish
therefrom, or be devoured by the wolf. And make this thy servant, whom
thou hast been graciously pleased to set over it as Abbot, worthy of thy
goodness; and adorn him with all virtues, that through his own deeds he
may offer a good example to those who are subject unto him; that they,
being moved to emulate his blameless life, may, with him, stand uncondemned before thy dread Judgment Seat.

For thine is the kingdom, and the power and the glory, of the Father,
and of the Son, and of the Holy Spirit, now, and ever, and unto ages of
ages.

Choir. Amen.

Bishop. Peace be with you all.

Choir. And with thy spirit.

Proto-Deacon. Bow your heads unto the Lord.

Choir. To thee, O Lord.

Then the Bishop saith, secretly, *the following Prayer:*

Incline thine ear, O Lord, and hear our prayers; and cause this
thy servant, the Abbot of this venerable habitation, to be a wise and
faithful steward of the reason-endowed flock which, through thy
grace, hath been entrusted unto him, working thy will in all things,
and becoming worthy of thy heavenly kingdom.

Through the grace, and bounties, and love towards mankind of thine
Only-begotten Son, with whom thou art blessed, together with thine
all-holy, and good, and life-giving Spirit, now, and ever, and unto
ages of ages. Amen.

Secretly.

Then the Proto-Deacon saith, loudly:

Command, Master.

And the Bishop, also, with a loud voice:

The grace of the all-holy Spirit, at the hands of our humble person, promoteth thee to be Abbot of the honourable habitation of our Lord and God, and Saviour, Jesus Christ, N. (*if the Temple be dedicated to him*); *or* of our most holy Sovereign Lady, the Mother of our Lord, N. (if the *Temple be dedicated to her*); *or* of Saint N. (*if the Temple be dedicated to a Saint*).

Then, laying his hand upon his head, the Bishop exclaimeth:

Axios!   (*Thrice.*)

And the Choir singeth:

Axios.   (*Thrice.*)

Then he who hath been invested with the office of Abbot kisseth the pall * of the Bishop on the right, and on the left shoulder: and being led away, he taketh his place with the other Abbots, according to their rank: and they enter the Sanctuary through the Holy Door; and he ministereth with the other clergy, according to the Ritual.

* See Appendix B, VIII (11).

THE OFFICE USED AT THE ELEVATION OF AN ARCHIMANDRITE

He who is to be installed as Archimandrite is led by the Proto-Deacon, or by two Deacons, to the Bishop, in the middle of the Church, where the Bishop standeth, at the time of the Little Entrance with the book of the Holy Gospels (see page 84), if the Bishop himself be the celebrant at the Divine Liturgy. But if not, then they bring to the Bishop his priestly stole, his gauntlets, and his pall, and he vesteth himself where he standeth. He who is to be installed as Archimandrite, being brought to his appointed place, boweth before the Bishop, even to his girdle, and bendeth his head. And the Bishop, sitting, maketh thrice, with his hand, the sign of the cross over his head. And if the Candidate for the rank of Archimandrite be already an Abbot, the Prayers at the Elevation of an Abbot are not used, and the Proto-Deacon saith only, aloud:

Command, Master:

And the Bishop saith, in a loud voice:

The grace of the all-holy Spirit, through our humility promoteth thee to be Archimandrite of the venerable habitation of our Lord, and God, and Saviour, Jesus Christ; *or* of our most holy Lady, the Birth-giver of God (*if the Temple be dedicated to her*); *or* of Saint N. (*if it be dedicated to a Saint*).

Then, laying his hand upon the head of him who is being elevated, the Bishop exclaimeth:

Axios! (*Thrice.*) *

Choir. Axios. (*Thrice.*)

And if a mitre is to be conferred upon an Archimandrite, then, after the Little Entrance from the Sanctuary, with the book of the Holy Gospels, the Archimandrite is led to the Bishop. And the Bishop saith no prayer, but only blesseth the Archimandrite with his hand. And the Archimandrite kisseth the hand of the Bishop, and the mitre; and the mitre is then put upon the Archimandrite. Then he is led away, and placed with the other Archimandrites and Abbots, according to his rank. And they enter the Sanctuary through the Holy Door, and minister with the Clergy who are celebrating, according to the Ritual.

And at the end of the Divine Liturgy the Bishop, giving the Archimandrite (or Abbot) his pastoral staff, saith:

Take this staff and with it establish and rule thy flock: seeing that thou must answer therefor to our Lord God, on the Day of Judgment.

Then the Bishop exhorteth him and his flock to the observance of their respective duties.

* See Appendix B, VIII (8).

THE ORDER OF ELECTING AND CONSECRATING A BISHOP *

When the time is come for electing a Bishop to a vacant Episcopal Throne, the Most Holy Synod taketh counsel as to who knoweth of a fitting incumbent of such a dignity; and when such person hath been selected, the Nomination of him who is designated to the Bishopric is made after the following manner:

When the time is come, the Bishops and Candidate-elect are summoned to the Most Holy Synod; and when they are assembled, the Presiding Bishop putteth on his priestly stole.

Then announcement is made to the Bishop-elect by the Chief Secretary in this wise:

Honourable Father Archimandrite (*or* Hiero-Monk), N.: Our Ruler, by an edict signed with his name, commandeth, and the Most Holy Synod assenteth thereto, that your Holiness shall be the Bishop of the God-saved cities, NN.

And thereto the Bishop-elect maketh answer:

Seeing that our Ruler, N., hath commanded my preferment, and that the Most Holy Governing Synod hath judged me worthy of this ministry, I return thanks, and accept, and say nothing contrary thereto.

Then the Presiding Bishop beginneth:

Blessed is our God always, now, and ever, and unto ages of ages.
Choir. Amen.

The others say:

O heavenly King, the Comforter, Spirit of Truth, who art in all places and fillest all things; Treasury of good things and Giver of life: Come, and take up thine abode in us, and cleanse us from every stain; and save our souls, O Good One.

O Holy God, Holy Mighty, Holy Immortal One, have mercy upon us. (*Thrice.*)

Glory to the Father, and to the Son, and to the Holy Spirit, now, and ever, and unto ages of ages.   Amen.

Our Father, who art in heaven, Hallowed be thy Name. Thy kingdom come. Thy will be done on earth, As it is in heaven. Give us this day our daily bread. And forgive us our trespasses, As we forgive those who trespass against us. And lead us not into temptation; But deliver us from the Evil One:

The Presiding Bishop. For thine is the kingdom and the power, and the glory, of the Father, and of the Son, and of the Holy Spirit, now, and ever, and unto ages of ages. Amen.

* Appendix B, VIII.

The others recite the following Hymn (Tropár):

Blessed art thou, O Christ-God, who hast revealed the fishers most wise, sending down upon them thy Holy Spirit, and thereby catching the universe as in a net.   Glory to thee, O thou who lovest mankind.

Glory to the Father, and to the Son, and to the Holy Spirit, now, and ever, and unto ages of ages.   Amen.

And the Collect-Hymn (Kondák):

When the Most High descended confounding the tongues, he dispersed abroad the nations: but when he distributed the tongues of fire, he called all men unto unity.   Wherefore, with one accord, we glorify the all-holy Spirit.

Then the Presiding Bishop reciteth this Litany:

Have mercy upon us, O God, according to thy great mercy, we beseech thee: hearken, and have mercy. ℞

Furthermore we pray for our most God-fearing Ruler, N.; and for all the Authorities. ℞

Furthermore we pray for the Most Holy Synod. ℞

Furthermore we pray for the all-honourable Archimandrite (*or* Hiero-Monk), N., the newly-elected Bishop of the God-saved cities, NN. ℞

Furthermore we pray for all the brotherhood, and for all Orthodox Christians. ℞

Choir. Lord, have mercy. (Thrice.)

Exclamation.

For thou art a merciful God, who lovest mankind, and unto thee do we ascribe glory, to the Father, and to the Son, and to the Holy Spirit, now, and ever, and unto ages of ages.

Choir. Amen.

Deacon. Wisdom!

Choir. More honourable than the Cherubim, and beyond compare more glorious than the Seraphim, thou who without defilement barest God the Word, true Birth-giver of God, we magnify thee.

Glory to the Father, and to the Son, and to the Holy Spirit, now, and ever, and unto ages of ages.   Amen.

Lord, have mercy.   (*Thrice.*)

Bless, Master.

And the BENEDICTION.

May he who, in the form of tongues of fire, sent down from heaven the Holy Spirit upon his Disciples and Apostles, Christ our true God; through the prayers of his all-pure Mother, of the honourable, glorious Prophet, the Forerunner and Baptist, John, and of Saint N. (*whose day it is*), and of all Saints, have mercy upon us and save us, for he is good and loveth man.

Then the Choir chanteth MANY YEARS *to the most God-fearing Ruler of the Land, (to the Most Blessed Patriarch): to the Most Holy Synod, and to the Bishop-elect. (See page 540.)*

And when this is finished, the Chief Bishop riseth and blesseth the Bishop-elect with the cross, and sprinkleth him with holy water, and each one of them then departeth to his own abode.

CONSECRATION

On the day when the Consecration is to take place, the bells are pealed for the Vigil Service, according to the Ritual: and at the Ninth Theme-Song of the Canon the great bell peals.

And the Bishops and others assemble in the Cathedral Church, and having vested themselves according to the Ritual, they ascend the tribune, preceded by the Archimandrite, the Abbot, and the Archpriest, and all the Clergy.

And in the middle of the Church, near the tribune, on the ecclesiastical carpet, there is placed the figure of a one-headed eagle, having its wings outspread, standing upright on its feet; and under its feet is a city with walls and towers, and the eagle, as it were, treading upon the towers thereof. And this is guarded so that no one may step upon the eagle. (12)

Then the Bishops command the Archpriest and the Proto-Deacon to summon him who is to receive consecration: and they, doing reverence and kissing the hands of the Bishops, take the Candidate for consecration, who is in the Sanctuary, clad in all the vestments of a Priest, and lead him upon the tail of the eagle; and he maketh three reverences. The Proto-Deacon first leadeth the Bishop-elect, proclaiming and saying, in an audible voice, these things following:

The most God-beloved, elect and confirmed Archimandrite (*or* Hiero-Monk), N., is led forth for consecration to the Bishopric of the God-saved city, N. (cities *NN.*).

And to the Bishop-elect, holding in his hands the holy writing of the Orthodox faith, the Chief Bishop saith:

Wherefore art thou come, and what dost thou ask of our meekness?

The Bishop-elect maketh answer, saying:

The laying-on of hands, unto the grace of the Bishop's office, Most Reverend Sirs.

And the Bishop questioneth him, saying:

And how believest thou?

And the Bishop-elect reciteth, aloud, THE SYMBOL OF THE FAITH:

I believe in one God the Father Almighty, Maker of heaven and earth, And of all things visible and invisible:

And in one Lord Jesus Christ, the Only-begotten Son of God, begotten of his Father before all worlds; Light of Light, Very God of very God; Begotten, not made; Being of one Essence with the Father; By whom all things were made; Who, for us men, and for our salvation, came down from heaven, And was incarnate by the Holy Ghost of the Virgin Mary, And was made man. And was crucified also for us under Pontius Pilate, and suffered and was buried. And the third day he rose again, according to the Scriptures. And ascended into heaven, And sitteth on the right hand of the Father. And he shall come again with glory to judge both the quick and the dead; Whose kingdom shall have no end.

And in the Holy Ghost, the Lord, the Giver of Life, Who proceedeth from the Father, Who with the Father and the Son together is worshipped and glorified, Who spake by the Prophets. In one Holy Catholic and Apostolic Church. I acknowledge one Baptism for the remission of sins. I look for the resurrection of the dead, And the Life of the world to come Amen.

And when he hath said this, the Bishop blesseth him with the sign of the cross, and saith:

The grace of God the Father, and of our Lord Jesus Christ, and of the Holy Spirit, be with thee.

The Bishop-elect is then led to the middle of the eagle, the Proto-Deacon proclaiming his being led, as was explained above:

The most God-beloved . . . is led . . . *and so forth, as before.*

And when the Bishop-elect hath been placed upon the centre of the eagle, the Chief Bishop directeth his words to him, and saith:

Reveal unto us more particularly how thou believest concerning the properties of the three Persons of the ineffable Godhead, and concerning the Incarnation of the Person of the Son and Word of God

And the Bishop-elect immediately readeth, aloud, *the* SECOND CONFESSION OF FAITH, *as followeth:*

I believe in one God, the Father Almighty, Maker of heaven and earth, and of all things visible and invisible; For he is without beginning, unbegotten, and without cause, but is himself the natural beginning and cause of the Son, and of the Spirit. And I believe in his Only-begotten Son, without mutation and without time begotten of him, being of one Essence with Him by whom all things were made. And I believe in the Holy Spirit, who proceedeth from the same Father, and with him is glorified as coeternal, being of one Essence with him, and equal in glory, and enthroned together with him, the Author of creation. I believe that one of the same super-substantial and life-giving Trinity, the Only-begotten Word, came down from heaven, for us men, and for our salvation, and was incarnate by the Holy Spirit of the Virgin Mary, and was made man; that is to say, was made perfect man, yet remaining God, and in nowise changing his divine essence by his participation in the flesh, neither being transmuted into anything else: but without mutation assuming man's nature, he therein endured suffering and death, being free in his divine nature from every suffering. And on the third day he rose again from the dead; and ascended into heaven, and sitteth on the right hand of his God and Father. And I believe those traditions and narrations concerning the one Catholic and Apostolic Church which we have received from

God and the men of God. I acknowledge one Baptism for the remission of sins. I look for the Resurrection of the dead, and the life of the world to come. Furthermore I confess the one Person, the Word made flesh; and I believe and proclaim that Christ is one and the same in two natures after his incarnation, preserving those things which were in them and from them. Therefore, also, I adore two wills, in that each nature retaineth its own special will and its own action. I reverence, relatively, but not in the way of worship, the images divine and reverence-worthy of Christ himself, and of the all-undefiled Mother of God, and of all the Saints, addressing to their originals the honour shown to them. I reject as ill-advised those who think otherwise. And I literally and truly confess our Sovereign Lady, Mary the Birth-giver of God, as having borne in the flesh one of the Trinity, even Christ our God. And may the same be my helper, protector, and defender all the days of my life. Amen.

And immediately the Bishop saith, blessing in the form of a cross him who is receiving Consecration:

The grace of the Holy Spirit be with thee, enlightening, strengthening and endowing thee with wisdom all the days of thy life.

Then the Bishop-elect is led upon the head of the eagle, and after the Proto-Deacon hath proclaimed his preferment, as above described, and hath placed him on the head of the eagle, the Bishop saith to him:

Declare unto us, also, what thou thinkest concerning the Canons of the holy Apostles and the holy Fathers, and the traditions and regulations of the Church.

And the Bishop-elect immediately readeth, in a loud voice, the THIRD CONFESSION OF FAITH:

In this my confession of the holy faith, I promise to observe the Canons of the holy Apostles, and of the Seven Œcumenical Councils, and of the pious Provincial Councils, the traditions of the Church, and the decrees, orders and regulations of the Holy Fathers. And all things whatsoever they have accepted I also accept; and whatsoever things they have rejected those will I also reject.

I promise also to preserve the peace of the Church, and firmly to hold and zealously to teach the people entrusted to me, and not to devise anything whatsoever which is contrary to the Orthodox Catholic Christian faith of the East all the days of my life; and that I will, in all things, follow and always obey the Most Blessed Patriarch and the Most Holy Synod; and to be, in all things, of one mind with the Most Blessed Patriarch and with the Most Reverend Metropolitans, Archbishops and Bishops, my brethren, and conjointly with them submissive to the divine law, and the sacred rules of the Holy Apostles and Holy Fathers; and with all sincerity to cherish towards them spiritual affection: and to regard them as brethren.

And I promise to rule the flock committed unto me in the fear of God and in devoutness of life; and with all diligent heed to guard it against all heresies of doctrine.

And I also confess, in this my written profession of faith, that neither by the promise nor by the gift of gold or of silver am I come to this ministry; but, on the contrary, I have received it by the election of the Most Holy Synod.

And herewith I promise also to do nothing through constraint, whether coerced by powerful persons, or by a multitude of the people, even though they should command me, under pain of death, to do something contrary to divine and holy laws: nor to celebrate the Divine Liturgy in another diocese than my own, nor to exercise any other priestly function without the permission of the Bishop of that diocese; and that I will not ordain either a Priest, or a Deacon, or any other ecclesiastic in another's diocese, nor receive such into my diocese without letters of dismissal from their own Bishops.

I will deal with the opponents of the Holy Church with reasonableness, uprightness and gentleness, according to the Apostle Paul; And the servant of the Lord must not strive, but be gentle unto all men, apt to teach, forbearing, in meekness instructing those who oppose themselves; if God, peradventure, will give them repentance to the acknowledging of the truth.

I promise to visit and watch over the flock now confided to me, after the manner of the Apostles, whether they remain true to the faith, and in the exercise of good works, more especially the Priests; and to inspect with diligence, and to exhort and inhibit, that there may be no schisms, superstitions and impious veneration, and that no customs contrary to Christian piety and good morals may injure Christian conduct.

And all those things, my bounden duty, which I have this day promised in word, I also promise to perform in deed unto my uttermost breath, for the sake of the covenanted good things to come. And may God, who seeth the heart, be the witness to my vow. And may our Saviour himself be my helper, in my sincere and zealous government and my performance thereof; and unto Him, together with the Father and the Holy Spirit, be glory and dominion, honour and worship, now, and ever, and unto ages of ages. Amen.

And when this is completed, the Presiding Bishop, blessing him, saith:

The grace of the Holy Spirit, through my humility, exalteth thee, most God-beloved Archimandrite (*or* Hiero-Monk), N., to be the Bishop-elect of the God-saved cities, NN.

And the Bishop-elect maketh three reverences to the Presiding Bishop; and the Proto-Deacon leadeth him to the Bishops. And he, delivering to the same the written statement of his faith and his promise, kisseth their right hands.

And thus he descendeth from the tribune (amvón), and maketh a reverence. And the Presiding Bishop, signing him with his hand, in the form of a cross, saith:

The grace of the Most Holy Spirit be with thee.

And they lead him upon the eagle, and the Choir chanteth MANY YEARS *to the Ruler of the Land, to the Synod, and to the newly-elected Bishop.*

(The Divine Liturgy is then begun, the Bishop-elect standing until his Consecration (or Ordination) in the Deacon's chapel (Diakónnik), or the chapel on the south of the Altar, fully vested as a Priest).

And after the THRICE-HOLY *hath been sung,* (13) *he who is to receive Ordination is led forth by the Archpriest and the Proto-Deacon, in front of the Holy Door (see page 87); and is received by the Bishops in the holy Sanctuary, before the Holy Altar. And he straightway kneeleth down on both knees, in the midst of the Bishops. And they take the book of the Holy Gospels, and opening it, they lay it, with the writing downward, upon his head, holding it here and there.* (14)

Then the Presiding Bishop saith, so that all may hear:

By the election and approbation of the most God-loving Bishops, and of all the consecrated Council,

The grace divine, which always healeth that which is infirm, and completeth that which is wanting, through the laying-on of hands elevateth thee, the most God-loving Archimandrite (*or* Hiero-Monk) N., duly elected, to be the Bishop of the God-saved cities, NN.

Wherefore let us pray for him, that the grace of the all-holy Spirit may come upon him.

And a Priest saith:

Let us pray to the Lord.   (*Thrice.*)

And while the Bishops hold the book of the Holy Gospels, the Presiding Bishop maketh three crosses above the head of him who is being consecrated, blessing him:

In the Name of the Father, and of the Son, and of the Holy Spirit, now, and ever, and unto ages of ages.

And while the Bishops lay their right hands upon his head, the Presiding Bishop saith this Prayer:

O Master, Lord our God, who through thine all-laudable Apostle Paul hast established for us an ordinance of degrees and ranks, unto the service and divine celebration of thine august and all-spotless Mysteries upon thy holy Altar; first, Apostles, secondly, Prophets, thirdly, teachers: Do thou, the same Lord of all, who also hast graciously enabled this chosen person to come under the yoke of the Gospel and the dignity of a Bishop through the laying-on of hands of us, his fellow Bishops here present, strengthen him by the inspiration and power and grace of thy Holy Spirit, as thou didst strengthen thy holy Apostles and Prophets; as thou didst anoint Kings; as thou hast consecrated Bishops: And make his Bishopric to be blameless; and adorning him with all dignity, present thou him holy, that he may be worthy to ask those things which are for the salvation of the people, and that thou mayest give ear unto him. For blessed is thy Name, and glorified thy Kingdom, of the Father, and of the Son, and of the Holy Spirit, now, and ever, and unto ages of ages. Amen.

And after the Amen, *one of the other consecrating Bishops reciteth the following petitions in a low voice, so that only the Prelates there present can hear and respond:*

In peace, let us pray to the Lord.

Lord, have mercy.

For the peace that is from above, and for the salvation of our souls: ℞

For the peace of the whole world; for the welfare of God's holy Churches, and for the union of all: ℞

For the Most Holy Synod, their holiness, succour, maintenance, peace, health and salvation, and for the work of their hands: ℞

For the servant of God, N., now ordained to be a Bishop, and for his salvation: ℞

That our God who loveth mankind will grant him to exercise his episcopal office without stain or blame: ℞

For our most God-fearing Ruler, N., and for all the Authorities; and for all their Council and their Army and Navy: ℞

For this city, and for every city, and for all those who entreat of God aid and protection: ℞

That he will deliver us from all tribulation, wrath and necessity: ℞

Secretly.

Response. let us pray to the Lord. Lord, have mercy.

Succour us, save us, have mercy upon us, and keep us, O God, by thy grace.

Lord, have mercy.

Calling to remembrance our most holy, all-undefiled, most blessed and glorious Lady, the Birth-giver of God and ever-virgin Mary, with all the Saints, let us commend ourselves, and each other, and all our life unto Christ our God.

To thee, O Lord.

And when these things have been said, the Presiding Bishop, who also hath his hand upon the head of him who is receiving Ordination, prayeth thus:

O Lord our God, who, forasmuch as it is impossible for the nature of man to endure the Essence of the Godhead, in thy providence hast instituted for us teachers of like nature with ourselves, to maintain thine Altar, that they may offer unto thee sacrifice and oblation for all thy people; Do thou, the same Lord, make this man also, who hath been proclaimed a steward of the episcopal grace, to be an imitator of thee, the true Shepherd, who didst lay down thy life for thy sheep; to be a leader of the blind, a light to those who are in darkness, a reprover of the unwise, a teacher of the young, a lamp to the world: that, having perfected the souls entrusted unto him in this present life, he may stand unashamed before thy throne, and receive the great reward which thou hast prepared for those who have contended valiantly for the preaching of thy Gospel.

For thine it is to show mercy, and to save us, O our God, and unto thee do we ascribe glory, to the Father, and to the Son, and to the Holy Spirit, now, and ever, and unto ages of ages.   Amen.

And after the Amen *they lay the book of the Holy Gospels upon the Altar.   And the Presiding Bishop then putteth the dalmatic (sákkos) and the other episcopal vestments upon him who hath received Consecration, saying:*

Axios! (15)

And the Choir singeth the same.

Then the Bishops kiss him who hath received consecration; and when the customary thanksgivings have been said, the Presiding Bishop proclaimeth the Peace *before the Epistle.   And the Bishops go to the episcopal seats in the apse, and sit there.*

And the celebration of the Divine Liturgy is continued.

And when it is finished, they unvest in the holy Sanctuary, and lead the newly-consecrated Bishop to the Presiding Bishop, who putteth upon him the cassock of a Bishop; also the pectoral holy image, the mantle and cowl, blessing him with his hand as he doeth it; and he giveth him the rosary.   Then the Bishops come forth from the Sanctuary, and ascend the dais (káthedra) which hath been prepared; and the Archpriest and the Proto-Deacon lead him who hath received Consecration upon the dais; and the Presiding Bishop delivereth to him the pastoral staff (pósokh), with an EXHORTATION.

Right Reverend Bishop N.: . . .

Or, when the Bishop delivereth the staff, he useth this brief Exhortation:

Receive thou the pastoral staff, that thou mayest feed the flock of Christ entrusted unto thee: and be thou a staff and support unto those who are obedient.   But lead thou the disobedient and the wayward unto correction, unto gentleness, and unto obedience; and they shall continue in due submission.

Then they depart to their abodes, the Archpriest and the Proto-Deacon escorting the newly-ordained Bishop to his home.

THE OFFICE OF HOLY UNCTION, SUNG BY SEVEN PRIESTS ASSEMBLED IN A CHURCH, OR IN A HOUSE *

(THE ORDER FOR THE VISITATION OF THE SICK)

A small table is prepared, upon which is set a vessel containing wheat: and on the wheat an empty shrine-lamp. And round about are set seven wands, wrapped with cotton for the Anointing, and thrust into the wheat: and the book of the Holy Gospels lieth there also: and tapers (2) are given to all the Priests. These stand round about the table vested in their chasubles. Then the first Priest taketh a censer with incense therein, and censeth round about the table of the Holy Oil and the whole church or house: and taking his stand before the table, with his face to the east, he beginneth:

Blessed is our God always, now, and ever, and unto ages of ages.
Choir. Amen.

And we begin:

O Holy God, Holy Mighty, Holy Immortal One, have mercy upon us. (*Thrice.*)

Glory to the Father, and to the Son, and to the Holy Spirit, now, and ever, and unto ages of ages. Amen.

O all-holy Trinity, have mercy upon us. O Lord, wash away our sins. O Master, pardon our transgressions. O Holy One, visit and heal our infirmities, for thy Name's sake.

Lord, have mercy. (*Thrice.*)

Glory to the Father, and to the Son, and to the Holy Spirit, now, and ever, and unto ages of ages. Amen.

Our Father, who art in heaven, Hallowed be thy Name. Thy kingdom come. Thy will be done on earth, as it is in heaven. Give us this day our daily bread. And forgive us our trespasses, As we forgive those who trespass against us. And lead us not into temptation; But deliver us from the Evil One:

Priest. For thine is the kingdom, and the power, and the glory, of the Father, and of the Son, and of the Holy Spirit, now, and ever. and unto ages of ages.

Choir. Amen.

Lord, have mercy. (*Twelve times.*) —— Glory . . . now, and ever . . .

O come, let us worship God our King. O come, let us worship and fall down before Christ, our King and our God. O come, let us worship and fall down before the Very Christ, our King and our God. (*Three reverences.*)

* See Appendix B, IX (1).

PSALM CXLIII.

Hear my prayer, O Lord, and consider my desire; hearken unto me for thy truth and righteousness' sake. And enter not into judgment with thy servant; for in thy sight shall no man living be justified. For the enemy hath persecuted my soul; he hath smitten my life down to the ground; he hath laid me in the darkness, as the men that have been long dead. Therefore is my spirit vexed within me; and my heart within me is desolate. Yet do I remember the time past; I muse upon all thy works; yea, I exercise myself in the works of thy hands. I stretch forth my hands unto thee; my soul gaspeth unto thee as a thirsty land. Hear me, O Lord, and that soon; for my spirit waxeth faint: hide not thy face from me, lest I be like unto them that go down into the pit. O let me hear thy loving-kindness betimes in the morning; for in thee is my trust; show thou me the way that I should walk in; for I lift up my soul unto thee. Deliver me, O Lord, from mine enemies; for I flee unto thee to hide me. Teach me to do the thing that pleaseth thee; for thou art my God; let thy loving Spirit lead me forth into the land of righteousness. Quicken me, O Lord, for thy Name's sake; and for thy righteousness' sake bring my soul out of trouble. And of thy goodness slay mine enemies, and destroy all them that vex my soul; for I am thy servant.

Glory . . . now, and ever, . . .

Alleluia, alleluia, alleluia; glory to thee, O Lord. (*Thrice.*)

And the Deacon reciteth the Little Litany:

Again, yet again, in peace let us pray to the Lord.

Choir. Lord, have mercy.

Succour us, save us, have mercy upon us, and keep us, O God, by thy grace.

Choir. Lord, have mercy.

Calling to remembrance our most holy, all-undefiled, most blessed and glorious Lady, the Birth-giver of God and ever-virgin Mary, with all the Saints, let us commend ourselves, and each other, and all our life unto Christ our God.

Choir. To thee, O Lord.

Priest. For unto thee are due all glory, honour and worship, to the Father, and to the Son, and to the Holy Spirit, now, and ever, and unto ages of ages.

Choir. Amen.

And immediately Alleluia, *in Tone VI., is sung.*

Verse (*Stikh*) 1: O Lord, rebuke me not in thine anger, neither chasten me in thy sore displeasure.

Verse 2: Have mercy upon me, O Lord, for I am weak.

Then the Hymns (*Tropari*):

Have mercy upon us, O Lord, have mercy upon us. For we sinners, void of all defence, do offer unto thee as unto our Master, this petition: Have mercy upon us.

Glory to the Father, and to the Son, and to the Holy Spirit.

Have mercy upon us, O Lord, for in thee have we trusted, and be not very wroth with us, neither call thou to remembrance our iniquities; but look down even now upon us, inasmuch as thou art of tender compassion, and deliver us from our enemies; for thou art our God, and we are thy people, we are all the work of thy hand, and we call upon thy Name.

Now, and ever, and unto ages of ages. Amen.

Open unto us the door of thy loving-kindness, O blessed Birth-giver of God. In that we set our hope on thee, may we not fail, but through thee may we be delivered from all adversities; for thou art the salvation of all Christian people.

PSALM LI.

Have mercy upon me, O God, after thy great goodness; according to the multitude of thy mercies do away mine offences. Wash me throughly from my wickedness, and cleanse me from my sin. For I acknowledge my faults, and my sin is ever before me. Against thee only have I sinned, and done this evil in thy sight; that thou mightest be justified in thy saying, and clear when thou art judged. Behold, I was shapen in wickedness, and in sin hath my mother conceived me. But lo, thou requirest truth in the inward parts, and shalt make me to understand wisdom secretly. Thou shalt purge me with hyssop, and I shall be clean; thou shalt wash me, and I shall be whiter than snow. Thou shalt make me hear of joy and gladness, that the bones which thou hast broken may rejoice. Turn thy face from my sins, and put out all my misdeeds. Make me a clean heart, O God, and renew a right spirit within me. Cast me not away from thy presence, and take not thy holy Spirit from me. O give me the comfort of thy help again, and stablish me with thy free Spirit. Then shall I teach thy ways unto the wicked, and sinners shall be converted unto thee. Deliver me from blood-guiltiness, O God, thou that art the God of my health; and my tongue shall sing of thy righteousness. Thou shalt open my lips, O Lord, and my mouth shall show thy praise. For thou desirest no sacrifice, else would I give it thee; but thou delightest not in burnt-offerings. The sacrifice of God is a troubled spirit: a broken and contrite heart, O God, shalt thou not despise. O be favourable and gracious unto Zion; build thou the walls of Jerusalem. Then shalt thou be pleased with the sacrifice of righteousness, with the burnt-offerings and oblations; then shall they offer young bullocks upon thine altar.

And the CANON, *of which the cross-acrostic is:* The Prayer of the Oil, a Song of Arsenius.

Canticle I., Tone IV.

Theme-Song (Irmós). When Israel of old had passed through the

Red Sea's abyss with foot unwet, through the cross-wise stretching forth of Moses' hands, they overthrew the host of Amalek in the wilderness.

Hymns (Tropari). O Master, who ever makest glad the souls, and likewise also the bodies of mortal men, with the oil of loving-kindness, and preservest also thy faithful by oil: Show compassion also unto those who now draw near unto thee through the Oil.

The whole earth is full of thy mercy, O Master: Wherefore we, in faith, do beseech thee, that thou wilt bestow upon us, who to-day shall be anointed with thy divine and precious Oil, thy mercy which passeth understanding.

Glory . . .

O thou who lovest mankind, who through thine Apostle didst mercifully give us a command to perform Holy Unction upon thy sick servants: Do thou, through the prayers of the same, have mercy upon us all, by thy seal.

Now, and ever, . . .

Hymn to the Birth-giver of God (Bogoróditchen). O only Pure One, who didst give birth to the fathomless Abyss of Peace: By thine unceasing prayers unto God deliver thou thy servant from infirmities and afflictions; that he (*she*) may unceasingly magnify thee.

Canticle III.

Theme-Song (Irmós). The Church rejoiceth in thee, O Christ, crying: Thou art my fortress, O Lord, my refuge and my strength.

Hymns (Tropari). Thou who alone art wonderful and merciful unto faithful men: Grant thy grace from on high unto thy servant who lieth in sore sickness, O Christ.

O Lord, who of old didst show forth an olive-branch unto the abating of the Flood, through thy divine command: Save the sufferer, through thy mercy.

Glory . . .

With the lamp of light divine, in thy mercy make bright, through this Unction, O Christ, him (*her*) who now, in faith, maketh haste to thy mercy.

Now, and ever, . . .

Hymn to the Birth-giver of God (Bogoróditchen). Graciously look down from on high, O Mother of the Creator of all men, and through thy prayers dispel the sufferer's bitter pangs.

Sitting-Hymn (Syedálen), in Tone VIII. Thou who art like a river divine of mercy, like a bottomless gulf of great loving-kindness, O Bountiful One; Show forth the god-like streams of thy mercy, and heal all men. Pour forth abundantly floods of wonders, and wash clean all men: For resorting ever unto thee, we fervently implore thy grace.

Another, in Tone IV. O Physician and Helper of the suffering, O Redeemer and Saviour of the sick: Do thou, the same Master and Lord of all, grant healing unto thy sick servant. Show compassion, have mercy upon him (*her*) who hath grievously sinned. And deliver him (*her*), O Christ, from his (*her*) iniquities, that he (*she*) may glorify thy might divine.

Canticle IV.

Theme-Song (*Irmós*). The Church, beholding thee uplifted upon the Cross, O Sun of Righteousness, standeth in its stateliness, worthily crying: Glory to thy might, O Lord.

Hymns (*Tropári*). O Saviour, who like unto chrism incorruptible dost empty thyself utterly in grace and purify the world: Show mercy and bounty, in god-like wise, upon the bodily wounds of him (*her*) who, with faith, is now about to receive Unction.

Forasmuch as, with the tranquillity of thy mercy's seal, thou hast now signed the senses of thy servant, O Master, make inaccessible, impenetrable the entrance of all adverse powers.

Glory . . .

Thou who hast commanded the ailing to summon thine inspired ministers, and to procure salvation through prayers, and the anointing with thy holy Oil by the same: Save the sufferer by thy mercy, O thou who lovest mankind.

Now, and ever, . . .

Hymn to the Birth-giver of God (*Bogoróditchen*). O Birth-giver of God, ever-virgin, all-pure, steadfast Refuge and Fortress, Haven and Wall, Ladder and battlemented Bulwark: Have mercy and show compassion upon this sick person; for unto thee alone hath he (*she*) fled for refuge.

Canticle V.

Theme-Song (*Irmós*). Thou art come, O my Lord, for a light to the world, a holy light, which turneth from the darkness of ignorance those who with faith sing praises unto thee.

Hymns (*Tropári*). O Good One, who art a great deep of mercy; through thy mercy divine, O Merciful One, show thou mercy upon this sufferer: For thou art tender of heart.

O Christ who, in wise ineffable, hast sanctified both our souls and bodies from on high, by the divine impress of thy seal: Heal us all by thy hand.

Glory . . .

O Lord, exceeding good, who, through thine unspeakable love, didst accept anointing with precious ointment at the hands of the woman who was a sinner: Have compassion upon thy servant.

Now, and ever, . . .

Hymn to the Birth-giver of God (*Bogoróditchen*). O all-lauded, pure, exceeding gracious Birth-giver of God, have mercy upon those who are now to be anointed with the Oil divine: and save thy servant.

Canticle VI.

Theme-Song (Irmós). I will sacrifice unto thee with the voice of thanksgiving, O Lord, the Church crieth aloud unto thee, in that she hath purified herself from the blood of demons by the blood which for the sake of mercy flowed from thy side.

Hymns (Tropari). O thou who lovest mankind, who didst institute anointment for kings by thy words, and by the hands of High Priests didst accomplish the same: Save also this sufferer by thy seal; forasmuch as thou art of great loving-kindness.

Let no interposition of malignant demons, O Saviour, touch the senses of him (*her*) who is marked with thine anointing divine; but hedge him (*her*) about with the bulwark of thy glory.

Glory . . .

Stretch forth thy hand from on high, O thou who lovest mankind, and having sanctified thine Oil, bestow it, O Saviour, on thy servant, unto healing, and unto release from all his (*her*) ills.

Now, and ever, . . .

Hymn to the Birth-giver of God (Bogoróditchen). Thou hast manifested thyself a fruitful olive-tree, in the abode of thy God, O Mother of the Creator, and thereby the world is seen to be filled with mercy. And thereby, also, save thou the pangs of thy sufferer by thy prayers.

Collect-Hymn (Kondák), in Tone II. O Fountain of mercy, who art exceeding good: Deliver thou from every adversity these persons who, with fervent faith, adore thy mercy unspeakable, O Tenderly-compassionate One; and taking away their maladies, vouchsafe thou unto them grace divine from on high.

Canticle VII.

Theme-Song (Irmós). The Abrahamic Children in the Persian furnace, fired rather by love of godliness than by the flame, cried aloud: Blessed art thou, O Lord, in the tabernacle of thy glory.

Hymns (Tropari). Thou who in thy mercies and compassions, O Saviour and only God, dost heal both the passions of the soul and the bodily afflictions of all men: Do thou, the same God, restore this person who suffereth from bodily infirmities, and heal thou him (*her*).

When the heads of all men are anointed with the oil of Unction, vouchsafe thou the joy of gladness unto this person, who seeketh the mercy of thy redemption, O Christ, bestowing the riches of thy grace, O Lord.

Glory . . .

Thy seal is a sword against demons, O Saviour, a fire that consumeth the passions of the soul, through the prayers of priests. Wherefore, we who have received healing, in faith, do sing praises unto thee.

Now, and ever, . . .

Hymn to the Birth-giver of God (Bogoróditchen). O Mother of God, who within thy womb, in god-like wise didst hold, and ineffably didst incarnate him who holdeth all things in the hollow of his hand, mercifully assuage the pangs of this sufferer, we beseech thee.

Canticle VIII.

Theme-Song (Irmós). Daniel stretched forth his hand, and stopped the gaping mouths of the lions in the pit. And the Holy Children, zealous in piety, girding themselves with virtue, quenched the raging fire, as they cried: O all ye works of the Lord, bless ye the Lord.

Hymns (Tropari). Thou showest mercy on all men, O Saviour, because of thy mercy infinite and divine: For which cause all we have assembled ourselves together, mystically representing the worship of thy bounties, and have brought in faith the anointing with the holy Oil unto thy servant: whom also do thou visit.

By the streams of thy mercy, O Christ, and through anointing by thy priests, wash away, in that thou art full of loving-kindness, O Lord, the pains and hurts, and the sudden assaults of suffering of him (*her*) who is tormented by the violence of passions; that he (*she*) may glorify thee with thanksgiving, in that he (*she*) hath been saved.

Glory . . .

Forasmuch as thy mercy divine hath been decreed to us from on high, O Master, as a token of condescension and of tranquillity: Take not away thy mercy, neither despise thou him (*her*) who, with faith, continually doth cry unto thee: O all ye works of the Lord, bless ye the Lord.

Now, and ever, . . .

Hymn to the Birth-giver of God (Bogoróditchen). Nature accepted thy divine birth-giving, O Pure One, as a crown exceeding glorious, which crushed the hosts of the adversary, and conquered their dominion. Wherefore, crowned with the joyful radiance of thy grace, we sing praises unto thee, O all-hymned Lady.

Canticle IX.

Theme-Song (Irmós). The Corner-stone unhewn by hands from thee was hewn, O Virgin Mount unquarried, even Christ, who hath bound together Nature that had been divided. Therefore, rejoicing, we magnify thee, O Birth-giver of God.

Hymns (Tropari). Look down from heaven, O Bountiful One, and show forth thy mercy upon all men. Give now thy succour and thy strength unto him (*her*) who draweth near unto thee through divine Unction at the hands of thy priests, O thou who lovest mankind.

O Saviour most good, rejoicing have we beheld the Oil divine, which by thy condescension inspired thou hast received, and above the merits of the participants hast symbolically imparted unto those who have shared in the laver divine.

Glory . . .

Show thy bounty, have mercy, O Saviour; deliver from terrors and pains, rescue from the darts of the Evil One the souls and bodies of thy servants: Forasmuch as thou art a merciful Lord, who healest by thy grace divine.

Now, and ever, . . .

Hymn to the Birth-giver of God (Bogoróditchen). As thou receivest the songs and supplications of thy servants, O Virgin, so also deliver thou from irksome ills and maladies, him (*her*) who, through us, fleeth unto thy divine protection, O All-pure One.

For meet is it, in truth, to bless thee, the Birth-giver of God, ever-blessed, and all-undefiled, and the Mother of our God. More honourable than the Cherubim, and beyond compare more glorious than the Seraphim, thou who without defilement barest God the Word, true Birth-giver of God, we magnify thee.

Exapostilárion.

In mercy, O Good One, cast thine eyes upon the petitions of us who to-day are come together in thy holy temple, to anoint thy sick servant(*s*) with thine Oil divine.

Then the Stanzas (Stikhíri), in Tone IV. Thou hast given thy grace, O thou who art easy to be entreated and lovest mankind, through thine apostles, by thy holy Oil, for the healing of the wounds, as also the infirmities of all men. Have mercy, therefore, upon him (*her*) who now, with faith, hath recourse unto thine Oil, and sanctify, and show mercy, in that thou art of tender compassion. Purge him (*her*) from every ailment, and vouchsafe unto him (*her*) thy food incorruptible, O Lord.

Look down from heaven, O Ineffable One, in that thou art of tender loving-kindness, who with thy hand invisible hast sealed our senses, O thou who lovest mankind, upon him (*her*) that, through thine Oil divine, in faith appealeth unto thee, and asketh remission of his (*her*) transgressions. And grant healing for both soul and body, that with love he (*she*) may glorify thee, magnifying thy sovereign power.

Through anointing with thine Oil, and the touch of thy priests, O thou who lovest mankind, sanctify thou from on high thy servant. Free him (*her*) from his (*her*) infirmities. Purge away his (*her*) spiritual vileness. Wash him (*her*), O Saviour, and deliver him (*her*) from greatly entangling temptations. Assuage his (*her*) maladies. Banish all obstacles. Utterly destroy thou all his (*her*) afflictions; forasmuch as thou art bountiful and full of loving-kindness.

Glory to the Father, and to the Son, and to the Holy Spirit, now, and ever, and unto ages of ages. Amen.

Hymn to the Birth-giver of God (Bogoróditchen). O most pure Palace of the King, O greatly extolled One, purify, I implore thee, my mind which is stained with all manner of sin, and make it the fair abode of the Trinity exceedingly divine; that, being saved, I, thine unprofitable servant, may magnify thy power, and thy boundless mercy.

O Holy God, Holy Mighty, . . . (*See page* 332.) Glory . . . now, and ever, . . . O all-holy Trinity . . . Lord, have mercy. (*Thrice.*) Glory. . . now, and ever, . . . Our Father, . . . For thine is the kingdom, . . .

Then the Hymn, in Tone IV. Thou who alone art a speedy succour, O Christ, manifest thy speedy visitation from on high upon thy sick servant; deliver him (*her*) from his (*her*) infirmities, and cruel pain; and raise him (*her*) up again to sing praises unto thee, and without ceasing to glorify thee: through the prayers of the Birth-giver of God, O thou who alone lovest mankind.

> *Then the Deacon, or the principal Priest, saith the following Litany:*

In peace, let us pray to the Lord.

Choir. Lord, have mercy.

For the peace that is from above, and for the salvation of our souls: ℞

For the peace of the whole world; for the welfare of God's holy Churches, and for the union of all: ℞

For this holy Temple, and for those who with faith, devoutness, and the fear of God have entered therein: ℞

That he will bless the Oil by the power, and operation, and descent of the Holy Spirit: ℞

For the servant of God, N., and for his (*her*) visitation in God; and that the grace of the Holy Spirit may come upon him (*her*): ℞

That he will deliver him (*her*) and us from all tribulation, wrath, and necessity: ℞

Choir. let us pray to the Lord. Lord, have mercy.

Succour us, save us, have mercy upon us, and keep us, O God, by thy grace.

Choir. Lord, have mercy.

Calling to remembrance our most holy, all-undefiled, most blessed and glorious Lady, the Birth-giver of God, and ever-virgin Mary, with all the Saints, let us commend ourselves, and each other, and all our life unto Christ our God.

Choir. To thee, O Lord.

> *Then the principal Priest reciteth the* PRAYER OF THE OIL *over the shrine-lamp. And in some churches, wine is poured into the shrine-lamp, with the oil, instead of water.* (3)

Let us pray to the Lord.

Lord, have mercy.

While the Prayer of the Oil is being said, the Choir singeth the following Hymns:

Tone IV.

Thou who alone art a speedy succour, O Christ, . . . (*See above.*)

The Priest, secretly.

O Lord who, in thy mercies and bounties, healest the disorders of our souls and bodies: Do thou, the same Master, *Secretly.*

Blind of my spiritual eyes, I come unto thee, O Christ, as did the man blind from his birth, in repentance crying unto thee: Have mercy upon me, O thou who illuminest with exceeding brightness them that are in darkness.

Tone III.

By thine intercession divine, O Lord, raise thou up my soul, which is cruelly paralyzed by all manner of sin, and by unseemly deeds, as thou aforetime didst raise up the paralytic; that, being saved, I may cry unto thee: Grant me healing, O compassionate Christ.

Tone II.

As a disciple* of the Lord, O Righteous One, thou didst receive the Gospel; as a Martyr, thou hast that which surpasseth utterance; as the brother of God thou hast boldness; as a hierarch, thou hast power in prayer. Implore thou Christ our God that he will save our souls.

sanctify this Oil, that it may be effectual for those who shall be anointed therewith, unto healing, and unto relief from every passion, every malady of the flesh and of the spirit, and every ill; and that therein may be glorified thy most holy Name, of the Father, and of the Son, and of the Holy Spirit, now, and ever, and unto ages of ages. Amen.

And the other Priests also recite the same Prayer, secretly, with him.

Secretly.

Tone IV.

The Only-begotten Word of God the Father, who in these latter days hath sojourned among us, ordained thee, O James divine, who was sent by God, to be the first shepherd and teacher of them that dwelt in Jerusalem, and a faithful steward of spiritual mysteries: Wherefore, O Apostle, we all revere thee.

Tone III.

To them of Mary, O Saint † thou didst reveal thyself as a minister of Holy Mysteries. For fulfilling the Gospel of Christ, O Venerable One, thou didst lay down thy life for thy people, and didst save the innocent from death. For which cause thou art canonized as a great Initiate in the grace of God.

Tone III.

The world hath found in thee a champion great in affliction, O Endurer of Pain, who didst put to flight the heathen. For like as thou didst humble Lyæus' pride, and encourage Nestor in his striving for the prize, even so, O Saint Demetrius, pray thou unto Christ our God, that he will grant unto us great mercy. (4)

* Saint James.　　　　　　† Saint Nicholas the Wonder-worker.

Tone III.

O holy Endurer of Pain, and Healer, Panteleimon, beseech thou the merciful God that he will grant remission of sins unto our souls. (5)

Tone VIII.

O sainted Unmercenaries and Wonder-workers, visit ye our infirmities. Freely ye have received, freely give ye unto us.

Tone II.

Thy grandeur, O Chaste One,* who shall declare? For thou aboundest in wonders, and pourest forth streams of healing, and intercedest for our souls, as learned in wisdom divine, and as the friend of Christ.

O fervent Intercession, and Wall Impregnable, O Fountain of Mercy, O Refuge of the world; unto thee we earnestly do cry: O Birth-giver of God, O Lady, come thou to our aid, and deliver us from adversity, O thou who alone art a speedy Intercessor.

Deacon. Let us attend.

Priest. Peace be with you all.

Choir. And with thy spirit.

Deacon. Wisdom! Let us attend.

Reader. The Gradual (*Prokímen*), in the First Tone. Let thy mercy be upon us, O Lord, even as we have put our trust in thee.

Verse (Stikh): Rejoice in the Lord, O ye righteous; for praise becometh the righteous.

Deacon. Wisdom!

Reader. The Lesson from the General Epistle of James.

Priest. Let us attend.

Deacon. (*James v. 10-17.*) Take, my brethren, the prophets, who have spoken in the name of the Lord, for an example of suffering affliction, and of patience. Behold, we count them happy which endure. Ye have heard of the patience of Job, and have seen the end of the Lord; that the Lord is very pitiful, and of tender mercy. But above all things, my brethren, swear not, neither by heaven, neither by the earth, neither by any other oath: but let your yea, be yea; and your nay, nay; lest ye fall into condemnation. Is any among you afflicted? let him pray. Is any merry? let him sing psalms. Is any sick among you? let him call for the elders of the church; and let them pray over him, anointing him with oil in the Name of the Lord: and the prayer of faith shall save the sick, and the Lord shall raise him up; and if he have committed sins, they shall be forgiven him. Confess your faults one to another, and pray one for another, that ye may be healed. The effectual fervent prayer of a righteous man availeth much.

First Priest. Peace be with thee.

Reader. And with thy spirit.

* St. John the Divine.

Deacon. Wisdom! Let us attend.

Reader. Alleluia, *in the Eighth Tone.*

Verse (Stikh): I will sing unto thee of mercy and judgment, O Lord.

Priest. Wisdom, O believers! Let us listen to the Holy Gospel. Peace be with you all.

People. And with thy spirit.

Priest. The Lesson from the holy Gospel of Luke.

Choir. Glory to thee, O Lord; glory to thee. —— *Deacon.* Let us attend.

The Priest then readeth the Gospel (Luke x. 25-38).

And behold, a certain lawyer stood up, and tempted him, saying, Master, what shall I do to inherit eternal life? He said unto him, What is written in the law? how readest thou? And he answering said, Thou shalt love the Lord thy God with all thy heart, and with all thy soul, and with all thy strength, and with all thy mind; and thy neighbour as thyself. And he said unto him, Thou hast answered right: this do, and thou shalt live. But he, willing to justify himself, said unto Jesus, And who is my neighbour? And Jesus answering, said, A certain man went down from Jerusalem to Jericho, and fell among thieves, which stripped him of his raiment, and wounded him, and departed, leaving him half dead. And by chance there came down a certain priest that way; and when he saw him, he passed by on the other side. And likewise a Levite, when he was at the place, came and looked on him, and passed by on the other side. But a certain Samaritan, as he journeyed, came where he was: and when he saw him, he had compassion on him, and went to him, and bound up his wounds, pouring in oil and wine, and set him on his own beast, and brought him to an inn, and took care of him. And on the morrow, when he departed, he took out two pence, and gave them to the host, and said unto him, Take care of him: and whatsoever thou spendest more, when I come again, I will repay thee. Which now of these three, thinkest thou, was neighbour unto him that fell among the thieves? And he said, he that showed mercy on him. Then said Jesus unto him, Go, and do thou likewise.

Choir. Glory to thee, O Lord; glory to thee.

Then the Deacon saith the Litany.

Have mercy upon us, O God, according to thy great mercy, we beseech thee; hearken, and have mercy.

Choir. Lord, have mercy. (*Thrice.*)

Furthermore we pray for mercy, peace, life, health, salvation and remission of sins for the servant of God, N. ℞

That he (*she*) may be pardoned his (*her*) every transgression, whether voluntary or involuntary, let us pray to the Lord. ℞

Exclamation.

Priest. For thou art a merciful God, who lovest mankind, and unto

thee do we ascribe glory, to the Father, and to the Son, and to the Holy
Spirit, now, and ever, and unto ages of ages.

Choir. Amen.

Deacon. Let us pray to the Lord.

Choir. Lord, have mercy.

Prayer.

Priest. O thou who art without beginning, eternal, the Holy of Holies,
who didst send down thine Only-begotten Son to heal every infirmity and
every wound, both of our souls and bodies: Send down thy Holy Spirit,
and sanctify this Oil; and cause it to be for thy servant, N., who is about
to be anointed therewith, unto perfect remission of his (*her*) sins, and unto
inheritance in the kingdom of heaven.

Some say this Prayer only thus far, adding here the Exclamation: For thy property
it is to show mercy . . . *Others recite it to the end.*

For thou art a great and marvellous God, who keepest thy covenant
and thy mercy towards them that love thee; who givest remission of sins
through thy Holy Child, Jesus Christ; who regeneratest us from sin by
holy Baptism, and sanctifiest us with thy Holy Spirit; who givest light
to the blind; who raisest up them that are cast down; who lovest the
righteous, and showest mercy unto sinners; who leadest us forth again out
of darkness and the shadow of death, and sayest unto them that are in
captivity: Come forth; and unto them that sit in darkness: Be ye unveiled.
For he shined in our hearts with the light of the knowledge of his presence
when, for our sakes, he revealed himself upon earth, and dwelt among
men; and unto as many as accepted him, to them gave he the power to
become the sons of God, vouchsafing unto us the adoption of sonship
through the laver of regeneration, and causing us to have no share in the
assaults of the Devil. And inasmuch as it hath not pleased thee that we
should be cleansed by blood, but by holy Oil, thou didst give unto us the
image of his Cross, that we might become the flock of Christ, a royal
priesthood, a holy nation; and didst purify us by water, and sanctify us
by thy Holy Spirit. Do thou, the same Master, O Lord, vouchsafe unto
us grace in this thy ministry, as thou didst vouchsafe it unto Moses, thy
servant, who found favour in thy sight; and unto Samuel, beloved of
thee; and unto John, thy chosen one; and unto all those who, from generation to generation, have been acceptable unto thee.   In like manner,
make us also to be ministers of the new Covenant of thy Son upon this
Oil, which thou hast acquired unto thyself through the precious blood of
thy Christ; that putting away earthly lusts, we may die unto sin, and live
unto righteousness, being clothed upon with him through the anointing
with sanctification of this Oil which we are about to summon to our aid.
Let this Oil, O Lord, become the oil of gladness, the oil of sanctification,
a royal robe, an armour of might, the averting of every work of the Devil,

the seal of immunity from snares, the joy of the heart, an eternal rejoicing; that they who shall be anointed with this Oil of regeneration may be terrible unto their adversaries, and may shine in the radiance of thy Saints, having neither spot nor wrinkle; and that they may attain unto thy rest everlasting, and receive the prize of their high calling.

For thy property it is to show mercy and to save us, O our God; and unto thee do we ascribe glory, together with thine Only-begotten Son, and thine all-holy, and good, and life-giving Spirit, now, and ever, and unto ages of ages.

Choir. Amen.

After the Prayer, the Priest taketh one of the wands, and dippeth it in the holy Oil, and anointeth the sick person, in cross-form; on the brow, the nostrils, the cheeks, the lips, the breast, and on both sides of the hands, repeating the while this Prayer:

O holy Father, Physician of souls and bodies, who didst send thine Only-begotten Son, our Lord Jesus Christ, which healeth every infirmity and delivereth from death: Heal thou, also, thy servant, N., from the ills of body and soul which do hinder him (*her*), and quicken him (*her*), by the grace of thy Christ; through the prayers of our most holy Lady, the Birth-giver of God and ever-virgin Mary; through the intercession of the honourable Bodiless Powers of Heaven; through the might of the precious and life-giving Cross; through the protection of the honourable, glorious Prophet, Forerunner and Baptist, John; of the holy, glorious and all-laudable Apostles; of the holy, glorious and right-victorious Martyrs; of our reverend and God-bearing Fathers; of the holy and healing Unmercenaries, Cosmas and Damian, Cyrus and John, Panteleimon and Hermolaus, Samson and Diomedes, Photius and Anicetas; of the holy and righteous Ancestors of God, Joachim and Anna; and of all the Saints.

For thou art the Fountain of healing, O our God, and unto thee do we ascribe glory, together with thine Only-begotten Son, and thy Spirit, one in essence, now, and ever, and unto ages of ages. Amen.

This Prayer is said by each of the Priests, after he hath read the Gospel and the accompanying Prayer, while he anointeth the person with the Oil.

Deacon. Let us attend.

Second Priest. Peace be with you all.

Choir. And with thy spirit.

Deacon. Wisdom! Let us attend.

Reader. The Gradual (*Prokímen*), in the Second Tone. The Lord is my fortress and my song, and shall be my salvation.

Verse (*Stikh*): In chastening hast thou chastened me, O Lord; yet hast not given me over unto death.

Deacon. Wisdom!

Reader. The Lesson from the Epistle of the holy Apostle Paul to the Romans.

Priest. Let us attend.

Deacon. (*Romans xv. 1–8.*) Brethren, we then that are strong ought to bear the infirmities of the weak, and not to please ourselves. Let every one of us please his neighbour for his good to edification. For even Christ pleased not himself; but, as it is written, The reproaches of them that reproached thee fell on me. For whatsoever things were written aforetime, were written for our learning, that we through patience and comfort of the scriptures might have hope. Now the God of patience and consolation grant you to be like-minded one toward another according to Christ Jesus: that ye may with one mind and one mouth glorify God, even the Father of our Lord Jesus Christ. Wherefore receive ye one another, as Christ also received us, to the glory of God.

Priest. Peace be with thee.

Reader. And with thy spirit.

Deacon. Wisdom! Let us attend.

Reader. Alleluia, *in the Fifth Tone.*

Verse (Stikh): I will sing of thy mercy, O Lord, forever.

Priest. Wisdom, O believers! Let us listen to the Holy Gospel. Peace be with you all.

Choir. And with thy spirit.

Second Priest. The Lesson from the holy Gospel of Luke.

Choir. Glory to thee, O Lord; glory to thee.

Deacon. Let us attend.

The Priest then readeth the Gospel (Luke xix. 1–11).

Then Jesus entered and passed through Jericho. And behold, there was a man named Zaccheus, which was the chief among the publicans, and he was rich. And he sought to see Jesus who he was; and could not for the press, because he was little of stature. And he ran before, and climbed up into a sycamore-tree to see him; for he was to pass that way. And when Jesus came to the place, he looked up, and saw him, and said unto him, Zaccheus, make haste, and come down: for to-day I must abide at thy house. And he made haste, and came down, and received him joyfully. And when they saw it, they all murmured, saying, That he was gone to be guest with a man that is a sinner. And Zaccheus stood, and said unto the Lord; Behold, Lord, the half of my goods I give to the poor; and if I have taken any thing from any man by false accusation, I restore him fourfold. And Jesus said unto him, This day is salvation come to this house, forasmuch as he also is a son of Abraham. For the Son of man is come to seek and to save that which was lost.

Choir. Glory to thee, O Lord; glory to thee.

Then the Deacon straightway reciteth the Litany: Have mercy upon us, O God, according to thy great mercy, . . . *with the Exclamation:* For thou art a merciful God, . . . (*See page* 343.)

Deacon. Let us pray to the Lord.——*Choir.* Lord, have mercy.

And the Second Priest saith the following Prayer:

O God great and supreme, who art adored by all created beings, Fountain of wisdom, Abyss of goodness in very truth unfathomable, and Sea illimitable of loving-kindness: do thou, the same Master who lovest mankind, the God of things eternal and of wonders, to the understanding of whom none among men by taking thought can attain, look down and hear us, thine unworthy servants, and wheresoever in thy great Name we shall bring this Oil, send thou down the gift of thy healing, and remission of sins: and heal him (*her*), in the multitude of thy mercies. Yea, O Lord who art easy to be entreated; who alone art merciful and lovest mankind; who repentest thee of our evil deeds; who knowest how that the mind of man is applied unto wickedness, even from his youth up; who desirest not the death of a sinner, but rather that he should turn again and live; who for the salvation of sinners didst become incarnate, yet still remain in God, and didst thyself become a created being for the sake of thy creatures; thou hast said: I am not come to call the righteous but sinners to repentance; thou didst seek the wandering sheep; thou didst diligently seek out the lost piece of silver, and having found it, thou didst say: He that cometh unto me I will in no wise cast out; thou didst not abhor the sinful woman who washed thy precious feet with her tears; thou didst say: As often as thou fallest arise, and thou shalt be saved; thou art he who didst say: There is joy in heaven over one sinner who repenteth. Do thou, O tender-hearted Master, look down from the height of thy sanctuary, overshadowing us sinners, who are also thine unworthy servants, with the grace of the Holy Spirit, at this hour, and take up thine abode in thy servant, N., who acknowledgeth his (*her*) iniquities, and draweth near unto thee in faith; and accepting him (*her*) because of thy love towards mankind, forgiving him (*her*) whatsoever he (*she*) hath done amiss, whether by word, or deed, or thought, forgive him (*her*), cleanse him (*her*), make him (*her*) pure from every sin; and abiding ever present with him (*her*), preserve him (*her*) all the remaining years of his (*her*) life; that, walking ever in thy statutes, he (*she*) may in no wise again become an object of malignant joy to the Devil; and thy holy Name may be glorified in him (*her*).

For thy property it is to show mercy and to save us, O Christ-God; and unto thee do we ascribe glory, together with thy Father who is from everlasting, and thine all-holy, and good, and life-giving Spirit, now, and ever, and unto ages of ages. Amen.

And straightway after this Prayer, the Second Priest taketh the second wand, and dipping it in the holy Oil, he anointeth the sick person, reciting the while the Prayer: O holy Father, Physician of souls and bodies, . . . (See page 345.)

Deacon. Let us attend.

Third Priest. Peace be with you all.

Choir. And with thy spirit.

Deacon. Wisdom! Let us attend.

Reader. The Gradual (*Prokímen*), in the Fourth Tone. The Lord is my light and my salvation; whom shall I fear?

Verse (Stikh): The Lord is the strength of my life; of whom shall I be afraid?

Deacon. Wisdom!

Reader. The Lesson from the Epistle of the holy Apostle Paul to the Corinthians.

Priest. Let us attend.

Deacon. (*1 Cor. xii. 27–xiii. 1–8.*) Brethren, now ye are the body of Christ, and members in particular. And God hath set some in the church, first apostles, secondarily prophets, thirdly teachers, after that miracles, then gifts of healings, helps, governments, diversities of tongues. Are all apostles? are all prophets? are all teachers? are all workers of miracles? Have all the gifts of healing? do all speak with tongues? do all interpret? But covet earnestly the best gifts. And yet shew I unto you a more excellent way. Though I speak with the tongues of men and of angels, and have not charity, I am become as sounding brass, or a tinkling cymbal. And though I have the gift of prophecy, and understand all mysteries, and all knowledge; and though I have all faith, so that I could remove mountains, and have not charity, I am nothing. And though I bestow all my goods to feed the poor, and though I give my body to be burned, and have not charity, it profiteth me nothing. Charity suffereth long, and is kind; charity envieth not; charity vaunteth not itself, is not puffed up, doth not behave itself unseemly, seeketh not her own, is not easily provoked, thinketh no evil. Rejoiceth not in iniquity, but rejoiceth in the truth; beareth all things, believeth all things, hopeth all things, endureth all things. Charity never faileth.

Third Priest. Peace be with thee.

Reader. And with thy spirit.

Deacon. Wisdom! Let us attend.

Reader. Alleluia, *in the Second Tone.*

Verse (Stikh): O Lord, in thee have I trusted: let me never be confounded.

Priest. Wisdom, O believers! Let us listen to the Holy Gospel. Peace be with you all.

Choir. And with thy spirit.

Third Priest. The Lesson from the holy Gospel of Matthew.

Choir. Glory to thee, O Lord; glory to thee.

Deacon. Let us attend.

The Third Priest then readeth the Gospel (Matt. x. 1, 5–9).

And when Jesus had called unto him his twelve disciples, he gave them power against unclean spirits, to cast them out, and to heal all manner of sickness, and all manner of disease. These twelve Jesus sent forth, and commanded them, saying, Go not into the way of the Gentiles, and into any city of the Samaritans enter ye not. But go rather to the lost sheep of the house of Israel. And as ye go, preach, saying, The kingdom of heaven is at hand. Heal the sick, cleanse the lepers, raise the dead, cast out devils: freely ye have received, freely give.

Choir. Glory to thee, O Lord; glory to thee.

And straightway the Deacon reciteth the Litany: Have mercy upon us, O God, . . . *with the Exclamation:* For thou art a merciful God, . . . (*See page* 343.)

Deacon. Let us pray to the Lord.

Choir. Lord, have mercy.

The Third Priest then saith the following Prayer:

O Master Almighty, O holy King, who chastenest and yet slayest not; who raisest up them that fall, and restorest them that are cast down; who relievest the bodily afflictions of men: We beseech thee, O our God, that thou wilt direct thy mercy upon this Oil, and upon all who shall be anointed therewith in thy Name; that it may be effectual unto the healing of their souls and bodies, and unto cleansing, and unto the putting away of every infirmity, and disease, and malady, and every defilement, both of body and spirit. Yea, Lord, send down from heaven thy healing might; touch the bodies; quench the fever: soothe the pangs, and banish every hidden ailment. Be thou the physician of thy servant, N. Raise him (*her*) up from his (*her*) bed of sickness, and from his (*her*) couch of suffering, and from his (*her*) bed of wasting disease, whole and perfectly restored to health, vouchsafing unto him (*her*), through thy Church, those things which are well-pleasing unto thee, and which work thy will.

For thy property it is to show mercy and to save us, O our God; and unto thee do we ascribe glory, to the Father, and to the Son, and to the Holy Spirit, now, and ever, and unto ages of ages. Amen.

And after this Prayer, the Third Priest dippeth the third wand in the holy Oil, and anointeth the sick person therewith, repeating the while the Prayer: O holy Father, Physician of souls and bodies, . . . (*See page* 345.)

Deacon. Let us attend.

Fourth Priest. Peace be with you all.

Choir. And with thy spirit.

Reader. The Gradual (*Prokímen*), in the Fourth Tone. Hear me speedily, O Lord, in that day when I shall call upon thee.

Verse (*Stikh*): O Lord, hear my prayer, and the voice of my crying.

Deacon. Wisdom!

Reader. The Lesson from the Epistle of the holy Apostle Paul to the Corinthians.

Priest. Let us attend.

Deacon. (*2 Cor. vi. 16–vii. 1.*) Brethren, ye are the temple of the living

God; as God hath said, I will dwell in them, and walk in them; and I will be their God, and they shall be my people. Wherefore come out from among them, and be ye separate, saith the Lord, and touch not the unclean thing; and I will receive you; and will be a Father unto you, and ye shall be my sons and daughters, saith the Lord Almighty. Having therefore these promises, dearly beloved, let us cleanse ourselves from all filthiness of the flesh and spirit, perfecting holiness in the fear of God.

Fourth Priest. Peace be with thee.

Reader. And with thy spirit.

Deacon. Wisdom! Let us attend.

Reader. Alleluia, *in the Second Tone.*

Verse (Stikh): I waited patiently for the Lord, and he heard me.

Fourth Priest. Wisdom, O believers! Let us listen to the Holy Gospel. Peace be with you all.

Choir. And with thy spirit.

Fourth Priest. The Lesson from the holy Gospel of Matthew.

Choir. Glory to thee, O Lord; glory to thee.

Deacon. Let us attend.

The Fourth Priest readeth the Gospel (Matt. viii. 14-24).

And when Jesus was come into Peter's house, he saw his wife's mother laid, and sick of a fever. And he touched her hand, and the fever left her: and she arose, and ministered unto them. When the even was come, they brought unto him many that were possessed with devils: and he cast out the spirits with his word, and healed all that were sick; that it might be fulfilled which was spoken by Esaias the prophet, saying, Himself took our infirmities and bare our sicknesses. Now when Jesus saw great multitudes about him, he gave commandment to depart unto the other side. And a certain scribe came, and said unto him, Master, I will follow thee whithersoever thou goest. And Jesus saith unto him, The foxes have holes, and the birds of the air have nests; but the Son of man hath not where to lay his head. And another of his disciples said unto him, Lord, suffer me first to go and bury my father. But Jesus said unto him, follow me; and let the dead bury their dead. And when he was entered into a ship, his disciples followed him.

Choir. Glory to thee, O Lord; glory to thee.

Then the Deacon saith the Litany: Have mercy upon us, O God, . . . *with the Exclamation:* For thou art a merciful God, . . . (*See page* 343.)

Deacon. Let us pray to the Lord.

Choir. Lord, have mercy.

Then the Fourth Priest prayeth:

O good Lord who lovest mankind, compassionate and exceeding merciful, plentiful in mercy, and rich in beneficence, the Father of bounties and God of all comfort, who through thy holy Apostles hast empowered

us to heal the infirmities of thy people by oil and prayer: Do thou confirm
this Oil unto the healing of those who shall be anointed therewith; unto
relief from every ailment, and from every malady; unto deliverance from
evils of those who await, in firm hope, salvation from thee.   Yea, O
Master, Lord our God, we beseech thee, O Almighty One, that thou wilt
save us all.   O only Physician of souls and bodies, sanctify us all.   O
thou who healest every infirmity, heal also thy servant, N. Raise him
(*her*) up from his (*her*) couch of sickness, through the mercies of thy goodness.   Visit him (*her*) with thy mercies and thy bounties.   Cast out of
him (*her*) every ailment and weakness; that, being raised up by thy
mighty hand, he (*she*) may serve thee with all thanksgiving; and that we
also, who now do share thine inexpressible love towards mankind, may
sing praises and glorify thee who performest deeds great and marvellous,
both glorious and transcendent.

For thy property it is to show mercy and to save us, O our God; . . .
(*See page* 345.)

> *And straightway after this Prayer, the Fourth Priest taketh the fourth wand, and
> dipping it in the holy Oil, he anointeth therewith the sick person, reciting the while
> the Prayer:* O holy Father, Physician of souls and bodies, . . . (*See page* 345.)

Deacon. Let us attend.

Fifth Priest. Peace be with you all. —— *Choir.* And with thy spirit.

Deacon. Wisdom!   Let us attend.

Reader. The Gradual (*Prokímen*), in the Fifth Tone.   Thou, O Lord,
shalt keep us and protect us, from this generation, forevermore.

Verse (*Stikh*): Save me, O Lord, for the righteous are become few.

Deacon. Wisdom!

Reader. The Lesson from the Epistle of the holy Apostle Paul to the
Corinthians.

Priest. Let us attend.

Deacon. (*2 Cor. i. 8–12.*) For we would not, brethren, have you ignorant of our trouble which came to us in Asia, that we were pressed out of
measure, above strength, insomuch that we despaired even of life: but we
had the sentence of death in ourselves, that we should not trust in ourselves, but in God which raiseth the dead: who delivered us from so great
a death, and doth deliver: in whom we trust that he will yet deliver us; ye
also helping together by prayer for us, that for the gift bestowed upon us by
the means of many persons, thanks may be given by many on our behalf.

Fifth Priest. Peace be with thee.

Reader. And with thy spirit.

Deacon. Wisdom!   Let us attend.

Reader. Alleluia, *in the First Tone.*

Verse (*Stikh*): I will sing praises unto thy mercy, O Lord, forever.

Fifth Priest. Wisdom, O believers!   Let us listen to the Holy Gospel.
Peace be with you all.

Choir. And with thy spirit.

Priest. The Lesson from the holy Gospel of Matthew.

Deacon. Let us attend.

Choir. Glory to thee, O Lord; glory to thee.

The Priest. (Matt. xxv. 1–14.) The Lord spake this parable: Then shall the kingdom of heaven be likened unto ten virgins, which took their lamps, and went forth to meet the bridegroom. And five of them were wise, and five were foolish. They that were foolish took their lamps, and took no oil with them: but the wise took oil in their vessels with their lamps. While the bridegroom tarried, they all slumbered and slept. And at midnight there was a cry made, Behold, the bridegroom cometh; go ye out to meet him. Then all those virgins arose, and trimmed their lamps. And the foolish said unto the wise, Give us of your oil: for our lamps are gone out. But the wise answered, saying, Not so; lest there be not enough for us and you: but go ye rather to them that sell, and buy for yourselves. And while they went to buy, the bridegroom came; and they that were ready, went in with him to the marriage: and the door was shut. Afterward came also the other virgins, saying, Lord, Lord, open unto us. But he answered and said, Verily, I say unto you, I know you not. Watch therefore, for ye know neither the day nor the hour wherein the Son of man cometh.

Choir. Glory to thee, O Lord; glory to thee.

Then the Deacon saith the Litany: Have mercy upon us, O God, . . . *with the Exclamation:* For thou art a merciful God, who lovest mankind, . . . (*See page* 343.)

Deacon. Let us pray to the Lord.

Choir. Lord, have mercy.

And the Fifth Priest saith the following Prayer: '

O Lord our God, who chastenest and again healest; who raisest up the beggar from the earth, and exaltest the poor man from the dunghill; O Father of orphans, and Haven of the tempest-tossed, and Physician of the ailing, who painlessly didst bear our weaknesses, and accept our infirmities; who showest mercy with gentleness, and passest over our wickedness, and takest away our unrighteousness; who art quick to help, and slow to wrath; who didst breathe upon thy disciples and say: Receive ye the Holy Spirit: whosesoever sins ye remit, they are remitted unto them; who acceptest the contrition of sinners, and hast power to pardon sins manifold and grievous, and bestowest healing upon all who continue in weakness and long-enduring sickness; who hast called me, also, thy humble, and sinful, and unworthy servant, entangled in manifold sins, and wallowing in the lusts of pleasures, to the holy and exceeding lofty degree of the Priesthood, and to enter in within the innermost veil, into the Holy of Holies, whither also the holy Angels desire to penetrate, and to hear the voice of the Lord God which announceth glad tidings, and to behold with mine eyes the presence of the sacred Oblation, and to take delight in the divine and sacred Liturgy: Thou who graciously enablest me to administer, as a priest, thy heavenly Mysteries, and to offer unto thee gifts and sacrifices for our sins, and for the ignorances of thy people, and to act as a mediator for thy speech-endowed sheep, that thou, through thy great and unspeakable love towards mankind, mayest cleanse them from their iniquities: Do thou, the same exceeding good King, give ear unto my prayer in this same hour and holy day, and at every time and place, and receive the voice of my supplication, and vouchsafe healing unto thy servant, N., who is weak both in soul and in body, granting unto him (*her*) remission of his (*her*) sins, and pardon of his (*her*) transgressions, both voluntary and involuntary. Heal thou his (*her*) incurable wounds, and every ailment, and every malady. Give health to his (*her*) soul, O thou who didst touch the mother-in-law of Peter, whereupon the fever left her, and she arose, and ministered unto thee. Do thou, the same Master, grant healing also to thy servant, N., and alleviation of every hurtful illness; and call to mind thy rich bounties and thy mercy. Call to mind how perpetually the mind of man inclineth unto evil, even from his youth up, and that not so much as one sinless man is to be found upon the earth; for thou alone art without sin, who didst come down and save the human race, and free us from bondage to the enemy. For if thou wilt enter into judgment with thy servants, none shall be found pure from stain, but every mouth shall be sealed, having nought to answer in extenuation; for like unto cast-off rags is all our righteousness in thy presence. Wherefore, O Lord, remember thou not the sins of our youth: For thou art the hope of the hopeless, and the rest of those who labour and are heavy-laden with iniquity. And unto thee do we ascribe glory, together with thy Father who is from everlasting, and thine all-holy, and good, and life-giving Spirit, now, and ever, and unto ages of ages.

Choir. Amen

And straightway after this Prayer, the Fifth Priest taketh the fifth wand, and dipping it in the holy Oil, he anointeth the sick person therewith, reciting the while the Prayer: O holy Father, Physician of souls and bodies, . . . *with the Exclamation.* (*See page* 345.)

Deacon. Let us attend.

Sixth Priest. Peace be with you all.

Choir. And with thy spirit.

Deacon. Wisdom! Let us attend.

Reader. The Gradual (*Prokímen*), in the Sixth Tone. Have mercy upon me, O God, according to thy great mercy.

Verse (*Stikh*): Make me a clean heart, O God, and renew a right spirit within me.

Deacon. Wisdom!

Reader. The Lesson from the Epistle of the holy Apostle Paul to the Galatians.

Priest. Let us attend.

Deacon. (*Gal. v. 22–vi. 1–2.*) Brethren, the fruit of the Spirit is love, joy, peace, long-suffering, gentleness, goodness, faith, meekness, temperance: against such there is no law.   And they that are Christ's have crucified the flesh, with the affections and lusts.   If we live in the Spirit, let us also walk in the Spirit.   Let us not be desirous of vain-glory, provoking one another, envying one another.   Brethren, if a man be overtaken in a fault, ye which are spiritual, restore such a one in the spirit of meekness; considering thyself, lest thou also be tempted.   Bear ye one another's burdens, and so fulfil the law of Christ.

Priest. Peace be with thee.

Reader. And with thy spirit.

Deacon. Wisdom! Let us attend.

Reader. Alleluia, *in the Sixth Tone*.

Verse (Stikh): Blessed is the man that feareth the Lord.   In his commandments he rejoiceth exceedingly.

Priest. Wisdom, O believers! Let us listen to the Holy Gospel.   Peace be with you all.

Choir. And with thy spirit.

Priest. The Lesson from the holy Gospel of Matthew.

Choir. Glory to thee, O Lord; glory to thee.

Deacon. Let us attend.

The Sixth Priest then readeth the Gospel (Matt. xiv. 21–29).

Then Jesus went thence, and departed into the coasts of Tyre and Sidon.   And behold, a woman of Canaan came out of the same coasts, and cried unto him, saying, Have mercy on me, O Lord, thou son of David; my daughter is grievously vexed with a devil.   But he answered her not a word.   And his disciples came and besought him, saying, Send her away; for she crieth after us.   But he answered and said, I am not sent but unto the lost sheep of the house of Israel.   Then came she and worshipped him, saying, Lord, help me.   But he answered and said, It is not meet to take the children's bread and to cast it to dogs.   And she said, Truth, Lord, yet the dogs eat of the crumbs which fall from their masters' table.   Then Jesus answered and said unto her, O woman, great is thy faith: be it unto thee even as thou wilt.   And her daughter was made whole from that very hour.

Choir. Glory to thee, O Lord; glory to thee.

Then the Deacon saith the Litany: Have mercy upon us, O God, . . . *with the Exclamation*.   (*See page* 343.)

Deacon. Let us pray to the Lord.

Choir. Lord, have mercy.

And the Sixth Priest saith the following Prayer:

We thank thee, O Lord our God, who art good and lovest mankind, the Physician of our souls and bodies, who painlessly hast borne our infirmities, by whose stripes we have all been healed, thou good Shepherd, who didst come to seek the wandering sheep; who givest consolation to the faint-hearted, and life unto those who are broken of heart; who didst heal the flow of the woman who had had an issue of blood twelve years; who didst free the daughter of the Canaanitish woman from the cruel demon; who forgavest their debt unto the two debtors, and didst grant remission of sins unto the woman that was a sinner; who didst vouchsafe healing unto the Paralytic, and likewise the remission of his sins; who didst justify the Publican by thy word, and didst accept the Thief at his last confession; who takest away the sins of the world, and wast nailed to the Cross: We beseech thee, and entreat thee, in thy goodness loose, remit, forgive, O God, the errors of thy servant, N., and his (*her*) iniquities, whether voluntary or involuntary, whether of knowledge or of ignorance, whether of excess or of disobedience, whether of the night or of the day; whether he (*she*) be under the ban of a priest, or the curse of father or mother; whether through the sight of his (*her*) eyes, or his (*her*) sense of smell; whether through the union of adultery or the taste of fornication, or through whatsoever impulse of the flesh and of the spirit he (*she*) hath departed from thy will, and from thy holiness. If we, also, have sinned in like manner, forgive; forasmuch as thou art a good God who rememberest not evil, and lovest mankind: and let not him (*her*) or us fall into evilness of life, neither run in hurtful ways. Yea, O Master, Lord, hearken unto me, a sinner, in this hour, on behalf of thy servant, N., and overlook all his (*her*) trespasses, forasmuch as thou art a God who rememberest not evil. Free him (*her*) from torment eternal; fill his (*her*) mouth with thy praise; open his (*her*) lips that he (*she*) may glorify thy holy Name; stretch forth his (*her*) hand to the performance of thy statutes. Guide his (*her*) feet aright in the way of thy Gospel, strengthening all his (*her*) members and his (*her*) thoughts, by thy grace. For thou art our God, who hast given us a commandment by thy holy Apostles, saying: Whatsoever ye bind on earth shall be bound in heaven, and whatsoever ye loose on earth shall be loosed in heaven. And again: Unto whomsoever ye remit sins, unto him they shall be remitted, and if ye retain them, they shall be retained. And as thou didst hearken unto Ezekiel in the sorrow of his soul, at the hour of his death, and didst not despise his supplications, so also, in like manner, give ear unto me, thy humble, and sinful, and unworthy servant at this hour. For thou art the Lord Jesus Christ, who didst command us to forgive the erring their sins, even unto seventy times seven, through thy goodness, and love towards mankind, and who repentest thee of our wickedness, and rejoicest over the return of those who have gone astray. For as is thy majesty, so also is thy mercy, and unto thee do we ascribe glory, together with thy Father who is from ever-lasting, and thine all-holy, and good, and life-giving Spirit, now, and ever, and unto ages of ages. —— *Choir.* Amen.

> *And after this Prayer, the Sixth Priest taketh the sixth wand, and dipping it in the holy Oil, he anointeth therewith the sick person, reciting the while the Prayer:* O holy Father, Physician of souls and bodies, . . . *with the Exclamation.* (*See page* 345.)

Deacon. Let us attend.

Seventh Priest. Peace be with you all. —— *Choir.* And with thy spirit.

Deacon. Wisdom! Let us attend.

Reader. The Gradual (*Prokímen*), in the Seventh Tone. O Lord, re-buke me not in thine anger, neither chasten me in thy sore displeasure.

Verse (*Stikh*): Have mercy upon me, O Lord, for I am weak.

Deacon. Wisdom!

Reader. The Lesson from the Epistle of the holy Apostle Paul to the Thessalonians.

Priest. Let us attend.

Deacon. (*1 Thes. v. 14–24.*) Now we exhort you, brethren, warn them that are unruly, comfort the feeble-minded, support the weak, be patient toward all men. See that none render evil for evil unto any man; but ever follow that which is good, both among yourselves, and to all men. Re-joice evermore. Pray without ceasing. In every thing give thanks: for this is the will of God in Christ Jesus concerning you. Quench not the spirit. Despise not prophesyings. Prove all things; hold fast that which is good. Abstain from all appearance of evil. And the very God of peace sanctify you wholly; and I pray God your whole spirit, and soul, and body, be preserved blameless unto the coming of our Lord Jesus Christ.

Seventh Priest. Peace be with thee.

Reader. And with thy spirit.

Deacon. Wisdom! Let us attend.

Reader. Alleluia, *in the Seventh Tone.*

Verse (*Stikh*): The Lord hear thee in the day of trouble; the Name of the God of Jacob defend thee.

Priest. Wisdom, O believers! Let us listen to the holy Gospel of Matthew. Peace be with you all. —— *Choir.* And with thy spirit.

Priest. The Lesson from the holy Gospel of Matthew.

Choir. Glory to thee, O Lord; glory to thee.

Deacon. Let us attend.

> *The Seventh Priest then readeth the Gospel* (Matt. ix. 9–14).

And as Jesus passed forth from thence, he saw a man named Matthew, sitting at the receipt of custom: and he saith unto him, Follow me. And he arose, and followed him. And it came to pass, as Jesus sat at meat in the house, behold, many publicans and sinners came and sat down with him and his disciples.   And when the Pharisees saw it, they said unto his disciples, Why eateth your Master with publicans and sinners?   But when Jesus heard that, he said unto them, They that be whole need not a physician, but they that are sick.   But go ye and learn what that meaneth, I will have mercy, and not sacrifice: for I am not come to call the righteous, but sinners to repentance.

Choir. Glory to thee, O Lord; glory to thee.

Then the Deacon saith the Litany: Have mercy upon us, . . . O God, *and the Exclamation.*   (*See page* 343.)

And the Seventh Priest saith the following Prayer:

O Master, Lord our God, thou art the Physician of souls and bodies, who assuagest temporal sufferings and healest every infirmity and every wound of men; who desirest that all men should be saved, and should come to the knowledge of the truth; who desirest not the death of a sinner, but that he should turn him again and live: for thou, O Lord, in the ancient Covenant, didst ordain repentance unto sinners, unto David and the Ninevites, and unto those who went before them, and likewise, at the advent of thy dispensation in the flesh, thou calledst not the righteous but sinners to repentance; who didst accept in repentance the Publican, the Woman who was a sinner, and the Thief, and great Paul the blaspheming Persecutor; and who didst accept in repentance great Peter, thy chief Apostle, who also thrice denied thee; and gavest unto him a promise, saying: Thou art Peter, and on this rock will I build my Church, and the gates of Hell shall not prevail against it; and I will give thee the keys of the kingdom of heaven.   For which cause, O Good One, who lovest mankind, we also have boldness, according to thy faithful promise, and we beseech thee, and implore thee, at this present hour: Give ear unto our supplication, and receive it as incense offered unto thee; and visit thy servant, N.; and if he (*she*) hath done aught amiss, either by word, or deed, or thought, either by night or by day; if he (*she*) hath fallen under the ban of a priest, or under his (*her*) own anathema; or hath been embittered by an oath, and hath cursed himself (*herself*): We beseech thee, and supplicate thee: loose, pardon, forgive him (*her*), O God, overlooking his (*her*) sins and wickednesses, both those which he (*she*) hath done knowingly, and those which he (*she*) hath committed in ignorance.   And if he (*she*) hath transgressed thy commandments, or hath sinned because he (*she*) beareth flesh, and dwelleth in the world, or through the wiles of the Devil, do thou, forasmuch as thou art a good God and lovest mankind, forgive; for there is no man who liveth and sinneth not.   For thou only art sinless, thy righteousness is righteousness to all eternity, and thy word is truth.   Because thou hast not created man for destruction, but for the keeping of thy commandments, and for the inheritance of life incorruptible; and unto thee do we ascribe glory, together with the Father, and the Holy Spirit, now, and ever, and unto ages of ages.   Amen.

And after this Prayer, the Seventh Priest taketh the seventh wand, and dipping it in the holy Oil, he anointeth therewith the sick person, reciting the while the Prayer: O holy Father, Physician of souls and bodies, . . . *with the Exclamation. (See page* 345.)

At the conclusion of the Anointing, the sick person, if he be able, shall himself go among the Priests; or, supported by his own people, he shall stand or sit among them.

But if he be not able, the Priests shall gather about him, as he lieth on his couch. And the principal Priest, taking the book of the Holy Gospels, and opening it, shall lay it, with the writing down, on the head of the sick person, the book being held by all the Priests.

And the principal Priest doth not lay on his hand, but reciteth, aloud, *this Prayer:* (7)

O holy King, compassionate and all-merciful Lord Jesus Christ, Son and Word of the living God, who desirest not the death of a sinner, but rather that he should turn from his wickedness and live: I lay not my sinful hand upon the head of him (*her*) who is come unto thee in iniquities, and asketh of thee, through us, the pardon of his (*her*) sins, but thy strong and mighty hand, which is in this, thy Holy Gospels, that is now held by my fellow-ministers, upon the head of thy servant, N. And with them I, also, beseech and entreat thy merciful compassion and love of mankind, which cherisheth no remembrance of evil, O God our Saviour, who by the hand of thy prophet Nathan didst give remission of his sins unto penitent David, and didst accept Manasses' prayer of contrition: Do thou, the same Lord, receive also with thy wonted tender love towards mankind, this thy servant, N., who repenteth him (*her*) of his (*her*) sore transgressions, regarding not all his (*her*) trespasses. For thou art our God, who hast commanded that we forgive, even unto seventy times seven, those who fall into sin. For as is thy majesty, so also is thy mercy: and unto thee are due all glory, honour and worship, now, and ever, and unto ages of ages. Amen.

Then, taking the book of the Holy Gospels from the head of the sick person, they give it to him to kiss.

And the Deacon straightway reciteth the Litany: Have mercy upon us, O God, . . . *with the Exclamation. (See page* 343.)

Then the Choir singeth: Glory to the Father, and to the Son, and to the Holy Spirit.

Hymn (Tropár), in Tone IV. Forasmuch as ye have a fountain of healing, O Unmercenary Ones, ye bestow healing upon all those who ask it, in that ye have been accounted worthy of exceeding great gifts from the Fountain ever-flowing, our Saviour. For the Lord hath said unto you, as unto zealous labourers, equal in zeal to the Apostles: Behold, I have given you power over unclean spirits, to cast them out, and to heal every infirmity, and every malady. Wherefore, as ye have nobly lived, according to his commandments, freely ye have received, and freely do ye give, healing the ills of our souls and bodies.

Now, and ever, and unto ages of ages.   Amen.

Hymn to the Birth-giver of God, in the same Tone. Regard the prayers of thy servants, O All-undefiled One, who quenchest the fierce attacks upon us, giving us release from every adversity: for thee alone have we as a support firm and assured, and have acquired thy protection, O Lady; and all we who call upon thee shall not be put to confusion. Make haste to the petitions of those who with faith cry unto thee: Hail, O Lady!   O Help of all men!   O Joy and Refuge, and Salvation of our souls!

Glory to the Father, and to the Son, and to the Holy Spirit, now, and ever, and unto ages of ages.   Amen.

Lord, have mercy.   (*Thrice.*)

Bless.

And the BENEDICTION.

May Christ our true God, through the prayers of his most pure Mother; by the might of the precious and life-giving Cross; of the holy, glorious and all-laudable James, the Apostle and the first Bishop of Jerusalem, the brother of God; and of all the Saints; save us and have mercy upon us, forasmuch as he is good, and loveth mankind.

And the Person who hath received Unction with Prayer maketh a reverence, saying:

Bless me, holy Fathers.   Pardon me, a sinner.   (*Thrice.*)

And having received their blessing and pardon, he goeth thence, giving thanks unto God.

THE OFFICE AT THE PARTING OF THE SOUL FROM THE BODY

The Abbot cometh to a monk, or his Father Confessor to a layman, and inquireth if there be any word or deed which hath been forgotten, or baseness, or any wrath against any brother, which hath remained unconfessed, or is unforgiven; he must search all there is, and interrogate the dying man concerning each one.

Then the Priest beginneth:

Blessed is our God always, now, and ever, and unto ages of ages. Amen.

O Holy God, Holy Mighty, Holy Immortal One, have mercy upon us. (*Thrice.*)

Glory to the Father, and to the Son, and to the Holy Spirit, now, and ever, and unto ages of ages. Amen.

O all-holy Trinity, have mercy upon us. O Lord, wash away our sins. O Master, pardon our transgressions. O Holy One, visit and heal our infirmities, for thy Name's sake.

Lord, have mercy. (*Thrice.*) Glory . . . now, and ever, . . .

Our Father, who art in heaven, Hallowed be thy Name. Thy kingdom come. Thy will be done on earth, As it is in heaven. Give us this day our daily bread. And forgive us our trespasses, As we forgive those who trespass against us. And lead us not into temptation; But deliver us from the Evil One:

For thine is the kingdom, and the power, and the glory, of the Father, and of the Son, and of the Holy Spirit, now, and ever, and unto ages of ages. Amen.

Lord, have mercy. (*Twelve times.*)

O come, let us worship God our King. O come, let us worship and fall down before Christ, our King and our God. O come, let us worship and fall down before the Very Christ, our King and our God. (*Three reverences.*)

PSALM LI.

Have mercy upon me, O God, after thy great goodness; according to the multitude of thy mercies do away mine offences. Wash me throughly from my wickedness, and cleanse me from my sin. For I acknowledge my faults, and my sin is ever before me. Against thee only have I sinned, and done this evil in thy sight; that thou mightest be justified in thy saying and clear when thou art judged. Behold I was shapen in wickedness, and in sin hath my mother conceived me. But lo, thou requirest truth in the inward parts, and shalt make me to understand wisdom secretly. Thou shalt purge me with hyssop, and I shall be clean; thou shalt wash me, and I shall be whiter than snow. Thou shalt make me hear of joy and gladness, that the bones which thou hast broken may rejoice. Turn thy face from my sins, and put out all my misdeeds. Make me a clean heart, O God, and renew a right spirit within me. Cast me not away from thy presence, and take not thy Holy Spirit from me. O give me the comfort of thy help again, and stablish me with thy free Spirit. Then shall I teach thy ways unto the wicked, and sinners shall be converted unto thee. Deliver me from blood-guiltiness, O God, thou that art the God of my health; and my tongue shall sing of thy righteousness. Thou shalt open my lips, O Lord, and my mouth shall show thy praise. For thou desirest no sacrifice, else would I give it thee; but thou delightest not in burnt-offerings. The sacrifice of God is a troubled spirit: a broken and contrite heart, O God, shalt thou not despise. O be favourable and gracious unto Zion: build thou the walls of Jerusalem. Then shalt thou be pleased with the sacrifice of righteousness, with the burnt-offerings and oblations: then shall they offer young bullocks upon thine altar.

A Canon of Prayer to the All-undefiled Birth-giver of God, with Theme-Songs (Irmosí) in the Sixth Tone, on behalf of a man whose soul is departing, and who cannot speak.

Canticle I.

Theme-Song (Irmós). When Israel passed on foot over the deep, as it had been dry land, and beheld their pursuer Pharaoh engulfed in the sea, they cried aloud: Let us sing unto God a song of victory.

Refrain. O all-holy Birth-giver of God, save us.*

Hymns (Tropari). Like drops of rain my evil days and few, dried up by summer's heat, already gently vanish: O Lady, save me.

Through thy tenderness of heart and thy many bounties, by nature inclined thereto, O Lady, in this dread hour intercede for me, O Helper Invincible!

Great terror now imprisoneth my soul, trembling unutterable and grievous, when forth from the body it must go: Comfort thou it, O All-undefiled One.

Glory to the Father, and to the Son, and to the Holy Spirit.

O Refuge renowned for the sinful and contrite, make thy mercy known upon me, O Pure One, and deliver me from the hands of demons: For many dogs have compassed me about.

Now, and ever, and unto ages of ages. Amen.

Lo, now is the hour for succour, lo, now the hour for thine intercession; lo, now, the time because of which, day and night I have bowed down before thee, and prayed fervently unto thee, O Lady.

Canticle III.

Theme-Song (Irmós). There is none holy like unto thee, O Lord, my God, who hast exalted the horn of thy faithful, O Good One, and hast established us upon the rock of thy confession.

* After each Irmós and Hymn, except the Collect-Hymn and the Ikos.

Hymns (Tropari). Inasmuch as I foresaw this day from afar, O Lady, meditating ever upon it as though it were come, with hot tears I have prayed unto thee that thou wouldst not forget me.

The assembly of the crafty, gaping, have compassed me round about, and seek to bear me away and bitterly torment me. Crush thou their teeth and jaws and save me, O Pure One.

For as an organ of speech I am altogether extinguished, and my tongue is bound, and mine eye closeth. In contrition of heart I entreat thee: O my Deliverer, save me.

Glory to the Father, and to the Son, and to the Holy Spirit.

Incline thine ear unto me, O Mother of Christ my God, from the height of thy great glory, O Good One; and hear my last groan, and give me thy hand.

Now, and ever, and unto ages of ages. Amen.

Turn not from me thy many bounties; shut not the bowels of thy love toward mankind, O Pure One: but intercede for me now, and in the hour of judgment remember thou me.

Canticle IV.

Theme-Song (Irmós). Christ is my strength, my God and my Lord, the august Church doth sing in God-befitting wise, crying aloud and out of a pure mind keeping festival unto the Lord.

Hymns (Tropari). Appoint thou now a washing for sin, a stream of tears, O Good One, receiving the contrition of my heart. In thee have I set my hope, O Good One, when thou deliverest me from frightful fiery torment; forasmuch as thou art the Fountain of Grace, O Birth-giver of God.

O Refuge which maketh not ashamed, and infallible unto all who are in need, Lady all-undefiled, be thou my defender in the hour of trial.

Stretch forth, O All-pure One, thine all-honourable hands, like unto the wings of a holy dove, under whose protection and shelter cover thou me, O Lady.

Glory.

O Conqueror and Tormentor of the fierce Prince of the air, O Guardian of the dread path, and Searcher of these vain words, help thou me to pass over unhindered, as I depart from earth.

Now, and ever, . . .

Lo, terror is come to meet me, O Lady, and I fear it; lo, a great ordeal hath seized hold upon me, wherein be thou my helper, O thou Hope of my salvation.

Canticle V.

Theme-Song (Irmós). With thy light divine, O Good One, illumine thou, I pray thee, the souls of those who wake early unto thee with love: that they may know thee, O Word of God, of the true God, who callest forth from the gloom of sin.

Hymns (Tropari). Forget me not, O Good One, neither turn thou away thy face from me, thy child; but hear me, for I am in trouble; and receive thou my soul, and deliver it.

Ye who are my kinsfolk in the flesh, and ye who are my brethren in the spirit, my friends and wonted acquaintance, weep ye, sigh, wail: For lo, now am I departing from you.

No one now delivereth, and, of a truth, there is none to aid. Succour thou me, O Lady; else as a helpless man shall I be captive in the hands of mine enemies.

Glory . . .

Having entered, O ye my holy Angels, as ye stand before the Judgment Seat of Christ, bending in thought your supersensual knees, cry ye with weeping unto him: Have mercy, O Maker of all men, upon the work of thy hands, O Good One; and cast it not away.

Now, and ever, . . .

Bowing down before the Sovereign Lady and all-pure Mother of my God, pray ye that she will bend her knees together with you; and she shall bend Him to mercy: For the true Mother and Nourisher will be heard.

Canticle VI.

Theme-Song (Irmós). Forasmuch as I behold the sea of life surging high with the tempest of temptations, I have fled to thy tranquil haven and cry aloud unto thee: Lead thou my life forth from corruption, O Most Merciful One.

Hymns (Tropari). My mouth is silent, and my tongue speaketh not, but my heart maketh utterance: For that fire of contrition which inwardly devoureth is kindled, and in tones inexpressible invoketh thee, O Virgin.

Look down upon me from on high, O Mother of God, and mercifully hearken now to my supplication; that having beheld thee I may go forth from the body rejoicing.

The destruction of ties, and the overthrow of nature's laws of union, and of the whole corporeal structure, cause me anguish and distress intolerable.

Glory . . .

To the holy and honourable arms of the holy Angels transfer me, O Lady; that covered with their wings I behold not the ignominious and revolting and gloomy forms of devils.

Now, and ever, . . .

O All-honourable Abode of God, grant unto me the heavenly, the supersensual abode, after that thou hast kindled my expiring and unradiant light by the holy oil of thy mercy.

Collect-Hymn (Kondák), in Tone VI.

Arise, O my soul, O my soul why sleepest thou? The end draweth near, and thou must speak. Arise, therefore, from thy sleep, and Christ our God, who is in all places and filleth all things, shall spare thee.

Ikos.

The Devil, when he beheld the healing of Christ thrown open, and the health which flowed therefrom unto Adam, being sore smitten as it were with a calamity, wailed and cried unto his friends: What shall I do unto the Son of Mary? The Bethlehemite, who is in all places and filleth all things, doth slay me.

Canticle VII.

Theme-Song (Irmós). An Angel made the fiery furnace to drop dew for the Holy Children, but the command of God, consuming the Chaldæans with fire, prevailed upon the tormentor to cry aloud: Blessed art thou, O God of our fathers!

Hymns (Tropari). The night of death, gloomy and moonless, hath overtaken me, still unready, sending me forth on that long and dreadful journey unprepared. But let thy mercy accompany me, O Lady.

Lo, all my days are vanished, of a truth, in vanity, as it is written, and my years also in vain; and now the snares of death, which of a truth are bitter, have entangled my soul, and have compassed me round about.

Let not the multitude of my sins conquer thy great tenderness of heart, O Lady. But let thy mercy compass me round about, and let it cover all my transgressions.

Glory . . .

They who shall lead me hence are come, and hem me in on every side; but my soul holdeth back and is dismayed, being filled with much rebellion; the which allay thou, O Pure One, by thy manifestation.

Now, and ever, . . .

Not one have I found who grieveth over my affliction, or who comforteth me, O Lady: For all my friends and acquaintance have now abandoned me. But do thou, O my Hope, in no wise forsake me.

Canticle VIII.

Theme-Song (Irmós). Out of the flames thou didst shed forth dew upon the Godly Ones, and with water didst kindle the sacrifice of the Righteous One. For thou doest all things which thou willest, O Christ. Thee will we exalt unto all the ages.

Hymns (Tropari). As the Mother loving mankind of the God who loveth mankind, look thou with calm and merciful eye when my soul from its body shall part; and I will glorify thee forever, O holy Birthgiver of God.

Vouchsafe that I may escape the hordes of bodiless barbarians, and rise through the abysses of the air, and enter into heaven; and I will glorify thee forever, O holy Birth-giver of God.

O thou who didst bear the Lord Almighty, banish thou far from me when I come to die, the chieftain of bitter torments who ruleth the universe; and I will glorify thee forever, O holy Birth-giver of God.

Glory . . .

When the last great trump shall sound unto the frightful and dread Resurrection of the Judgment Day, and all shall rise from the dead; then remember thou me, O holy Birth-giver of God.

Now, and ever, . . .

O lofty Palace of Christ our Master, who hast sent down thy grace from on high, aid thou me now, in the day of wrath; and I will glorify thee forever, O holy Birth-giver of God.

Canticle IX.

Theme-Song (Irmós). It is not possible that men should see God, upon whom the Orders of the Angels dare not gaze: but through thee, O All-pure One, was the Word Incarnate manifested unto men; Whom magnifying, together with the Heavenly Hosts, we call thee blessed.

Hymns (Tropari). Oh, how shall I look upon the invisible? How shall I endure its vision dread? How shall I dare mine eyes to open? How shall I dare to gaze upon my Master, whom I have not ceased, from my youth up, ever to grieve?

O Holy Maiden, Birth-giver of God, look with mercy upon my meekness. Receive this my propitiatory and final prayer, and from the fire that tortureth to all eternity make thou haste to deliver me.

I, who have defiled the holy temples, on quitting this vile temple of the body, do beseech thee, O all-honourable Temple of God, Maiden, Virgin Mother, that my soul may escape outer darkness, and the burning of fierce Gehenna.

Glory . . .

Forasmuch as I now behold the end of my life draw near, and am a worker of unseemly thoughts and deeds, O All-pure One, I am cruelly smitten with the stings of conscience, O Maker of my soul. But do thou mercifully incline unto me; and be thou my Intercessor.

Now, and ever, . . .

The Son will give himself unto us for mercy, the Son of God and King of the Angels, the Man Eternal, coming forth from thy pure blood; Whom do thou propitiate, O Maiden, on behalf of my passion-tossed soul, which is cruelly wrested from my body accursed.

Meet is it, in truth, to bless thee, the Birth-giver of God, ever-blessed and all-undefiled, and the Mother of our God. More honourable than the Cherubim, and beyond compare more glorious than the Seraphim, thou who without defilement barest God the Word, true Birth-giver of God, we magnify thee.

The Prayers said by the Priest at the Departure of a Soul.

O Lord God Almighty, the Father of our Lord Jesus Christ, who willest that all men should be saved, and should come unto the knowledge of the truth; who desirest not the death of a sinner, but that he should turn again and live: We pray thee and implore thee, absolve thou the soul of thy servant, N., from every bond, and deliver him (*her*) from every curse. Pardon his (*her*) transgressions, both of knowledge and of ignorance, both of deed and of word, which he (*she*) hath committed from his (*her*) youth up, and hath cleanly confessed or hath concealed, either through forgetfulness or through shame. For thou alone loosest those things which are bound, and guidest aright the contrite, and art the hope of the despairing, and mighty to remit the sins of every man who putteth his trust in thee. Yea, O Lord who lovest mankind, give thou command, and he shall be released from the bonds of the flesh and of sin; and receive thou in peace the soul of this thy servant, N., and give it rest in the everlasting mansions, with thy Saints; through the grace of thine Only-begotten Son, our Lord, and God, and Saviour Jesus Christ: with whom also thou art blessed, together with thine all-holy, and good, and life-giving Spirit, now, and ever, and unto ages of ages. Amen.

Or: Let us pray to the Lord.

Lord, have mercy.

O Master, Lord our God Almighty, who willest that all men should be saved and should come to a knowledge of the truth; who desirest not the death of a sinner, but that he should turn again and be saved: We pray thee and beseech thee, deliver thou the soul of thy servant, N., from every bond, free it from every curse. For thou art he who delivereth them that are bound, and guideth aright them that are cast down, O Hope of the hopeless. Wherefore, O Master, command that the soul of thy servant, N., may depart in peace, and may rest in thine everlasting mansions with all thy Saints; through thine Only-begotten Son, with whom thou art blessed, together with thine all-holy, and good, and life-giving Spirit, now, and ever, and unto ages of ages. Amen.

Another Prayer for a Person who hath suffered long, and is on the point of death.

O Lord our God, who in thine ineffable wisdom hast created man, fashioning him out of the dust, and adorning him with comeliness and goodness, as an honourable and heavenly acquisition, to the exaltation and magnificence of thy glory and kingdom, that thou mightest bring him into this image and likeness; but forasmuch as he sinned against the command of thy statute, having accepted the image but preserved it not, and because, also, evil shall not be eternal: Thou hast ordained remission unto the same, through thy love toward mankind; and that this destructible bond, which as the God of our fathers thou hadst sanctified by thy divine will, should be dissolved, and that his body should be dissolved from the elements of which it was fashioned, but that his soul should be translated to that place where it shall take up its abode until the final Resurrection. Therefore we pray unto thee, the Father who is from everlasting, and immortal, and unto thine Only-begotten Son, and unto thine all-holy Spirit, that thou wilt deliver N. from the body unto repose, entreating, also, forgiveness of thine ineffable goodness if he (*she*) in any wise, whether of knowledge or in ignorance, hath offended thy goodness, or is under the ban of a priest, or hath embittered his (*her*) parents, or hath broken a vow, or hath fallen into devilish imaginations and shameful sorceries, through the malice of the crafty demon: Yea, O Master, Lord our God, hearken unto me a sinner and thine unworthy servant in this hour, and deliver thy servant, N., from this intolerable sickness which holdeth him (*her*) in bitter impotency, and give him (*her*) rest where the souls of the righteous dwell. For thou art the repose of our souls and of our bodies, and unto thee do we ascribe glory, to the Father, and to the Son, and to the Holy Spirit, now, and ever, and unto ages of ages. Amen.

THE ORDER FOR THE BURIAL OF THE DEAD
(LAYMEN) (1) *

When an Orthodox believer dieth, his relatives straightway give notice thereof unto the Priest, who, when he is come to the house in which the remains of the dead man lie, and hath put on his priestly stole (epitrakhíl), and hath placed incense in the censer, censeth the body of the dead, and those present; and beginneth as usual:

Blessed is our God always, now, and ever, and unto ages of ages. Amen.

And those who stand there begin:

O Holy God, Holy Mighty, Holy Immortal One, have mercy upon us. (*Thrice.*)

Glory to the Father, and to the Son, and to the Holy Spirit, now, and ever, and unto ages of ages. Amen.

O all-holy Trinity, have mercy upon us. O Lord, wash away our sins. O Master, pardon our transgressions. O Holy One, visit and heal our infirmities, for thy Name's sake.

Lord, have mercy. (*Thrice.*) Glory . . . now, and ever, . . .

Our Father, who art in heaven, Hallowed be thy Name. Thy kingdom come. Thy will be done on earth, As it is in heaven. Give us this day our daily bread. And forgive us our trespasses, As we forgive those who trespass against us. And lead us not into temptation; But deliver us from the Evil One:

Priest. For thine is the kingdom, and the power, and the glory, of the Father, and of the Son, and of the Holy Spirit, now, and ever, and unto ages of ages. Amen.

And immediately the following Hymns (Tropárĭ), in Tone IV., are sung:

With the souls of the righteous dead give rest, O Saviour, to the soul of thy servant, preserving it unto the life of blessedness which is with thee, O thou who lovest mankind.

In the place of thy rest, O Lord, where all thy Saints repose, give rest also to the soul of thy servant; for thou only lovest mankind.

Glory . . .

Thou art the God who descended into Hell, and loosed the bonds of the captives. Do thou give rest also to the soul of thy servant.

Now, and ever, . . .

O Virgin alone Pure and Undefiled, who without seed didst bring forth God, pray thou that his (*her*) soul may be saved.

* For explanations, indicated by numbers, see Appendix, B, X.

Deacon. Have mercy upon us, O God, according to thy great mercy, we beseech thee: hearken, and have mercy.

Choir. Lord, have mercy. (*Thrice.*)

Furthermore we pray for the repose of the soul of the servant of God departed this life, N.; and that thou wilt pardon all his (*her*) sins both voluntary and involuntary. ℞

That the Lord God will establish his (*her*) soul where the just repose. ℞

The mercies of God, the kingdom of heaven, and the remission of his (*her*) sins, we entreat of Christ, our King Immortal and our God.

Choir. Grant it, O Lord.

Deacon. Let us pray to the Lord.

Choir. Lord, have mercy.

And the Priest, meanwhile, saith, secretly, the following Prayer:

O God of spirits, and of all flesh, who hast trampled down Death, and overthrown the Devil, and given life unto thy world: Do thou, the same Lord, give rest to the soul of thy departed servant, N., in a place of brightness, a place of verdure, a place of repose, whence all sickness, sorrow and sighing have fled away. Pardon every transgression which he (*she*) hath committed, whether by word, or deed, or thought. For thou art a good God, and lovest mankind; because there is no man who liveth and sinneth not: for thou only art without sin, and thy righteousness is to all eternity, and thy word is true.

Secretly.

Exclamation. For thou art the Resurrection, and the Life, and the Repose of thy departed servant, N., O Christ our God, and unto thee we ascribe glory, together with thy Father who is from everlasting, and thine all-holy, and good, and life-giving Spirit, now, and ever, and unto ages of ages. · Amen.

Deacon. Wisdom!

Choir. More honourable than the Cherubim, and beyond compare more glorious than the Seraphim, thou who without defilement barest God the Word, true Birth-giver of God, we magnify thee.

Lord, have mercy. (*Thrice.*)

Glory to the Father, and to the Son, and to the Holy Spirit, now, and ever, and unto ages of ages. Amen. —— Bless.

And straightway the Priest giveth the BENEDICTION.

May Christ, our true God, who hath dominion over the living and the dead: through the prayers of his all-holy Mother; of our righteous and God-bearing Fathers; and of all his Saints, establish the soul of his servant, N., departed from us, in his holy mansions, and number him (*her*) among the just; and have mercy upon us: Forasmuch as he is good and loveth mankind.

And if all things are now ready for the departure, the Priest beginneth again:
Blessed is our God ... (*See page* 368.)

And we begin to sing, with all awe and emotion: O Holy God, Holy Mighty, (2) ...
(*See page* 368.)

And taking up the mortal remains of the departed, we come, bearing tapers, unto the Church, preceded by the Priest, and by the Deacon with the censer. And when we come to the Church, the remains are deposited in the porch (or in the Church, as is the custom in Russia). And the beginning is:

PSALM XCI.

Whoso dwelleth under the defence of the Most High, shall abide under the shadow of the Almighty. I will say unto the Lord, Thou art my hope, and my stronghold; my God, in him will I trust. For he shall deliver thee from the snare of the hunter, and from the noisome pestilence. He shall defend thee under his wings, and thou shalt be safe under his feathers; his faithfulness and truth shall be thy shield and buckler. Thou shalt not be afraid for any terror by night, nor for the arrow that flieth by day; for the pestilence that walketh in darkness, nor for the sickness that destroyeth in the noon-day. A thousand shall fall beside thee, and ten thousand at thy right hand; but it shall not come nigh thee. Yea, with thine eyes shalt thou behold, and see the reward of the ungodly. For thou, Lord, art my hope; thou hast set thine house of defence very high. There shall no evil happen unto thee, neither shall any plague come nigh thy dwelling. For he shall give his angels charge over thee, to keep thee in all thy ways. They shall bear thee in their hands, that thou hurt not thy foot against a stone. Thou shalt go upon the lion and adder: the young lion and the dragon shalt thou tread under thy feet. Because he hath set his love upon me, therefore will I deliver him; I will set him up, because he hath known my Name. He shall call upon me, and I will hear him; yea, I am with him in trouble; I will deliver him, and bring him to honour. With long life will I satisfy him, and show him my salvation.
Blessed art thou, O Lord: teach me thy statutes.

Then the first portion of PSALM CXIX. *is chanted, in Tone VI.:* Blessed are those that are undefiled in the way, and walk in the law of the Lord.

PSALM CXIX.*

Blessed are those that are undefiled in the way, and walk in the law of the Lord. ℞
Refrain. Alleluia.
Blessed are they that keep his testimonies, and seek him with their whole heart. ℞
For they who do no wickedness, walk in his ways. ℞
Thou hast charged that we shall diligently keep thy commandments. ℞
O that my ways were made so direct, that I might keep thy statutes! ℞

* For the abbreviated form generally used, see page 377.

So shall I not be confounded, while I have respect unto all thy commandments. ℞

I will thank thee with an unfeigned heart, when I shall have learned the judgments of thy righteousness. ℞

I will keep thy ceremonies; O forsake me not utterly. ℞

Wherewithal shall a young man cleanse his way? even by ruling himself after thy word. ℞

With my whole heart have I sought thee; O let me not go wrong out of thy commandments! ℞

Thy words have I hid within my heart, that I should not sin against thee. ℞

Blessed art thou, O Lord; O teach me thy statutes! ℞

With my lips have I been telling of all the judgments of thy mouth. ℞

I have had as great delight in the way of thy testimonies, as in all manner of riches. ℞

I will talk of thy commandments, and have respect unto thy ways. ℞

My delight shall be in thy statutes, and I will not forget thy word. ℞

O do well unto thy servant; that I may live, and keep thy word. ℞

Open thou mine eyes; that I may see the wondrous things of thy law. ℞

I am a stranger upon earth; O hide not thy commandments from me! ℞

My soul breaketh out for the very fervent desire that it hath alway unto thy judgments. ℞

Thou hast rebuked the proud; and cursed are they that do err from thy commandments. ℞

O turn from me shame and rebuke; for I have kept thy testimonies. ℞

Princes also did sit and speak against me; but thy servant is occupied in thy statutes. ℞

For thy testimonies are my delight, and my counsellors. ℞

My soul cleaveth to the dust; O quicken thou me, according to thy word. ℞

I have acknowledged my ways, and thou heardest me: O teach me thy statutes! ℞

Make me to understand the way of thy commandments; and so shall I talk of thy wondrous works. ℞

My soul melteth away for very heaviness; comfort thou me according unto thy word. ℞

Take from me the way of lying, and cause thou me to make much of thy law. ℞

I have chosen the way of truth, and thy judgments have I laid before me. ℞

I have stuck unto thy testimonies; O Lord, confound me not! ℞

I will run the way of thy commandments, when thou hast set my heart at liberty. ℞

Teach me, O Lord, the way of thy statutes, and I shall keep it unto the end. ℞

Give me understanding, and I shall keep thy law; yea, I shall keep it with my whole heart. ℞

Make me to go in the path of thy commandments; for therein is my desire. ℞

Incline mine heart unto thy testimonies, and not to covetousness. ℞

O turn away mine eyes, lest they behold vanity; and quicken thou me in thy way. ℞

O stablish thy word in thy servant, that I may fear thee. ℞

Take away the rebuke that I am afraid of; for thy judgments are good. ℞

Behold, my delight is in thy commandments; O quicken me in thy righteousness. ℞

Let thy loving mercy come also unto me, O Lord, even thy salvation, according unto thy word. ℞

So shall I make answer unto my blasphemers; for my trust is in thy word. ℞

O take not the word of thy truth utterly out of my mouth; for my hope is in thy judgments. ℞

So shall I alway keep thy law; yea, forever and ever. ℞

And I will walk at liberty; for I seek thy commandments. ℞

I will speak of thy testimonies also, even before kings, and will not be ashamed. ℞

And my delight shall be in thy commandments, which I have loved. ℞

My hands also will I lift up unto thy commandments, which I have loved; and my study shall be in thy statutes. ℞

O think upon thy servant, as concerning thy word, wherein thou hast caused me to put my trust. ℞

The same is my comfort in my trouble; for thy word hath quickened me. ℞

The proud have had me exceedingly in derision: yet have I not shrinked from thy law. ℞

For I remembered thine everlasting judgments, O Lord, and received comfort. ℞

I am horribly afraid, for the ungodly that forsake thy law. ℞

Thy statutes have been my songs, in the house of my pilgrimage. ℞

I have thought upon thy Name, O Lord, in the night-season, and have kept thy law. ℞

This I had, because I kept thy commandments. ℞

Thou art my portion, O Lord; I have promised to keep thy law. ℞

I made my humble petition in thy presence with my whole heart; O be merciful unto me, according to thy word. ℞

I called mine own ways to remembrance, and turned my feet unto thy testimonies. ℞

I made haste, and prolonged not the time, to keep thy commandments. ℞

The congregations of the ungodly have robbed me; but I have not forgotten thy law. ℞

At midnight I will rise to give thanks unto thee, because of thy righteous judgments. ℞

I am a companion of all them that fear thee, and keep thy commandments. ℞

The earth, O Lord, is full of thy mercy: O teach me thy statutes! ℞

O Lord, thou hast dealt graciously with thy servant, according unto thy word. ℞

O learn me true understanding and knowledge; for I have believed thy commandments. ℞

Before I was troubled, I went wrong; but now have I kept thy word. ℞

Thou art good and gracious; O teach me thy statutes! ℞

The proud have imagined a lie against me; but I will keep thy commandments with my whole heart. ℞

Their heart is as fat as brawn; but my delight hath been in thy law. ℞

It is good for me that I have been in trouble; that I may learn thy statutes. ℞

Alleluia. Glory . . . alleluia. Now, and ever . . . alleluia.

Deacon. Again, yet again, in peace let us pray to the Lord.

Choir. Lord, have mercy. *And the rest, page* 369, *ending with the Exclamation.*

The law of thy mouth is dearer unto me than thousands of gold and silver.

Refrain. Have mercy upon thy servant.

Thy hands have made me and fashioned me: O give me understanding, that I may learn thy commandments. ℞

They that fear thee will be glad when they see me; because I have put my trust in thy word. ℞

I know, O Lord, that thy judgments are right, and that thou of very faithfulness hast caused me to be troubled. ℞

O let thy merciful kindness be my comfort, according to thy word unto thy servant. ℞

O let thy loving mercies come unto me, that I may live; for thy law is my delight. ℞

Let the proud be confounded, for they go wickedly about to destroy me; but I will be occupied in thy commandments. ℞

Let such as fear thee, and have known thy testimonies, be turned unto me. ℞

O let my heart be sound in thy statutes, that I be not ashamed. ℞

My soul hath longed for thy salvation, and I have a good hope because of thy word. ℞

Mine eyes long sore for thy word; saying, O when wilt thou comfort me? ℞

For I am become like a bottle in the smoke; yet do I not forget thy statutes. ℞

How many are the days of thy servant? when wilt thou be avenged of them that persecute me? ℞

The proud have digged pits for me, which are not after thy law. ℞

All thy commandments are true: they persecute me falsely; O be thou my help. ℞

They had almost made an end of me upon earth; but I forsook not thy commandments. ℞

O quicken me after thy loving-kindness; and so shall I keep the testimonies of thy mouth. ℞

O Lord, thy word endureth forever in heaven. ℞

Thy truth also remaineth from one generation to another; thou hast laid the foundation of the earth, and it abideth. ℞

They continue this day according to thine ordinance; for all things serve thee. ℞

If my delight had not been in thy law, I should have perished in my trouble. ℞

I will never forget thy commandments; for with them thou hast quickened me. ℞

I am thine: O save me, for I have sought thy commandments. ℞

The ungodly laid wait for me, to destroy me; but I will consider thy testimonies. ℞

I see that all things come to an end, but thy commandment is exceeding broad. ℞

Lord, what love have I unto thy law! all the day long is my study in it. ℞

Thou, through thy commandments, hast made me wiser than mine enemies; for they are ever with me. ℞

I have more understanding than my teachers; for thy testimonies are my study. ℞

I am wiser than the aged; because I keep thy commandments. ℞

I have refrained my feet from every evil way, that I may keep thy word. ℞

I have not shrunk from thy judgments; for thou teachest me. ℞

O how sweet are thy words unto my throat; yea, sweeter than honey unto my mouth! ℞

Through thy commandments I get understanding; therefore I hate all evil ways. ℞

Thy word is a lantern unto my feet, and a light unto my paths. ℞

I have sworn, and am steadfastly purposed, to keep thy righteous judgments. ℞

I am troubled above measure: quicken me, O Lord, according to thy word. ℞

Let the free-will offerings of my mouth please thee, O Lord; and teach me thy judgments. ℞

My soul is alway in my hand; yet do I not forget thy law. ℞

The ungodly have laid a snare for me; but yet I swerved not from thy commandments. ℞

Thy testimonies have I claimed as mine heritage for ever; and why? they are the very joy of my heart. ℞

I have applied my heart to fulfil thy statutes alway, even unto the end. ℞

I hate them that imagine evil things; but thy law do I love. ℞

Thou art my defence and shield; and my trust is in thy word. ℞

Away from me, ye wicked; I will keep the commandments of my God. ℞

O stablish me according to thy word, that I may live; and let me not be disappointed of my hope. ℞

Hold thou me up, and I shall be safe; yea, my delight shall be ever in thy statutes. ℞

Thou hast trodden down all them that depart from thy statutes; for they imagine but deceit. ℞

Thou puttest away all the ungodly of the earth like dross; therefore I love thy testimonies. ℞

My flesh trembleth for fear of thee; and I am afraid of thy judgments. ℞

I deal with the thing that is lawful and right; O give me not over unto mine oppressors! ℞

Make thou thy servant to delight in that which is good, that the proud do me no wrong. ℞

Mine eyes are wasted away with looking for thy health, and for the word of thy righteousness. ℞

O deal with thy servant according unto thy loving mercy, and teach me thy statutes. ℞

I am thy servant; O grant me understanding, that I may know thy testimonies. ℞

It is time for thee, Lord, to lay to thine hand; for they have destroyed thy law. ℞

For I love thy commandments above gold and precious stones. ℞

Therefore hold I straight all thy commandments; and all false ways I utterly abhor. ℞

Thy testimonies are wonderful; therefore doth my soul keep them. ℞

When thy word goeth forth, it giveth light and understanding unto the simple. ℞

I opened my mouth, and drew in my breath; for my delight was in thy commandments. ℟

Glory . . . Have mercy upon thy servant. Now, and ever. . . . Have mercy upon thy servant.

Deacon. Again, yet again, in peace let us pray to the Lord. (*See page 369, ending with the Exclamation.*)

O look thou upon me, and be merciful unto me, as thou usest to do unto those that love thy Name. —— *Refrain.* Alleluia.

Order my steps in thy word; and so shall no wickedness have dominion over me. ℟

O deliver me from the wrongful dealings of men; and so shall I keep thy commandments. ℟

Show the light of thy countenance upon thy servant, and teach me thy statutes. ℟

Mine eyes gush out with water, because men keep not thy law. ℟

Righteous art thou, O Lord; and true is thy judgment. ℟

The testimonies that thou hast commanded are exceeding righteous and true. ℟

My zeal hath even consumed me; because mine enemies have forgotten thy words. ℟

Thy word is tried to the uttermost, and thy servant loveth it. ℟

I am small and of no reputation; yet do I not forget thy commandments. ℟

Thy righteousness is an everlasting righteousness, and thy law is the truth. ℟

Trouble and heaviness have taken hold upon me; yet is my delight in thy commandments. ℟

The righteousness of thy testimonies is everlasting: O grant me understanding, and I shall live. ℟

I call with my whole heart; hear me, O Lord; I will keep thy statutes. ℟

Yea, even unto thee do I call; help me, and I shall keep thy testimonies. ℟

Early in the morning do I cry unto thee; for in thy word is my trust. ℟

Mine eyes prevent the night watches; that I might be occupied in thy words. ℟

Hear my voice, O Lord, according unto thy loving-kindness; quicken me, according as thou art wont. ℟

They draw nigh that of malice persecute me, and are far from thy law. ℟

Be thou nigh at hand, O Lord; for all thy commandments are true. ℟

As concerning thy testimonies, I have known long since, that thou hast grounded them forever. ℟

O consider mine adversity, and deliver me, for I do not forget thy law. ℟

Avenge thou my cause, and deliver me; quicken me according to thy word. ℞

Health is far from the ungodly; for they regard not thy statutes. ℞

Great is thy mercy, O Lord; quicken me, as thou art wont. ℞

Many there are that trouble me, and persecute me; yet do I not swerve from thy testimonies. ℞

It grieveth me when I see the transgressors; because they keep not thy law. ℞

Consider, O Lord, how I love thy commandments; O quicken me according to thy loving-kindness. ℞

Thy word is true from everlasting; all the judgments of thy righteousness endure for evermore. ℞

Princes have persecuted me without a cause; but my heart standeth in awe of thy word. ℞

I am as glad of thy word, as one that findeth great spoils. ℞

As for lies, I hate and abhor them; but thy law do I love. ℞

Seven times a day do I praise thee; because of thy righteous judgments. ℞

Great is the peace that they have who love thy law; and they are not offended at it. ℞

Lord, I have looked for thy saving health, and done after thy commandments. ℞

My soul hath kept thy testimonies, and loved them exceedingly. ℞

I have kept thy commandments and testimonies; for all my ways are before thee. ℞

Let my complaint come before thee, O·Lord; give me understanding according to thy word. ℞

Let my supplication come before thee; deliver me according to thy word. ℞

My lips shall speak of thy praise, when thou hast taught me thy statutes. ℞

Yea, my tongue shall sing of thy word; for all thy commandments are righteous. ℞

Let thine hand help me; for I have chosen thy commandments. ℞

I have longed for thy saving health, O Lord; and in thy law is my delight. ℞

O let my soul live, and it shall praise thee; and thy judgments shall help me. ℞

I have gone astray like a sheep that is lost; O seek thy servant, for I do not forget thy commandments. ℞

(Abbreviated alternative.) *

PSALM CXIX. 1–71.   *Tone VI.*

Blessed are those that are undefiled in the way, and walk in the law of the Lord.

* Generally all is omitted, except the first and last verses of each portion, as here shown; or selected verses (with the Refrains) only are used.

Refrain. Alleluia.

Blessed are they that keep his testimonies, and seek him with their whole heart. ℟

For they who do no wickedness, walk in his ways. ℟

. . . .

It is good for me that I have been in trouble: that I may learn thy statutes. ℟

Glory to the Father, and to the Son, and to the Holy Spirit, now, and ever, and unto ages of ages. Amen. Alleluia. *And the Priest re-*

Deacon. Again, yet again, in peace let us pray *citeth,* secretly, *the* to the Lord. *Prayer: O God of*

Choir. Lord, have mercy. (*Thrice.*) *spirits, . . .(See p. 369.)*

Again we pray for the repose of the soul of the servant of God, N., departed this life; and that he (*she*) may be pardoned all his (*her*) sins, both voluntary and involuntary. ℟

That the Lord God will establish his (*her*) soul where the Just repose. ℟

The mercy of God, the kingdom of heaven, and the remission of his (*her*) sins, we entreat of Christ, our King Immortal and our God.

Choir. Grant it, O Lord.

Deacon. Let us pray to the Lord.

Choir. Lord, have mercy.

Then the abbreviated second portion of PSALM CXIX. (*verses 72–131*). *Refrain at the end of each verse:* Have mercy upon thy servant.

The law of thy mouth is dearer unto me than thousands of gold and silver.

Refrain. Have mercy upon thy servant.

Thy hands have made me and fashioned me: O give me understanding, that I may learn thy commandments. ℟

. . . .

Thy testimonies are wonderful; therefore doth my soul keep them. ℟

When thy word goeth forth; it giveth light and understanding unto the simple. ℟

I opened my mouth, and drew in my breath; for my delight was in thy commandments. ℟

Glory . . . Have mercy upon thy servant. Now, and ever, . . .

Deacon. Again, yet again, . . . (*And the rest, as above.*)

And the Priest, in the meanwhile, saith the Prayer: O God of spirits, . . . (*See page 369.*)

Then the abbreviated third portion of PSALM CXIX. (*verse 132 to the end of Psalm*). *Refrain at the end of each verse:* Alleluia.

O look thou upon me and be merciful unto me, as thou usest to do unto those that love thy Name.

Refrain. Alleluia.

O let my soul live, and it shall praise thee; and thy judgments shall help me. ℞ . . . .

I have gone astray like a sheep that is lost; O seek thy servant, for I do not forget thy commandments. ℞

Refrain. Blessed art thou, O Lord: teach me thy statutes.

The Choir of the Saints have found the Fountain of Life and the Door of Paradise. May I also find the right way, through repentance. I am a lost sheep. Call me, O Saviour, and save me.

Refrain. Blessed art thou, O Lord: teach me thy statutes.

Ye who preached the Lamb of God, and like unto lambs were slain, and are translated unto the life eternal, which waxeth not old; ye holy Martyrs, pray ye unto him that he will vouchsafe us remission of our sins. ℞

Ye who have trod the narrow way most sad; all ye who, in life, have taken upon you the Cross as a yoke, and have followed Me through faith, draw near: Enjoy ye the honours and the crowns which I have prepared for you. ℞

I am an image of thy glory ineffable, though I bear the brands of transgressions: Show thy compassions upon thy creature, O Master, and purify him (*her*) by thy loving-kindness; and grant unto me the home-country of my heart's desire, making me again a citizen of Paradise. ℞

O thou who of old didst call me into being from nothingness, and didst honour me with thine image divine, but because I had transgressed thy commandments hast returned me again unto the earth from which I was taken: Restore thou me to that image, and to my pristine beauty. ℞

Give rest, O Lord, to the soul of thy servant, and establish him (*her*) in Paradise. Where the choirs of the Saints, O Lord, and of the Just, shine like the stars of heaven, give rest to thy servant who hath fallen asleep, regarding not all his (*her*) transgressions.

Glory to the Father, and to the Son, and to the Holy Spirit.

Devoutly do we hymn the triune Effulgence of the one Godhead, crying aloud: Holy art thou, O Father, who art from everlasting, O Son co-eternal, and Spirit divine! Illumine us who, with faith, do worship thee; and rescue us from fire eternal.

Now, and ever, and unto ages of ages. Amen.

Hail, O August One, who for the salvation of all men didst bring forth God in the flesh; through whom, also, mankind hath found salvation. Through thee have we found Paradise, O pure, most blessed Birth-giver of God. —— Alleluia. (*Thrice.*)

Deacon. Again, yet again, . . . (*See page* 378.)

And the rest, as before, while the Priest saith the Prayer: O God of spirits, . . . (*See page* 369.)

Then the following Hymn, in Tone V., is sung:

Give rest with the Just, O our Saviour, unto thy servant, and establish him (*her*) in thy courts, as it is written: Regarding not, in that thou art good, his (*her*) sins, whether voluntary or involuntary, and all things committed either with knowledge or in ignorance, O thou who lovest mankind.

Glory . . .

And all things, committed either with knowledge or in ignorance, O thou who lovest mankind.

Now, and ever, . . .

Hymn to the Birth-giver of God (*Bogoróditchen*).

O Christ-God, who from a Virgin didst shine forth upon the world, through her making us children of the light, have mercy upon us.

Then shall be read Psalm li.

Have mercy upon me, O God, after thy great goodness; according to the multitude of thy mercies do away mine offences. Wash me throughly from my wickedness, and cleanse me from my sin. For I acknowledge my faults, and my sin is ever before me. Against thee only have I sinned, and done this evil in thy sight; that thou mightest be justified in thy saying, and clear when thou art judged. Behold, I was shapen in wickedness, and in sin hath my mother conceived me. But lo, thou requirest truth in the inward parts, and shalt make me to understand wisdom secretly. Thou shalt purge me with hyssop, and I shall be clean; thou shalt wash me, and I shall be whiter than snow. Thou shalt make me hear of joy and gladness, that the bones which thou hast broken may rejoice. Turn thy face from my sins, and put out all my misdeeds. Make me a clean heart, O God, and renew a right spirit within me. Cast me not away from thy presence, and take not thy Holy Spirit from me. O give me the comfort of thy help again, and stablish me with thy free Spirit. Then shall I teach thy ways unto the wicked, and sinners shall be converted unto thee. Deliver me from blood-guiltiness, O God, thou that art the God of my health; and my tongue shall sing of thy righteousness. Thou shalt open my lips, O Lord, and my mouth shall show thy praise. For thou desirest no sacrifice, else would I give it thee; but thou delightest not in burnt-offerings. The sacrifice of God is a troubled spirit: a broken and contrite heart, O God, shalt thou not despise.

O be favourable and gracious unto Zion: build thou the walls of Jerusalem. Then shalt thou be pleased with the sacrifice of righteousness, with the burnt-offerings and oblation: then shall they offer young bullocks upon thine altar.

Then the Canon *is sung.* (*Composed by Theophanus.*)
Canticle I., Tone VI.

Theme-Song (*Irmós*). When Israel passed on foot over the deep as it had been dry land, and beheld their pursuer Pharaoh engulfed in the sea, they cried aloud: Let us sing unto God a song of victory.

Hymns (*Tropart*). In the heavenly mansions the valiant Martyrs continually do pray with fervour unto thee, O Christ. Graciously enable him (*her*) whom thou hast called as a faithful one from earth, to obtain eternal good things.

Thou who adornest all things hast created within me a blended creature, half-abject, half-august. Wherefore, O Saviour, give rest to the soul of thy servant.

Glory . . .

A citizen and husbandman of Paradise didst thou create me in the beginning; but when I transgressed thy commandment thou didst drive me forth. Wherefore, O my Saviour, give rest to the soul of thy servant.

Now, and ever, . . .

HYMN TO THE BIRTH-GIVER OF GOD (*Bogoródilchen*).

He who aforetime fashioned the first mother of our race, Eve, from a rib, assumed flesh through thy most holy womb, and thereby, O Pure One, he destroyed the power of Death.

Canticle III.

Theme-Song (*Irmós*). There is none holy like unto thee, O Lord my God, who hast exalted the horn of thy faithful, O Good One, and hast established us upon the rock of thy confession.

Hymns. Thy martyrs lawfully contended, O Life-giver, and being by thee adorned with the crown of victory, they eagerly adjudge unto the dead who is departed hence in faith redemption everlasting.

After that, with many signs and wonders, thou hadst first chastened me who had gone astray, thou didst, at the last, empty thyself, forasmuch as thou art of tender compassion: and didst seek, and find, and save.

Glory . . .

Mercifully vouchsafe, O Good One, that he (*she*) who from the transitory, unstable things of corruption hath passed over unto thee, may dwell with joy in the heavenly mansions, O God, being justified by faith and by grace.

Now, and ever, . . .

There is none undefiled, like unto thee, O most pure Mother of God: for thou alone, in all the ages, hast conceived in thy womb the true God, who hath shattered the power of Death.

Deacon. Again, yet again, in peace let us pray to the Lord.

Again we pray . . .

(*And the rest; see page* 378; *while the Priest saith the Prayer:* O God of spirits, . . .)

Sitting-Hymn (*Syedálen*), in Tone VI.

Of a truth, all things are vanity, and life is but a shadow and a dream. For in vain doth every one who is born of earth disquiet himself, as saith the Scriptures. When we have acquired the world, then do we take up our abode in the grave, where kings and beggars lie down together. Wherefore, O Christ our God, give rest to thy servant departed this life; forasmuch as thou lovest mankind.

Glory to the Father, and to the Son, and to the Holy Spirit, now, and ever, and unto ages of ages. Amen.

HYMN TO THE BIRTH-GIVER OF GOD (*Bogoróditchen*).

O all-holy Birth-giver of God, forsake me not all the days of my life, and give me not over to the mediation of mortal man.. But do thou thyself succour me, and show mercy upon me.

The Litany: Again, yet again: *and the Prayer:* O God of spirits, . . . (*See page* 369.)

Canticle IV.

Theme-Song (Irmós). Christ is my strength, my God, and my Lord, the august Church doth sing in God-befitting wise, crying aloud, and out of a pure mind keeping festival unto the Lord.

Hymns. In that thou didst reveal a great token of wisdom, and through the abundance of gifts the fulness of perfection of thy goodness, O August Master, thou didst unite the company of the Martyrs unto the Angels.

Mercifully enable him (*her*) who hath now appeared before thee to obtain thy glory unspeakable, O Christ, where is the abode of those who rejoice, and the voice of gladness pure.

Glory . . .

Him (*her*) who singeth thy majesty divine; him (*her*) whom thou hast taken away from earth, receive thou, making him (*her*) a child of the light, and cleansing him (*her*) from the gloom of sin, O exceeding-merciful One.

Now, and ever, . . .

HYMN TO THE BIRTH-GIVER OF GOD.

O Receptacle most pure, O Temple all-undefiled, O Ark all-holy, O virgin Place of sanctification: the Lord hath chosen thee, the Excellency of Jacob.

Canticle V.

Theme-Song (Irmós). With thy light divine, O Good One, illumine thou, through love, I pray thee, the souls of those who wake early unto thee: that they may know thee, O Word of God, of the true God, who callest forth from the gloom of sin.

Hymns. The Martyrs, in that they offered themselves unto God all-glorified, as it were a sacred whole burnt-offering and the first-fruits of the human race, perpetually intercede for our salvation.

To the faithful member of thy household who hath fallen asleep before us, vouchsafe, O Lord, a heavenly abiding-place, a meed of thy gifts, granting unto him (*her*) redemption from his (*her*) sins.

Glory . . .

O thou who art the sole Author of life; who art by nature, in truth, a fathomless abyss of goodness: graciously bestow upon the departed thy heavenly kingdom, O Bountiful, Only Immortal One.

Now, and ever, . . .

HYMN TO THE BIRTH-GIVER OF GOD.

He who was born in the world of thee, O Lady, is become the strength, and the song, and the salvation of the lost, delivering from the gates of Hell those who, with faith, do call thee blessed.

Canticle VI.

Theme-Song (Irmós). Forasmuch as I behold the sea of life surging high with the tempest of temptations, I have fled to thy tranquil haven and cry aloud unto thee: Lead thou my life forth from corruption, O Most Merciful One.

Hymns. When thou wast nailed to the Cross, thou didst gather unto thyself the company of the Martyrs who imitated thy Passion, O Blessed One. We beseech thee, therefore: Give rest unto him (*her*) who hath now been translated to thy presence.

When thou shalt come terribly, in thy glory ineffable in the clouds, to judge the whole world, graciously enable him (*her*) whom thou hast taken from the earth, thy faithful servant, to meet thee, the Redeemer, in brightness.

Glory . . .

O Lord, who art the Fountain of life through thy manhood divine; who settest at liberty them that are bound: establish thou in the bliss of Paradise thy servant who, in faith, hath departed unto thee.

Now, and ever, . . .

HYMN TO THE BIRTH-GIVER OF GOD.

We have returned back to the earth because we have sinned against the commandments divine of God. But through thee, O Virgin, we have ascended from earth unto heaven, shaking off the corruption of death.

Deacon. Again, yet again, in peace, let us pray to the Lord. ℞

Again we pray . . . (*See page* 378.)

(*And the rest; while the Priest saith the Prayer:* O God of spirits, . . . *See page* 369.)

The Collect Hymn (Kondák), in Tone III.

With the Saints give rest, O Christ, to the soul of thy servant, where there is neither sickness, nor sorrow, nor sighing, but life everlasting.

The Ikos.

Thou only art immortal, who hast created and fashioned man. For out of the earth were we mortals made, and unto the earth shall we return again, as thou didst command when thou madest me, saying unto me: For earth thou art, and unto the earth shalt thou return. Whither, also, all we mortals wend our way, making of our funeral dirge the song: Alleluia.

(*Then the Litany:* Again, yet again: *and the Prayer:* O God of spirits, . . . *See page* 369.)

Canticle VII.

Theme-Song (Irmós). An Angel made the fiery furnace to drop dew for the Holy Children, but the command of God consuming the Chaldæans with fire prevailed upon the tormentor to cry aloud: Blessed art thou, O God of our fathers.

Hymns. Thy Martyrs, redeemed by thy blood from the primal transgression, were stained with their own blood, and plainly image forth thy sacrifice. Blessed art thou, O God of our fathers.

Thou didst slay Death the insolent, O Life-originating Word. Accept thou now him (*her*) who now hath fallen asleep and with faith doth glorify thee, and doth say, O Christ: Blessed art thou, O God of our fathers.

Glory . . .

O Master, most truly God, who hast animated me, a man, with thy breath divine, graciously grant thou unto the dead thy kingdom, that he (*she*) may sing unto thee, O Saviour: Blessed art thou, O God of our fathers.

Now, and ever, . . .

Hymn to the Birth-giver of God.

Thou wast made more excellent than every created being, O All-undefiled One, when thou didst conceive God, who destroyed the gates of Death, and burst the bars. For which cause, we faithful do magnify thee in songs as the Mother of God, O Pure One.

Canticle VIII.

Theme-Song (Irmós). Out of the flames thou didst shed forth dew upon the Godly Ones, and with water didst kindle the sacrifices of the Righteous One. For thou doest all things which thou willest, O Christ. Thee will we exalt unto all the ages.

Hymns. When ye were shown as having steadfastly contended for the prize, ye Martyrs of Christ, as conquerors were ye adorned with the crown of victory, crying: We exalt thee, O Christ, unto all the ages.

Those who have continued faithful in godly living, and now are translated unto thee, do thou accept, O Master. Graciously give rest, forasmuch as thou art of tender compassion, unto those who exalt thee unto all the ages.

Glory . . .

Graciously vouchsafe, O Saviour, to establish now in the land of the meek all those who have fallen asleep before us, who having been justified through faith in thee and through grace exalt thee unto all the ages.

Now, and ever, . . .

Hymn to the Birth-giver of God.

We all do call thee blessed, O All-blessed One, which didst bring forth the Word, Who in very truth is blessed; Who, for our sake, became flesh; Whom also we will exalt unto all the ages.

Canticle IX.

Theme-Song (Irmós). It is not possible that men should see God, upon whom the Orders of the Angels dare not gaze. But through thee, O All-pure One, was the Word Incarnate manifested unto men: whom magnifying, together with the Heavenly Hosts, we call thee blessed.

Hymns. Hope made strong the company of the Martyrs, and incited them ardently toward thy love, thereby foreshadowing the future rest, which, in very truth, cannot be shaken: Unto which, O Good One, grant that he (*she*) may attain who hath been taken hence.

Graciously vouchsafe, O Christ, that he (*she*) who hath departed in the faith may receive of thy dazzling radiance divine; granting unto him (*her*) rest in Abraham's bosom; forasmuch as thou only art merciful; and vouchsafing unto him (*her*) blessedness eternal.

Glory . . .

O thou who art of nature gracious and loving-kind, and desirest mercy, and art an abyss of loving-kindness; who, also, O Saviour, hast translated him (*her*) from this place of affliction and the shadow of death: In that place where thy light shineth establish thou him (*her*).

Now, and ever, . . .

HYMN TO THE BIRTH-GIVER OF GOD.

We know thee, O Pure One, that thou art the holy Tabernacle, and the Ark, and the Table of the Law of grace: for through thee was redemption given unto those who are justified by the blood of him who was made flesh through thy womb, O All-undefiled One.

Deacon. Again, yet again, in peace let us pray to the Lord. ℟.

Again we pray for the repose . . . (*See page* 378.)

(And the rest, while the Priest saith the Prayer: O God of spirits, . . . *See page* 369.)

Then the Anthem, by John, the Monk of Damascus, is begun:

Tone I. What earthly sweetness remaineth unmixed with grief? What glory standeth immutable on earth? All things are but shadows most feeble, but most deluding dreams: yet one moment only, and Death shall supplant them all. But in the light of thy countenance, O Christ, and in the sweetness of thy beauty, give rest unto him (*her*) whom thou hast chosen: forasmuch as thou lovest mankind.

Tone II. Woe is me! What manner of ordeal doth the soul endure when from the body it is parted! Woe is me! how many then are its tears; and there is none to show compassion! It turneth its eyes to the Angels; all unavailing is its prayer. It stretcheth out its hands to men; and findeth none to succour. Wherefore, my brethren beloved, meditating on the brevity of our life, let us beseech of Christ rest for him (*her*) who hath departed hence: and for our souls great mercy.

Tone III. All mortal things are vanity and exist not after death. Riches endure not, neither doth glory accompany on the way: for when death cometh, all these things vanish utterly. For which cause let us cry unto Christ the immortal: Give rest, in the abode of those who are glad, to the dead translated from among us.

Tone IV. Where is earthly predilection? Where is the pomp of the ephemeral creatures of a day? Where are the gold and the silver? Where is the multitude of household servants and their clamour? All dust, all ashes, all shadows. But come, let us cry aloud unto the deathless King: O Lord, of thine eternal good things vouchsafe thou unto him (*her*) who hath been translated from among us, giving unto him (*her*) rest in thy blessedness which waxeth not old.

Tone V. I called to mind the Prophet, how he cried: I am earth and ashes; and I looked again into the graves, and beheld the bones laid bare; and I said: Who then is the king or the warrior, the rich man or the needy, the upright or the sinner? Yet give rest with thy Saints unto thy servant, O Lord.

Tone VI. Thy creating command was my origin and my foundation: for thy pleasure it was out of nature visible and invisible to fashion me, a living creature. From the earth thou didst shape my body, and didst give me a soul by thy divine and quickening breath. Wherefore, O Christ, give rest to thy servant in the land of the living, in the habitations of the Just.

Tone VII. When, in the beginning, thou hadst created man after thine own image and likeness, thou didst set him in Paradise to reign over thy creatures. But when, beguiled by the malice of the Devil, he tasted of the food, he became a transgressor of thy commandments. For which cause, O Lord, thou didst condemn him to return again unto the earth whence he was taken, and to entreat repose.

Tone VIII. I weep and I wail when I think upon death, and behold our beauty, fashioned after the image of God, lying in the tomb disfigured, dishonoured, bereft of form. O marvel! What is this mystery which doth befall us? Why have we been given over unto corruption, and why have we been wedded unto death? Of a truth, as it is written, by the command of God, who giveth the departed rest.

The Beatitudes. Tone VI.

Remember us, O Lord, when thou comest into thy kingdom.

Blessed are the poor in spirit: for theirs is the kingdom of heaven.

Blessed are they that mourn: for they shall be comforted.

Blessed are the meek: for they shall inherit the earth.

Blessed are they that do hunger and thirst for righteousness' sake: for they shall be filled.

Blessed are the merciful: for they shall obtain mercy.

O Christ, who, because of his repentance, didst pronounce in anticipation a citizen of Paradise the Thief that upon the Cross cried unto thee: Remember me! Make thou me, a sinner, worthy also of the same.

Blessed are the pure in heart: for they shall see God.

O thou who reignest over life and death, in the courts of thy Saints grant rest unto him (*her*) whom thou hast removed from temporal things. And remember me also, when thou comest into thy kingdom.

Blessed are the peacemakers: for they shall be called the children of God.

O thou who rulest over souls and bodies, in whose hand is our breath, the Consolation of the afflicted: In the land of the Just give rest unto thy servant whom thou hast taken from us.

Blessed are they which are persecuted for righteousness' sake: for theirs is the kingdom of heaven.

May Christ give thee rest in the land of the living, and open unto thee the gates of Paradise, and make thee a citizen of his kingdom; and give thee remission of those things wherein thou in life hast sinned, O thou who lovest Christ.

Blessed are ye when men shall revile you, and persecute you, and shall say all manner of evil against you, falsely, for my sake.

Let us go forth, and gaze into the tombs: for man is naked bones, food for the worms, and stench; and we shall learn what are riches, and comeliness, and beauty, and strength.

Rejoice, and be exceeding glad: for great is your reward in heaven: for so persecuted they the prophets which were before you.

Let us hearken unto what the Almighty crieth: Woe unto those who seek to behold the terrible day of the Lord! For lo, it is darkness: for all men shall be tried by fire.

Glory . . .

Him who hath no beginning in birth or cause, the Father who bestoweth birth, I worship; the Son, who is born, I glorify; unto the Holy Spirit, who shineth together with the Father and the Son, I sing praises.

Now, and ever, . . .

HYMN TO THE BIRTH-GIVER OF GOD.

How dost thou press milk in abundance from thy breasts, O Virgin? How dost thou nourish the Nourisher of creation? He knoweth it who made the water to well forth from the rock; streams of water for a people that were athirst, as it was written.

Deacon. Let us attend.

Priest. Peace be with you all.——*Choir.* And with thy spirit.

Deacon. Wisdom!

Reader. The Gradual (*Prokímen*), in the Sixth Tone. Blessed is the way in which thou shalt walk to-day, O soul; for a place of rest is prepared for thee.

Verse (*Stikh*): Unto thee will I cry, O Lord, my strength: think no scorn of me: lest if thou make as though thou hearest not, I become like them that go down into the pit.

And the Choir sing the Gradual, as usual.

Deacon. Wisdom!

Reader. The Lesson from the Epistle of the holy Apostle Paul to the Thessalonians.

Deacon. Let us attend.

Reader. (*1 Thess. iv. 13–18.*) Brethren: I would not have you to be ignorant concerning them which are asleep, that ye sorrow not, even as others which have no hope. For if we believe that Jesus died and rose again, even so them also which sleep in Jesus will God bring with him. For this we say unto you by the word of the Lord, that we which are alive and remain unto the coming of the Lord shall not prevent them which are asleep. For the Lord himself shall descend from heaven with a shout, with the voice of the archangel, and with the trump of God: and the dead in Christ shall rise first: then we which are alive and remain shall be caught up together with them in the clouds, to meet the Lord in the air: and so shall we ever be with the Lord.

Priest. Peace be with thee.

Reader. And with thy spirit.

Deacon. Wisdom!

Reader. Alleluia. (*Thrice.*)

Verse, in Tone VI.: Blessed is he whom thou hast chosen and taken, O Lord.

Deacon. Wisdom, O believers! Let us listen to the Holy Gospel.

Priest. Peace be with you all.

Choir. And with thy spirit.

Priest. The Lesson from the holy Gospel of John.

Choir. Glory to thee, O Lord; glory to thee.

Priest. (*John v. 24–30.*) The Lord said to the Jews which came unto him: Verily, verily, I say unto you, He that heareth my word and believeth on him that sent me, hath everlasting life, and shall not come into condemnation, but hath passed from death unto life. Verily, verily, I say unto you, The hour is coming, and now is, when the dead shall hear the voice of the Son of God: and they that hear shall live. For as the Father hath life in himself, so hath he given to the Son to have life in himself; and hath given him authority to execute judgment also, because he is the Son of man. Marvel not at this: for the hour is coming, in the which all that are in the graves shall hear his voice, and shall come forth; they that have done good, unto the resurrection of life; and they that have done evil, unto the resurrection of damnation. I can of mine own self do nothing: as I hear, I judge: and my judgment is just; because I seek not mine own will, but the will of the Father which hath sent me.

Choir. Glory to thee, O Lord; glory to thee.

Then the Deacon saith the Litany:

Have mercy upon us, O God, . . .
Choir. Lord, have mercy. (*Thrice.*)
Furthermore we pray for the repose . . . (*And the rest; see page* 369.)
Deacon. Let us pray to the Lord.
Choir. Lord, have mercy.

And when this is finished, the principal Priest, or the Bishop, if one be present, shall say, in a loud voice, as he standeth near the dead, while all the Priests present do the same, the Prayer: O God of spirits, . . . (*See page* 369.)

Whenever the Deacon reciteth the Litany, the Priests each, secretly, *recite, the while, according to his rank, this Prayer, standing near the dead. And the Exclamation shall be made,* aloud: For thou art the Resurrection, and the Life: *and the rest.* (*See page* 369.)

Then the principal Priest, or the Bishop, shall recite, aloud, *the Prayer which he hath said above:* O God of spirits, . . .

And after the Exclamation, the last kiss is given, and the following Stanzas, in Tone II., are sung:

Come, brethren, let us give the last kiss unto the dead, rendering thanks unto God. For he (*she*) hath vanished from among his (*her*) kin, and presseth onward to the grave, and vexeth himself (*herself*) no longer concerning vanities, and concerning the flesh, which suffereth sore distress. Where are now his (*her*) kinsfolk and his (*her*)friends? Lo, we are parted. Let us beseech the Lord that he will give him (*her*) rest.

What is this parting, O brethren? What is this wailing, what this weeping at the present hour? Come ye, therefore, let us kiss him (*her*) who was but lately with us; for he (*she*) is committed to the grave; he (*she*) is covered with a stone; he (*she*) taketh up his (*her*) abode in the gloom; he (*she*) is interred among the dead, and now is parted from all his (*her*) kinsfolk and his (*her*) friends. Let us beseech the Lord that he will give unto him (*her*) eternal rest.

Now is life's artful triumph of vanities destroyed. For the spirit hath vanished from its tabernacle; its clay groweth black. The vessel is shattered, voiceless, bereft of feeling, motionless, dead: Committing which unto the grave, let us beseech the Lord that he will give him (*her*) eternal rest.

What is our life like unto? Unto a flower, a vapour, and the dew of the morning, in very truth. Come ye, therefore, let us gaze keenly at the grave. Where is the beauty of the body, and where its youth? Where are the eyes and the fleshly form? Like the grass all have perished, all have been destroyed. Come ye, therefore, let us prostrate ourselves at the feet of Christ with tears.

A great weeping and wailing, a great sighing and agony, and Hell and destruction is the departure of the soul. This transitory life is a shadow unreal and an illusive dream; the trouble of the life of earth is a phantasm importunate. Let us, then, flee afar from every earthly sin, that we may inherit heavenly things.

As we gaze on the dead who lieth before us, let us all accept this example of our own last hour. For he (*she*) vanisheth from earth like the smoke; like a flower he (*she*) is faded; like the grass he (*she*) is cut down. Swathed in a coarse garment he (*she*) is concealed in the earth. As we leave him (*her*) hidden from sight, let us beseech Christ that he will give unto him (*her*) eternal rest.

Draw nigh, ye descendants of Adam, let us gaze upon him (*her*) who is laid low in the earth, made after our own image, all comeliness stripped off, dissolved in the grave by decay, by worms in darkness consumed, and hidden by the earth. As we leave him (*her*) hid from sight, let us beseech Christ that he will give unto him (*her*) eternal rest.

When the soul from the body is about to be rent with violence by Angels dread, it forgetteth all its kinsfolk and acquaintance, and is troubled concerning its appearance before the judgment which shall come upon the things of vanity and much-toiling flesh. Come ye, then, importuning the Judge let us implore that the Lord will pardon him (*her*) all his (*her*) deeds which he (*she*) hath done.

Come, O brethren, let us gaze into the grave upon the dust and ashes from which we are made. Whither go we now? What are we become? Who is poor, who rich? Who is the master? Who a freeman? Are not we all ashes? The beauty of the countenance is mouldered, and Death hath withered up all the flower of youth.

Vanity and corruption, of a truth, are all the illusions, the inglorious things of life. For all we shall pass away: all we shall die, kings and princes, judges and rulers, rich and poor, and every mortal creature. For now they who were erst alive are cast down into the grave. Wherefore, let us beseech the Lord that he will give rest.

Now are all the bodily organs seen to be idle, which so little while ago were filled with motion; all useless, dead, unconscious. For the eyes have withdrawn inward, the feet are bound, the hands lie helpless, and the ears withal; the tongue is imprisoned in silence, committed to the tomb. Of a verity, all mortal things are vanity.

Hymn to the Birth-giver of God.

O thou who savest those who fix their hope on thee, the Mother of the Sun that knoweth no setting, O Progenetrix of God; With thy prayers entreat, we beseech thee, the God exceeding good, that unto him (*her*) who hath now been translated he will give repose where the souls of the righteous rest. Manifest him (*her*) an heir of good things divine, in the courts of the Just, unto everlasting memory, O All-undefiled One.

Glory to the Father, and to the Son, and to the Holy Spirit.

Tone VI. As ye behold me lie before you all speechless and bereft of breath, weep for me, O friends and brethren, O kinsfolk and acquaintance. For but yesterday I talked with you, and suddenly there came upon me the dread hour of death. But come, all ye who loved me, and kiss me with the last kiss. For nevermore shall I walk or talk with you. For I go hence unto the Judge with whom is no respect of persons. For slave and master stand together before him, king and warrior, the rich and the poor, in honour equal. For according to his deeds shall every man receive glory or be put to shame. But I beg and implore you all, that ye will pray without ceasing unto Christ-God, that I be not doomed according to my sins, unto a place of torment; but that he will appoint unto me a place where is the light of life.

Now, and ever, and unto ages of ages. Amen.

HYMN TO THE BIRTH-GIVER OF GOD, *in the same Tone.*

Through the prayers of her who gave thee birth, O Christ; and of thy Forerunner; of the Apostles, Prophets, Hierarchs, Holy Ones, of the Just, and of all the Saints: Give rest unto thy servant who is fallen asleep.

O Holy God, Holy Mighty, . . . (*See page* 368.) Glory . . . now, and ever, . . . O all-holy Trinity, . . . Lord, have mercy. (*Thrice.*) Glory . . . now, and ever, . . . Our Father, . . . For thine is the kingdom, . . .

Then: With the souls of the righteous dead . . . (*See page* 368.) *And the rest. And the Deacon saith the Litany:* Have mercy upon us, O God, . . . (*See page* 369.) *While the Priest saith,* secretly, *the Prayer:* O God of spirits, . . . (*See page* 369.)

And after the Exclamation: Glory . . . now, and ever, . . .

And the BENEDICTION.

May he who rose again from the dead, Christ our true God; through the prayers of his all-pure Mother; of the holy, glorious and all-laudable Apostles; of our holy and God-bearing Fathers, and of all the Saints, establish in the mansions of the righteous the soul of his servant, N., who hath been taken from us; give him (*her*) rest in Abraham's bosom, and number him (*her*) with the Just; and have mercy upon us, forasmuch as he is good and loveth mankind.

Choir. Amen.

Then the Bishop or the principal Priest saith, thrice:

Eternal be thy memory, O our brother, who art worthy to be deemed happy and ever-memorable.

Or: Give rest eternal in blessed falling asleep, O Lord, to the soul(*s*) of thy servant(*s*), N. (*NN.*), departed this life, and make his (*her, their*) memory to be eternal.

And the Choir singeth:

Memory eternal! (*Thrice.*)

Then straightway the Bishop, if one be present, or the Priest, reciteth, aloud, the PARTING PRAYER:

May the Lord Jesus Christ our God, who gave his divine commands to his holy Disciples and Apostles, that they should bind and loose the sins of the fallen (we, in turn, having received from them the right to do the same) pardon thee, O spiritual child, all thy deeds done amiss in this life, both voluntary and involuntary: Now, and ever, and unto ages of ages. Amen.

But in place of this prayer, the following, called the PRAYER OF ABSOLUTION, *is now generally read: and being printed separately, when the Priest hath finished it, he layeth it in the dead person's hand.*

Our Lord Jesus Christ, by his divine grace, as also by the gift and power vouchsafed unto his holy Disciples and Apostles, that they should bind and loose the sins of men: (For he said unto them: Receive ye the Holy Spirit: Whosesoever sins ye remit, they are remitted; and whosesoever sins ye retain they are retained. And whatsoever ye shall bind or loose upon earth shall be bound or loosed also in heaven.) By that same power, also, transmitted unto us from them, this my spiritual child, N., is absolved, through me, unworthy though I be, from all things wherein, as mortal, he (*she*) hath sinned against God, whether in word, or deed, or thought, and with all his (*her*) senses, whether voluntarily or involuntarily; whether wittingly or through ignorance. If he (*she*) be under the ban or excommunication of a Bishop, or of a Priest; or hath incurred the curse of his (*her*) father or mother; or hath fallen under his (*her*) own curse; or hath sinned by any oath; or hath been bound, as man, by any sins whatsoever, but hath repented him (*her*) thereof, with contrition of heart: he (*she*) is now absolved from all those faults and bonds. May all those things which have proceeded from the weakness of his (*her*) mortal nature be consigned to oblivion, and be remitted unto him (*her*): Through His loving-kindness; through the prayers of our most holy, and blessed, and glorious Lady, the Mother of our Lord and ever-virgin Mary; of the holy, glorious and all-laudable Apostles, and of all Saints. Amen.

Then taking up the remains we go forth to the grave, followed by all the people, and preceded by the Priest, and singing:

O Holy God, Holy Mighty, . . . Glory . . . now, and ever, . . . O all-holy Trinity, . . . Lord, have mercy. (*Thrice.*) Glory . . . now, and ever, . . . Our Father, . . . For thine is the kingdom, . . . (*Page* 368.)

And the mortal remains are buried with thanksgiving and with joy: and with the song: Open, O earth, and receive that which was made from thee. *Then the body is laid in the grave, and the Bishop or the Priest, taking a shovelful of dust, streweth it crosswise upon the remains, saying:*

The earth is the Lord's, and the fulness thereof: the round world, and they that dwell therein.

Then he poureth upon the body oil from the shrine-lamp, (3) and streweth ashes (4) from the censer upon it. And thereafter the grave is filled up in the usual way, while these Hymns are sung.

With the souls of the righteous dead, give rest, O Saviour, to the soul of thy servant, preserving it unto the life of blessedness which is with thee, O thou who lovest mankind.

In the place of thy rest, O Lord, where all thy Saints repose, give rest, also, to the soul of thy servant: For thou only lovest mankind.

Glory to the Father, and to the Son, and to the Holy Spirit.

Thou art the God who descended into hell, and loosed the bonds of the captives: Do thou give rest, also, to the soul of thy servant.

Now, and ever, and unto ages of ages. Amen.

O Virgin alone Pure and Undefiled, who without seed didst bring forth God, pray thou unto him that his (*her*) soul may be saved.

THE ORDER FOR THE BURIAL OF THE DEAD
(PRIESTS) (1)*

When one of the Secular Clergy departeth unto the Lord, three Priests come and undress him and (2) rub him with pure oil. Then they array him in his customary garments; (3) and over them, in his priestly vestments; and they cover his face with a chalice-veil, and lay the book of the Holy Gospels on his breast. Then come the Priests, vested in their priestly robes. And the Senior Priest beginneth:

Blessed is our God always, . . . (*And the rest, as at the Burial of Laymen. See page* 368). O Holy God, Holy Mighty, . . . Glory . . . now, and ever, . . . O all-holy Trinity, . . . Lord, have mercy. (*Thrice.*) Glory . . . now, and ever, . . . Our Father, . . . For thine is the kingdom, . . . With the souls of the righteous dead, . . . In the place of thy rest, . . . Glory . . . Thou art the God . . . now . . . and ever . . . O Virgin, alone Pure . . . *The Litany:* Have mercy upon us, O God, . . . *and the Prayer:* O God of spirits, . . . (*page* 369). For thou art the Resurrection, . . . More honourable than the Cherubim, . . . Lord, have mercy. (*Thrice.*) Glory . . . now, and ever, . . . Bless. *The Benediction:* May Christ, our true God, . . .

Then they take up the remains of the Priest, and bear them to the porch (or the body) of the Church; and the book of the Holy Gospels (which hath been borne in front of them) is laid upon them, as hath already been said; and candlesticks, with their tapers, are set round about, in cross-form. And a Chanter beginneth, in Tone VI., Psalm cxix.:

Blessed are those that are undefiled in the way, . . . Alleluia. (*And the rest, as at the Burial of Laymen (see page* 371), *to the end of the Hymn:* O Christ-God, who from a Virgin didst shine forth upon the world, through her making us children of the light, have mercy upon us. *See page* 380.)

Then the Degrees (Stepénni) of Antiphon I., in Tone VI.

I will lift up mine eyes unto the heavens, unto thee, O Word. Show thy bounty upon me, that I may live unto thee.

Have mercy upon us who are humble of heart, making us thy vessels meet for thy service, O Word.

Glory to the Father, and to the Son, and to the Holy Spirit.

The Holy Spirit is of all things the all-redeeming Source. If upon any man he breatheth because the same is worthy, quickly doth He take him from earthly objects, endueth him with wings, raiseth him up, and establisheth him on high.

Now, and ever, and unto ages of ages. Amen.

* For explanations, indicated by numbers, see Appendix B, XI.

Deacon. Let us attend.

Priest. Peace be with you all.

Choir. And with thy spirit.

Deacon. Wisdom!

Reader. The Gradual (*Prokímen*), in the Sixth Tone: Blessed is the way in which thou shalt walk to-day, O soul; for a place of rest is prepared for thee.

Verse (Stikh): Return thou unto thy rest, O my soul, for the Lord hath dealt graciously with thee.

Deacon. Wisdom!

Reader. The Lesson from the Epistle of the holy Apostle Paul to the Thessalonians.

Deacon. Let us attend.

Reader. (*1 Thess. iv. 13–18.*) Brethren: I would not have you to be ignorant concerning them which are asleep, that ye sorrow not, even as others which have no hope. For if we believe that Jesus died and rose again, even so them also which sleep in Jesus will God bring with him. For this we say unto you by the word of the Lord, that we which are alive and remain unto the coming of the Lord shall not prevent them which are asleep. For the Lord himself shall descend from heaven with a shout, with the voice of the archangel, and with the trump of God: and the dead in Christ shall rise first: then we which are alive and remain shall be caught up together with them in the clouds, to meet the Lord in the air: and so shall we ever be with the Lord.

Priest. Peace be with thee.

Reader. And with thy spirit.

Deacon. Wisdom!

Reader. Alleluia, *in the Eighth Tone.* (*Thrice.*) Blessed is he whom thou hast chosen and taken, O Lord.

Deacon. Wisdom, O believers! Let us listen to the Holy Gospel.

Priest. Peace be with you all.——*Choir.* And with thy spirit.

Priest. The Lesson from the holy Gospel of John.

Choir. Glory to thee, O Lord; Glory to thee.

Priest. (*John v. 24–30.*) The Lord said to the Jews which came unto him: Verily, verily, I say unto you, He that heareth my word, and believeth on him that sent me, hath everlasting life, and shall not come into condemnation; but is passed from death unto life. Verily, verily, I say unto you, The hour is coming, and now is, when the dead shall hear the voice of the Son of God: and they that hear shall live. For as the Father hath life in himself; so hath he given to the Son to have life in himself; and hath given him authority to execute judgment also, because he is the Son of man. Marvel not at this: for the hour is coming, in the which all that are in the graves shall hear his voice, and shall come forth; they that have done good, unto the resurrection of life; and they that have done evil, unto the resurrection of damnation. I can of mine own self do nothing; as I hear, I judge: and my judgment is just; because I seek not mine own will, but the will of the Father which hath sent me.

Choir. Glory to thee, O Lord; glory to thee.

Deacon. Let us pray to the Lord.

Choir. Lord, have mercy.

And the Priest saith this Prayer:

O Master, Lord our God, who alone hast immortality, and dwellest in light unapproachable; who slayest and makest alive; who castest down into Hell, and again raisest up; Thou who in wisdom hast created man, and returnest him to the earth again, exacting the spiritual debt: Receive, we beseech thee, the soul of thy servant, and grant him rest in the bosom of Abraham, and Isaac, and Jacob; and give him the crown of thy righteousness, the portion of the saved, in the glory of thine elect. And for those things which in this world he hath wrought for thy Name's sake, may he receive a rich reward in the mansions of thy Saints; through the grace, and bounties, and love toward mankind of thine Only-begotten Son, our Lord Jesus Christ. Amen.

Hymn, Tone II. To-day part I from my kinsfolk, and flee unto thee, the Only Sinless One. In the mansions of the righteous with thine elect grant me rest.

Then PSALM XXIII. is recited.

The Lord is my shepherd; therefore can I lack nothing.

Refrain. Alleluia. (*Thrice.*)

He shall feed me in a green pasture, and lead me forth beside the waters of comfort. ℞ (*Thrice.*)

He shall convert my soul, and bring me forth in the paths of righteousness for his Name's sake. ℞ (*Thrice.*)

Yea, though I walk through the valley of the shadow of death, I will fear no evil; for thou art with me; thy rod and thy staff comfort me. ℞ (*Thrice.*)

Thou shalt prepare a table before me against them that trouble me; thou hast anointed my head with oil, and my cup shall be full. ℞ (*Thrice.*)

But thy loving-kindness and mercy shall follow me all the days of my life; and I will dwell in the house of the Lord forever. ℞ (*Thrice.*)

Then, in Tone VI., this Sitting-Hymn (Syedálen):

Forasmuch as we all are constrained to that same dread abode, and shall hide ourselves beneath a gravestone like to this, and shall ourselves shortly turn to dust, let us implore of Christ rest for him who hath been translated hence. For such is our life here, brethren, a mockery upon the earth; when we have no being, to receive it, and when we have being to dissolve into corruption. We are a fleeting dream; a breath which endureth not; the flight of a passing bird; a ship which leaveth no trace upon the sea. Wherefore, let us cry aloud unto the King Immortal: Deem him worthy of thy bliss never-ending, O Lord.

(The prefaces to the Gradual, and the Epistle, as usual. See page 395.)

Reader. The Gradual (*Prokímen*), in the Sixth Tone. Blessed is he whom thou hast chosen and taken, O Lord.

Verse: Unto thee belongeth song, O God, in Zion.

Reader. The Lesson from the Epistle of the holy Apostle Paul to the Romans.

(Rom. v. 13–22.) Wherefore, brethren, as by one man sin entered into the world, and death by sin; and so death passed upon all men, for that all have sinned. (For until the law, sin was in the world: but sin is not imputed when there is no law. Nevertheless, death reigned from Adam to Moses, even over them that had not sinned after the similitude of Adam's transgression, who is the figure of him that was to come. But not as the offence, so also is the free gift. For if through the offence of one many be dead, much more the grace of God, and the gift by grace, which is by one man, Jesus Christ, hath abounded unto many. And not as it was by one that sinned, so is the gift. For the judgment was by one to condemnation, but the free gift is of many offences unto justification. For if by one man's offence death reigned by one; much more they which receive abundance of grace, and of the gift of righteousness, shall reign in life by one, Jesus Christ.) Therefore, as by the offence of one judgment came upon all men to condemnation, even so by the righteousness of one the free gift came upon all men unto justification of life. For as by one man's disobedience many were made sinners, so by the obedience of one shall many be made righteous. Moreover the law entered, that the offence might abound. But where sin abounded, grace did much more abound: that as sin hath reigned unto death, even so might grace reign through righteousness unto eternal life by Jesus Christ our Lord.

Priest. Peace be with thee.

Reader. And with thy spirit.

Deacon. Wisdom!

Reader. Alleluia, *in the Fourth Tone.* (*Thrice.*)

Verse (Stikh): Blessed is he whom thou hast chosen and taken, O Lord.

(And the prefaces to the Gospel, as usual. See page 395.)

(John v. 17–25.) The Lord said to the Jews which came unto him: My Father worketh hitherto, and I work. Therefore the Jews sought the more to kill him, because he not only had broken the sabbath, but said also, that God was his Father, making himself equal with God. Then answered Jesus, and said unto them, Verily, verily, I say unto you, The Son can do nothing of himself, but what he seeth the Father do: for what things soever he doeth, these also doeth the Son likewise. For the Father loveth the Son, and showeth him all things that himself doeth: and he

will show him greater works than these, that ye may marvel. For as the Father raiseth up the dead, and quickeneth them, even so the Son quickeneth whom he will. For the Father judgeth no man; but hath committed all judgment unto the Son: that all men should honour the Son, even as they honour the Father. He that honoureth not the Son, honoureth not the Father which hath sent him. Verily, verily, I say unto you, he that heareth my word, and believeth on him that sent me, hath everlasting life, and shall not come into condemnation; but is passed from death unto life.

Choir. Glory to thee, O Lord; glory to thee.

Deacon. Let us pray to the Lord.

Choir. Lord, have mercy.

Priest. We give thanks unto thee, O Lord our God, for thou only hast life immortal, and thy glory is ineffable, and thy love toward mankind is unutterable, and thy kingdom faileth not forever, and with thee there is no respect of persons; for unto all men thou hast appointed a common debt of life, whose measure must be fulfilled. Wherefore we entreat thee, O Lord our God: Give rest in the bosom of Abraham, and Isaac, and Jacob unto thy servant, N., erstwhile a priest and our fellow-minister, who hath fallen asleep in the hope of resurrection unto life eternal. And as thou didst appoint him to be a minister of thy Church on earth, so also do thou make him the same at thy heavenly altar, O Lord. As thou hast adorned him with spiritual honour among men, so also receive thou him uncondemned into the glory of the Angels. Thou thyself hast dignified his life upon the earth; in like manner, also, make thou glorious the exit of his life at his entrance among thy holy Saints, and number his soul with all those who from all the ages have been well-pleasing in thy sight. For thou art the Resurrection, and the Life, and the Rest of thy servant, N., who hath fallen asleep, O Christ our God; and unto thee do we ascribe glory, to the Father, and to the Son, and to the Holy Spirit, now, and ever, and unto ages of ages. Amen.

Antiphon II.

If the Lord had not been on our side, we had not been able to withstand the assaults of the enemy: hence they who conquer shall be exalted.

Let not my soul be caught like a bird, in their teeth, O Word. Woe is me! How shall I escape from the enemy, wedded as I am unto sin?

Glory to the Father, and to the Son, and to the Holy Spirit.

Through the Holy Spirit unto all men come adoration, good will, wisdom, peace and blessing: For equally with the Father and the Son he hath effectual power.

Now, and ever, and unto ages of ages. Amen.

Through the Holy Spirit . . . (*Repeat.*)

Then PSALM XXIV.

The earth is the Lord's, and all that therein is; the compass of the world, and they that dwell therein.

Refrain. Alleluia. (*Thrice.*)

For he hath founded it upon the seas, and prepared it upon the floods. ℞ (*Thrice.*)

Who shall ascend into the hill of the Lord? or who shall rise up in his holy place? ℞ (*Thrice.*)

Even he that hath clean hands, and a pure heart; and that hath not lift up his mind unto vanity, nor sworn to deceive his neighbour. ℞ (*Thrice.*)

He shall receive the blessing from the Lord, and righteousness from the God of his salvation. ℞ (*Thrice.*)

This is the generation of them that seek him; even of them that seek thy face, O Jacob. ℞ (*Thrice.*)

Lift up your heads, O ye gates; and be ye lift up, ye everlasting doors; and the King of Glory shall come in. ℞ (*Thrice.*)

Who is the King of Glory? It is the Lord, strong and mighty, even the Lord mighty in battle. ℞ (*Thrice.*)

Lift up your heads, O ye gates; and be ye lift up, ye everlasting doors; and the King of Glory shall come in. ℞ (*Thrice.*)

Who is the King of Glory? Even the Lord of Hosts, he is the King of Glory. ℞ (*Thrice.*)

Glory to the Father, and to the Son, and to the Holy Spirit. Alleluia. Now, and ever, and unto ages of ages. Amen. Alleluia.

Then the Hymn, in Tone II.

In faith, and hope, and love, in meekness and purity and in priestly worth uprightly hast thou discharged thy sacred functions, O Ever-memorable One. For which cause the God eternal, whom thou hast served, shall himself establish thy spirit in a place of brightness, and of beauty, where the Righteous rest; and thou shalt receive pardon and great mercy at the Judgment Day of Christ.

Sitting-Hymn (Syedálen), in Tone V.

Thou knowest, O our God, that we are born in sin; Wherefore we entreat thee: Give rest unto him who hath departed this life, regarding not, forasmuch as thou art good, the iniquities which in life he, as man and mortal, hath committed; through the prayers of the Birth-giver of God, O thou who alone lovest mankind.

(*Then the prefaces to the Gradual, as usual.*)

Reader. The Gradual (*Prokímen*), in the Sixth Tone. Blessed is he whom thou hast chosen and taken, O Lord.

Verse: His remembrance is from generation to generation.

(And the prefaces, as usual, to the Epistle.)

The Lesson from the Epistle of the holy Apostle Paul to the Corinthians.

(1 Cor. xv. 1–12.) Brethren: I declare unto you the gospel which I preached unto you, which also ye have received, and wherein ye stand; by which also ye are saved, if ye keep in memory what I preached unto you, unless ye have believed in vain. For I delivered unto you first of all, that which I also received, how that Christ died for our sins according to the scriptures; and that he was buried, and that he rose again the third day according to the scriptures: and that he was seen of Cephas, then of the twelve: after that, he was seen of above five hundred brethren at once; of whom the greater part remain unto this present, but some are fallen asleep. After that, he was seen of James; then of all the apostles. And last of all he was seen of me also, as of one born out of due time. For I am the least of the apostles, that am not meet to be called an apostle, because I persecuted the church of God. But by the grace of God I am what I am: and his grace which was bestowed upon me, was not in vain; but I laboured more abundantly than they all: yet not I, but the grace of God which was with me. Therefore whether it were I or they, so we preach, and so ye believed.

Alleluia. Blessed is he whom thou hast chosen and taken, O Lord.

(Then the customary preface to the Gospel.)

The Lesson from the holy Gospel of John.

(John vi. 35–39.) The Lord said to the Jews which came unto him: I am the bread of life: he that cometh to me, shall never hunger; and he that believeth on me, shall never thirst. But I said unto you, That ye also have seen me, and believe not. All that the Father giveth me, shall come to me; and him that cometh to me, I will in no wise cast out. For I came down from heaven, not to do mine own will, but the will of him that sent me. And this is the Father's will which hath sent me, that of all which he hath given me, I should lose nothing, but should raise it up again at the last day.

Choir. Glory to thee, O Lord; glory to thee.
Deacon. Let us pray to the Lord.
Choir. Lord, have mercy.

And the Priest saith this Prayer:

O Lord of Hosts, who art the consolation of the afflicted, and the comfort of those who mourn, and the succour of all those who are fainthearted: Comfort, through thy loving-kindness, those who are distressed with weeping for him who hath fallen asleep, and heal every pain that doth oppress their hearts. And give rest in Abraham's bosom unto thy servant, N., who hath fallen asleep in the hope of resurrection unto life eternal. For thou art the Resurrection, and the Life, and the Repose of thy servant, N., O Christ our God; and unto thee do we ascribe glory, with thy Father who is from everlasting, and thine all-holy, and good, and life-giving Spirit, now, and ever, and unto ages of ages. Amen.

Antiphon III.

Those who put their trust in the Lord are terrible unto their enemies, and wonderful unto all men, for their eyes are fixed on high.

The Assembly of the Just, in that they have thee, O Saviour, for their helper, will not lift up their hands unto iniquity.

Glory to the Father, and to the Son, and to the Holy Spirit.

The dominion of the Holy Spirit is over all men. Before him the heavenly hosts bow down, together with everything that hath breath here below.

Now, and ever, and unto ages of ages. Amen.

The dominion of the Holy Spirit . . . (*Repeat.*)

Then PSALM LXXXIV.

O how amiable are thy dwellings, thou Lord of hosts!

Refrain. Alleluia. (*Thrice.*)

My soul hath a desire and longing to enter into the courts of the Lord; my heart and my flesh rejoice in the living God. ℞ (*Thrice.*)

Yea, the sparrow hath found her an house, and the swallow a nest, where she may lay her young; even thy altars, O Lord of hosts, my King and my God. ℞ (*Thrice.*)

Blessed are they that dwell in thy house; they will be always praising thee. ℞ (*Thrice.*)

Blessed is the man whose strength is in thee; in whose heart are thy ways. ℞ (*Thrice.*)

Who going through the vale of misery use it for a well; and the pools are filled with water. ℞ (*Thrice.*)

They will go from strength to strength, and unto the God of gods appeareth every one of them in Zion. ℞ (*Thrice.*)

O Lord God of hosts, hear my prayer; hearken, O God of Jacob. ℞ (*Thrice.*)

Behold, O God our defender, and look upon the face of thine Anointed. ℞ (*Thrice.*)

For one day in thy courts is better than a thousand. ℞ (*Thrice.*)

I had rather be a door-keeper in the house of my God, than to dwell in the tents of ungodliness. ℞ (*Thrice.*)

For the Lord God is a light and defence; the Lord will give grace and worship; and no good thing shall he withhold from them that live a godly life. ℞ (*Thrice.*)

O Lord God of hosts, blessed is the man that putteth his trust in thee. ℞ (*Thrice.*)

Then the Hymn (Tropár), in Tone VI.

My brethren beloved, forget me not when ye sing unto the Lord, but call to mind our brotherhood, and pray ye fervently unto God, that with the righteous the Lord will give me rest.

Hymn, in Tone VI.

Suddenly hath Death come upon me, and severed me from mine own this day. But do thou who hast called me hence, O Christ, in places of refreshing grant me rest.

Glory . . .

Have mercy upon us, O Lord, have mercy upon us; for devoid of all defence we sinners offer unto thee, as unto our Sovereign Lord, the prayer: Have mercy upon us.

Have mercy upon us, O Lord, for in thee have we trusted, and be not very wroth with us, neither call thou to remembrance our iniquities; but look down even now upon us, inasmuch as thou art of tender compassion; and deliver us from our enemies; for thou art our God, and we are thy people, we are all the work of thy hands, and we call upon thy Name.

Now, and ever, . . .

HYMN TO THE BIRTH-GIVER OF GOD (*Bogoróditchen*).

Open unto us the door of thy loving-kindness, O blessed Birth-giver of God. In that we set our hope on thee may we not fail, but through thee may we be delivered from adversities; for thou art the salvation of all Christian people.

(Then the customary prefaces to the Gradual.)

Reader. The Gradual (*Prokímen*), in the Sixth Tone. In the courts of the blessed shall his soul be established.

Verse: Unto thee, O Lord, will I cry: Think no scorn of me, O Lord, my strength.

(The customary prefaces to the Epistle.)

The Lesson from the Epistle of the holy Apostle Paul to the Corinthians.

(*1 Cor. xv. 20–29.*) Brethren: Now is Christ risen from the dead, and become the first-fruits of them that slept. For since by man came death, by man came also the resurrection of the dead. For as in Adam all die, even so in Christ shall all be made alive. But every man in his own order: Christ the first-fruits; afterward they that are Christ's at his coming. Then cometh the end, when he shall have delivered up the kingdom to God, even the Father; when he shall have put down all rule, and all authority, and power. For he must reign, till he hath put all enemies under his feet. The last enemy that shall be destroyed is death. For he hath put all things under his feet. But when he saith all things are put under him, it is manifest that he is excepted which did put all things under him. And when all things shall be subdued unto him, then shall the Son also himself be subject unto him that put all things under him, that God may be all in all. Else what shall they do, which are baptized for the dead, if the dead rise not at all? why are they then baptized for the dead?

Alleluia. Blessed is the man that feareth the Lord.

Verse: His seed shall be mighty in the earth.

(Then the customary prefaces to the Gospel.)

The Lesson from the holy Gospel of John.

(John vi. 40–44.) The Lord said to the Jews which came unto him, And this is the will of him that sent me, that every one which seeth the Son, and believeth on him, may have everlasting life: and I will raise him up at the last day. The Jews then murmured at him, because he said, I am the bread which came down from heaven. And they said, Is not this Jesus the son of Joseph, whose father and mother we know? how is it then that he saith, I came down from heaven? Jesus therefore answered and said unto them, Murmur not among yourselves. No man can come to me, except the Father which hath sent me draw him: and I will raise him up at the last day.

Then the Beatitudes. Tone II.

In thy kingdom remember us, O Lord, when thou comest into thy kingdom.

Blessed are the poor in spirit: for theirs is the kingdom of heaven.

Blessed are they that mourn: for they shall be comforted.

Blessed are the meek: for they shall inherit the earth.

Blessed are they which do hunger and thirst after righteousness: for they shall be filled.

Blessed are the merciful: for they shall obtain mercy.

For when Adam, of old, had eaten of the tree which was for food, he was driven forth from Paradise. But when the Thief, as he hung upon the cross, confessed thee God, he was made a citizen of Paradise. And we, who have been saved by thy Passion, O Master, imitating the Thief, with faith do cry: Remember us, also, when thou comest into thy kingdom.

Blessed are the pure in heart: for they shall see God.

Taking clay from the earth, He who created me, fashioned my body through his will divine; and having breathed into it a soul with his life-bearing breath, he laid upon it a holy command. Therefore hast thou called me, who am subject to the corruption of sin, O thou who lovest mankind, because of thy boundless tenderness of heart. But grant rest with thy Saints, O God, unto him whom thou hast called.

Blessed are the peacemakers: for they shall be called the children of God.

When the soul from the body is parted, fearful is the mystery and terrible to all men; for the soul goeth forth lamenting, and the body is committed to the earth, and hidden from sight. Wherefore, in that we, also, have learned our final end, let us make appeal unto the Saviour.

crying aloud, with tears: Remember us also, O Lord, when thou comest into thy kingdom.

Blessed are they which are persecuted for righteousness' sake: for theirs is the kingdom of heaven.

Why mourn ye me so violently, O men? Why clamour ye so vainly? he who is called hence proclaimeth unto all. Death is a rest unto all men. Therefore let us listen to the voice of Job, when he saith: Death is rest unto man. But grant rest with thy Saints, O God, unto him whom thou hast taken.

Blessed are ye when men shall revile you, and shall persecute you, and shall say all manner of evil against you, falsely, for my sake.

Paul, all-wise, clearly did foretell translation hence, teaching all men that the dead shall rise again incorruptible, and we shall be changed by command divine. Then shall the trumpet ring out with dreadful clang, and they who in all the ages have gone unto their rest shall arise from their sleep. But grant rest with thy Saints, O God, unto him whom thou hast taken.

Rejoice, and be exceeding glad: for great is your reward in heaven.

He who is gone hence and lieth dead in the grave, in gracious reconciliation crieth unto all: Come unto me, ye earth-born; behold the beauty of the body all turned to blackness. Wherefore, O brethren, forasmuch as we have learned therefrom the end, unto the Saviour let us make appeal, crying with tears: Grant rest with thy Saints, O God, unto him whom thou hast taken.

Glory . . . now, and ever, . . .

Hymn to the Birth-giver of God.

In supernatural wise, O Lady, without seed thou didst conceive in thy womb the God who was before all the ages, and didst bear him in the flesh, both God and man, without change of Essence, and with Essence still unmingled. Wherefore, we acknowledge thee ever as the Birth-giver of God, and unto the God who was born of thee with faith we cry: Remember us, also, in thy kingdom.

(The customary prefaces to the Gradual.)

The Gradual (Prokímen), in the Sixth Tone. Blessed is he whom thou hast chosen and taken, O Lord.

Verse: Among the blessed shall his soul take up its abode

(The customary prefaces to the Epistle.)

The Lesson from the Epistle of the holy Apostle Paul to the Romans.

(Rom. xiv. 6-9) Brethren: He that regardeth the day, regardeth it unto the Lord: and he that regardeth not the day, to the Lord he doth not regard it. He that eateth, eateth to the Lord, for he giveth God thanks; and he that eateth not to the Lord he eateth not, and giveth God thanks. For none of us liveth to himself, and no man dieth to him-

self. For whether we live, we live unto the Lord; and whether we die, we die unto the Lord: whether we live therefore, or die, we are the Lord's.

Alleluia, *in the Sixth Tone.*

Blessed is he whom thou hast chosen and taken, O Lord.

Verse: Among the blest shall his soul take up its abode.

(The customary prefaces to the Gospel.)

The Lesson from the holy Gospel of John.

(John vi. 48–54.) The Lord said to the Jews which came unto him, I am that bread of life. Your fathers did eat manna in the wilderness, and are dead. This is the bread which cometh down from heaven, that a man may eat thereof, and not die. I am the living bread which came down from heaven: if any man eat of this bread, he shall live forever: and the bread that I will give is my flesh, which I will give for the life of the world. The Jews therefore strove among themselves, saying, How can this man give us his flesh to eat? Then Jesus said unto them, Verily, verily, I say unto you, Except ye eat the flesh of the Son of man, and drink his blood, ye have no life in you. Whoso eateth my flesh, and drinketh my blood, hath eternal life; and I will raise him up at the last day.

Then Psalm li. (see page 380). And the Canon. Tone VI. Canticle I.

Theme-Song (Irmós). The children of those that were saved hid under the earth him who, of old, drowned in the waves of the sea the tormentor pursuing. But let us like the virgins sing unto the Lord: For he hath gloriously glorified himself.

Refrain. Unto the soul of thy departed servant give rest, O Lord.

Hymns (Tropari). With burning tears fall we down before thee, O Beneficent One, Christ the Lord of all, and utter forth with wailing this funeral song: Give rest to thy faithful servant, in that thou art full of loving-kindness.

Graciously grant, O Word, that he may stand in holiness with thine elect on thy right hand, in the hope of resurrection from the dead. O thou who lovest mankind, we fervently entreat thee with the voice of praise.

Graciously grant, O thou who lovest mankind, that thy chosen servant, who hath been taken from earth, may radiantly rejoice in thy heavenly, august kingdom; regard not his spiritual transgressions, forasmuch as thou art of tender loving-kindness.

Glory . . .

Woe is me! For earthly glory hath suddenly sprung up like the grass, and straightway hath withered. What is rank in the grave? What is comeliness or beauty there? Therefore, O Lord, spare thou thy servant, forasmuch as thou art full of loving-kindness.

Now, and ever, . . .

HYMN TO THE BIRTH-GIVER OF GOD (*Bogoróditchen*).

As is our bounden duty, we all with love sing praises unto thee ever, O Mary, Virgin all-undefiled, the Mother of God, in that we have the sleepless eye of thy prayers. From sin deliver us now, and from the condemnation of death.

Canticle III.

Theme-Song. There is none holy like unto thee, O Lord my God, who hast exalted the horn of thy faithful, O Good One, and hast established us upon the rock of thy confession.

Hymns. There is no man upon the earth who sinneth not, O Word. Accept, therefore, the petition of us humble ones; and pardon, remit, O Saviour, all the iniquities of thy servant.

And who is full of love toward mankind like unto thee, O merciful Lord, who with great power forgivest sins both to the living and also to the dead? Wherefore, save thou thy servant, by the same power.

Glory . . .

Of thy heavenly calling, O Saviour, make thou an heir him who, in faith, hath been translated hence, accepting this last tearful prayer, O only Sinless One.

Now, and ever, . . .

Hymn to the Birth-giver of God. Cease not thou, who art our true Lady, O Virgin most holy, to implore God whom thou hast borne, that unto him who hath departed this life in the faith he will mercifully vouchsafe his heavenly kingdom.

Sitting-Hymn (*Syedálen*), in Tone VI.

Of a truth, all things are vanity, and life is but a shadow and a dream. For in vain doth every one who is born of earth disquiet himself, as saith the Scriptures. When we have acquired the world, then do we take up our abode in the grave, where kings and beggars lie down together. Wherefore, O Christ our God, give rest to thy servant departed this life; forasmuch as thou lovest mankind.

Canticle IV.

Theme-Song. When Habakkuk, by anticipation, beheld thine exhaustion divine upon the Cross, in amaze he cried: Thou hast destroyed the dominion of the mighty, O Good One, in that thou hast joined thyself unto the company of those who were in hell; For thou art almighty.

Hymns. Forasmuch as the judgment of that dread day of wrath is not to be endured, let us diligently entreat of Christ remission of all iniquities for him who hath departed this life in faith and in the hope of resurrection.

Mercifully vouchsafe, O Christ, unto this thy servant, who, **through** repentance ere his death burned before thee as a bright light thy **man**sions of light, O Master, Saviour, tenderly compassionate.

Glory . . .

When thou shalt reveal all secrets, and shalt convict us of our sins, O Christ, spare him whom thou hast taken unto thyself, calling to mind his confession, O Good One.

Now, and ever, . . .

Hymn to the Birth-giver of God. Forget not all us who, with wailing, diligently do call upon thee, O holy Birth-giver of God, the consolation of all men. Entreat thou, O Good One, that thy faithful servant departed this life may obtain rest.

Canticle V.

Theme-Song. When Isaiah beheld the light which knoweth no setting of thy divine manifestation, that was graciously made unto us, O Christ, his soul longed for thee in the night-season, and he cried: The dead shall rise, and those who lie in the grave shall arise and all the earth-born shall rejoice.

Hymns. In the assembly of the Elect, and the delights of Paradise, O Bountiful One, establish thou him whom in the faith thou hast translated from us. For thou hast appointed, O our Saviour, godly-inspired repentance unto all us sinning mortals. Forasmuch as thou art the Lord, unto this man also graciously vouchsafe thy heavenly kingdom.

Through thy power as God, in sovereign wise dost thou show mercy, O Lord, upon thy creatures whom thou hast brought into subjection to mortal law, O thou who alone lovest mankind. Wherefore, O Saviour, pardon, remit, forgive the sins of him who in the faith hath departed this life; and vouchsafe unto the same thy kingdom.

Glory . . .

None shall escape there the dread judgment of thy throne. Side by side with their slaves stand all the mighty kings, and the terrible voice of the Judge ordereth sinful men to the condemnation of Gehenna; from the which deliver thou thy servant, O Christ.

Now, and ever, . . .

Hymn to the Birth-giver of God. Of thee, in supernatural wise, was the Redeemer born after the nature of men: Whom also do thou diligently entreat, O Virgin unwedded, that from all torments, and from fierce, dread pains in hell, he will deliver and will save him who now in the faith hath departed from us.

Canticle VI.

Theme-Song. The nethermost abyss of sin hath compassed me about, and unable longer to endure the billows thereof, like Jonah I cry aloud unto thee, O Master: Lead me forth from corruption.

Hymns. Death and the grave await us, and the judgment, which shall reveal all deeds. Deliver thou therefrom thy servant whom thou hast taken hence, O thou who lovest mankind.

Unto him who is gone hence, O my Saviour, open thou, we beseech thee, the door of thy mercy, O Christ; that he may rejoice in glory, as he partaketh of the joys of thy realm.

Glory . . .

Through thy mercy deliver thou from his iniquities, O Saviour, thy servant whom thou hast now translated hence in the faith. For out of the things which he hath done in the body shall now man be justified, O thou who lovest mankind.

Now, and ever, . . .

Hymn to the Birth-giver of God. O Progenetrix of God, in the flesh hast thou borne the Destroyer of Death, and the Release from the curse, the Creator who saveth all them that die in the faith, forasmuch as he is good and loveth mankind.

The Litany.

Deacon. Again, yet again, in peace let us pray to the Lord.

Choir. Lord, have mercy. *(Thrice.)*

Again we pray for the repose of the soul of N., the servant of God who hath fallen asleep; and that he may be pardoned every transgression, whether voluntary or involuntary. ℞

And the Priest, meanwhile, saith the Prayer: O God of spirits, . . *(See page 369, BURIAL OF LAYMEN.)*

That the Lord God will establish his soul where the Just repose. ℞

The mercies of God, the kingdom of heaven, and the remission of his sins let us ask of Christ, our King Immortal, and our God.

Choir. Grant it, O Lord.

The Collect-Hymn (Kondák), in Tone VIII.

Give rest with the Saints, O Christ, to the soul of thy servant, where there is neither sickness, nor sorrow, nor sighing, but life everlasting.

The Ikos.

Thou only art immortal, who hast created and fashioned man. For out of the earth were we mortals made, and unto the earth shall we return again, as thou didst command when thou madest me, saying unto me: For earth thou art, and unto the earth shalt thou return. Whither, also, we mortals wend our way, making of our funeral dirge the song: Alleluia.

In thought I implore ye, hearken unto me: For with difficulty do I announce these things. For your sakes have I made moan; perchance it may profit one of you. But when ye shall sing these things make mention, now and then, of me whom ye once knew. For often have we walked together, and together in the house of God have sung: Alleluia.

Rise now, all ye, and make ready, and when ye are set, hearken ye unto the word. Terrible, my brethren, is the Judgment Seat before which all we must appear. There is neither bondman nor freeman there; there is neither small nor great; but we shall all stand naked there. Wherefore, it is good ofttimes to sing together the psalm: Alleluia.

Let us all be consumed with tears, when we behold the earthly remains lying low; and when we shall all draw near to kiss, and peradventure to utter such things as these: Lo! thou hast abandoned us who love thee. Thou speakest no more with us, O friend. Why speakest thou not, as thou wert wont to speak, but holdest thus thy peace who before with us didst say: Alleluia.

Why these bitter words of the dying, O brethren, which they utter as they go hence? I am parted from my brethren. All my friends do I abandon, and go hence. But whither I go, that understand I not, neither what shall become of me yonder; only God, who hath summoned me knoweth. But make commemoration of me with the song: Alleluia.

But whither now go the souls? How dwell they now together there? This mystery have I desired to learn, but none can impart aright. Do they call to mind their own people, as we do them? Or have they forgotten all those who mourn them and make the song: Alleluia?

Accompany ye the dead, O friends, and come ye to the grave with heed, and there gaze ye steadfastly, with understanding; and make ready your feet. All youth is fallen to dissolution there; there all the flower of life is faded; there are dust, and ashes, and worms; there all is silence; and there no man saith: Alleluia.

Lo! now behold we him who lieth here, but ne'er shall lie before us more. Lo! already is his tongue stilled, and lo! his mouth hath ceased to speak. Fare ye well, O my friends, my children. Fare ye well, O brethren! Fare ye well, O my comrades; for I go forth upon my way. But make commemoration of me with the song: Alleluia.

None of the dwellers yonder have returned to life to tell us how there they fare, our erstwhile brethren and our kinsfolk gone before us to the Lord. Wherefore, again and oft we say: Shall we see each other there? Shall we see our brethren there? Shall we there again together say the psalm: Alleluia?

We go forth on the path eternal, and as condemned, with downcast faces, present ourselves before the only God eternal. Where then is comeliness? Where then is wealth? Where then is the glory of this world? There shall none of these things aid us, but only to say oft the psalm: Alleluia.

Why dost thou untimely vex thyself, O man! Yet one hour, and all things shall pass away. For in Hell there is no repentance, nor further remission there. There is the worm that sleepeth not; there is the land, all dark and gloomy, where I must be judged. For I made not haste to say oft the psalm: Alleluia.

Naught is so easily forgot as mortal from his brother-mortal parted. If for a brief space we call to mind, yet straightway forget we Death, as we had not ourselves to die. Parents, also, utterly forget their children, whom from their own bodies they have borne and reared; and they have dropped tears with the song: Alleluia.

I will remember ye, O my brethren; and my children, and my friends, forget me not, when unto the Lord ye pray. I entreat, I beseech, I implore, that ye learn by heart this thing, and mourn for me night and day. As said Job unto his friends, so say I also unto you: Sit ye again and say: Alleluia.

Leaving all things behind us, forth we go, and naked and grieving must present ourselves to God. For like the grass doth beauty fade, and we men only are allured therewith. Naked wast thou born, O wretched one, and naked there must every man appear. Dream not, O mortal, of sweetness in this life, but only groan ever with the moan: Alleluia.

If thou hast shown mercy unto man, O man, that same mercy shall be shown thee there; and if on an orphan thou hast shown compassion, the same shall there deliver thee from want. If in this life the naked thou hast clothed, the same shall give thee shelter there, and sing the psalm: Alleluia.

Toilsome the way in which I must go hence, the which, in truth, I never yet have trod; and unknown is that land, and no one knoweth ought of me there. Awesome is it to behold my guides; most terrible he who hath called me, the Ruler of life and death, who also calleth us, when he willeth, thither: Alleluia.

If journeying from a home-land we stand in need of guides, what shall we do when forth we fare to a land to us still all unknown? Many leaders wilt thou then require, many prayers to accompany thee, to save the wretched sinner's soul; until thou come to Christ and say to him: Alleluia.

They who are in thrall to the material passions shall find no pardon whatsoever there. For there are the dread accusers; there, also, the books are opened. Where, then, around about thee wilt thou gaze, O man? And who then shall succour thee? Unless thou hast led an upright life, and hast done good to the needy, singing: Alleluia.

Youth and the beauty of the body fade at the hour of death, and the tongue then burneth fiercely, and the parched throat is inflamed. The beauty of the eyes is quenched then, the comeliness of the face all altered, the shapeliness of the neck destroyed; and the other parts have become numb, nor often say: Alleluia.

Hush, then; be dumb. Henceforward keep ye silence before him who lieth there, and gaze upon the mighty mystery; for terrible is this hour. Be silent, that the soul may issue forth in peace. For it to a great ordeal is constrained, and in fear doth oft petition make to God: Alleluia.

I have beheld a dying child, and I have mourned my life. For he was all agitated, and trembled greatly when the hour was come, and cried, O father, help me! O mother, save me! And no one then could succour him, but only stood helpless as they gazed on him, and wept for him in the grave: Alleluia.

How many suddenly are snatched to the tomb even from the plighting of their troth, and united by a bond eternal; and without avail have made their moan unending, and have not risen from that bridal chamber! But there was both marriage and the grave, both union and disunion, both laughter and weeping, and the psalm: Alleluia.

With ecstasy are we inflamed if we but hear that there is light eternal yonder; that there is the fountain of our life, and there delight eternal; that there is Paradise, wherein every soul of Righteous Ones rejoiceth. Let us all, also, enter into Christ, that all we may cry aloud thus unto God: Alleluia.

Hymn to the Birth-giver of God. O all-holy Virgin unwedded, who hast brought forth the Light Ineffable, I make petition never ceasing, and beseech thee, and entreat thee: Implore thou the Lord perpetually for thy servant who hath fallen asleep, O most pure One; that he may find there remission of his iniquities in the Day of Judgment, O All-pure One. For thou, O Lady, hast boldness ever to beseech thy Son: Alleluia.

The Collect-Hymn.

Give rest with the Saints, O Christ, to the soul of thy servant, where there is neither sickness, nor sorrow, nor sighing, but life everlasting.

The Ikos. Thou only art immortal, . . . (*See page* 383.)

Canticle VII.

Theme-Song. O marvel unutterable! He who delivered the Holy Children in the fiery furnace from the flames is laid dead, bereft of breath, in the grave, for the salvation of us who sing: O God our Redeemer, blessed art thou.

Hymns. From the fires of Hell and the dread sentence of condemnation deliver thou, O Christ, forasmuch as thou lovest mankind, thy servant whom thou hast now taken hence in the faith. And grant that thy servant may sing unto thee: O God our Redeemer, blessed art thou.

O God, who hast been graciously pleased to establish in the land of the meek, in the delights of Paradise, in the marvellous tabernacle of glory, thy servant who in faith hath fallen asleep, grant that he may sing unto thee: O God, our Redeemer, blessed art thou.

Glory . . .

Great is the judgment, and indescribable is the distress of Hell, O my brethren: for the souls of sinners are burned therein, together with their bodies. And with pain do they weep, unable to cry: O God our Redeemer, blessed art thou.

Now, and ever, . . .

Hymn to the Birth-giver of God. O Birth-giver of God all-undefiled, encompass thou ever with thy prayers the living who with understanding sing praises unto thee as, beyond a doubt, the Mother of God; and deliver thou from bitter torments those who have departed this life; that they may cry aloud unto Christ: O God our Redeemer, blessed art thou.

Canticle VIII.

Theme-Song. Fear with trembling, O ye heavens, and let the foundations of the earth be shaken. For lo! he who dwelleth on high is numbered among the dead, and is lodged in the narrow grave. Ye Children, bless; ye Priests, sing praises; ye People, magnify him unto all the ages.

Hymns. What a dread hour awaiteth sinners, O brethren! O what is the terror then, when Hell's fire unquenchable shall consume and torture evermore! Wherefore, O Christ, bountiful Master, deliver thou from the dread ban him who this day hath been translated from us, that he may escape the torments of Hell forevermore.

O the joy of the Righteous, which they shall receive when the Judge shall come! For there a mansion is prepared, and Paradise, and all Christ's kingdom: wherein establish thou thy servant, making him glad with the Saints, O Christ, forevermore.

Glory . . .

Who shall withstand, O Christ, the dread menace of thy coming again? For then shall the heavens be rolled up like a scroll, in terrible wise; and the stars shall fall; and all creation shall quake with fear; and the light shall suffer sombre change. But in that day, O Word, spare thou him who hath been translated from us.

Now, and ever, . . .

Hymn to the Birth-giver of God. He who, in more than mortal wise, was incarnate of thee as thy Son, O Pure One, the same is the Judge both of the quick and of the dead, and judgeth all the earth, and saveth from torment whomsoever he willeth: More especially those who, with love, do worship him in his manifestations, and who sing praises unto thee, O Birth-giver of God, unto all the ages.

Canticle IX.

Theme-Song. Lament not for me, O Mother, when thou beholdest in the grave thy Son whom, without seed, thou didst conceive in thy womb. For I shall rise again and glorify myself; and in that I am God, I will raise in glory that hath no ending those who, with faith and love, do magnify thee.

Hymns. Mourn not all ye who have died in the faith: for Christ hath endured for us the flesh, the cross, and the grave, making children of immortality all those who cry aloud unto him: Enter thou not into judgment with thy servant.

Let us fervently entreat Christ, O ye faithful, that he will establish in the abode of the blessed our brother who hath fallen asleep in the faith, and in the hope of resurrection. For there is the stern judgment seat, and the dread trial, and none can aid himself; but only good deeds and the united prayers of the faithful. And so let us cry aloud: Enter thou not into judgment with thy servant, O Lord.

Glory . . .

In thy glory which waxeth not old, in the sweetness of Paradise, establish thou now, O Good One, him who hath been translated from us; forasmuch as in the true belief and in repentance he hath hastened unto thee in faith.   And make him an elect defender of thy kingdom.

Now, and ever, . . .

Hymn to the Birth-giver of God.   Thee, as the Mother of the Life, and in more than mortal wise the Virgin Birth-giver of God, we faithful devoutly magnify.   For through thee we, who before were dead, have become immortal; we have found life, and lo! unto thee do we make this song.

Then the Litany: Again, yet again (*see page* 378): *with the Prayer:* O God of spirits, . . . (*See page* 369).

Exapostilárion

Now am I at rest, and have found great release, in that I have been translated from corruption and have passed over into life.   Glory to thee, O Lord.

The People. Verse (Stikh): Man is like the grass, his days are as the flower of the field.

Verse: For his spirit goeth forth from him, and he ceaseth to be.

Verse: But the truth of the Lord abideth forever.

And after each Verse the Exapostilárion is repeated.

Glory to the Father, and to the Son, and to the Holy Spirit, now, and ever, and unto ages of ages.   Amen.

Now have I chosen the Maiden Mother of God: for Christ, the Redeemer of all men, was born of her: Glory to thee, O God.

And then immediately PSALM CL.

O praise God in his holiness: praise him in the firmament of his power.

Refrain. To thee, O God, is due a song.

Praise him in his noble acts: praise him according to his excellent greatness. ℞

Praise him in the sound of the trumpet: praise him upon the lute and harp. ℞

Praise him in the cymbals and dances: praise him upon the strings and pipe. ℞

Praise him upon the well-tuned cymbals: praise him upon the loud cymbals. ℞

Let every thing that hath breath praise the Lord. ℞

Then the Stanzas (Stikhíri), in Tone VI.

Thy godly minister, made a partaker of the nature divine in his translation hence, through thy life-giving mystery, O Christ, is now come unto thee.   Receive thou his soul in thy hand, as it were a bird, O Saviour. Establish thou him in thy courts, and in the choir of the Angels; and because of thy great mercy, O Lord, give rest unto him whom thou hast taken by thy command.

Strange is the mystery of death: for it cometh to all untimely. Nature is dissolved by force. It taketh old men, abbots and learned men; it slayeth the teachers of vain philosophies, bishops and pastors, and every nature of mortals. But let us cry aloud, with tears: Because of thy great mercy, O Lord, give rest unto him whom thou hast taken by thy command.

He who lived in godliness, and was adorned as thy priest, O Christ, the sacrificer and minister of thy mysteries divine, by thy divine command hath passed over from life's clamour unto thee. Save him whom, as Priest, thou didst accept, O Saviour; and because of thy great mercy, give unto him rest with the Just.

Glory . . . now, and ever, . . .

Hymn to the Birth-giver of God. We have come to the knowledge of God who was incarnate of thee, O Virgin Birth-giver of God: Entreat thou him that he will save our souls.

Then shall be read:

Glory be to God on high, and on earth peace, good will towards men. We praise thee, we bless thee, we worship thee, we glorify thee, we give thanks to thee for thy great glory, O Lord God, heavenly King, God the Father Almighty. O Lord, the Only-begotten Son Jesus Christ, and the Holy Spirit; O Lord God, Lamb of God, Son of the Father, that takest away the sins of the world, have mercy upon us. Thou that takest away the sins of the world, receive our prayer. Thou that sittest at the right hand of God the Father, have mercy upon us. For thou only art holy; thou only art the Lord; thou only, O Jesus Christ, with the Holy Spirit, art most high in the glory of God the Father. Amen.

Every day will I give thanks unto thee, and praise thy Name forever and ever. Lord, thou hast been our refuge from one generation to another. I said, Lord, be merciful unto me; heal my soul, for I have sinned against thee. I flee unto thee. Teach me to do thy will; for thou art my God. For with thee is the well of life, and in thy light shall we see light. O continue forth thy loving-kindness unto them that know thee. Vouchsafe, O Lord, to keep us this day without sin. Blessed art thou, O Lord God of our fathers, and praised and glorified be thy holy Name forever.

Let thy merciful kindness, O Lord, be upon us, as we do put our trust in thee.

Blessed art thou, O Lord: O teach me thy statutes. (*Thrice.*)

Lord, thou hast been our refuge from one generation to another. I said: Lord, be merciful unto me: heal my soul, for I have sinned against thee.

Lord, I flee unto thee. O teach me to do the thing that pleaseth thee; for thou art my God. For with thee is the well of life, and in thy light shall we see light. O continue forth thy loving-kindness unto those who know thee.

Then the following Stanzas (Stikhíri), by St. John of Damascus. Tone I.

What earthly sweetness remaineth unmixed with grief? What glory standeth immutable on earth? All things are but shadows most feeble, but most deluding dreams: yet one moment only, and Death shall supplant them all. But in the light of thy countenance, O Christ, and in the sweetness of thy beauty, give rest unto him whom thou hast chosen: forasmuch as thou lovest mankind.

Verse (Stikh): The Lord is my shepherd, I shall not want.

In very deed, O my Saviour, dost thou show forth that thou art the Resurrection of all men, who, by thy word, O Word, didst raise up Lazarus from the dead. Then were the bars shattered, and the gates of Hell were confounded. Then was man's death shown to be but a sleep. But do thou, who art come to save thy creation, and not to condemn it, give rest unto him whom thou hast chosen: forasmuch as thou lovest mankind.

Glory . . . now, and ever, . . .

Hymn to the Birth-giver of God. Thou hast manifested thyself a fervent Intercessor for all men, O Birth-giver of God; the Protector of all men, and the Power of God to those who have recourse unto thee; the Succour of those who are in need; a speedy Deliverance unto those who are captive. For Christ hath appointed thee to be an Avenger and a Champion against the barbarian, and a Wall indestructible, and a Fortress impregnable for the weak; and the Bestower of peace upon our souls.

Stanzas (Stikhíri), in Tone II. Woe is me! What manner of ordeal doth the soul endure when from the body it is parted! Woe is me! how many then are its tears; and there is none to show compassion! It turneth its eyes to the Angels; all unavailing is its prayer. It stretcheth out its hands to men; and findeth none to succour. Wherefore, my brethren beloved, meditating on the brevity of our life, let us beseech of Christ rest for him who hath departed hence; and for our souls great mercy.

Verse: I called upon the Lord when I was in trouble, and he heard me.

Come, let us all gaze upon the marvel that is past understanding: he who but yesterday was with us now lieth dead. Come, let us learn how that, in a little while, we also shall end in the swathing-bands of death. How lie they in stench, who were anointed with sweet-smelling spices! How lie they who erst bedecked themselves with gold, now unadorned, bereft of form! Wherefore, my brethren beloved, let us meditate upon the brevity of our life, and entreat of Christ rest for him who hath been translated hence; and for our souls great mercy.

Verse: Deliver my soul, O Lord, from the mouths of the ungodly.

Farewell, vain life! Farewell, all ye, my kinsfolk, friends and children! For I tread a way wherein I ne'er have walked. But come, remembering my love for you, follow me, and commit this, my mortal clay, unto the grave: And make entreaty with tears, unto Christ who shall judge my humble soul, that he will snatch me from the fire unquenchable.

Glory . . . now, and ever, ...

Hymn to the Birth-giver of God. Thou Gate Impassable, mystically sealed, O blessed Virgin Birth-giver of God, accept thou our petitions, and bear them unto thy Son and God; that through thee he may save our souls.

Stanzas, in Tone III. Lo, here I lie, my brethren beloved, silent and voiceless amid you all. My mouth is idle, my tongue is stopped, and my lips are curbed; my hands are bound, and my feet are fettered; my semblance is changed, mine eyes are quenched, and behold not those who make moan; mine ears receive not the wail of the mourners, my nose perceiveth not the sweet fragrance of the incense. But true love can in no wise die. Wherefore I beseech all my dear ones: Remember me before the Lord in the Day of Judgment, that I may find mercy at that dread Judgment Seat.

Verse: I will lift up mine eyes unto the hills, whence cometh my help.

All mortal things are vanity, and exist not after death. Riches endure not, neither doth glory accompany on the way: for when death cometh, all these things vanish utterly. For which cause let us cry unto Christ the Immortal: To him who hath been translated from among us, give thou rest where is the abode of those who are glad.

Verse: The Lord shall preserve thy going out and thy coming in, from this time forth, even forevermore.

O men, why vex we ourselves in vain? Swift and grievous is the course we run. Life is a smoke, and vapour, and ashes, and clay; and soon shall we be dust, and like a flower shall we wither away. Wherefore, unto Christ, the King Immortal, let us cry: To him who hath been translated from among us, give thou rest where is the abode of all who are glad.

Glory . . . now, and ever, . . .

Hymn to the Birth-giver of God. Thee as a Haven of salvation, O Virgin Birth-giver of God, have we who are tempest-tossed on the sea of life. Wherefore, entreat thou him who, without seed, was incarnate of thee, and in wise ineffable was made man, that he will save our souls.

Stanzas, in Tone IV. Where is earthly predilection? Where is the pomp of the ephemeral creatures of a day? Where are the gold and the silver? Where is the multitude of household servants and their clamour? All dust, all ashes, all shadows. But come, let us cry aloud unto the King Immortal: O Lord, thine eternal good things vouchsafe thou unto him who hath been translated from us, giving him rest in thy blessedness which waxeth not old.

Verse: I rejoiced when they said unto me: Let us go into the house of the Lord.

Death came like a robber; he came, the corrupter, and laid me low;

he came, the corrupter, and made me as one that existeth not; he came, and being earth, I lie as though I were not. Of a truth are we mortals a dream; of a truth are we a vision. But come, unto the King Immortal let us cry: Thine eternal good things vouchsafe thou, O Lord, unto him who hath been translated from us, granting him rest in the life which waxeth not old.

Glory . . . now, and ever, . . .

Hymn to the Birth-giver of God. O Virgin alone Pure and Undefiled, who without seed didst bring forth God: Pray thou that our souls may be saved.

Stanzas, in Tone V. I called to mind the Prophet, how he cried: I am earth and ashes; and I looked again into the graves, and beheld the bones laid bare; and I said: Who then is the king or warrior, the rich man or the needy, the upright or the sinner? Yet give rest with thy Saints, unto thy servant, O Lord.

Verse: Our feet have stood in thy courts, O Jerusalem.

Thou hast said, O Christ, that he who believeth on thee shall not see death; and forasmuch as I, from the Light in the Light, am the Light, so also shall ye be illumined with me in my glory. For, being very God, I am come to save those who, in true right belief, do honour me, the only Lord God, twofold in nature, of flesh and Godhead, but one in Person. Wherefore, in the light of thy countenance, with the Saints, give rest unto this thy faithful servant, who hath confessed me: forasmuch as thou lovest mankind.

Glory . . . now, and ever, . . .

Hymn to the Birth-giver of God. We entreat **thee,** as the Mother of God, O Blessed One: Beseech thou him that he will save us.

Stanzas, in Tone VI. Thy creating command was my origin and my foundation: for thy pleasure it was, out of nature visible and invisible, to fashion me, a living creature. From the earth thou didst shape my body, and didst give me a soul by thy divine and quickening breath. Wherefore, O Christ, give rest to thy servant, in the land of the living, in the habitations of the Just.

Verse: Unto thee have I lifted up mine eyes, O thou who dwellest in the heavens.

With thine own image hast thou honoured the work of thy hands, O Word, depicting in material form the likeness of thine Essence supersensual; whereof, also, thou hast made me a participant, placing me on earth to rule with independent lordship over created things. Wherefore, O Saviour, give rest unto thy servant, in the land of the living, in the habitations of the Just.

Glory . . . now, and ever, . . .

Hymn to the Birth-giver of God. We have come to the knowledge of God who was incarnate of thee, O Virgin Birth-giver of God. Entreat thou him that he will save our souls.

Stanzas, in Tone VII. When, in the beginning, thou hadst created man after thine own image and likeness, thou didst set him in Paradise to reign over thy creatures. But when, beguiled by the malice of the Devil, he tasted of the food, he became a transgressor of thy commandments. For which cause, O Lord, thou didst condemn him to return again unto the earth whence he was taken, and to entreat repose.

Verse: How amiable are thy tabernacles, O Lord of hosts.

Death which looseth every sorrow is granted unto the race of Adam. For we became subject unto corruption through the eating of the fruit; for we know that, as we were made of earth, dust shall we be again, and ashes, as we were before. Wherefore, with the voice of entreaty, let us beseech the Creator that he will grant pardon and mercy unto him who hath been translated hence.

Glory . . . now, and ever, . . .

Hymn to the Birth-giver of God. We faithful have thee, O Birth-giver of God, for a Wall impregnable and a steadfast Hope. Wherefore, cease thou not, O Lady, to entreat for thy servants who have fallen asleep in the faith that they may receive pardon at the Judgment Day, when thy Son and God shall sit as Judge (for thou knowest our nature, how that of every manner of sin are we now commingled); that we may all bless thee.

Stanzas, in Tone VIII. I weep and I wail when I think upon death, and behold our beauty, fashioned after the image of God, lying in the tomb, disfigured, dishonoured, bereft of form. O marvel! What is this mystery which doth befall us? Why have we been given over unto corruption, and why have we been wedded unto death? Of a truth, as it is written, by the command of God, who giveth the departed rest.

How are we become subject unto corruption, we who have borne the image of the Incorruptible, and have received a soul immortal through the breath divine, and so are become of blended nature, as it is written? How have we sinned against the commands of God? O marvel! How have we, abandoning the food of God, eaten the fruit which begetteth death and bitterness? How, being led astray, have we bereft ourselves of life divine? Henceforth let us cry unto Christ: In thy courts establish thou him whom thou hast translated hence.

Glory . . . now, and ever, . . .

Hymn to the Birth-giver of God. Thy protection, O Virgin Birth-giver of God, is spiritual healing. For having recourse thereunto, we are released from our spiritual ills.

Stanzas in Tone VIII. Measureless is the torment of those who have lived lewdly; gnashing of teeth and wailing unconsoled; gloom unlightened and outer darkness, the worm that sleepeth not, tears unavailing, and judgment without mercy. For which cause, ere the end shall come, let us cry aloud and say: Unto this man whom thou hast chosen, O Lord Christ, give rest with thine elect.

The trump shall thunder forth its sound, and the dead shall rise as it were from sleep, desiring with great longing to receive the heavenly life, setting their hope on thee, their Creator and their Lord.   Condemn thou not, therefore, thy servant, O Immortal One, who for our sake didst become mortal.   For which cause, ere the end shall come, let us cry aloud and say: Unto this man whom thou hast chosen, O Lord Christ, give rest with thine elect.

Lo! the elements and heaven and earth shall be changed; and all creation shall put on immortality, and mortality shall be destroyed; and darkness shall flee away at thy coming.   For thou shalt come again in glory, as it is written, to requite unto every man according to what he hath done.   Unto this man whom thou hast chosen, O Lord Christ, give rest with thine elect.

Glory . . . *Tone VI.*

Come ye all, and behold a sight strange and terrible, familiar unto all, the image to-day beheld; and vex yourselves no longer about temporal things.   To-day is the soul severed from the body, and translated to the world eternal; for it setteth out upon a path which it hath never trod, and goeth to the Judge who respecteth not persons, where the Angelic Hosts stand round about.   For terrible, O my brethren, is that Judgment Seat, where all we naked must appear.   For some shall be put to shame, and some shall receive crowns.   Wherefore, let us cry unto the King Immortal: When thine it shall be to try the secret things of man, spare thy servant whom thou hast taken, O Lord who lovest mankind.

Now, and ever, ...

Hymn to the Birth-giver of God. By the prayers of her who bare thee, O Christ, and of thy Forerunner; of the Apostles, Prophets, Hierarchs, Holy Ones, and Just, and of all the Saints: Give rest unto thy servant who hath fallen asleep.

Then PSALM XCII.

It is a good thing to give thanks unto the Lord, and to sing praises unto thy Name, O Most Highest: to tell of thy loving-kindness early in the morning, and of thy truth in the night-season; upon an instrument of ten strings, and upon the lute; upon a loud instrument, and upon the harp.   For thou, Lord, hast made me glad through thy works; and I will rejoice in giving praise for the operations of thy hands.   O Lord, how glorious are thy works! thy thoughts are very deep.   An unwise man doth not well consider this, and a fool doth not understand it.   When the ungodly are green as the grass, and when all the workers of wickedness do flourish, then shall they be destroyed forever; but thou, Lord, art the Most Highest for evermore.   For lo, thine enemies, O Lord, lo, thine enemies shall perish; and all the workers of wickedness shall be destroyed. But mine horn shall be exalted like the horn of an unicorn; for I am anointed with fresh oil. Mine eye also shall see his lust of mine enemies, and mine ear shall hear his desire of the wicked that arise up against me. The righteous shall flourish like a palm-tree, and shall spread abroad like a cedar in Libanus. Such as are planted in the house of the Lord, shall flourish in the courts of the house of our God. They also shall bring forth more fruit in their age, and shall be fat and well-liking; that they may show how true the Lord my strength is, and that there is no unrighteousness in him.

O Holy God, Holy Mighty, . . . Glory . . . now, and ever, . . . O all-holy Trinity, . . . Lord, have mercy. (*Thrice.*) Glory . . . now, and ever, . . . Our Father, . . . For thine is the kingdom, . . . (*See the Burial of Laymen, page* 368.)

Give rest with the Just, O Saviour, unto thy servant, and establish him in thy courts, as it is written: Regarding not, in that thou art good, his sins, whether voluntary or involuntary, and all things committed either with knowledge or in ignorance, O thou who lovest mankind.

In the place of thy rest, O Lord, where all thy Saints repose, give rest also to the soul of thy servant: for thou only lovest mankind.

O Holy Mother of the Light Ineffable, with songs angelic honouring, devoutly do we magnify thee.

Then the Litany: Have mercy upon us: *and the Prayer:* O God of spirits, . . . (*See page* 369.)

And after the Exclamation, the last kiss is given, while the Choir singeth:

Come, brethren, let us give the last kiss unto the dead, rendering thanks unto God. For he hath vanished from among his kin, and presseth onward to the grave, and vexeth himself no longer concerning vanities, and concerning the flesh, which suffereth sore distress. Where are now his kinsfolk and his friends? Lo, we are parted. Let us beseech the Lord that he will give him rest.

What is this parting, O brethren? What is this wailing, what this weeping at the present hour? Come ye, therefore, let us kiss him who was but lately with us; for he is committed to the grave; he is covered with a stone; he taketh up his abode in the gloom; he is interred among the dead, and now is parted from all his kinsfolk and his friends. Let us beseech the Lord that he will give unto him eternal rest.

Now is life's artful triumph of vanities destroyed. For the spirit hath vanished from its tabernacle; its clay groweth black. The vessel is shattered, voiceless, bereft of feeling, motionless, dead. Committing which unto the grave, let us beseech the Lord that he will give him rest eternal.

What is our life like unto? Unto a flower, a vapour, and the dew of the morning, in very truth. Come ye, therefore, let us gaze keenly at the grave.   Where is the beauty of the body, and where its youth?   Where are the eyes and the fleshly form?   Like the grass all have perished, all have been destroyed.   Come ye, therefore, let us prostrate ourselves at the feet of Christ with tears.

A great weeping and wailing, a great sighing and agony, and Hell and destruction is the departure of the soul.   This transitory life is a shadow unreal and an illusive dream; the trouble of the life of earth is a phantasm importunate.   Let us, then, flee afar from every earthly sin, that we may inherit heavenly things.

As we gaze on the dead who lieth before us, let us all accept this example of our own last hour.   For he vanisheth from earth like the smoke; like a flower he is faded; like the grass he is cut down.   Swathed in a coarse garment he is concealed in the earth.   As we leave him hidden from sight, let us beseech Christ that he will give unto him eternal rest.

Draw nigh, ye descendants of Adam, let us gaze upon him who is laid low in the earth, made after our own image, all comeliness stripped off, dissolved in the grave by decay, by worms in darkness consumed, and hidden by the earth.   As we leave him hid from sight, let us beseech Christ that he will give unto him eternal rest.

When the soul from the body is about to be rent with violence by Angels dread, it forgetteth all its kinsfolk and acquaintance, and is troubled concerning its appearance before the judgment which shall come upon the things of vanity and much-toiling flesh.   Come ye, then, importuning the Judge, let us implore that the Lord will pardon him all his deeds which he hath done.

Come, O brethren, let us gaze into the grave upon the dust and ashes from which we are made.   Whither go we now?   What are we become?   Who is poor, who rich?   Who is the master?   Who a freeman?   Are not we all ashes?   The beauty of the countenance is mouldered, and Death hath withered up all the flower of youth.

Vanity and corruption, of a truth, are all the illusions and the inglorious things of life.   For all we shall pass away: all we shall die, kings and princes, judges and rulers, rich and poor, and every mortal creature. For now they who were erst alive are cast down into the grave.   Wherefore, let us beseech the Lord that he will give rest.

Now are all the bodily organs seen to be idle, which so little while ago were filled with motion; all useless, dead, unconscious.   For the eyes have withdrawn inward, the feet are bound, the hands lie helpless, and the ears withal; the tongue is imprisoned in silence, committed to the tomb.   Of a verity, all mortal things are vanity.

Hymn to the Birth-giver of God. O thou who savest those who fix their hope on thee, the Mother of the Sun that knoweth no setting, O Progenetrix of God; With thy prayers entreat, we beseech thee, the God exceeding good, that unto him who hath now been translated, he will give repose where the souls of the righteous rest. Manifest him an heir of divine good things in the courts of the Just, unto everlasting memory, O All-undefiled One.

Glory to the Father, and to the Son, and to the Holy Spirit.

Tone VI. As ye behold me lie before you all speechless and bereft of breath, weep for me, O friends and brethren, O kinsfolk and acquaintance. For but yesterday I talked with you, and suddenly there came upon me the dread hour of death. But come, all ye who loved me, and kiss me with the last kiss. For nevermore shall I walk or talk with you. For I go hence unto the Judge with whom is no respect of persons. For slave and master stand together before him, king and warrior, the rich and the poor, in honour equal. For according to his deeds shall every man receive glory or be put to shame. But I beg and implore you all, that ye will pray without ceasing unto Christ-God, that I be not doomed according to my sins, unto a place of torment; but that he will appoint unto me a place where is the light of life.

Now, and ever, and unto ages of ages. Amen.

He who hath been translated hence hath crossed life's ever-troubled sea, and hath sailed into thy haven through faith; but in thy tranquillity and sweetness immortal, with the Saints instructing him, give rest, O Christ, to the soul of thy servant.

Tone IV. To-day is fulfilled the all-praised word of devout David, who said: Man is like the grass, his days are as the flower of the field when it is withered. For erstwhile we beheld him living and speaking; lo, now he lieth dead, motionless, bereft of breath. He is gone forth, and hath departed from present things, thither where is the recompense of his deeds; thither, where is the joy of all the Saints. With the same give rest, O God, unto him that is gone hence: in that thou art merciful and lovest mankind.

Tone VIII. Give rest, O Lord Almighty, to the soul of thy servant, in the mansions of the Just, where the light of thy countenance shineth upon all that are worthy, O thou who alone lovest mankind.

I have vanished from among my kin, and have abandoned the residue of my life, and have fled unto thee, O Lord: Save me.

Through the prayers of the Birth-giver of God, give peace to the life of us who cry unto thee: O Life-giver, glory to thee!

O Holy God, Holy Mighty, . . . (*see page* 391), *and the rest to the end of the Prayer:* Our Lord Jesus Christ by his divine grace, . . . (*See page* 392.)

Then, as they go forth to the grave, the Priests sing the Theme-Songs (Irmosí) of the GREAT CANON OF ST. ANDREW OF CRETE.

A helper and protector hath revealed himself to me unto salvation; He is my God, and Him will I glorify; the God of my fathers, and Him will I exalt: For greatly hath he glorified himself.

Hear, ye heavens; I will proclaim and sing praises unto Christ, come in the flesh through a Virgin.

On the rock immovable of thy statutes, O Christ, establish thou my thoughts.

The prophet heard of thy coming, O Lord, and was affrighted, that thou shouldest will to be born of a Virgin, and to reveal thyself unto men: and he said: I have heard thy tidings, and was sore afraid: Glory to thy might, O Lord.

I have longed for thee in the night-season, O thou who lovest mankind; illumine me, I beseech thee, and guide me in thy commandments.   And teach me, O Saviour, to do thy will.

With my whole heart cried I unto God, rich in mercies, and he heard me from the nethermost hell, and led forth my life from corruption.

We have sinned, we have dealt unlawfully, we have wrought evil in thy sight, neither have we observed, neither have we done those things which thou hast commanded us: yet cast us not away utterly, O God of our fathers.

Him whom all the Hosts of heaven glorify, before whom tremble Cherubim and Seraphim, praise ye, bless ye, and magnify forever, everything that hath breath and every creature.

Passing understanding is the Nativity of seedless conception, incorruptible is the fruit of the mother unwedded; for the birth of God reneweth nature: Wherefore all generations, and we with them, right gloriously do magnify thee, as Bride and Mother of our God.

O Holy God, . . . Glory . . . now, and ever, . . . O all-holy Trinity, . . . Lord, have mercy.   (*Thrice.*)   Glory . . . now, and ever, . . . Our Father, . . . For thine is the kingdom, . . . In the place of thy rest, . . . Thou art the God who didst descend into Hell, . . . O Only Pure and Spotless Virgin, . . . (*page* 368).   *And the Litany:* Have mercy upon us, O God: *with the Prayer:* O God of spirits, . . . (*page* 369) *and the rest, as at the Burial of Laymen.   (See page* 391.)

> *With this difference: That in the Benediction, and in the "Eternal memory," the name of the Priest is mentioned.   The Prayer of Absolution is read by the Bishop (if one be present), or by the Principal Priest; and it is then placed in the hand of the dead Priest in the coffin by his Confessor.*

THE ORDER FOR THE BURIAL OF A CHILD *

The Priest. Blessed is our God always, now. and ever, and unto ages of ages.

Choir. Amen.

> *Then Psalm xci.:* Whoso dwelleth under the defence of the Most High, shall abide under the shadow of the Almighty. Alleluia, *in Tone V.* (*See page* 370, *the Burial of Laymen.*)

Verse (Stikh): Blessed is he whom thou hast chosen and taken, O Lord.

Choir. Alleluia, *in Tone VIII.*

Verse: And his remembrance is from generation to generation.

Choir. Alleluia.

O Holy God, Holy Mighty, . . . Glory . . . now, and, ever, . . . O all-holy Trinity, . . . Lord, have mercy. (*Thrice.*) Glory . . . now, and ever, . . . Our Father, . . . For thine is the kingdom, . . . (*See page* 368, *Burial of Laymen.*)

O Thou who, with wisdom profound, mercifully orderest all things, and givest that which is expedient unto all men, thou Only Creator: Give rest, O Lord, to the soul of thy servant who hath fallen asleep; For he (*she*) hath set his (*her*) hope on thee, our Maker, the Author of our being and our God.

Glory to the Father, and to the Son, and to the Holy Spirit.

For he (*she*) hath set his (*her*) hope on thee, our Maker, the Author of our being, and our God.

Now, and ever, and unto ages of ages. Amen.

Thee have we as a Wall and a Defence, and a Mediatrix well-pleasing unto God whom thou hast borne, O Virgin Birth-giver of God, the salvation of the faithful.

> *Then Psalm li.*, Have mercy upon me, O God, . . . (*See page* 380.)

> *And after that beginneth the* CANON FOR THE DEAD, *over the departed child.*

> *Canticle I., Tone VIII.*

Theme-Song (Irmós). When Israel had passed through the water as it had been dry land, and had escaped from the malice of the Egyptians, they cried: Let us sing praises unto our deliverer and our God.

Refrain. Give rest to the child, O Lord.

Hymns. O Word of God, who didst humble thyself even unto the flesh, and wast graciously pleased to become a babe, yet without change:

---

* The Order for the Burial of a Child under seven years of age differeth from that of Burial of Adults, inasmuch as it is celebrated over innocent, sinless beings.

Ordain thou that this child whom thou hast accepted may be received into Abraham's bosom, we beseech thee.

Thou wast beheld a little child, thou who existest before all the ages, and forasmuch as thou art good, unto children hast promised thy kingdom: Number therein this child here present.

Glory to the Father, and to the Son, and to the Holy Spirit.

Thou hast taken unto thyself, O Christ the Saviour, this spotless child, ere he (*she*) had been tempted of earthly pleasures, bestowing upon him (*her*) thine eternal good things; forasmuch as thou lovest mankind.

Now, and ever, and unto ages of ages. Amen.

Hymn to the Birth-giver of God. O thou who, in wise inexpressible, didst bear the Wisdom and Word of the Father, heal thou the cruel wound of my soul, and soothe the pang of my heart.

Canticle III.

Theme-Song (Irmós). O Lord Supreme and Creator of the vault of heaven, and Founder of the Church, establish thou me in thy love, O thou who alone lovest mankind; the Summit of desire, the Confirmation of the faithful.

Refrain. Give rest to the child, O Lord.

O Word all-perfect, who as perfect child didst manifest thyself, thou hast translated unto thyself this child of stature unfulfilled. Give him (*her*) rest with all the just who are well-pleasing unto thee, O thou who alone lovest mankind.

This uncorrupted child, whom thou hast translated through thy command divine, torn hence ere he (*she*) had tasted the sweets of earth, show thou forth a partaker of super-mundane good things, we beseech thee, O Beneficent One.

Glory . . .

A partaker of heavenly mansions, and of radiant rest, and of the holy Choir of the Saints, make thou, O Lord, this child most pure, whom it hath seemed good to thee, O Saviour, to call unto thyself.

Now, and ever, . . .

Hymn to the Birth-giver of God. Bereft of all things I flee to thy sole shelter, O Lady Most Pure: Succour thou me. For I have heaped up a treasure of iniquity, and am all filled with poverty of virtues.

Then the Theme-Song: O Lord Supreme and Creator . . .

Then the Priest reciteth the following Litany:

Again, yet again, in peace let us pray to the Lord.

Choir. Lord, have mercy.

Furthermore we pray for the repose of this blessed child, N. And that, according to his word, He will graciously vouchsafe unto him (*her*) his heavenly kingdom.

Choir. Lord, have mercy. (*Thrice.*)

That the Lord our God will appoint his (*her*) soul where all the Just repose.

Choir. Lord, have mercy. (*Thrice.*)

The mercies of God, the kingdom of heaven, and rest with the Saints, for him (*her*) and for ourselves, let us beseech of Christ, our King Immortal and our God.

Choir. Grant it, O Lord.

Priest. Let us pray to the Lord.

Choir. Lord, have mercy.

O Lord Jesus Christ our God, who hast promised to bestow the kingdom of heaven upon them that have been born of water and of the Spirit, and in spotlessness of life have been translated unto thee, and hast said, Suffer the little children to come unto me, for of such is the kingdom of heaven: We humbly entreat thee that thou wilt give unto thy servant, the spotless child, N., now departed from us, the inheritance of thy kingdom, according to thine unfailing promise. And grant that we may continue in innocency of living, and make a Christian ending of our life, and attain to an abode in the heavenly mansions, with all thy Saints.

For thou art the Resurrection, and the Life, and the Repose of all thy servants, and of thy servant, this child, N., now taken from us, O Christ our God; and unto thee do we ascribe glory, together with thy Father who is from everlasting, and thine all-holy, and good, and life-giving Spirit, now, and ever, and unto ages of ages.

Choir. Amen.

Hymn. Of a truth, all things are vanity, and life is but a shadow and a dream. For in vain doth every one who is born of earth disquiet himself, as saith the Scriptures. When we have acquired the world, then do we take up our abode in the grave, where kings and beggars lie down together. Wherefore, O Christ our God, give rest to thy servant departed this life; forasmuch as thou lovest mankind.

Canticle IV.

Theme-Song (Irmós). I have heard the mystery of thy dispensation, O Lord, and have considered thy works, and have glorified thy divinity.

Refrain. Give rest to the child, O Lord.

Hymns. Let us not mourn the child, but rather weep heavily for ourselves who sin always; that we may be delivered from Gehenna.

Thou hast deprived the child of earthly joys, O Master. Grant unto him (*her*) thy heavenly good things; forasmuch as thou art he who judgeth righteously.

Glory . . .

A citizen of Paradise, O truly blessed child, shall he make thee who hath summoned thee from earth, and numbereth thee with the company of the Saints.

Now, and ever, . . .

Hymn to the Birth-giver of God. All we who are illumined know thee, O Birth-giver of God most pure. For thou hast borne the Sun of Righteousness, O Ever-Virgin One.

Canticle V.

Theme-Song (Irmós). Wherefore hast thou cast me away from thy countenance, O Light which knowest no setting? And why hath hostile darkness encompassed me, the wretched one? But turn thou me again, and guide thou my paths in the light of thy commandments, I beseech thee.

Refrain. Give rest to the child, O Lord.

Hymns. By thy righteous judgment hast thou mowed down, ere like a green shoot it had put forth buds, the child whom thou has called to thyself, O Lord. But in that thou hast led the same unto the mount of blessings everlasting, implant thou him (*her*) firmly there, O Word.

The sword of death hath come and cut thee off like a tender branch ere thou hadst tasted earthly joys, O Blessed One. But lo! Christ doth open unto thee the heavenly gates, numbering thee with the elect. For he is full of loving-kindness.

Glory . . .

Grieve ye not for me, for he hath ordained nothing worthy of grief. But weep ye rather always for yourselves who have sinned sore, O kin and friends, the dead child crieth: that when ye shall be proved ye receive not chastisement.

Now, and ever, . . .

Hymn to the Birth-giver of God. Of myself do I despair, when I look upon the multitude of my deeds. But when I take thought of thee, who beyond understanding didst bear the Lord, O Mother of God, I am refreshed with hope. For thee alone do we possess as our Mediatrix.

Canticle VI.

Theme-Song (Irmós). I will pour out my petition unto the Lord, and unto him will I proclaim my grief. For evil hath filled my soul, and my life hath drawn nigh unto the pit; and like Jonah will I pray: Lead me forth from corruption, O God.

Refrain. Give rest to the child, O Lord.

Hymns. As a child thou wast laid in a manger, and didst yield thyself to the embrace of an aged man who had begotten babes in his loins. And ere this child had attained unto his (*her*) full stature, thou has translated him (*her*) into life. For which cause we glorify thee with thanksgiving.

Thou didst cry unto the Apostles, O Word: Suffer the little children to come unto me, for unto such as are like unto them in spirit is my kingdom given. Grant, therefore, thy light unto the child who hath been translated unto thee.

Glory . . .

Thou hast despoiled thy child of earthly good things, that thou mightest manifest him (*her*) a partaker of thy heavenly good things, inasmuch as he (*she*) hath not offended against thy commands divine.   Let us glorify the depth immeasurable of thy providence, O Blessed One.

Now, and ever, . . .

Hymn to the Birth-giver of God. Thee have we as a vast wall of refuge, O Maiden, and an all-perfect salvation for our souls, and an abiding-place in sorrow; and in thy light will we rejoice evermore.   O Lady, save us now from our griefs and woes.

Then the Theme-Song: I will pour out my petition . . .

Then the Priest reciteth the Litany: Again, yet again: *with the Prayer:* O Lord Jesus Christ our God, . . . *and the Exclamation.   (See page 425.)*

Then is sung the Collect-Hymn (Kondák), in Tone VIII.

With the Saints give rest, O Christ, to the soul of thy servant, where there is neither sickness, nor sorrow, nor sighing, but life everlasting.

The Ikos.

Thou only art immortal, who hast created and fashioned man.   For out of the earth were we mortals made, and unto the earth shall we return again, as thou didst command when thou madest me, saying unto me: For earth thou art, and unto the earth shalt thou return.   Whither, also, all we mortals wend our way, making of our funeral dirge the song: Alleluia.

Also the following Ikosi:

Naught is more pitiable than a mother, naught more wretched than a father; for their affections are sore distressed when they send their children forth before them to the grave.   Great, also, is the pang of their hearts because of their children, and yet the more when these are sweet of speech, as they call to mind their sayings with the song: Alleluia.

Oft do they beat their breasts before the grave and say: O my son, and sweetest child, hearest thou not what thy mother crieth unto thee?   Behold, also, the womb that bare thee.   Why speakest thou not with us, as thou wert wont to speak, but thus holdest thy peace, and sayest not with us: Alleluia.

O God, O God, who has called me hence, be thou the consolation of my household now; for a great affliction hath befallen them.   For all hold their gaze fixed steadfastly on me, having me as their only-begotten one. But do thou, who wast born of a Virgin Mother, refresh the bowels of my mother, and water with dew the heart of my father, even with this: Alleluia.

Then the Collect-Hymn, in Tone VIII.

With the Saints give rest, O Christ, to the soul of thy servant, where there is neither sickness, nor sorrow, nor sighing, but life everlasting.

Canticle VII.

Theme-Song (Irmós). The Hebrew Children in the furnace trod boldly on the flames, and the fire was transformed into dew as they cried: Blessed art thou, O Lord God, forevermore.

Refrain. Give rest to the child, O Lord.

Hymns. Inscribe thy child in the Book of the Redeemed, in that thou lovest mankind, O Bountiful One; that, rejoicing, he may cry aloud to the majesty of thy glory: Blessed art thou.

With the radiant light of thy countenance illumine thou, O Word, thy child who, in the faith, hath been translated unto thee in unripe age, and singeth unto thee: O Lord God, blessed art thou.

Glory . . .

A cause of woe doth thy going hence now seem to those who love thee; but of a surety to thee a cause of joy and gladness. For thou, O child, hast inherited life unto all the ages.

Now, and ever, . . .

Hymn to the Birth-giver of God. Behold, O Virgin, the affliction which the multitude of my evil deeds hath brought upon me; and ere I go hence, give me refreshing with thy maternal prayers, that God may show mercy upon me.

Canticle VIII.

Theme-Song (Irmós). With seven-fold heat did the Chaldæan tyrant in his rage cause the furnace to be heated for the Godly Ones; but when he beheld them saved by a better power, he cried aloud unto their Maker and Redeemer: Ye Children, bless; ye Priests sing praises; ye People exalt him unto all the ages.

Refrain. Give rest to the child, O Lord.

Hymns. In Abraham's bosom, in the mansions of rest, where abideth ever the joy of those who make glad; in the places of refreshing where is the water of life, may Christ establish thee, in that he himself became a little child for the sake of us who continually do cry unto him: Ye Priests, sing praises; ye People, exalt him forevermore.

Thy going hence is, of a truth, the all-sufficent and ever-memorable cause of our grief and of our tears. For ere thou hadst tasted the pleasant things of this present life, thou hast left the earth, and thy parents' bosom. But Abraham's bosom shall receive thee; for thou art but a little child, and hast no part in any stain.

Glory . . .

Why mourn ye me, the child translated hence? he crieth invisibly, as dead he lieth. There is no cause for grief. For unto children who have committed no deeds worthy of tears is appointed the joy of all the Righteous. For unto Christ they sweetly sing: Ye Priests, sing praises; ye People exalt him forevermore.

Now, and ever, . . .

Hymn to the Birth-giver of God. Arise to my succour, O Birth-giver of God. Receive my supplications, and deliver me from condemnation dread, from rigorous searching-out, from outer darkness, and fire, and from gnashing of teeth; from the spiteful abuse of demons, and from every distress, O Hope of the hopeless, O Life of the despairing.

Canticle IX.

Theme-Song (Irmós). Heaven was affrighted, and the ends of the earth were amazed: For God revealed himself unto men in the flesh, and thy womb became more spacious than the heavens. For which cause the chieftains of men and of Angels do glorify thee, O Birth-giver of God.

Refrain. Give rest to the child, O Lord.

Hymns. O Christ, who didst become a little child, yet without change of essence; and of thine own good will didst unite thyself unto the Cross; and with pity didst look upon the maternal sorrows of her who gave thee birth: Assuage thou the sadness and sore grief of the faithful parents of the dead child: that unto thy majesty we may sing praises.

O King of all men, in that thou hast sent from on high, and taken this blessed child, like a pure little bird, to its heavenly nest, thou hast saved this soul from snares of many kinds, O Lord, and hast united it with the spirits of the righteous who enjoy the delights of thy kingdom.

Glory . . .

Thou hast bestowed a heavenly abode, O Word of God, upon children who have wrought no evil: for thus hath it seemed good in thy sight, O Blessed One. With the same number thou also thy creature, the child who is now come unto thee. Assuage thou the grief of his (*her*) parents; forasmuch as thou art pitiful, and lovest mankind.

Now, and ever, . . .

Hymn to the Birth-giver of God. With the eye of the heart gazing ever steadfastly unto thee, who makest supplication maternal to him who was born of thee, I implore thee, O all-blameless One: Quench thou the passions of my soul; move me betimes to penitence, O Virgin, and illumine me with thy light.

Then the Litany: Again, yet again: *with the Prayer:* O Lord Jesus Christ our God, . . . *and the Exclamation.* (*See page* 425.)

Exapostilárion.

Now am I at rest, and have found great release; for I have been translated from corruption, and have passed over into life. Glory to thee, O Lord.

(*And the Choir repeateth the same after each of the following Verses.*)

Verse (Stikh): Man is as the grass: his days are as the flower of the field. ℟

Verse: For his spirit goeth forth from him, and he ceaseth to be. ℟

Verse: But the truth of the Lord endureth forever. ℞

Glory to the Father, and to the Son, and to the Holy Spirit, now, and ever, and unto ages of ages. Amen.

Now have I chosen the Maiden Mother of God; for Christ, the Redeemer of all men was born of her. Glory to thee, O Lord.

And straightway the Priest shall exclaim:

For holy art thou, O Lord our God, and restest in the Saints; and unto thee do we ascribe glory, to the Father, and to the Son, and to the Holy Spirit, now, and ever, and unto ages of ages.

Choir. Amen.

O Holy God, Holy Mighty, Holy Immortal One, have mercy upon us. (*Thrice.*)

Deacon. Let us attend.

Priest. Peace be with you all.

Reader. And with thy spirit.

Deacon. Wisdom!

Reader. The Gradual (*Prokímen*), in the Sixth Tone. Blessed is the way in which thou shalt walk to-day, O soul; for a place of rest is prepared for thee.

And the Choir repeateth this.

Verse: Return thou unto thy rest, O my soul, for the Lord hath dealt graciously with thee.

Deacon. Wisdom!

Reader. The Lesson from the Epistle of the holy Apostle Paul to the Corinthians.

Deacon. Let us attend.

(*1 Cor. xv. 39–46.*) Brethren: All flesh is not the same flesh: but there is one kind of flesh of men, another flesh of beasts, another of fishes, and another of birds. There are also celestial bodies, and bodies terrestrial: but the glory of the celestial is one, and the glory of the terrestrial is another. There is one glory of the sun, and another glory of the moon, and another glory of the stars; for one star differeth from another star in glory. So also is the resurrection of the dead. It is sown in corruption, it is raised in incorruption; it is sown in dishonour, it is raised in glory: it is sown in weakness, it is raised in power: it is sown a natural body, it is raised a spiritual body. There is a natural body, and there is a spiritual body. And so it is written, The first man Adam was made a living soul, the last Adam was made a quickening spirit.

Priest. Peace be with thee.

Reader. And with thy spirit.

Deacon. Wisdom! —— *Reader.* Alleluia. (*Thrice.*)

Verse: Blessed is he whom thou hast chosen and taken, O Lord.

Verse: Among the blessed shall his soul take up its abode.

Priest. Wisdom, O believers! Let us listen to the Holy Gospel. Peace be with you all.

Choir. And with thy spirit.

Deacon. The Lesson from the holy Gospel of John.

Choir. Glory to thee, O Lord; glory to thee.

Priest. Let us attend.

(*John vi. 35–40.*) The Lord said unto the Jews which came unto him: I am the bread of life: he that cometh unto me shall never hunger, and he that believeth on me shall never thirst. But I said unto you, that ye also have seen me and believe not. All that the Father giveth me shall come to me: and him that cometh unto me, I will in no wise cast out. For I came down from heaven, not to do mine own will, but the will of him that sent me. And this is the Father's will, which hath sent me, that of all which he hath given me, I should lose nothing, but should raise it up again at the last day.

Priest. Peace be unto thee, who hast announced the good tidings.

Choir. Glory to thee, O Lord; glory to thee.

And straightway the last kiss is given, while the Choir singeth the following Stanzas (Stikhiri):

Tone VIII. Who would not weep, my child, thy lamentable translation from this life! For a babe immature from thy mother's arms, like a birdling small, now hast thou flown swiftly hence, and hast fled unto the Creator of all men. Who would not wail, O child, beholding thy rosy face so early faded, which before was beautiful as the crimson lily of the field? O, who would not wail, my child, and cry aloud with weeping, because of thy great comeliness, and the beauty of thy pure life? For like some ship that leaveth no wake behind, with equal swiftness hast thou vanished from my sight. Come ye, my friends, my kinsfolk, and my neighbours, and with me kiss ye him (*her*) whom we are committing to the tomb.

Death is a release for babes; for they are not accounted sharers in life's evil, and have attained unto rest and heavenly gladness; and in Abraham's bosom they rejoice, and now with choirs divine of holy children they make glad, and faithfully exult: because from sin's corruption pure have they escaped.

Glory . . .

Tone VI. Painful to Adam of old in Eden was the tasting of the tree, when the serpent belched forth his poison. For thereby did Death universal enter in, which devoureth man. But then the Master came, subdued the dragon, and gave us rest. For which cause let us cry aloud unto him: Spare, O Saviour, and give rest among the Saints to him (*her*) whom thou hast taken.

Now, and ever, . . .

Hymn to the Birth-giver of God. Thou who art the Consolation of mourners; thou Deliverance of the weak, O Virgin Birth-giver of God: save thou the city and its people, O thou Peace of those who battle, thou Calm of the tempest-tossed, and sole Defender of the faithful.

O Holy God, Holy Mighty, . . . Glory . . . now, and ever, . . . O all-holy Trinity, . . . Lord, have mercy. (*Thrice.*) Glory . . . now, and ever, . . . Our Father, . . . For thine is the kingdom, . . . (*See page* 368, *Burial of Laymen*).

Then the Hymn.

With the souls of the righteous dead give rest, O Saviour, to the soul of thy servant, preserving it unto the blessedness which is with thee, O thou who lovest mankind.

Then the Litany: Again, yet again, . . . (*See page* 425.)

Priest. Let us pray to the Lord.

Choir. Lord, have mercy.

Then the Priest, bowing his head, readeth, secretly, *this Prayer:* O Lord Jesus Christ our God, . . . (*See page* 426.)

Aloud. For thou art the Resurrection, . . . (*See page* 426.)

Choir. Amen.

Deacon. Wisdom!

Choir. More honourable than the Cherubim, and beyond compare more glorious than the Seraphim, thou who without defilement barest God the Word, true Birth-giver of God, we magnify thee.

Glory to the Father, and to the Son, and to the Holy Spirit, now, and ever, and unto ages of ages. Amen.

Lord, have mercy. (*Thrice.*) Bless.

And the Priest bestoweth the BENEDICTION.

Do thou who rose again from the dead, and hast dominion over both the quick and the dead, Christ our very God, through the prayers of thy most holy Mother, and of all thy Saints; establish in thy holy tabernacles the soul of the child, N., who hath now been translated from us; and number him (*her*) among the Righteous: Forasmuch as thou art good and lovest mankind.

Choir. Amen.

And after the Benediction the Priest saith:

Eternal be thy memory, O N., worthily-blessed and ever-memorable child!

And the Choir singeth: Memory eternal! (*Thrice.*)

Thereupon the Priest saith the following Prayer:

Deacon. Let us pray to the Lord.

Choir. Lord, have mercy.

Priest. O Lord, who guardest little children in this present life, and hast prepared for them in the life which is to come a spacious place, even Abraham's bosom, and angelic abodes brightly radiant which befit their purity, wherein the souls of the righteous dwell: Do thou, the same Lord Christ, receive the soul of thy servant, the child, N., with peace. For thou hast said: Suffer the little children to come unto me, for of such is the kingdom of heaven. For unto thee are due all glory, honour and worship, with the Father and the Holy Spirit, now, and ever, and unto ages of ages. Amen.

And taking up the body, they go forth to the grave, preceded by the Priest, the Deacon, and the Choir, all singing:

O Holy God, Holy Mighty, Holy Immortal One, have mercy upon us. (*Thrice.*)

And when the body hath been laid in the grave, the Senior Priest, taking the shovel, scattereth earth into the grave, saying:

The earth is the Lord's, and the fulness thereof: the round world, and they that dwell therein.

And so they depart, giving thanks unto God.

THE ORDER FOR THE BURIAL OF THOSE WHO DIE AT HOLY EASTER, AND DURING THE WHOLE OF THE BRIGHT WEEK *

It must be known that if any one is called unto God at Holy Easter, or on any day of the Bright Week, up to St. Thomas's Sunday, very little of the customary Office for the Dead is sung, because of the majesty and honour of the joyful Feast of the Resurrection: for it is the festival of joy and gladness, not of lamentation. And as all who have died in the risen Christ, in the hope of resurrection and of life eternal, have been taken unto God through Christ's Resurrection from the sorrowful things of this world to things joyful and blissful, the Church proclaimeth the hymns of Resurrection over these dead. And by a few fitting hymns, litanies and prayers we bear testimony that the dead person hath died in penitence; but if he hath not made satisfaction for his sins, they are remitted to him through the prayers of the Church, and he is freed from detention.

When the Priest is come, with his assistants, to the house where the body of the dead person lieth, and hath put on his priestly stole and chasuble, and hath censed the remains, he maketh the customary beginning: Blessed is our God. *And the Choir chanteth:* Christ is risen *(see page 226), in Tone V. And the Priest saith the customary verses, to wit:* Let God arise *(see page 226): and the rest. And when these have been sung, the Priest sprinkleth the body of the dead person with holy water; as also his coffin, both within and without. And the dead person is immediately laid therein. And when the singing is finished, the Deacon saith the customary litany for the dead. And the Priest reciteth, secretly, the Prayer:* O God of spirits, . . . *(See page 369.)*

After the Exclamation: In that we have beheld the resurrection of Christ, *is read, taking up the remains of the dead, they go forth to the Church, the Priest leading, and the Deacon and all the Choir and the laymen following. And as they go, the ecclesiastics and the Choir chant the Easter Canon, that is to say:* The Day of Resurrection! *(see page 227), in regular order, as much as they will, until the Church is reached.*

At the Church, after the remains have been set down, they finish the Canon which hath been begun, the Priest censing according to the custom. And at the fourth Theme-Song there is the usual Litany, with the Prayer.

Exclamation. For thou art the Resurrection, and the Life, . . . *(See page 369.)*

Then: When they who with the Marys came, . . . *(See page 228.)*

Then the fourth Theme-Song is sung, in due order. After the sixth Theme-Song, there is the usual Litany for the dead, with the Prayer.

Exclamation. For thou art the Resurrection, and the Life, . . . *(See page 369.)*

Then the Collect-Hymn: With the Saints give rest, . . . *And the Ikos:* Thou only art immortal, . . . *(See page 428.)*

And in place of: O Holy God, Holy Mighty, . . . As many as have been baptized into Christ have put on Christ.

The Epistle for the Day, from the Acts of the Apostles.

* The full text of the litanies, prayers and hymns will be found in the other Burial Orders and in the Easter Service.

Alleluia, *in Tone II.*

The Gospel for the first Sunday.

And then: In that we have beheld the Resurrection of Christ (*see page* 230): *and the rest of the Songs of the Canon.*

And when the Canon is completed, the Exapostilárion is read or sung: After that thou hadst fallen asleep in the flesh, . . . (*Twice.*) (*See page* 233.)

Then is sung: Blessed art thou, O Lord; teach me thy statutes. The company of the Angels was amazed, . . . (*See page* 28.)

Then the Easter Canticles (Stikhíri), with their Verses. (*See page* 233.)

Glory . . . now, and ever, . . . The Day of Resurrection, . . . (*Thrice.*) (*See page* 227.) *And:* Christ is risen . . . (*Thrice*)

And when these Canticles have been sung, there is the customary kissing of the dead, as they say: Christ is risen.

And after the Canticles, the usual Litany for the dead, with the Prayer, which is read aloud, close to the dead person, by the Bishop or Priest.

Exclamation.   For thou art the Resurrection, and the Life, . . . (*See page* 369.)

Then the customary Benediction. (*See page* 391.)

Then the concluding Prayer: May the Lord Jesus Christ our God, . . . (*See page* 392.)

And we go forth to the grave, bearing the body of the dead for burial. And the Priest, and all the Choir, going before the remains, chant: Christ is risen from the dead, trampling down Death by death, and upon those in the tomb bestowing life.

And the body is buried, with thanksgiving and joy, all things having been done and said which are written in the Burial of a Layman.

And the Hymn (Tropár) having been sung: Open, O earth, and receive that which was made from thee.

THE REQUIEM OFFICE FOR THE DEAD *

(PANIKHÍDI)

The Parastása, that is to say, the Great Requiem Service (1) for all our fathers and brethren who have fallen asleep in the Lord, and for all Orthodox Christians departed this life.

(And the Office for Orthodox Warriors, who have died in battle for the Faith and the Fatherland; celebrated on August 29 (September 11, N. S.).)

The Priest, vested in his stole and chasuble, and the deacon in his dalmatic, come forth from the sanctuary to the porch, preceded by a Reader bearing a light. And they stand in their wonted places, on either side of a table, upon which is a dish of kóliva. (2)

Then the Deacon saith:

Bless, Master.

And the Priest, taking the censer with the incense, exclaimeth:

Blessed is our God always; now, and ever, and unto ages of ages.
Choir. Amen.

Then, preceded by the Deacon with the light, he shall cense the kóliva, in the usual manner, in the form of a cross, while the Reader reciteth:

O Holy God, Holy Mighty, Holy Immortal One, have mercy upon us. (*Thrice.*)

Glory to the Father, and to the Son, and to the Holy Spirit, now, and ever, and unto ages of ages. Amen.

O all-holy Trinity, have mercy upon us. O Lord, wash away our sins. O Master, pardon our transgressions. O Holy One, visit and heal our infirmities, for thy Name's sake.

Lord, have mercy. (*Thrice.*)

Glory . . . now, and ever, . . .

Our Father, who art in heaven, Hallowed be thy Name. Thy kingdom come. Thy will be done on earth, As it is in heaven. Give us this day our daily bread. And forgive us our trespasses, As we forgive those who trespass against us. And lead us not into temptation; But deliver us from the Evil One:

Priest. For thine is the kingdom, and the power, and the glory, of the Father, and of the Son, and of the Holy Spirit, now, and ever, and unto ages of ages.

Choir. Amen.

Reader. Lord, have mercy. (*Twelve times.*) Glory, now, and ever, . . .

O come, let us worship God our King. O come, let us worship and

* For explanations, indicated by numbers in the text, see Appendix B. XII.

fall down before Christ, our King and our God. O come, let us worship and fall down before the Very Christ, our King and our God. (*Three reverences.*)

Psalm xci.

Whoso dwelleth under the defence of the most High, shall abide under the shadow of the Almighty. I will say unto the Lord, Thou art my hope, and my strong hold; my God, in him will I trust. For he shall deliver thee from the snare of the hunter, and from the noisome pestilence. He shall defend thee under his wings, and thou shalt be safe under his feathers; his faithfulness and truth shall be thy shield and buckler. Thou shalt not be afraid for any terror by night, nor for the arrow that flieth by day; for the pestilence that walketh in darkness, nor for the sickness that destroyeth in the noon-day. A thousand shall fall beside thee, and ten thousand at thy right hand; but it shall not come nigh thee. Yea, with thine eyes shalt thou behold, and see the reward of the ungodly. For thou, Lord, art my hope; thou hast set thine house of defence very high. There shall no evil happen unto thee, neither shall any plague come nigh thy dwelling. For he shall give his angels charge over thee, to keep thee in all thy ways. They shall bear thee in their hands, that thou hurt not thy foot against a stone. Thou shalt go upon the lion and adder; the young lion and the dragon shalt thou tread under thy feet. Because he hath set his love upon me, therefore will I deliver him; I will set him up, because he hath known my Name. He shall call upon me, and I will hear him; yea, I am with him in trouble; I will deliver him, and bring him to honour. With long life will I satisfy him, and show him my salvation.

Glory . . . now, and ever, . . . Alleluia. (*Thrice.*)

Glory to thee, O God. (*Thrice.*)

Then the Deacon, taking the censer from the Priest, censeth before the table, reciting the Great Litany.

In peace let us pray to the Lord.

Choir. Lord, have mercy.

For the peace that is from above, and for the salvation of our souls, let us pray to the Lord. ℟

For the remission of the sins of him (*her*) who hath (*those who have*) departed this life in blessed memory, let us pray to the Lord. ℟

And if the souls of all our fathers and brethren are prayed for:

For the souls of all our fathers and brethren who, from all time, have fallen asleep in the true faith, and in hope of the Resurrection, and of life everlasting: and of the blessed wardens and benefactors of this holy Temple (*or* habitation), let us pray to the Lord. ℟

But if only a certain number are to be prayed for:

For the ever-memorable servant of God, N. (*or* servants of God, NN.);

for his (*her, their*) repose, tranquillity and blessed memory, let us pray to the Lord. ℟

[For the repose, tranquillity and blessed memory of the ever-memorable servants of God, the Orthodox Warriors who have valiantly contended: and for all who have laid down their life in battle for the Faith and the Fatherland, let us pray to the Lord. ℟] *Orthodox Warriors.*

That he will pardon him (*her, them*) every transgression, whether voluntary or involuntary: ℟

That he (*she, they*) may present himself (*herself, themselves*) blameless before the dread throne of the Lord of glory: ℟

For the sorrowing and the sick who have set their hope in the consolation of Christ: ℟

That he will release him (*her, them*) from all sickness, sorrow and sighing, and make him (*her, them*) glad where the light of God's countenance shall visit him (*her, them*). ℟

That the Lord our God will establish his (*her*) soul (*their souls*) in a place of brightness, a place of verdure, a place of rest, where all the Righteous dwell: ℟

That he (*she, they*) may be numbered with those who are in the bosom of Abraham, and Isaac, and Jacob: ℟

That he will deliver us from all tribulation, wrath and necessity: ℟

Choir. Lord, have mercy. *let us pray to the Lord.*

Succour us, save us, have mercy upon us, and keep us, O God, by thy grace.

Choir. Lord, have mercy.

Having implored for him (*her, them*) the mercies of God, the kingdom of heaven, and remission of sins, let us commend ourselves, and each other, and all our life unto Christ our God.

Choir. To thee, O Lord.

And when the Litany is finished, the Priest shall recite, secretly, while all stand with bowed heads, the following Prayer:

O God of spirits, and of all flesh, who hast trampled down Death, and overthrown the Devil, and given life unto thy world: Do thou, the same Lord, give rest to the soul of thy departed servant, N. (*servants, NN.*), in a place of brightness, a place of verdure, a place of repose, whence all sickness, sorrow and sighing have fled away. Pardon every transgression which he (*she*) hath (*they·have*) committed, whether by word, or deed, or thought. For thou art a good God, and lovest mankind; because there is no man who liveth and sinneth not; for thou only art without sin, and thy righteousness is to all eternity, and thy word is true. *Secretly.*

Exclamation.

Priest. For thou art the Resurrection, and the Life, and the Repose of thy departed servant, N. (*servants, NN.*), O Christ our God, and unto thee we ascribe glory, together with thy Father who is from everlasting, and thine all-holy, and good, and life-giving Spirit, now, and ever, and unto ages of ages. —— *Choir.* Amen.

[For thou art the Resurrection, and the Life, and the Repose of the **Orthodox** ever-to-be-commemorated Orthodox Warriors who have fallen **Warriors.** asleep, and of all those who have laid down their life in battle for the Faith and the Fatherland, O Christ our God: (*and the rest, as above*).]

Alleluia. (*Thrice.*) *In Tone VIII.*
Verses (*Stikhí*) 1: Blessed is he whom thou hast chosen and taken, O Lord. — Alleluia. (*Thrice.*)
2: The remembrance of them is from generation to generation. — Alleluia. (*Thrice.*)
3: Their souls shall dwell with the blessed. — Alleluia. (*Thrice.*)

Then the Hymn, in Tone VIII.

O Thou who, with wisdom profound, mercifully orderest all things, and givest that which is expedient unto all men, thou Only Creator: Give rest, O Lord, to the soul of thy servant, N., who hath (*souls of thy servants, NN., who have*) fallen asleep; For he (*she*) hath (*they have*) set his (*her, their*) hope on thee, our Maker, the Author of our being, and our God.

Glory to the Father, and to the Son, and to the Holy Spirit.

For he (*she*) hath set his (*her, they have set their*) hope on thee, our Maker, the Author of our being, and our God.

Now, and ever, and unto ages of ages.   Amen.

HYMN TO THE BIRTH-GIVER OF GOD.

Thee have we as a Wall and a Refuge, and a Mediatrix well-pleasing unto God whom thou hast borne, O Virgin Birth-giver of God, the salvation of the faithful.

Then shall be sung Psalm cxix., in two portions. (But in the briefer Office for Ortho-dox Warriors it is omitted.)

Blessed are those that are undefiled in the way, and walk in the law of the Lord.

Refrain. Remember, O Lord, the soul(s) of thy servant(s).

Blessed are they that keep his testimonies, and serve him with their whole heart.

Refrain. Remember, O Lord, the soul(s) of thy servant(s).   (*To verse 94*).

(*For the remainder of the Psalm see the* ORDER FOR THE BURIAL OF LAYMEN, *page* 370.)

Then the LITANY FOR THE DEPARTED *shall be said.*

Deacon. Again, yet again, in peace let us pray to the Lord.

Choir. Lord, have mercy.

Furthermore we pray for the repose of the soul of the servant(s) of God, N. (*NN.*), departed this life: and that he (*she, they*) may be pardoned all his (*her, their*) sins, both voluntary and involuntary.

Choir. Lord, have mercy.

[Furthermore we pray for the repose of the souls of the servants of God who have fallen asleep, Orthodox Warriors, and of all who Orthodox have laid down their life in battle for the Faith and the Father- Warriors. land: and that He will pardon them every sin, both voluntary and involuntary.]

Choir. Lord, have mercy.

That the Lord God will establish his (*her, their*) soul(s) where the Just repose.

Choir. Lord, have mercy.

The mercies of God, the kingdom of heaven, and the remission of his (*her, their*) sins let us entreat of Christ, our King Immortal, and our God.

Choir. Grant it, O Lord.

Deacon. Let us pray to the Lord.

Choir. Lord, have mercy.

Then the Priest saith, secretly, *the Prayer:* O God of spirits, . . . (*See page* 439.)

And the Third Priest maketh the Exclamation, as usual (see page 439). *or for Warriors:* For thou art the Resurrection, . . . (*See page* 440.)

Then the second portion of Psalm cxix.; from verse 94, page 374, to the end.

I am thine, O save me, for I have sought thy commandments.

Refrain. Give rest, O Lord, to the soul(s) of thy servant(s).

The ungodly laid wait for me, to destroy me: but I will consider thy testimonies.

Refrain. Give rest, O Lord, to the soul(s) of thy servant(s).

And the same Refrain shall be sung after every verse. (*See the* ORDER FOR THE BURIAL OF LAYMEN, *page* 378.)

O let my soul live, and it shall praise thee: and thy judgments shall help me. I have gone astray like a sheep that is lost; O seek thy servant for I do not forget thy commandments. (*Thrice.*)

Give rest, O Lord, to the soul(s) of thy servant(s).

Then shall be sung the Requiem-Hymns, in Tone V.

Refrain. Blessed art thou. O Lord: teach me thy statutes. (*To each Hymn.*)

The Choir of the Saints . . . (*See the* ORDER FOR THE BURIAL OF LAY-MEN, *page* 379). ℞

Ye who preached the Lamb of God, . . . ℞

Ye who have trod the narrow way . . . ℞

I am an image of thy glory . . . ℞

O thou who of old . . . ℞

Give rest, O Lord, to the soul(s) of thy servant(s) and establish it (*them*). Alleluia. (*Thrice.*) Glory to thee, O God. ℞

Glory to the Father, and to the Son, and to the Holy Spirit.

Devoutly do we hymn the triune Effulgence . . .

Now, and ever, and unto ages of ages. Amen.

Hail, O August One, . . . Alleluia. (*Thrice.*) Glory to thee, O God. (*Thrice.*)

Then the Deacon saith the Litany: Again, yet again, in peace . . . (*See page* 441.)

While the Third Priest saith, secretly, *the Prayer:* O God of spirits: *and the Fourth Priest maketh the Exclamation:* For thou art the Resurrection: *or for Orthodox Warriors.*

Then shall be sung, in Tone V., the Hymns. (*See the* ORDER FOR THE BURIAL OF LAYMEN, *page* 380.)

Give rest with the Just, . . . Glory . . .

And all things . . . Now, and ever, . . .

O Christ our God, who from a Virgin . . .

Then Psalm li. is read: Have mercy upon me, O God, . . . (*See page* 380.)

Then the Canon for those who have fallen asleep is sung. Its Acrostic being:

Unto those who have died in the faith I will sing the eighth song.

THE CANON. *Tone VIII.*

(*A separate Canon is used for Orthodox Warriors. See page* 449.)

Canticle I.

Theme-Song (Irmós). When Israel had passed through the water as it had been dry land, and had escaped from the malice of the Egyptians, they cried: Let us sing praises unto our deliverer and our God.

Refrain. Wonderful is God in his Saints, the God of Israel.

Hymns (Tropari). Having imitated in their deaths the death of Christ, and in their passions the precious Passion of Christ, all the Martyrs divine and blessed have received life and now pray for the salvation of our souls.

Refrain. Give rest, O Lord, to the soul(s) of thy servant(s).

Regarding not the sins in youth of thy servant(s) who hath (*have*) fallen asleep before us, and passing over his (*her, their*) iniquities, number thou him (*her, them*) among thine elect, O Christ our Saviour.

Glory to the Father, and to the Son, and to the Holy Spirit.

O all-merciful One, who didst receive glory and gladness when thou hadst acquired an existence of bliss: Grant rich reward unto thy servant(s), whom thou hast taken.

Now, and ever, and unto ages of ages. Amen.

HYMN TO THE BIRTH-GIVER OF GOD.

Thou didst conceive the Word of the Father, uniting Its essence to the flesh which is from thee, O Virgin all-undefiled, triumphing over Hell with might divine. Beseech thou the Same that he will give life unto him (*her, them*) who hath (*have*) died in the faith.

Canticle III.

Theme-Song (Irmós). O Master and Creator of the vault of heaven, and Founder of the Church, establish thou me in thy love, O Summit of desires, O Confirmation of the faithful, who alone lovest mankind.

Hymns. Having washed away the fall of our forefather of old by baptism and a new birth, and having been sprinkled with streams of your blood, ye shall reign in Christ, O Blessed Ones.

Thou who, of thine own good will, didst lay thyself dead in the grave, and didst call forth those who lay in the graves, O Saviour: Be graciously pleased to establish him (*her, them*) whom thou hast taken from us, in the mansions of thy Righteous Ones.

Glory . . .

Thou who art entreated of thy loving-kindness divine, and who, instructed by thy dual nature, art moved to mercy, O Master: Grant remission of his (*her, their*) sins unto thy servant(s), O Saviour; and give him (*her, them*) rest.

Now, and ever, . . .

Intercede, we beseech thee, O Birth-giver of God, with him who was incarnate in thy womb, and was made man: and who, especially, in that he alone loveth mankind, doth save man from the gates of death; that he will grant repose with his saints to the soul(s) of his servant(s) who hath (*who have*) fallen asleep.

Then the Theme-Song is repeated, and the Deacon saith the Litany: Again, yet again, . . . (*See page* 441.) *While the Priest saith,* secretly, *the Prayer:* O God of spirits, . . . (*see page* 439), *and the Fourth Priest maketh the Exclamation:* For thou art the Resurrection, . . . (*See page* 439.)

Then the Sitting-Hymn (Syedálen), in Tone VI.

Of a truth, all things are vanity, and life is but a shadow and a dream. For in vain doth every one who is born of earth disquiet himself, as saith the Scriptures. When we have acquired the world, then do we take up our abode in the grave, where kings and beggars lie down together. Wherefore, O Christ our God, give rest to thy servant(s) departed this life; forasmuch as thou lovest mankind.

Glory to the Father, and to the Son, and to the Holy Spirit, now, and ever, and unto ages of ages. Amen.

HYMN TO THE BIRTH-GIVER OF GOD (*Bogoróditchen*).

O all-holy Birth-giver of God, forsake me not all the days of my life, and give me not over to the mediation of mortal man. But do thou thyself succour me, and show mercy unto me.

Canticle IV.

Theme-Song. Thou art my fortress, O Lord, and thou art my strength: Thou art my God, thou art my joy. Thou didst not leave the bosom of the Father, yet hast thou visited our wretchedness. Wherefore, with the prophet Habakkuk cry I unto thee: Glory to thy might, O thou who lovest mankind.

Hymns. May thy Martyrs divine, O Lord, who with patience have endured every manner of torment, radiantly behold and in heaven receive the brightness of thy glory, as they sing unto thee, O Christ: Glory to thy might, O thou who lovest mankind.

Many are thy mansions, O Saviour, meted out in inheritance unto all men according to their merits. Wherefore, O Bountiful One, graciously vouchsafe to fill the same with those who have departed this life in thy faith, devoutly crying unto thee: Glory to thy might, O thou who lovest mankind.

Glory . . .

As a man like unto us hast thou revealed thyself, O Immortal One; and like unto all men hast thou suffered death, and hast shown us the way of life. Unto him (*her, them*) who hath (*have*) departed this life grant remission of his (*her, their*) sins: forasmuch as thou lovest mankind, and as Master supreme bestowest gifts and givest participation in the light.

Now, and ever, . . .

Thou art the boast of the faithful, O Unwedded One; thou art the Intercessor, and the Refuge of Christians, a Wall of defence and a Stronghold. Thou bearest petitions to thy Son, O All-undefiled One, and savest from adversity those who, with faith and love, acknowledge thee to be the pure Birth-giver of God. Entreat thou now the Same that unto this person who hath (*these persons who have*) departed this life in the faith, he will grant rest with the Saints.

Canticle V.

Theme-Song. Why hast thou cast me away from thy countenance, O Light which knowest no setting, and why hath strange darkness covered me, the accursed one? But turn thou me, and guide my paths in the light of thy commandments, I beseech thee.

Hymns. Mercifully grant thy glory ineffable, and thy blessedness which words cannot express, in the mansions of the Saints, where fair is the voice of those who keep high festival, unto him (*her, them*) who hath (*have*) departed hence; recompensing him (*her, them*) unto the life that knoweth no passion, O thou who alone lovest mankind.

Where the Angelic hosts, where the assembly of the Righteous rejoice, in the bosom of Abraham, grant an abode to thy servant(s), O Saviour; and graciously vouchsafe that with boldness he (*she, they*) may stand before thy throne dread and divine, O Compassionate One.

Glory . . .

As purification and righteousness and deliverance hast thou revealed thyself unto us; and by thy wounds hast thou healed our infirmities. Wherefore, O Bountiful One, forasmuch as thou art gracious, establish in the delights of Paradise him (*her*) who hath (*those who have*) departed hence.

Now, and ever, . . .

Mercifully, O Merciful One, didst thou accept the stature of mankind; and having endued flesh in a Virgin's womb, inspired by the word, and having thereby overthrown Death, thou givest life unto the faithful. Wherefore, through the intercessions of her who bare thee, grant thou rest with the Saints unto him (*her, those*) who hath (*have*) fallen asleep.

Canticle VI.

Theme-Song. Purge me, O Saviour, for mine iniquities are manifold; and lead me forth from the abyss of evil, I beseech thee: For I have cried unto thee. And hear me, O God of my salvation.

Thy Martyrs, O Christ, endured many pains, being wounded in soul by the love of thee, O Holy One, and desiring thy glory everlasting, and thy sweet communion. Wherefore, through their prayers, grant repose unto the soul(s) of him (*her, them*) who hath (*have*) fallen asleep.

Thou didst rend the belly of the enemy by death, O Saviour, and didst raise again all those who were held captive therein, bestowing life upon them. Grant the same also unto him (*her, them*) who is (*are*) gone from us, O Beneficent One.

Glory . . .

From the tears and the sighing which are in Hell deliver thy servant(s), O Saviour: For thou alone art of tender mercy, and hast wiped away all tears from the faces of all those who, with faith, do bless thee.

Now, and ever, . . .

He who is the Creator of all Nature doth beget in thy womb: he who is full, in that he is God, doth empty himself, O All-undefiled One. The Only Immortal One dieth the death for the salvation of all men, and giveth life unto those who die in the faith.

Purge me, O Saviour . . .

Then the Deacon saith the Litany: Again, yet again, . . . (*See page* 441.) *While the Priest saith*, secretly, *the Prayer:* O God of spirits, . . . (*see page* 439); *and the Fifth Priest saith*, aloud, *the Exclamation:* For thou art the Resurrection, . . . *see page* 438; *or the Exclamation for Orthodox Warriors.* (*See page* 439.)

The Collect-Hymn (*Kondák*).

With the Saints give rest, O Christ, to the soul(s), of thy servant(s), where there is neither sickness, nor sorrow, nor sighing, but life ever-lasting.

The Ikos.

Thou only art immortal, who hast created and fashioned man. For out of the earth were we mortals made, and unto the earth shall we return again, as thou didst command when thou madest me, saying unto me: For earth thou art, and unto the earth shalt thou return. Whither also all we mortals wend our way, making of our funeral dirge the song: Alleluia.

Canticle VII.

Theme-Song. The Hebrew Children in the furnace trod boldly upon the flames, and the fire was transmuted into dew as they sang: Blessed art thou, O Lord God, forevermore.

Hymns. All the desire of the Martyrs reached out unto the only Lord, in love united unto him, and singing: Blessed art thou, O Lord God, forevermore.

O thou who givest unto those who have departed this life in faith the brightness of thy kingdom divine, grant also the robe of incorruption unto those who cry aloud: Blessed art thou, O Lord God, forever-more.

Glory . . .

Fill with joy and gladness thy servant(s) whom thou hast taken from this life, O Bountiful One, who hast enabled him (*her, them*) to call upon thee, and to sing: Blessed art thou, O Lord God, forevermore.

Now, and ever, . . .

Annulling the curse of Eve, thou didst take up thine abode in a Virgin undefiled, pouring forth a fountain of blessing upon those who cry aloud: Blessed, O most holy One, is the fruit of thy womb.

Canticle VIII.

Theme-Song. The Three Children obeyed not when the instruments of music sounded in harmony, and thousands numberless of people bowed down before the image on Dura's plain; but praised and magnified the Lord unto all the ages.

Hymns. The Martyrs true, having passed through earthly feats of might and received heavenly crowns, cry aloud unto thee unceasingly: Praise ye the Lord, and magnify him unto all the ages.

When thou hadst descended into the nethermost pit, thou didst raise again, through thy life-giving palm, those who abode in the grave. Grant rest, also, by the same, we beseech thee, unto thy servant(s) who before us hath (*have*) fallen asleep in the faith, O Bountiful One.

Let us praise the Father, and the Son, and the Holy Spirit, the Lord.

Forasmuch as thou art the Fountain of Life everflowing and a stream of sweetest pleasures, grant that thy servant(s) who hath (*have*) been translated to thy presence may devoutly praise and magnify thee unto all the ages.

Now, and ever, . . .

O Mary, Virgin, Birth-giver of God, who didst bear God the Saviour. as man, in the flesh: Save thou those who, with faith, do laud thy birth-giving, and extol thee throughout all the ages.

Canticle IX.

Theme-Song. Every ear hath been amazed at the unutterable condescension of God; for of his own good will, the Most High hath condescended even unto the flesh, becoming man by a Virgin's womb. For which cause we faithful do extol the most holy Birth-giver of God.

Hymns. The Martyrs of Christ, having a stronghold impregnable and invincible, brought to naught the godless commands of their tormentors; and while yet in the flesh were visibly granted the kingdom of heaven, being illumined by the beams of the Trinity who is all-worthy of praise.

Hell the bitter was destroyed when thou didst destroy it, O Thou who lovest mankind, when thou didst die, and didst raise from the dead those who, throughout all the ages, had lain asleep therein. But do thou now, also, mercifully grant unto him (*her, them*) who is (*are*) come unto thee, in that thou art gracious, thy light which knoweth no setting, O Tenderly-loving One.

Glory . . .

Thou art all sweetness, O Saviour; thou art all desire and love, in very truth inexhaustible; thou art all goodness unspeakable. Wherefore deign thou to admit him (*her, those*) who hath (*have*) now appeared before thee to delight in thy beauty; and grant thou unto him (*her, them*) thy goodness divine.

Now, and ever, . . .

Save me, O Mother of God, who hast borne Christ my Saviour, both God and man, two in nature but not in essence, the Only-begotten of the Father and of thee, the First-born of all created beings. And forasmuch as thou art the Mother who loveth mankind, entreat thou him that he will grant unto him (*her, them*) who hath (*have*) departed this life repose with his Saints.

And after the Ninth Canticle the Priest saith:

The Birth-giver of God and Mother of the world let us magnify in song.
Choir. The spirits and souls of the righteous bless thee, O Lord.

And the Theme-Song: Every ear hath been amazed, . . . O Holy God, Holy Mighty, . . . *and the rest.* (*See page* 437.) *Exclamation. The Priest.* For thine is the kingdom, . . .

Then the Hymns, in Tone IV.

With the souls of the righteous dead, give rest, O Saviour, to the soul(s) of thy servant(s), preserving it (*them*) unto the life of blessedness which is with thee, O thou who lovest mankind.

In the place of thy rest, O Lord, where all thy Saints repose, give rest also unto the soul(s) of thy servant(s); for thou only lovest mankind.

Glory to the Father, and to the Son, and to the Holy Spirit.

Thou art the God who descended into Hell, and loosed the bonds of the captives: Do thou give rest also to the soul(s) of thy servant(s).

Now, and ever, and unto ages of ages.   Amen.

Hymn to the Birth-giver of God. O Virgin alone Pure and Undefiled, who without seed didst bring forth God, pray thou that his (*her*) soul (*their souls*) may be saved.

Then the Litany.

Have mercy upon us, O God, according to thy great mercy, we beseech thee: hearken, and have mercy.

Choir. Lord, have mercy. (*Thrice.*)

Again we pray for the repose of the soul of N. (*NN.*), the servant(s) of God, departed this life, and that he (*she, they*) may be pardoned all his (*her, their*) sins, both voluntary and involuntary. ℟

That the Lord God will establish his (*her*) soul (*their souls*) where the Just repose. ℟

The mercies of God, the kingdom of heaven, and remission of his (*her, their*) sins, let us ask of Christ, our King immortal and our God.

Choir. Grant it, O Lord.

And the Priest saith, aloud, *the Prayer:* O God of spirits, . . . (*See page* 439.)

And the Senior Priest maketh the Exclamation: For thou art the Resurrection, and the Life, . . . *see page* 439, or *exclamation for Warriors; see page* 440.

A Priest or the Deacon saith: Wisdom!

Choir. More honourable than the Cherubim, and beyond compare more glorious than the Seraphim, thou who without defilement barest God the Word, true Birth-giver of God, we magnify thee.

Senior Priest. Glory to thee, O Christ-God, our hope; glory to thee.

Choir. Glory to the Father, and to the Son, and to the Holy Spirit, now, and ever, and unto ages of ages.   Amen.

Lord, have mercy. (*Thrice.*)   Bless.

The BENEDICTION.

Priest. May he who rose again from the dead, Christ our true God, through the prayers of his all-pure Mother; of the holy, glorious and all-laudable Apostles; of our holy and God-bearing Fathers, and of all the Saints, establish in the mansions of the righteous the soul(s) of his servant(s), N. (*NN.*), who hath (*have*) been taken from us (*or the souls of his servants, the Orthodox Warriors who have fallen asleep, and of all those who have laid down their life in battle for the Faith and the Fatherland*); give him (*her, them*) rest in Abraham's bosom, and number him (*her, them*) with the Just; and have mercy upon us, forasmuch as he is good and loveth mankind.

And after the Benediction the Deacon proclaimeth:

Give rest eternal in blessed falling asleep, O Lord, to the soul(*s*) or thy servant(*s*) N. (*NN.*), departed this life (*or* of his servants, the Orthodox Warriors who have fallen asleep, and of all those who have laid down their life for the Faith and the Fatherland); and make his (*her, their*) memory to be eternal.

And the Choir singeth:

Memory Eternal! (*Thrice.*)

And when there is no Deacon, the Choir singeth:

To N. (*NN.*), the servant(*s*) of God, Memory eternal!

THE CANON FOR ORTHODOX WARRIORS SLAIN ON THE FIELD OF BATTLE FOR THE FAITH AND THE FATHERLAND.

Canticle I., Tone VIII.

Theme-Song (*Irmós*). When Israel had passed through the water as it had been dry land, and had escaped from the malice of the Egyptians, they cried: Let us sing praises unto our deliverer and our God.

Verse (*Stikh*): Give rest, O Lord, to the souls of thy servants who have fallen asleep.

Hymns. Having opened my mouth, O Saviour, give me speech to pray, O Compassionate One, for those who have wrought valiant deeds of the Faith and the Fatherland; and give rest to their souls, O Master.

Do thou who wast dead in the flesh, O Saviour, and wast laid in the grave with the dead, give rest unto the souls of thy servants in a place of verdure; forasmuch as thou art compassionate.

Glory to the Father, and to the Son, and to the Holy Spirit.

Receive thou the voice of our supplication, O Triune God, and establish thou the souls of thy servants in Abraham's bosom, O Redeemer.

Now, and ever, and unto ages of ages. Amen.

HYMN TO THE BIRTH-GIVER OF GOD (*Bogoróditchen*).

O most holy Birth-giver of God, who didst give birth after that thou hadst conceived without having known man, entreat thou thy Son that he will grant rest unto thy servants ever worthy of remembrance.

Canticle III.

Theme-Song. O Master and Creator of the vault of heaven, and Founder of the Church, establish thou me in thy love, O thou who alone lovest mankind; the Summit of desire, the Confirmation of the faithful.

Hymns. In a place of verdure, a place of repose, where the company of the Saints rejoice, give rest, O Christ, to the souls of thy servants who have valiantly wrought for the Holy Church and their Fatherland, O only Merciful One.

Where the company of the Saints abide, O Master, establish thou those who have served thee for thy Holy Church with all their hearts, and have borne thy yoke upon their shoulders: For thou alone art Lord over life and death.

Glory . . .

O heavenly Father Almighty, and Only-begotten Son, and Holy Spirit issuing forth: Regard thou not the transgressions of these dead, but establish them as first-fruits in thy Church; that they may glorify thee, together with all those who are acceptable in thy sight.

Now, and ever, . . .

Forasmuch as thou art the Holy Mother of the Most Holy God, the Lady of all, Mary the Bearer of the Lord, pray thou unto him, together with all the Saints, that he will give rest in heavenly mansions unto the souls of thy servants.

Theme-Song: O Master and Creator, . . . , *the Litany (see page 441), with the Prayer and Exclamation. (See page 439.)*

Canticle IV.

Theme-Song. I have heard the mystery of thy providence, O Lord; I have understood thy deeds, and have magnified thy Godhead.

Hymns. When thou hadst descended into the nethermost depths, O Christ, thou didst raise up again with thee all those who were dead. Give rest, also, O Saviour, to those who have been translated from among us, forasmuch as thou art bountiful.

There is none without sin, save only thee, O Master. Wherefore pardon thou the sins of those who have suffered for thy Holy Church and the Fatherland; and establish the same in Paradise.

Glory . . .

Give ear, O holy Trinity, to the voices of supplication which are offered unto thee in the Church for those who have perished in battle for the sake of thy Holy Church. And illumine, with thy divinely sovereign light, their souls which have been darkened by affection for earthly vanities.

Now, and ever, . . .

Without seed of man thou didst give birth, O Virgin most pure, unto him who, both perfect God and perfect man, doth take away our sins. Intercede thou with him, O Lady, that unto thy servants who have suffered death he will give rest.

Canticle V.

Theme-Song. Enlighten us with thy precepts, O Lord, and with thy lofty arm give us thy peace, O Merciful One.

Hymns. O Christ our God, who hast power over life and death, grant rest unto those who have been translated from among us: For thou art the Saviour, and the Rest, and the Life of all men.

Upon thee, O Saviour, did they set their hope who have suffered for thy Holy Church and the Fatherland, and now have departed from us. Be thou bountiful unto them, O Lord, forasmuch as thou art a very merciful God.

Glory . . .

Illumine thou, O thrice-holy and praised Lord, us who entreat thee that we may receive thy heavenly peace. And establish thou in the abodes of peace the souls of those who have departed from things temporal in the hope of life eternal.

Now, and ever, . . .

Entreat thou thy Son, O Lady, that he will deliver the dead from condemnation to stand at his left hand: For thou art the Mother of our Saviour and our God.

Canticle VI.

Theme-Song. I will pour out my petition unto the Lord, and unto him will I confide my grief. For my soul is filled with sorrow, and my life hath drawn nigh unto Hell; and like unto Jonah will I pray: Lead thou me forth from corruption, O God.

Hymns. Thou didst overthrow Hell, O Lord; thou didst raise up those who lay dead from all the ages. Those who have died for thy Holy Church establish thou in Abraham's bosom, O Lord, remitting all their transgressions; forasmuch as thou art of tender compassion.

If we have sinned, O God, against the commandment which thou gavest us, and have become subject unto death, nevertheless do thou, the God who didst descend into the grave, and hast raised up thence the souls of all the ages, revive us not unto torment, but unto rest. O Lord, those who have died for thy Holy Church and the Fatherland cry unto thee through us, O thou who art full of mercy.

Glory . . .

We entreat thee, O Father, who art from everlasting, and O Son and O Holy Spirit, reject thou not into the abyss of Hell the souls of those who were infected by the plague of the soul-attainting world, and now are come unto thee, the Creator, O God our Saviour.

Now, and ever, . . .

From heaven did Christ our God descend upon thee, O most Pure One, like the dew upon the fleece, slaking the thirst of all the world, and drying up every godless water-spring, and flooding the whole earth with his wisdom, O Ever-virgin One. Entreat thou him that unto the souls of thy servants who have suffered death he will give rest.

Theme-Song: I will pour out my petition . . . , *the Litany (see page* 441), *with the Prayer and Exclamation. (See page* 439.)

The Collect-Hymn (Kondák), in Tone VIII.

With the Saints give rest, O Christ, to the soul(s) of thy servant(s), where there is neither sickness, nor sorrow, nor sighing, but life everlasting.

The Ikos.

Thou only art immortal, who hast created and fashioned man. For out of the earth were we mortals made, and unto the earth shall we return again, as thou didst command when thou madest us, saying unto me: For earth thou art, and unto earth shalt thou return. Whither, also, all we mortals wend our way, making of our funeral dirge the song: Alleluia.

Canticle VII.

Theme-Song. The Holy Children, sprung from the Jews of yore, in Babylon, through the faith of the Trinity did trample under foot the fiery furnace, singing: O God of our fathers, blessed art thou.

Hymns. O Master, Christ our God, when thou shalt come to judge the world, spare thou the souls of thy servants who have suffered for thy Holy Church and the Fatherland, and whom thou hast taken from us, crying: O God of our fathers, blessed art thou.

In the pastures of Paradise, where abide the souls of the Righteous who have served thee, number thou also, with them, O Christ, the souls of thy servants who sing unto thee: O God of our fathers, blessed art thou.

Glory . . .

O thou who didst save the three Hebrew Children from the fire, and in Three Persons art exalted, deliver from fire eternal the dead who in faith do laud thee: O God of our fathers, blessed art thou.

Now, and ever, . . .

Isaiah called thee the Sceptre, O most Pure One; and Daniel, the Mount Uncloven; and Ezekiel, the Door whence issued forth Christ. And we also, naming thee the true Mother of God, do magnify thee.

Canticle VIII.

Theme-Song. With a furnace seven times heated did the Chaldæan tormentor fiercely scorn the God-fearing Ones; but when he beheld the same saved by a better power, unto their Maker and Deliverer he cried: Ye Children, bless; ye Priests, sing praises; ye People, magnify forevermore.

Hymns. They who have finished their course, and have fled for refuge unto thee, O Lord, and have suffered for thy Holy Church, now cry aloud unto thee: Pardon our iniquities, O Christ our God, and condemn not, when thou shalt come to judge all men, us who with faith have cried unto thee: O all ye works of the Lord, praise ye the Lord and magnify him forevermore.

Establish thou, O Lord, those who have borne upon their shoulders, though it be not always, thy yoke and thy burden which are light. Yea, in the place of thy Saints, establish thou the souls of those who sing praises unto thee, O Christ our God: Ye Children, bless; ye Priests, sing praises; ye People, magnify forevermore.

Let us bless the Father, and the Son, and the Holy Spirit, the Lord.

O holy Trinity, who art from everlasting, God the Father, the Son, and the Holy Spirit, in the company of the blessed number thou the souls of thy servants who have suffered; and deliver them from fire eternal, that they may laud thee, and sing praises unto thee forever. Ye Children, bless; ye Priests, sing praises; ye People, magnify forevermore.

Now, and ever, . . .

The company of the prophets foretold thee, O Virgin: for beholding thee with vision perspicacious, one called thee the Sceptre; another, the Door of the East; another, the Mount Uncloven of Man. And we, also, confess thee to be the true Mother of the Lord, who hast borne the God of all men. Beseech thou him that unto those who have suffered in all the ages he will give rest.

Canticle IX.

Theme-Song. The heavens marvelled thereat, and the ends of the earth were amazed, when God manifested to men himself incarnate; and thy womb was more spacious than the heavens. For which cause the chieftains of Angels and of men do magnify thee, O Birth-giver of God.

Hymns. O Jesus, God and Saviour, thou didst take upon thee Adam's sin, and didst taste of death, that thou mightest deliver men therefrom, O Compassionate One. For which cause we beseech thee, O Merciful One: In the courts of thy Saints give rest unto those who have suffered, in that thou art gracious: For thou only art good, and lovest mankind.

There is none among men who sinneth not, O Compassionate One, save only thee, O Jesus Christ, who takest away the sins of the whole world. Wherefore, after that thou hast purged thy servants from their iniquities, establish thou them in the courts of thy Saints: For thou art the Life, and the Rest, and the Light, and the Joy of all who are well-pleasing in thy sight.

Glory . . .

All mortal nature marvelled thereat, that thou, the Only-begotten Son of the Father who is from everlasting, from a Virgin, through the operation of the Holy Spirit didst take flesh, and as man didst suffer, and didst give life unto those who were dead. Wherefore, we fervently entreat thee, forasmuch as thou art good: In the land of the living establish thou those who have suffered for thy Holy Church and the Fatherland.

Now, and ever, . . .

We call thee the Bride of the Father Invisible, O most Pure One, and Mother of the Son who by the Holy Spirit was incarnate of thee: And we offer unto thee our supplications on behalf of those who have suffered for the Church of thy Son, and for their Fatherland. For in thee we, who are of the earth, have a Mediatrix. and singing with love thy praises, we magnify thee.

THE OFFICE FOR RECEIVING INTO THE ORTHO-DOX FAITH SUCH PERSONS AS HAVE NOT PRE-VIOUSLY BEEN ORTHODOX,

BUT HAVE BEEN REARED FROM INFANCY OUTSIDE THE ORTHODOX CHURCH, YET HAVE RECEIVED VALID BAPTISM, IN THE NAME OF THE FATHER, AND OF THE SON, AND OF THE HOLY SPIRIT *

The power of granting absolution to such persons, and of uniting them to the Church, properly devolveth on a Bishop. Nevertheless, that the converts to Orthodoxy may not be tempted to return to their heresy by reason of delay, it is wiser and more expedient that the Bishop should delegate his power, and grant his blessing therewith, to a Priest well versed in divine lore, and who is competent to instruct such a person in the articles of the Orthodox faith, and to correct his erroneous opinions.

Therefore, first of all, the penitent shall be examined with due caution (either by the Bishop or by the person to whom he hath delegated his authority) as to the particulars of his errors.

Then must he be convinced of them. •

Thereafter, he shall be instructed in the doctrine of the Orthodox faith, and confirmed therein.

And when the appointed examination and instruction have been completed, with all precaution shall the Bishop require from the penitent the confession of all his sins, which he can recall, from his youth up.

And the Bishop shall not immediately thereafter grant him absolution; but after the confession and exhortation, he shall go with him into the Church, and shall place him before the church doors, in the church porch.

And the Bishop, vested in his priestly stole and pall (omofór) and mitre, and having in his left hand his pastoral staff, shall take his seat upon his throne (but if a Priest holding power to this end from the Bishop officiate, he shall be vested in his priestly stole and chasuble, and shall stand at the door of the Church).

And if the convert cometh to the Orthodox Faith from the Roman-Latin Confession (or from a Protestant Confession), the Bishop shall question him, and shall say:

Wilt thou renounce the errors and false doctrines of the Roman-Latin (*or* Armenian, *or* Lutheran, *or* Reformed) Confession?

And he shall reply: I will.

Then the Bishop demandeth of him, from whatever confession he may come:

Dost thou desire to enter into and abide in the communion of the Orthodox-Catholic Faith?

Answer. I do.

Then the Bishop, rising, signeth him with his right hand, in the form of a cross saying:

In the Name of the Father, and of the Son, and of the Holy Spirit. Amen.

---

* The Office for the Reception of Jews, Saracens and Heathens will be found on page 467.

And laying his hand upon the bowed head of the convert, he shall recite the following Prayer:

The Deacon saith: Let us pray to the Lord.

The Choir. Lord, have mercy.

In thy Name, O Lord God of truth, and in the Name of thine Only-begotten Son, and of thy Holy Spirit, look upon thy servant, N., whom thou hast graciously enabled to have recourse unto thy Holy Orthodox Church, and to take refuge under the shadow of her wings. Remove far from him (*her*) his (*her*) former errors, and fill him (*her*) with the true faith, and hope, and love which are in thee. Enable him (*her*) to walk in all thy commandments, and to fulfil those things which are well-pleasing unto thee; for if a man do these things, he shall also find life in them. Inscribe him (*her*) in thy Book of Life, and unite him (*her*) to the flock of thine inheritance: and may thy holy Name be glorified in him (*her*), together with that of thy beloved Son, our Lord Jesus Christ, and of thy Life-giving Spirit. Let thine eyes ever look upon him (*her*) with mercy, and let thine ears alway receive the voice of his (*her*) supplication. Make him (*her*) to rejoice in the work of his (*her*) hands, and in all his (*her*) generation, that he (*she*) may confess thee, worshipping thee and glorifying thy great and exalted Name, and magnify thee alway, all the days of his (*her*) life.

·   *Exclamation.* For all the Powers of heaven sing praises unto thee, and thine is the glory, of the Father, and of the Son, and of the Holy Spirit, now, and ever, and unto ages of ages. Amen.

After the Prayer, the Bishop (*or Priest*) *shall say to the convert:*

Wherefore renounce now, with all thy heart, thine errors, and false doctrines, and mistakes of judgment, and confess the Orthodox-Catholic Faith.

(*or, without specific renunciation:* Hast thou renounced: *page* 457.)

And the Bishop questioneth the convert from the Roman-Latin Confession.

Dost thou renounce the false doctrine that, for the expression of the dogma touching the Procession of the Holy Spirit, the declaration of our Saviour Christ himself: "who proceedeth from the Father": doth not suffice; and that the addition, of man's invention: "and from the Son": is required?

Answer. I do.

Dost thou renounce the erroneous belief that it doth not suffice to confess our Lord Jesus Christ as the head of the Universal Church; and that a man, to wit, the Bishop of Rome, can be the head of Christ's Body, that is to say, of the whole Church?

Answer. I do.

Bishop. Dost thou renounce the erroneous belief that the holy Apostles did not receive from our Lord equal spiritual power, but that the holy Apostle Peter was their Prince: And that the Bishop of Rome alone is his·successor: And that the Bishops of Jerusalem,

Roman-Latin.

Alexandria, Antioch and others are not, equally with the Bishop of Rome, successors of the Apostles?

Answer. I do.

Bishop. Dost thou renounce the erroneous belief of those who think that the Pope of Rome is superior to the Œcumenical Councils, and infallible in faith, notwithstanding the fact that several of the Popes have been heretics, and condemned as such by the Councils?

Answer. I do.

Bishop. Dost thou renounce all the other doctrines of the Western Confession, both old and new, which are contrary to the Word of God, and to the true tradition of the Church, and to the decrees of the seven Œcumenical Councils?

Answer. I do.

The convert from the Armenian Confession is questioned as follows by the Bishop:

Dost thou renounce the erroneous belief that in our Lord Jesus Christ there are not two natures, Divine and human, but one only; the human nature being swallowed up by the Divine?

Answer. I do.

The Bishop questioneth the convert from the Lutheran Confession thus:

Dost thou renounce the false doctrine that, for the expression of the dogma touching the Procession of the Holy Ghost the declaration of our Saviour Christ himself: "who proceedeth from the Father": doth not suffice; and that the addition, of man's invention: "and from the Son": is required?

Answer. I do.

Bishop. Dost thou renounce the erroneous belief that in the Sacrament of the Holy Eucharist the bread is not transmuted into the Body of Christ, and doth not become the Body of Christ; and that the wine is not transmuted into the Blood of Christ, and doth not become the Blood of Christ; but that the presence of Christ's Body only for a short time doth touch the bread, which remaineth simple bread?

Answer. I do.

Bishop. Dost thou renounce the erroneous belief of the teachers who do not accept as Sacraments Chrismation, Marriage, Anointing with Oil, and the Priesthood itself, which administereth the other Sacraments, and presume to administer Baptism and the Eucharist, never having received, through the laying-on of hands by a Bishop, that Ordination which hath been transmitted from one to another, even from the holy Apostles?

Answer. I do.

Bishop. Dost thou renounce the erroneous belief of the teachers who receive not the traditions of the Holy Church, reverence not the Saints, and deprive the dead of spiritual aid and the living of spiritual consolation, in that they reject prayers for the dead?

Answer. I do.

The Bishop questioneth the convert from the Reformed Confession after this wise:

Dost thou renounce the false doctrine that, for the expression of the dogma touching the Procession of the Holy Spirit, the declaration of our Saviour Christ himself: "who proceedeth from the Father": doth not suffice; and that the addition, of man's invention: "and from the Son": is required?

Answer. I do.

Bishop. Dost thou renounce the false doctrine, that the predestination of men to their salvation, or their rejection, is not in accordance with the Divine foreknowledge of the faith and good works of the former, or of the unbelief and evil deeds of the latter; but in accordance with some arbitrary destiny, by reason of which faith and virtue are robbed of their merit, and God is held accountable for the perdition of sinners?

Answer. I do.

Bishop. Dost thou renounce the erroneous belief that in the Sacrament of the Holy Eucharist the bread and wine are not transmuted into the Body and Blood of Christ, and are merely emblems of the Body and Blood of Christ?

Answer. I do.

Bishop. Dost thou renounce the erroneous belief of the Reformed teachers, who reject five Sacraments: Chrismation, Confession, Marriage, Anointing with Oil, and the Priesthood itself, which administereth the other Sacraments, and presume to administer Baptism and the Eucharist, never having received, through the laying-on of hands by a Bishop, that Ordination which hath been transmitted from one to another, even from the holy Apostles?

Answer. I do.

Bishop. Dost thou renounce the erroneous belief of the Reformed teachers who receive not the traditions of the Holy Church, reverence not the Saints, and deprive the dead of spiritual aid, and the living of consolation, in that they reject prayers for the dead?

Answer. I do.

And after these special questions, appointed for the converts from different Confessions, the Bishop shall proceed with the catechizing which is common to all, and shall ask:

Bishop. Hast thou renounced all ancient and modern heresies and false doctrines which are contrary to the teachings of the Holy Orthodox-Catholic Eastern Church?

Answer. I have.

Bishop. Dost thou desire to be united unto the Holy Orthodox-Catholic Eastern Church?

Answer. I desire it with all my heart.

Bishop. Dost thou believe in one God, who is adored in the holy Trinity, the Father, the Son, and the Holy Spirit: and dost thou worship him as thy King and thy God?

Answer. I believe in one God who is glorified and adored in the Trinity, the Father, the Son, and the Holy Spirit; and I worship him as my King and my God.

Then he maketh one lowly reverence, kneeling and bowing his head to the earth, and reciteth the Creed.

I believe in one God the Father Almighty, Maker of heaven and earth, And of all things visible and invisible:

And in one Lord Jesus Christ, the only-begotten Son of God, Begotten of his Father before all worlds; Light of Light, Very God of very God, Begotten, not made; Being of one Essence with the Father; By whom all things were made; Who, for us men, and for our salvation, came down from heaven, And was incarnate by the Holy Ghost of the Virgin Mary, And was made man. And was crucified also for us under Pontius Pilate, and suffered and was buried. And the third day he rose again, according to the Scriptures. And ascended into heaven, And sitteth on the right hand of the Father. And he shall come again with glory to judge both the quick and the dead; Whose kingdom shall have no end.

And in the Holy Ghost, the Lord and Giver of Life, Who proceedeth from the Father, Who with the Father and the Son together is worshipped and glorified, Who spake by the Prophets. In one Holy Catholic and Apostolic Church. I acknowledge one Baptism for the remission of sins. And I look for the Resurrection of the dead, And the Life of the world to come. Amen.

Bishop. Blessed is God, who enlighteneth every man that cometh into the world.

And again the Bishop saith:

Dost thou accept the Apostolical and Ecclesiastical Canons framed and established at the Seven Holy Universal and Provincial Councils, and the other traditions and ordinances of the Orthodox Church?

Answer. I do.

Bishop. Dost thou acknowledge that the Holy Scriptures must be accepted and interpreted in accordance with the belief which hath been handed down by the Holy

Or the Bishop (or Priest) may, at his discretion, use the Shorter Office, as followeth:

Tell us of the other dogmas of our Orthodox Church, its traditions and ordinances; how thou holdest concerning them?

And he replieth:

I accept and confess the Apostolic and Ecclesiastical Canons, established at the Seven Holy Œcumenical and Provincial Councils, and the other traditions of the

Fathers, and which the Holy Orthodox Church, our Mother, hath always held and still doth hold?

Answer. I do.

Bishop. Dost thou believe and confess that there are seven Sacraments of the New Testament, to wit: Baptism, Chrismation, the Eucharist, Confession, the Priesthood, Marriage, and Anointing with Oil, instituted by the Lord Christ and his Church, to the end that, through their operation and reception, we may obtain blessings from on high?

Answer. I believe and confess it.

Bishop. Dost thou believe and confess that in the Divine Liturgy, under the mystical forms of the holy bread and wine, the faithful partake of the Body and Blood of our Lord Jesus Christ, unto the remission of sins, and unto life eternal?

Answer. I believe and confess it.

Bishop. Dost thou believe and confess that it is proper to reverence and invoke the Saints who reign on high with Christ, according to the interpretation of the Holy Orthodox Church; and that their prayers and intercessions before God avail with the beneficent God unto our salvation: and that it is well-pleasing in the sight of God that we should do homage to their relics, glorified through incorruption, as precious memorials of their virtue?

Answer. I believe and confess it.

Bishop. Dost thou confess that the images of our Saviour Christ; and of the Ever-virgin Mother of God, and of the other Saints are worthy of being possessed and

Holy Orthodox-Catholic Apostolic Church of the East, its rules and ordinances; and I likewise will accept and understand Holy Scripture in accordance with the interpretation which the Holy Orthodox-Catholic Church of the East, our Mother, hath held, and doth hold.

I believe and confess that there are Seven Sacraments of the New Testament, to wit: Baptism, Chrismation, the Eucharist, Confession, the Priesthood, Marriage, and Anointing with Oil, instituted by the Lord Christ and his Church, to the end that, through their operation and reception, we may receive blessings from on high.

I believe and confess that, in the Divine Liturgy, under the mystical forms of bread and wine, the faithful partake of the ·true Body and Blood of our Lord Jesus Christ, unto the remission of their sins, and unto life eternal.

I believe and confess that it is proper to reverence and invoke the Saints who reign on high with Christ, according to the interpretation of the Holy Orthodox-Catholic Church of the East; and that their prayers and intercessions avail with the beneficent God unto our salvation: Likewise that it is well-pleasing in the sight of God that we should do homage to their relics, glorified through incorruption, as the precious memorials of their virtues.

I acknowledge that the images of our Saviour Christ, and of the Ever-virgin Mother of God, and of other Saints are worthy to be possessed and honoured; not unto idolatry, but that, through con-

honoured; not unto idolatry, but that, through contemplation thereof, we may be incited unto piety, and unto emulation of the deeds of the holy persons represented by these images?

Answer. I do.

Bishop. Dost thou confess that the prayers of the faithful which are offered up to God, and more especially when accompanied by the oblation of the unbloody sacrifice, for the salvation of those who have departed this life in the faith, are favourably received, through the mercy of God?

Answer. I do.

Bishop. Dost thou believe and confess that power hath been given by our Saviour Christ unto the Orthodox-Catholic Church to bind and to loose: and that whatsoever, by virtue of that power, is bound or loosed on earth will be bound or loosed in heaven?

Answer. I believe and confess it.

Bishop. Dost thou believe and confess that the Foundation, Head, and Great High Priest and Chief Shepherd of the Holy Orthodox-Catholic Church is our Lord Jesus Christ; and that Bishops, Pastors and Teachers are appointed by him to rule the Church; and that the Guide and Pilot of this Church is the Holy Spirit?

Answer. I believe and confess that this Church is the Bride of Christ, and that therein is true

templation thereof, we may be incited unto piety, and unto emulation of the deeds of the holy persons represented by those images.

I confess that the prayers of the faithful, which are offered up to God for the salvation of those who have departed this life in the faith, are favourably received, through the mercy of God.

I believe and confess that power hath been given by our Saviour Christ unto the Holy Orthodox-Catholic Church, to bind and to loose: and that whatsoever, by virtue of that power, is bound or loosed on earth will be bound or loosed in heaven.

I believe and confess that the Foundation, Head, and Great High Priest and Chief Shepherd of the Holy Orthodox-Catholic Church is our Lord Jesus Christ: and that Bishops, Pastors and Teachers are appointed by him to rule the Church: and that the Guide and Pilot of this Church is the Holy Spirit.

I confess that this Church is the Bride of Christ, and that therein is true salvation.

I promise true obedience, unto my life's end, to the Most Holy Synod (*if it be in a Diocese, then the Bishop of that Diocese is named*), as the true Pastor of the Orthodox Church, and to the Priests appointed by them.

---

salvation, which was in the Ark of Noah at the Flood.

Bishop. Dost thou promise true obedience, unto thy life's end, in guidance which is salutary unto the soul, to the Most Holy Synod; to the Most Holy Patriarch, the Equal-of-the-Apostles (*or* to the Ecclesiastical Authorities of the Autocephalous Provincial Church); and to the

Bishop of this Diocese, as the true Pastors appointed by the Holy Spirit; and to the Priests ordained by them?

Answer. I promise it, with heart unfeigned.

Then the Bishop giveth him the end of his pall (omofór) (if a Priest officiate, he giveth him the end of his priestly stole (epitrakhíl)) in his right hand, saying:

Enter thou into the Orthodox Church; and cast away all the errors and false doctrines wherein thou hast dwelt: and honour the Lord God, the Father Almighty, and his Only-begotten Son Jesus Christ, and the Holy Spirit, one true and living God, the holy Trinity, one in Essence and indivisible.

And having thus spoken, he leadeth the convert into the Church, holding the end of the pall (or of the priestly stole), and placeth him in front of the tribune, where, upon a table, is laid the book of the Holy Gospels: and when he hath taken his place, the convert immediately looseth the end of the pall from his hand. And as they enter the Church, the Reader shall read:

PSALM LXVII.

God be merciful unto us, and bless us, and show us the light of his countenance, and be merciful unto us; that thy way may be known upon earth, thy saving health among all nations. Let the people praise thee, O God; yea, let all the people praise thee. O let the nations rejoice and be glad; for thou shalt judge the folk righteously, and govern the nations upon earth. Let the people praise thee, O God; yea, let all the people praise thee. Then shall the earth bring forth her increase; and God, even our own God, shall give us his blessing. God shall bless us; and all the ends of the world shall fear him.

And when the Psalm is finished, the Bishop commandeth the convert to kneel down before the Holy Gospels.

And when he hath done this, the Bishop reciteth the following Verses:

Send thy Holy Spirit, and they shall be created; and renew the face of the earth.

Turn again, O Lord, how long? And be entreated for thy servant.

The crooked places shall be made straight, and the rough ways plain.

O Lord my God, save thy servant, who putteth his trust in thee.

Be thou unto him, O Lord, a pillar of strength against the face of the enemy.

Let the enemy in nowise prevail against him, and let not the son of iniquity go about to offend him.

Hear my prayer, O Lord, and let the voice of my cry come unto thee.

Then immediately the Deacon shall say:

Let us pray to the Lord. —— *Choir.* Lord, have mercy.

And the Bishop, with all devoutness, shall recite the following Prayer:

O Lord God Almighty, who alone art holy, and restest in the Saints; who, because of thy great and incalculable love toward mankind, dost alway offer unto them that have sinned divers manners of repentance, and dost show unto them that have wandered from the truth the right path unto knowledge of thee, the only true God, who art glorified and adored in the Trinity, that not one of them should perish, but that all may be saved, and come unto the knowledge of the truth: We thank thee, we glorify thee, and we magnify thee, for that thou hast now shed down into the heart of this, thy reason-endowed creature, N., the light which is unto the knowledge of thy truth; and hast graciously enabled him (*her*) to have recourse unto thy Holy Apostolic Orthodox-Catholic Church. Illumine his (*her*) heart, O Lord, we humbly beseech thee, with the perfect light of the grace of thy Holy Spirit unto the enlightening of his (*her*) mind in the truth of thy Holy Gospel. Grant that he (*she*) may unfeignedly, irrevocably and without hypocrisy unite himself (*herself*) unto thy Holy Catholic Church, and truly accept and confess the Orthodox-Catholic faith. Number him (*her*) with thy chosen flock, and unite him (*her*) to the body of thy Holy Church. Make him (*her*) a vessel of honour, and the temple of thy Holy Spirit; that, being ever nourished and guided by the Same, he (*she*) may keep thy saving commandments; and that doing thy gracious, acceptable and perfect will, he (*she*) may be counted worthy to receive thy heavenly good things, together with all those who are well-pleasing in thy sight. For thou art the God of mercy and compassion and love toward mankind, and willest that all men should be saved; and unto thee do we ascribe glory, to the Father, and to the Son, and to the Holy Spirit, now, and ever, and unto ages of ages. ——*Choir*. Amen.

And after the Prayer, the Bishop commandeth him to stand, saying:

Rise, and stand aright: stand with fear.

And he, rising, saith:

This true faith of the Holy Orthodox-Catholic Church, which I now voluntarily confess and unfeignedly hold, I will firmly maintain and confess whole and in its fulness and integrity, until my last breath, God being my helper; and will teach it and proclaim it, so far as in me lieth; and will strive to fulfil its obligations cheerfully and with joy, preserving my heart in purity and virtue. And in confirmation of this, my true and sincere profession of faith, I now kiss the word and cross of my Saviour. Amen.

Then the Bishop giveth him the Holy Gospels and the cross to kiss. And after he hath kissed them, he saith:

Blessed is God, who willeth that all men should be saved, and should come unto the knowledge of the truth: Blessed is he forevermore.

Choir. Amen.

Then he saith to the convert:

Bow thy knees before the Lord God, whom thou hast confessed, and receive remission of thy sins.

And the convert kneeleth down and boweth his head, having his eyes cast down.   Then the Bishop (or he who hath received this power from him), pronounceth the absolution thus:

(The form of absolving such a convert from Excommunication, and from his sins, and of joining him unto the Holy Catholic Church.)

Our Lord and God Jesus Christ committed unto his Apostles the keys of the kingdom of heaven, and bestowed upon them full power through his grace, both to bind and to loose a man from his sins upon earth: May the same, through his unspeakable mercy, pardon and absolve thee.   And I, by his almighty power, given unto me, an unworthy Bishop (*or* Priest), through his holy Apostles and their successors, do pardon and absolve thee, my child (N.), from all thy sins: and do unite thee unto the fellowship of the faithful, and unto the body of Christ's Church: and do communicate thee with the Divine Sacraments of the Church: In the Name of the Father, and of the Son, and of the Holy Spirit.   Amen.

Then the Bishop saith to him:

Rise, brother (*sister*), and as a faithful servant of Jesus Christ pray thou unto him with us, that he will vouchsafe unto thee, through anointment with the holy Chrism, to receive the grace of the Holy Spirit.

And rising, the convert standeth with all emotion.

THE OFFICE OF ANOINTMENT WITH THE HOLY CHRISM INTO THE ORTHODOX FAITH OF THOSE WHO HAVE BEEN CONVERTED AND HAVE UNITED THEMSELVES WITH THE HOLY ORTHODOX-CATHOLIC CHURCH OF THE EAST

When the foregoing Office hath been completed, one of the Priests, or a Proto-Deacon (if the Bishop himself celebrate these Offices), taking the vessel with the holy Chrism, and a sponge, and a wand and, in a small vessel, warm water for wetting the sponge, that the places anointed with the holy Chrism may be wiped off, setteth them on the table which hath been prepared, upon which, also, the book of the Holy Gospels shall be laid, and the Life-giving Cross; and on which, also, shall be placed two lighted tapers, in candlesticks.
And when these things have been made ready, the Bishop (or the Priest) maketh three reverences toward the east, as do all those who are present.

The Deacon saith:

Bless, Master.

Priest. Blessed is the kingdom of the Father, and of the Son, and of the Holy Spirit. —— *Choir.*   Amen.

Then shall be sung, in Tone VI.

O heavenly King, the Comforter, Spirit of Truth, who art in all places and fillest all things; Treasury of good things and Giver of life: Come, and take up thine abode in us, and cleanse us from every stain; and save our souls, O Good One.

And when the singing is finished, the Deacon straightway saith the Litany of Holy Chrismation.

In peace let us pray to the Lord. —— *Choir.* Lord, have mercy.

For the peace that is from above, and for the salvation of our souls: ℟

For the peace of the whole world; for the welfare of God's holy Churches, and for the union of all: ℟

For our Most Holy Synod (*or* Patriarch); for our Bishop (*or* Archbishop, *or* Metropolitan), N.; for the honourable Presbytery, the Diaconate in Christ; for all the clergy and the laity: ℟

Here follow petitions for the Ruler of the Land and for all the Authorities, according to the elements and nationalities of which the Parish is constituted.

Furthermore we pray, that through anointment with the all-holy, beneficent and all-perfect Chrism, divine power may be vouchsafed unto the servant of God, N., who is now united unto the Holy Orthodox-Catholic Church; unto the overcoming and the treading down of all adverse wiles of the Devil, and of the assaults which come through the flesh and the world. ℟

That he (*she*) may be a valiant and victorious soldier of Christ our God, through the power, and effectual operation, and grace, and descent of the Holy Spirit: ℟

That he (*she*) may remain steadfast, and strong, and immovable in the Orthodox Faith, and in love and hope, through anointment with the most holy Chrism, all the days of his (*her*) life: ℟

That grace may be granted unto him (*her*), through anointment with the most holy Chrism, to the end that with boldness, without fear, and unashamed, he (*she*) may confess the Name of Christ our God before all men, and ever be ready, for his sake, lovingly to suffer and to die: ℟

That he (*she*) may increase in all virtues, and prosper in the commandments of Christ our God, through anointment with the all-holy Chrism: ℟

That with holy fear he (*she*) may preserve his (*her*) soul in purity and truth, through anointment with the all-holy Chrism: ℟

That he (*she*) may ripen unto the perfect man, unto the measure of the stature of the fulness of Christ, by the power, and effectual operation, and grace, and indwelling of the Holy Spirit: ℟

That he (*she*) and we, with him (*her*), may be delivered from all tribulation, wrath, and necessity: and that we may all attain unto the unity of the faith, and unto the knowledge of the Son of God: ℟

Calling to remembrance our most holy, all-undefiled, most blessed and glorious Lady, the Birth-giver of God and ever-virgin Mary, with all the Saints, let us commend ourselves, and each other, and all our life unto Christ our God.

let us pray to the Lord. *Choir.* Lord, have mercy.

Choir. To thee, O Lord.

Exclamation.

Priest. For unto thee are due all glory, honour and worship, to the Father, and to the Son, and to the Holy Spirit, now, and ever, and unto ages of ages. ———— *Choir.* Amen.

Deacon. Let us pray to the Lord. ———— *Choir.* Lord, have mercy.

Then the Priest reciteth this Prayer, aloud, with all attention:

Blessed art thou, O Lord God Almighty, Source of all good things, Sun of Righteousness, who sheddest forth upon them that were in darkness the light of salvation, through the manifestation of thine Only-begotten Son and our God; and who hast given unto us, unworthy though we be, blessed purification through hallowed water, and divine sanctification through life-giving Chrismation; who now, also, art graciously pleased to regenerate this thy servant, N., that hath newly received Illumination by water and the Holy Spirit, to know thy truth, and in repentance to have recourse unto thy mercy; and unite himself (*herself*) to thine elect flock and grantest unto him (*her*) remission of sins, through me, thine unworthy servant; Do thou, the same Master of all men, compassionate King of kings, grant also unto him (*her*) the seal of the gift of thy holy, almighty and adorable Spirit, and participation in the holy Body and precious Blood of thy Jesus Christ. Keep him (*her*) in thy sanctification; confirm him (*her*) in the Orthodox faith; deliver him (*her*) from the Evil One, and from all machinations of the same. And preserve his (*her*) soul in purity and uprightness, through the saving fear of thee; that he (*she*) may please thee in every deed and word, and may be a child and heir of thy heavenly kingdom.

For thou art our God, the God whose property it is to show mercy and to save; and unto thee do we ascribe glory, to the Father, and to the Son, and to the Holy Spirit, now, and ever, and unto ages of ages.

Choir. Amen.

Deacon. Let us pray to the Lord. ———— *Choir.* Lord, have mercy.

And after this Prayer, the Priest straightway anointeth the Convert with the holy Chrism, making the sign of the cross upon his brow and eyes, and nostrils and lips, and on both ears, and breast, and hands and feet, saying:

The seal of the gift of the Holy Spirit. Amen.

And when this hath been done, he saith the following Prayer:

O Lord our God, who hast graciously vouchsafed to show this thy servant, N., perfect, through the true faith which is in thee, and through the seal of the gift of the Holy Spirit, in thy holy and most heavenly anointing: Do thou, O Lord of all, maintain in him (*her*) the true faith; train him (*her*) in righteousness and verity; and adorn him (*her*) with all thy gifts.

For thou art our God, and unto thee do we ascribe glory, to the Father, and to the Son, and to the Holy Spirit, now, and ever, and unto ages of ages.

Choir. Amen.

Then, taking the sponge, and dipping it in the warm water, he wipeth the places which have been anointed with the holy Chrism, saying:

Thou art justified. Thou art illumined. Thou art sanctified; in the Name of our Lord Jesus Christ, and by the Spirit of our God. Thou hast received anointment with the holy Chrism, in the Name of the Father, and of the Son, and of the Holy Spirit, now, and ever, and unto ages of ages.

Choir. Amen.

Priest. Peace be with you all.

Choir. And with thy spirit.

Deacon. Bow your heads unto the Lord.

Choir. To thee, O Lord.

And all bow their heads, and the Priest reciteth, secretly, the following Prayer:

He (*she*) who hath put on thee, O Christ and our God, now boweth his (*her*) head with us unto thee. Keep him (*her*) always a warrior invincible in every attack of those who assail him (*her*) and us: and make us all victors even unto the end, through thy crown incorruptible.

Exclamation.

For thy property it is to show mercy and to save ; and unto thee do we ascribe glory, together with thy Father who is from everlasting, and thine all-holy, and good, and life-giving Spirit, now, and ever, and unto ages of ages.

Choir. Amen.

Then the Litany.

Have mercy upon us, O God, according to thy great mercy, we beseech thee: hearken, and have mercy.

Choir. Lord, have mercy. (*Thrice.*)

Furthermore we pray for our most God-fearing Ruler, N.; and for all the Authorities; and for all their Council and Army and Navy: ℞

Furthermore we pray for the Most Holy Synod: ℞

Furthermore we pray for mercy, life, peace, health, salvation and remission of sins of the servant of God, N., the sponsor: ℞

Furthermore we pray for the newly illumined servant of God, N.: That he (*she*) may be preserved in the faith of a pure confession, in all godliness, and in the fulfilling of the commandments of Christ all the days of his (*her*) life: ℞

let us pray to the Lord. *Choir.* Lord, have mercy. (*Thrice.*)

For thou art a merciful and compassionate God, and unto thee do we ascribe glory, to the Father, and to the Son, and to the Holy Spirit, now, and ever, and unto ages of ages.   Amen.

Choir. Amen.

Priest. Glory to thee, O Christ-God, our hope; glory to thee.

Choir. Glory to the Father, and to the Son, and to the Holy Spirit, now, and ever, and unto ages of ages.   Amen.

Lord, have mercy. (*Thrice*.)   Bless.

And the Priest pronounceth the Benediction.

He who hath received Anointment with the holy Chrism is blessed unto the reception of the Most Holy Sacrament of the Body and Blood of the Lord at the Divine Liturgy.   For these things are done before the Liturgy.

(There are several differences in this Office, as celebrated in the Greek Church; but they are not important.)

THE OFFICE FOR THE RECEPTION INTO THE ORTHODOX CHURCH OF JEWS, MAHOMETANS (SARACENS) AND HEATHENS

Differeth from that for persons who have already received holy Baptism.

After the Choir hath sung PSALM XXXIV.:

I will alway give thanks unto the Lord; his praise shall ever be in my mouth My soul shall make her boast in the Lord; the humble shall hear thereof, and be glad.   O praise the Lord with me, and let us magnify his Name together.   I sought the Lord, and he heard me; yea, he delivered me out of all my fear.   They had an eye unto him, and were lightened; and their faces were not ashamed.   Lo, the poor crieth, and the Lord heareth him; yea, and saveth him out of all his troubles.   The angel of the Lord tarrieth round about them that fear him, and delivereth them.   O taste, and see, how gracious the Lord is: blessed is the man that trusteth in him.   O fear the Lord, ye that are his saints; for they that fear him lack nothing.   The lions do lack, and suffer hunger; but they who seek the Lord shall want no manner of thing that is good.   Come, ye children, and hearken unto me; I will teach you the fear of the Lord.   What man is he that lusteth to live, and would fain see good days?   Keep thy tongue from evil, and thy lips, that they speak no guile.   Eschew evil, and do good; seek peace, and ensue it.   The eyes of the Lord are over the righteous, and his ears are open unto their prayers.   The countenance of the Lord is against them that do evil, to root out the remembrance of them from the earth.   The righteous cry, and the Lord heareth them, and delivereth them out of all their troubles.   The Lord is nigh unto them that are of a contrite heart, and will save such as be of an humble spirit.   Great are the troubles of the righteous; but the Lord delivereth him out of all.   He keepeth all his bones, so that not one of them is broken.   But misfortune shall slay the ungodly; and they that hate the righteous shall be desolate.   The Lord delivereth the souls of his servants; and all they that put their trust in him shall not be destitute.

The Bishop, or Priest, inquireth, at the door of the Church:

Who art thou?

Answer. I am one who desireth to know the true God, and seeketh salvation.

Priest. Why art thou come to the Holy Church?

Answer. That I may learn from her the true faith, and unite myself unto her.

Priest. What profit dost thou hope to receive from the true faith?

Answer. Life eternal and blessed.

The Catechumen is then asked to renounce his errors and confess his belief.

The Jew renounceth: The blasphemies of the Jews against Jesus Christ our Saviour, his most holy Mother and his Saints; circumcision; the observance of Saturday, and all Jewish festivals and ceremonies; the Rabbinical interpretation of the Scriptures contained in the Talmud and ancient and modern writings; the doctrine that the Messiah is not yet come; and the vain expectation of his coming. *[Jews.]*

(*The Jew accepteth the belief: That the Father, the Son, and the Holy Spirit are one God, divided in three Persons, but in Essence undivided; that Jesus Christ, the Only-begotten Son of God, was incarnate by the Holy Spirit of the Virgin Mary for the sake of our salvation, and became very man, yet remaining very God, one in Essence, but in two Persons, divine and human; that our Lord Jesus Christ, of his own free will, in very truth, and not in appearance only, suffered for us in the flesh, but not in his divinity, and, having died and been buried as man, rose again by virtue of his divinity, and ascended into heaven in the flesh; that the Virgin Mary was and remained truly Virgin, and truly is worthy of reverence as the chief intercessor for us with God; and that the Cross of Christ was the instrument and emblem of our salvation.*)

The Mahometan renounceth: The Mahometan faith, and its Sophistries; Mahomet, as being a false prophet; the Koran and all false legends, laws and traditions therein contained; the pilgrimage to Mecca for worship, as salutary to the soul; the inculcation of polygamy in this life, and the teaching as to sensual pleasures in Paradise; and the blasphemies which Mahometans utter touching Christ our Saviour, his most holy Mother, and Christians. *[Mahometans.]*

(*He accepteth all the points set forth for the Jew, and in addition the belief that the Holy Scriptures contained in the Old and New Testaments, as accepted by the Church, are the Word of God, given for our salvation, and were written by the holy men of God who were illumined by the Holy Spirit; that the traditions, regulations and prayers which have come down from the Apostles and the holy Fathers of the Church are salutary for the soul; and that the Apostles, Martyrs, and all the Saints revered by the Holy Church are, in very truth, Saints of God, abide with Christ in the kingdom of heaven, and pray for us sinners.   He also professeth belief touching the holy images (see page 459) required from all converts.*)

The Heathen renounceth: Heathen superstitions; the adoration of created things; the worship of material statues, and bowing down to idols; the offering and eating of sacrifices unto idols; idolatrous priests and magicians, and their superstitious deeds and soothsaying.

Heathens.

(*He accepteth the same as the Mahometan.*)

The Convert then maketh oath of allegiance.

I, N., who to-day am come to enter the Christian faith from Judaism (*Mahometanism, Heathenism*) to the Christian faith, take my oath before omniscient God, that I renounce the false doctrine of the Jews (*Mahometans, Heathens*), and all the heresies and calumnies therein contained, and enter the saving faith of Christ, not because of any compulsion or fear, nor because of the oppression of my fellow-believers, and not for the sake of gain, neither by reason of any hidden guilt on my part, but solely for the salvation of my soul.   Being convinced of the very truth of this faith, and drawn by the love of my heart unto Christ the Saviour, I desire to become a Christian, and that holy Baptism may be vouchsafed unto me. And if I now assert these things through hypocrisy, and come not unto Christ my God through the desire of my heart; and if I shall hereafter dare to renounce the Christian faith, and return unto Judaism (*Mahometanism, Heathenism*), may the wrath of God and everlasting damnation befall me.

And after this, he receiveth Baptism, Chrismation and the Holy Communion.

THE LESSER BLESSING OF WATER

A small table, covered with a cloth, is placed in the centre of the church, at the customary spot, and water thereon in a vessel. And the Priest, putting on his priestly stole and his chasuble, and holding in his hand the precious cross and a sprinkler for the holy water, is preceded by the Deacon with the censer, and by two taper-bearers with tapers. And when he cometh to the table, he layeth the cross thereon, and taking the censer, he censeth the water in cross-form, and maketh the usual beginning. (See page 479: Blessed is our God . . . to end of the Lord's Prayer.) And after the Priest hath pronounced the blessing, the Deacon beginneth:

PSALM CXLIII.

Reader. Hear my prayer, O Lord, and consider my desire; hearken unto me for thy truth and righteousness' sake. And enter not into judgment with thy servant; for in thy sight shall no man living be justified. For the enemy hath persecuted my soul; he hath smitten my life down to the ground; he hath laid me in the darkness, as the men that have been long dead. Therefore is my spirit vexed within me, and my heart within me is desolate. Yet do I remember the time past: I muse upon all thy works; yea, I exercise myself in the works of thy hands. I stretch forth my hands unto thee; my soul gaspeth unto thee as a thirsty land. Hear me, O Lord, and that soon; for my spirit waxeth faint: hide not thy face from me, lest I be like them that go down into the pit. O let me hear thy loving-kindness betimes in the morning; for in thee is my trust: show thou me the way that I should walk in; for I lift up my soul unto thee. Deliver me, O Lord, from mine enemies; for I flee unto thee to hide me. Teach me to do the thing that pleaseth thee; for thou art my God: let thy loving Spirit lead me forth into the land of righteousness. Quicken me, O Lord, for thy Name's sake, and for thy righteousness' sake bring my soul out of trouble. And of thy goodness slay mine enemies, and destroy all them that vex my soul; for I am thy servant.

Deacon. God is the Lord, and hath revealed himself unto us. Blessed is he that cometh in the Name of the Lord. *(Thrice.) In Tone IV.*

And these Hymns (Tropari), in Tone IV.

Unto the Birth-giver of God let us sinners and humble ones now diligently have recourse, and let us bow down, in penitence exclaiming, from the bottom of our souls: O Sovereign Lady, help us, having compassion upon us! Make haste to help, for we perish with the multitude of our sins; turn not thy servants empty away: for we have thee as our only hope. *(Twice.)* Glory . . . now, and ever . . .

Never, O Birth-giver of God, will we unworthy ones cease to proclaim thy powers: for if thou didst not come to our aid, making intercession. who would deliver us from our manifold adversities? Who would have pre-served us free unto this day? We will not forsake thee, O Lady: for thou ever savest thy servants from all ruthless foes.

Then Psalm li.: Have mercy upon me, O God, . . . (*See page 380.*)

Then the following Hymns (Tropari) are sung, in Tone VI.

O Virgin who didst receive from the Angel "Hail!" and didst there-after give birth to thy Creator, save thou those who magnify thee.

(This First Hymn is sung twice.)

We sing thy Son, O Birth-giver of God, and cry aloud: From all ad-versities save thou thy servants, O Lady all-pure.

The Eulogy of kings, prophets, apostles and martyrs art thou, and Intercessor for the world, O All-undefiled One.

Every tongue of right believers laudeth, and blesseth, and glorifieth thine all-pure birth-giving, O Mary, Bride of God.

Give unto me also, though unworthy, O my Christ, remission of my trespasses, I beseech thee, through the prayers of her who hath borne thee, in that thou art compassionate.

Upon thee have I set my trust, O Birth-giver of God: save me by thy prayers, granting unto me remission of my sins.

Quicken me, O thou who hast borne the Life-giver and Saviour: save, through thy prayers, O Blessed Hope of our souls.

O Virgin undefiled, who didst conceive in thy womb the Creator of all men, through thy prayers, save thou our souls.

O Birth-giver of God all-lauded, who through the word of the Angel, in manner which no word can utter, didst give birth to the Word, pray thou the Same that he will save our souls.

Through thy prayers, O Lady, make thou thy Son to be a merciful judge of me who am a sinner above all other men.

In duty bound we cry aloud unto thee: Hail, O pure Birth-giver of God ever-virgin! Through thy prayers are saved those who pray.

Deliver me from fire eternal, and the torments which await me, O Birth-giver of God, forasmuch as I magnify thee.

Despise not the petitions of thy servants, we beseech thee, O All-praised Lady, that we may be delivered from every assault.

From infirmities and every malady deliver thou us, who have recourse to thy holy protection.

Marvellous was the wonder shown in thee, O Birth-giver of God: For for our sakes the Creator of all and our God was born of thee, and like unto us.

Thy temple, O Birth-giver of God, was shown forth a remedy without price for ills, and a consolation for wounded souls.

O Birth-giver of God all-holy, who hast borne the Saviour, save thou thy servants from all adversities and from all other necessities.

Deliver thy servants from every ban under which they lie, and from every ailment, both spiritual and bodily, O Lady all-holy.

Through thy prayers, O Virgin Birth-giver of God, save thou all who have recourse unto thee; and deliver them from all necessity and sorrow.

Who that hath recourse unto thy temple, O Birth-giver of God, doth not receive speedy healing, both of soul and of body, O All-pure One?

Entreated by all the high and holy Heavenly Powers, O Bountiful One, through her who hath borne thee, cleanse thou me.

Spare, O Saviour, the souls of our brethren who have died in the hope of life; and loose, remit their sins.

Hail, O Virgin, Mercy-seat of the world! Hail, thou Haft and Candelabrum all-golden, thou Manna and Light Divine, O Bride of God!

We sing thee, One God in Three Persons, crying aloud the Thrice-Holy song, entreating that we may receive salvation.

Glory to the Father, and to the Son, and to the Holy Spirit.

O Virgin, who hast borne the Saviour, and Sovereign and Lord of the world, pray thou him that he will save our souls.

Now, and ever, and unto ages of ages. Amen.

Hail, O Mount! Hail, O Bush that burned and yet was not consumed! Hail, O Gate! Hail, O Ladder! Hail, O Altar divine! Hail, O Sovereign Lady, the helper of all men.

Through the prayers of thine all-holy Mother, and of all thy Saints, O Merciful One, grant thy mercies unto thy people.

Through the prayers of the glorious Archangels, and Angels, and of the Heavenly Hosts, preserve thou mightily thy servants, O Christ my Saviour.

Through the prayers of thine honourable and glorious Baptist, Prophet and Forerunner, and of all thy Saints, grant thou thy mercies unto thy people.

Through the prayers of the glorious Apostles and Martyrs, and of all thy Saints, grant thou thy mercies unto thy people.

Through the prayers of the glorious Unmercenaries, O Birth-giver of God, preserve thou thy servants, in that thou art the Intercessor and the Confirmation of the world.

Glory to the Father, and to the Son, and to the Holy Spirit.

The Father, and the Son, and the Holy Spirit do we glorify, saying: O Holy Trinity, save thou our souls.

Now, and ever, and unto ages of ages. Amen.

O Virgin, who in wise ineffable didst, in the latter days, conceive and bring forth thy Creator, save thou those who magnify thee.

Then: Open unto us the door of thy loving-kindness, O Blessed Birth-giver of God. In that we set our hope on thee may we not fail, but through thee may we be delivered from all adversities; for thou art the salvation of all Christian people.

Then: Let us pray to the Lord.

Priest. For holy art thou, O our God, and unto thee are due all glory, honour and worship, to the Father, and to the Son, and to the Holy Spirit, now, and ever, and unto ages of ages.

Choir. Amen.

Then these Hymns (Tropari), in Tone VI.

Now is drawn nigh the time which sanctifieth all men, and a just Judge awaiteth us; but turn thou, O my soul, unto repentance, like the adulteress crying with tears: Have mercy upon me, O Lord.

O Christ, the Fountain, who dost bedew with the waters of healing, in the all-honourable temple of the Virgin, thou to-day, through the sprinkling of thy blessing, dost expel the maladies of the ailing, O thou Physician of our souls and bodies.

As a Virgin who had not known man thou didst give birth, and as Mother unwedded a Virgin didst remain, O Mary, Birth-giver of God: Entreat thou Christ our God that he will save us.

O all-holy Virgin Birth-giver of God, guide thou aright the works of our hands, and entreat thou pardon for our transgressions, when we chant the angelic song: —

O Holy God, Holy Mighty, Holy Immortal, have mercy upon us.

And when the Thrice-Holy hath been sung, in the usual manner, the Deacon saith: Let us attend.

Priest. Peace be with you all. —— *Choir.* And with thy spirit.

Reader. The Gradual (*Prokimen*), in the Third Tone. The Lord is my light and my Saviour; whom shall I fear?

Verse: The Lord is the defender of my life; of whom shall I be afraid?

Reader. The Lesson from the Epistle of the holy Apostle Paul to the Hebrews.

(*Heb. ii. 11–18.*) Brethren: Both he that sanctifieth and they who are sanctified are all of one: for which cause he is not ashamed to call them brethren; saying, I will declare thy name unto all my brethren; in the midst of the church will I sing praises unto thee. And again, I will put my trust in him. And again, Behold I and the children which God hath given me. Forasmuch then as the children are partakers of flesh and blood, he also himself likewise took part of the same; that through death he might destroy him that had the power of death, that is, the devil: and deliver them who through fear of death were all their life-time subject to bondage. For verily he took not on him the nature of angels; but he took on him the seed of Abraham. Wherefore in all things it behoved him to be made like unto his brethren, that he might be a merciful and faithful high priest in things pertaining to God, to make reconciliation for the sins of the people. For in that he himself hath suffered being tempted, he is able to succour them that are tempted.

Priest. Peace be with thee. —— *Reader.* And with thy spirit.

Deacon. Wisdom!

Alleluia, *in the Sixth Tone.*

Verse 1: My heart is inditing of a good matter.

Verse 2: I will tell my deeds unto the king.

Priest. Wisdom, O believers! Let us listen to the Holy Gospel. Peace be with you all.

People. And with thy spirit.

Deacon. The Lesson from the holy Gospel of John.

Choir. Glory to thee, O Lord; glory to thee.

(*John v. 1–4.*) At that time Jesus went up to Jerusalem. Now there is at Jerusalem by the sheep market, a pool, which is called in the Hebrew tongue Bethesda, having five porches. In these lay a great multitude of impotent folk, of blind, halt, withered, waiting for the moving of the water. For an angel went down at a certain season into the pool, and troubled the water: whosoever then first after the troubling of the water stepped in, was made whole of whatsoever disease he had.

Choir. Glory to thee, O Lord; glory to thee.

Then the Deacon saith the Litany (*Ekténiya*).

In peace let us pray to the Lord.

Choir. Lord, have mercy.

For the peace that is from above, and for the salvation of our souls: ℞

For the peace of the whole world; for the welfare of God's holy Churches, and for the union of all: ℞

For this holy Temple, and for those who with faith, devoutness, and in the fear of God have entered therein: ℞

For our Most Holy Synod (*or* Patriarch); for our Bishop (*or* Archbishop, *or* Metropolitan), N.; for the honourable Presbytery, the Diaconate in Christ; for all the clergy and the laity: ℞

Here follow petitions for the Ruler of the Land and for all the Authorities, according to the elements and nationalities of which the Parish is constituted.

That he will aid them and subdue under their feet every foe and adversary: ℞

For this city (*if in a monastery*, for this holy habitation), and for those who with faith dwell therein: ℞

For healthful seasons; for abundance of the fruits of the earth, and for peaceful times: ℞

For those who travel by sea or by land; for the sick and the suffering; for those who are in captivity, and for their salvation: ℞

That these waters may be sanctified by the power, and effectual operation, and descent of the Holy Spirit: ℞

That there may descend upon these waters the cleansing operation of the super-substantial Trinity: ℞

let us pray to the Lord. *Choir.* Lord, have mercy.

That this water may be unto the healing of souls and bodies, and unto the banishing of every hostile power: ℞

That the Lord God will send down the blessing of Jordan, and sanctify these waters: ℞

For all those who entreat of God aid and protection: ℞

That he will illumine us with the light of understanding, with the consubstantial Trinity: ℞

That the Lord our God will show us forth sons and heirs of his kingdom, through partaking of and sprinkling with these waters: ℞

That he will deliver us from all tribulation, wrath and necessity: ℞

let us pray to the Lord. Choir. Lord, have mercy.

Succour us, save us, have mercy upon us, and keep us, O God, by thy grace.——*Choir*. Lord, have mercy.

Calling to remembrance our most holy, all-undefiled, most blessed and glorious Lady, the Birth-giver of God and ever-virgin Mary, with all the Saints, let us commend ourselves, and each other, and all our life unto Christ our God.

Choir. To thee, O Lord.

Exclamation.

For unto thee are due all glory, honour and worship, to the Father, and to the Son, and to the Holy Spirit, now, and ever, and unto ages of ages.

Choir. Amen.

Then this Prayer:

O Lord our God, who art mighty in counsel, and wonderful in thy deeds, the Creator of all things, who keepest thy covenant and thy mercy unto those who love thee and keep thy commandments, and receivest the contrite tears of all who are in distress: (For for this cause thou didst come in the similitude of a servant, scorning not our image, but giving true health to the body, and saying: Lo, thou art healed, sin no more; and with clay thou didst make the man's eyes whole, and having commanded him to wash, didst make him, by thy word, to rejoice in the light, putting to confusion the floods of passion of enemies, and drying up the bitter sea of the life of the same, and subduing the waves of sensual desires heavy to be endured): Do thou, the same King who lovest mankind, who hast granted unto us to clothe ourselves in the garment of snowy whiteness, by water and the Spirit, send down upon us thy blessing, through partaking of this water, and through sprinkling therewith, washing away the defilement of passions. Yea, we beseech thee, visit thou our weakness, O Good One, and heal our infirmities, both spiritual and bodily, by thy mercy; Through the prayers of our all-pure, most blessed Lady, the Birth-giver of God and ever-virgin Mary; through the might of the honourable and life-giving Cross; through the intercession of the honourable Bodiless Powers of heaven; of the honourable, glorious Prophet, Forerunner and Baptist, John; of the holy, glorious and all-laudable Apostles; of our holy and God-bearing Fathers; of our Fathers among the Saints, the great Hierarchs and Œcumenical Teachers, Basil the Great, Gregory the Theologian and John Chrysostom; of our Fathers among the Saints Athanasius and Kyril, Patriarchs of Alexandria; of our Father among the Saints, Spiridon, the Wonder-worker of Trimethuetus; of our Father among the Saints, Nicholas, the Wonder-worker, Archbishop of Myra in Lycia; (of our Holy Fathers of All-Russia, Wonder-workers, Peter, Alexis, Jonah and Philip); of the holy and glorious great martyr, George the Victorious; of the holy and glorious great martyr, Demetrius the exhaler of chrism; of the holy right-victorious Martyrs; of the holy and righteous Ancestors of God, Joachim and Anna; of the holy, glorious and wonder-working Unmercenaries, Cosmas and Damian, Kir and John, Panteleimon and Ermolaus, Samson and Diomid, Mokius and Anikita, Thalaleus and Tryphon; and of Saint N., whom we commemorate; and of all thy Saints.

And preserve, O Lord, thy servant, our most God-fearing Ruler, N. (*Thrice.*) And all the Authorities.

Save, O Lord, and have mercy upon the Most Holy Synod (*or* the Patriarch, N.) granting unto it (*him*) health, spiritual and bodily; and be merciful in all things unto this Christian habitation which laboureth for thee. Have in remembrance, O Lord, every Bishopric over the Orthodox, which rightly administereth the word of thy truth, and every priestly and monastic Order, and their salvation. Have in remembrance, O Lord, both those who hate us, and those who love us, the brethren who serve with us, the people who are here present, and those who for a cause worthy of blessing have gone forth and have empowered us, unworthy though we be, to pray for them. Have in remembrance, O Lord, our brethren who are in captivity and affliction, and show mercy upon them, according to thy great mercy, delivering them from all distress. For thou art the Fountain of healing, O Christ our God, and unto thee do we ascribe glory, together with thy Father who hath no beginning, and with thine all-holy, and good, and life-giving Spirit, now, and ever, and unto ages of ages.

Choir. Amen.

Priest. Peace be with you all.——*Choir.* And with thy spirit.

Deacon. Bow your heads unto the Lord.

Choir. To thee, O Lord.

And the Priest saith, secretly, *this Prayer:*

Bow thine ear, and hearken unto us, O Lord, who didst deign to be baptized in Jordan, and didst sanctify the water: and bless all of us who by the bowing of our necks do show forth our apprehension that we are thy servants; and grant that we may be filled with thy sanctification, through partaking of this water; and let it be to us, O Lord, for the health of soul and body.

Secretly.

Exclamation.

For thou art our sanctification, and unto thee do we ascribe glory, and thanksgiving, and worship, together with thy Father who hath no beginning, and thine all-holy, and good, and life-giving Spirit, now, and ever, and unto ages of ages.

Choir. Amen.

Then, taking the honourable cross, he blesseth the water thrice, in cross-form, dipping it and moving it in due fashion, and chanting the following Hymn (Tropár) in Tone I. (Thrice.)

O Lord, save thy people and bless thine inheritance, granting to the most God-fearing Ruler, N., victory over all adversaries, and by thy Cross preserving thine Estate.

Then the following Hymn, in Tone II., is sung:

Make us worthy of thy gifts, O Virgin Birth-giver of God, disregarding our transgressions, and bestowing healing, through faith, upon those who accept thy blessing, O All-pure One.

Then the Priest kisseth the honourable cross, and so do likewise all the people; and he sprinkleth them all with the holy water, and all the Sanctuary and the Church. And the people sing the following Hymns (Tropari), in Tone IV.:

O holy Unmercenaries, who have a fountain of healing, give ye healing unto all who ask it, in that ye have been vouchsafed gifts most excellent from the everflowing fountain our Saviour. For the Lord saith unto you, as unto your fellow-zealots the Apostles: Lo, I have given unto you power over unclean spirits, that ye may drive them out, and heal every infirmity, and every wound. Wherefore, abiding fully in that command, freely ye have received, freely do ye give, healing the passions of our souls and bodies.

Have regard to the prayers of thy servants, O All-undefiled One, allaying the fierce risings against us, assuaging our every woe; for in that we have thee as a confirmation certain and renowned, and have acquired thy intercession, we shall not be put to shame, O Lady, when we call upon thee. Strive thou earnestly for the petition of those who faithfully cry unto thee: Hail, O Lady, O Help of all men, O Joy and Protection and Salvation of our souls.

Receive, O Lady, the prayers of thy servants, and deliver us from every distress and sorrow.

And after the Sprinkling, the Litany (Ekténiya).

Have mercy upon us, O God, according to thy great mercy, we beseech thee: hearken, and have mercy.

Choir. Lord, have mercy. (*Thrice.*)

Furthermore we pray that he will preserve this city and this holy Temple, and every city and land from pestilence, famine, earthquake, flood, fire, the sword, the invasion of enemies, and from civil war: and that our good God, who loveth mankind, will be graciously favourable and easy to be entreated, and will turn away from us all the wrath stirred up against us, and deliver us from all his righteous chastisement which impendeth against us, and have mercy upon us.

Choir. Lord, have mercy. (*Forty times.*)

Then the Priest exclaimeth:

Hear us, O God our Saviour, the hope of all the ends of the earth, and of those who are far off upon the sea; and show mercy, show mercy, O Master, upon our sins, and be merciful unto us.

For thou art a merciful God and lovest mankind, and unto thee we ascribe glory, to the Father, and to the Son, and to the Holy Spirit, now, and ever, and unto ages of ages.

Choir. Amen.

Priest. Peace be with you all.

Choir. And with thy spirit.

Deacon. Let us bow our heads unto the Lord.

Choir. To thee, O Lord.

Then the Priest readeth, in a loud voice, the following Prayer:

O greatly merciful Master, Lord Jesus Christ our God, favourably fulfil our prayer; through the prayers of our all-pure Birth-giver of God and ever-virgin Mary; through the might of the honourable and life-giving Cross; through the intercession of the honourable Bodiless Powers of heaven; of the honourable, glorious Prophet, Forerunner and Baptist, John; of the holy, glorious and all-laudable Apostles; of the holy, glorious and righteous Martyrs; of our holy and God-bearing Fathers and Œcumenical great teachers and saints, Basil the Great, Gregory the Theologian, and John Chrysostom; of our Father among the Saints, Nicholas, Archbishop of Myra in Lycia, the Wonder-worker; (of our Holy Fathers of All-Russia, Wonder-workers, Peter, Alexis, Jonah and Philip); of the righteous Ancestors of God, Joachim and Anna (*and of the Patron Saint of the Temple*); and of all thy Saints: Grant us remission of our sins.   Cover us with the shelter of thy wing; root out from us every foe and adversary; render tranquil our life; have mercy upon us, and thy world, O Lord, and save our souls, forasmuch that thou art gracious and lovest mankind.

Choir. Amen.

Then the BENEDICTION.

May Christ, our true God, through the prayers of his all-holy Mother, and of all the Saints, have mercy upon us and save us, for he is good and loveth mankind.

THE OFFICE USED AT THE FOUNDING OF A CHURCH

(THE LAYING OF THE CORNER-STONE)

No one may found a church, either of stone or of wood, except the Bishop himself, or an Archpriest or one of the Priests whom it shall please him to send, with his special blessing, for that purpose. But if any one shall dare to begin the building of a church without the Bishop's blessing, he shall incur the penalty of being deposed, as a contemner of the Bishop's authority.

And the Founding shall be after this wise: If the church is to be of stone, trenches are dug at the place where the corner-stone is to be laid, and stones and mortar shall be prepared; and on one square stone there shall be depicted or carved a cross; and below the cross (if the Bishop or his representative so desireth), a place shall be prepared for the insertion of Holy Relics. And the following inscription shall be put on the stone: In the Name of the Father, and of the Son, and of the Holy Spirit this church is founded, in honour and memory of (*here the name of a Feast, or of the Patron Saint of the Temple is inserted*); in the rule of the most God-fearing Ruler, N. *If it be in a foreign land, the title and name of the Ruler are here inserted*); in the Episcopacy of the Right (*or* Most) Reverend N., of N.; in the Year of the World . . . , and from the Birth in the flesh of God the Word . . . (*with the month and day*).

A church may be founded without the Relics of a Saint and the above-mentioned inscription, but not without the square stone. In addition to this, a large wooden cross is prepared, and this cross is planted in a trench dug at the spot where the altar is to be.

But if the church is to be of wood, no excavations are made, with the exception of one under the wall of the Sanctuary, at the eastern extremity, wherein to set the square stone, and another for the planting of the cross at the spot where the altar is to be. The beams, or planks whereon the church is to rest, are also prepared.

All these preparations having been made, the Bishop or his representative, having vested himself in the church which is nearest the place where the Laying of the corner-stone is to be, cometh forth with all the clergy, preceded by a Deacon with the censer, and a Priest with the cross, two and two. And the clergy chant the Stanzas (Stikhíri) of the Litiyá for the Temple of the future church. And on arriving at the place, they lay upon the table there prepared the book of the Holy Gospels, and the cross; and the Rector, having taken the censer, and having censed therewith the table, in cross-form, thrice, the Deacon saith:*

Bless, Master.

And the Rector beginneth, as usual:

Blessed is our God always, now, and ever, and unto ages of ages.

Choir. Amen.

O heavenly King, the Comforter, Spirit of Truth, who art in all places and fillest all things; Treasury of good things and Giver of life: Come, and take up thine abode in us, and cleanse us from every stain; and save our souls, O Good One.

* See the Services for the Feasts.

And until the singing is finished, the Rector standeth in front of the book of the Holy Gospels, censing it. Then he censeth all the trenches, where the foundation is to lie, beginning from the first wall of the Sanctuary, and proceeding against the sun, until he cometh back to the place whence he began. Then he censeth the Clergy and the People. And the Reader readeth:

O Holy God, Holy Mighty, Holy Immortal One, have mercy upon us. (*Thrice.*)

Glory to the Father, and to the Son, and to the Holy Spirit, now, and ever, and unto ages of ages. Amen.

O all-holy Trinity, have mercy upon us. O Lord, wash away our sins. O Master, pardon our transgressions. O Holy One, visit and heal our infirmities, for thy Name's sake.

Lord, have mercy. (*Thrice.*)

Glory . . . now, and ever, . . .

Our Father, who art in heaven, Hallowed be thy Name. Thy kingdom come. Thy will be done on earth, As it is in heaven. Give us this day our daily bread. And forgive us our trespasses, As we forgive those who trespass against us. And lead us not into temptation; But deliver us from the Evil One:

Priest. For thine is the kingdom, and the power, and the glory, of the Father, and of the Son, and of the Holy Spirit, now, and ever, and unto ages of ages.

Choir. Amen.

O come, let us worship God our King. O come, let us worship and fall down before Christ, our King and our God. O come, let us worship and fall down before the Very Christ, our King and our God.

PSALM CXLIII.

Hear my prayer, O Lord, and consider my desire; hearken unto me for thy truth and righteousness' sake. And enter not into judgment with thy servant; for in thy sight shall no man living be justified. For the enemy hath persecuted my soul; he hath smitten my life down to the ground; he hath laid me in the darkness, as the men that have been long dead. Therefore is my spirit vexed within me, and my heart within me is desolate. Yet do I remember the time past; I muse upon all thy works; yea, I exercise myself in the works of thy hands. I stretch forth my hands unto thee; my soul gaspeth unto thee as a thirsty land. Hear me, O Lord, and that soon; for my spirit waxeth faint: hide not thy face from me, lest I be like unto them that go down into the pit. O let me hear thy loving-kindness betimes in the morning; for in thee is my trust: show thou me the way that I should walk in; for I lift up my soul unto thee. Deliver me, O Lord, from mine enemies; for I flee unto thee to hide me. Teach me to do the thing that pleaseth thee; for thou art my God: let thy loving Spirit lead me forth into the land of righteousness. Quicken me, O Lord, for thy Name's sake; and for thy righteousness'

sake bring my soul out of trouble.   And of thy goodness slay mine enemies, and destroy all them that vex my soul; for I am thy servant.

Glory to the Father, and to the Son, and to the Holy Spirit, now,
and ever, and unto ages of ages.   Amen.

Alleluia.   (*Thrice.*)

And the Deacon saith this Litany:

In peace let us pray to the Lord.

Choir.   Lord, have mercy.

For the peace that is from above, and for the salvation of our
souls: ℟

For the peace of the whole world; for the welfare of God's holy
Churches, and for the union of all: ℟

For this holy Temple, and for those who, with faith, devoutness,
and in the fear of God have entered therein: ℟

For our Holy Synod (*or* Patriarch); for our Bishop (*or* Archbishop, *or* Metropolitan), N.; for the honourable Presbytery, the
Diaconate in Christ; for all the clergy and the laity: ℟

*Here follow petitions for the Ruler of the Land and for all the Authorities, accord-
ing to the elements and nationalities of which the Parish is constituted.*

That he will aid them and subdue under their feet every foe and
adversary: ℟

For this city (*if it be in a monastery*, for this holy habitation), for
every city and land, and for those who with faith dwell therein: ℟

For healthful seasons; for abundance of the fruits of the earth,
and for peaceful times: ℟

For those who travel by sea or by land; for the sick and the suffering; for those who are in captivity, and for their salvation: ℟

That he will look graciously upon this place chosen for the foundation of a church to the glory of his all-holy Name, and will bless it
with his heavenly blessing: ℟

That he will bless this good intention and work of his servants
(*or* of his servant, N., *and the Wardens of the church are commemorated*): ℟

That he will bless the commencement of founding this building,
and that its beginning may be successfully laid, to the glory of his
Name, and continued with speed and without hindrance unto its
conclusion, through the power, and effectual operation, and grace
of the all-holy Spirit: ℟

That he will prosper the labourers who work thereon in all things,
and grant them to accomplish the work of their hands, and through
the power, and descent and grace of the all-holy Spirit, to carry it
to a speedy ending: ℟

That he will prosper this blessed labour of his servants, NN. (*or*

let us pray to the Lord.   Choir.   Lord, have mercy.

of his servant, N.), with all abundance, through the power, and effectual operation, and grace of the all-holy Spirit: ℞

That he will appoint to this work, and to the promoters thereof, his holy guardian Angel, who shall invisibly repel all assaults of enemies, both seen and unseen; and that in everything he will grant prosperity and wisdom unto its erection, and strength for its completion: through the power, and effectual operation, and grace of the all-holy Spirit: ℞

That he will deliver us from all tribulation, wrath and necessity: ℞

let us pray to the Lord. Choir. Lord, have mercy.

Succour us, save us, have mercy upon us, and keep us, O God, by thy grace.

Choir. Lord, have mercy.

Calling to remembrance our most holy, all-undefiled, most blessed and glorious Lady, the Birth-giver of God and ever-virgin Mary, with all the Saints, let us commend ourselves, and each other, and all our life unto Christ our God.

Choir. To thee, O Lord.

And the Rector maketh the Exclamation:

For unto thee are due all glory, honour and worship, to the Father, and to the Son, and to the Holy Spirit, now, and ever, and unto ages of ages.

Choir. Amen.

And the Choir chanteth:

God is the Lord, and hath revealed himself unto us. . . . (*And the Verses. See page* 515.)

If the Temple is to be named after the Lord, this is sung in the Tone of the Hymn for the Feast; and after the Hymn for the Day, at the Glory . . . *the Hymn of the Feast of Foundation is sung: at the* Now, and ever, . . . *the Hymn of the Feast.*

But if the Temple is not to be named after the Lord, then the God is the Lord *is sung in Tone II., and the Hymn of Foundation:*

O God, the Maker and Creator of all things, speedily guide aright with thy blessing the work of our hands, which hath been begun unto thy glory, and through thy might bring thou the same presently unto completion; forasmuch as thou alone art almighty, and alone lovest mankind.

But if the Temple is to be named after the Birth-giver of God, the Hymn of Foundation is sung twice, repeating at the Glory . . . *the Hymn of the Temple.*

And if it is to be called after any one of the Saints, then the Hymn of Foundation, and at the Glory . . . *to the Saint.* Now, and ever, . . . *the Hymn to the Birth-giver of God, in the Tone of the Hymn to the Saint. And immediately after the Hymns, Psalm li. is read:* Have mercy upon me, O God, after thy great goodness: . . . (*See page* 380.)

Then two vessels are brought and placed on the table, one containing pure water and the other oil. And when the Psalm is finished, the following Hymn is sung, in Tone VI., thrice:

Send down grace from heaven, O Life-giver, and sanctify this water, and show it to be a purification of all uncleanness.

Deacon. Let us pray to the Lord.

Choir. Lord, have mercy.

The Rector readeth over the water the following Prayer:

O God greatly-exalted, the Father of our Lord Jesus Christ, who alone workest wonders which cannot be numbered: whose voice is on many waters, and beholding whom the waters are afraid, and the deeps are thrown into confusion, and the water roareth greatly; whose way is in the sea, and his path in the great waters, and his footsteps are not known; Who, through the baptism of thine Only-begotten Son incarnate, and the descent upon him of the all-holy Spirit in the form of a dove, and thy voice as the Father hast sanctified the streams of Jordan: To thee do we, thine unworthy servants, now make our supplications, and implore thee; Send thou the grace of the all-holy Spirit upon this water, and with thy heavenly benediction bless, purify and hallow it, and give unto it the grace and the blessing of Jordan, and the might which purifieth all uncleanness, and healeth every infirmity, and expelleth the assaults of all demons and their snares. And show it forth through the power, and effectual operation, and grace of the all-holy Spirit, unto all thy servants who, with faith, shall drink of the same, receive it, and be sprinkled therewith, to be for a remission of sins, a release from passions, an expelling of every evil thing, an increase of virtue, a healing of infirmity, and a blessing to homes and to every place, a driving away of all hurtful and pernicious breezes, and the acquirement of thy grace. For thou art he who blesseth and sanctifieth all things, O our God, and unto thee do we ascribe glory, together with thine Only-begotten Son, and thine all-holy, good, and life-giving Spirit, now, and ever, and unto ages of ages.

Choir. Amen.

Priest. Peace be with you all.

Choir. And with thy spirit.

Deacon. Bow your heads unto the Lord.

Choir. To thee, O Lord.

And the Priest readeth, secretly, *this Prayer:*

Incline thine ear, O Lord, and hear me, thou who didst sanctify the waters of Jordan by the manifestation of thy Christ; and bless all us who, by the bending of our necks, express obedience unto thee; and enable us to fulfil thy sanctification by the reception of this water; and may the same be unto us for health to our souls and bodies. *Secretly.*

Exclamation. For thou art our sanctification, and unto thee do we ascribe glory, together with thine Only-begotten Son, and thine all-holy, and good, and life-giving Spirit, now, and ever, and unto ages of ages.

Choir. Amen.

And the Rector, taking the cross, dippeth it in the water, in cross-form, chanting the Hymn, in Tone VIII.:

O Lord, save thy people and bless thine inheritance, granting to our most God-fearing Ruler, N., victory over all adversaries, and by thy Cross preserving thine Estate.   (*Thrice.*)

Then he blesseth the oil, thrice, with his right hand, saying:

In the Name of the Father, and of the Son, and of the Holy Spirit. Amen.

Deacon. Let us pray to the Lord. —— *Choir.* Lord, have mercy.

The Priest then reciteth this Prayer:

O Lord God of our fathers, unto whom the pouring out of the oil that Jacob poured upon the stone, which he set up for a pillar and called the house of God, was well-pleasing and acceptable: Look thou now also, in mercy, we beseech thee, upon this oil, and bless it with thy heavenly blessing, and sanctify it and bestow upon it power through the grace of thine all-holy Spirit, that everything which shall be anointed therewith to thy glory may be consecrated and blessed, well-pleasing and acceptable unto thee: Through the bounties of thine Only-begotten Son, with whom thou art glorified, together with thine all-holy, and good, and life-giving Spirit, now, and ever, and unto ages of ages.

Choir. Amen.

Then the Rector taketh the holy water, and sprinkleth therewith the place where the cross is to be planted, saying:

Graciously vouchsafe, O Lord Jesus Christ our God, with the dread emblem and might of thy Cross to guard this place, to the glory of thee, our crucified God, and of thy Father who is from everlasting, and of thine all-holy Spirit: and may the all-pernicious Angel and adverse powers withdraw therefrom.   For thine is the majesty, and thine are the kingdom and the power and the glory of our great God and Saviour Jesus Christ, now, and ever, and unto ages of ages.   Amen.

And the Priests, taking the cross, plant it in the place which hath been prepared for it, chanting, with the Rector, this Hymn, in Tone II.:

Through the planting of the cross on earth hath the assault of foes perished and been utterly annulled: and man, who before was cast out, entereth again into Paradise: But glory to thee, our only God, for so was it well-pleasing unto thee.

Then they sing the Collect-Hymn (Kondák) for the Foundation, in Tone VI.:

O thou who art speedy to succour and strong to help, manifest thyself now through the grace of thy might, and having blessed, strengthen, and bring to an auspicious conclusion the works of thy servants: For whatsoever things thou willest thou canst perform, in that thou art God Almighty.

Glory to the Father, and to the Son, and to the Holy Spirit, now, and ever, and unto ages of ages.   Amen.

O Protection of Christians that maketh not ashamed, O Mediatrix never-failing with the Creator: Despise not the sinners' voice of supplication; but in that thou art good, come speedily to the aid of us who faithfully call upon thee; make haste to our petition and further our prayer, O Birth-giver of God, who ever protectest them that do thee honour.

Deacon. Let us pray to the Lord.

Choir. Lord, have mercy.

The Rector then readeth the following Prayer, in front of the cross which hath been planted, looking toward the east the while:

O Lord God Almighty, who didst foreshadow by the staff of Moses the precious and life-giving Cross of thy beloved Son, our Lord Jesus Christ: Do thou, the same Lord, bless and sanctify this place, through the power and effectual operation of that precious and life-giving Tree (upon which thou hast bestowed a sprinkling of the precious blood of thy Son), unto the expelling of demons, and of every adverse power, preserving this place, and those who shall serve thee here unhurt of every evil thing; through the prayers of our all-glorious Birth-giver of God and ever-virgin Mary, and of Saint N. (*the Saint who is to be the Patron of the Temple*).

For blessed and glorified be thy kingdom, of the Father, and of the Son, and of the Holy Spirit, now, and ever, and unto ages of ages.

Choir. Amen.

The Rector then goeth to the trench where the laying of the corner-stone is to take place, and the square stone which hath been prepared lieth before him on a table.   And the Choir singeth:

PSALM LXXXIV.

O how amiable are thy dwellings, thou Lord of hosts! My soul hath a desire and longing to enter into the courts. of the Lord; my heart and my flesh rejoice in the living God.   Yea, the sparrow hath found her an house, and the swallow a nest, where she may lay her young; even thy altars, O Lord of hosts, my King and my God.   Blessed are they that dwell in thy house; they will be alway praising thee.   Blessed is the man whose strength is in thee; in whose heart are thy ways. Who going through the vale of misery use it for a well; and the pools are filled with water.   They will go from strength to strength, and unto the God of gods appeareth every one of them in Zion.   O Lord God of hosts, hear my prayer; hearken, O God of Jacob.   Behold, O God our defender, and look upon the face of thine Anointed.   For one day in thy courts is better than a thousand. I had rather be a door-keeper in the house of my God, than to dwell in the tents of ungodliness. For the Lord God is a light and defence; the Lord will give grace and worship; and no good thing shall he withhold from them that live a godly life. O Lord God of hosts, blessed is the man that putteth his trust in thee.

Glory to the Father, and to the Son, and to the Holy Spirit, now, and ever, and unto ages of ages. Amen.

Alleluia. (*Thrice.*)

Deacon. Let us pray to the Lord.

Choir. Lord, have mercy.

The Rector then readeth over the stone this Prayer:

O Lord Jesus Christ, Son of the living God, who art the true God and the Brightness and Image of the Father which is from everlasting, and the Life Everlasting; and art the Corner-stone, hewn without the aid of seed of man from the Virgin Mount; as also the Foundation immovable of thy Church; who also, through the shedding of thy precious blood, hast founded thy Church, and hast raised it up by thy death, and perfected it by thy Resurrection and blessed it by thine Ascension, and hast sanctified and enlarged it by the descent of thy Holy Spirit: Unto thee do we now humbly pray: Send down the grace of thy Holy Spirit, and bless the laying of this stone, and all the foundation of the building which is now begun to the glory of thine all-holy Name (*and if it be a Feast of the Lord, he saith:*) and in honour and memory of thy holy (Nativity, *or whatever it may be; or:* of the Falling-asleep (Assumption) of thine all-holy Mother, *or of whatsoever other Feast of the Birth-giver of God or Saint it may be, mentioning it by name*). And be thou, who art the Alpha and the Omega, the beginning and the end, who from eternity hast created all things, the beginning, the increase, and the completion of this work; bless the wardens and the workers, and prosper thou the work of their hands, and by thy divine providence abundantly multiply all things necessary for the building and completion of this Temple: that the Temple may be perfect and filled with thy glory, and that in it may be glorified thy great and all-holy Name, together with thy Father and thine all-holy Spirit, always, now, and ever, and unto ages of ages.

Choir. Amen.

And the Principal Priest, taking the holy water, sprinkleth the stone therewith, saying:

This stone is blessed through the sprinkling of this holy water, unto the foundation imperishable of the Temple erected in the Name of the Father, and of the Son, and of the Holy Spirit. Amen.

And if the relics of Saints are to be inserted, one of the Priests readeth the inscription, and layeth the relics in the place prepared for them, saying:

O praise God in his saints, praise him in the firmament of his power. For the righteous shall praise thee in glory, and shall rejoice on their beds.

*And when he hath said this, he covereth them.   But if there be no relics, nothing of this
is done.   And the Rector, taking the stone in his hands, layeth it in the mortar
which is prepared in the trench, saying:*

This Church is founded to the glory of our great God and Saviour
Jesus Christ, in honour and memory of (*the name of the Feast of the Lord, or
of the Birth-giver of God, or of the Patron Saint of the Temple*), in the Name
of the Father, and of the Son, and of the Holy Spirit.   Amen.

Then, taking the oil, he saith:

The Most High God, who hath founded this Church, is in the midst of
it, and it shall not be removed.   God shall help it, and that right early.

And he poureth the oil on the stone, set in its place, saying:

Blessed and illustrious be this place for a house of prayer, to the
honour and glory of God, glorified in the Holy Trinity, of the Father, and
of the Son, and of the Holy Spirit.   Amen.

Then, with the whole Choir, he singeth the following, in Tone VI.:

Jacob rose up early in the morning, and took the stone that he had put
for his pillow, and set it up for a pillar, and poured oil upon the top of it,
and said: Surely, the Lord is in this place, and I knew it not; how dreadful
is this place! this is none other but the house of God, and this is the gate
of heaven.
Alleluia, alleluia, alleluia.

*If the foundation be for a wooden church, when all the foregoing hath been performed,
the Rector, taking an axe, smiteth it thrice into the central beam of the Sanctuary,
saying:*

This work is begun in the Name of the Father, and of the Son, and
of the Holy Spirit, and in honour and memory of (*the name of* **Wooden**
the Feast or of the Saint).   Amen.   **Church.**

*Then he beginneth to sprinkle all the foundations round about, starting from the
northern side, against the sun, and saying:*

In the Name of the Father, and of the Son, and of the Holy Spirit·
Amen.

While the Choir singeth PSALM LXXXVII·

Her foundations are upon the holy hills: the Lord loveth the gates of
Zion more than all the dwellings of Jacob.   Very excellent things are
spoken of thee, thou city of God.   I will think upon Rahab and Babylon,
with them that know me.   Behold, yea the Philistines also, and they of
Tyre, with the Morians; lo, there was he born.   And of Zion it shall be
reported that he was born in her; and the Most High shall stablish her.
The Lord shall rehearse it, when he writeth up the people, that he was
born there.   The singers also and trumpeters shall he rehearse: All my
fresh springs shall be in thee.

And the workmen shall immediately begin their labour with speed, in the Name of the Lord. And when the Rector hath passed over the first portion of the foundation, on the northern side, he shall stand with his face to the north; and when the Psalm is finished, and the Deacon hath said: Let us pray to the Lord: *and the Choir hath answered:* Lord, have mercy:

The Rector shall read this Prayer:

O Lord our God, who hast made the North and the sea, and all things; whom heaven and earth are not able to contain; who didst deign to have for thyself on earth a Temple for the perpetual praise of thine all-holy Name: Humbly falling down before thee we entreat thy loving-kindness: bless thou the foundations of this Temple, and its whole edifice; and establish it by thy might, and make it immovable and impregnable, to the glory of thee, the only God glorified in the Trinity, to the Father, and to the Son, and to the Holy Spirit, now, and ever, and unto ages of ages.

Choir. Amen.

Wooden Church. *And after the Prayer, if the church is to be of wood, he taketh the axe again, and smiteth therewith the central beam, saying the same as at the first smiting.*

Then he goeth on, sprinkling the second portion of the foundation, and saying:

In the Name of the Father, and of the Son, and of the Holy Spirit. Amen.

And the Choir chanteth PSALM CXXVII

Except the Lord build the house, their labour is but lost that build it. Except the Lord keep the city, the watchman waketh but in vain.   It is but lost labour that ye haste to rise up early, and so late take rest, and eat the bread of carefulness; for so he giveth his beloved sleep.   Lo, children, and the fruit of the womb, are an heritage and gift that cometh of the Lord.   Like as the arrows in the hand of the giant, even so are the young children.   Happy is the man that hath his quiver full of them; they shall not be ashamed when they speak with their enemies in the gate.

And having come to the western side, and standing with his face toward the west, after the Psalm is finished, and the Deacon hath said: Let us pray to the Lord: *and the Choir hath responded:* Lord, have mercy: *the Rector reciteth the following Prayer:*

O Lord our God, whose Name is praised from the rising of the sun even unto the going down of the same, and who, by thy divine providence, hast chosen this place for an abode for thyself: Send now, we humbly pray thee, thy heavenly blessing upon it, and bless the beginning of this building, and strengthen and establish it, and bring it to successful completion.   For thou art he who doeth all things for the profit of our souls, and unto thee do we ascribe glory, to the Father, and to the Son, and to the Holy Spirit, now, and ever, and unto ages of ages.

Choir. Amen.

And after this Prayer, he again smiteth thrice with the axe, if the church is to **Wooden**
be of wood, saying the same as before.   **Church.**

Then he goeth and sprinkleth the third part of the foundation, and saith:

In the Name of the Father, and of the Son, and of the Holy Spirit.
Amen.

And the Choir singeth, the while, PSALM CXXII.

I was glad when they said unto me, We will go into the house of the
Lord.   Our feet shall stand in thy gates, O Jerusalem.   Jerusalem is
built as a city that is at unity in itself.   For thither the tribes go up,
even the tribes of the Lord, to testify unto Israel, to give thanks unto
the Name of the Lord.   For there is the seat of judgment, even the seat
of the house of David.   O pray for the peace of Jerusalem, they shall
prosper that love thee.   Peace be within thy walls, and plenteousness
within thy palaces.   For my brethren and companions' sakes I will wish
thee prosperity.   Yea, because of the house of the Lord our God I will
seek to do thee good.

*And coming to the southern side of the foundation, and standing with his face to the
south, when the Psalm is finished, and the Deacon hath said:* Let us pray to the
Lord: *and the Choir hath responded:* Lord, have mercy: *the Rector reciteth this
Prayer:*

O Lord Jesus Christ our God, who didst come from the south for our
salvation, and from the shady Virgin Mount as holy didst reveal thyself,
and didst dwell among men: Look with mercy, we beseech thee, upon
the wardens of the Temple, the building whereof hath been begun in thy
Name, and bless them in all things; and give them strength and steadfastness, together with vigour and abundance of health, and prosper
them in all ways, unto the completion of the work which hath been begun
to thy glory.   For thou art the God of mercy, and bounties, and of love
toward mankind, and unto thee do we ascribe glory, together with thy
Father who is from everlasting, and thine all-holy, and good, and life-
giving Spirit, now, and ever, and unto ages of ages.

Choir. Amen.

*After this Prayer he doth as before.   And he goeth and sprinkleth the fourth portion
of the foundation, saying:*

In the Name of the Father, and of the Son, and of the Holy Spirit.
Amen.

While the Choir chanteth PSALM CXXXII.

Lord, remember David, and all his trouble: how he sware unto the
Lord, and vowed a vow unto the Almighty God of Jacob; I will not come
within the tabernacle of mine house, nor climb up into my bed; I will
not suffer mine eyes to sleep, nor mine eyelids to slumber; neither the
temples of my head to take any rest; until I find out a place for the temple of the Lord; an habitation for the Mighty God of Jacob.   Lo, we
heard of the same at Ephrata, and found it in the wood.   We will go

into his tabernacle, and fall low on our knees before his footstool. Arise, O Lord, into thy resting-place; thou, and the ark of thy strength. Let thy priests be clothed with righteousness; and let thy saints sing with joyfulness. For thy servant David's sake, turn not away the presence of thine Anointed. The Lord hath made a faithful oath unto David, and he shall not shrink from it; of the fruit of thy body shall I set upon thy seat. If thy children will keep my covenant, and my testimonies that I shall learn them; their children also shall sit upon thy seat for-evermore. For the Lord hath chosen Zion to be an habitation for him-self; he hath longed for her. This shall be my rest forever; here will I dwell, for I have a delight therein. I will bless her victuals with increase: and will satisfy her poor with bread. I will deck her priests with health, and her saints shall rejoice and sing. There shall I make the horn of David to flourish: I have ordained a lantern for mine Anointed. As for his enemies, I shall clothe them with shame; but upon himself shall his crown flourish.

And when he is come to the place where he began to sprinkle, he stoppeth, and standing in front of the cross planted in the earth, with his face toward the east, when the Psalm is finished, the Rector beginneth, with all emotion, to sing, accompanied by all the Choir:

O heavenly King, the Comforter, Spirit of Truth, who art in all places and fillest all things; Treasury of good things and Giver of life: Come, and take up thine abode in us, and cleanse us from every stain; and save our souls, O Good One.

Deacon. Let us pray to the Lord.

Choir. Lord, have mercy.

Then the Rector readeth this Prayer:

O Lord our God, who hast deigned at this place, and upon the stone laid thereon and blessed in thy Name, to found for thyself a Church, mercifully accept those who bring unto thee thine own of thine own, for the erection to thy glory of the Temple which hath been founded in honour and memory of N. (*the Feast or the Saint*): Requite thou the same with the multitude of thy heavenly and earthly good things; grant-ing also unto all who shall lend their aid in the building and completion of this church bodily health and spiritual salvation. Strengthen the labourers, preserving them unharmed of every evil thing; and preserve these foundations indestructible and immovable, and bring this thy Temple speedily to completion: that therein unceasingly, with all-exalting hymns and praises and unbloody sacrifices, we may glorify and sing thee, our only true God. For unto thee are due all glory, honour and worship, to the Father, and to the Son, and to the Holy Spirit, now, and ever, and unto ages of ages.

Choir. Amen.

The Rector. Peace be with you all. —— *Choir.* And with thy spirit.

And the Deacon, with all emotion, saith:

Again, yet again, on bended knees let us pray to the Lord.

Choir. Lord, have mercy. (*Thrice.*)

And all kneel down.   And the Rector, himself kneeling, readeth with emotion this Prayer:

We praise thee, O Lord God of hosts, our Saviour, that because of the great multitude of thy goodness and loving-kindness toward mankind, thou hast chosen and sanctified this place, and hast founded thereon a church to the glory of thine all-holy Name, through us, thine unworthy servants.   Wherefore, bowing the knees of our souls and bodies, we humbly beseech thee: Graciously vouchsafe to found also upon this place an Altar for the offering up of the unbloody sacrifice of the all-holy Body and the precious Blood of thy Christ, unto thy glory, and unto the salvation of our souls.   And bring thou this Temple, and this Altar, which have now been begun, speedily to completion by thy divine might; that therein and thereon, even until the end of the ages, the praise of thine all-holy Name, and thine unbloody, supersensual sacrifices may be offered up and performed unto thee unceasingly without hindrance, by thine Orthodox people: For with thee all things are possible; and unto thee do we ascribe glory, together with thine Only-begotten Son, and thine all-holy, and good, and life-giving Spirit, now, and ever, and unto ages of ages.

Choir. Amen.

And all standing, the Deacon saith this Litany:

Have mercy upon us, O God, according to thy great mercy, we beseech thee: hearken, and have mercy: ℞

Here follow petitions for the Ruler of the Land and for all the Authorities, according to the elements and nationalities of which the Parish is constituted.

Furthermore we pray for our Most Holy Synod (*or* Patriarch); for our Bishop (*or* Archbishop *or* Metropolitan), N., for the honourable Presbytery, the Diaconate in Christ; for all the clergy and the laity: ℞

Furthermore we pray that the Lord our God will hearken unto the voice of our petition, and will bless the work of our hands: and let us all say: O Lord, hearken, and have mercy. ℞

Furthermore we pray for the God-fearing Wardens, and for the founders to the glory of God, of the Temple, N., which hath been begun and is to be built to the glory of God; and for the prosperous forwarding of their holy work, and for their health, salvation, and the remission of their sins: and let us all say: O Lord, hearken, and have mercy. ℞

Furthermore we pray that he will appoint to this holy work an Angel, a guardian against every evil assault of foes both visible and invisible, who shall deliver from impediments, and shall defend and strengthen the labourers: and let us all say: O Lord, hearken, and have mercy. ℞

Choir. Lord, have mercy. (Thrice.)

And the Rector exclaimeth:

Hear us, O God our Saviour, the hope of all the ends of the earth, and of those who are far off upon the sea; and show mercy, show mercy, O Master, unto us sinners, and be merciful unto us, and unto the founders of this Temple: For thou art a merciful God and lovest mankind, and unto thee we ascribe glory, to the Father, and to the Son, and to the Holy Spirit, now, and ever, and unto ages of ages.

Choir. Amen.

And he pronounceth the Benediction appropriate to the Temple. And having blessed the People, the Bishop or the Archpriest, if he hath come with the Litiyá, as said above, returneth also with the Litiyá to the Church whence he hath come, while the Choir sing the Stanzas of the Temple, or whatsoever else they wish, to the glory of God.

THE OFFICE AT THE CONSECRATION OF A CHURCH WHEN PERFORMED BY A BISHOP (1) *

When the Church is finished, there cometh a person, sent from the Bishop, one day or more beforehand, and prepareth those things which are necessary for the Consecration, not only within the Sanctuary, but also in all the Church. And especially he is careful that the Altar shall stand upon four columns, with a fifth column bearing a small coffer, in the middle; and the coffer must be in the centre, under the Altar, about fourteen inches high, and the Altar thirty-eight inches in height, and its width in proportion to the Sanctuary, and the top of the Altar in proportion to the Altar.

The Table of Oblation, also, shall be of the same height, width and length, in proportion to the Sanctuary. In the top of the Altar-columns cavities are hollowed out, a couple of inches in depth, where the wax-mastic is to be: in these same columns, six inches from the floor, notches shall be cut for holding the cord; and round about the table of the Altar, a couple of inches from the top, other such notches shall be cut, for holding the cord; and holes are to be bored in the corners of the tables for the Altar and the Table of Oblation where the nails are to be, and hollow spaces shall be prepared where the heads of the nails are to be, so that the heads of the nails may lie on a level with the table of the Altar; and the columns are to be pierced in such a manner that the nails shall enter them straight. The following things are required: For making fast the table of the Altar, four nails, and as many more are required for the Table of Oblation; four stones, wherewith to drive the nails; one altar-cloth for draping the Altar, and another for the Table of Oblation; upper altar-cloths, for covering the Altar and the Table of Oblation; veils; cloths wherewith to wipe the Altar; a curtain for the Holy Door; two palls, for the Altar and the Table of Oblation; one glass each of rose-water and of church wine; holy Chrism, and an anointing brush; a sponge for the corporal; a sponge for the sacred chalice; a small leaden box for the holy relics under the Altar; tapers for the Bishop, and for distribution among the other Ecclesiastics and the laity; incense, both of the finest sort, and also of the ordinary sort; two large tapers, for carrying in procession; the church banners, if there be any. And round about the Church it must be clean.

Then the table-board shall be taken from the Altar, and placed against the wall, on the right-hand side, and note must be taken beforehand of the position in which it lay upon the Altar columns.

Then a table is placed in front of the Holy Door, and upon it is spread an altar-cloth: And the book of the Holy Gospels, and the precious cross, and the sacred vessels are set thereon; the spoon, the spear, the altar-cloths, together with the veils, the cord, the covering of the Altar and of the Table of Oblation, the nails, and the sponges; and they are covered with an altar-cloth; and four candlesticks are set there, one at each corner; and another small table is placed within the Sanctuary, near the Bishop's throne, and an altar-cloth is spread thereon; and upon this table are placed the holy Chrism, the church-wine and the rose-water in their glasses, an anointing-brush, an aspergillus, the stones wherewith the nails are to be driven, and the wax-mastic.

And the holy relics are placed upon the paten, covered with the star-cover and the veil, and on the eve of the Consecration are set upon a lectern before the holy picture of the Saviour, by the side of the Holy Door, in the Church itself; and outside the Sanctuary

* See Appendix B, XIII.

is celebrated the VIGIL OFFICE, *by whomsoever the Bishop shall appoint. And before the blessing of the water, the relics shall be borne thence, with all reverence, to a neighbouring Church, after an early Liturgy, and there placed upon the holy Altar; and the book of the Gospels shall be placed from the east over the holy relics; and a candlestick shall be placed before the holy relics. But if there be no other church in the vicinity, then they shall stand in the same spot until they are used.*

THE BEGINNING OF THE CONSECRATION

When the time for the Divine Liturgy is come, and the Bishop hath entered the Church which is to be consecrated, he vesteth himself in his episcopal robes, and addeth thereto a special white garment (sratchítza). (2) And thus arrayed he entereth the holy Sanctuary; and the Priests who are to serve, wearing similar garments over their priestly vestments, bear before the Bishop the table with all things needful for the Consecration, and set it on the right-hand side. And the Bishop, giving his pastoral staff to a Sub-Deacon as he cometh to the Holy Doors, entereth the Sanctuary: and after he hath prayed, he maketh the sign of the cross in blessing over those who are serving, on both sides. At this time the Deacon bringeth holy water (3) to the Bishop, and the Bishop, taking the aspergillus, sprinkleth the columns with the holy water. Then the Sacristan bringeth the hot wax-mastic to the Bishop, and the Bishop sprinkleth the wax-mastic with holy water, and taketh the vessel with the wax-mastic, and poureth it upon the columns, in the form of a cross, to the requisite amount, compassing them about; then he giveth the vessel to the Sacristan, and again sprinkleth the columns with holy water, that the wax-mastic may harden quickly; and the Priests breathe upon the columns where the wax-mastic is, until it is hard. (4)

And when this is finished, the Archdeacon saith:

Let us pray to the Lord.

The Priests. Lord, have mercy.

And the Bishop reciteth this Prayer, in the hearing of all:

O Lord God our Saviour, who createst all things and makest the race of man for salvation, accept the prayer of us, thine unworthy servants; and enable us at this present hour without condemnation to accomplish the consecration of this Temple, founded to thy praise in the name of Saint N.; and to consummate the erection therein of an Altar.

Exclamation. For unto thee are due all glory, honour and worship, to the Father, and to the Son, and to the Holy Spirit, now, and ever, and unto ages of ages.——*Priests.* Amen.

Then the Priests bring the table of the Altar, and the Bishop sprinkleth it on all sides, and layeth it upon the columns of the Altar.

And while this is being done, the following Psalm is sung:

PSALM CXLV.

I will magnify thee, O God, my King; and I will praise thy Name forever and ever. Every day will I give thanks unto thee; and praise thy Name forever and ever. Great is the Lord, and marvellous worthy to be praised; there is no end of his greatness. One generation shall praise thy works unto another, and declare thy power. As for me, I will be talking of thy worship, thy glory, thy praise, and wondrous works; so that men shall speak of the might of thy marvellous acts; and I will also tell of thy greatness. The memorial of thine abundant kindness shall be showed; and men shall sing of thy righteousness. The Lord is gracious and merciful; long-suffering, and of great goodness. The Lord is loving unto every man; and his mercy is over all his works. All thy works praise thee, O Lord; and thy saints give thanks unto thee. They show the glory of thy kingdom, and talk of thy power; that thy power, thy glory, and mightiness of thy kingdom, might be known unto men. Thy kingdom is an everlasting kingdom, and thy dominion endureth throughout all ages. The Lord upholdeth all such as fall, and lifteth up all those that are down. The eyes of all wait upon thee, O Lord; and thou givest them their meat in due season. Thou openest thine hand, and fillest all things living with plenteousness. The Lord is righteous in all his ways, and holy in all his works. The Lord is nigh unto all them that call upon him; yea, all such as call upon him faithfully. He will fulfil the desire of them that fear him; he also will hear their cry, and will help them. The Lord preserveth all them that love him; but scattereth abroad all the ungodly. My mouth shall speak the praise of the Lord; and let all flesh give thanks unto his holy Name forever and ever.

And when the Psalm is finished, the Bishop saith:

Blessed is our God always, now, and ever, and unto ages of ages.
The Priests. Amen.

And when the wax-mastic hath become hard, and the places upon which it flowed have been cleaned, they say PSALM XXIII.

The Lord is my shepherd; therefore can I lack nothing. He shall feed me in a green pasture, and lead me forth beside the waters of comfort. He shall convert my soul, and bring me forth in the paths of righteousness for his Name's sake. Yea, though I walk through the valley of the shadow of death, I will fear no evil; for thou art with me; thy rod and thy staff comfort me. Thou shalt prepare a table before me against them that trouble me; thou hast anointed my head with oil, and my cup shall be full. But thy loving-kindness and mercy shall follow me all the days of my life; and I will dwell in the house of the Lord forever.

Then the Bishop:

Blessed is our God always, now, and ever, and unto ages of ages.
Priests. Amen.

The Sacristan bringeth four nails, and layeth them on the Altar; (5) and the Bishop sprinkleth them with holy water and placeth them in the columns. Again, the Sacristan bringeth the four stones; and the Bishop having taken one stone and the officiating ecclesiastics the others, they make firm the Altar. And when the Altar hath been established, the carpet is immediately spread before the Holy Door, and (the Holy Door being now opened), the upper end is laid in place. And when the Bishop is come forth from the Sanctuary, the Deacon shall exclaim:

Again, yet again, on bended knees, let us pray to the Lord.

And the Priests within the Sanctuary chant: Lord, have mercy.   *(Thrice.)* After *which the Bishop, kneeling, saith the following Prayer:*

O God, without beginning and eternal, who callest all things into being from nothingness; who dwellest in light unapproachable, and hast the heavens for thy throne, and the earth for thy footstool; who didst give a law and pattern unto Moses, and didst inspire Bezaleel with the spirit of wisdom, and didst enable them to complete the perfect building of the Tabernacle of thy Covenant, wherein ordinances of divine worship were instituted, which were the images and types of the true; who didst bestow upon Solomon breadth and greatness of heart, and thereby didst rear of old the Temple; and upon thy holy and all-laudable Apostles didst renew the service in the Spirit, and the grace of the true Tabernacle, and through the same, O Lord of Hosts, didst plant thy churches and thine altars in all the earth, that there might be offered unto thee consecrated and unbloody sacrifices; who, also, hast graciously been pleased to found this Temple, in the name of Saint N., to thy glory, and to the glory of thine Only-begotten Son, and of thine all-holy Spirit: Do thou, the same immortal and munificent King, call to mind thy bounties and thy mercies, which are from everlasting, and abhor not us who are defiled with a multitude of sins, neither annul thou thy Covenant because of our uncleanness; but disregard thou now our iniquities, and strengthen us with the grace and inspiration of thy life-giving and holy Spirit, that without condemnation we may accomplish the renewal of this Temple, and fulfil the consecration of the Altar(*s*) therein; that therein blessing thee in Psalms, and songs, and mystical rites we may always magnify thy loving-kindness.   Yea, O Master, Lord our God, the hope of all the ends of the earth, hear us sinners who make our supplications unto thee, and send down thine all-holy, and adorable, and almighty Spirit, and sanctify this Temple and this Altar (*these Altars*): Fill it (*them*) with the light everlasting: elect it (*them*) for thy dwelling-place; make it (*them*) the abode of thy glory.   Adorn it (*them*) with thy divine and supernal gifts.   Appoint it (*them*) for a haven of the tempest-tossed, for a healing of passions, for a refuge of the weak, for an expelling of evil spirits.   Let thine eyes be open upon it (*them*) day and night, and let thine ears be heedful of the prayer of those who shall enter therein in thy fear and in devoutness, and shall call upon thine all-honourable and adorable Name; that whatsoever they shall ask of thee, thou wilt hear it in heaven above, and wilt show mercy and be gracious unto them.   Preserve it indestructible even unto the end of the ages, and show forth the holy Altar(*s*) therein, the Altar(*s*) of thy Holy Things through the power and effectual operation of thy Holy Spirit.   Glorify it (*them*) above the Mercy-Seat according to the Law; that the holy offices which shall be celebrated thereon may attain unto thy holy, and most heavenly, and supersensual Altar.

and obtain for us the grace of thy most pure over-shadowing; for we trust not in the service of our unworthy hands, but in thine unspeakable goodness.

And when the Prayer is finished, the Bishop standeth, and goeth into the Sanctuary, to the holy Altar; and the Proto-Deacon, within the holy Sanctuary, saith (the Holy Door being closed):

Succour us, save us, have mercy upon us, and keep us, O God, by thy grace.

The Priests. Lord, have mercy.

For the peace that is from above, and for the salvation of our souls: ℞

For the peace of the whole world; for the welfare of God's holy Churches, and for the union of all: ℞

For the Most Holy Governing Synod (*or* Patriarch), and for the Right Reverend Bishop N., and for the works of his hands; and for the Priests and Deacons who are with him: ℞

That he will sanctify this holy Temple, and the Altar that is (*the Altars that are*) therein, through the descent and might of the Holy Spirit: ℞

Here follow petitions for the Ruler of the Land and for all the Authorities, according to the elements and nationalities of which the Parish is constituted.

For this city, and for every city and land, and for those who with faith dwell therein: ℞

That he will deliver us from all tribulation, wrath, and necessity: ℞

Response. Lord, have mercy. let us pray to the Lord.

Calling to remembrance our most holy, all-undefiled, most blessed and glorious Lady, the Birth-giver of God and ever-virgin Mary, with all the Saints, let us commend ourselves, and each other, and all our life unto Christ our God.

Choir. To thee, O God.

Exclamation.

For holy art thou, O our God, who restest upon the Martyrs who have suffered for thee; and unto thee we ascribe glory, to the Father, and to the Son, and to the Holy Spirit, now, and ever, and unto ages of ages.

The Priests. Amen.

Then a porringer is brought, filled with warm water, and red wine and rose-water. And the Proto-Deacon saith:

Let us pray to the Lord.

And the Bishop, bowing his head, saith this Prayer over the water and the wine:

O Lord our God, who didst sanctify the streams of Jordan by thy redeeming manifestation: Do thou, the same Lord, send down now also the grace of thy Holy Spirit; and bless this water and this wine, unto the sanctification and completion of this thine Altar (*these thy Altars*): For blessed art thou unto ages of ages.   Amen.

And after the Prayer, he poureth the warm water, thrice, upon the Altar, saying:

In the Name of the Father, and of the Son, and of the Holy Spirit. Amen.

And mingling the red wine and the rose-water, he poureth them into one vessel.

Then the Sacristan bringeth four cloths. And the Bishop, taking one of them, blesseth his fellow-ministers to take the others; and they wipe the Altar therewith.

And when these things are finished, PSALM LXXXIV. *is said.*

O how amiable are thy dwellings, thou Lord of Hosts!   My soul hath a desire and longing to enter into the courts of the Lord; my heart and my flesh rejoice in the living God.   Yea, the sparrow hath found her an house, and the swallow a nest, where she may lay her young; even thy altars, O Lord of Hosts, my King and my God.   Blessed are they that dwell in thy house; they will be alway praising thee.   Blessed is the man whose strength is in thee; in whose heart are thy ways.   Who going through the vale of misery use it for a well; and the pools are filled with water.   They will go from strength to strength, and unto the God of gods appeareth every one of them in Zion.   O Lord God of Hosts, hear my prayer; hearken, O God of Jacob.   Behold, O God our defender, and look upon the face of thine Anointed.   For one day in thy courts is better than a thousand.   I had rather be a door-keeper in the house of my God, than to dwell in the tents of ungodliness.   For the Lord God is a light and defence; the Lord will give grace and worship; and no good thing shall he withhold from them that live a godly life.   O Lord God of Hosts, blessed is the man that putteth his trust in thee.

And when the Altar hath been washed and wiped, the Bishop saith:

Glory to our God unto ages of ages.
Priests. Amen.

The Bishop then taketh from the Sacristan the red wine mingled with rose-water, and poureth it upon the Altar, thrice, in cross-form, liberally, and they wet the Altar abundantly, stretching forth their hands: and with this same mixture the Bishop sprinkleth the other holy corporals. (6) *And as he doth this, he saith at each sprinkling:*

Thou shalt sprinkle me with hyssop, and I shall be clean: thou shalt wash me, and I shall be whiter than snow.

And after the Altar and the corporals have been sprinkled, the following shall be added (PSALM LI. verses 8–19):

Thou shalt make me hear of joy and gladness, that the bones which thou hast broken may rejoice.   Turn thy face from my sins, and put out all my misdeeds.   Make me a clean heart, O God, and renew a right

spirit within me.   Cast me not away from thy presence, and take not
thy holy Spirit from me.   O give me the comfort of thy help again, and
stablish me with thy free Spirit.   Then shall I teach thy ways unto the
wicked, and sinners shall be converted unto thee.   Deliver me from
blood-guiltiness, O God, thou that art the God of my health; and my
tongue shall sing of thy righteousness.   Thou shalt open my lips, O Lord,
and my mouth shall show thy praise.   For thou desirest no sacrifice,
else would I give it thee; but thou delightest not in burnt-offerings.   The
sacrifice of God is a troubled spirit: a broken and contrite heart, O God,
shalt thou not despise.   O be favourable and gracious unto Zion; build
thou the walls of Jerusalem.   Then shalt thou be pleased with the sacrifice of righteousness, with the burnt-offerings and oblations; then shall
they offer young bullocks upon thine altar.

*Then the Sacristan bringeth the sponges.   The Bishop taketh one sponge, and his
fellow-ministers take the others; and they wipe the Altar with the sponges.   Then
they spread the corporal (or the corporals) at the upper edge of the Altar.   Then the
Bishop saith:*

Blessed is our God always, now, and ever, and unto ages of ages.
Priests. Amen.

*Then the Sacristan bringeth the holy Chrism.   The Bishop, taking the brush, anoint-
eth the Altar, in cross-form.   The Proto-Deacon saith, for the Altar, and for each
corporal:* Let us attend.   *The Bishop maketh upon the Altar three crosses, one in
the middle, and one on each side, a little lower down, saying:* Alleluia, thrice, at
each.   *And he anointeth also the pillars of the Altar, on two sides, and on the middle, and on the edges.   Thereafter the Priests take the corporal (corporals) and lay
it (them) on the Altar, one by one, below the crosses, which are traced with the holy
Chrism, that these crosses be not erased.   The Bishop maketh three crosses on each
corporal (antimins) (7) with the holy Chrism, which is on the Altar.   And when
this is accomplished,* PSALM CXXXIII. *is read:*

Behold, how good and joyful a thing it is, brethren, to dwell together
in unity!   It is like the precious ointment upon the head, that ran down
unto the beard, even unto Aaron's beard, and went down to the skirts
of his clothing.   Like as the dew of Hermon, which fell upon the hill of
Zion.   For there the Lord promised his blessing, and life forevermore.

Then the Bishop saith:

Glory to thee, O Holy Trinity our God, unto ages of ages.
The Priests. Amen.

*And they place the corporal (or the corporals) on the salver.   Then the Priests bring
the first covering of the Altar; (8) the Bishop sprinkleth it without and within with
holy water, and they put it on the Altar.   Then the cord is brought. (9)   The
Bishop sprinkleth the cord, and they bind the Altar about therewith; and this is the
manner of the binding.   The Bishop holdeth the cord upon the right side, at the
first pillar, and they all go with the cord round to the second pillar towards the east,
whence it is carried to the bottom of the third pillar, and goeth to the bottom of the
fourth pillar, and is carried again to the middle of the first pillar, and fastened to*

the end which the Bishop holdeth; and again it is carried to the bottom of the second pillar, and passeth, low down, to the third pillar, and is taken thence to the top of the fourth pillar, and from the fourth pillar is carried to the bottom of the first pillar, so that a cross is formed at the front. And from the first pillar it goeth to the bottom of the second pillar, and thence is carried to the top of the third pillar, so that a cross is formed towards the east. And from the third pillar it is carried to the bottom of the fourth pillar, so that there is a cross upon the north side; and from the fourth pillar it goeth to the bottom of the first pillar. And from the bottom of the first pillar it goeth to the top of the second pillar; and so there is formed a cross on the south side. And it passeth round in such manner that there are three cords at the top, and the second end of the rope is bound to the first end at the first pillar.

And when these things are accomplished, that is to say, when the Altar hath been robed in the first covering and bound about with the cord, PSALM CXXXII. *is said, once, twice, and thrice.*

Lord, remember David, and all his trouble: how he sware unto the Lord, and vowed a vow unto the Almighty God of Jacob; I will not come within the tabernacle of mine house, nor climb up into my bed; I will not suffer mine eyes to sleep, nor mine eyelids to slumber; neither the temples of my head to take any rest; until I find out a place for the temple of the Lord; an habitation for the mighty God of Jacob. Lo, we heard of the same at Ephrata, and found it in the wood. We will go into his tabernacle, and fall low on our knees before his footstool. Arise, O Lord, into thy resting-place; thou, and the ark of thy strength. Let thy priests be clothed with righteousness; and let thy saints sing with joyfulness. For thy servant David's sake, turn not away the presence of thine Anointed. The Lord hath made a faithful oath unto David, and he shall not shrink from it; of the fruit of thy body shall I set upon thy seat. If thy children will keep my covenant, and my testimonies that I shall learn them; their children also shall sit upon thy seat forevermore. For the Lord hath chosen Zion to be an habitation for himself; he hath longed for her. This shall be my rest forever: here will I dwell, for I have a delight therein. I will bless her victuals with increase, and will satisfy her poor with bread. I will deck her priests with health, and her saints shall rejoice and sing. There shall I make the horn of David to flourish: I have ordained a lantern for mine Anointed. As for his enemies, I shall clothe them with shame; but upon himself shall his crown flourish.

And when this is finished, the Bishop saith:

Glory to our God unto ages of ages.

Then the Priests bring the upper covering (the indítia). (10) The Bishop sprinkleth it with holy water within and without, and they put it on the holy Altar, and spread the pall (the ilitón), (11) and upon it place the corporal (corporals), and the book of the Holy Gospels, and the precious cross upon the Altar, and cover them with the altar-cloth; and all these things are sprinkled with holy water. And all these things being accomplished, PSALM XCIII. *is read:*

The Lord is King, and hath put on glorious apparel; the Lord hath

put on his apparel, and girded himself with strength. He hath made
the round world so sure, that it cannot be moved. Ever since the world
began hath thy seat been prepared: thou art from everlasting. The
floods are risen, O Lord, the floods have lift up their voice; the floods
lift up their waves. The waves of the sea are mighty, and rage horribly;
. but yet the Lord, who dwelleth on high, is mightier. Thy testimonies,
O Lord, are very sure: holiness becometh thine house forever.

And after the Psalm the Bishop saith:

Blessed is our God always, now, and ever, and unto ages of ages.
The Priests. Amen.

*Then the Bishop commandeth the chief of the officiating clergy to array the Table of
Oblation, with sprinkling of holy water; and they place the vessels, and the veils
thereon, and cover them with an altar-cloth, saying nothing, but only sprinkling
them with holy water. Then the Bishop is divested of the special white garment;
and the Proto-Deacon bringeth the censer to the Bishop. And the Bishop censeth
the Altar and the Table of Oblation round about, and all the Sanctuary; and the
Proto-Deacon goeth before him with a taper, reciting PSALM XXVI.:*

Be thou my Judge, O Lord, for I have walked innocently: my trust
hath been also in the Lord, therefore shall I not fall. Examine me, O
Lord, and prove me; try out my reins and my heart. For thy loving-
kindness is ever before mine eyes; and I will walk in thy truth. I have
not dwelt with vain persons; neither will I have fellowship with the
deceitful. I have hated the congregation of the wicked; and will not
sit among the ungodly. I will wash my hands in innocency, O Lord;
and so will I go to thine altar; that I may show the voice of thanksgiving;
and tell of all thy wondrous works. Lord, I have loved the habitation
of thy house, and the place where thine honour dwelleth. O shut not
up my soul with the sinners, nor my life with the blood-thirsty; in whose
hands is wickedness, and their right hand is full of gifts. But as for me,
I will walk innocently: O deliver me, and be merciful unto me. My
foot standeth right: I will praise the Lord in the congregations,

many times, until the Sanctuary and the whole Church have been censed.

*And as the Bishop censeth, two Archimandrites, or Abbots, or Priests, follow him.
One sprinkleth the walls with holy water; the second, holding the vessel of the holy
Chrism, anointeth them with the brush, in cross-form, dipping it in the Chrism,
first in the Sanctuary over the Bishop's seat, above the window; then over the western
doors of the church; then on the south side and the north side over the doors; and if
they be lofty, steps are used.*

*And when the censing and the Psalm are finished, the Bishop entereth the Sanctuary
and saith:*

Glory to the Father, and to the Son, and to the Holy Spirit, now, and
ever, and unto ages of ages. Amen.

And the Proto-Deacon taketh the censer and censeth the Bishop thrice. Then he saith, in front of the Altar, on the left side, the Little Litany.

Again, yet again, in peace let us pray to the Lord.

Choir. Lord, have mercy.

Succour us, save us, have mercy upon us and keep us, O God, by thy grace.

Choir. Lord, have mercy.

Calling to remembrance our most holy, all-undefiled, most blessed and glorious Lady, the Birth-giver of God and ever-virgin Mary, with all the Saints, let us commend ourselves, and each other, and all our life unto Christ our God.

Choir. To thee, O Lord.

And the Bishop doth not make the Exclamation, but the Proto-Deacon:

Let us pray to the Lord.

Then the Bishop's mitre is removed. And standing in front of the holy Altar, he saith, very loudly, the following Prayer:

O Lord of heaven and earth, who with wisdom ineffable hast founded thy holy Church, and hast appointed the Order of the Priesthood upon the earth for an antitype of the Angels' service in heaven: Do thou, O munificent Lord, receive also us who now make our petitions unto thee, not as being worthy to ask such great things of thee, but that the exceeding excellence of thy goodness may be manifested; for thou hast not ceased in manifold wise to be gracious unto mankind.   And, as the chiefest of thy benefits, thou hast bestowed upon us the coming in the flesh of thine Only-begotten Son, who was seen upon earth, and shedding forth the light of salvation upon them that sat in darkness, did offer himself a sacrifice for us, and became a propitiation for the whole world, making us to be partakers of his Resurrection; and after that he had ascended into heaven, he endued his Apostles and Disciples, as he had promised, with power from on high, which is the Holy Spirit, adored and almighty, who proceedeth from thee, our God and Father; through whom, also, they became mighty in deed and in word, administered Baptism unto the adoption of sonship, builded churches, established Altars, and instituted the laws and precepts of the Priesthood.   And we sinners, having preserved the tradition thereof, do fall down before thee, the everlasting God, and implore thee, O Loving-kind One: Fill with thy glory divine this Temple erected to thy praise, and show thou forth the holy Altar(s) therein set up as the Holy of Holies; that we who stand before it (*them*), as before the dread throne of thy kingdom, may serve thee uncondemned, sending up unto thee petitions for ourselves and for all the people, and offering the unbloody sacrifice to thy goodness, unto the remission of sins both voluntary and involuntary, unto the governing of our life, the attainment of a good conversation, and the fulfilling of all righteousness.

For blessed be thine all-holy Name, of the Father, and of the Son, and of the Holy Spirit, now, and ever, and unto ages of ages.

Priests. Amen.

And the Bishop saith:

Peace be with you all. —— *Priests.* And with thy spirit.

Proto-Deacon. Bow your heads unto the Lord.

To thee, O Lord.

And the Bishop saith, secretly, *the following Prayer:*

We thank thee, O Lord God of Hosts, for that thou hast graciously vouchsafed to continue also even unto us sinners and thine unworthy servants, because of thy great love toward mankind, that grace which thou hast poured out upon thy holy Apostles, and upon our sainted fathers. Wherefore we pray thee, O all-merciful Lord: Fill with glory, and holiness, and grace this Altar (*these Altars*), that the unbloody sacrifices which shall thereon be offered unto thee may be transmuted into the most pure Body and precious Blood of thine Only-begotten Son, who is our Lord, and God, and Saviour Jesus Christ, unto the salvation of all thy people, and of our unworthiness.

Secretly.

Exclamation. For thou art our God, the God whose property it is to show mercy and to save; and unto thee we ascribe glory, to the Father, and to the Son, and to the Holy Spirit, now, and ever, and unto ages of ages.

Priests. Amen.

*And thereupon there is brought to the Bishop a candlestick, and therein a new, unlighted taper, which the Bishop lighteth with his own hands, (12) and placeth on the High Place (the Bishop's seat) behind the Altar.**

Then the Sacristan directeth how they are to go to another church, with the cross, for the holy relics: the Bishop giveth the book of the Holy Gospels and the cross to the Priests, and distributeth the tapers in the Sanctuary to those present, and issuing forth from the Sanctuary upon the tribune, to the laity. Then the Bishop entereth the Sanctuary: and preceded by the priests, the Bishop goeth forth from the Sanctuary through the church doors for the holy relics, taking his pastoral staff at the Holy Door from a Chanter, and saith:

Let us go forth in peace.

Then they go for the holy relics, according to the ritual: in front are borne the church banners, and the holy pictures (ikóni), as is done in processions of the cross. The Bishop is supported by two Deacons. And the Priests walk before the Bishop, bearing the book of the Holy Gospels and the cross, and the Proto-Deacon and the Deacon cense.

The Singers chant the Hymn, in Tone IV.

Thy Church which, in all the world, thou hast adorned with the blood of thy martyrs, as it were purple and fine linen, crieth aloud through them unto thee, O Christ-God: Send down thy bounties upon thy people, giving grace unto thine Estate, and great mercy unto our souls.

* Note that up to this point no tapers have been lighted in the Sanctuary.

Glory to the Father, . . . now, . . . (*Tone VIII.*)

The universe offereth unto thee, O Lord, the God-bearing martyrs, the first-fruits of nature, as to the Founder of Creation: Through the prayers of the same, and of the Birth-giver of God, O merciful One, preserve in peace profound thy Church, which is thine Estate.

And when the Bishop cometh to the Temple where the holy relics are placed, he entereth the Sanctuary through the Holy Door, with two of the Ecclesiastics there present. And at the Holy Door he giveth his pastoral staff to an acolyte. And the Bishop and Ecclesiastics do reverence to the holy relics; and the Bishop maketh the sign of the cross over those who stand there.

Then the Proto-Deacon, standing in front of the Holy Door, reciteth the Little Litany. (See page 502.)

Again, yet again, in peace . . .

And the Priests outside the Sanctuary respond:

Lord, have mercy.

And after the Litany, the Bishop pronounceth the Exclamation in front of the Altar:

For holy art thou, O our God, who restest on the honourable Martyrs, which have suffered for thee; and unto thee do we ascribe glory, to the Father, and to the Son, and to the Holy Spirit, now, and ever, and unto ages of ages.

Choir. Amen.

O Holy God, Holy Mighty, Holy Immortal One, have mercy upon us. (*Thrice.*)

Proto-Deacon. Let us pray to the Lord.

Choir. Lord, have mercy.

And the Bishop is divested of his mitre, which is laid upon the salver. And he saith the following Prayer:

O Lord our God, faithful in thy words, and steadfast in thy promises, who hast enabled thy holy Martyrs to fight the good fight and to fulfil the course of godliness, and to keep the faith of the true confession: Be thou, the same all-holy Lord, entreated of their prayers, and vouchsafe unto us thine unworthy servants to have a part and inheritance with them; that being followers of them, we also may obtain the good things which await them.

Exclamation. Through the mercy and love toward mankind of thine Only-begotten Son, with whom thou art blessed, together with thine all-holy, and good, and life-giving Spirit, now, and ever, and unto ages of ages.

Choir. Amen.

Bishop. Peace be with you all.

Choir. And with thy spirit.

Proto-Deacon. Bow your heads unto the Lord.

Choir To thee, O Lord.

And the Bishop saith, secretly, *the following Prayer:*

O Lord our God, through the prayers of our most holy Lady, the Birth-giver of God, and of all thy Saints, direct thou the works of the hands of us, thine unworthy servants; and vouchsafe that we may, in all things, prove acceptable unto thy goodness.

Exclamation. Blessed and all-glorified be the majesty of thy kingdom, of the Father, and of the Son, and of the Holy Spirit, now, and ever, and unto ages of ages.

Choir. Amen.

The Bishop then taketh the censer from the Proto-Deacon, and censeth the holy relics thrice three times; and giving the censer to be held, and taking the holy paten with the holy relics, covered with a veil over the star-cover, he setteth it upon his head, and goeth out through the Holy Door, supported by the chief Ecclesiastics. But the Bishop himself holdeth the paten with both hands. And thus they go forth, according to their rank. In front are borne the church banners, and the holy image (ikóna) of the Temple. Before the holy image go the Singers; then the Priests, then the Taper-bearer with the pastoral staff; and the mitre is borne in the middle.

Then the Proto-Deacon and a Deacon go with censers and cense the holy relics and the Bishop; and over the paten Deacons bear two or four sacramental fans. Before the Bishop Sub-Deacons bear the double-branched and triple-branched candlesticks (dikíri and trikíri).

Then the Singers chant the Hymn, in Tone III.:

O Good·One, who didst found thy Church upon the rock of faith, direct thou aright our petitions therein; and accept thou the people who, in faith, do cry unto thee: Save us, O our God, save us.

If there be time, they sing also the following Theme-Songs (Irmosí):

Tone III., Song III.

O Lord, the Confirmation of those who set their hope on thee, confirm thou thy Church, which thou hast bought with thy precious blood.

Tone VIII., Song III.

O Master and Creator of the vault of heaven, and Founder of the Church, establish thou me in thy love, O thou who alone lovest mankind; the Summit of desire, the Confirmation of the faithful.

Tone V., Song III.

Thou who upon nothing, by thy command, didst erect the earth, and didst suspend it, hanging unsupported: Upon the rock immovable of thy commandments, O Christ, establish thou thy Church, O thou who alone art good and lovest mankind.

When they come to the Church which is to be consecrated, they circle round about it from the western door to the southern side, and so on to the east; (13) And a Priest goeth before, and sprinkleth the Church with holy water. And when they come in front of the great door of the Church, the Singers chant the Hymns, in Tone VII.:

O holy Martyrs, who fought the good fight and have received your crowns: Entreat ye the Lord that our souls may be saved.

Glory to thee, O Christ-God, the Apostles' boast, the Martyrs' joy, whose preaching was the consubstantial Trinity.

Then the Bishop taketh from his head the paten with the holy relics, and setteth it on the table prepared in front of the church doors. And he doeth reverence to the holy relics thrice: and putteth on his mitre, and signeth the Priests on either side with the sign of the cross. And while the Singers chant the Hymns, they enter the Temple.

And the doors being shut or screened with a curtain, the Clergy stand with the holy images, the Gospels and the cross, behind the table which is in front of the door, turning toward the west; and on the table is spread an altar-cloth, and at the corners stand four candlesticks, or two; and the Deacons hold the sacramental fans over the holy relics.

Then the Proto-Deacon bringeth the censer to the Bishop. And the Bishop, taking it, censeth the holy paten thrice three times, as also the book of the Holy Gospels, and the cross, and the holy images (ikóni), on the right and on the left; and also the Clergy.

And after the censing, the Proto-Deacon taketh the censer from the Bishop, and censeth the Bishop thrice.

And the Bishop, standing before the holy relics, saith:

Blessed art thou always, O Christ our God, now, and ever, and unto ages of ages.

And the Singers within the Temple respond: Amen.

Then the Bishop saith:

Receive your princes, O ye gates, and be ye lifted up, ye everlasting doors, and the King of Glory shall come in.

And the Singers within the Temple sing:

Who is this King of Glory?

And again, for the second time, the Bishop proclaimeth:

Receive your princes, O ye gates, and be ye lifted up, ye everlasting doors, and the King of Glory shall come in.

Singers. Who is this King of Glory?

Proto-Deacon. Let us pray to the Lord.

Singers. Lord, have mercy.

The Bishop's mitre is then removed, and he saith, in a loud voice, this Prayer:

Blessed be thou forever, O God and Father of our Lord Jesus Christ, who through the veil of his flesh hath consecrated for us an entrance into the Church of the first-born, who are written in heaven, where is the abode of those who rejoice, and the voice of gladness: Do thou, the same Lord who lovest mankind, look upon us, thy sinful and unworthy servants, who now celebrate the renewal of the honourable Temple of N., after the pattern of thy most holy Church, that is, of our own body, which thou hast vouchsafed unto us by thine all-laudable Apostle Paul to call thy Temple (and members of thy Christ); and establish thou it immovable unto the end of time, and glorified in thee.   And vouchsafe that without condemnation we may offer therein praises and exaltations unto thy glory, and unto thine Only-begotten Son, our Lord Jesus Christ, and thy Holy Spirit, with understanding, and with all emotion; and that those who worship thee in thy fear may show themselves worthy of thy divine bounties; and that these prayers offered up by us and by all thy people unto thine ineffable loving-kindness may be acceptable unto thy goodness: Through the prayers of our most holy Lady, the Birth-giver of God, and ever-virgin Mary.

Exclamation.

For holy art thou, O our God, who restest on the Saints.   And unto thee do we ascribe glory, to the Father, and to the Son, and to the Holy Spirit, now, and ever, and unto ages of ages.

Choir. Amen.

Bishop. Peace be with you all.

Choir. And with thy spirit.

Proto-Deacon. Bow your heads unto the Lord.

Choir. To thee, O Lord.

And the Bishop reciteth, secretly, *this Prayer of the Entrance.*

O Master, Lord our God, who hast appointed in heaven, ranks and hosts of Angels and Archangels for the ministry of thy glory: Cause that with our entrance may enter also the holy Angels, with us serving thee and with us glorifying thy goodness. *Secretly.*

Exclamation.

For unto thee are due all glory, honour and worship, to the Father, and to the Son, and to the Holy Spirit, now, and ever, and unto ages of ages.

Choir. Amen.

Then the Bishop taketh the paten with the holy relics, and signeth the doors of the Church in cross-form, saying:

The Lord of Hosts, he is the King of Glory.

And the Choir singeth:

The Lord of Hosts, he is the King of Glory.

And while the Choir singeth this for the last time, the table is removed, and the Bishop setteth the paten with the holy relics on his head; and they enter the Temple.   At that moment the Choir singeth the Hymn in Tone IV.

Forasmuch as thou hast shown forth the splendour of the firmament on high, and the beauty of the holy habitation of thy glory here below, O Lord: Establish thou the same forever, and accept our petitions continually offered unto thee therein; through the Birth-giver of God, O thou who art the life and the Resurrection of all men.

And the Bishop goeth into the holy Sanctuary, through the Holy Door, and setteth the paten with the holy relics on the holy Altar, and doeth reverence to the holy relics. And the Bishop's mitre is put upon him. Then the Proto-Deacon bringeth the censer to the Bishop, and the Bishop taketh it, and censeth the holy relics thrice three times, and his fellow-clergy, on both sides. And the Proto-Deacon, taking the censer from the Bishop, censeth the Bishop thrice.

The Bishop prayeth, and blesseth his fellow-ministers, and taketh the veil and star-cover from the paten; and the Sacristan bringeth the holy Chrism, and the coffer for the holy relics, which is beneath the Altar. After him the Sub-Deacon bringeth the wax-mastic, somewhat cooled. And the Bishop taketh the holy relics, unfolding them from the paper in which they have been wrapped, in three portions, encased in wax, and placeth them in the coffer, having first anointed them with the holy Chrism; and poureth of the wax-mastic, and giveth the coffer to the Sacristan.

And the Sacristan, taking it, and kissing the holy hand of the Bishop, closeth the coffer, and layeth it under the Altar, in the central pillar.

Then the Bishop layeth the prepared particles in the corporal (or corporals), having first anointed inside a little bag in the centre of each corporal with the holy Chrism, and maketh them fast with wax-mastic with a special small paddle. (14)

[When there is no other church in the vicinity of the Temple to be consecrated, the holy relics are set, in the same manner, on the preceding evening, upon a lectern in front of the holy picture (ikóna) of the Saviour, in the Temple which is to be conse-crated. And when the time is come to go for the holy relics, the Bishop issueth forth from the doors of the Church, and standeth over against the relics, on his eagle rug, and praying, he blesseth his fellow-clergy; and the Bishop taketh the censer, and censeth the holy relics thrice: and the Choir singeth the Hymn already set forth (page 503): Thy Church which, in all the world, . . . Glory . . . now, . . .; and the Collect-Hymn: The universe offereth unto thee, O Lord, . . . (See page 504.)

And when the Choir hath finished singing, the Proto-Deacon saith the Little Litany: Again, yet again, . . . (page 502) before the holy relics, and all things are done according to the ritual, as herein before set forth. And the Bishop taketh the holy relics on his head, and goeth with the cross round about the Church, according to the ritual. And when it is in no wise possible to make the circuit of the Church with the holy relics, then they go forth before the great door of the Temple, and the Bishop setteth the holy relics on the table there made ready, and doeth reverence to the holy relics, and taketh the censer from the Proto-Deacon, and censeth the holy relics three times; and everything is done according to the order already prescribed. And after all hath been accomplished, the Bishop setteth the holy relics on his head, and having blessed therewith the great door of the church, he setteth them again upon his head; and entering the Sanctuary, he maketh the circuit of the Sanctuary once with the holy relics, instead of going round about the Temple, as should have been done; and he setteth the holy relics upon the holy Altar, and layeth them in the coffer, and in the corporals, and doth the rest, according to the order set forth above.]

And when this hath been accomplished, the Proto-Deacon saith:

Let us pray to the Lord.
Priests. Lord, have mercy.

The Bishop saith the following Prayer:

O Lord our God, who hast bestowed upon the holy Martyrs which suffered for thy sake this glory also, that their relics should be sown abroad in all the earth, in thy holy churches, and should bring forth fruits of healing: Do thou, the same Master, who art the giver of all good things, through the intercessions of the saints whose relics thou hast graciously permitted to be placed in this thy most honourable Altar (*these thy most honourable Altars*), enable us uncondemned to offer unto thee thereon the unbloody sacrifice: And grant us all those petitions which are unto salvation, vouchsafing also to the relics therein of those who have suffered for thy holy Name, that they may work miracles unto our salvation.

Exclamation.

For thine are the kingdom and the power and the glory, of the Father, and of the Son, and of the Holy Spirit, now, and ever, and unto ages of ages.

The Priests. Amen.

Then the Proto-Deacon saith:

Again, yet again, on bended knees, let us pray to the Lord.

And the Bishop, kneeling (and the people there present in the Temple kneel also) reciteth, in the hearing of all, this Prayer:

O Lord our God, who by thy word alone didst bring into existence creation, and who in unutterable wise didst adorn it diversely, and didst send down thy Holy Spirit, gathering it together, and hast poured forth this light of the sun unto its renewal; who didst inspire Moses, well-pleasing in thy sight, to add unto thine exceedingly good creation a certain special praise, and to say: Thou didst behold the light, that it was good, and didst call it Day: which, also, we have beheld, even this most radiant sun that every day reneweth creation, and do glorify thee, the Sun of the true day, and thy light which hath no setting; Who, through thy Son, hast commanded us to renew our nature by thy Holy Spirit, that through the gift thereof thy Saints may shine like the sun: We pray thee, and beseech thee, the Father of the Word, our Lord and our God (forasmuch as, through thine unutterable love toward mankind and thy boundless mercy, creation and the ancient covenant, — which was the image of the new covenant, — in thy divine revelation of thyself on Mount Sinai, and that wondrous Bush that burned, and the tabernacle of assembly, and the exceeding beautiful Temple of Solomon, received renewal): with merciful eyes look thou upon us, thy sinful and unworthy servants, who are here present in this house like unto heaven, which is the praise of the universe, a true altar of thine ineffable glory. And send down upon us, and upon thine inheritance thy most Holy Spirit, and after the manner of the divine David renew within our hearts a right spirit, and establish us with thy sovereign Spirit. And grant unto our most God-fearing Ruler, N., victories and conquests over enemies both visible and invisible; and unto us peace and concord. And give remission of sins to those who have diligently completed this building and consecration of a temple out of love to thee, O God: Grant them those petitions which are unto salvation; stir them up to do thy commandments; vouchsafe unto them the renewal of the gift of thy Holy Spirit, that uncondemned they may worship thee, the only true God, and Jesus Christ whom thou hast sent: Through the prayers of the Birth-giver of God (*and of N., the Saint to whom the Church is dedicated*), and all of thy Saints.   Amen.

And after the Prayer the Bishop riseth, as do likewise the others, and the Proto-Deacon saith:

Succour us, save us, have mercy upon us, raise us up, and keep us, O God, by thy grace.

(*And the rest of the Little Litany.   See page 502.*)
The Ascription: The Bishop.

For holy art thou, O our God, and restest on the holy, honourable Martyrs, who have suffered for thy sake; and unto thee do we ascribe glory, to the Father, and to the Son, and to the Holy Spirit, now, and ever, and unto ages of ages. —— *Choir.* Amen.

Then the Bishop goeth to the place where he is vested, if such a place there be, with his pastoral staff.   But if there be no vesting-place, he standeth on the tribune in front of the Sanctuary.   And the Priests take their stand on either side, according to the ritual.   And when the Bishop hath stood there and prayed, he blesseth those present.
The Proto-Deacon reciteth the Litany.

Have mercy upon us, O God, according to thy great mercy, we beseech thee: hearken, and have mercy. ℞

Here follow petitions for the Ruler of the Land and for all the Authorities, according to the elements and nationalities of which the Parish is constituted.

Furthermore we pray for our Most Holy Synod (*or* Patriarch); for our Bishop (*or* Archbishop, *or* Metropolitan), N.: ℞

Furthermore we pray for all their Christ-loving Army and Navy. ℞

Furthermore we pray for the blessed and ever-memorable founders of this holy Temple. ℞

Furthermore we pray for mercy, life, peace, health, salvation, forgiveness and remission of sins for the servants of God, our brethren of this holy Temple. ℞

Furthermore we pray for those who bear fruit and do good work in this holy and all-honourable Temple: for those who labour in its service; for the singers, and for the people here present, who await in firm hope the great and rich mercies which are from thee. ℞

Choir. Lord, have mercy.   (Thrice.)

And the Bishop maketh the Exclamation.

For thou art a merciful God, who lovest mankind, and unto thee do we ascribe glory, to the Father, and to the Son, and to the Holy Spirit, now and ever, and unto ages of ages.

Choir. Amen.

Then the Sacristan bringeth to the Bishop a cross upon a salver. And the Bishop taketh the cross, and standing on that same vesting-place (or on the tribune before the Sanctuary) blesseth thrice with the cross, on all four sides: to the east, and the west, and the south, and the north. And the Proto-Deacon censeth over against the cross thrice on each side, and passing over, saith: Let us all say, Lord, have mercy. *(Thrice.)*

Choir. Lord, have mercy. *(Thrice.)*

After the blessing, the Proto-Deacon saith: Wisdom!

And the Bishop, laying the cross upon the Sacristan's salver, goeth (if he hath been standing upon the vesting-place) to the tribune before the Sanctuary, bearing his pastoral staff, saying:

O most holy Birth-giver of God, save us.

Choir. More honourable than the Cherubim, and beyond compare more glorious than the Seraphim, thou who without defilement barest God the Word, true Birth-giver of God, we magnify thee.

Bishop. Glory to thee, O Christ-God our hope; glory to thee.

Choir. Glory . . . now, and ever, . . . Lord, have mercy. *(Thrice.)* Master, bless.

And the Bishop, ascending the tribune, and giving his pastoral staff, again taketh the cross, and giveth the Benediction with the cross. And after the Benediction the Proto-Deacon proclaimeth Many years. *And after the* Many years, *the Deacon bringeth the Bishop holy water. And the Bishop sprinkleth with the holy water the wall, west, north and south. After the sprinkling, the Bishop himself kisseth the precious cross, and after him the other Ecclesiastics and the People kiss it likewise; and he sprinkleth each of them with holy water. And while the People salute it, the Choir singeth:* Many Years. *(See page 549.)*

And when this hath been sung, the Hours are begun. At the Liturgy, the Gradual (Prokimen) of the Consecration and of the Saint of the Temple are used. The Epistle is: Hebrews ix. 1–8, *and that of the Temple. The Gospel is:* John x. 22–27, *and that of the Temple.*

A SERVICE OF THANKSGIVING FOR AN ANSWER TO PRAYER, AND FOR EVERY FAVOUR FROM GOD

Every Orthodox Christian should know in what manner he is bound to return thanks to God our Benefactor, for every answer to prayer, and for every favour received at his hands, whether for the soul or body; either individually or for all the people; either privately in his own chamber or publicly in church.

If the following Thanksgiving is to be celebrated, not in connection with the Liturgy but after the Matins or Vesper Service, the Priest, vested in his stole and chasuble, and standing in front of the holy Altar after having censed the same in the form of a cross, beginneth as follows:

Glory to the Holy, and Consubstantial, and Undivided Trinity, always, now, and ever, and unto ages of ages.

Choir. Amen.

Then is read:

O heavenly King, the Comforter, Spirit of Truth, who art in all places and fillest all things; Treasury of good things and Giver of life: Come, and take up thine abode in us, and cleanse us from every stain; and save our souls, O Good One.

O Holy God, Holy Mighty, Holy Immortal One, have mercy upon us. (*Thrice.*)

Glory to the Father, and to the Son, and to the Holy Spirit, now, and ever, and unto ages of ages. Amen.

O all-holy Trinity, have mercy upon us. O Lord, wash away our sins. O Master, pardon our transgressions. O Holy One, visit and heal our infirmities, for thy Name's sake.

Lord, have mercy. (*Thrice.*)

Our Father, who art in heaven, Hallowed be thy Name. Thy kingdom come. Thy will be done on earth, As it is in heaven. Give us this day our daily bread. And forgive us our trespasses, As we forgive those who trespass against us. And lead us not into temptation; But deliver us from the Evil One:

For thine is the kingdom, and the power, and the glory, of the Father, and of the Son, and of the Holy Spirit, now, and ever, and unto ages of ages.

Choir. Amen.

O come, let us worship God our King. O come, let us worship and fall down before Christ, our King and our God. O come, let us worship and fall down before the Very Christ, our King and our God. O come, let us worship and fall down before him. (*Three reverences.*)

Psalm CXVIII.

O give thanks unto the Lord, for he is gracious: because his mercy endureth forever. Let Israel now confess that he is gracious, and that his mercy endureth forever. Let the house of Aaron now confess that his mercy endureth forever. Yea, let them now that fear the Lord confess that his mercy endureth forever. I called upon the Lord in trouble, and the Lord heard me at large. The Lord is on my side, I will not fear what man doeth unto me. The Lord taketh my part with them that help me, therefore shall I see my desire upon mine enemies. It is better to trust in the Lord than to put any confidence in man. It is better to trust in the Lord than to put any confidence in princes. All nations compassed me round about; but in the Name of the Lord will I destroy them. They kept me in on every side, they kept me in, I say, on every side, but in the Name of the Lord will I destroy them. They came about me like bees, and are extinct even as the fire among the thorns; for in the Name of the Lord will I destroy them. Thou hast thrust sore at me, that I might fall: but the Lord was my help. The Lord is my strength and my song, and is become my salvation. The voice of joy and health is in the dwellings of the righteous: the right hand of the Lord bringeth mighty things to pass. The right hand of the Lord hath the preëminence; the right hand of the Lord bringeth mighty things to pass. I shall not die, but live, and declare the works of the Lord. The Lord hath chastened and corrected me, but he hath not given me over unto death. Open me the gates of righteousness, that I may go into them, and give thanks unto the Lord. This is the gate of the Lord: the righteous shall enter into it. I will thank thee, for thou hast heard me, and art become my salvation. The same stone which the builders rejected is become the head-stone in the corner. This is the Lord's doing, and it is marvellous in our eyes. This is the day the Lord hath made: we will rejoice and be glad in it. Help me now, O Lord: O Lord, send us now prosperity. Blessed be he that cometh in the Name of the Lord. We have wished you good luck, ye that are of the house of the Lord. God is the Lord who hath showed us light: bind the sacrifice with cords, yea, even unto the horns of the altar. Thou art my God, and I will thank thee. O give thanks unto the Lord, for he is gracious, and his mercy endureth forever.

Glory to the Father, and to the Son, and to the Holy Spirit, now, and ever, and unto ages of ages. Amen.

Alleluia, alleluia, alleluia. Glory to thee, O God. (*Thrice.*)

Then the Deacon reciteth the customary Litany.

In peace let us pray to the Lord.
Choir. Lord, have mercy.

For the peace that is from above, and for the salvation of our souls: ℞

For the peace of the whole world; for the welfare of God's holy Churches, and for the union of all: ℞

For this holy Temple, and for those who with faith, devoutness, and in the fear of God have entered therein: ℞

For our Most Holy Synod (*or* Patriarch); for our Bishop (*or* Archbishop, *or* Metropolitan), N.; for the honourable Presbytery, the Diaconate in Christ; for all the clergy and the laity: ℞

Here follow petitions for the Ruler of the Land and for all the Authorities, according to the elements and nationalities of which the Parish is constituted.

That he will aid them in all things, and subdue under their feet every foe and adversary: ℞

For this city, and for every city and land; and for those who with faith dwell therein. ℞

For healthful seasons, for abundance of the fruits of the earth, and for peaceful times: ℞

For those who travel by sea or by land; for the sick and suffering; for those who are in captivity, and for their salvation: ℞

That he will graciously accept this present thanksgiving and supplication of us unworthy sinners on his most heavenly Altar, and in his compassion have mercy upon us: ℞

That he will not despise the thanksgiving of us his unprofitable servants, which we offer with humble hearts for the benefits that we have received from him; but that it may be acceptable unto him as sweet-smelling incense, and a whole burnt-offering: ℞

That he will hearken now unto the voice of petition of us, his unworthy servants, and will always fulfil the good intention and desire of his faithful, as may be most expedient for them; and, in that he is bountiful, may always bestow his benefits upon us, and grant unto his holy Church and unto every faithful servant of his their petitions: ℞

That he will deliver his holy Church (and his servants, NN.; *or* his servant, N.) and us all from every tribulation, wrath, peril and necessity, and from all enemies, both visible and invisible; and that he will always hedge about his faithful people with health, long life, and peace, and the host of his holy Angels: ℞

Succour us, save us, have mercy upon us, and keep us, O God, by thy grace.

Choir. Lord, have mercy.

Calling to remembrance our most holy, all-undefiled, most blessed and glorious Lady, the Birth-giver of God and ever-virgin Mary, with all the Saints, let us commend ourselves, and each other, and all our life unto Christ our God.

let us pray to the Lord. Choir. Lord, have mercy.

Choir. To thee, O Lord.

Priest. For unto thee are due all glory, honour and worship, to the Father, and to the Son, and to the Holy Spirit, now, and ever, and unto ages of ages.

Choir. Amen.

Then: God is the Lord, and hath revealed himself unto us. Blessed is he that cometh in the Name of the Lord.

Verse (Stikh) 1: O give thanks unto the Lord, for he is gracious; because his mercy endureth forever.

Verse 2: All the nations compassed me about, but in the Name of the Lord have I driven them back.

Verse 3: I shall not die, but live, and declare the works of the Lord.

Verse 4: The stone which the builders rejected, the same is become the head of the corner. This is the Lord's doing, and it is marvellous in our eyes.

And the following Hymns (Tropari), in Tone IV.:

We, thine unworthy servants, O Lord, grateful for thy great benefits which thou hast showed upon us, glorifying thee do praise, bless, give thanks, sing, and magnify thy loving-kindness, and with love do cry aloud unto thee in humble submissiveness: O our Benefactor and our Saviour, glory to thee.

Glory to the Father, and to the Son, and to the Holy Spirit. (*Tone III.*)

O Master, who hast freely vouchsafed thy benefits and gifts unto thine unprofitable servants, zealously resorting unto thee, we offer unto thee thanksgiving according to our strength, and glorifying thee as our Benefactor and our Creator, we cry aloud: Glory to thee, O God most bountiful.

Now, and ever, and unto ages of ages. Amen. (*Tone III.*)

O Birth-giver of God, the Helper of Christians, having acquired thy protection, we thy servants gratefully do cry aloud unto thee: Hail, most pure Virgin Birth-giver of God! And from all calamities deliver thou us always by thy prayers, O thou who alone art a speedy Helper in trouble.

Deacon. Let us attend.

Priest. Peace be with you all.——*Reader.* And with thy spirit.

Deacon. Wisdom! Let us attend.

Reader. The Gradual (*Prokímen*), in the Fourth Tone. I will sing praises unto the Lord, because he hath dealt so lovingly with me, yea I will praise the Name of the Lord Most Highest.

Verse: My heart shall rejoice in thy salvation.

Then the Epistle is read:

(*Ephesians v. 8–21.*) Brethren, walk ye as children of the light (for the fruit of the Spirit is in all goodness and righteousness and truth);

proving what is acceptable unto the Lord. And have no fellowship with the unfruitful works of darkness, but rather reprove them. For it is a shame even to speak of those things which are done of them in secret. But all things that are discovered are made manifest by the light: for whatsoever doth make manifest is light. Wherefore he saith, Awake thou that sleepest, and arise from the dead, and Christ shall give thee light. See then that ye walk circumspectly, not as fools, but as wise, redeeming the time, because the days are evil. Wherefore be ye not unwise, but understanding what the will of the Lord is. And be not drunk with wine, wherein is excess; but be filled with the Spirit; speaking to yourselves in psalms and hymns and spiritual songs, singing and making melody in your heart to the Lord; giving thanks always for all things unto God and the Father, in the name of our Lord Jesus Christ; submitting yourselves one to another in the fear of God.

[On Days commemorating Victories:

(*2 Cor. ii. 14–16.*) Now, brethren, thanks be unto God, which always causeth us to triumph in Christ, and maketh manifest the savour of his knowledge to us in every place. For we are unto God a sweet savour of Christ, in them that are saved, and in them that perish: To the one we are the savour of death unto death; and to the other the savour of life unto life. And who is sufficient for these things?

(*1 Tim. i. 17.*) Now unto the King eternal, immortal, invisible, the only wise God, be honour and glory unto ages of ages. Amen.]

Priest. Peace be unto thee.
Reader. And to thy spirit.
Deacon. Wisdom!
Reader. Alleluia, *in the Fourth Tone.*
Deacon. And that he will graciously vouchsafe unto us to hear his Holy Gospel, let us pray to the Lord.
Choir. Lord, have mercy. (*Thrice.*)
Deacon. Wisdom, O believers!   Let us listen to the Holy Gospel.
Priest. Peace be with you all.
Choir. And with thy spirit.
Deacon. Let us attend.
Priest. The Lesson from the holy Gospel of Luke.
Choir. Glory to thee, O Lord; glory to thee.

The Priest then readeth the Gospel.

(*Luke xvii. 12–19.*) And as Jesus entered into a certain village, there met him ten men that were lepers, which stood afar off: and they lifted up their voices, and said, Jesus, Master, have mercy on us. And when he saw them, he said unto them, Go show yourselves unto the priests. And it came to pass, that, as they went, they were cleansed. And one of them, when he saw that he was healed, turned back, and with a loud voice glorified God. And fell down on his face at his feet, giving him thanks: and he was a Samaritan. And Jesus answering said, Were there not ten cleansed? but where are the nine? There are not found that returned to give glory to God, save this stranger. And he said unto him, Arise, go thy way: thy faith hath made thee whole.

Choir. Glory to thee, O Lord; glory to thee.

And immediately the Deacon reciteth the following Litany:

Have mercy upon us, O God, according to thy great mercy, we beseech thee: hearken, and have mercy. ℟

Returning thanks with fear and trembling, as unprofitable servants, unto thy loving-kindness, O Lord, our Saviour and our Master, for thy benefits which thou hast poured out abundantly upon thy servants, we fall down in worship, and offer unto thee praise as God, and with fervour do cry aloud unto thee: Deliver thou thy servants from all calamities, and in that thou art merciful fulfil thou always the desires of us all as may be expedient for us, we diligently entreat thee: hearken, and have mercy. ℟

In that thou now hast mercifully hearkened unto the supplications of thy servants, O Lord, and hast manifested upon us the tender compassion of thy love for mankind, so also, in time to come, despising us not, do thou fulfil, unto thy glory, all good desires of thy faithful people, and reveal unto us all thy rich mercy, disregarding all our iniquities, we beseech thee: hearken, and have mercy. ℟

And may this our thanksgiving be as sweet-smelling incense, as a fat whole burnt-offering before the majesty of thy glory, O all-gracious Master; and send thou down always upon thy servants, in that thou art beneficent, thy rich mercies and bounties; and deliver from all assaults of enemies, both visible and invisible, thy holy Church, and this city; and grant unto all thy people length of days, sinless and healthful, and increase in all virtue, we beseech thee, O all-bountiful King: mercifully hearken, and speedily show mercy. ℟

Choir. Lord, have mercy. (*Thrice.*)

Exclamation.

Priest. Hear us, O God our Saviour, the hope of all the ends of the earth, and of those who are far off upon the sea; and show mercy, show mercy, O Master, upon us sinners, and be merciful unto us.

For thou art a merciful God who lovest mankind, and unto thee we ascribe glory, to the Father, and to the Son, and to the Holy Spirit, now, and ever, and unto ages of ages.

Choir. Amen.

And making three reverences before the holy Altar, the Deacon saith:

Let us pray to the Lord

Choir. Lord, have mercy.

Then the Priest, with all heed and devoutness, readeth the following Prayer, aloud:

O Lord Jesus Christ our God, the God of all mercies and bounties, whose mercy is immeasurable, and whose love for mankind is an unfathomable deep: falling down in adoration before thy majesty, with fear and trembling, as unprofitable servants, and now humbly rendering thanks unto thy loving-kindness for thy benefits bestowed upon thy servants, NN. (*or* upon thy servant, N.), we glorify thee, we praise thee, we sing thee, and we magnify thee as our Lord, and Master, and Benefactor; and again falling down before thee, we humbly thank thee, supplicating thy boundless and inexpressible mercy. And in that thou hast now graciously vouchsafed to accept the petitions of thy servants and to fulfil them, so also grant that henceforth thy holy Church and this city may be delivered from every hostile assault, and may be vouchsafed peace and tranquillity, and that increasing in true love of thee, and in all virtues, all thy faithful people may receive all thy benefits; and that we may ever offer thanksgiving unto thee, together with thy Father who is from everlasting, and thine all-holy, and good, and lifegiving Spirit, God glorified in one Person; and that we may say exceeding good things, and sing:

And immediately he exclaimeth, in a very loud voice:

Glory to thee, O God our Benefactor, unto ages of ages.

And standing in the centre of the Church, the Choir singeth: Amen.

Then immediately is sung the Great Anthem of Praise: Glory be to God on high (*see page 34*): *Or instead, the Anthem of St. Ambrose, Bishop of Milan, is sung:* We praise thee, O God, . . . (*See page 539.*)

And when it is finished, the Deacon saith:

Wisdom!

Reader. More honourable than the Cherubim, and beyond compare more glorious than the Seraphim, thou who without defilement barest God the Word, true Birth-giver of God, we magnify thee.

Glory to the Father, and to the Son, and to the Holy Spirit, now, and ever, and unto ages of ages. Amen. Lord, have mercy. (*Thrice.*) Bless.

And the Priest pronounceth the customary BENEDICTION

May Christ, our true God, through the prayers of his most holy Mother, of Saint N. (*the Saint for the day*), and of all the Saints, have mercy upon us and save us, forasmuch as he is good and loveth mankind.

And blessing the People with his hand, he saith:

May the blessing of the Lord, through his grace, and bounties, and love of mankind, be upon you always, now, and ever, and unto ages of ages. Amen.

A SERVICE OF PRAYER WHEN CHILDREN BEGIN THEIR INSTRUCTION

The Priest beginneth: Blessed is our God, always, now, and ever, and unto ages of ages.

Choir. O heavenly King, . . .

Reader. O Holy God, Holy Mighty, . . . Glory . . . now, and ever, . . . O all-holy Trinity, . . . Lord, have mercy. (*Thrice.*) Glory, . . . now, and ever, . . . Our Father, . . . For thine is the kingdom, . . . O come, let us worship . . . (*See page* 512.)

PSALM XXXIV.

I will alway give thanks unto the Lord; his praise shall ever be in my mouth. My soul shall make her boast in the Lord; the humble shall hear thereof, and be glad. O praise the Lord with me, and let us magnify his Name together. I sought the Lord, and he heard me; yea, he delivered me out of all my fear. They had an eye unto him, and were lightened; and their faces were not ashamed. Lo, the poor crieth, and the Lord heareth him; yea, and saveth him out of all his troubles. The angel of the Lord tarrieth round about them that fear him, and delivereth them. O taste, and see, how gracious the Lord is: blessed is the man that trusteth in him. O fear the Lord, ye that are his saints; for they that fear him lack nothing. The lions do lack, and suffer hunger; but they who seek the Lord shall want no manner of thing that is good. Come, ye children, and hearken unto me; I will teach you the fear of the Lord. What man is he that lusteth to live, and would fain see good days? Keep thy tongue from evil, and thy lips, that they speak no guile. Eschew evil, and do good; seek peace, and ensue it. The eyes of the Lord are over the righteous, and his ears are open unto their prayers. The countenance of the Lord is against them that do evil, to root out the remembrance of them from the earth. The righteous cry, and the Lord heareth them, and delivereth them out of all their troubles. The Lord is nigh unto them that are of a contrite heart, and will save such as be of an humble spirit. Great are the troubles of the righteous; but the Lord delivereth him out of all. He keepeth all his bones, so that not one of them is broken. But misfortune shall slay the ungodly; and they that hate the righteous shall be desolate. The Lord delivereth the souls of his servants; and all they that put their trust in him shall not be destitute.

Glory to the Father, and to the Son, and to the Holy Spirit, now, and ever, and unto ages of ages. Amen. Alleluia. (*Thrice.*)

And the usual Litany: In peace let us pray to the Lord, . . . *and the rest (see page 514), to the end of the petition:* For those who travel by sea or by land, . . . *after which the following petitions are added:*

That he will send down upon these children the spirit of wisdom and understanding, and will open their minds and their lips, and enlighten their hearts, unto the receiving of precepts of good instruction, let us pray to the Lord.

Choir. Lord, have mercy.

That he will implant in their hearts his godly fear, which is the beginning of wisdom, and will thereby expel from their hearts the turbulence of youth, and enlighten their minds, that they may turn aside from evil and do that which is good: ℞

That he will open their minds to receive, and to understand, and to remember all instruction which is good and profitable for the soul: ℞

That he will grant them the wisdom which abideth with his throne, and will implant it in their hearts, so that he may teach them that which is well-pleasing in his sight: ℞

That he will prosper them in wisdom and in stature, to the glory of God: ℞

That they may have a wise and virtuous life, and prosperity in the Orthodox faith, and may be a joy and consolation to their parents, and pillars of the Orthodox-Catholic Church: ℞

That they and we may be delivered from all tribulation, wrath, peril and necessity: ℞

Succour us, save us, have mercy upon us and keep us, O God, by thy grace. —— *Choir.* Lord, have mercy.

Calling to remembrance our most holy, all-undefiled, most blessed and glorious Lady, the Birth-giver of God and ever-virgin Mary, with all the Saints, let us commend ourselves, and each other, and all our life unto Christ our God.

Choir. To thee, O Lord.

right margin: let us pray to the Lord. *Choir.* Lord, have mercy.

Exclamation.

For unto thee are due all glory, honour and worship, to the Father, and to the Son, and to the Holy Spirit, now, and ever, and unto ages of ages.

Choir. Amen.

Then the following Hymns (Tropari) are read.   Tone VI.:

As thou didst come into the midst of thy Disciples, O Saviour, bestowing upon them peace, so also come thou unto us, and save us.

Of thine unlettered Disciples thy Holy Spirit made teachers, O Christ-God; and by the commingling of tongues He annulled idolatry in that He is almighty.

Glory to the Father, and to the Son, and to the Holy Spirit. (*Tone VIII.*)

Blessed art thou, O Christ our God, who hast revealed fishers most wise, sending down upon them the Holy Spirit, and thereby catching the universe as in a net. O Christ our God, who lovest mankind, glory to thee.

Now, and ever, and unto ages of ages. Amen.

O Protection of Christians that maketh not ashamed, O Mediatrix never-failing with the Creator: Despise not the sinners' voice of supplication; but in that thou art good, come speedily to the aid of us who faithfully call upon thee; make haste to our petition and further our prayer, O Birth-giver of God, who ever protectest them that do thee honour.

Deacon. Let us attend.

Priest. Peace be with you all.

Reader. And with thy spirit.

Deacon. Wisdom! Let us attend.

Reader. The Gradual (*Prokímen*), in the Fourth Tone: Out of the mouths of babes and sucklings hast thou ordained praise.

Verse: My heart shall rejoice in thy salvation.

Then the Reader readeth the Epistle.

(*Ephesians i. 16–19; iii. 16–21.*) Brethren: I cease not to give thanks for you, making mention of you in my prayers; that the God of our Lord Jesus Christ, the Father of glory, may give unto you the spirit of wisdom and revelation in the knowledge of him: the eyes of your understanding being enlightened; that ye may know what is the hope of his calling, and what the riches of the glory of his inheritance in the saints, and what is the exceeding greatness of his power to usward who believe, according to the working of his mighty power. And that ye may know the love of Christ which passeth knowledge, that ye might be filled with all the fulness of God. Now unto him who is able to do exceeding abundantly above all that we ask or think, according to the power that worketh in us, unto him be glory in the Church by Christ Jesus, throughout all ages, world without end. Amen.

Then the Deacon saith:

Wisdom, O believers! Let us listen to the Holy Gospel.

Priest. Peace be with you all.

Choir. And with thy spirit.

Priest. The Lesson from the holy Gospel of Luke.

Deacon. Let us attend.

Choir. Glory to thee, O Lord; glory to thee.

(*Mark x. 13–16.*) At that time they brought young children to him, that he should touch them: and his disciples rebuked those that brought them. But when Jesus saw it, he was much displeased, and said unto them, Suffer the little children to come unto me, and forbid them not; for of such is the kingdom of God. Verily I say unto you, Whosoever shall not receive the kingdom of God as a little child, he shall not enter therein. And he took them up in his arms, put his hands upon them, and blessed them.

Choir. Glory to thee, O Lord; glory to thee.

Then the Deacon reciteth the Augmented Litany as far as: Furthermore we pray for all their Christ-loving Army and Navy. (*See page* 90.)

Then: Furthermore we pray unto the Lord our God, that he will look graciously upon these children, and will send down into their hearts, their minds, and their lips the spirit of wisdom, and of understanding, and of piety, and of his fear; and that he will illumine them with the light of his knowledge, and will bestow upon them strength and steadfastness, that they may quickly apprehend and speedily become wonted to the instruction in his Divine Law, and to all good and profitable learning: furthermore, that he will prosper them in wisdom and understanding, and in all good works to the glory of his holy Name, and will give them health, and make them long-lived, unto the building up and the glory of his Church, let us all say: O Lord, hearken and mercifully have mercy.

Choir. Lord, have mercy. (*Twelve times.*)

Then the Priest exclaimeth: Hear us, O God our Saviour, . . . (*See page* 517.)

Choir. Amen.

Deacon. Let us pray to the Lord.

Choir. Lord, have mercy.

And the Priest, with all heed and emotion, readeth, aloud, the following Prayer:

O Lord our God and Creator, who hast honoured us men with thine own image; who hast taught thine elect, so that most wise are they who give heed to thy teaching; who revealest wisdom unto babes; who hast imparted thy teaching unto Solomon and unto all who have sought thy wisdom: Open thou the hearts, the minds, and the lips of these thy servants, that they may receive the power of thy law, and successfully apprehend the useful precepts which shall be taught them, to the glory of thine all-holy Name, to the profit and building up of thy holy Church, and that they may understand thy good and perfect will. Deliver them from every hostile oppression; preserve them in Orthodoxy and the faith, and in all uprightness and purity all the days of their life, that they may advance in wisdom, and in the fulfilling of thy commandments: that, being thus prepared, they may glorify thine all-holy Name, and become heirs of thy kingdom. For thou art God mighty in mercy, and gracious in strength; and unto thee is due glory, to the Father, and to the Son, and to the Holy Spirit, now, and ever, and unto ages of ages. Amen.

Deacon. Wisdom!

Choir. More honourable than the Cherubim, and beyond compare more glorious than the Seraphim, thou who without defilement barest God the Word, true Birth-giver of God, we magnify thee.

Priest. Glory to thee, O Christ-God, our hope; glory to thee.

Choir. Glory to the Father, and to the Son, and to the Holy Spirit, now, and ever, and unto ages of ages. Amen.

Lord, have mercy. (*Thrice.*) Bless.

And the customary BENEDICTION.

May Christ, our true God, through the prayers of his all-holy Mother; of the holy, glorious and all-laudable Apostles; of the holy, righteous Ancestors of God, Joachim and Anna; and of all the Saints, have mercy upon us, and save us, forasmuch as he is good, and loveth mankind.

Then the Priest, blessing the Children with the cross, saith:

The blessing of the Lord, with his grace, and bounties, and love toward mankind, be upon you always, now, and ever, and unto ages of ages. Amen.

Then the Children kiss the holy cross, and the Priest sprinkleth them with holy water.

THE RITE OF BLESSING FOR A JOURNEY

The Priest, vested in his priestly stole and chasuble, if the rite be said apart from the Liturgy, beginneth as usual:

Blessed is our God always, now, and ever, and unto ages of ages.

Reader. O heavenly King, . . . O Holy God, Holy Mighty, . . . Our Father, . . . Lord, have mercy. (*Twelve times.*) Glory . . . now and ever, . . . O come, let us worship . . . (*Thrice.*) (*See page* 512.)

PSALM CXLIII.

Hear my prayer, O Lord, and consider my desire; hearken unto me for thy truth and righteousness' sake. And enter not into judgment with thy servant; for in thy sight shall no man living be justified. For the enemy hath persecuted my soul; he hath smitten my life down to the ground; he hath laid me in the darkness, as the men that have been long dead. Therefore is my spirit vexed within me, and my heart within me is desolate. Yet do I remember the time past: I muse upon all thy works; yea I exercise myself in the works of thy hands. I stretch forth my hands unto thee; my soul gaspeth unto thee as a thirsty land. Hear me, O Lord, and that soon; for my spirit waxeth faint: hide not thy face from me, lest I be like unto them that go down into the pit. O let me hear thy loving-kindness betimes in the morning; for in thee is my trust: show thou me the way that I should walk in; for I lift up my soul unto thee. Deliver me, O Lord, from mine enemies; for I flee unto thee to hide me. Teach me to do the thing that pleaseth thee; for thou art my God: let thy loving Spirit lead me forth into the land of righteousness. Quicken me, O Lord, for thy Name's sake; and for thy righteousness' sake bring my soul out of trouble. And of thy goodness slay mine enemies, and destroy all them that vex my soul; for I am thy servant.

Glory to the Father, and to the Son, and to the Holy Spirit, now, and ever, and unto ages of ages. Amen.

Alleluia, alleluia, alleluia. Glory to thee, O God. (*Thrice.*)

And the Deacon, if there be one, or the Priest himself, readeth the Litany:

In peace let us pray to the Lord.

Choir. Lord, have mercy. (*See page* 80.)

And the rest, as far as:

For those who travel by sea or by land; for the sick and the suffering; for those who are in captivity, and for their salvation: ℞

That he will show mercy upon his servant(s), and pardon him (*her, them*) every sin, both voluntary and involuntary, and bless his (*her, their*) journey: ℞

That he will send him (*her, them*) an Angel of Peace, as fellow-traveller and guide, to guard, defend and succour him (*her, them*), and preserve him (*her, them*) unharmed of every evil assault: ℞

That he will shield him (*her, them*) from all attacks and assaults of enemies, and bring him (*her, them*) to his (*her, their*) journey's end and home again unharmed: ℞

That he will give him (*her, them*) a sinless and peaceful journey, and a prosperous return in health, and in all piety and honour: ℞

That he will preserve him (*her, them*) unharmed and invincible against all foes, both visible and invisible, and from the wrath of wicked men: ℞

That he will bless his (*her, their*) good intention, and prosper it, through his grace, unto spiritual and bodily profit: ℞

let us pray to the Lord. Choir. Lord, have mercy.

Succour us, save us, have mercy upon us, and keep us, O God, by thy grace.

Choir. Lord, have mercy.

Calling to remembrance our most holy, all-undefiled, most blessed and glorious Lady, the Birth-giver of God and ever-virgin Mary, with all the Saints, let us commend ourselves, and each other, and all our life unto Christ our God.

Choir. To thee, O Lord.

Exclamation.

For unto thee are due all glory, honour and worship, to the Father, and to the Son, and to the Holy Spirit, now, and ever, and unto ages of ages. —— *Choir.* Amen.

Then: God is the Lord, and hath revealed himself unto us. Blessed is he that cometh in the Name of the Lord. (*Tone II. And the Verses. See page* 515.)

And this Hymn (Tropár).

O Christ, who art the Way and the Truth, send now thine Angel as a fellow-traveller to thy servant(s), preserving him (*her, them*) like Tobias of old, and guarding him (*her, them*) unharmed of every evil thing, and in all prosperity, unto thy glory: through the prayers of the Birth-giver of God, O thou who alone lovest mankind.

In the same Tone.

Glory to the Father, and to the Son, and to the Holy Spirit.

O Saviour, who didst accompany Luke and Cleopas unto Emmaus, accompany thou now also thy servant who is (*servants who are*) minded to travel, delivering him (*her, them*) from every evil assault: For thou canst do all things whatsoever thou wilt, in that thou lovest mankind.

Now, and ever, and unto ages of ages. Amen.

O Protection of Christians that maketh not ashamed, O Mediatrix never-failing with the Creator: . . . (*See page 521.*)

Deacon. Let us attend.

Priest. Peace be with you all.

Deacon. Wisdom! Let us attend.

The Choir singeth the Gradual (Prokímen). Tone IV.

Teach me thy way, O Lord, and I will walk therein, for unto thee have I lifted up my soul.

Verse: Deliver me from mine enemies, O Lord; unto thee have I fled for refuge.

The Epistle: Acts viii. 26–39. And in those days the Angel of the Lord spake unto Philip, saying, Arise, and go toward the south, unto the way that goeth down from Jerusalem unto Gaza, which is a desert. And he arose and went: and, behold, a man of Ethiopia, an eunuch of great authority under Candace, Queen of the Ethiopians, who had the charge of all her treasure, and had come to Jerusalem for to worship, was returning; and sitting in his chariot, read Esaias the prophet. Then the Spirit said unto Philip, Go near, and join thyself to this chariot. And Philip ran thither to him, and heard him read the prophet Esaias, and said, Understandest thou what thou readest? And he said, How can I, except some man should guide me? And he desired Philip that he would come up and sit with him. The place of the scripture which he read was this, He was led as a sheep to the slaughter; and like a lamb dumb before his shearer, so opened he not his mouth: in his humiliation his judgment was taken away: and who shall declare his generation? for his life is taken from the earth. And the eunuch answered Philip, and said, I pray thee, of whom speaketh the prophet this? of himself, or of some other man? Then Philip opened his mouth, and began at the same scripture, and preached unto him Jesus. And as they went on their way, they came unto a certain water: and the eunuch said, See, here is water; what doth hinder me to be baptized? And Philip said, If thou believest with all thine heart, thou mayest. And he answered and said, I believe that Jesus Christ is the son of God. And he commanded the chariot to stand still: and they went down both into the water, both Philip and the eunuch; and he baptized him. And when they were come up out of the water the Spirit of the Lord caught away Philip, that the eunuch saw him no more; and he went on his way rejoicing.

Alleluia. (*According to the Tone.*)

Verse 1: The footsteps of a man are guided by the Lord: he hath longed greatly for his ways.

Verse 2: Reveal thy path unto the Lord, and trust in him, and he shall bring it to pass.

Deacon. Wisdom, O believers!   Let us listen to the Holy Gospel.

Priest. Peace be with you all.

Choir. And with thy spirit.

Deacon. The Lesson from the holy Gospel according to John.

Choir. Glory to thee, O Lord; glory to thee.

Priest. Let us attend.

(*John xiv. 1–10.*) The Lord said unto his disciples: Let not your heart be troubled: ye believe in God, believe also in me.   In my Father's house are many mansions: if it were not so I would have told you.   I go to prepare a place for you.   And if I go and prepare a place for you, I will come again, and receive you unto myself; that where I am, there ye may be also.   And whither I go ye know, and the way ye know. Thomas saith unto him, Lord, we know not whither thou goest, and how can we know the way?   Jesus saith unto him, I am the way, and the truth, and the life: no man cometh unto the Father, but by me.   If ye had known me, ye should have known my Father also: and from henceforth ye know him, and have seen him.   Philip saith unto him, Lord, show us the Father, and it sufficeth us.   Jesus saith unto him, Have I been so long time with you, and yet hast thou not known me, Philip? he that hath seen me hath seen the Father; and how sayest thou then, Show us the Father?   Believest thou not that I am in the Father, and the Father in me?

Choir. Glory to thee, O Lord; glory to thee.

And after the Gospel the Deacon or the Priest saith this Litany (Ekténiya).

O Lord, who dost guide the footsteps of man, graciously look upon thy servant, N. (*servants, NN.*); and pardoning him (*her, them*) every sin, both voluntary and involuntary, bless the good intention of his (*her, their*) counsel, and guide his (*her, their*) goings out and comings in on the journey, we earnestly pray: hearken, and have mercy. R̤

O Lord, who didst most gloriously deliver Joseph from the wrath of his brethren, and didst lead him to Egypt, and through the blessing of thy goodness didst make him to prosper in all things: Bless also this thy servant (*these thy servants*) who purposeth (*purpose*) to travel, and cause his (*her, their*) journey to be tranquil and prosperous, we pray thee: hearken, and have mercy. R̤

O thou who didst send an Angel as companion on their way unto Isaac and Tobias, and thereby didst ensure unto them a peaceful and prosperous journey, and return: Send now also, O Most Gracious One, thine Angel of Peace unto thy servant who through us entreateth (*servants who entreat*) thee, that he may guide him (*her, them*) unto every good deed; and deliver him (*her, them*) from enemies

Choir. Lord, have mercy.

both visible and invisible, and from every evil assault; and enable him (*her, them*) to return in safety, peace and prosperity, unto thy glory, we earnestly pray thee: hearken and have mercy. ℟

O thou who didst accompany Luke and Cleopas on the way to Emmaus, and didst make them to return rejoicing unto Jerusalem through that most glorious knowledge of thee: Accompany thou now also, with thy grace and thy blessing divine, this thy servant who earnestly prayeth (*these thy servants who earnestly pray*) with us; and prosper him (*her, them*) in every good work, to the glory of thine all-holy Name, preserving him (*her, them*) in health and well-being, and bringing him (*her, them*) back again in due season, we pray unto thee, as unto an all-bountiful benefactor: hearken, and have mercy. ℟

And the Priest exclaimeth: Hear us, O God our Saviour, . . . (*See page* 517.)

Deacon. Bowing our heads and our knees devoutly unto the Lord, let us pray to the Lord.

Choir. Lord, have mercy. (*Thrice.*)

And all kneeling, the Priest turneth toward them; and the Holy Door being open, he readeth, in a loud voice, this Prayer:

O Lord Jesus Christ our God, the true and living Way, who didst deign to journey with thine ostensible father Joseph, and thine All-pure Virgin Mother, into Egypt, and didst accompany Luke and Cleopas on their way to Emmaus: We now humbly entreat thee, O all-holy Master, accompany now with thy grace this thy servant (*these thy servants*). And send unto him (*her, them*), as unto thy servant Tobias, an angel guardian and guide, preserving and delivering him (*her, them*) from every evil assault of enemies both visible and invisible; and directing him (*her, them*) unto the fulfilment of thy commandments; and prospering him (*her, them*) in peace, happiness and health; and bringing him (*her, them*) back again in safety and tranquillity. And grant that he (*she, they*) may fulfil all his (*her, their*) good purpose unto thy good pleasure, and favourably to thy glory. For thine it is to show mercy and to save us, and unto thee do we ascribe glory, together with thy Father who hath no beginning, and thine all-holy, and blessed, and life-giving Spirit, now, and ever, and unto ages of ages.

Choir. Amen.

Then the Priest, taking the holy cross, giveth it to him (her, them) *to kiss, and sprinkleth him with holy water, saying:*

May the Lord bless thee (*you*) out of Zion; and so shalt thou (*shall ye*) behold the good things of Jerusalem all the days of thy (*your*) life: and may he direct thy (*your*) journey in peace, unto the glory of his holy Name. Amen.

And immediately he pronounceth the customary Benediction for the day.

Choir. Lord, have mercy.

THE RITE OF BLESSING THOSE WHO ARE ABOUT TO TRAVEL BY WATER

The Priest, vested in his stole and chasuble, beginneth as usual:

Blessed is our God always, now, and ever, and unto ages of ages.
Choir. Amen.
Reader. O heavenly King, . . . (*See page* 512.)   O Holy God, Holy Mighty, . . . Glory . . . now, and ever, . . . Our Father, . . . For thine is the kingdom, . . . Lord, have mercy. (*Twelve times.*)   Glory . . . now, and ever.
O come, let us worship Christ our King.   O come, let us worship and fall down before Christ, our King and our God.   O come, let us worship and fall down before the Very Christ, our King and our God.

Then PSALM CXXI

I will lift up mine eyes unto the hills, from whence cometh my help. My help cometh even from the Lord, who hath made heaven and earth. He will not suffer thy foot to be moved, and he that keepeth Israel shall neither slumber nor sleep.   The Lord himself is thy keeper: the Lord is thy defence upon thy right hand: so that the sun shall not burn thee by day, neither the moon by night.   The Lord shall preserve thee from all evil; yea, it is even he that shall keep thy soul.   The Lord shall preserve thy going out and thy coming in, from this time forth, even forevermore.
Glory to the Father, and to the Son, and to the Holy Spirit, now, and ever, and unto ages of ages.   Amen.
Alleluia, alleluia, alleluia.   Glory to thee, O God.   (*Thrice.*)

And the Deacon saith the Great Litany.

In peace let us pray to the Lord.
Choir. Lord, have mercy.   (*See page* 80.)

And the rest, as far as:

For those who travel by sea or by land; for the sick and the suffering; for those who are in captivity, and for their salvation: let us pray to the Lord.
Choir. Lord, have mercy.
That he will be merciful, and condescending, and easy to be entreated toward his servant, who now, through us, maketh his (*her*) (*servants who now make their*) earnest supplications unto him; and pardoning all his

(*her*, *their*) sins, both voluntary and involuntary, will bless his (*her*, *their*) voyage on the sea: ℟

That, in that he is merciful, he will lull the tempest, restrain the winds, and will grant unto him (*her*, *them*), as unto his Apostles of old, tranquil seas for a voyage undisturbed: ℟

That he will send him (*her*, *them*) his Guardian Angel to guide him (*her*, *them*), and to shield him (*her*, *them*) from every malice of foes both visible and invisible, and to deliver him (*her*, *them*) from drowning in the watery tempest: ℟

That he will bring him (*her*, *them*) over in peace and safety, and conduct him (*her*, *them*) back again in health and tranquillity: ℟

That he will bless the purpose of his (*her*, *their*) counsel and his (*her*, *their*) deeds, unto expedient fulfilment of the same, to the glory of his all-holy Name, and to his (*her*, *their*) spiritual and bodily profit: ℟

That by the might of his grace he will deliver him (*her*, *them*) from all calamities and distress, both of soul and of body; and from sickness, and from sudden death, and from all mortal wounds: and that he will graciously grant him (*her*, *them*), in due season, restoration to his (*her*) home (*their homes*), in health and safety: ℟

Succour us, save us, have mercy upon us, and keep us, O God, by thy grace. —— *Choir*. Lord, have mercy.

Calling to remembrance our most holy, all-undefiled, most blessed and glorious Lady, the Birth-giver of God and ever-virgin Mary, with all the Saints, let us commend ourselves, and each other, and all our life unto Christ our God.

Choir. To thee, O Lord.

Exclamation.

For unto thee are due all glory, honour and worship, to the Father, and to the Son, and to the Holy Spirit, now, and ever, and unto ages of ages.

Choir. Amen.

Then: God is the Lord, and hath revealed himself unto us. Blessed is he that cometh in the Name of the Lord. (*Tone II.*)

(*And the rest. See page* 515.)
And the following Hymns (*Tropari*):

Despise not, O Saviour, those who have recourse unto thee, and who seek from thine omnipotent right hand, as from their Creator and their Master, both aid and blessing. But forasmuch as of old thou didst, by thy word, give unto thine Apostles tranquillity upon the sea, in like manner give thou now also unto this person (*these persons*) a calm and untroubled voyage, and good health: through the prayers of the Birth-giver of God, O thou who alone lovest mankind.

[right margin:] let us pray to the Lord. *Choir*. Lord, have mercy.

Glory to the Father, and to the Son, and to the Holy Spirit. (*Tone V.*)

O Saviour, be thou the helper and deliverer of him (*her*) who hath (*them who have*) set all his (*her, their*) hope on thee: and bless the good purpose of his (*her, their*) deed, as also his (*her, their*) journey; that we all may glorify thee, the sole Giver of all good things.

Now, and ever, and unto ages of ages. Amen.

We flee unto thy protection, O Virgin Birth-giver of God. Despise not thou our prayers in affliction, but from distress deliver us, O only Pure and Blessed One.

Deacon. Let us attend.

Priest. Peace be with you all.

Choir. And with thy spirit.

Deacon. Wisdom! Let us attend.

Reader. The Gradual (*Prokimen*), in the Fourth Tone. Though I walk through the valley of the shadow of death, I will fear no evil, for thou art with me.

Verse: And thy mercy shall follow me all the days of my life.

The Epistle, from the Acts of the Apostles.

(*Acts xxi. 1-7.*) And in those days it came to pass, that after we were gotten from them, and had launched, we came with a straight course unto Coos, and on the day following unto Rhodes, and from thence to Patras. And finding a ship sailing over unto Phenicia, we went aboard, and set forth. Now when we had discovered Cyprus, we left it on the left hand, and sailed unto Syria, and landed at Tyre: for there the ship was to unlade her burden. And finding disciples, we tarried there seven days: who said unto Paul by the Spirit, that he should not go up to Jerusalem. And when we had accomplished those days, we departed and went our way, and they all brought us on our way, with wives and children, till we were out of the city: and we kneeled down on the shore and prayed. And when we had taken our leave one of another, we took ship; and they returned home again. And when we had finished our course from Tyre, we came to Ptolemais, and saluted the brethren, and abode with them one day.

Alleluia. (*According to the Tone.*)

Verse 1: Deliver me from them that hate me, and from the deep waters.

Verse 2: Let not the watery tempest drown me, neither let the deep swallow me up.

Deacon. Wisdom, O believers! Let us listen to the Holy Gospel.

Priest. Peace be with you all.

Choir. And with thy spirit.

Deacon. The Lesson from the holy Gospel according to Mark.

Choir. Glory to thee, O Lord; glory to thee.

Priest. Let us attend.

(*Mark iv. 35–41.*) The Lord said unto his disciples, Let us pass over unto the other side. And when they had sent away the multitude, they took him even as he was in the ship: and there were also with him other little ships. And there arose a great storm of wind, and the waves beat into the ship, so that it was now full. And he was in the hinder part of the ship, asleep on a pillow: and they awake him, and say unto him, Master, carest thou not that we perish? And he arose, and rebuked the wind, and said unto the sea, Peace, be still. And the wind ceased, and there was a great calm. And he said unto them, Why are ye so fearful? how is it that ye have no faith? And they feared exceedingly, and said one to another, What manner of man is this, that even the winds and the sea obey him?

Choir. Glory to thee, O Lord; glory to thee.

Then the Priest or the Deacon saith the Augmented Litany.

Have mercy upon us, O God, according to thy great mercy, we beseech thee: hearken, and have mercy.

Choir. Lord, have mercy. (*Thrice.*)

And the rest (see page 90). To this he addeth:

Do thou, who of old didst rebuke the winds and the sea, and unto the ship tossed by the waves didst give calm by thy word; and didst render thy disciples untroubled: Regard now, also, O Merciful One, the prayers of thy servant who diligently worshippeth (*servants who diligently worship*) thee, and bless his (*her, their*) voyage, granting unto him (*her, them*) a calm, peaceful and untroubled journey, we beseech thee: hearken, and have mercy. ℟

O Saviour, who didst walk upon the water as upon dry land, and didst deliver Peter from drowning by thy right hand almighty: Deliver thou, O Lord, him (*her*) who in faith hath (*those who in faith have*) recourse unto thee, and is directing his (*her*) (*are directing their*) steps to a journey, from all calamities and stormy winds; mercifully granting unto him (*her, them*) a favourable journey and restoration to his (*her, their*) home(s), we beseech thee, O all-bountiful Lord: hearken, and have mercy. ℟

Send thine Angel, O all-merciful Lord, to accompany him (*her, them*) on the way, and to be the guardian of his (*her*) soul and body (*their souls and bodies*), preserving him (*her, them*), and sheltering him (*her, them*) from all enemies, both visible and invisible; and by thy might divine delivering him (*her, them*) from all tribulation, calamity and necessity, from sickness and from mortal wounds; and in due season restore thou him (*her, them*) again to his (*her*) home (*their homes*) in safety: to the glory of thine all-holy Name, we beseech thee, O omnipotent Master: mercifully hearken, and have mercy. ℟

Choir. Lord, have mercy. (Thrice.)

And the Priest maketh the Exclamation:

Hear us, O God, our Saviour, . . . (*See page* 517.)

And the Deacon saith:

Bowing our knees and our heads devoutly unto the Lord, let us pray to the Lord.

Choir. Lord, have mercy. (*Thrice.*)

Then, as all kneel, the Priest, turning to the west and standing at the door of the Church, saith, in a loud voice, this Prayer:

O Master, Lord Jesus Christ our God, who didst walk upon the waters as upon dry land, and didst deign to have thy holy Disciples and Apostles as thy fellow-voyagers in the ship; and didst rebuke the stormy wind, and command the waves of the sea to be still: Be pleased now also (we humbly entreat thee, O Saviour), to sail with this thy servant (*these thy servants*) in this ship (*or* boat), allaying every contrary wind and tempest: And raise up special and timely winds for a prosperous voyage, being thyself ever unto him (*her, them*) a pilot, and a saving, untempestuous and tranquil haven unto the same, and unto his (*her, their*) ship (*or* boat). And as thou didst save Peter from drowning, so also, in sovereign wise, deliver thou this person (*these persons*) from all assaults of enemies, both visible and invisible, and from calamity, and distress, and fear, by thy right hand omnipotent: And graciously vouchsafe that he (*she, they*) may return in peace to his (*her*) home (*their homes*) in health and happiness, having accomplished his (*her, their*) purpose and good undertaking, richly bestowing upon all his (*her, their*) deeds thy rich and inexhaustible grace, and preserving the vessel whole and unharmed. For thou art the Saviour, the Deliverer, and the rich Giver of all good things, both heavenly and earthly, and unto thee do we ascribe glory, to the Father, and to the Son, and to the Holy Spirit, now, and ever, and unto ages of ages.

Choir. Amen.

Then taking the honourable cross, the Priest giveth it to the person(s) to kiss; and he sprinkleth the person(s) with holy water, saying:

May the Lord bless thee (*you*) out of Zion; and so shalt thou (*shall ye*) behold the good things of Jerusalem all the days of thy (*your*) life: and may he direct thy (*your*) journey in peace, unto the glory of his holy Name. Amen.

And immediately he pronounceth the usual Benediction for the day.

THE OFFICE OF THANKSGIVING AT THE NEW YEAR

After the Liturgy is ended, the Deacon saith:

Bless, Master.

Priest. Blessed is the kingdom of the Father, and of the Son, and of the Holy Spirit, now, and ever, and unto ages of ages.

Choir. Amen.

Reader. O come, let us worship God our King. O come, let us worship and fall down before Christ, our King and our God. O come, let us worship and fall down before the Very Christ, our King and our God. O come, let us worship and fall down before him. (*Three reverences.*)

And PSALM LXV.

Thou, O God, art praised in Zion; and unto thee shall the vow be performed in Jerusalem. Thou that hearest the prayer, unto thee shall all flesh come. My misdeeds prevail against me: O be thou merciful unto our sins. Blessed is the man whom thou choosest, and receivest unto thee: he shall dwell in thy court, and shall be satisfied with the pleasures of thy house, even of thy holy temple. Thou shalt show us wonderful things in thy righteousness, O God of our salvation; thou that art the hope of the ends of the earth, and of them that remain in the broad sea. Who in his strength setteth fast the mountains, and is girded about with power. Who stilleth the raging of the sea, and the noise of his waves, and the madness of the people. They also that dwell in the uttermost parts of the earth shall be afraid at thy tokens, thou that makest the out-goings of the morning and evening to praise thee. Thou visitest the earth and blessest it; thou makest it very plenteous. The river of God is full of water: thou preparest their corn, for so thou providest for the earth. Thou waterest her furrows; thou sendest rain into the little valleys thereof; thou makest it soft with the drops of rain, and blessest the increase of it. Thou crownest the year with thy goodness; and thy clouds drop fatness. They shall drop upon the dwellings of the wilderness, and the little hills shall rejoice on every side. The folds shall be full of sheep; the valleys also shall stand so thick with corn, that they shall laugh and sing.

Glory to the Father, and to the Son, and to the Holy Spirit, now, and ever, and unto ages of ages. Amen. Alleluia, alleluia, alleluia. Glory to thee, O God. (*Thrice.*)

Then the Deacon saith the following Litany:

In peace let us pray to the Lord.——*Choir.* Lord, have mercy.

For the peace that is from above, and for the salvation of our souls: ℞

For the peace of the whole world; for the welfare of God's holy Churches, and for the union of all: ℞

For this holy Temple, and for those who with faith, devoutness, and in the fear of God have entered therein: ℞

For our Most Holy Synod (*or* Patriarch); for our Bishop (*or* Archbishop, *or* Metropolitan), N.; for the honourable Presbytery, the Diaconate in Christ; for all the clergy and the laity: ℞

Here follow petitions for the Ruler of the Land and for all the Authorities, according to the elements and nationalities of which the Parish is constituted.

. That he will aid them in all things, and subdue under their feet all nations who are hateful unto Christ, and every foe and adversary: ℞

For this city, and for every city and land, and for those who with faith dwell therein: ℞

That he will graciously accept this present thanksgiving and supplication of us unworthy sinners on his most heavenly Altar, and in his compassion have mercy upon us: ℞

That our prayers may be well-pleasing in his sight, and that he will forgive us and all his people their transgressions, both voluntary and involuntary, which we have wickedly committed in the year that is past: ℞

That he will bless the beginning and continuance of this year with the grace of his love for mankind: and will grant unto us peaceful times and favourable seasons, and that we may live without sin, in health and plenty: ℞

That he will turn aside from us his wrath, which hath been justly kindled against us because of our sins: ℞

That he will banish from us all soul-destroying passions and corrupting usages: and that he will implant in our hearts his divine fear, unto the fulfilment of his commandments: ℞

That he will renew a right spirit within us, and confirm us in the Orthodox faith; and make us to be zealous in the performance of good deeds, and the fulfilment of all his commandments: ℞

That he will overthrow all heresies and schisms, and everywhere plant right belief and piety, and convert all who have departed from the true faith unto a knowledge of his truth, and unite them all unto his holy Orthodox Church: ℞

That he will deliver his holy Church, and us all, from every tribulation, wrath and necessity, and from all enemies, both visible and invisible; and that he will always hedge about his faithful people with health, long life and peace, and the host of his holy Angels: ℞

let us pray to the Lord. Choir. Lord, have mercy.

Succour us, save us, have mercy upon us and keep us, O God, by thy grace.

Choir. Lord, have mercy.

Calling to remembrance our most holy, all-undefiled, most blessed and glorious Lady, the Birth-giver of God and ever-virgin Mary, with all the Saints, let us commend ourselves, and each other, and all our life unto Christ our God.

Choir To thee, O Lord.

Exclamation.

Priest. For unto thee are due all glory, honour and worship, to the Father, and to the Son, and to the Holy Spirit, now, and ever, and unto ages of ages.

Choir. Amen.

Then: God is the Lord, and hath revealed himself unto us. Blessed is he that cometh in the Name of the Lord.

Verse (Stikh) 1: O give thanks unto the Lord, for he is gracious, because his mercy endureth forever.

Verse 2: All the nations compassed me about, but in the Name of the Lord have I driven them back.

Verse 3: I shall not die but live, and declare the works of the Lord.

Verse 4: The stone which the builders rejected, the same is become the head of the corner. This is the Lord's doing, and it is marvellous in our eyes.

And the following Hymns, in Tone IV.:

We, thine unworthy servants, O Lord, grateful for thy great benefits which thou hast showed upon us, glorifying thee do praise, bless, give thanks, sing and magnify thy loving-kindness, and cry aloud unto thee in humble submissiveness: O our Benefactor and our Saviour, glory to thee.

Glory to the Father, and to the Son, and to the Holy Spirit. (*Tone III.*)

O Master, who hast freely vouchsafed thy benefits and gifts unto thine unprofitable servants, zealously resorting unto thee, we offer unto thee thanksgiving according to our strength, and glorifying thee as our Benefactor and our Creator, we cry aloud: Glory to thee, O God most bountiful.

Now, and ever, and unto ages of ages. Amen. (*Tone II.*)

O thou Author of all created things, who hast set the seasons and the years in thy power, bless thou the crown of the year with thy goodness, O Lord, preserving in peace our Ruler and thy city, through the prayers of the Birth-giver of God; and save us.

Deacon. Let us attend.

Priest. Peace be with you all.

Reader. And with thy spirit.

Deacon. Wisdom! Let us attend.

Reader. The Gradual (*Prokímen*), in the Fourth Tone.   I will sing praises unto the Lord because he hath dealt so lovingly with me, yea, I will praise the Name of the Lord Most Highest.

Verse (*Stikh*): My heart shall rejoice in thy salvation.

Then he readeth the Epistle.

(*I Timothy ii. 1–6.*) My son Timothy, I exhort thee, that, first of all, supplications, prayers, intercessions, and giving of thanks be made for all men.   For kings and for all that are in authority; that we may lead a' quiet and peaceable life in all godliness and honesty.   For this is good and acceptable in the sight of God our Saviour; who will have all men to be saved, and to come to the knowledge of the truth.   For there is one God and one mediator between God and men, the man Jesus Christ; who gave himself a ransom for all.   To him be honour and glory unto ages of ages.   Amen.

Priest. Peace be unto thee.

Reader. And to thy spirit.

Deacon. Wisdom!

Reader. Alleluia, *in the Fourth Tone.*

Then the Deacon:

And that he will graciously vouchsafe unto us to hear his Holy Gospel, let us pray to the Lord God.

Choir. Lord, have mercy.   (*Thrice.*)

Deacon. Wisdom, O believers!   Let us listen to the Holy Gospel.

Priest. Peace be with you all. —— *Choir.* And with thy spirit.

Deacon. Let us attend.

Priest. The Lesson from the holy Gospel of Luke.

Choir. Glory to thee, O Lord; glory to thee.

And immediately the Priest readeth the Gospel.

(*Luke iv. 16–22.*) Then came Jesus to Nazareth, where he had been brought up: and as his custom was, he went into the synagogue on the Sabbath day, and stood up for to read.   And there was delivered unto him the book of the prophet Esaias.   And when he had opened the book, he found the place where it was written, The spirit of the Lord is upon me, because he hath anointed me to preach the gospel to the poor; he hath sent me to heal the broken-hearted, to preach deliverance to the captives, and recovering of sight to the blind, to set at liberty them that are bruised, to preach the acceptable year of the Lord.   And he closed the book, and he gave it again to the minister, and sat down.   And the eyes of all them that were in the synagogue were fastened on him.   And he began to say unto them, This day is this scripture fulfilled in your ears. And all bare him witness, and wondered at the gracious words which proceeded out of his mouth.

Choir. Glory to thee, O Lord; glory to thee.

Then immediately the Deacon saith the following Litany:

Let us all say, with all our soul and with all our mind let us say,
Choir. Lord, have mercy. (*Thrice.*)

O Lord Almighty, the God of our fathers, we beseech thee: hearken, and have mercy. ℞

Have mercy upon us, O God, according to thy great mercy, we beseech thee: hearken, and have mercy. ℞

Here follow petitions for the Ruler of the Land and for all the Authorities, according to the elements and nationalities of which the Parish is constituted.

For our Holy Synod (*or* Patriarch); for our Bishop (*or* Archbishop *or*, Metropolitan), N.; for the honourable Presbytery, the Diaconate in Christ; and for all our brethren in Christ: ℞

Returning thanks with fear and trembling, as unprofitable servants, unto thy loving-kindness, O Lord, our Saviour and our Master, for thy benefits, which thou hast poured out abundantly upon thy servants, we fall down in worship, and offer unto thee praise as God, and with fervour do cry aloud unto thee: Deliver thou thy servants from all calamities, and in that thou art merciful fulfil thou always the desires of us all, as may be expedient for us, we diligently entreat thee: hearken, and have mercy. ℞

That thou wilt bless the crown of the coming year with thy goodness, and quench among us all enmities, discords and civil strife; that thou wilt give us peace, love steadfast and unfeigned, as also a seemly disposition and virtuous life, we beseech thee, O all-gracious Lord: hearken, and have mercy. ℞

That thou wilt not call to mind our innumerable transgressions and evil actions, which we have committed during the year which is past, and that thou wilt not requite us according to our deeds; but that thou wilt remember us in mercy and bounty, we beseech thee, O tenderly-compassionate Lord: hearken, and have mercy. ℞

That thou wilt give rain in due season, both the early and the latter rains, fruitful dew, temperate and healthful breezes; and that thou wilt illumine with the warmth of the sun, we beseech thee, O all-bountiful Lord: hearken, and have mercy. ℞

That thou wilt call to mind thy holy Church, and strengthen and establish it, enlarge it, and give it peace, and preserve it unscathed by the gates of hell, and impregnable against all assaults of enemies both visible and invisible forever, we beseech thee, O all-sovereign Lord: hearken, and have mercy. ℞

That thou wilt root out and extinguish every blasphemous impiety of the pagan world and speedily destroy its kingdom, and give it into the hand of the right believers, we beseech thee, O all-powerful Lord: hearken, and have mercy. ℞

That thou wilt deliver us through the coming year, and all the days

Choir. Lord, have mercy. (Thrice.)

of our life, from pestilence, famine, earthquake, flood, hail, fire, the sword, the invasion of enemies, and from civil war, and from all death-dealing wounds, calamity and distress, we beseech thee, O tenderly-compassionate Lord: hearken, and have mercy.

Choir. Lord, have mercy. (*Thrice.*)

Hear us, O God our Saviour, the hope of all the ends of the earth, and of those who are far off upon the sea; and show mercy, show mercy, O Master, upon us sinners, and be merciful unto us.

For thou art a merciful God who lovest mankind, and unto thee we ascribe glory, to the Father, and to the Son, and to the Holy Spirit, now, and ever, and unto ages of ages.—— *Choir.* Amen.

Deacon. Again, yet again, on bended knees let us pray to the Lord.

Choir. Lord, have mercy. (*Thrice.*)

And the Priest readeth the following Prayer:

O Master, Lord our God, the Source of life and of immortality, the Author of all created things both visible and invisible, who hast placed all seasons and years in thy power, and dost direct all things with thy most-wise and all-gracious providence: We thank thee for thy bounties, which thou hast poured out upon us during our life that is past, and we entreat thee, O all-bountiful Lord!   Bless the crown of the coming year with thy goodness: preserve thy beloved servants, our Ruler, N., and all the Authorities; Multiply the days of their life in health unalterable, and grant them progress in all virtues.   Bestow thy good things from above upon all thy people, as also health and salvation, and good furtherance in all things.   Deliver thy holy Church, this city, and all cities and lands from every evil assault, and vouchsafe unto them peace and tranquillity; and grant that we may always offer thanksgiving unto thee, the Father who is from everlasting, together with thine Only-begotten Son, and thine all-holy, and good, and life-giving Spirit, God glorified in one Essence, and to hymn thine all-holy Name.

Exclamation.

Glory to thee, O God, our Benefactor, unto ages of ages.

Choir. Amen.

Then is sung: Glory be to God on high: (*See page 34.*)   *Or, in place of it, the Hymn of St. Ambrose, Bishop of Milan:*

We praise thee, O God; we acknowledge thee to be the Lord.   All the earth doth worship thee, the Father everlasting.   To thee all Angels cry aloud; the Heavens, and all the Powers therein.   To thee Cherubim and Seraphim continually do cry, Holy, Holy, Holy, Lord God of Sabaoth; heaven and earth are full of the Majesty of thy Glory.   The glorious company of the Apostles praise thee.   The goodly fellowship of the Prophets praise thee.   The noble army of Martyrs praise thee.   The holy Church throughout all the world doth acknowledge thee; the Father of an infinite Majesty; thine adorable, true, and only Son; also the Holy Ghost, the Comforter. Thou art the King of Glory, O Christ. Thou art the everlasting Son of the Father. When thou tookest upon thee to deliver man, thou didst humble thyself to be born of a Virgin. When thou hadst overcome the sharpness of death, thou didst open the Kingdom of Heaven to all believers. Thou sittest at the right hand of God, in the glory of the Father. We believe that thou shalt come to be our Judge. We therefore pray thee, help thy servants, whom thou hast redeemed with thy precious blood. Make them to be numbered with thy Saints, in glory everlasting. O Lord, save thy people, and bless thine heritage. Govern them, and lift them up forever. Day by day we magnify thee; and we worship thy Name, ever, world without end. Vouchsafe, O Lord, to keep us this day without sin. O Lord, have mercy upon us, have mercy upon us. O Lord, let thy mercy be upon us, as our trust is in thee. O Lord, in thee have I trusted; let me never be confounded.

And when it is finished, the Deacon saith:

Wisdom!

Priest. O most holy Birth-giver of God, save us.

Choir. More honourable than the Cherubim, and beyond compare more glorious than the Seraphim, thou who without defilement barest God the Word, true Birth-giver of God, we magnify thee.

Priest. Glory to thee, O Christ-God, our hope; glory to thee.

Choir. Glory to the Father, and to the Son, and to the Holy Spirit. now, and ever, and unto ages of ages. Amen.

Lord, have mercy. (*Thrice.*) Bless.

Priest. May Christ, our true God, who for our salvation condescended to be circumcised in the flesh, through the prayers of his most holy Mother, and of all the Saints, have mercy upon us and save us, forasmuch as he is gracious and loveth mankind.

The Deacon then proclaimeth:

Grant, O Lord, a prosperous and peaceful life, health and safety, and furtherance in all things, as also conquest and victory over his enemies, unto our most God-fearing Ruler, N., and to all the Authorities (*and to the Ruler of the Land, mentioning him by his title, if it be in a foreign country*): and preserve them for many years.

And the Choir singeth: Many years.

THE OFFICE OF PRAISE AND THANKSGIVING TO THE LORD GOD*

SUNG IN RUSSIA ON THE DAY OF THE BIRTH OF OUR SAVIOUR JESUS CHRIST: IN COMMEMORATION OF THE DELIVERANCE OF THE CHURCH AND THE RUSSIAN EMPIRE FROM THE INVASION OF THE GAULS AND THE TWELVE NATIONS

When the Divine Liturgy hath been said, the Clergy come forth from the Sanctuary, and take their stand in the middle of the Temple; and making three reverences, they begin:

Deacon. Bless, Father.

Priest. Glory to the Holy, Consubstantial, Life-giving and Undivided Trinity always, now, and ever, and unto ages of ages. —— *Choir.* Amen.

O heavenly King, the Comforter, Spirit of Truth, who art in all places and fillest all things; Treasury of good things and Giver of life: Come, and take up thine abode in us, and cleanse us from every stain; and save our souls, O Good One.

Reader. O Holy God, Holy Mighty, Holy Immortal One, have mercy upon us. (*Thrice, and three reverences.*)

Glory to the Father, and to the Son, and to the Holy Spirit, now, and ever, and unto ages of ages. Amen.

O all-holy Trinity, have mercy upon us. O Lord, wash away our sins. O Master, pardon our transgressions. O Holy One, visit and heal our infirmities, for thy Name's sake.

Lord, have mercy. (*Thrice.*)

Our Father, who art in heaven, Hallowed be thy Name. Thy kingdom come. Thy will be done on earth, As it is in heaven. Give us this day our daily bread. And forgive us our trespasses, As we forgive those who trespass against us. And lead us not into temptation; But deliver us from the Evil One:

Priest. For thine is the kingdom, and the power, and the glory, of the Father, and of the Son, and of the Holy Spirit, now, and ever, and unto ages of ages.

Reader. Amen. Lord, have mercy. (*Twelve times.*) Glory . . . now, and ever . . .

O come, let us worship God our King. O come, let us worship and fall down before Christ, our King and our God. O come, let us worship and fall down before the Very Christ, our King and our God. O come, let us worship and fall down before him. (*Three reverences.*)

* This service was prohibited, during the World War, by the Holy Synod of Russia. It is retained in this edition as being of historical and liturgical interest.

Then the Choir singeth the Prophecy of the holy Prophet Isaiah (viii., ix.):

God is with us: Understand, ye nations, and submit yourselves: For God is with us.

Reader. Hear ye, even unto the uttermost ends of the earth: ℞
Submit yourselves, ye mighty: ℞
If again ye shall rise up in your might, again shall ye be overthrown: ℞
And if any take counsel together, them shall the Lord destroy: ℞
And the word which ye shall speak shall not abide in you: ℞
For we fear not your terror, neither are we troubled: ℞
But the Lord our God, he it is to whom we will ascribe holiness, and him will we fear: ℞
And if I put my trust in him, he shall be my sanctification: ℞
I will set my hope on him, and through him shall I be saved: ℞
Lo, I and the children whom God hath given me: ℞
The people that walked in darkness have seen a great light: ℞
And they that dwelt in the land of the shadow of death, on them hath the light shined: ℞
For unto us a son is born, unto us a child is given: ℞
And the government shall be upon his shoulder: ℞
And of his peace there shall be no end: ℞
And his Name shall be called the great Council of the Angels: ℞
Wonderful, Counsellor: ℞
The Mighty God, the Everlasting Father, the Prince of Peace: ℞
The Father of the world to come: ℞
God is with us: Understand, ye nations, and submit yourselves: ℞
Glory to the Father, and to the Son, and to the Holy Spirit: ℞
God is with us: Understand, ye nations, and submit yourselves: ℞
Now, and ever, and unto ages of ages. Amen.

For God is with us.

Choir. God is with us: Understand, ye nations, and submit yourselves: For God is with us.

Reader. Alleluia, alleluia, alleluia. Glory to thee, O God. (*Thrice.*)

Deacon. In peace let us pray to the Lord. —— *Choir.* Lord, have mercy.

For the peace that is from above, and for the salvation of our souls: ℞
For the peace of the whole world; for the welfare of God's holy churches, and for the union of all: ℞
For this holy Temple, and for those who with faith, devoutness, and in the fear of God have entered therein: ℞
For the Most Holy Synod of Russia, and for our Bishop (*or* Archbishop), N., of N.; for the honourable Presbytery; for the Diaconate in Christ; and for all the clergy and laity: ℞
For our most God-fearing Ruler, N., for his Council and his Army.

let us pray to the Lord. Choir. Lord, have mercy.

That he will aid them in all things, and subdue under their feet every foe and adversary: ℞

For this city, and for every city and land; and for those who with faith dwell therein: ℞

For healthful seasons; for abundance of the fruits of the earth, and for peaceful times: ℞

For those who travel by sea or by land; for the sick and the suffering; for those who are in captivity, and for their salvation: ℞

That this our prayer may be set forth as incense before our God and Saviour, and these free will offerings of our hearts and lips may be accepted from us who have rendered thanks, in the day of salvation, unto the Lord who heard us in the day of trouble: ℞

Choir. Lord, have mercy. let us pray to the Lord.

That he will look with benignity and mercy upon our most God-fearing Ruler, and his conquering Empire, who now lay their crowns of victory before the footstool of Him who hath the nations for His inheritance, and the uttermost parts of the earth for His possession, the King of kings and Lord of lords; falling down in worship before whom let us pray.

Choir. Lord, have mercy.

That he will give unto us grace, with faith and love, henceforth and forever to proclaim salvation, and the might and the kingdom of our God, and the dominion of his Christ, let us beseech the Lord, who hath granted the power to his kingdom, and requiteth us with the joy of his salvation.

Choir. Lord, have mercy.

That he will deliver us from all tribulation, wrath and necessity.

Choir. Lord, have mercy.

Succour us, save us, have mercy upon us, and keep us by thy grace.

Choir. Lord, have mercy.

Calling to remembrance our most holy, all-undefiled, most blessed and glorious Lady, the Birth-giver of God, and ever-virgin Mary, with all the Saints, let us commend ourselves, and each other, and all our life unto Christ our God.

Choir. To thee, O Lord.

Exclamation.

Priest. For unto thee are due all glory, honour and worship, to the Father, and to the Son, and to the Holy Spirit, now, and ever, and unto ages of ages.

Choir. Amen.

God is the Lord, and hath revealed himself unto us. Blessed is he that cometh in the Name of the Lord.

Verse (Stikh) 1: O give thanks unto the Lord, for he is gracious, because his mercy endureth forever.

Verse 2: All the nations compassed me about, but in the Name of the Lord have I driven them back.

Verse 3: I shall not die but live, and declare the works of the Lord.

Verse 4: The stone which the builders rejected, the same is become the head of the corner. This is the Lord's doing, and it is marvellous in our eyes.

Then the following shall be sung, in Tone VI.:

Choir I. Glory be to God on high, and on earth peace. To-day doth Bethlehem receive him who sitteth with the Father forever enthroned. To-day Angels majestically magnify the Child who is born. Glory be to God on high, and on earth peace, good will toward men.

Choir II. (*Tone II.*) Glory be to God on high, and on earth peace. Behold, the Lamb of Bethlehem hath crushed under his feet the lion and the adder for us, and hath given peace unto his world. Wherefore, unto the Child who is the Sovereign Lord of the universe, do we, together with the Angels, offer glorious praise. Glory be to God on high, and on earth peace, good will toward men.

Choir I. (*Tone I.*) Glory to the Father, and to the Son, and to the Holy Spirit.

O Lord, save thy people, and bless thine inheritance, granting to our most God-fearing Ruler, N., victory over all adversaries, and by thy Cross preserving thine Estate.

Now, and ever, and unto ages of ages. Amen.

HYMN TO THE BIRTH-GIVER OF GOD (*Bogoróditchen*). Tone I.

Let us sing the praises of Mary, Virgin, Door of heaven, Glory of all the world, sprung forth from man, who also bare the Lord; the Song of the Bodiless Powers, and the Enriching of the faithful. For she revealed herself as Heaven and the Temple of the Godhead. She destroyed the bulwarks of enmity, and ushered in peace, and threw open the kingdom. Wherefore, in that we possess this confirmation of our faith, we have a Defender, even the Lord who was born of her. Be bold, therefore, ye people of God, be bold, for he, the All-Powerful, will vanquish your foes.

Deacon. Let us attend.

Priest. Peace be with you all.

Reader. And with thy spirit.

The following Parable (Paremiyá) is then read by the Reader or a Deacon:

Principal Deacon. Wisdom!

Deacon or Reader. The Lesson from the Prophecy of Isaiah.

Principal Deacon. Let us attend.

(*Isaiah xiv. 13–18; 24–28.*) Thus saith the Lord to the King of Babylon: For thou hast said in thy heart, I will ascend into heaven, I will exalt my throne above the stars of God: I will sit also upon the mount of the congregation, in the sides of the north: I will ascend above the heights of the clouds; I will be like the Most High. Yet thou shalt be brought down to hell, to the sides of the pit. They that see thee shall narrowly look upon thee, and consider thee, saying, Is this the man that made the earth to tremble, that did shake kingdoms: that made the world as a wilderness, and destroyed the cities thereof: that opened not the house of his prisoners? The Lord of hosts hath sworn, saying, Surely as I have thought, so shall it come to pass; and as I have purposed, so shall it stand: that I will break the Assyrian in my land, and upon my mountains tread him under foot: then shall his yoke depart from off them, and his burden depart from off their shoulders. This is the purpose that is purposed upon the whole earth: and this is the hand that is stretched out upon all the nations. For the Lord of hosts hath purposed, and who shall disannul it? and his hand is stretched out, and who shall turn it back?

Deacon. Let us attend.

Priest. Peace be with you.

Reader. And with thy spirit.

Deacon. Wisdom!

Reader. The Gradual (*Prokímen*), in the Seventh Tone. Who is so great a God as our God? Thou art God, and doest wonders.

Verse (Stikh) 1: Thou hast declared thy power among the nations.

Verse 2: I said: To-day have I begotten thee. These are the rewards of the right hand of the Most High.

Verse 3: I have remembered the works of the Lord; for I recall thy marvels from the beginning.

And again: Who is so great a God as our God? Thou art God, and doest wonders.

Deacon. Wisdom!

Reader. The Lesson from the Epistle of the holy Apostle Paul to the Hebrews.

Deacon. Let us attend.

Reader. (*Heb. xi. 32–35; xii. 1–2.*) Brethren: What shall I say more? for the time would fail me to tell of Gedeon, and of Barak, and of Samson, and of Jephthae, of David also, and Samuel, and of the prophets: who through faith subdued kingdoms, wrought righteousness, obtained promises, stopped the mouths of lions, quenched the violence of fire, escaped the edge of the sword, out of weakness were made strong, waxed valiant in fight, turned to flight the armies of the aliens. Wherefore, seeing we also are compassed about with so great a cloud of witnesses, let us lay aside every weight, and the sin which doth so easily beset us, and let us run with patience the race that is set before us, looking unto Jesus the author and finisher of our faith.

Priest. Peace be unto thee.

Reader. And to thy spirit.

Deacon. Wisdom!

Reader. Alleluia. (*Tone VII.*) The Lord shall give strength unto his people: the Lord shall give his people the blessing of peace.

Deacon. That he will mercifully vouchsafe unto us to hear his Holy Gospel, let us pray to the Lord God.

Choir. Lord, have mercy. (*Thrice.*)

Deacon. Wisdom, O believers; let us listen to the Holy Gospel!

Priest. Peace be with you all.

People. And with thy spirit.

Priest. The Lesson from the holy Gospel of Matthew.

Choir. Glory to thee, O Lord; glory to thee.

Deacon. Let us attend.

Priest. (*Matt. xxiv. 6–8, 21–23.*) Jesus said unto his disciples: Ye shall hear of wars, and rumours of wars: see that ye be not troubled: for all these things must come to pass, but the end is not yet. For nation shall rise against nation, and kingdom against kingdom: and there shall be famines, and pestilences, and earthquakes in divers places. For then shall be great tribulation, such as was not since the beginning of the world to this time, no, nor ever shall be. And except those days should be shortened, there should no flesh be sáved: but for the elect's sake those days shall be shortened.

Choir. Glory to thee, O Lord; glory to thee.

Then straightway the Deacon reciteth this Litany:

Let us all say, with all our soul and with all our mind let us say,

Choir. Lord, have mercy.

O Lord Almighty, the God of our fathers, we beseech thee: hearken, and have mercy.

Choir. Lord, have mercy.

Have mercy upon us, O God, according to thy great mercy, we beseech thee: hearken, and have mercy. ℟

Again we pray for our most God-fearing Ruler, N., for his might, victory, maintenance, peace, health, salvation; and that the Lord our God will abundantly aid and prosper him in all things, and subdue under his feet every foe and adversary. ℟

Again we pray (*for the Ruler of the Land, by his title, if it be in a foreign country*). ℟

Again we pray for our Most Holy Synod (*or* Patriarch); for our Bishop (*or* Archbishop, *or* Metropolitan), N., of N.; and for all our brethren in Christ. ℟

Furthermore we pray for all their Christ-loving Army and Navy. ℟

Furthermore we pray that our Lord and Saviour will accept the confession and thanksgiving of us, his unworthy servants: for he hath not dealt with us according to our sins, neither rewarded us according to our iniquities. But in the hour of trial also, which came upon all the world, he delivered us; and when our enemies compassed us round about, he revealed unto us his salvation. ℟

O thou who, at the hand of Melchisedec, didst accept the tithe of

Choir. Lord, have mercy. (*Thrice.*)

Abraham, after that he had overthrown four kings, and had set free the captives; and when Pharaoh together with his host was engulfed in the Red Sea, didst give heed from the cloudy pillar to the Song of Moses and Miriam, to the trumpets also and dancing; and didst teach David, the king after thine own heart, to write Psalms of triumph unto thee alone: Do thou, the same Lord of Hosts, now, also, in that thou hast overcome him who was an enemy and alien from thee, and hast saved thine Anointed, and glorified the majesty of Russia, and established the Church, as out of the mouths of babes make the praises out of the mouths of all us acceptable unto thee; receive into thy salvation as a burnt-offering our souls which had vanished away. Hearken to the voice of our rejoicing; and, as of old, we fervently beseech thee show mercy upon us in the day of trouble. ℞

Choir. Lord, have mercy. (Thrice.)

Furthermore we pray for our victorious chieftains and warriors, and for all those zealous defenders of the Faith and of righteousness, who have laid down their lives for their brethren in the year of tribulation: that the King of Glory will recompense them, in the day of his just requiting, with life everlasting and the crown which fadeth not away; and that he will confirm us all in their spirit, and in faith and concord. ℞

Hear us, O God our Saviour, the hope of all the ends of the earth, and of those who are far off upon the seas; and show mercy, show mercy, O Master, upon us sinners, and be merciful unto us.

For thou art a merciful God who lovest mankind, and unto thee we ascribe glory, to the Father, and to the Son, and to the Holy Spirit, now, and ever, and unto ages of ages.

Choir. Amen.

Deacon. Let us attend, and in lowliness of heart bowing the knees of our souls and bodies, let us pray to the Lord.

Then the Priest, kneeling down (as doth also the whole congregation), shall recite, aloud, with all fervour and emotion, the following Prayer:

O God, great and inscrutable, O Father, who hast no beginning, O Son who likewise hast no beginning, and Spirit who equally existest from everlasting; who bringest into being that which had no being, and savest those who are ready to perish, and givest life to the dead, working after thy will among the heavenly hosts, and in the dwellings of earth, and by thy marvellous Providence directing all things! Incline thine ear from thy holy place on high, and accept from us, thy humble and unworthy servants, upon whom thou hast manifested thy great salvation from calamity and utter destruction, these prayers of gratitude, praise and thanksgiving which we offer unto thee with our heart, and with our lips. For not according to our transgressions hast thou dealt with us, O Lord, neither rewarded us according to our iniquities. Thou didst say of old unto the

Children of Israel, that if they would not hearken unto thy voice to keep and to do all thy commandments, thou wouldest send upon them the heathen shameless of countenance, who should crush them in their cities, until also their walls should be cast down; and we have seen how this terrible word came upon us, and upon our fathers. Yet fearing not thy warning, and despising thy compassion, we departed from the way of thy righteousness, and walked after the lusts of our own hearts, and strove not to have in our hearts thee, the God of minds and of hearts; and heeding not the traditions of our fathers, we angered thee through strangers. For which cause, also, like unto the Children of Israel of old, a fierce host encompassed us round about, and those in whose customs we were zealous, these same turbulent and brutal-natured ones have we had as our enemies. But thou, O Lord God, who art pitiful and merciful, long-suffering and rich in loving-kindness, and faithful, keeping righteousness and showing mercy unto thousands, taking away iniquities and transgressions, after that thou hadst departed from us for a little space, with great mercy hast been merciful unto us: and having visited our wrong-doings with thy rod, like as a father is bountiful unto his children, even so hast thou been bountiful unto us. For thou hast regarded our affliction and the wasting away of the Imperial City, wherein, from ancient days, thy Name hath been invoked, and our supplications which, trusting not in our own righteousness but in thy great bounties, we have laid at thy feet, O Lord. And thou hast given us the ascendency over our ungodly adversaries; thou hast crowned our most God-fearing Emperor, Alexander Pávlovitch, with the panoply of thy favour, that vanishing thine enemies might vanish before the face of thy Christ even as the smoke, and that they who love thee might shine even as the rising sun in his splendour. We have seen, O Lord, we have seen, and all nations have seen in us, that thou art God, and that there is none beside thee. Thou slayest and makest alive; thou smitest and healest, and there is none who shall wrest us out of thy hand. Therefore is our heart fixed upon our Lord, who hath exalted our horn in our God, and we have rejoiced in thy salvation. We thank thee, O Lord, that thou hast chastised us for a little space, but hast not given us over unto death forever. Enable us, O Lord, unceasingly and steadfastly to bear within us the memory of this, thy glorious visitation, unto the establishment in us of filial fear, together with love and faith in thee. And vouchsafe that, compassed about by thy protection, we may ever henceforth, as this day, praise and magnify thy holy Name. Confirm thy good will upon our most God-fearing Ruler, N., and may thy blessed spirit abide upon him evermore. Grant in his godly dominion: To the Pastors, holiness; to the Rulers, judgment and uprightness; to the People, peace and quietness; to the law, strength; and to the faith, advancement. O most merciful Lord! satisfy with thy mercy those who have known thee; and unto those who are not seeking thee, reveal thou thyself; and turn thou also the hearts of our enemies unto thee; and be thou known unto all tribes and nations in thine only true Christ. And let all the peoples, from the rising of the sun even unto the going down of the same, cry aloud with praise unto thee, in every tongue, with the voice of rejoicing.

Then he proclaimeth, with a loud voice:

Glory to thee, O God, Saviour of all, unto ages of ages!

Choir. Amen.

Then is sung the GREAT HYMN OF PRAISE (*The Gloria in Excelsis. See page* 34), *or* We praise thee, O God; . . . (*See page* 539.)

And the following BENEDICTION *is pronounced:*

May he who, like a lamb, did lie in the manger at Bethlehem, who also, like a lion, doth overthrow the power of the enemy and doth lead his own faithful sheep in the way of righteousness and salvation, and doth guide and feed the world, Christ our true God and Saviour; through the intercessions of his most holy Mother, and of all the Saints, have mercy upon us and save us, in that he is gracious and loveth mankind.

Then the Deacon proclaimeth:

Grant, O Lord, a prosperous and peaceful life, health and safety, and furtherance in all things, as also conquest and victory over his enemies, unto our most God-fearing Ruler, N. (*and to the Ruler of the Land, mentioning him by his title, if it be in a foreign country*): and preserve them for many years.

Choir. Many years.

Deacon. Unto thy departed servant, our most God-fearing Sovereign, the Emperor Alexander the First, grant repose eternal in the assumption of the blessed, O Lord; and make his memory to be eternal.

Choir. Memory eternal! (*Thrice.*)

To the victorious, Christ-loving Army of Russia, Many years.

Choir. Many years. (*Thrice.*)

And when the Many years *hath been sung, the bells begin to peal, and so continue, until Vespers.*

THE GREAT OFFICE OF THANKSGIVING
(TE DEUM)

FOR OCCASIONS OF SOLEMN THANKSGIVING

Priest. Blessed is the kingdom of the Father, and of the Son, and of the Holy Spirit, now, and ever, and unto ages of ages.

Choir. Amen.

O heavenly King, the Comforter, Spirit of Truth, who art in all places and fillest all things; Treasury of good things and Giver of life: Come, and take up thine abode in us, and cleanse us from every stain; and save our souls, O Good One.

O Holy God, Holy Mighty, Holy Immortal One, have mercy upon us. (*Thrice, and three reverences.*)

Glory to the Father, and to the Son, and to the Holy Spirit, now, and ever, and unto ages of ages. Amen.

O most Holy Trinity, have mercy upon us. O Lord, wash away our sins. O Master, pardon our transgressions. O Holy One, visit and heal our infirmities, for thy Name's sake.

Lord, have mercy. (*Thrice.*)

Our Father, who art in heaven, Hallowed be thy Name. Thy kingdom come. Thy will be done on earth, As it is in heaven. Give us this day our daily bread. And forgive us our trespasses, As we forgive those who trespass against us. And lead us not into temptation; But deliver us from the Evil One:

Priest. For thine is the kingdom, and the power, and the glory, of the Father, and of the Son, and of the Holy Spirit, now, and ever, and unto ages of ages.

Choir. Amen. Lord, have mercy. (*Twelve times.*)

Priest. O come, let us worship God our King. O come, let us worship and fall down before Christ, our King and our God. O come, let us worship and fall down before the Very Christ, our King and our God. O come, let us worship and fall down before him. (*Three reverences.*)

Then the Choir chanteth the Imperial Psalm:

PSALM XXI.

The King shall rejoice in thy strength, O Lord; exceeding glad shall he be of thy salvation. Thou hast given him his heart's desire, and hast not denied him the request of his lips. For thou shalt prevent him with the blessings of goodness, and shalt set a crown of pure gold upon his head.

He asked life of thee, and thou gavest him a long life, even for ever and ever.   His honour is great in thy salvation: glory and great worship shalt thou lay upon him.   For thou shalt give him everlasting felicity, and make him glad with the joy of thy countenance.   And why?   Because the King putteth his trust in the Lord; and in the mercy of the Most Highest he shall not miscarry.   All thine enemies shall feel thine hand: thy right hand shall find out them that hate thee.   Thou shalt make them like a fiery oven in the time of thy wrath; the Lord shall destroy them in his displeasure, and the fire shall consume them.   Their fruit shalt thou root out of the earth, and their seed from among the children of men. For they intended mischief against thee, and imagined such a device as they are not able to perform.   Therefore shalt thou put them to flight, and the strings of thy bow shalt thou make ready against the face of them.   Be thou exalted, O Lord, in thine own strength: so will we sing and praise thy power.

Glory to the Father, and to the Son, and to the Holy Spirit, now, and ever, and unto ages of ages.   Amen.

Alleluia, alleluia, alleluia.   Glory to thee, O God.   (*Thrice.*)

Then the Deacon saith the Litany:

In peace let us pray to the Lord.   ℟

For the peace that is from above, and for the salvation of our souls: ℟

For the peace of the whole world; for the welfare of God's holy Churches, and for the union of all: ℟

For this holy Temple, and for those who with faith, devoutness and in the fear of God have entered therein: ℟

For the Most Holy Synod, and for our Bishop, N., of N.; for the honourable Presbytery; for the Diaconate in Christ; and for all the clergy and laity: ℟

For our most God-fearing Ruler, N., and all the Authorities: ℟

That his authority may be strengthened by the right hand of the Most High: ℟

That he may receive from heaven strength and wisdom, unto rule and righteous judgment: ℟

That he may receive prosperity in all things, and length of rule: ℟

That the Lord God will hear him in the day of trouble, and that the Name of the God of Jacob may defend him: ℟

That the Lord will send him help from his holy dwelling-place, and defend him out of Zion: ℟

That the Lord will give him the desire of his heart, and fulfil all his counsel: ℟

That he will preserve free from venality and partiality the judges who are subject unto him: ℟

let us pray to the Lord.   Choir.   Lord, have mercy.

That the Lord of hosts will ever strengthen his armed hosts: ℟

That he will subdue under his feet every foe and adversary: ℟

For this city, and for every city and land; and for those who with faith dwell therein: ℟

For healthful seasons; for abundance of the fruits of the earth, and for peaceful times: ℟

For those who travel by sea or by land; for the sick and the suffering; for those who are in captivity, and for their salvation: ℟

That he will deliver us from all tribulation, wrath and necessity: ℟

let us pray to the Lord. Choir. Lord, have mercy.

Succour us, save us, have mercy upon us, and keep us, O God, by thy grace.

Choir. Lord, have mercy.

Calling to remembrance our most holy, all-undefiled, most blessed and glorious Lady, the Birth-giver of God and ever-virgin Mary, with all the Saints, let us commend ourselves, and each other, and all our life unto Christ our God.

Choir. To thee, O Lord.

Exclamation.

Priest. For unto thee are due all glory, honour and worship, to the Father, and to the Son, and to the Holy Spirit, now, and ever, and unto ages of ages.

Choir. Amen.

Then: God is the Lord, and hath revealed himself unto us. Blessed is he that cometh in the Name of the Lord.

Verse (Stikh) 1: O give thanks unto the Lord, for he is gracious; because his mercy endureth forever.

Verse 2: All the nations compassed me about, but in the Name of the Lord have I driven them back.

Verse 3: I shall not die but live, and declare the works of the Lord.

Verse 4: The stone which the builders rejected, the same is become the head of the corner. This is the Lord's doing, and it is marvellous in our eyes.

And these Hymns (Tropari), in Tone IV.

We, thine unworthy servants, O Lord, grateful for thy great benefits which thou hast shown upon us, glorifying thee, do praise, bless, give thanks, sing, and magnify thy loving-kindness, and do cry aloud unto thee in loving submissiveness: O our Benefactor and our Saviour, glory to thee!

Tone I. Glory to the Father, and to the Son, and to the Holy Spirit.

O Lord, save thy people, and bless thine inheritance, granting to the most God-fearing Ruler, N., victory over all adversaries, and by thy Cross preserving thine Estate.

Tone II. Now, and ever, and unto ages of ages. Amen.

Do thou who, of thine own good will, upon the Cross wast lifted up, bestow thy bounties upon the new State which is called by thy Name, O Christ-God; make glad with thy might our most God-fearing Ruler, N., granting victory over his adversaries unto him who hath thine aid, which is a panoply of peace, a trophy invincible.

Deacon. Let us attend.

Priest. Peace be with you all.

Reader. And with thy spirit.

The Gradual (Prokímen), in Tone IV.: The King shall rejoice in thy strength, O Lord; exceeding glad shall he be of thy salvation.

Verse (Stikh): Thou hast given him his heart's desire, and hast not denied him the request of his lips.

Deacon. Wisdom!

Reader. The Lesson from the Epistle of the holy Apostle Paul to the Romans.

Deacon. Let us attend.

Reader. (Rom. xiii. 1–8.) Brethren: Let every soul be subject unto the higher powers. For there is no power but of God: the powers that be are ordained of God. Whosoever, therefore, resisteth the power resisteth the ordinance of God: and they that resist shall receive to themselves damnation. For rulers are not a terror to good works, but to the evil. Wilt thou then not be afraid of the power? do that which is good, and thou shalt have praise of the same. For he is the minister of God to thee for good. But if thou do that which is evil, be afraid; for he beareth not the sword in vain: for he is the minister of God, a revenger to execute wrath upon him that doeth evil. Wherefore ye must needs be subject, not only for wrath, but also for conscience sake. For this cause pay ye tribute also: for they are God's ministers, attending continually upon this very thing. Render therefore to all their dues: tribute to whom tribute is due; custom to whom custom; fear to whom fear; honour to whom honour. Owe no man anything, but to love one another: for he that loveth another hath fulfilled the law.

Alleluia. (*Thrice.*)

Deacon. Wisdom, O believers! Let us listen to the Holy Gospel.

Priest. Peace be with you all. —— *Choir.* And with thy spirit.

Priest. The Lesson from the holy Gospel of Matthew.

Choir. Glory to thee, O Lord; glory to thee.

Deacon. Let us attend.

Priest. (Matt. xxii. 15–22.) Then went the Pharisees and took counsel how they might entangle him in his talk. And they sent out unto him their disciples, with the Herodians, saying, Master, we know that thou art true, and teachest the way of God in truth, neither carest thou for any man; for thou regardest not the person of men. Tell us, therefore, What thinkest thou? Is it lawful to give tribute unto Cæsar, or not? But

Jesus perceived their wickedness, and said, Why tempt ye me, ye hypocrites? Show me the tribute money. And they brought unto him a penny. And he saith unto them, Whose is this image and superscription? They say unto him, Cæsar's. Then saith he unto them, Render therefore unto Cæsar the things which are Cæsar's, and unto God the things that are God's. When they had heard these words, they marvelled, and left him, and went their way.

Choir. Glory to thee, O Lord; glory to thee.

Deacon. Have mercy upon us, O Lord, according to thy great mercy, we beseech thee: hearken, and have mercy.

Choir. Lord, have mercy. (*Thrice.*)

Again we pray for our most God-fearing Ruler, N.; for his might, victory, maintenance, peace, health, salvation; and that the Lord our God will abundantly aid and prosper him in all things, and subdue under his feet every foe and adversary. ℟

Furthermore we pray for all the Authorities (*and for the Ruler of the Land, by his title, if it be in a foreign country*). ℟

Furthermore we pray for the Most Holy Synod (*or* Patriarch); for our Bishop (*or* Archbishop, *or* Metropolitan), N., of N.; and for all our brethren in Christ. ℟

Furthermore we pray for all their Christ-loving Army and Navy. ℟

Returning thanks with fear and trembling, as unprofitable servants, unto thy loving-kindness, O Lord, our Saviour and our Master, for thy benefits, which thou hast poured out abundantly upon thy servants, we fall down in worship, and offer unto thee praise as God, and with fervour do cry aloud unto thee: Deliver thou thy servants from all calamities, and in that thou are merciful fulfil thou always the desires of us all, as may be expedient for us, we diligently entreat thee: hearken, and have mercy. ℟

O Lord our God, inscrutable in mercy, grant unto thy servant, our most God-fearing Ruler, whom thou hast appointed to rule over us, the prosperity vouchsafed to Moses, the valour of David, and the wisdom of Solomon, to the glory of thy Name, we beseech thee, O King all-Holy: hearken, and have mercy. ℟

O Master, who art the Creator of all wisdom and the Ruler of all created things, establish thou the Supremacy of thy servant, our Ruler, N. Fulfil the desire and petitions of his heart; and exalt the horn of thy Christ, we beseech thee: hearken, and have mercy. ℟

Choir. Lord, have mercy. (*Thrice.*)

Exclamation.

Priest. Hear us, O God our Saviour, the hope of all the ends of the earth, and of those who are far off upon the sea; and show mercy, show mercy, O Master, upon us sinners, and be merciful unto us.

For thou art a merciful God who lovest mankind, and unto thee we ascribe glory, to the Father, and to the Son, and to the Holy Spirit, now, and ever, and unto ages of ages.

Choir. Amen.

Deacon. Again, yet again, in peace let us pray to the Lord.

Then the Bishop or the Priest, kneeling down, shall recite this Prayer:

O God, great and wonderful, who by thine inscrutable goodness and rich providence rulest all things; by whose all-wise yet unsearchable judgments the life and sojourn upon earth of mankind receiveth different bounds: With gratitude we acknowledge that not according to our iniquities hast thou dealt with us, neither according to our sins hast thou rewarded us. We have sinned, O Lord, we have wrought evil, and have rendered ourselves worthy of thine extreme displeasure. But thou, O Ineffable Loving-kindness! art merciful and long-suffering, and grievest over the wickedness of men, O Master. Having chastened us with a brief visitation of sorrow, lo! thou hast filled our hearts abundantly with joy and gladness, in that thou hast appointed to rule over us thy beloved servant, our most God-fearing Ruler, N. Wherefore, endue thou him with wisdom, and direct thou him, that without hindrance he may discharge this great service unto thee. Grant him reason and understanding, that he may judge thy people uprightly; and preserve this thine inheritance in tranquillity, and without affliction. Make him victorious over his enemies; terrible to evil-doers, gracious unto those who are good and worthy to be trusted. Kindle his heart unto consideration of the needy, unto hospitality to strangers, unto the defence of those who are assailed; that, guiding those who are subject to his rule in the way of truth and of righteousness, and putting aside all dissembling and venality, he may maintain in loyalty unfeigned all the people whom thou hast committed to his authority. Make him to be a joyful father of children, and show forth thy marvellous mercies upon us. Multiply thou the days of his life in health unalterable and prosperity unchangeable. Vouchsafe, also, in his day and unto us all peace, tranquillity and prosperity, favourable seasons, abundance of the fruits of the earth, and all things necessary to life both temporal and eternal. O our Lord all-merciful, the God of Bounties, and Father of all consolation! turn not thy face from us, and put not to confusion in our sure hope us, who, in firm expectation, make our supplications unto thee, and entreating thee, do set our trust upon thy bounties. For thou only knowest our necessities, and givest before we ask, and confirmest thy gifts: and every good gift and every perfect gift is from above, and cometh down from thee, the Father of lights. Unto thee be glory and dominion, together with thine Only-begotten Son, and thine all-holy, and good, and life-giving Spirit, now, and ever, and unto ages of ages.

Choir. Amen.

Then immediately is sung the Great Hymn of Praise: Glory be to God on high, . . .
(See page 34.)

Or, in its stead, the Anthem of St. Ambrose, Bishop of Milan:

We praise thee, O God; we acknowledge thee to be the Lord. . . .
(See page 539.)

And when it is finished, the Priest bestoweth the customary BENEDICTION.

May Christ, our true God, through the prayers of his most holy
Mother; of Saint N. *(the Saint of the day)*; and of all the Saints, have
mercy upon us and save us, forasmuch as he is gracious, and loveth mankind.

And after the Benediction, the Deacon proclaimeth

MANY YEARS (LONG LIFE)

To the Ruler as followeth:

Unto our most God-fearing Ruler, N., grant, O Lord, length of days,
a peaceful life, health, salvation and prosperity in all things; as also, conquest and victory over his enemies; and preserve him for many years.

Choir. Many years.

PRAYERS

AT THE FOUNDING OF A HOUSE

Let us pray to the Lord.

O God Almighty, who hast made the heavens with wisdom, and hast established the earth upon its firm foundations, the Creator and Author of all men: Look upon thy servant, N., to whom it hath seemed good to set up a house for his dwelling in the dominion of thy power, and to rear it by building. Establish thou the same upon a stable rock, and found it according to thy divine word in the Gospel, so that neither wind nor flood nor any other thing shall be able to harm it. Graciously grant that he may bring it to an ending; and deliver all those who shall wish to dwell therein from every attack of the enemy.

For thine is the dominion, and thine are the kingdom and the power and the glory, of the Father, and of the Son, and of the Holy Spirit, now, and ever, and unto ages of ages. Amen.

WHEN ONE IS ABOUT TO TAKE UP HIS ABODE IN A NEW HOUSE

O God our Saviour, who didst deign to enter under the roof of Zaccheus, unto the salvation of the same and of all who were in the house: Do thou, the same Lord, keep safe also from all harm those who have now desired to dwell here, and who together with us unworthy ones do offer unto thee prayers and supplications; blessing this their dwelling, and preserving their life free from aspersion. For unto thee are due all glory, honour and worship, together with thy Father who hath no beginning, and thine all-holy, and good, and life-giving Spirit, now, and ever, and unto ages of ages. Amen.

FOR THE BLESSING OF ANY OBJECT

After the customary beginning: The Thrice-Holy (O Holy God, Holy Mighty). Then: Our Father, . . . (See page 559.) And after the Exclamation, the Priest saith:

Let us pray to the Lord. Lord, have mercy.

And he readeth this Prayer:

O Creator and Author of the human race, Giver of spiritual graces and Bestower of eternal salvation: Do thou, the same Lord, send down thy Holy Spirit with a blessing from on high upon this object; that fortified by the might of heavenly protection, it may be potent unto bodily salvation and succour and aid, unto all who shall desire to make use of it, through Jesus Christ our Lord.   Amen.

He then sprinkleth the object thrice with holy water, and pronounceth the customary Benediction.

A GENERAL SERVICE OF PRAYER

(MOLIÉBEN)

Deacon. Bless, Master.

Priest. Blessed is our God always, now, and ever, and unto ages of ages.

Choir. Amen.

O heavenly King, the Comforter, Spirit of Truth, who art in all places and fillest all things; Treasury of good things and Giver of life: Come, and take up thine abode in us, and cleanse us from every stain; and save our souls, O Good One.

Reader. O Holy God, Holy Mighty, Holy Immortal One, have mercy upon us. (*Thrice.*) Glory to the Father, and to the Son, and to the Holy Spirit, now, and ever, and unto ages of ages. Amen. O all-holy Trinity, have mercy upon us; O Lord, wash away our sins; O Master, pardon our transgressions; O Holy One, visit and heal our infirmities, for thy Name's sake.

Lord, have mercy. (*Thrice.*)

Glory to the Father, and to the Son, and to the Holy Spirit, now, and ever, and unto ages of ages. Amen.

Our Father, who art in heaven, Hallowed be thy Name. Thy kingdom come. Thy will be done on earth, As it is in heaven. Give us this day our daily bread. And forgive us our trespasses, As we forgive those who trespass against us. And lead us not into temptation; But deliver us from the Evil One:

Priest. For thine is the kingdom, and the power, and the glory, of the Father, and of the Son, and of the Holy Spirit, now, and ever, and unto ages of ages.

Choir. Amen.

Lord, have mercy. (*Twelve times.*)

Glory . . . now, and ever . . .

Deacon. God is the Lord, and hath revealed himself unto us. Blessed is he who cometh in the Name of the Lord.

Verse 1: O give thanks unto the Lord, for he is gracious; because his mercy endureth forever.

Verse 2: All the nations compassed me about, but in the Name of the Lord have I driven them back.

Verse 3: I shall not die but live, and declare the works of the Lord.

Verse 4: The stone which the builders rejected, the same is become the head of the corner. This is the Lord's doing, and it is marvellous in our eyes.

Choir. God is the Lord, . . . (*as above*).

And if it be a Prayer Service to the Saviour, this Hymn:

We do homage to thy pure image, O Good One, entreating forgiveness of our transgressions, O Christ our God: for of thine own good will thou wast graciously pleased to ascend the Cross in the flesh, that thou mightest deliver from bondage to the enemy those whom thou hadst fashioned. For which cause we cry aloud unto thee with thanksgiving: With joy hast thou filled all things, O our Saviour, in that thou didst come to save the world.

If it be a Prayer Service to the Birth-giver of God, this Hymn (Bogoródilchen):

Unto the Birth-giver of God let us sinners and humble ones now diligently have recourse; and let us fall down in penitence exclaiming, from the bottom of our souls: O Sovereign Lady, help us, having compassion on us! Show zeal, for we perish with the multitude of our sins; turn not thy servants empty away; for we have thee as our only hope.

If it be a Prayer Service to a Saint, the Hymn (Tropár) of the Saint to whom appeal is being made.

Refrains.

Priest and Deacon. (*To the Saviour.*) Glory to thee, our God; glory to thee.

Priest and Deacon. (*To the Birth-giver of God.*) O most holy Birth-giver of God, save us.

Priest and Deacon. (*To a Saint.*) O holy Saint N.; pray unto God for us.

Priest and Deacon. Glory to the Father, and to the Son, and to the Holy Spirit.

Choir. Now, and ever, and unto ages of ages. Amen.

Then they sing:

(*To the Saviour.*) Deliver from distress thy servants, O greatly-merciful One; for we have diligent recourse unto thee, the merciful Deliverer of all men, O Lord Jesus Christ.

(*To the Birth-giver of God.*) Deliver from distress thy servants, O Birth-giver of God; for unto thee in God we have recourse, as to a Wall Impregnable, and to thy intercession. Look with benignity, O all-hymned Birth-giver of God, upon my dire bodily suffering, and heal thou the sickness of my soul.

(*To a Saint.*) Pray thou unto God for us, O holy N.; for we diligently have recourse unto thee, who art a speedy help and intercessor for our souls.

Deacon. Have mercy upon us, O God, according to thy great mercy, we beseech thee: hearken, and have mercy.

Choir. Lord, have mercy. (*Thrice.*)

Furthermore we pray for our most God-fearing Ruler, N.; for his might, victory, maintenance, peace, health, salvation; and that the Lord our God will abundantly aid and succour him in all things, and subdue under his feet every foe and adversary; (*and for the Ruler of the Land, if it be in a foreign country*). ℞

Furthermore we pray for the Most Holy Synod (*or* Patriarch) and for our Bishop (*or* Archbishop, *or* Metropolitan), N.; and for all our brethren in Christ. ℞

Furthermore we pray for the mercy, life, peace, health and salvation of the servants of God, NN., and for the persons who are here present, and who pray. ℞

Furthermore we pray for all the brethren and for all Christians. ℞

Choir. Lord, have mercy. (*Thrice.*)

Exclamation.

Priest. For thou art a merciful God who lovest mankind, and unto thee do we ascribe glory, to the Father, and to the Son, and to the Holy Spirit, now, and ever, and unto ages of ages.

Choir. Amen.

The Refrains (see page 560) are then repeated.

The LITTLE LITANY.

Deacon. Again, yet again, in peace let us pray to the Lord.

Choir. Lord, have mercy.

Succour us, save us, have mercy upon us, and keep us, O God, by thy grace.

Choir. Lord, have mercy.

Calling to remembrance our most holy, all-undefiled, most blessed and glorious Lady, the Birth-giver of God, and ever-virgin Mary, with all the Saints, let us commend ourselves, and each other, and all our life unto Christ our God.

Choir. To thee, O Lord.

Exclamation.

Priest. For blessed be thy Name, and glorified be thy kingdom, of the Father, and of the Son, and of the Holy Spirit, now, and ever, and unto ages of ages.

Choir. Amen.

Deacon. Let us attend.

Priest. Peace be with you all.

Deacon. Wisdom! The Gradual (*Prokimen*).

To the Saviour: Lord, we will walk in the light of thy countenance and rejoice in thy Name forevermore.

To the Birth-giver of God: I will call upon thy name from generation to generation.

To a Saint: Right dear in the sight of the Lord is the death of **his** Saints.

The Choir then singeth the Gradual, in the usual manner.

Deacon. Let us pray to the Lord.

Choir. Lord, have mercy.

Exclamation.

Priest. For holy art thou, O our God, and restest in the Saints, **and** unto thee do we ascribe glory, to the Father, and to the Son, and to **the** Holy Spirit, now, and ever, and unto ages of ages.

Choir. Amen.

Deacon. Let everything that hath breath praise the Lord.

Verse: Praise the Lord from heaven, praise him in the heights.

The Choir repeateth the same. (Thrice.)

Deacon. And that he will vouchsafe us grace to listen to the Holy Gospel, let us pray to the Lord God.

Choir. Lord, have mercy. *(Thrice.)*

Priest. Peace be with you all.

Choir. And with thy spirit.

Priest. The Lesson from the holy Gospel **according to N.**

Choir. Glory to thee, O Lord; glory to thee.

Deacon. Let us attend.

Here the Gospel is read, appropriate to the Saint, or to the petition, Matt. vii. 8–11. If the Service is to the Saviour, Matt. xii. 27–30. If to the Birth-giver of God, Luke i. 39–49, 56.

Then the Choir. Glory to thee, O Lord; glory to thee.

Then again the Refrains, as above.

Then the Choir singeth: Meet is it of a truth to bless thee, O Birth-giver of God, ever-blessed, and all-undefiled, and Mother of our God. More honourable than the Cherubim, and beyond compare more glorious than the Seraphim, thou who without defilement barest God the Word, true Birth-giver of God, we magnify thee.

Deacon. Have mercy upon us, O God, according to thy great mercy, . . . *(See pages 560–561.)*

Exclamation.

Priest. Hear us, O God our Saviour, the hope of all the ends of the earth, and of those who are far off upon the sea; and show mercy, show mercy, O Master, upon us sinners, and be merciful unto us.

For thou art a merciful God who lovest mankind, and unto thee we ascribe glory, to the Father, and to the Son, and to the Holy Spirit, now, and ever, and unto ages of ages.

Choir. Amen.

Deacon. Wisdom!

Priest. O most holy Birth-giver of God, save us.

Choir. More honourable than the Cherubim, and beyond compare more glorious than the Seraphim, thou who without defilement barest God the Word, true Birth-giver of God, we magnify thee.

Priest. Glory to thee, O Christ-God our hope; glory to thee.

Choir. Glory to the Father, and to the Son, and to the Holy Spirit, now, and ever, and unto ages of ages. Amen. Lord, have mercy. (*Thrice.*) Bless.

Priest. May Christ our true God, through the prayers of his most pure Mother; of Saint N. (*the Patron Saint of the Temple*); (of Saint N., *to whom the Service is said*); and of all the Saints, have mercy upon us and save us, forasmuch as he is good and loveth mankind.

Choir. Lord, have mercy. (*Thrice.*)

And the Priest holdeth the cross to be kissed.

THE GENERAL PANIKHÍDA OR REQUIEM SERVICE

(This service is celebrated, as a rule, in the centre of the Church, in front of a movable stand, whereon are placed a vessel containing rice, and lighted tapers. The censing continueth, almost uninterruptedly, throughout the service.)

Deacon. Bless, Master.

Priest. Blessed is our God always, now, and ever, and unto ages of ages.

Choir. Amen.

The Litany.

Deacon. In peace let us pray to the Lord.

Choir. Lord, have mercy.

For the peace that is from above, and for the salvation of our souls: ℞

For the remission of the sins of those who have departed this life in blessed memory: ℞

For the ever-memorable servants of God, NN.; for their repose, tranquillity and blessed memory: ℞

That he will pardon them every transgression, whether voluntary or involuntary: ℞

That they may present themselves blameless before the dread throne of the Lord of glory: ℞

For the sorrowing and the sick who have set their hope in the consolation of Christ: ℞

That he will release them from all sickness, sorrow and sighing, and make them glad where the light of God's countenance shall visit them: ℞

That the Lord our God will establish their souls in a place of verdure, a place of rest, where all the Righteous dwell: ℞

That they may be numbered with those who are in the bosom of Abraham and Isaac and Jacob: ℞

That he will deliver us from all tribulation, wrath and necessity: ℞

[*℞ = let us pray to the Lord. Choir. Lord, have mercy.*]

Succour us, save us, have mercy upon us, and keep us, O God, by thy grace.

Choir. Lord, have mercy.

Having implored for them the mercies of God, the kingdom of heaven, and remission of sins, let us commend ourselves, and each other, and all our life unto Christ our God.

Choir. To thee, O Lord.

And when the Litany is finished the Priest, bowing his head, readeth, secretly, the Prayer:

O God of spirits, and of all flesh, who hast trampled down Death, and overthrown the Devil, and given life unto thy world: Do thou, the same Lord, give rest to the souls of thy departed servants, NN., in a place of brightness, a place of verdure, a place of repose, whence all sickness, sorrow and sighing have fled away.   Pardon every transgression which they have committed, whether by word, or deed, or thought.   For thou art a good God and lovest mankind; because there is no man who liveth and sinneth not: for thou only art without sin, and thy righteousness is to all eternity, and thy word is true.

Secretly.

Exclamation. For thou art the Resurrection, and the Life, and the Repose of thy departed servants, NN., O Christ our God, and unto thee do we ascribe glory, together with thy Father who is from everlasting, and thine all-holy, and good, and life-giving Spirit, now, and ever, and unto ages of ages.

Choir. Amen.

Deacon. Alleluia (*thrice*), *in the Eighth Tone.*

Verse 1: Blessed are those whom thou hast chosen and taken, O Lord.

Verse 2: The remembrance of them is from generation to generation.

Verse 3: Their souls shall dwell with the blessed.

Choir. Alleluia.   (*Thrice.*)

O Thou who, with wisdom profound, mercifully orderest all things, and who givest that which is expedient unto all men, thou Only Creator: Give rest, O Lord, to the souls of thy servants who have fallen asleep; For they have set their hope on thee, our Maker, the Author of our being, and our God.

Glory to the Father, and to the Son, and to the Holy Spirit, now, and ever, and unto ages of ages.   Amen.

Thee have we as a Wall and a Refuge, and a Mediatrix well-pleasing unto God whom thou hast borne, O Virgin Birth-giver of God, the salvation of the faithful.

Then the Requiem Hymns (Tropari), with the following Refrain:

Blessed art thou, O Lord; teach me thy statutes.

The Choir of the Saints have found the Fountain of Life and the Door of Paradise.   May I also find the right way, through repentance.   I am a lost sheep.   Call me, O Saviour, and save me. ℞

Ye who preached the Lamb of God, and like unto lambs were slain, and are translated unto the life eternal, which waxeth not old: ye holy Martyrs, pray ye unto him that he will vouchsafe us remission of our sins. ℞

Ye who have trod the narrow way most sad; all ye who, in life, have taken upon you the Cross as a yoke, and have followed Me through faith, draw near: Enjoy ye the honours and the crowns which I have prepared for you. ℟

I am an image of thy glory ineffable, though I bear the brands of transgressions: Show thy compassions upon thy creature, O Master, and purify him by thy loving-kindness; and grant unto me the home-country of my heart's desire, making me again a citizen of Paradise. ℟

O thou who of old didst call me into being from nothingness, and didst honour me with thine image divine, but because I had transgressed thy commandments hast returned me again unto the earth from which I was taken: Restore thou me to that image, and to my pristine beauty. ℟

Give rest, O Lord, to the souls of thy servants, and establish them in Paradise. Where the choirs of the Saints, O Lord, and of the Just, shine like the stars of heaven, give rest to thy servants who have fallen asleep, regarding not all their transgressions. ℟

Glory to the Father, and to the Son, and to the Holy Spirit.

Devoutly do we hymn the triune Effulgence of the one Godhead, crying aloud: Holy art thou, O Father who art from everlasting, O Son coeternal, and Spirit divine! Illumine us who, with faith, do worship thee and rescue us from fire eternal.

Now, and ever, and unto ages of ages. Amen.

Hail, O August One, who for the salvation of all men didst bring forth God in the flesh; through whom, also, mankind hath found salvation. Through thee have we found Paradise, O pure, most-blessed Birth-giver of God.

Alleluia, alleluia, alleluia. Glory to thee, O God. (*Thrice.*)

The Litany.

Deacon. Again, yet again, in peace let us pray to the Lord.

The Priest meanwhile reciteth, secretly, the Prayer: O God of spirits, . . . (*See page* 565.)

Choir. Lord, have mercy.

Again we pray for the repose of the souls of the servants of God, NN., departed this life: and that they may be pardoned all their sins, both voluntary and involuntary.

Choir. Lord, have mercy.

That the Lord God will establish their souls where the Just repose.

Choir. Lord, have mercy.

The mercies of God, the kingdom of heaven, and remission of their sins, let us entreat of Christ, our King Immortal and our God.

Choir. Grant it, O Lord.

Deacon. Let us pray to the Lord.

Exclamation.

Priest. For thou art the Resurrection, and the Life, . . . (*See page* 565.)

Choir. Amen.

Give rest with the Just, O our Saviour, unto thy servants, and establish them in thy courts, as it is written: Regarding not, in that thou art good, their sins, whether voluntary or involuntary, and all things, committed either with knowledge or in ignorance, O thou who lovest mankind.

O Christ our God, who from a Virgin didst shine forth upon the world, through her making us children of the light, have mercy upon us.

The Refrain.

Priest and Deacon chant: Give rest, O Lord, to the souls of thy servants dep rted this life.

The Choir repeateth the same.

Priest and Deacon. Glory to the Father, and to the Son, and to the Holy Spirit.

Choir. Now, and ever, and unto ages of ages.   Amen.

(Twice.)

The Theme-Song (Irmós) of the Sixth Canticle of the Canon at the Parting of the Soul from the Body.

Forasmuch as I behold the sea of life surging high with the tempest of temptations, I have fled to thy tranquil haven and cry aloud unto thee: Lead thou my life forth from corruption, O Most Merciful One.

The Litany.

Deacon. Again, yet again, in peace . . . (*See page* 566.)

The Priest meanwhile reciteth, secretly, the Prayer: O God of spirits, . . . (*See page* 565.)

Exclamation.

Priest. For thou art the Resurrection, and the Life, . . . (*See page* 565.)

Choir. Amen.

With the Saints give rest, O Christ, to the souls of thy servants, where there is neither sickness, nor sorrow, nor sighing, but life everlasting.

Thou only art immortal, who hast created and fashioned man. For out of the earth were we mortals made, and unto the earth shall we return again, as thou didst command when thou madest me, saying: For earth thou art, and unto the earth shalt thou return.   Whither also all we mortals wend our way, making of our funeral dirge the song.   Alleluia.

Refrain. Give rest, O Lord, to the souls of thy servants departed this life.

The Theme-Song of the Ninth Canticle of the Canon at the Parting of the Soul from the Body.

It is not possible that men should see God, upon whom the Orders of the Angels dare not gaze: but through thee, O All-pure One, was the Word Incarnate manifested unto men: Whom magnifying, together with the Heavenly Hosts, we call thee blessed.

Reader. O Holy God, Holy Mighty, Holy Immortal One, have mercy upon us.   (*Thrice.*)

Glory . . . O all-holy Trinity, . . . Lord, have mercy.   (*Thrice.*)

Glory . . . now, and ever, . . .

Our Father, . . . (*See page* 559.)

Priest. For thine is the kingdom, and the power, and the glory, of the Father, and of the Son, and of the Holy Spirit, now, and ever, and unto ages of ages.

Choir. Amen.

With the souls of the righteous dead, give rest, O Saviour, to the souls of thy servants, preserving them unto the life of blessedness which is with thee, O thou who lovest mankind.

In the place of thy rest, O Lord, where all thy Saints repose, give rest also to the souls of thy servants: For thou only lovest mankind.

Glory to the Father, and to the Son, and to the Holy Spirit.

Thou art the God who descended into hell, and loosed the bonds of the captives: Do thou give rest, also, to the souls of thy servants.

Now, and ever, and unto ages of ages.   Amen.

O Virgin alone Pure and Undefiled, who without seed didst bring forth God, pray thou unto him that their souls may be saved.

The Litany.

Deacon. Have mercy upon us, O God, according to thy great mercy, we beseech thee: hearken, and have mercy. ℞

Again we pray for the repose of the souls of NN., the servants of God departed this life: and that they may be pardoned all their sins, both voluntary and involuntary. ℞

That the Lord God will establish their souls where the Just repose. ℞

Choir. Lord, have mercy. (Thrice.)

The mercies of God, the kingdom of heaven, and the remission of their sins, let us entreat of Christ, our King Immortal and our God.

Choir. Grant it, O Lord.

Deacon. Let us pray to the Lord.

Choir. Lord, have mercy.

Priest. For thou art the Resurrection, and the Life, . . . (*See page* 565.)

The Priest meanwhile reciteth, secretly, the Prayer: O God of spirits, . . . (*See page* 565.)

Choir. Amen.

Deacon. Wisdom!

Priest. O most holy Birth-giver of God, save us.

Choir. More honourable than the Cherubim, and beyond compare more glorious than the Seraphim, thou who without defilement barest God the Word, true Birth-giver of God, we magnify thee.

Priest. Glory to thee, O Christ-God, our hope; glory to thee.

Glory to the Father, and to the Son, and to the Holy Spirit, now, and ever, and unto ages of ages.   Amen.

Lord, have mercy.   (*Thrice.*)   Bless.

The Priest bestoweth the BENEDICTION.

May he who hath power over both the living and the dead, who himself rose again from the dead, Christ our very God: through the prayers of his all-pure Mother; of the holy, glorious and all-laudable Apostles; of our holy and God-bearing Fathers; and of all the Saints, establish in the mansions of the righteous the souls of his servants who have been taken from us; give them rest in Abraham's bosom, and number them among the Just; and have mercy upon us, forasmuch as he is good and loveth mankind.

Deacon. Give rest eternal, in blessed falling-asleep, O Lord, to the souls of thy servants, NN., departed this life; and make their memory to be eternal.

Choir. Memory eternal!   (*Thrice.*)

PRAYERS IN PREPARATION FOR THE HOLY COMMUNION

(A SELECTION)

I.

A PRAYER OF ST. BASIL THE GREAT.

O Master, Lord Jesus Christ our God, the Fountain of life and of immortality, the Author of all creation, both visible and invisible, the Son coeternal with the Father and equally without beginning, as is the Father which hath no beginning, who through thy great goodness hast, in these latter days, endued flesh, and hast suffered crucifixion and burial for us ungrateful and evil-natured men, and hast renewed with thy blood our nature which was become corrupt through sin: Do thou accept, O King immortal, the repentance of me, a sinner; incline thine ear unto me, and give heed unto my words: for I have sinned, O Lord, I have sinned against heaven and before thee, and am not worthy to look upon the loftiness of thy glory. I have affronted thy goodness, in that I have transgressed thy commandments, and have not obeyed thy behests. But thou, O Lord, inasmuch as thou art not vengeful, but long-suffering and of great mercy, hast not delivered me over unto destruction with my transgressions, for that thou didst, at every moment, await my return. For, O thou who lovest mankind, thou hast said, by the mouth of thy prophet: I desire not the death of the sinner, but that he should turn again and live. Thou dost not desire, O Master, to destroy the work of thy hands, neither desirest thou the destruction of the human race, but willest that all men should be saved, and should come to the knowledge of the truth. Wherefore I, also, albeit I am unworthy of heaven and of earth and of this transitory life, in that I have made myself all sin, and have become a slave to sensual things, and have defiled thine image; yet, inasmuch as I am thy creature and the work of thy hands, I despair not of my salvation, accursed though I be, and I draw near with confident hope to thine illimitable compassion. Accept me also, O Lord who lovest mankind, as thou didst accept the sinning woman, the thief, the publican, the prodigal Son; take thou my heavy burden of sin, O thou who hast borne the sins of the world, who healest human infirmities, who invitest to thyself, and givest rest unto, those who labour and are heavy-laden; who didst come to call not the righteous but sinners to repentance. Purify me from all uncleanness, both bodily and spiritual, and teach me to fulfil holiness in thy fear; that having received a portion of thy Holy Things with the testimony of my pure conscience, I may be united unto thy holy Body and Blood, and may possess thee, dwelling within me and abiding with the Father and thy Holy Spirit. Yea, O Lord Jesus Christ my God, let the communion of thine All-pure and Life-giving Mysteries be not unto me for condemnation, and let me not be infirm in body and soul because I have partaken thereof unworthily. But grant that, even unto my last breath, I may partake uncondemned of thy Holy Things, unto communion with the Holy Spirit, unto a viaticum for life eternal, unto an acceptable defence at thy dread Judgment Seat. And let me, together with all thine elect, be a partaker of the incorruptible good things which thou hast prepared, O Lord, for those who love thee; in whom, also, thou art glorified forever. Amen.

II.

A Prayer of St. John Chrysostom.

I know, O Lord my God, that I am unworthy and am not meet that thou shouldest enter beneath the roof of the temple of my soul, because it is all empty and dead; and there is in me no worthy place wherein thou mayest lay thy head. But inasmuch as thou from thy loftiness didst humble thyself for our sake, so likewise do thou now humble thyself unto my humility: and as it seemed good unto thee to lie in the cavern and in the manger of dumb beasts, so also now graciously vouchsafe to lie in the manger of my dumb soul, and to enter into my defiled body. As thou didst not disdain to enter into the house of Simon the leper, and there to sit at meat with sinners, so also graciously vouchsafe to enter into the house of my humble soul, which is leprous and sinful. As thou didst not reject the woman, a harlot and a sinner like unto me, who came and touched thee, so also show thou mercy upon me, a sinner, who now come unto thee and touch thee. As thou didst feel no loathing for the polluted lips of the woman which kissed thee, so also loathe thou not my even more defiled and polluted lips and unclean tongue. But may the fiery coal of thine all-pure Body and of thy precious Blood be unto the sanctification, enlightenment and health of my humble soul and body, unto the lightening of the burden of my many sins, unto preservation from every operation of the Devil, unto the expulsion and interdiction of my evil and wicked manner of life, unto the mortification of passions, unto instruction in thy commandments, unto the acquiring of thy divine grace, unto the inheritance of thy kingdom. For I come unto thee, O Christ-God, not with disdain, but trusting in thine unspeakable goodness, and in order that through long absenting of myself from communion with thee I be not seized by the invisible wolf. Wherefore I pray thee, in that thou alone art holy, O Master: Sanctify thou my soul and body, my mind and heart, my belly and my reins, and renew thou me altogether. Establish thy fear in my members, and make thy sanctification to be inalienable from me. Be thou my helper and defender, guiding my life in peace, enabling me to stand at thy right hand with thy Saints: through the prayers and supplications of thy Mother; of thy bodiless servitors, the all-pure heavenly hosts; and of all the saints who, in all the ages, have been well-pleasing unto thee. Amen.

III.

A Prayer of Simeon Metaphrastes.

Like as I were now standing before thy dread and upright Judgment Seat, O Christ-God, receiving sentence and rendering an accounting of the sins I have committed, so also now, ere that day of my condemnation be come, standing before thee at thy holy Altar and before thy terrible and holy angels, convicted by mine own conscience, I offer as a sacrifice unto thee my evil and iniquitous deeds, declaring and condemning them. Look upon my humility, O Lord, and pardon all my sins. Behold, mine iniquities have exceeded the number of the hairs upon my head. For what evil is there that I have not done? What sin is there that I have not committed? What evil thing is there that I have not meditated in my soul? I am guilty of fornication and of adultery, of pride, arrogance, condemnation of others, censure, idle conversation, unworthy laughter, drunkenness, gluttony, hatred, envy, cupidity, avarice, usury, self-love, ambition, rapacity; of untruthfulness, unjust acquisition, jealousy, calumny, and of impiety. I have polluted, corrupted and rendered lewd all my senses and members, in all things fulfilling the will of the Devil. I know, O Lord, that mine iniquities are gone over my head; but thy bounties are immeasurable, thy benignant goodness is unutterable, and there is no sin which can overcome thy love of mankind. Wherefore, O King most marvellous, O Lord benign, reveal thy mercies also upon me, a sinner; show forth the power of thy clemency; manifest the might of thine ineffable tenderness of heart, and accept me, a sinner, who now have recourse unto thee. Accept me as thou didst accept the prodigal son, as thou didst accept the thief and the woman who was a sinner. Accept me, who have beyond measure sinned against thee in word, in deed, in unlawful desires and in foolish thoughts. As thou didst receive those who came unto thee at the eleventh hour, and had done nothing worthy, so also receive thou me, a sinner; for I have sinned greatly, I have defiled myself, I have offended thy Holy Spirit, and have grieved thy love both in deed, and in word, and in thought, both by day and by night, both secretly and openly, both voluntarily and involuntarily. I know, O Lord, that thou wilt set my sins before me as they were committed by me, and wilt demand of me an accounting of that wherein I have unpardonably transgressed. But O Lord, Lord! Convict me not at thy just Judgment, neither condemn me in thine anger, and chastise me not with thy wrath; Have mercy upon me, O Lord, for I am not only helpless, but I am also the work of thy hands. Thou, O Lord, hast confirmed thy fear upon me, yet I have done evil in thy sight. Against thee only have I sinned; but I entreat thee: Enter thou not into judgment with thy servant: for if thou, Lord, wilt regard iniquity, Lord, who shall stand? I am an abyss of sin, and unworthy to look up and behold the heights of heaven because of my many sins, which are without number. For in me there is no lack of every sort of misdoing, neither of guile, nor of satanic wiliness, of presumption, of sinful thoughts, and of many other passions. With what sins have not I defiled myself! Unto what evil habits have not I been in bondage! I have committed every sin, I have filled my soul with every sort of uncleanness, and have become worthless for thee, my God, and for men. Who shall reëstablish me, who have fallen into such evil and countless transgressions? O Lord, my God, on thee do I set my trust! If it be possible for me to hope for salvation, if the multitude of my iniquities are vanquished by thy love for mankind, — then be thou unto me a Saviour: according to thy bounties and thy mercies, loose, remit unto me, forgive all things wherein I have sinned against thee, seeing that my soul is filled with many sins and there is no hope of salvation in me. Have mercy upon me, O God, according to thy great mercy; requite me not according to my deeds; judge me not according to my acts; but turn thou me again; be thou my defender; deliver thou my soul from mine increasing iniquities and from my frightful imaginations. Save me for thy mercy's sake, that where sin was multiplied there also may thy grace abound. And I will laud and glorify thee forever, all the days of my life; for thou art the God of the penitent and the Saviour of those who have sinned; and unto thee do we ascribe glory, together with thy Father who hath no beginning, and thine all-holy, and good, and life-giving Spirit, now, and ever, and unto ages of ages. Amen.

IV.

A Prayer of Simeon, the New Theologian.

From lips defiled, from heart iniquitous, from tongue impure, from soul polluted, receive thou my prayer, O my Christ, and despise not my words, imaginations and presumption. Vouchsafe that I may speak boldly, O my Christ, that which I desire. Teach me, moreover, that which I ought to do and to say. I have sinned above the sinning woman who, having learned where the Lord was, and having bought ointment, came fearlessly to anoint thy feet, my God, my Master and my Christ. As thou didst not repulse her, when she came from the impulse of her heart, so also despise thou not me, O Word, and grant that I, also, may clasp thy feet and kiss them and fearlessly anoint them with floods of tears, as with precious ointment. Wash me and purify me with my tears, O Word; remit my transgressions and grant me pardon. Thou knowest the multitude of my evil-doings; thou knowest also my scars; thou seest my wickedness. But thou knowest also my faith, and beholdest my earnest desire, and hearest my sighing. Not a single tear-drop, nor even a single portion of a drop, is hidden from thee, O my God, my Maker, my Deliverer. Thine eyes behold also that which I have not yet done: in thy book is written also that which, as yet, is not performed. Thou seest my humility, thou seest my infirmities and all my sins. Remit them, O God of all men, that with a pure heart, with trembling mind and contrite soul I may partake of thine undefiled and all-holy Mysteries, wherewith is quickened and made a participant of the divine every man who eateth and drinketh thereof with a pure heart. Thou hast said, O my Lord: Every one who eateth my flesh and drinketh my blood abideth in me, and I in him. True is every word of my Lord and God. Partaking of the divine Mysteries which make men like unto God, I am no longer alone, but abide O, my Christ, with thee, the all-effulgent Light which illumineth, the world. And I shall not be left without thee, the Life-giver, my Breath, my life, my joy, the salvation of the world. Wherefore I draw near unto thee, as thou seest, with tears and a contrite soul, and implore thee that thou wilt vouchsafe unto me to receive remission of my transgressions, and to partake, uncondemned, of thy spotless and life-giving Mysteries. Abide with me, the greatly-accursed one, as thou hast promised, that the Evil One may not craftily tempt me, and having tempted, may not lead me astray from thy precepts which render god-like. And therefore I fall down before thee, and I cry fervently unto thee: As thou didst accept the prodigal son, as thou didst accept the sinning woman who came unto thee, so also receive thou me, who am a prodigal and vile, O Bountiful One! Having now recourse unto thee with a contrite soul, I know, O my Saviour, that no other man hath so sinned against thee as have I, no other man hath wrought such deeds as have I. But I know, also, that neither the magnitude of the transgression, nor the multitude of the sins can transcend the great long-suffering and unutterable love toward mankind of my God. According to thy mercy and condescension thou cleansest those who repent with their whole heart; thou cleansest and enlightenest them, and makest them participants of the light, and sharers of thy Divinity. And, albeit it is strange for angels and men to comprehend, thou ofttimes holdest converse with them as with thy true friends. All this doth render me bold, all this doth give me wings, O my Christ. And confidently setting my hope on thy rich mercy to usward, both with joy and trembling, I partake of fire, being myself but grass. And — O marvellous wonder!— I am not consumed but am sprinkled with dew, as was of old the bush which burned yet was not consumed. Now, with grateful thoughts, with grateful heart, with grateful members both of my soul and of my body, I bow in worship, I laud and glorify thee, O my God, who art blessed now and forevermore.

V.

A Prayer of St. John of Damascus.

I stand before the doors of thy temple, yet refrain not from wicked thoughts. But O Christ-God, who didst justify the publican, and didst show mercy upon the woman of Cana, and didst open the doors of Paradise to the thief, — open thou unto me also thy loving-kindness, and accept thou me, who am come and who touch thee, as thou didst accept also the woman who was a sinner, and the woman who had an issue of blood. One of them, through touching the hem of thy garment, received perfect healing; and the other, clasping thine all-pure feet, carried away the forgiveness of her sins. And let me not be consumed, accursed though I be, through daring to receive thy Body. But accept thou me, as thou didst accept them, and illumine my spiritual senses, consuming my sinful offences: through the prayers of Her who bore thee without seed, and of the heavenly Powers: For blessed art thou, unto ages of ages. Amen.

VI.

A Prayer of St. John Chrysostom.

I believe, O Lord, and I confess, that thou art in very truth the Christ, the Son of the living God, who didst come into the world to save sinners, of whom I am chief. And I believe that this is, of a truth, thine all-pure Body, and that this is thine own precious Blood. Wherefore, I beseech thee, have mercy upon me, and forgive my transgressions, whether voluntary or involuntary: whether of word or of deed: whether committed with knowledge or in ignorance. And vouchsafe that I may partake without condemnation of thine all-pure Mysteries, unto the remission of my sins, and unto life eternal. Amen.

APPENDIX A

Hymns for: Lord, I have cried unto thee.
Hymns to the Birth-giver of God (Dogmátiki).
Tropari (Hymns for the Day), Bogoróditchny (Hymns to the Birth-giver of God),
Kondaki (Collect-Hymns), and Canons: In the Eight Tones.

TONE I.

Hymns for: Lord, I have cried unto thee.

Accept our evening petitions, O holy Lord, and grant us remission of our sins: For thou only revealest Resurrection unto the world.

Go ye round about Zion, ye people, and encompass her, and give glory therein to him who is risen from the dead: For he is our God who delivereth us from our sins.

O come, ye people, let us sing praises and worship Christ, glorifying his Resurrection from the dead: For he is our God, who delivereth the world from the wiles of the enemy.

Glory to the Father, and to the Son, and to the Holy Spirit, now, and ever, and unto ages of ages.   Amen.

Hymn to the Birth-giver of God (Dogmátik). Let us sing the praises of Mary, Virgin, Door of heaven, Glory of all the world, sprung forth from man, who also bare the Lord; the Song of the Bodiless Powers, and the Enriching of the faithful.   For she revealed herself as Heaven and the Temple of the Godhead.   She destroyed the bulwarks of enmity, ushered in peace, and threw open the kingdom.   Wherefore, in that we possess this confirmation of our faith we have a defender, even the Lord who was born of her.   Be bold, therefore, be bold, ye people of God, for he, the All-Powerful, will vanquish your foes.

Hymn (Tropár). While the stone was sealed by the Jews, and soldiers stood on guard over thy body undefiled, thou didst rise on the third day, O Saviour, who givest life unto the world.   For which cause the Heavenly Powers cried aloud unto thee, O Giver of Life: Glory to thy resurrection, O Christ!   Glory to thy kingdom!   Glory to thy providence, O thou who alone lovest mankind!

Glory to the Father, and to the Son, and to the Holy Spirit, now, and ever, and unto ages of ages.   Amen.

Hymn to the Birth-giver of God (Bogoróditchen). As Gabriel proclaimed unto thee, O Virgin: Hail!   With that cry did the Lord of all become incarnate in thee, the Holy Tabernacle, as spake the righteous David: Thou hast manifested thyself more spacious than the heavens, in that thou hast borne thy Creator. Glory to him who abode in thee! Glory to him who came forth from thee! Glory to him who through thy birth-giving hath set us free!

Collect-Hymn (Kondák). As God thou didst arise from the grave in glory, and with thee didst raise the world; and the race of men singeth praises unto thee as God; and Death hath vanished; and Adam leapeth for joy, O Lord; and Eve, now released from her bonds, exulteth, crying: Thou art he who giveth Resurrection unto all men, O Christ.

THE CANON

Canticle I. (Founded on Exodus xv. 1–20.)

Theme-Song (Irmós). In godlike wise hath thy victorious right arm been glorified in strength; for in that it was all-powerful, O Immortal One, it shattered the adversaries, and made for the Israelites a new path through the deep.

Refrain. Glory to thy holy Resurrection, O Lord.

Hymns (Tropari). Thou who, with hands most pure, in the beginning, in that thou art God, divinely created me out of the dust, didst stretch forth thine arms upon the cross, summoning from the earth my corrupti-ble body, which thou thyself also didst accept from a Virgin. ℞

Unto dissolution thou didst subject thyself for my sake, and didst yield up thy soul unto death, O thou who with thy divine in-breathing didst infuse into me a soul. And when thou hadst rent asunder the bonds which were from everlasting, and with thee didst raise up the dead, thou wert glorified in incorruption. ℞

Hymn to the Birth-giver of God (Bogoróditchen). Hail, O Fount of Grace! Hail, O Ladder, and Gate of Heaven! Hail! O Candlestick and Golden Jar, and Mount Unhewn, who gavest birth to Christ, the Life-giver of the world!

(Canticle II. is generally omitted.)

Canticle III. (Founded on 1 Samuel ii. 1–11.)

Theme-Song (Irmós). O thou who alone knowest the frailty of man's nature, and in tender compassion didst transform thyself into his like-ness: Gird me with might from on high, that I may cry aloud unto thee, O Holy One: Inspired is the temple of thine ineffable glory, O thou who lovest mankind.

Refrain. Glory to thy holy Resurrection, O Lord.

(And the other Hymns (Tropari), appointed, as after the first Theme-Song.)

Canticle IV. (Founded on Habakkuk iii. 2.)

Theme-Song (Irmós). When Habakkuk, with vision prophetic, beheld thee as a Mount overshadowed by the grace of God, he proclaimed in anticipation that from thee should come forth the Holy One of Israel, for our salvation and regeneration.

(Refrain as before, and the appointed Hymns.)

Canticle V. (Founded on Isaiah xxvi. 9–20.)

Theme-Song (Irmós). Thou who, by the brightness of thy coming, hast illumined, and by thy Cross hast enlightened the uttermost parts of the universe, O Christ: Enlighten with the light of thy wisdom divine the hearts of true believers who hymn thy praises.

(Refrain as before, and the appointed Hymns.)

Canticle VI. (Founded on Jonah ii. 2–7.)

Theme-Song (Irmós). The nethermost pit hath compassed us about. There is none that delivereth; we are accounted as sheep for the slaughter. Save thy people, O God, for thou art the strength of the weak and their restoration.

(Refrain as before, and the appointed Hymns.)

Canticle VII. (Founded on Daniel iii. 26–56.)

Theme-Song (Irmós). Upon thee, as a supersensual furnace, do we faithful fix our eyes, O Birth-giver of God; for as he, the greatly-exalted, saved the Three Children, so also did he, the God of our fathers, worthy of praise and exceeding glorious, wholly renew the world through thy womb.

(Refrain as before, and the appointed Hymns.)

Canticle VIII. (Founded on Daniel iii. 57–72 (Apocrypha).)

We praise, bless and adore the Lord, singing praises and exalting him unto ages of ages.

Theme-Song (Irmós). In the furnace, as in a smelting-forge, did the Hebrew Children shine with the beauty of godliness more pure than gold, saying: O all ye works of the Lord, bless ye the Lord: praise him and magnify him unto all the ages.

(Refrain as before, and the appointed Hymns.)

Canticle IX. (Founded on Exodus iii. 2–4.)

Theme-Song (Irmós). The bush that burned with fire yet was not consumed, showed forth the type of thy pure birth-giving. Quench now, also, we beseech thee, the fiery furnace of the fierce temptations which assail us, that we may perpetually magnify thee, O Birth-giver of God.

(Refrain as before, and the appointed Hymns.)

TONE II.

Verses and Hymns (Stikhíri) for: Lord, I have cried unto thee.

O come, let us worship him who was begotten of the Father before the ages, the Word of God incarnate of the Virgin Mary; for when he had endured the cross he was delivered over to the tomb, for his own good will it was so to do; and when he rose again from the dead he saved me, the man who had gone astray.

Christ our Saviour, when he had nailed to the cross the handwriting against us, brought it to naught and annihilated the dominion of death. We adore his awakening again from death on the third day.

With the Archangels let us sing the Resurrection of Christ: for he is the Redeemer and Saviour of our souls; and he shall come again, in glory most terrible, in power most mighty, to judge the world which he hath made.

Glory to the Father, and to the Son, and to the Holy Spirit, now, and ever, and unto ages of ages. Amen.

Hymn to the Birth-giver of God (Dogmátik). The shadow of the Law passed away when grace came; for as the bush burned with fire yet was not consumed, even so as a Virgin didst thou bring forth yet remainedst Virgin still. In place of the pillar of fire there rose the Sun of Righteousness; in place of Moses, Christ, the Salvation of our souls.

Hymn (Tropár). When thou didst condescend unto death, O Life Immortal, thou didst slay Hell with the lightning flash of thy divinity. When also thou didst raise up the dead from the subterranean abodes, all the Powers of heaven cried aloud: O Life-giver, Christ our God, glory to thee!

Hymn to the Birth-giver of God (Bogoróditchen). Beyond the power of thought, exceeding glorious are all thy mysteries, O Birth-giver of God; sealed in purity and preserved in virginity, thou art acknowledged to be, in very truth, the Mother who didst bring forth the true God; wherefore entreat thou him that our souls may be saved.

Collect-Hymn (Kondák). Thou didst rise from the tomb, O Saviour almighty, and Hell was affrighted when it beheld the marvel; and the dead arose; Creation, also, beholding, exulted with thee, and Adam rejoiced exceedingly. And the world, O my Saviour, singeth thy praises forevermore.

THE CANON

Theme-Songs (Irmós). I. In the deep, aforetime, did the overwhelming force overthrow all the host of Pharaoh; and the Word, when it became incarnate, utterly annihilated sin most pernicious. Exceeding glorious is the Lord, for he hath triumphed gloriously.

Refrain. Glory to thy holy Resurrection, O Lord.

(Then the appointed Hymns, composed after the model of those shown in Tone I.)

III.* The desert hath blossomed like the lily of the field, O Lord, as also the barren church of the Gentiles, through thy coming, wherein, also, my heart is established. *(Refrain and appointed Hymns.)*

IV. From a Virgin didst thou come forth; neither as an Ambassador nor as Angel, but the very Lord himself made flesh, and didst wholly save me, a man. For which cause I cry aloud unto thee: Glory to thy might, O Lord. *R. and Hs.*

* As already explained, Theme-Song II. is usually omitted.

V. As Mediator between God and man didst thou come, O Christ-God; for through thee, O Lord, we have access from the night of ignorance unto thy Father, the Author of Light. *R. and Hs.*

VI. Wallowing in the abyss of sin, I appeal unto the abyss unfathomable of thy loving-kindness. Raise thou me up from corruption, O God. *R. and Hs.*

VII. The impious command of the cruel tyrant forced the flame on high; but Christ bore unto the God-fearing Children spiritual dew. Blessed and most glorious is he. *R. and Hs.*

VIII. The fiery furnace of old in Babylon divided in twain its action, by the command of God consuming the Chaldæans, but sprinkling with dew the faithful who sang: O all ye works of the Lord, bless ye the Lord. *R. and Hs.*

IX. The Son of the Begetter who hath no beginning, both God and the Lord, hath revealed himself unto us incarnate of a Virgin, to illumine those who sat in darkness, and to gather together those who were scattered abroad: for which cause we magnify the all-hymned Birth-giver of God. *R. and Hs.*

TONE III.

Verses and Hymns for: Lord, I have cried unto thee.

By thy cross, O Christ our Saviour, the dominion of death hath been destroyed and the delusion of the Devil overthrown; the generation of men also, being saved by faith, doth offer unto thee a perpetual song.

All things have been illumined by thy Resurrection, O Lord, and Paradise hath been opened once again; and all creation extolling thee doth offer unto thee a perpetual song.

I glorify the might of the Father, and of the Son, and of the Holy Spirit I sing the power; the Godhead, undivided, uncreated, the Trinity of one Essence, who reigneth unto ages of ages.

Glory to the Father, and to the Son, and to the Holy Spirit, now, and ever, and unto ages of ages. Amen.

Hymn to the Birth-giver of God (Dogmátik). How can we refrain from wonder at thy human-divine birth-giving, O All-august One? For though thou receivedst not the embrace of man, O All-undefiled One, yet didst thou bear, without a father, a son in the flesh born of the Father without mother before the ages: who suffered no change, neither mingling nor division, but preserved intact the peculiar natures of both. Wherefore, O Maiden Mother, Sovereign Lady, beseech thou him that the souls of those may be saved who, in the true faith, confess thee to be the Birth-giver of God.

Hymn (Tropár). Let the heavens rejoice and let the earth be glad, for the Lord hath showed strength with his arm; he hath trampled down Death by death; he is become the first-born of the dead; from the womb of Hell hath he delivered us, and unto the world hath he vouchsafed great mercy.

Hymn to the Birth-giver of God (Bogoróditchen). Thee, who wast the Mediatrix of the salvation of our race, we sing, O Birth-giver of God and Virgin. For in the flesh assumed from thee, after that he had suffered the passion of the cross, thy Son and our God delivered us from corruption, in that he loveth mankind.

Collect-Hymn (Kondák). To-day art thou risen from the tomb, O Bountiful One, and hast led us forth from the gates of death; to-day Adam exulteth and Eve rejoiceth, and the Prophets, together with the Patriarchs, continually do sing the power divine of thy might.

THE CANON

Theme-Songs (Irmosí). I. He who of old, by his gesture divine, did gather together into one mass the waters and cleave the sea for the people of Israel, the same is our God exceedingly glorious: To him alone will we make our song, for he hath glorified himself.

Refrain. Glory to thy holy Resurrection, O Lord.

(Then the appointed Hymns, composed after the model of those shown in Tone I.)

III. O thou who from nothingness didst call forth all things created by the Word, and perfected by thy Spirit, O Ruler of the Universe: Stablish thou me in thy love. *R. and Hs.*

IV. Thou hast established a steadfast love to usward, O Lord; for thine Only-begotten Son hast thou given unto death for us. Wherefore we cry aloud with thanksgiving unto thee: Glory to thy might, O Lord. *R. and Hs.*

V. Right early do I wake unto thee, O Maker of all things, the Peace which passeth understanding; for thy commandments are the light: Guide thou me therein. *R. and Hs.*

VI. The nethermost abyss of sins hath compassed me about, and my soul forsaketh me. But stretch forth thy lofty arm, O Lord, and save me, as thou savedst Peter of old, O my Pilot. *R. and Hs.*

VII. As thou of old didst refresh with dew the three godly Children in the Chaldæan flames, even so illumine thou with the radiant fire of the Godhead us who cry unto thee: Blessed art thou, O God of our fathers. *R. and Hs.*

VIII. When the godly Children were thrust into the fire intolerable, yet remained without hurt from the flame, they sang the song divine: O all ye works of the Lord, bless ye the Lord and exalt him unto all the ages. *R. and Hs.*

IX. A marvel new and befitting the Godhead! Through the closed gates of a Virgin the Lord passeth forth to sight; naked at his going-in, and at his coming-forth a bearer of the flesh did God manifest himself, and the gate remaineth closed: Her, who in wise ineffable is the Mother of God, we magnify. *R. and Hs.*

TONE IV.

Hymns for: Lord, I have cried unto thee.

Unceasingly do we adore thy life-giving Cross, O Christ our God, and glorify thy Resurrection on the third day; for thereby, O Almighty One, thou didst renew the nature of man, which had become corrupt, and didst restore to us the way to heaven: For thou only art good and lovest mankind.

Thou hast done away with the penalty of the tree of disobedience, O Saviour, in that thou, of thine own good will, wast nailed to the tree of the Cross; and when thou hadst descended into Hell, O Mighty One, thou didst break the bonds of death, in that thou wert God: For which cause we worship thy Resurrection from the dead, joyfully crying unto thee: O Lord Almighty, glory to thee.

Thou hast destroyed the gates of Hell, O Lord, and by thy death hast annihilated the kingdom of Death, and hast freed the human race from corruption, giving life and incorruption and great mercy unto the world.

Glory to the Father, and to the Son, and to the Holy Spirit, now, and ever, and unto ages of ages. Amen.

Hymn to the Birth-giver of God (Dogmátik). The Prophet David who, through thee, was the forefather of God, did prophesy in melody concerning thee, to him who wrought mighty things for thee: Upon thy right hand did stand the Queen. For God, who was graciously pleased without father to become incarnate of thee, hath manifested thee as the Mother and Ambassador of life, that he might restore again his image, which had become corrupted by passions; and that Christ, who is great and rich in mercy, when he had found the sheep which was gone astray wandering on the mountains, and had laid it on his shoulders, might bring it to his Father, and according to his will unite it to the heavenly powers, and save the world, O Birth-giver of God.

Hymn (Tropár). When the Women Disciples of the Lord had learned from the Angels the glad tidings of the Resurrection, and had cast away the condemnation of their forefathers, they spake exultingly to the Apostles: Death is no more; Christ-God is risen, granting unto the world great mercy.

Hymn to the Birth-giver of God (Bogoróditchen). The mystery which was hidden from everlasting and was unknown of the Angels, through thee, O Birth-giver of God, was revealed to those who dwell upon earth, in that God having become incarnate in unblended union, of his own good will accepted the Cross for our sakes; whereby he raised again the first created and hath saved our souls.

Collect-Hymn (Kondák). My Saviour and Redeemer from the grave, in that he was God, rose from earth-born bonds, and shattered the gates of Hell; and in that he was the Lord, he rose again on the third day.

THE CANON. .

St. John of Damascus.

Theme-Songs (Irmosi). I. When Israel of old had passed through the Red Sea's abyss with foot unwet, through the cross-wise stretching forth of Moses' hands, they overcame the host of Amalek in the wilderness.

Refrain. Glory to thy holy Resurrection, O Lord.

(Then the appointed Hymns, composed after the model of those shown in Tone I.)

III. Thy Church rejoiceth in thee, O Christ, crying: Thou art my fortress, O Lord, my refuge and my strength. *R. and Hs.*

IV. The Church, beholding thee uplifted upon the Cross, O Sun of Righteousness, standeth in its stateliness, worthily crying: Glory to thy might, O Lord. *R. and Hs.*

V. Thou art come, O my Lord, for a light to the world, a holy light, which turneth from the darkness of ignorance those who with faith sing praises unto thee. *R. and Hs.*

VI. I will sacrifice unto thee with the voice of thanksgiving, O Lord, the Church crieth aloud unto thee, in that she hath purified herself from the blood of demons by the blood which for the sake of mercy flowed from thy side. *R. and Hs.*

VII. The Abrahamic Children in the Persian furnace, fired rather by love of godliness than by the flame, cried aloud: Blessed art thou, O Lord, in the tabernacle of thy glory. *R. and Hs.*

VIII. Daniel stretched forth his hand, and stopped the gaping mouths of the lions in the pit. And the Holy Children, zealous in piety, girding themselves with virtue, quenched the raging fire, as they cried: O all ye works of the Lord, bless ye the Lord. *R. and Hs.*

IX. The Corner-stone unhewn by hands from thee was hewn, O Virgin, Mount unquarried, even Christ, who hath bound together Nature that had been divided. Therefore, rejoicing, we magnify thee, O Birth-giver of God. *R. and Hs.*

TONE V.

Hymns for: Lord, I have cried unto thee.

By thy precious Cross, O Christ, thou didst put to shame the Devil, and by thy Resurrection thou didst dull the sting of sin, and save us from the gates of death: We glorify thee, O Only-begotten One.

He who giveth Resurrection to the generation of men was led as a sheep to the slaughter. The Princes of Hell were terrified by him, and the gates of lamentation were lifted up. For Christ, the King of Glory, entered in, saying unto those who were in bonds: Go forth; and to those who were in darkness: Unveil yourselves.

O mighty marvel! The Creator of things invisible, through his love toward mankind, after having suffered in the flesh, is risen again immortal. Come, ye subjects of the nations, let us bow in worship before him. For in that, through his tender loving-kindness, we have been delivered from going astray, we have learned to sing the praises of the One God in three Persons.

Glory to the Father, and to the Son, and to the Holy Spirit, now, and ever, and unto ages of ages. Amen.

Hymn to the Birth-giver of God (Dogmátik). In the Red Sea of old was set forth the type of the Bride unwedded: there Moses was the divider of the water; but here Gabriel was the minister of the miracle. Then Israel passed over the deep with foot unwet; but now a Virgin hath, without seed, given birth to Christ. The sea, after Israel had passed over, remained impassable; the Blameless One, after the conception of Emmanuel, remained undefiled. Thou who Art, and who from ever-lasting Art, hast revealed thyself in fashion as a man: Have mercy upon us, O God.

Hymn (Tropár). The Word, who with the Father and the Spirit hath no beginning, and who, for our salvation, was born of a Virgin, let us faithful believers hymn and adore. For it was his good pleasure to ascend the cross in the flesh, and to suffer death, and through his own glorious Resurrection to raise the dead.

Hymn to the Birth-giver of God (Bogoróditchen). Hail, O impassable Gate of the Lord! Hail, Wall and Shelter of those who flee unto thee! Hail, Haven unvexed of storms and Unwedded One who didst bring forth in the flesh thy Maker and thy God! Abate not thine entreaties on behalf of those who sing thy praises and do homage to thy birth-giving.

Collect-Hymn (Kondák). Into Hell thou didst descend, O my Saviour, and when thou hadst destroyed its gates, in that thou art almighty, thou didst raise again with thee those who were dead, in that thou art the Creator; and thou didst destroy the sting of death, O Christ, and didst release Adam from the curse, O thou who lovest mankind. Wherefore we all do cry aloud: Save us, O Lord.

THE CANON.

Theme-Songs (Irmosí). I. The horse and its rider did Christ cast into the Red Sea, shattering the hosts thereof with his lofty arm: But he saved Israel, who sang a song of victory.

Refrain. Glory to thy holy Resurrection, O Lord.

(Then the appointed Hymns, composed after the model of those shown in Tone I.)

III. Thou who upon nothing by thy command didst erect the earth, and didst suspend it, hanging unsupported: Upon the rock immovable of thy commandments, O Christ, establish thou thy Church, O thou who alone art good and lovest mankind. *R. and Hs.*

IV. When Habakkuk, with vision prophetic, meditated upon thy

Divine Emptying, O Christ, he cried aloud with trembling unto thee: For the salvation of thy people and to save thine anointed ones art thou come. *R. and Hs.*

V. O thou who arrayest thyself with light as it were a garment, unto thee do I wake right early, and I cry unto thee: Illumine thou my darkened soul, O Christ, in that thou only art compassionate. *R. and Hs.*

VI. Lull to tranquillity, O Lord Christ, the sea infuriated by the soul-destroying billows of my passions, and in that thou art compassionate lead me forth from corruption. *R. and Hs.*

VII. The greatly exalted Lord of our Fathers quenched the fire and sprinkled with dew the Children, who sang with one accord: O God, blessed art thou. *R. and Hs.*

VIII. Unto thee, the Maker of all things, the Children in the furnace, weaving a choral universal, did sing: O all ye works of the Lord, bless ye the Lord and exalt him unto all the ages. *R. and Hs.*

IX. Rejoice, O Isaiah! A Virgin is with child, and shall bear a Son, Emmanuel, both God and Man: and Orient is his name; whom magnifying, we call the Virgin blessed. *R. and Hs.*

TONE VI.

Hymns for: Lord, I have cried unto thee.

In that thou didst possess the victory over Hell, O Christ, thou didst ascend the cross, that thou who art free among the dead mightest raise up with thee those who sat in the shadow of death. O Saviour Almighty, who from thine own light dost shed forth life, have mercy upon us.

To-day is Christ risen, as he foretold, having trampled Death under foot and given joy to the world, that crying aloud in song we all may say: O Fountain of Life, O Light unapproachable, O Saviour Almighty, have mercy upon us.

From thee, O Lord, who art present in all creation, whither shall we sinners flee? To heaven? Thou thyself dwellest there. To Hell? Thou didst trample Death under foot. To the depths of the sea? There, also, is thy hand, O Lord. Unto thee do we flee, and bowing down before thee, we make our petition: O thou who didst rise from the dead, have mercy upon us.

Glory to the Father, and to the Son, and to the Holy Spirit, now, and ever, and unto ages of ages. Amen.

Hymn to the Birth-giver of God (Dogmátik). Who is there that doth not bless thee, O all-holy Virgin? Who is there that singeth not thy undefiled birth-giving? The Only-begotten Son, who shone forth before all ages from the Father, the same came forth from thee, O Pure One, having in wondrous wise become incarnate, being by nature God, and becoming by nature a man, for our sake; not being divided in two persons, but known in two natures, yet unmerged. Him do thou beseech, O Pure, All-blessed One, that he will have mercy on our souls.

Hymn (Tropár). The Angelic Powers were in thy sepulchre, and the guards became as dead men, and Mary stood by the tomb seeking thy most pure body. Thou didst lead captive Hell, yet wert not tempted thereby; thou who art the bestower of life didst come to meet the Woman. Glory to thee, O Lord, who didst rise again from the dead.

Hymn to the Birth-giver of God (Bogoróditchen). Thou who didst call thy Mother blessed, of thine own good will didst come unto thy passion, shining radiantly upon the cross, desiring to seek out Adam, and saying unto the Angels: Rejoice with me, for I have found the piece of silver which was lost. O our God, who with wisdom hast ordered all things, glory to thee.

Collect-Hymn (Kondák). When Christ-God, the Life-giver of all things, had by his life-bestowing palm raised up from the valleys of gloom those who were dead, he adjudged Resurrection unto the race of men. For he is the Saviour of all, and the Resurrection, and the Life, and the God of all.

THE CANON.

Theme-Songs (Irmosí). I. When Israel passed on foot over the deep, as it had been dry land, and beheld their pursuer Pharaoh engulfed in the sea, they cried aloud: Unto God let us sing a song of victory.

Refrain. Glory to thy holy Resurrection, O Lord.

(Then the appointed Hymns, composed after the model of those shown in Tone I.)

III. There is none holy like unto thee, O Lord my God, who hast exalted the horn of thy faithful, O Good One, and hast established us upon the rock of thy confession. *R. and Hs.*

IV. Christ is my strength, my God, and my Lord, the august Church doth sing in God-befitting wise, crying aloud and out of a pure mind keeping festival unto the Lord. *R. and Hs.*

V. With thy light divine, O Good One, illumine thou, I beseech thee, the souls of those who wake early unto thee with love; that they may know thee, O Word of God, as the true God, who callest forth from the gloom of sin. *R. and Hs.*

VI. Forasmuch as I behold the sea of life surging high with the tempest of temptations, I have fled to thy tranquil haven, and cry aloud unto thee: Lead thou my life forth from corruption, O Most Merciful One. *R. and Hs.*

VII. An Angel made the fiery furnace to drop dew for the Holy Children, but the command of God, consuming the Chaldæans with fire, prevailed upon the tormentor to cry aloud: Blessed art thou, O God of our fathers. *R. and Hs.*

VIII. Out of the flames thou didst shed forth dew upon the Godly Ones, and with water didst kindle the sacrifice of the Righteous One. For thou doest all things which thou willest, O Christ. Thee will we exalt unto all the ages. *R. and Hs.*

IX. It is not possible that men should see God, upon whom the Orders of the Angels dare not gaze: but through thee, O All-pure One, was the Word Incarnate manifested unto men: Whom magnifying, together with the Heavenly Hosts, we call thee blessed. *R. and Hs.*

TONE VII.

Hymns for: Lord, I have cried unto thee.

O come, let us rejoice in the Lord, who hath destroyed the power of death, and illumined the generation of men, crying with the Bodiless Ones: O our Maker and Saviour, glory to thee.

For our sake, O Saviour, thou didst endure the cross and burial; and by death didst thou slay Death, in that thou art God. For which cause we adore thy Resurrection on the third day: Glory, O Lord, to thee.

When the Apostles beheld the Resurrection of their Maker they were amazed, and sang the angelic hymn of praise: This is the glory of the Church, this is the riches of the kingdom: O Lord, who didst suffer for our sake, glory to thee.

Glory to the Father, and to the Son, and to the Holy Spirit, now, and ever, and unto ages of ages. Amen.

Hymn to the Birth-giver of God (Dogmátik). A Mother in more than human wise art thou acknowledged, O Birth-giver of God; yet thou didst remain Virgin beyond speech and beyond understanding; and the marvel of thy birth-giving can no tongue declare. Most glorious in the nature of thy conception, O Pure One, incomprehensible likewise is the manner of thy true birth-giving: for when God so willeth the order of nature is conquered. Wherefore, in that we perceive thee to be the Mother of God, with diligence we all beseech thee that our souls may be saved.

Hymn (Tropár). By thy cross thou didst destroy death; thou didst open paradise to the Thief; thou didst change the funeral wail of the Myrrh-bearing Women, and didst command them to announce unto thine Apostles that thou wert risen from the dead, O Christ our God, who bestowest on the world great mercy.

Hymn to the Birth-giver of God (Bogoróditchen). In that thou art the Treasury of our Resurrection, lead thou forth from the pit and deep of transgressions those who set their hope on thee, O All-hymned One! For thou hast saved those who were guilty of sin, in that thou didst give birth to our Salvation: O thou who before birth-giving wast Virgin, and in birth-giving wast Virgin, and after birth-giving remainest Virgin still.

Collect-Hymn (Kondák). No longer can the power of death hold mortals in captivity; for Christ hath descended, shattering and bringing to naught its powers. Hell is fettered; the Prophets with one accord rejoice, saying: The Saviour hath appeared unto those who believe: Come forth, ye faithful, unto the Resurrection.

THE CANON.

Theme-Songs (Irmost). I. At thy nod, O Lord, the nature of water which hitherto had flowed freely, was transmuted into terrestrial form: Wherefore Israel, journeying with foot unwet, doth sing unto thee a hymn of victory.

Refrain. Glory to thy holy Resurrection, O Lord.

(Then the appointed Hymns, composed after the model of those shown in Tone I.)

III. Thou who in the beginning didst establish the heavens by thine almighty word, O Lord our Saviour, and all the might thereof by thy Spirit all-creating and divine: Establish thou me upon the rock immovable of thy confession. *R. and Hs.*

IV. Thou didst not leave the bosom of the Father, yet didst come down upon earth, O Christ our God. I have heard the mystery of thy dispensation, and have glorified thee, who alone lovest mankind. *R. and Hs.*

V. The night is devoid of light for unbelievers, O Christ, but for the faithful there is illumination in the sweetness of thy words: For which cause I wake early unto thee, and hymn thy divinity. *R. and Hs.*

VI. As I sail over the surges of earthly cares, drowning because of my shipload of sins, and flung to the soul-destroying beast, like Jonah cry I unto thee, O Christ: From the death-dealing deep, O lead thou me forth. *R. and Hs.*

VII. The Children of God aforetime showed forth the fiery furnace to be dew-dropping, as they sang the praises of the one God, and said: All-exalted is the God of our fathers and all-glorious. *R. and Hs.*

VIII. The bush which on Sinai burned with fire yet was not consumed revealed God unto Moses, slow and halting of speech; and zeal for God made the Three Children invincible in the fire as they sang: O all ye works of the Lord, bless ye the Lord and exalt him unto all the ages. *R. and Hs.*

IX. O Mother who hast not known man, Virgin Birth-giver of God, thou who, without having tasted of corruption, wast with child and didst lend flesh unto the all-creating Word, Receptacle of the Illimitable, Abode of thine infinite Artificer, we hymn thee. *R. and Hs.*

TONE VIII.

Hymns for: Lord, I have cried unto thee.

Our evening song and reasonable service we offer unto thee, O Christ, in that thou hast graciously been pleased to show mercy upon us through thy Resurrection.

O Lord, Lord, cast us not away from thy presence, but graciously be pleased to show mercy upon us through thy Resurrection.

Hail, O Zion the holy, Mother of the Churches, the Abode of God! For thou, first of all, didst receive remission of sins through the Resurrection.

Glory to the Father, and to the Son, and to the Holy Spirit, now, and ever, and unto ages of ages. Amen.

Hymn to the Birth-giver of God (Dogmátik). The King of Heaven, because of his love toward mankind, hath appeared upon earth and dwelt among men: for he was incarnate of a pure Virgin, and came forth from her through that incarnation, the Only Son, twofold in nature but not in Essence. Wherefore, proclaiming him, in very truth, perfect God and perfect man, we confess Christ to be our true God: Whom do thou implore, O Mother unwedded, that he will have mercy on our souls.

Hymn (Tropár). Thou didst descend from on high, O Tender-hearted One; thou didst endure the three-days' burial, that thou mightest free us from our passions, O our Life and Resurrection. Glory, O Lord, to thee.

Hymn to the Birth-giver of God (Bogoróditchen). Thou who for our sake wast born of a Virgin, and didst suffer crucifixion, O Good One, and didst despoil Death through death, and as God didst reveal Resurrection: Despise not those whom thou hast created with thine own hand; show forth thy love for mankind, O Merciful One; accept the Birth-giver of God who bare thee, and who entreateth thee for us; and save thy despairing people, O our Saviour.

Collect-Hymn (Kondák), When thou didst rise again from the tomb, thou didst waken the dead and didst raise up Adam. Eve also exulteth in thy Resurrection, and all the ends of the earth which are risen from the dead in thy rising do celebrate the festival, O All-compassionate One.

THE CANON.

Theme-Songs (Irmosí). I. The wonder-working rod of Moses aforetime, when therewith he smote the sea in the form of a cross and divided it, submerged Pharaoh and his chariots; but Israel did it save, as the same fared forth on foot, singing unto God as they fled a song of victory.

Refrain. Glory to thy holy Resurrection, O Lord.

(Then the appointed Hymns, composed after the model of those shown in Tone I.)

III. Thou who in the beginning didst establish the heavens with wisdom, and didst found the earth upon the waters: Upon the rock of thy commandments, O Christ, establish thou me; for there is none holy save thee, O thou who alone lovest mankind. *R. and Hs.*

IV. Thou art my fortress, O Lord, thou art also my might, and thou art my God; thou art my joy: Without leaving the bosom of the Father thou hast visited our wretchedness. Wherefore with the Prophet Habakkuk will I cry unto thee: Glory to thy might, O thou who lovest mankind. *R. and Hs.*

V. Wherefore hast thou cast me away from thy presence, O Light which knowest no setting? And why hath hostile darkness encompassed me, the wretched one? But turn thou me again, and guide thou my paths in the light of thy commandments, I beseech thee. *R. and Hs.*

VI. Cleanse thou me, O my Saviour, for many are my transgressions; and lead me forth from the abyss of iniquity, I beseech thee, for unto thee have I cried: And hear me, O God of my salvation. *R. and Hs.*

VII. The fire in Babylon of old was put to shame by God's coming-down; for which cause the Children dancing in the furnace with joyful feet as in a flowery mead, did sing with exultation: Blessed art thou, O God of our fathers. *R. and Hs.*

VIII. With seven-fold heat did the Chaldæan tyrant in his rage cause the furnace to be heated for the Godly Ones; but when he beheld them saved by a better power, he cried aloud unto their Maker and Deliverer: Ye Children, bless; ye Priests, sing praises; ye People, exalt him unto all the ages! *R. and Hs.*

IX. Heaven was affrighted, and the ends of the earth were amazed: For God revealed himself unto men in the flesh, and thy womb became more spacious than the heavens. For which cause the chieftains of men and of Angels do glorify thee, O Birth-giver of God. *R. and Hs.*

APPENDIX B

I.

THE ALL–NIGHT VIGIL OFFICE.

(1) The Holy Orthodox-Catholic Apostolic Church of the East reckons its day after the pattern of the Jewish Church, from sunset. Therefore the worship of God begins with the Evening Service, which typifies, in general, the Old Testament times, as foreshadowing our Lord Jesus Christ and his life on earth, and precedes the Divine Liturgy of the morning, wherein is typified the life of our Lord as set forth in the New Testament and his life in heaven.

On ordinary evenings, Great or Lesser Vespers is used. On Saturday evening, and on the eves of the Great Feasts, is celebrated the Vigil Service, which consists of portions of Great Vespers, combined with Matins. In the early Church, the Vigil Service lasted all night, as its name, the "All-Night Vigil Service," denotes; and at the present day, in the monasteries of the East, where the service is read and chanted slowly, and in its completeness, it so lasts. In the monasteries, also, are used the Great and Lesser Later Evensong (Compline), and the various midnight services.

At the Saturday evening Vigil Service, the Resurrection of our Lord is more particularly commemorated and exalted.

On Christmas Eve, and on the Eves of the Epiphany and sometimes of the Annunciation, the All-Night Vigil Office consists of Great Later Evensong (Grand Compline) and Matins.

THE SYMBOLISM OF GREAT VESPERS.

(2) This Exclamation the Priest utters after the Deacon has said to the brethren who have assembled for Divine Service, and are seated: "Stand," and asks from him a blessing on the service: "Bless, Master."

(3) By these acts of devotion the thoughts of the Christian are carried back to the epoch of the Creation of the world, to the blissful state of our first parents. The censing typifies the saying of Genesis, that at the Creation the Spirit of God, the true Light and Incense unto the elect, moved over the face of the waters. The opening of the Holy Doors signifies that, from the creation of the world, man was appointed to dwell in Paradise. But the blissful condition of mankind was of brief duration. As a token of the fact that men were banished from Paradise after the Fall, the Holy Doors are closed after the Temple has been censed.

(4) The Priest stands before the Holy Doors, which are closed, and reads secretly the Prayers of Light, thereby typifying Adam sorrowing in repentance before the gates of Paradise. The Priest reads these

prayers with uncovered head, in token of penitence and humility. In the Service Books of the Church these prayers are called "The Prayers of Light" because in them the Priest glorifies the Lord, who dwelleth in Light ineffable, for the gift of material light, and prays for illumination of soul.

(5) All the Exclamations pronounced by the Priest after the Litanies bear a close relation either to the preceding litanies, to the prayers read secretly by the Priest, or to the chants of the singers.

(6) "Kafísma" signifies "sitting." The term may have had its rise in the fact that sitting was appointed while certain parts of the Kafísma were being read, verse by verse; but at some points standing was enjoined. In ancient times these verses were chanted.

(7) These verses express two thoughts: Adam's repentance for his sins, with his regret for the Paradise which he has lost; and the exhortation from the mouth of Adam to his posterity that they shall utterly obey the will of God.

(8) The *Bogoróditchny* (Hymns to the Birth-giver of God) are called "Dogmátiki," from the Greek word *dogma*, or doctrine; so that, together with the praise of the All-holy Birth-giver of God, they contain dogmatic teaching concerning the person of Jesus Christ, and in particular concerning the incarnation of the Lord and the union in his person of two natures — the divine and the human. The Hymn to the Birth-giver of God is sung at this point to remind us that she was the Mediatrix through whom, by the birth of her Holy Son, the life of those who were under the dispensation of the law was assuaged.

(9) The Entrance typifies in action that which is expressed by the chant: "O gladsome radiance"; that is to say, that the Gladsome Radiance has shone for men in the person of the Saviour, who, for the sake of men's infirmities, humbled the immortal glory of the heavenly Father, and came down from heaven.

The Holy Doors are opened, in token that with the coming of the Lord the Paradise of God was opened to men. The Priest comes forth from the Sanctuary standing erect, with his chasuble hanging straight, to typify humility and majesty. The Deacon precedes the Priest, as if he were the Forerunner, holding the censer in his hand. The censer with its incense signifies that, through the mediation of the Lord, our prayers are borne upward to God like incense, and that the Holy Spirit is present in the Temple. The Deacon is preceded by a taper, which denotes the spiritual light brought by the Lord to earth.

(10) The Gradual (*Prokímen*) (from the Greek, signifying that which precedes), is the verse which precedes the Lessons from Holy Scripture, namely, the Parables (*Paremíí*), the Epistle and the Gospel, and serves as a preface to the Lesson. The Gradual, generally in the words of Holy Writ, expresses either the contents and application of the Lesson which

follows it, or the significance of the day; that is, of the prayers and hymns which relate to the day.

(11) The Lessons from Holy Scripture of the Old Testament (and also sometimes from the New Testament) are called Parables (*Paremií*), and contain the prophecies of the event commemorated on the day; or explain the force of the Feast, and the intent with which it was established; or set forth the praise of the Saint whose festival it is.

(12) The *Litiyá* (from the Greek, *Liti*, *litomai*, — a fervent prayer). The fervent prayer is expressed in the "Lord, have mercy" many times repeated. The *Litiyá* is sometimes performed in the porch of the Temple, or on the steps; sometimes inside the Temple. It reminds us of the ancient Processions of the Cross in the streets, more especially by night; and of the fervent petitions which the early Christians offered up during those processions, on the occasion of divers public calamities. This going forth into the porch for the *Litiyá*, at the All-Night Vigil, after the Entrance and the Evening Litany (*Ekténiya*), on the one hand, typifies for those who stand in the porch (the penitents) the same thing as is typified for those who stand in the Temple by the Entrance at Vespers; that is to say, that our Lord Jesus Christ, the Gladsome Radiance, came down to us here below; that they who stand in the porch may expect mercy from the Lord, and the remission of sins. On the other hand, the going-forth of the faithful to the porch, the place of catechumens and penitents, denotes the profound humility of the Faithful, who are ready to put themselves in the place of the learners and penitents, and pray in company with them.

(13) At the Blessing of the Loaves God's blessing is asked on the fertility of the earth for the nourishment of men. In the early Church, when the All-Night Vigil lasted until the morning, it was customary to distribute the common offerings of bread, wine and oil after the Vespers; to the end that the Faithful who intended to remain throughout the service might be strengthened and refreshed thereby. After the Priest had pronounced the final Benediction upon the people, he and the Deacon descended from the Sanctuary, and sitting down with the people, they consumed with them the food which had thus been blessed. During this time selections from the Acts of the Apostles, or from the Epistles, were read aloud. This custom is still observed in certain monasteries, notably in those on Mount Athos. The distribution of the blessed bread during Grand Matins, to the Faithful who have received the benediction by the anointing with the blessed oil, commemorates this in ordinary churches.

II.

MATINS.

(1) Thereby expressing that those present, in their prayers, have sincere faith and love towards the Lord Jesus Christ; like the Wise Men, who

brought unto him offerings of frankincense and myrrh, and so honoured God in the flesh.

(2) The Six Psalms represent the wretched condition of the human race in the Old Testament days, which the Offices preceding the Divine Liturgy chiefly set forth: and the hope of a Saviour from on high.

(3) When our Lord Jesus Christ revealed himself to the people assembled beside the Jordan, John the Baptist hailed him with joy and reverence. Therefore the Priest, or the Deacon, now solemnly makes proclamation, beholding, as it were, our Lord himself come to minister to the world.

(4) During Fasts *Alleluia* is sung four times instead of: "God is the Lord and hath revealed himself unto us."

(5) Thereby reminding us of the time when the Holy Women bearing spices, and other Disciples of the Lord, came early to his sepulchre, even before the dawn, and there learning of our Saviour's Resurrection, imparted to his remaining Disciples the glad tidings. The incense typifies the sweet spices which the women brought to the tomb of the Lord; the taper typifies the light and joy of the glad tidings of the Resurrection, and the light of faith therein, and in our future life. The procession of the Priest about the Temple typifies the return of the Holy Women and the Disciples from the sepulchre of the Saviour, bringing the tidings to the remaining Disciples.

(6) It is so called from the Greek words *poli* (much) and *elea* (oil or mercy); because the latter word — mercy — is frequently repeated in these Psalms; and from the lighting of the shrine-lamps filled with pure oil, while the Psalms are being sung.

(7) Our Lord Jesus Christ, after that he was risen from the dead, speedily manifested himself to his Disciples. Wherefore the Church, by the reading of the Gospel after the Song of the Holy Women, announces to the People one of the ten Manifestations of the risen Saviour to his Disciples. The appointed Gospels for Matins in their order will be found on p. xxi. All the eleven Lessons from the Gospels, appointed to be read in rotation, refer to the Resurrection of our Lord on the third day.

(8) While the Choir sings, the Priest and Deacon first salute the Holy Gospels. And after them the people, in the presence of the Priest, as it were of the Angel-Messenger of the Resurrection, joyfully do homage to the Holy Book, as to Christ himself, and kiss it, in that it contains the redeeming tidings of the Resurrection.

(9) On Feast Days, the holy image of the Feast or of the Saint is saluted in token of devotion and gratitude to God for his mercy; and the Priest bestows the blessing, signing each one of the Faithful on the brow, in the form of a cross (with the oil which has been blessed at the Vespers) in the Name of the Holy Trinity, for the enlightenment and sanctification of their minds and hearts, and protection against all evil.

(10) As joy expresses itself in song, so the Holy Church has appointed to be sung, after the salutation of the Book of the Gospels, the Nine Songs of the Canon, which represent the Hymns of praise, at the Resurrection, of the nine Ranks of the heavenly Hierarchy. The Canon contains, also, the Hymns of those godly persons in the Old Testament, from Moses to Zacharias, who magnified the Lord God in spiritual songs. This is in conformity with the teachings of our Lord himself, who, after his Resurrection, expounded unto his Disciples the things in all the Scriptures concerning himself; and each Song (*Irmós*), in the vast number of Canons in the Holy Orthodox Church, is inspired by the Hymn of Scripture appointed to precede it. But these Scripture hymns are generally omitted, with the exception of the Song of the Holy Birth-giver of God, which precedes Song IX. Many of the Hymns which follow each song are also sometimes omitted. The second Hymn of Holy Scripture (Deuteronomy xxxiii.) is not, properly speaking, so much a hymn as a denunciation of God's judgments upon the Israelites. Therefore it is said only on the Tuesdays of the Great Fast. In imitation of this, the Second Song of every Canon also consists of denunciations of God's wrath upon the disobedient, and is also omitted.

(11) The Hymns of Light (*Svyetílny*) are also called the "Exapostilárion"; "Hymns of Light," because their subject is chiefly the illumination of the soul from on high, and because the singing of them at Matins precedes the break of day and the *Gloria in excelsis;* "Exapostilárion," because in ancient times a chanter was sent out into the centre of the church to sing them. (Greek: *Exapostilárion*, one who is sent forth.)

(12) In ancient times the singing of the Canon lasted until the dawn. Therefore it is still the custom, at the present day, for the Priest, shortly after the Canon is finished, to make this Exclamation, in an outburst of joy and thanksgiving, beholding, as it were, the dawn of day.

III.

THE HOURS.

In the *First Hour* we thank God for the light of day which he has given to us, and pray him that we may pass the day without sin. According to the ecclesiastical reckoning, the First Hour corresponds with the present seven o'clock in the morning.

In the *Third Hour* we commemorate the Descent of the Holy Spirit upon the Apostles on the day of Pentecost. It corresponds to the present nine o'clock in the morning.

In the *Sixth Hour*, corresponding to twelve o'clock (noon), the Crucifixion of Jesus Christ is commemorated.

The *Ninth Hour*, corresponding to three o'clock in the afternoon, commemorates the death of Jesus Christ, our Lord.

The Hours for Easter consist of the Hymns only, all the Psalms being omitted.

The Imperial Hours, used at Christmas and Good Friday, consist of all the Hours, and special Psalms, read consecutively; each Hour being augmented by the reading of Lessons from the Old Testament, from the Epistles, and from the Gospels, and the singing of special Hymns.

The Typical Psalms in their prayers and songs typify the Divine Liturgy. They are sometimes used in place of the Liturgy. They are also used as the continuation and conclusion of the Hours (during the Great Fast), and of the Imperial Hours.

IV.

THE LITURGY: ST. JOHN CHRYSOSTOM, ST. BASIL, PONTIFICAL.

(1) As the Sanctuary symbolically represents the kingdom of heaven, the drawing aside of the curtain during Divine Services typifies, in general, the revelation to mankind of the mysteries of salvation, which had been hidden from the foundation of the world and were revealed at the incarnation of the Lord; through whom, also, was revealed unto men the kingdom of heaven, forfeited by our first parents. The opening of the Holy Door typifies, in general, the opening of the way to the places where the Saviour of the world abode, or of the gates of Paradise; and, sometimes, the entrance into the kingdom of heaven.

(2) They thus ask forgiveness for any offences which they may have committed against their fellow-men; and the Choirs and the People express their pardon by bowing in return.

(3) All this and the whole Office of Oblation are said while the clergy are vesting, in a low voice, by the Priest, behind the image-screen (*ikonostás*), which corresponds to the chancel-rail in the Western Church. At the point duly indicated, after the Priest and Deacon have vested themselves, the Reader (in front of the image-screen), begins to read the Hours; the Priest (behind the image-screen), making aloud the exclamations and benedictions, as shown in the Hours.

(4) Five *prosforí* are generally used in preparing the holy Communion, in commemoration of the five loaves wherewith our Lord fed the five thousand people. But any one who wishes to have a living or a dead friend prayed for at the appointed place in the Liturgy, sends to the Chapel of Oblation a similar *prosforá* (an Altar-bread, — that is, "an offering"), with the Christian name only of the person written on a paper, or in a book kept for that purpose. At the end of the Liturgy the *prosforá* is returned to the sender, a particle having been removed, in token that the offering has been accepted. But the particles thus taken from these private offerings for the living and the dead do not form a part of the Communion, because they are not transubstantiated. The Ruler and the Government, the Holy Synod, or Patriarch, and other persons in authority are prayed for here and at other points in the service (which explains

the frequent recurrence of those petitions), not only in their official capacity, but also as representing benefactors of the Church and the people in general.   In the early Church people brought bread, wine, oil and the other things required for the sustentation of the Church and for the services, on behalf of themselves or of living friends, or as memorials of their dead friends; and all such persons were prayed for, in detail, by name. With the growth of the Church this special mention of innumerable individuals became burdensome, and rendered the services oppressively long. Therefore the present abbreviated and representative form (the Rulers) was adopted.

(5) The Altar, which represents the tomb of Christ and the throne of God, the holy pictures (*ikóni* — images), and the People are censed by the Deacon at the end of the Office of Oblation, in order that the Faithful may thereby be incited to a more fervent offering up of prayers.   The withdrawal of the curtain here typifies the revelation to the world of the secrets of salvation, hidden from eternity.

(6) These words, and the briefer form, the "Eis pollá eti, Déspota," at Pontifical services, as well as the "Axios" and "Kyrie eleison" in the Ordination Offices, are retained in the original Greek as an acknowledgment of the Russian Church's origin in and oneness with the Greek Church.

(7) This opening of the Holy Door signifies that the heavens were opened at the Baptism of our Lord Jesus Christ, and a voice proceeding thence testified to him.   The *Little Entrance* typifies the entrance of our Lord upon his work of preaching to the world, and his drawing near to men. The book of the Holy Gospels represents Christ our Lord, and the taper borne before it signifies that the teaching of the Gospels — that is, our Lord himself — is the Light of the world.   He who bears the taper represents John the Baptist.   The censer, with its glowing embers, typifies the Divine Ember, Christ himself, the God-Man, who united himself to mortal flesh, and, burning with divine love towards the human race, did utterly consume himself upon the altar of the Cross, in the savour of a sweet fragrance unto the everlasting Father.

(8) The exclamation, "Wisdom, O believers!" always has the object of calling the people's attention to some especially edifying or sacred portions of the service.   "Wisdom!" points directly to this edifying lesson, hymn or action.

(9) The *Thrice-Holy* is sung as follows: First the Choir sings the whole hymn thrice.   Then: "Glory . . . now, and ever, . . . Holy Immortal One, have mercy upon us."   Then the whole hymn, very slowly.

(10) This hymn is sung in the same manner as the preceding.   It is used at these Feasts because, in the early Church, converts to Christianity were chiefly baptized at these seasons.   By its use at the present day, the holy Church reminds us that we are bound to fulfil the vows made for us in Baptism.

(11) The Bishop takes his seat upon the "High Place," or Throne, because he represents our Lord Jesus Christ.

(12) The Gradual (*Prokimen*), a verse which precedes the Lesson of Scripture, is sung thus: The Reader reads it; the Choir sings it. The Reader reads the Verse, or Verses, while the Choir repeats the Gradual proper. The Reader then reads the first half of the Gradual, and the Choir sings the last half.

(13) This censing of the Temple, in preparation for listening to the reading of the Holy Gospel, draws the thoughts of the worshippers on high, and typifies the grace of the Holy Spirit, which is shed abroad in all the world, giving to the heart of man the savour of the sweetness of Christ (2 Cor. ii. 15). It is also a sign of prayerful reverence and homage to the Holy Gospel, as a symbol of the Holy Spirit, which is bestowed upon the world through the Gospel.

(14) If there is to be a sermon, the Priest may preach it immediately after the reading of the Gospel, or at the end of the Liturgy.

(15) After this clear announcement of God's Word in Christ, it is meet and right that men should repeat their petitions, and pray to him with redoubled fervour for all things necessary both for their souls and bodies. Therefore it is ordered that the *Litany of Fervent Supplication* shall now be said.

(16) The Catechumens in the early Church were not considered to be sufficiently instructed to look upon the Holy Mysteries without incurring the danger of misunderstanding them.

(17) In the middle of the *Cherubimic Hymn* the *Great Entrance* is made: that is to say, the Holy Gifts are brought from the Chapel (or Table) of Oblation to the Altar. In the days of the early Church, during this Great Entrance, all persons who-had brought or sent offerings for the use of the Church were mentioned by name. But as this detailed commemoration was extremely long and difficult, it was ordered that only the chief personages in rank and power should thereafter be mentioned by name; all others being included under the honourable title of "all Orthodox Christians." If it be a Pontifical Liturgy, the Bishop washes his hands at this point, thus ceremonially purifying himself for the sacred office which he is about to exercise.

The Great Entrance typifies our Lord's going to his Passion and death. Therefore it is customary for the Faithful to do homage to the Holy Gifts at this point, although these are not yet consecrated.

(18) In the early Church the Deacons, Sub-Deacons and Sacristans were wont to guard the doors, that no heathen or unworthy person might enter in, and that no one should go out during the solemn celebration of the Holy Sacrament. At the present time, the words, "The Doors!" warn us to guard the doors of our souls against all evil thoughts, as we prepare to confess our faith by the Creed, and to give heed to the Holy Mysteries.

(19) The Deacon here binds his stole about him in the form of a cross, to represent the wings of the Cherubim, who stand about the throne of God; as he himself represents an angel.

(20) The Greek letters: ИC, XC; NI, KA mean: Jesus Christ the Conqueror.

(21) The sacred warm water represents the water which came forth from the side of our Lord, with the Blood, showing that, although he was dead, his Body was not devoid of divine virtue; that is, the warmth and vitality of the Holy Spirit. The union of the Holy Elements is symbolical of our Lord's Resurrection.

(22) All persons, both Infants and Adults, are communicated alike; that is to say, with the mingled holy Body and Blood, by the sacred spoon. Infants receive the holy Communion by virtue of their having received holy Chrismation immediately following their Baptism, which holy Chrismation makes them full members of the Church. Until they reach the age of seven years they receive the holy Communion without the (otherwise) indispensable preface of the Sacrament of Confession.

(23) This represents the appearances of our Lord to his Disciples after his Resurrection; also his Ascension into heaven.

(24) The *Antidóron* (literally, "in place of the Gifts") consists of that part of the first Altar-bread which remains on the Table of Oblation after the Sacred Lamb has been taken therefrom to be consecrated. It came to be the custom to distribute this blessed bread from the following causes: First, it was given as a memorial of those Love-feasts which were held, in ancient times, immediately after the Divine Liturgy; and again, it was given to Christians in place of the Holy Gifts (as its name indicates), when they came fasting to the Liturgy, but had not prepared themselves, by reason of human frailty, to receive the holy Sacrament. Sometimes the last two breads are brought out (after the prescribed particles have been removed) at the end of the service, and given to persons of distinction who may be present.

V.

THE OFFICE OF THE DIVINE LITURGY OF THE PRESANCTIFIED (GIFTS).

(1) At the Liturgy of the Presanctified (Gifts), *there is no consecration of the Sacred Elements*, but those who desire to communicate receive the Holy Gifts which have been consecrated at a previous service.

It is used only during the *Great Fast (Lent)*, on *Wednesdays* and *Fridays;* in the fifth week of Great Fast, on *Thursday;* and in *Passion* (Holy) *Week,* on *Monday, Tuesday* and *Wednesday.* It was instituted in the first ages of Christianity, but received its present form from Gregory the Great, Bishop of Rome in the sixth century.

The Fathers of the Church regarded it as unbefitting the contrition of Lent that the full Liturgy (of St. John Chrysostom or of St. Basil the

Great) should be celebrated. Therefore the complete Liturgy is allowed during the Great Fast only on Saturday, Sunday, the Feast of the Annunciation, and Holy Thursday. The Sacred Elements are consecrated at the Liturgy on those days, and thereafter are preserved in the tabernacle, on the holy Altar.

The *Liturgy of the Presanctified* consists of *Vespers*, with special Prayers together with a *portion of the ordinary Liturgy*, omitting its most important part, namely, the consecration of the Holy Gifts; and the *Third, Sixth and Ninth Hours* (with the Typical Psalms) are used in a particular manner at the beginning.

(2) The Minéya is a set of twelve volumes containing the services for every day in the year, with the proper Hymns for the Saints of the day, and so forth. In addition, there are the Minéya of the Feasts, and the Pentecostárion (with the services for Easter-tide); and the Triódion, which contains the services, day by day, for the Great Fast.

(3) The Priest by his exclamation sets forth, as it were, that our forefathers the Prophets, from whose writings we have heard and shall hear Lessons, were illumined by the same light which still enlightens all men.

(4) As in the early Church there were always some among the Catechumens who were soon to be baptized (illumined), that is to say, in Easter week, this special Litany was inserted for them in the Liturgy of the Presanctified (where alone it is used) after Mid-Fast, or the Adoration of the Cross. But on Saturdays and Sundays, at the Liturgy of St. John Chrysostom, or of St. Basil the Great, it is not used.

(5) At the Liturgy of the Presanctified Gifts, after the Grand Entrance, the curtain is, as a rule, not completely, but only half drawn; because it is fully drawn at the full Liturgy after the Grand Entrance. The Entrance commemorates the Lord's going to his suffering, which is the inconceivable mystery of men's salvation, and had been hid from many ages and generations (Col. i. 26). At this time the Presanctified Gifts are on the Altar, and the people (when the curtain is drawn aside), beholding the sacrifice offered for the sins of the world, with boldness call upon God, the heavenly Father, and say: "Our Father."

(6) At the Liturgy of the Presanctified Gifts there is no elevation of the Body of Christ; because, as it represents the elevation of the Lord upon the Cross, it has already been made during the Liturgy at which the Gifts were consecrated.

VI.

THE RITE OF HOLY BAPTISM AND HOLY CHRISMATION.

(1) It will be observed that this rite remains in its ancient form; that is to say, as arranged for adults — the Catechumens being all adults in the early Church.

The removal of the Catechumen's garment signifies the putting off of the old man and of his sinful life, inasmuch as this Order is required only in the baptism of adults; that is, of persons above seven years of age, who are received only after due examination and their own expressed desire to be baptized.   With such, also, the procedure differs, according as they may be Jews, Mahometans, or members of some other non-Christian body; in which case, each must specifically renounce the errors of his former belief.   But the rite is alike for all Infants (that is, persons under seven years of age), whether they be of Orthodox or non-Orthodox parents; and of them, through their Sponsor, only the third catechizing, to which the answer is the Symbol of the Faith (the Nicene Creed), is required.

Three tapers are lighted and placed upon the font itself to typify the Holy Trinity, in whose name Baptism is administered.   The Sponsors also hold tapers, to signify their faith in the illumination which the Holy Mystery (Sacrament) confers upon the soul of the person baptized: that the baptized person passes from darkness into light, and becomes a child of the light.   For this reason, also, Baptism is called "Illumination."

The font typifies Noah's ark.

Holy Baptism is a Sacrament through which a man is born once only in spiritual birth; therefore it is not repeated, if it has been regularly performed, through triple immersion, in the Name of the Father, and of the Son, and of the Holy Spirit.   •

If any doubt exists as to whether it has previously been performed or not, the formula "if not already baptized" must be interpolated.   The rule is that it shall be administered in church; but in case of necessity it may be administered in a private house.   In extremity, a layman may baptize; and the Baptism is not repeated, though the Chrismation is afterwards performed, if the child live.   Though immersion is prescribed, a child may be baptized by affusion in case of extreme weakness or mortal danger; and those baptized by affusion in such cases (or persons who have been so baptized in other Christian Churches, when they join the Eastern Catholic Church) are not rebaptized, but are only anointed with the holy Chrism.

It is not customary for either father or mother to be present at the baptism; though it is not forbidden for the father.   Provided forty days have elapsed since the birth of the child, the mother is permitted to be present.

For a man or boy, one sponsor (male) not younger than fifteen years of age is indispensable.   For a woman or girl one female sponsor not younger than thirteen years of age is indispensable.   The Church does not forbid other sponsors.   The sponsor ought to be a member of the Holy Orthodox Apostolic Church of the East; but if a member of another Church should, for any reason, stand sponsor, he (she) is required to recite the Symbol of the Faith of the Orthodox Church.   In such case a non-Orthodox man or woman may stand as additional sponsor.

(2) That is to say, endowed with reason and speech, in contradistinction to the dumb animals.

(3) From the west comes darkness; and Satan, who is darkness, and whom the Catechumen must renounce, has his dominion there. The uplifted hands of the Catechumen indicate the realm of the evil spirits of the air.

(4) The Catechumen turns his face to the east, because light proceeds thence. The white vestments and the lights typify spiritual joy in the illumination of the person through holy Baptism.

(5) This is called "the oil of gladness" because the person baptized is thereby engrafted into the good olive-tree, Jesus Christ, having been, as it were, a branch wrested from a wild olive-tree. As the Lord sent to the people in Noah's ark a twig of olive by a dove, in token of reconciliation and salvation, so the sign of the cross is made above the water with the oil, in token that the waters of baptism serve to reconcile man with God, through the mercy of God therein manifested, and save from the taint of sin (Rom. xi. 17).

(6) Anointment with the holy Chrism (Chrismation) is a Sacrament whereby the recipient, through the anointing of various parts of the body in the name of the Holy Spirit, receives the gifts of the Holy Spirit, to rear and strengthen him in the spiritual life, and to render him strong, firm and invincible in faith, in love and hope; in boldness, that without fear he may confess before all men the name of Christ: that he may grow in all virtues, free himself from the Evil One and all his guile, and preserve his soul in purity and righteousness (1 John ii. 20; 2 Cor. i. 21, 22). After anointment with the holy Chrism the child is a member of Christ's Church, and receives the holy Communion, without preliminary confession, until he reaches the age of seven years. Beginning with that age confession is obligatory.

(7) The circle typifies eternity. Therefore the triple circling of the font with lighted tapers signifies that the newly baptized (illumined) person has entered into eternal union with Christ, the Light of the world.

(8) The three Offices — (a) Prayers at the Reception of a Catechumen; (b) Holy Baptism and Chrismation; and (c) Ablution, which were formerly celebrated separately — are now commonly joined together in one service. In the early Church the Catechumen wore his robe of purity for eight days, which he spent in fasting and prayer.

(9) The words of the Apostle (1 Cor. vi. 11).

(10) The shearing of the hair signifies that the newly baptized person has dedicated himself to the service of God, and to obedience; because the cutting of the hair has always been the symbol of submission and servitude. It is also symbolical of the scriptural offering of the first-fruits.

VII.
THE RITE OF HOLY MATRIMONY.

(1) Tapers are given to those who plight their troth and to bridal pairs to symbolize the purity of their lives, which shine with the light of virtue (John iii. 20–21). The morning, immediately after the celebration of the Divine Liturgy, is regarded by the Church as the proper time for the solemnization of Marriage (although this time is not obligatory), in order that the bridal pair may receive this Sacrament fasting. The rite is not solemnized on all days of the year, but is forbidden during Fasts; on the Eves of Great Feasts; during Easter week; and on some other days.

(2) The rubric prescribes a gold ring for the man, to typify his greater worth and authority; and a silver ring for the woman, to typify her scriptural subjection to her husband, as the head of the wife. In modern practice the rings are, as a rule, both of gold; and the bridal pair themselves make the prescribed exchange in the Russian Church, but not in the Greek Church.

(3) It is customary, at the beginning of this Office, to lead the bridal pair upon a piece of new, rose-coloured material (or a new rug), which is spread before the lectern. In olden days the Russian Tzars and their brides were led upon a piece of flowered silken material and sable skins (sometimes as many as forty in number), which were intended as emblems of happiness and plenty in the new path upon which they were entering. This is the significance in general.

(4) The crowns represent the honour and reward bestowed upon the wedded pair for the purity of their lives. In Greece the crowns are woven of olive leaves (emblematic of fruitfulness), or of laurel, interwined with flowers. But in Russia, metal crowns are kept in the churches. They are adorned with holy pictures (*ikóni*); that of our Lord Jesus Christ being upon the crown of the bridegroom, and that of his holy Mother upon that of the bride.

(5) Wine is used in the Sacrament of Marriage, because at the marriage in Cana of Galilee, which our Lord blessed with his presence, the water converted into wine by a miracle was served. The "common cup" of weal and woe is given to the bride and bridegroom in token that they ought to dwell in unbroken concord, hold and use, undivided, their acquisitions, and share equally the cup of joy and sorrow. In Greece they are given bread soaked in wine, having the same significance.

(6) The circle typifies eternity. By this circling round the lectern, upon which lie the book of the Gospels and the cross, the bridal pair signify their oath forever to preserve their marriage bond, until death shall break it. The triple circling is in honour of the Holy Trinity, which is invoked to bear witness to their oath.

(7) Saint Constantine and Saint Helena are invoked because they were

the disseminators (in the tenth century) of the Orthodox faith; and Saint Procopius is invoked because he instructed the twelve women to go to their death of martyrdom as to a marriage feast. The Exhortation is generally made immediately after this Benediction, instead of at the point originally prescribed. (*See page 293.*)

(8) In the early Church, the crowns (of olive leaves) were worn for a week.

(9) This second Order of Marriage is used only when both bride and bridegroom have been previously wedded. When either is now married for the first time, the preceding Order is used. The holy Church permits second and even third marriages, but unwillingly. Nicephorus, Patriarch of Constantinople, commanded that persons who entered into a second marriage should not be crowned, and should be deprived of the holy Communion for the space of two years. Persons who entered into a third marriage were debarred from the Communion for five years. This rule is not observed at the present day, but explains this separate Order for Second Marriage.

VIII.

ORDINATIONS.

(1) The Sub-Deacon in his service typifies the service of the angels. Accordingly, at his ordination he is invested with the stole, which he girds about him crosswise, thereby symbolizing the wings with which the Cherubim veil their faces as they stand before the throne of God.

(2) As no man is ordained to the Diaconate unless he be already a Sub-Deacon, it is now customary (if he be not already a Sub-Deacon) to ordain him to that degree on the same day upon which he receives the Laying-on of Hands to the Diaconate. As he cannot marry after he has received this degree (of Sub-Deacon), he must be already married if he is to become a parish priest; that is, unless he has elected to become a monk. As he does not celebrate the Sacrament of the Eucharist but only serves at it, he is ordained after the consecration of the Holy Gifts.

(3) The first "command" is addressed to the people, the second to the clergy, and the third to the Bishop. In the early days of Christianity the people and the clergy of the local church had a voice in the election of Bishops, Priests and Deacons, in the sense that the choice made by the Bishops was announced to them, with the object of obtaining their testimony in regard to the qualities of the candidates, and of giving them an opportunity to declare for or against the choice. Later on, owing to difficulties, the influence of the people upon the selection of their Bishops was restricted. In the choice of Priests and Deacons the people never had as much to say as in that of their Bishops. The "command" addressed to them preserves the tradition of their right to pronounce upon the candidate's fitness.

(4) Hereby he announces his intention to devote himself always to the service of God's altar.

(5) He thereby signifies his gratitude and respect for him at whose hands the grace of God is invoked upon him. The three hymns which are chanted while he is making this triple circuit of the Altar are symbolical: The Martyrs invoked in the first are to serve the candidate as an example for the preservation of his faith and purity; the second proclaims that the subject of the candidate's preaching (like that of the Apostles and Martyrs) is to be the Trinity, one in Essence and Undivided; the third denotes that the foundation of the priesthood and of the Church was the coming of the Saviour, who must be magnified, while the holy Virgin is blessed.

(6) In token that the fulness of the sacred ministry is not conferred upon the Deacon, but only a portion thereof.

(7) This denotes that he who is thus receiving Ordination is preparing himself to share the pastoral burden.

(8) *Kyrie eleison* (Lord, have mercy), like *Axios* (worthy), is left in the original Greek, in order to show whence the Russian Church derived its Holy Orders. *Axios* signifies that he who through the Laying-on of Hands has received the grace of the Holy Spirit, is become worthy to perform the sacred office entrusted to him.

(9) The kissing signifies the mutual greeting upon the entry of the new ecclesiastic upon his new ministry, and the love and union of all the participants.

(10) The Ordination of a Priest takes place after the Holy Gifts have been borne from the Credence Table to the Altar, in order that he may take part in their consecration. In token that he is finishing his service as Deacon, he bears the air (*vózdukh*) on his head during the Great Entrance. He kneels at the Altar on both knees, to denote that he is receiving a greater ministry and a higher gift than the Deacon. The rest of the symbolism is the same as at the Ordination of a Deacon.

(11) Because the Abbot is set over the flock of God in the Monastery, he kisses the Bishop's stole, which is the emblem of the wandering sheep that the Good Shepherd took upon his shoulder, and which the Bishop wears to denote his charge over the flock of Christ. The rest of the symbolism is the same as at the Ordination of a Deacon.

THE CONSECRATION OR ORDINATION OF A BISHOP.

(12) This "Eagle" is a very large rug, upon which is depicted a single-headed eagle hovering over a city with battlemented walls and towers. Similar rugs, or "eagles," of a smaller size, are used for the Bishop (or more exalted Prelate) to stand upon when he celebrates any service. The city is a symbol of his episcopal authority over the cities of his diocese; the eagle symbolizes his pure and lofty and upright theological teaching.

in imitation of that eagle which is depicted with St. John the Divine. The same significance is attached to the halo round the eagle's head, which typifies theological attainments and the gift of grace.

(13) The Consecration takes place at this point because the Little Entrance typifies the coming to earth of the Lord incarnate, who suffered for us, and rose again, and was received up into heaven. Thereafter the Holy Spirit consecrated the first successors of the Saviour, and revealed them as enthroned and reigning with Christ. Therefore, when the Chief Bishop enters the Sanctuary, as it were heaven, with the other ecclesiastics, the candidate for Consecration is led thither, and the Sacrament of Laying-on of Hands is conferred upon him before they all take their places on the episcopal thrones, as it were on the heavenly thrones; and thus he, also, becomes a throned Bishop, and sits with them as their equal.

(14) The book of the Gospels represents Christ the Lord, the source of all things. It is placed on the Bishop's neck to show that he should rule his flock after the pattern of Christ, bending his neck lightly under the yoke of Christ, and must do nothing contrary to His will. For under the form of the Gospels he has taken upon his head and neck the Church of the Lord.

(15) *Axios* is said only when the *omofór* or Bishop's stole (pall) is laid upon his shoulders; because he already possesses all the vestments of a Priest. It was made of wool in former days, and represents the wandering sheep which the Good Shepherd found and laid across his shoulders. It is adorned with crosses to signify that, as Christ bore his cross upon his shoulders, so all who desire to follow him must bear their cross on their shoulders. Many traditions quoted by ancient writers affirm that the clergy and all the people, by uttering this word "Axios" (worthy), at the Consecration of Bishops and at the Ordinations of Priests and Deacons, thereby gave their testimony to the blameless life and good morals of him who had received the laying-on of hands. St. Clement instituted in the Primitive Church, in the name of the Apostles, a law that such testimony should be exacted *especially* at the Consecration of Bishops, in reply to the definite question, thrice put to the people: "Is he, in truth, worthy of this ministry?"

IX.

HOLY UNCTION.

(1) Anointing with the holy Oil is a Sacrament in which, through the anointing of the body, the grace of God is invoked upon the sick person; because that grace heals all ills, both those of the soul and those of the body. It is performed only over sick persons (James v. 14, 15), with one exception: In the Cathedral of the Falling-asleep of the Birth-giver of God (Assumption) in Moscow, on Holy Thursday, the Bishop anoints all per-

sons who desire it, after the Divine Liturgy; because, on the evening of Great and Holy Thursday Christ instituted a new Covenant with his Body and Blood. Therefore it is not unfitting that a well man should partake also of this Sacrament, since he knows not the day and hour of his death. The warrant for this is the saying of St. James, taken in its broadest sense to include those who suffer from spiritual ills — grief, despondency, and the like — as well as from those of the body.

The sick person who receives this Sacrament must be of the Orthodox faith, and must prepare himself by repentance and confession; and before or after this Sacrament he receives the Sacrament of the Holy Communion. Holy Unction, being in the nature of a healing remedy, may be repeated; and even the young need not fear to receive it, under the erroneous impression that, having received it, they cannot, thenceforth, eat meat or marry. It is performed in church, in the presence of an assembly, if the sick person be able to leave his bed; or at home, before an assembly of people. Seven Priests are appointed to perform it, because there are seven Lessons from the Epistles, seven from the Gospels, and seven Prayers; the number seven being chosen as symbolical of the Seven Gifts of the Holy Spirit, and in conformity with the number seven connected with the Shunammite woman's child and Prophet Elisha (2 Kings iv. 35);* of the reopening of the skies by the Prophet Elijah, after they had been shut up for three years and a half (1 Kings xviii. 43); of Naaman's dipping himself in the waters of the Jordan, after which he was cleansed. But in case of need the holy Church permits one Priest to perform the Office, if he does so in the name of the whole assembly. A shorter form of the Office is appointed for use over those in danger of immediate death. Another name for the Sacrament is "Prayer-Oil."

(2) Seven tapers are lighted round about the shrine-lamp or other vessel which contains the wine and oil, as images of the Seven Gifts of the Holy Spirit. It is customary for all those who are present to hold tapers not only during the reading of the Gospels, but also during all the residue of the Office, in token of their fervent prayers for the salvation of the sick person.

The wheat serves as the emblem of the embryo of a new life — of healing and of life after the death of the body — of resurrection (John xii. 24; 1 Cor. xv. 36–38). The oil is the visible token of the grace of healing (Mark xvi. 18). The wine is used as a symbol of the blood of Christ shed upon the cross for the salvation of men. The oil must be pure olive oil, without any admixture.

(3) The oil symbolizes God's mercy; the wine, the blood which flowed from the side of our Lord upon the cross. The union of the oil and wine is made after the pattern of the remedy which was used by the Good Samaritan.

* *Slavonic:* "he stretched himself upon the child seven times."

(4) The Great Martyr, Demetrius († at Thessalonica, A.D. 306), whose bones still exude chrism, and are famous throughout the Orient as healing to the sick. Nestor was a young Christian of Thessalonica who visited St. Demetrius in prison (where the latter was suffering for the faith) to receive his blessing before engaging in conflict with the Emperor's favourite gladiator. Demetrius predicted that Nestor would conquer, but would suffer martyrdom in consequence; and so it came to pass.

(5) St. Panteleimon, of Nicomedia, was a Christian physician, who suffered martyrdom for the faith A. D. 296. He performed many miraculous cures during his lifetime, and was beheaded, after many vain efforts to kill him by various torturing assaults, in which God protected him from harm.

(6) "Unmercenaries" is the title applied to disinterested benefactors, who alleviated the pangs both of the soul and body; more especially to physicians of the early Church.

(7) In this act the Church imitates the Prophet Elisha, who sent his staff to the Shunammite woman (2 Kings iv. 29). As the Gospels contain the accounts of many miracles wrought by Jesus Christ, they are laid upon the sufferer's head, with the printed pages down, in the hope that he will receive like physical and spiritual healing; and in order to strengthen the faith in the written word of our Lord in the minds of those present. Christ, in performing his miracles of healing, laid his almighty hand upon the sick. Therefore his priests, in this Office, lay their hands upon (or hold) the Gospels, in token of reconciliation.

X.

·THE BURIAL OF THE DEAD (LAYMEN).

(1) When an Orthodox layman dies his body is washed, after the custom of Apostolic times (Acts ix. 37), out of irespect to the dead and a desire that he shall present himself clean before the presence of God, in the resurrection. Then the body is clothed in new garments, which symbolize our new garment of incorruption (1 Cor. xv. 53). The garments thus used correspond to the calling or rank of the departed. They denote that in the resurrection every man must render an accounting to God of the manner in which he has fulfilled his duty in that state of life to which he was called. Thus a monk is dressed in monastic garb, and wrapped in his mantle, which is cut a little, in order that it may be laid about him in the form of a cross; and his face is covered, to denote that in the earthly life he was estranged from the things of this world.

The Psalter is read over the body of an Orthodox believer until the time is come to bury him. This reading comforts those who are mourning the departed, and inclines them to prayer. Inasmuch as the Psalter is designed chiefly to represent prayers for him who has fallen asleep in the

Lord, it is interrupted by a commemoration of the dead, with special prayerful petitions to God wherein the dead person is mentioned by name. It is customary to repeat this after each division of the Psalter, as indicated by the Doxology.

Upon the brow of the dead is placed the *chaplet*, a strip of material upon which are depicted our Lord Jesus Christ, his holy Mother, and St. John the Baptist; together with the *Thrice-Holy* (O Holy God, Holy Mighty, Holy Immortal, have mercy upon us). The dead Christian is thus adorned with the wreath like an athlete who, with honour, has left the field of contest; or like a warrior who has won a victory. The figures printed thereon signify that he who has run his earthly career hopes to receive the crown for his deeds solely through the mercy of the Triune God and the mediation of the Mother of our Lord and of his Forerunner.

In the hand of the dead is placed a holy picture (*ikóna*) of the Saviour, in token that he has believed in Christ and has surrendered his soul to him; that in life he beheld the Lord by anticipation, and now is gone to see him face to face in blessedness, with the Saints. The body of the dead is covered with a holy pall, in token that, as one who has been a believer and has been sanctified by the Sacraments, he is under the protection of Christ.

At funerals four standard candlesticks are placed at the four sides of the coffin, forming a cross. Those present, both at funerals and at Requiem Services (*Panikhídi*), hold tapers, thereby typifying the light divine wherewith the Christian is enlightened at baptism, and the fervour of his prayers. The taper also serves as an image of the world to come, of the light which knows no setting.

(2) This, the song of the Archangels in honour of the Holy Trinity, is sung because the dead person is now being accompanied into the realm of the Angels, who sing continually the Thrice-Holy hymn.

(3) That is to say, if the Sacrament of Holy Unction has been performed upon the deceased during his lifetime, the oil and wine which remained therefrom are poured over his dead body. This anointment is Christ's token, and a seal of confirmation that they who die in Christ have wrought for Christ, in the sanctification of their bodies, and have lived uprightly in this earthly life.

(4) The ashes typify the same thing as the unconsumed oil — the life which is extinguished on earth, yet acceptable unto God; like the sweet spices of the censer.

(5) If anyone departs this life on holy Easter Day, or on any day of the Bright Week which intervenes between that day and the Sunday of All Saints following, less than the customary funeral songs are sung, because of the majesty and honour due to the joyful Feast of the Resurrection; for it is a festival of joy and gladness, not of mourning. And since all who have died in the hope of resurrection and of life eternal

through Christ are, by Christ's resurrection, translated from the sorrowful things of this world to things glad and joyful, the Church proclaims this by songs of resurrection over the dead. By this diminution of the songs, litanies and prayers ordinarily appropriate to those who have fallen asleep, we are assured that he who dies in penitence, even if he have not yet given satisfaction for his sins, has pardon for them, through the prayers of the Church, and is freed from their bonds.

XI.

THE BURIAL OF THE DEAD (PRIESTS).

(1) At the burial of Prelates, Hiero-monks, Archimandrites and Priests, when the body is borne from the house to the church, during the reading of the Prayer of Absolution, and on the way to the grave, the church bells are rung, as they are when the holy cross is brought forth from the Sanctuary, on September 14, (27), August 1 (14), in Mid-Lent, on Good Friday, and on Holy Saturday. That is to say, each bell is struck once, and the order is repeated thrice, or oftener; after which all the bells are struck together, once.

At the burial of a Bishop the body is carried round the church on its way to the grave, and a brief service is celebrated at each side of the church.

Deacons are buried like laymen; because in the Order for the Burial of Priests the sacerdotal rank of the latter is specifically mentioned. A censer is placed in the hand of the dead Deacon.

(2) A dead Bishop, after he has been rubbed with oil by means of a sponge, is arrayed in all his sacerdotal vestments while "Thy soul shall delight itself in the Lord" is being sung; and the censers, sacramental fans, together with the double and triple branched candlesticks (*dikiri*, *trikiri*) are used. When the vesting is completed he is seated in an armchair, and the Proto-Deacon proclaims: "Send forth thy light"; after which the body is laid upon a table, and the face is covered with a sacramental veil. The veil denotes that the dead was a minister of the Sacraments of God, more especially of the Holy Mysteries of the Body and Blood of Christ, and it is buried with him. If he has at any time received the Sacrament of Holy Unction, the oil remaining therefrom is used to anoint his body for burial, as is the case also with Priests.

(3) In token that he proclaimed unto men the teachings of the Gospels, a cross is generally placed in the hands of a dead Bishop or Priest; because it is the emblem of salvation, both of the living and the dead. The book of the Holy Gospels is buried with him, and the cross also. Over the remains of a dead Bishop or Priest the Gospels are read instead of the Psalter, "in order to propitiate God," says Simeon of Thessalonica. "For what other offering can be made unto God, to propitiate him on behalf of him that lieth there, if not this, to wit, the proclamation of the

Incarnation of God, of his teachings, his Sacraments, and the gift of the remission of sins, his redeeming Passion for us, his life-creating death and resurrection?"

XII.

THE REQUIEM OFFICE FOR THE DEAD (PANIKHÍDI).

(1) The origin of the Service of the Dead (*Panikhídi*) is as follows: St. Macarius of Alexandria once inquired from the Angels who accompanied him an explanation of the Church's custom to celebrate the third, ninth, and fortieth days after a death by religious services. And the Angel told him: "When, on the third day, the body is brought to the Temple, the Soul of the dead man receiveth from his Guardian Angel relief from the grief which he feeleth at parting from his body. This he receiveth because of the oblation and praise which are offered for him in God's Church, whence there ariseth in him a blessed hope. For during the space of two days the Soul is permitted to wander at will over the earth, with the Angels which accompany it. Therefore the Soul, since it loveth its body, sometimes hovereth around the house in which it parted from the body; sometimes around the coffin wherein its body hath been placed: and thus it passeth those days like a bird which seeketh for itself a nesting-place. But the beneficent Soul wandereth through those places where it was wont to perform deeds of righteousness.

"On the third day He who rose again from the dead commandeth that every Soul, in imitation of his own Resurrection, shall be brought to heaven, that it may do reverence to the God of all. Wherefore the Church hath the blessed custom cf celebrating oblation and prayers on the third day for the Soul.

"After the Soul hath done reverence to God, He ordereth that it shall be shown the varied and fair abodes of the Saints and the beauty of Paradise. All these things the Soul vieweth during six days, marvelling and glorifying God, the Creator of all. And when the Soul hath beheld all these things, it is changed, and forgetteth all the sorrow which it felt in the body. But if it be guilty of sins, then, at the sight of the delights of the Saints, it beginneth to wail, and to reproach itself, saying: 'Woe is me! How vainly did I pass my time in the world! Engrossed in the satisfaction of my desires, I passed the greater part of my life in heedlessness, and obeyed not God as I ought, that I, also, might be vouchsafed these graces and glories. Woe is me, poor wretch!' After having thus viewed all the joys of the Just for the space of six days, the Angels lead the Soul again to do reverence to God. Therefore the Church doth well, in that she celebrateth service and oblation for the Soul on the ninth day.

"After its second reverence to God, the Master of all commandeth that the Soul be conducted to Hell, and there shown the places of torment, the different divisions of Hell; and the divers torments of the ungodly, which cause the souls of sinners that find themselves therein to groan continually, and to gnash their teeth. Through these various places of torment the Soul is borne during thirty days, trembling lest it also be condemned to imprisonment therein.

"On the fortieth day the Soul is again taken to do reverence to God: and then the Judge determineth the fitting place of its incarceration, according to its deeds. Thus the Church doth rightly in making mention, upon the fortieth day, of the baptized dead."

It is also customary to have the Requiem Office celebrated on the anniversaries of the birth-day, name-day, and death-day of the departed.

(2) It is customary, at the Requiem Office (*Panikhídi*), to place upon a small table in the church a dish of *kutiyá* or *kolíva:* that is, boiled wheat, mixed with honey, to which raisins are sometimes added. The *kolíva* serves to remind us of the resurrection of the dead. As grain, in order that it may form ears and give fruit, must be buried in the earth, and moulder there; so, also, the body of the dead must be committed to the earth, in order that it may rise to life eternal. The honey typifies the sweetness of bliss of the future life. In the grain is set upright a lighted taper, which symbolizes the light wherewith the Christian is illumined in baptism; and also the light of the world to come, which knows no setting.

(3) Thereby offering unto God, as it were, a sacrifice of propitiation for the dead person, and in honour of the Sovereign Lord over life and death.

XIII.

THE CONSECRATION OF A CHURCH.

(1) The Canon of the Holy Orthodox-Catholic Apostolic Church of the East orders that the Consecration of a Church must be performed by a Bishop. If, however, this be not possible, the Bishop sends a corporal (*antimíns*) which has been consecrated to the Church that is to be consecrated, and delegates his authority of consecration to an Archimandrite, an Abbot, an Archpriest, or a Priest. In that case a briefer Office is used than the one here given. In substance, the two Offices are identical; but the most important part of the Office as performed by a Bishop, namely, the consecration of the corporal, is of necessity omitted. Relics are placed in the Altar only in case a Bishop consecrates the church. If the Altar is of stone, all the portions of the service prescribed for a wooden Altar are omitted.

(2) This garment (Exodus xxviii. 4) is white in colour, and is trebly girt: about the neck of the officiating ecclesiastic, in token of wisdom and obedience to God; about the body, beneath the breast, to symbolize the Word; about the loins, as a symbol of purity and strength. If a Bishop celebrate, the apron-like garment should be of silk; if a Priest, of cotton cloth.

(3) The Office of Consecration proper is preceded by the Blessing of Water, in a form which greatly resembles that appointed for the Feast of the Epiphany.

(4) As the Altar represents the sepulchre of our Lord Jesus Christ, so the mastic, mingled with fragrant spices, represents the sweet-smelling spices wherewith Joseph of Arimathea and Nicodemus anointed the body of our Lord when they laid him in the tomb.

As the Temple is fashioned after the image of our bodies, which are the temple of God (2 Cor. vi. 16) and members of Christ (1 Cor. xii. 27), that rite which is performed at the Consecration of a Church is analogous to the rite by which every believer is made a member of the Church, and the Consecration resembles holy Baptism and holy Chrismation. Therefore, at a Consecration, rose-water, the holy Chrism, white garments and tapers are used: and the building, like the font, is compassed about in procession, in the circle which is the emblem of Eternity.

(5) The affixing of the table to the Altar with four nails commemorates the nailing of our Lord to the cross. The stones thus used are not thrown away, but are generally laid beneath the Altar.

(6) Moses, by the Lord's command, anointed the Tabernacle and the Altar at the dedication of the Temple (Exodus xl. 9, 10), as the Altar is here first anointed, and the Sanctuary afterwards. The three places anointed are those where, during the Divine Liturgy, the book of the Holy Gospels, the paten and the chalice are to stand.

(7) The corporal (*antimíns*) is, as it were, the Altar itself, and takes the place of an Altar when, by reason of storm or any other cause, the Altar falls into ruin; or when it is necessary to celebrate the Divine Liturgy in the absence of a duly consecrated Altar. It consists of a silken cloth, whereon is depicted our Lord Jesus Christ in the sepulchre. (*See page* xxvii.)

(8) The double vesting of the Altar indicates its double significance: as the tomb of Christ and the throne of God. The first altar-cloth represents the winding-sheet wherein the body of our Lord Jesus Christ was wrapped for burial.

(9) The cord typifies the cord wherewith our Lord was bound, when he was led before Annas and Caiaphas.

(10) The second covering of the Altar, the *indítia*, of rich and brilliant material, typifies the glory of God's throne.

(11) This, the *ilitón*, represents the swaddling-clothes wherein the infant Christ was wrapped at his birth; our Lord's winding-sheet in the tomb; and the napkin which was bound about his head in the tomb. (Here, as in certain other instances, there are several explanations of the symbolism, upon which the authorities occasionally differ.)

(12) This typifies, as in holy Baptism, spiritual illumination.

(13) This signifies that the Church is consecrated forever to God; because the circle is the symbol of eternity.

(14) The holy relics placed in the Altar or under the corporal (*anti-mins*) bear witness to the special presence there of God.   They remind the Christian that when he is in church he is in a place sprinkled with the blood of the Saints; and he rejoices with holy gladness, recalling the words of St. John: "That ye, also, may have fellowship with us" (1 John i. 3).

The holy relics are anointed with the holy Chrism as for burial, in token of the close bond between the Martyrs and Christ.   The relics of the Saints which remain incorruptible on earth assure us of the special prayers for us on the part of the Saints thus honoured with immortality of body ere the coming of the Kingdom of Glory (Rev. vi. 9, 10).

The Riverside Press
CAMBRIDGE · MASSACHUSETTS
PRINTED IN THE U.S.A.

8335004R00363

Printed in Great Britain
by Amazon.co.uk, Ltd.,
Marston Gate.